Building ASP.NET
Server Controls

DALE MICHALK AND ROB CAMERON

Building ASP.NET Server Controls
Copyright © 2004 by Dale Michalk and Rob Cameron

ISBN (pbk): 1-59059-140-2

Printed and bound in the United States of America 10987654321

Trademarked names may appear in this book. Rather than use a trademark symbol with every occurrence of a trademarked name, we use the names only in an editorial fashion and to the benefit of the trademark owner, with no intention of infringement of the trademark.

Technical Reviewer: Larry Wall

Editorial Board: Dan Appleman, Craig Berry, Gary Cornell, Tony Davis, Steven Rycroft, Julian Skinner, Martin Streicher, Jim Sumser, Karen Watterson, Gavin Wray, John Zukowski

Assistant Publisher: Grace Wong

Copy Editor: Nicole LeClerc

Production Manager: Kari Brooks

Proofreader: Linda Seifert

Compositor: Diana Van Winkle, Van Winkle Design Group

Indexer: Kevin Broccoli

Artist: April Milne

Cover Designer: Kurt Krames

Manufacturing Manager: Tom Debolski

Distributed to the book trade in the United States by Springer-Verlag New York, Inc., 175 Fifth Avenue, New York, NY 10010 and outside the United States by Springer-Verlag GmbH & Co. KG, Tiergartenstr. 17, 69112 Heidelberg, Germany.

In the United States: phone 1-800-SPRINGER, email orders@springer-ny.com, or visit http://www.springer-ny.com. Outside the United States: fax +49 6221 345229, email orders@springer.de, or visit http://www.springer.de.

For information on translations, please contact Apress directly at 2560 Ninth Street, Suite 219, Berkeley, CA 94710. Phone 510-549-5930, fax 510-549-5939, email info@apress.com, or visit http://www.apress.com.

The source code for this book is available to readers at http://www.apress.com in the Downloads section. You will need to answer questions pertaining to this book in order to successfully download the code.

To my loving wife, Melissa, and beautiful daughter, Grace,
who make my life whole and fulfilling.
—Dale Michalk

To my beautiful wife, Ally, and daughters Amanda and Anna,
who bring so much joy to my life.
—Rob Cameron

Contents at a Glance

Contents

Foreword

IN THE EARLY DAYS of the web it was great fun to craft web pages by hand, carefully placing each HTML tag onto the page. As time has gone on, we've acquired a wealth of new technologies, including CSS, JavaScript, and the full gamut of HTML standards, including XHTML and DHTML. These advances bring freedom but also complexity and an almost overwhelming array of choices. Few developers can intimately know all of these technologies, and even if they could, browser compatibility issues are often significant enough to humble the most hard-core developer.

However, even with these new technologies, we still often feel that we're reinventing the wheel each time we build a website. For example, when we create image buttons that change when the mouse pointer rolls over them, we're writing fresh JavaScript script. That script has to be written and tested, but it also adds potentially unhelpful complexity when we come to change the page later. Then when we want to reuse the script, we have to figure out how to transplant it neatly, and then go through the whole test cycle again to make sure we didn't break it. And if the user interface element is more complex—for instance, a pop-up menu, a navigational toolbar, or a rich form control—we disappear into a deep, dark pit of DHTML and script, and it may not be clear whether the work is worthwhile.

So really we've reached a point at which we have all these wonderful technologies, but it takes a great deal of time and energy to make use of them. But you know what? That isn't the problem. The problem is that it takes a lot of effort *every time* we use the code, as reuse and customization of reused code is hard. What would make a huge difference is if we could write a fancy user interface widget and know we've invested our time in something that can be reused again and again in future projects. It's time to solve problems in a new way by applying the concepts of software reuse to web user interfaces. That then frees us up to solve *new problems*, and that's what we're all here for. Rather than doing the same stuff we did last week, we should be exploring new frontiers and taking on new programming challenges. And, most important, we should be encapsulating the solutions to those programming challenges in pieces of reusable code.

Of course ASP.NET is a revolutionary platform for many reasons, but I think perhaps the greatest is the server control architecture because it helps us do exactly this: create reusable code. It enables us to take user interface elements and wrap them up as components that can be used over and over again, even those containing JavaScript, DHTML, and CSS. And even better, while doing that we can account for the needs of different web browsers and also provide a range of properties and methods on the control that allow developers to customize it any way they wish when they use it in future.

Dale and Rob have done a fantastic job of bringing detailed and extremely thorough coverage of this cornerstone of modern web development to our bookshelves. I commend them highly for the work they've done—they've written a book that is a vital part of the mass migration of developers to these new and exciting ways of building better web applications. Don't just build, reuse! Read on and let Dale and Rob show you how.

Ollie Cornes
CEO, RichTextBox.com
ASP.NET MVP, MCSE, MCP, BSc

About the Authors

Dale Michalk is employed with Microsoft Corporation in Dallas, Texas. He has been with Microsoft since 2001. He helps promote .NET as a development platform and assists companies interested in migrating to new technologies such as ASP.NET. A former U.S. Army officer and West Point graduate, he spends his free time chasing after his 2-year-old daughter, who keeps him extremely busy.

Rob Cameron is employed with Microsoft Corporation in Atlanta, Georgia. He has been with Microsoft since 2000 working as a development consultant providing developer advisory services and escalation management to Fortune 500 enterprise development teams. Prior to his employment at Microsoft, he worked as an independent consultant developing software on the Microsoft platform for over 5 years. He has a master's degree in information technology management and a bachelor's degree in computer science. A former U.S. Navy officer and Naval Academy graduate, he enjoys spending his free time with his wife and two daughters.

Acknowledgments

WRITING A BOOK is a long and incredible journey that requires the support and care of a lot of people. First and foremost, we would like to recognize our families. Without their support and patience with all those long hours on the computer, this book would have never come to pass. The same goes to our respective coauthor. This nights-and-weekends project wouldn't have been completed without this partnership. Thanks also go to Ollie Cornes for getting this book project started in the first place and putting together the Foreword. A sharper individual in the ASP.NET community you will not find.

Apress is a fantastic company to work for as an author, as evidenced by their care and feeding in getting this book produced. This is a publishing house run by those who actually write for a living—they understand the balance in ensuring high quality versus meeting deadlines. Thanks especially to Gary Cornell for all the patience in our slipped schedules and author changes. Thanks to the editing folks from Apress, Grace Wong, Nicole LeClerc, Kari Brooks, Jessica Dolcourt, and Hollie Fischer, as well as to those who we don't know by name but whose efforts helped make this book possible. We would also like to thank the folks who reviewed the book and provided technical assistance and support: Larry Wall, Drew Dials, Joel Reyes, and Roger Lamb.

A final thanks is owed to the ASP.NET product team, who provided the Microsoft web development community with an awesome product and are busy at work on a second version that will reach new heights.

Introduction

WITH THE EXPLOSION of the Internet in the mid-1990s, web development tools
evolved as a combination of HTML and a scripting language such as ASP or Perl to
generate dynamic output. With the advent of Microsoft's .NET Framework, ASP.NET
turned web development on its head by combining a design-time interface similar
to Visual Basic with an HTML and JavaScript output that requires nothing more
than a web browser for rendering.

At the core of ASP.NET is server control technology. From the `Page` class to the
`Label` control, all objects in ASP.NET are server controls. Server controls combine
server-side execution in a well-defined life cycle with browser-friendly rendering
that includes down-level browsers and a plethora of mobile clients. Regardless of
the target output, server controls behave in a similar manner. Understanding this
technology and how to leverage it in your own development efforts is the subject
of this book.

What This Book Covers

This book is about server control technology as the underlying foundation of
ASP.NET. It will provide you with a deep understanding of how server control technology works and how to build your own custom server controls as part of a web
development project or for resale in the component marketplace.

The first part of the book presents an introduction to server control technology.
Here we also discuss different ways to build a server control, including inheritance
from a base control such as `Control` or `WebControl`, encapsulation or composite controls, and inheritance from an existing or rich control such as the `TextBox` server
control.

The second part of the book dives deep into a discussion on critical topics
such as state management, server-side event handing, templates, data binding,
client-side script integration, and validation controls. A common theme in all
these discussions is how the topic relates to the control life cycle. Understanding
the control life cycle is critical to server control development and to ASP.NET
development in general. Of course, we offer copious amounts of code to support
our discussions as well.

The third part of the book covers mobile control development. We first provide background on mobile control server control technology, highlighting the similarities to and differences with mobile development when compared to development targeting a desktop browser. After covering the basics, we dive into the various ways you can customize mobile server controls, including building a custom mobile control.

The last part of the book covers design-time support in detail. Many of the controls built in earlier chapters include design-time support; however, we centralize discussion of the design-time support capabilities in ASP.NET and server controls to facilitate understanding without cluttering up the earlier chapters. We round out the book with a discussion on licensing, globalization, and localization.

Who This Book Is For

The target audience for this book is developers with an intermediate to advanced experience level looking to deepen their understanding of ASP.NET and its underlying server control architecture. The example code in this book is written in C#, but if you're a VB .NET developer the examples translate pretty easily because ASP.NET development is language agnostic. The .NET Framework and the ASP.NET object model are what's important, not the language.

If you're a developer in need of learning a particular technique, each major facet of control development is presented with simple example code to highlight that particular topic. For example, if you're looking for information on how to add events to your server controls, or how to understand how events work in ASP.NET, you can drill down into that chapter to get the details.

If you're a developer looking for full-featured example code, the templates and data-binding example shows how to implement data binding and templates that can connect to a database back-end. A demonstration in the last part of the book pulls together the techniques described throughout the book into a holistic example on how to build a rich, complex server control that is fully localized and includes licensing support.

Source Code Download

You can find all the source code presented in this book in the Downloads area of the Apress website at http://www.apress.com. Please don't hesitate to send us your feedback.

We hope that you benefit from the information we present on building custom server controls and use the understanding you gain from this book in your own web development efforts with the .NET Framework and ASP.NET.

CHAPTER 1

User Interface Reuse

IN THIS CHAPTER, we highlight the challenges inherent to web application development and discuss the state of web development up to the release of Visual Studio .NET. Next, we compare ASP to ASP.NET, highlighting the advantages of ASP.NET and the modularity that ASP.NET server controls can provide in web development efforts.

The Primitive Nature of Web Development

Up until recently, the rapid march to web application development was not matched by improvements in the frameworks and development environments used to build them. In fact, many web developers use Notepad or Emacs as their development environment of choice, shunning more advanced tools for the simple pleasure (and often the speed) of authoring tags directly in a text editor. However, the rapid growth of the Web and demand for "web-enabled" applications is driving development managers in search of more productive development models.

The Growth of the Web

The rapid growth of the Internet has driven the requirements for building web applications ever higher in complexity. Web application development projects demand rapid time-to-market, near 100% uptime, and accessibility by a wide audience. Putting aside the hype of the dot-com boom and bust of the late 1990s, corporate business processes steadily continue to move to the Web. The reasons behind this continued migration to web-enabled processes is well documented elsewhere. The point we want to make here is that demand for web applications that are quickly developed, reliable, and maintainable continues to grow.

The simple truth is that web development has remained in a somewhat primitive state compared to traditional Windows application development. In the next section, we investigate this primordial state of web development in light of the Microsoft-recommended and commonly used multitier architecture.

The Multitier Architecture

The architecture most web developers on the Windows platform would agree upon uses multiple layers or tiers to separate the major concerns of an application: presentation, business logic, and data access.

The presentation layer handles interaction with the end user and takes the form of a Hypertext Markup Language (HTML) page generated by an Active Server Pages (ASP) script on the web server. The HTML user interface can be simple and effective by supporting the basic HTML 3.2 specification, or richer and more interactive by supporting dynamic HTML (DHTML) and JavaScript in higher-version browsers. In the current ASP model, there is not much available in the development environment to support code reuse, abstraction, or modularity.

 NOTE *Easily creating a highly interactive presentation layer is where ASP.NET server controls shine. This book focuses on developing new, and extending exisiting, server controls.*

To build up web page content, an ASP script running on Internet Information Services (IIS) typically calls upon the business layer to do work, which is usually implemented as COM+-enabled objects that represent the business rules and logic. The next level of abstraction is provided by the data access layer, which leverages stored procedures or dynamically generated SQL statements fronting a back-end relational database. These layers work together to make up the heart of the application, as shown in Figure 1-1.

Figure 1-1. A typical three-tier architecture

The development of reusable COM components and stored procedures in the business and data layers of the multitier application architecture has made significant headway into the hearts and minds of web application architects. This model increases code maintainability, provides abstraction between layers, and offers encapsulation of application logic that can be reused in other applications. This model still holds true in the .NET world when building multitier applications with ASP.NET.

Unfortunately, the presentation layer of the ASP three-tier web architecture has not received the same benefits of componentization or reuse. A portion of the blame can be laid on web developers and the almost unreasonable time demands of modern development projects; most of the blame can be placed on the rudimentary support for componentization in the presentation layer of the development platform itself.

The ASP Development Model

HTML rendering environments such as ASP are a minimal layer of abstraction over a stream generation engine. ASP comes packaged as an Internet Server Application Programming Interface (ISAPI) extension for IIS that handles requests for files with the .asp filename extension. Internally, it takes the ASP page content and parses it to produce interpreted script code that sends the content to the output stream by executing logic provided within script tags and sending the raw HTML directly down to the browser. The model is simple and flat in its design (see Figure 1-2), as there is no way to plug into the parsing process and/or effectively modularize the script content beyond a script function block.

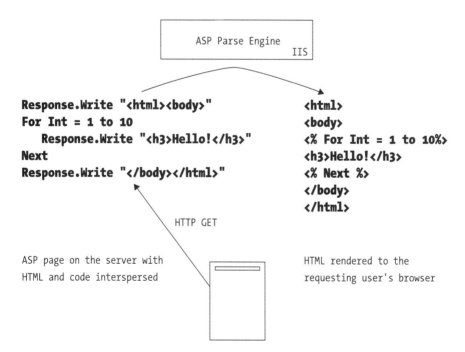

Figure 1-2. The ASP parsing and rendering process

Programmers are forced to do quite a few things manually when delivering content and function to users in the ASP model of development. This model requires programmers to have complete exposure to the intricacies of HTML tags and the functionality of Hypertext Transfer Protocol (HTTP). To construct client-side state or have HTML elements remember their contents, programmers must manipulate cookies and hidden variables, or form post information programmatically by hand to read the returned information from the client, as well as generate the correct HTML based on the logic of the application back to the client.

Implementation of client-side validation required tedious, time-consuming manipulation of JavaScript emitted into the output stream that can easily obfuscate the logical view of the ASP page. Building database-backed HTML content requires manual iteration through Recordset rows and calls to `Response.Write` to build the output. Many tasks required by a web development project are accomplished through duplicated code time and time again.

Listing 1-1 shows some of the manual work required with ASP development. The code calls upon a script function that returns an ADO Recordset from the SQL Server sample Northwind database and then loops through the result set to display an HTML table. The code also implements an HTML input text box for maintaining search filter expressions through an HTTP POST cycle to the web server. To accomplish the task, the script code must manually set the value of the `<INPUT type="text">` tag during the postback process. The manual steps required to add additional functionality are not provided by the ASP system; the system provides little relief beyond its simple object model to get and return content.

Listing 1-1. Customers.asp Code for Searching the Northwind Customers Table

```
<html>
  <body>
    <form method="post" action="Customers.asp">
      <%
      Function GetCustomersRS(Name)
          Dim RS
          Dim Conn
          Set Conn = Server.CreateObject("ADODB.Connection")
          Conn.Open "Provider=SQLOLEDB.1;Integrated Security=SSPI;" & _
              "Initial Catalog=Northwind;Data Source=(local);"

          Set RS = Server.CreateObject("ADODB.Recordset")
        SQL = "SELECT ContactName, CompanyName FROM Customers WHERE ContactName
LIKE '%" & Trim(Name) & "%'"
          RS.CursorLocation = 3 'adUseClient
          RS.CursorType = 3     'adOpenStatic
          RS.ActiveConnection = Conn
```

```
      RS.Open SQL
      Set RS.ActiveConnection = Nothing
      Set GetCustomersRS = RS
            Conn.Close
      End Function
      Dim CustName
      CustName = Request("custname")
      Dim CustRS

%>
      <br>
      <h3>Customer Search</h3>
      ContactName<br>
      <input id=name name=custname type="text" value="<%= CustName  %>"><br>
      <input type="submit">
      <br>
      <h4>Results</h4>
      <table border="1" cellspacing="0" style="border-width:1px;border-style:solid
;border-collapse:collapse;">
        <tr>
          <td><b>ContactName</b></td>
          <td><b>CompanyName</b></td>
        </tr>
        <%
      If CustName <> "" THen
          Set CustRS = GetCustomersRS(CustName)
          If Not CustRS.EOF Then
              Do While Not CustRS.EOF
%>
        <tr>
          <td><%= CustRS("ContactName") %></td>
          <td><%= CustRS("CompanyName") %></td>
        </tr>
        <%
                  CustRS.MoveNext
              Loop
%>
      </table>
      <%
        End If
      End If
%>
    </form>
  </body>
</html>
```

Figure 1-3 shows the execution results of our simple ASP page.

Figure 1-3. Customers.asp execution results

Early Attempts at Presentation Layer Code Reuse

When it comes to ASP development, packaging content or code is as primitive as the rendering process. The IIS *include* directive is a popular means of reusing script and HTML content in multiple ASP pages. Unfortunately, it does not create a new namespace for the included content, which leads to inevitable name clashes with global variables and script functions. Because it is an outside mechanism that is performed as a simple input/output (I/O) operation by IIS, there is no way to find out how many include files are referenced within a page or a means of programmatically working with them. For include files with large numbers of script functions, it is difficult to find the names or correct parameters for a function. At some point, external documentation or text searches through include files are necessary to make sense of what is inside. Obviously, this does not promote maintainable code.

As a web application grows in complexity, ASP development becomes increasingly complex, leading toward poor separation between user interface (UI) and programming logic due to its flat nature and lack of componentization. The scripting code ends up getting interspersed with HTML tags in a nearly undecipherable manner, which results in a unique appearance called *spaghetti code,* something near and dear to ASP coders. Programmers get lulled into the free-flow modifications of the scripted environment and forget to apply software engineering best practices such as a consistent coding style. The resulting modifications made to the original HTML to produce dynamic code also make it difficult for the UI designer to redesign the web site without the help of a skilled programmer to ensure the logic is not broken for a simple UI change.

The Visual Basic Model of Development

Comparing the travails of web application development to the model of Visual Basic
Windows application development makes it look like a step backward in many respects.
Visual Basic revolutionized the Windows development world by providing a rapid application development (RAD) environment with a WYSIWYG ("What You See Is What You
Get"), integrated development environment (IDE) and drag-and-drop form control
editing (see Figure 1-4). This opened up Windows development to a much wider developer base by permitting developers to create UIs without having to forge into
the tedious world of handcrafted Win32 C code.

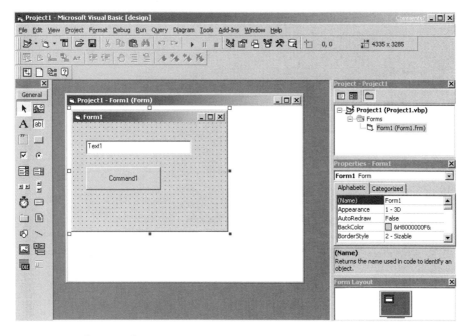

Figure 1-4. The Visual Basic IDE

The Visual Basic runtime hides the grunge details of graphical user interface (GUI)
programming from programmers, allowing them to concentrate on implementing the
major UI features and business logic. No need to worry about Win32 application programming interface (API) constructs such as `WNDCLASS`, `WNDPROC`, and device contexts to
get a simple window displayed on the screen. Instead, programmers can concentrate
on wiring up UI events and writing business logic and data access code. Though Visual
Basic was initially derided as a toy language not capable of real-world development,
almost all modern programming environments, including those in the C++ camp, have
incorporated at least a portion of Visual Basic's groundbreaking concepts into their
implementations.

Beyond hiding the grunge work of Windows programming, Visual Basic helped solidify the use of controls as a means of packaging UI elements. Instead of programmers trying to reinvent the UI wheel, or widget, with each application, they could pass controls from project to project to achieve the Holy Grail of code reuse.

Initially a consumer of controls built in other development environments, Visual Basic eventually gained the capability to create controls inside its RAD environment. This promotion of control development to the rapid development environment of Visual Basic gave rise to a cottage industry of control vendors supporting Visual Basic development that is still going strong today.

Taking a page from the Visual Basic playbook, several attempts have been made to move the control model to the surface of the web browser. Unfortunately, the two main initiatives, Java applets and ActiveX controls, failed to gain momentum in the web developer community. Applets ran into installation hassles around installation of the correct Java Virtual Machine (JVM) version on the client and significant performance problems for effective UI interaction. ActiveX controls have registration hassles because they install as COM objects into a machine's registry.

Still, the demand for a rich UI experience on the Web led to developers seeking alternative development models. This resulted in much of the applet and ActiveX control thunder being stolen by DHTML. DHTML allowed for a rich, interactive UI environment via the browser that satiated the UI demand to a degree but still failed to provide a robust vehicle for UI reuse.

A New Paradigm of Web Development

The state of web development described in the previous section required a new technical architecture to raise the bar of abstraction, modularity, and power to what was available already in the Windows client development world. ASP.NET provides just such an architecture, which we describe in the following sections.

The ASP.NET Development Model

The architects of ASP.NET at Microsoft had the previous experience of ASP to draw upon, and they sought to correct its deficiencies in abstraction and modularity while retaining its hallmark flexibility and simplicity. It is quite apparent that the ASP.NET team members had as part of their vision the desire to bring the power and ease of Visual Basic development to the Web. ASP.NET provides state management, cross-browser support, separation of code from HTML script, and many other benefits with ease that previously required hand coding in ASP. At the heart of the amazing ASP.NET architecture is server control technology, which we focus on throughout this book.

ASP.NET Server Controls

Server-side controls encapsulate the details of page layout and HTML tags by representing them with an easy-to-understand, consistent object model that adds a welcome layer of abstraction. Server controls in the .NET Framework also provide the following capabilities:

- The controls are smart enough to figure out whether or not they can emit DHTML for rich display or JavaScript to validate data on the client. They are also smart enough to realize when to use Cascading Style Sheets (CSS)–style attributes or explicit HTML style tags for down-level browsers.

- Controls remember their previous content by emitting their state into a hidden variable mechanism called ViewState that is automatically handled by ASP.NET in a tamper-proof manner.

- Controls provide extensive customization through style attributes and the use of templates. Templates allow web developers to insert content that gets included with the final output of the control. We discuss templates in more detail in Chapter 7.

- Server controls inherit the concept of data binding from the world of Visual Basic development. *Data binding* takes a data source and attaches it to a control. Then the control renders its output according to the data. This saves time by avoiding tedious looping constructs and doing manual `Response.Writes` of the formatted data as in ASP. We discuss how to implement data biding in server controls in Chapter 7.

- Controls raise events in conjunction with the HTTP postback mechanism, providing a clean development model over ASP. Events allow controls to behave in a similar manner to their brethren from the world of Visual Basic and provide a more intuitive system for directing UI activities and executing business logic. We discuss how to implement events in Chapter 5.

- Controls support drag-and-drop functionality, visual placement, and property-sheet editing inside the Visual Studio .NET Web Form Designer. The WYSIWYG support of the Designer allows web developers to build ASP.NET web applications at the same speed as Visual Basic developers built Windows applications in the past, without paying a huge premium in performance or functionality.

- Controls can be bundled up and packaged for reuse. This allows for the development of third-party control libraries such as those that exist for ActiveX control and Visual Basic desktop development.

How ASP.NET Works: A Brief Overview

An ASP.NET Web Form executes within a parsing process much like an ASP page, but instead of generating flat, procedural code executed by a script engine, it generates strongly typed compiled code that represents the page as a tree of control objects that support properties, methods, and events that are visible and accessible by code during server-side processing (see Figure 1-5).

```
<%@ Page language="c#" %>          ⊞   __PAGE  System.Web.UI.Page
<html>
 <body>                               .......   ctr10  System.Web.UI.LiteralControl
  <form runat=server>
   Enter :                         ⊞   ctr11  System.Web.UI.HtmlControls.HtmlForm
   <asp:TextBox runat=server />
  </form>                            .......   ctr13  System.Web.UI.LiteralControl
 </body>
</html>                              .......   ctr14  System.Web.UI.WebControls.TextBox

                                     .......   ctr15  System.Web.UI.LiteralControl

                                     .......   ctr12  System.Web.UI.LiteralControl
```

Figure 1-5. The ASP.NET page-parsing process and server-control hierarchy

All the content on a page, such as server tags, HTML elements, and so forth, is encapsulated as a control that inherits from the root System.Web.UI.Control base class, making the use of polymorphic and dynamic control building and processing very efficient and accessible. No longer is the web page a black box; it is now a transparent entity that can be programmatically manipulated to meet the needs of web developers.

You can think of the control tree of an ASP.NET web page as a server-side object model (or a document object model [DOM], for those who work with HTML/XML). It can have nodes (server controls) added, removed, or manipulated to create the final content necessary to render the desired output. This fully programmatic access to the web page makes building completely dynamic, modular web applications easy and efficient.

ASP.NET and Code-Behind

The default design pattern chosen by the Visual Studio .NET IDE aids developers in achieving modularity and abstraction of web development through the use of code-behind. *Code-behind* separates UI layout from page code logic without giving up any power or flexibility. This separates the concerns of the UI designer, who works with the visual appearance in the HTML tag file, from those of the programmer, who works on wiring up the UI to back-end business/database logic and handles events in a code-behind class file (see Figure 1-6).

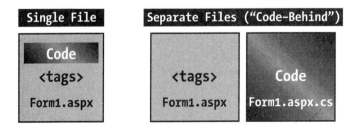

Figure 1-6. The ASP.NET code-behind model

The elegant design of the model uses inheritance to bring the two entities together at compile time and allows programmatic access to tags from the code-behind file in a manner with performance identical to that of a single .aspx page design with inline code.

The code-behind technique of developing ASP.NET web pages is not a requirement. The ASP.NET parser supports inline code that is similar to the development model of ASP. We use the code-behind system in all examples in this book, as created by the default Web Form creation process in Visual Studio .NET. We believe that the code-behind technique provides nice task separation that most developers will want to leverage. If you prefer the inline technique, you can easily port all of the samples without losing any functionality.

ASP vs. ASP.NET: The Customers Table Example Revisited

In Listing 1-2 we revisit the original ASP code in Listing 1-1 and bring it forward to the new world of ASP.NET. The ASP.NET code in Listing 1-2 produces identical output to the original version, querying the contents of the Customers table in the SQL Server Northwind database. The most obvious difference between the two listings is the split of the original ASP page into an .aspx Web Form page and a code-behind class file shown in Listing 1-3. The code-behind class, while adding a small amount of textual bulk through the class and control variable declaration syntax, gives us the undeniable advantage of a separation of tasks between UI design and programming logic.

Listing 1-2. CustDemo.aspx Tag Page for Searching the Northwind Customers Table

```
<%@ Page language="c#" Codebehind="CustDemo.aspx.cs" AutoEventWireup="false"
 Inherits="ControlsBookWeb.Ch01.CustDemo" %>
<%@ Register TagPrefix="apressUC" TagName="ControlsBookHeader"
Src="..\ControlsBookHeader.ascx" %>
<%@ Register TagPrefix="apressUC" TagName="ControlsBookFooter"
Src="..\ControlsBookFooter.ascx" %>
<!DOCTYPE HTML PUBLIC "-//W3C//DTD HTML 4.0 Transitional//EN" >
<HTML>
  <HEAD>
    <title>Customers</title>
    <meta name="GENERATOR" Content="Microsoft Visual Studio 7.0">
    <meta name="CODE_LANGUAGE" Content="C#">
    <meta name="vs_defaultClientScript" content="JavaScript">
    <meta name="vs_targetSchema"
content="http://schemas.microsoft.com/intellisense/ie5">
  </HEAD>
  <body>
    <form id="Customers" method="post" runat="server">
      <apressUC:ControlsBookHeader id="Header" runat="server" ChapterNumber="1"
ChapterTitle="User Interface Reuse" />
      <h3>CustDemo</h3>
      <h3>Customer Search</h3>
      ContactName<BR>
```

```
        <asp:textbox id="CustName" runat="server"></asp:textbox><BR>
        <asp:button id=""QueryButton" runat="server" Text="Submit Query">
</asp:button><BR>
     <BR>
     <H4>Results</H4>
     <asp:datagrid id="DataGrid1" runat="server" />
     <apressUC:ControlsBookFooter id="Footer" runat="server" />
   </form>
  </body>
</HTML>
```

Listing 1-3. Customers.aspx.cs Code-Behind Class File for Searching the Northwind Customers Table

```
using System;
using System.Collections;
using System.ComponentModel;
using System.Data;
using System.Drawing;
using System.Web;
using System.Web.SessionState;
using System.Web.UI;
using System.Web.UI.WebControls;
using System.Web.UI.HtmlControls;
using System.Data.SqlClient;

namespace ControlsBookWeb.Ch01
{
   public class CustDemo : System.Web.UI.Page
   {
      protected System.Web.UI.WebControls.DataGrid DataGrid1;
      protected System.Web.UI.WebControls.Button QueryButton;
      protected System.Web.UI.WebControls.TextBox CustName;

      private void Page_Load(object sender, System.EventArgs e)
      {

      }

      #region Web Form Designer generated code
      override protected void OnInit(EventArgs e)
      {
         //
         // CODEGEN: This call is required by the ASP.NET Web Form Designer.
         //
         InitializeComponent();
         base.OnInit(e);
      }
```

```
        /// <summary>
        /// Required method for Designer support - do not modify
        /// the contents of this method with the code editor.
        /// </summary>
        private void InitializeComponent()
        {
            this.QueryButton.Click += new System.EventHandler(this.QueryButton_Click);
            this.Load += new System.EventHandler(this.Page_Load);

        }
        #endregion

        private SqlDataReader GetCustomersReader(string name)
        {
            SqlConnection conn =
                new SqlConnection("Server=(local);Database=Northwind;
Integrated Security=true;");
            conn.Open();

            SqlCommand cmd =
                new SqlCommand("SELECT ContactName, CompanyName FROM Customers WHERE
ContactName LIKE '%" + name.Trim() + "%'",
                conn);

            SqlDataReader rdr =
                cmd.ExecuteReader(CommandBehavior.CloseConnection);

            return rdr;
        }

        private void QueryButton_Click(object sender, System.EventArgs e)
        {
            DataGrid1.DataSource = GetCustomersReader(CustName.Text);
            DataGrid1.DataBind();
        }
    }
}
```

All of the coding logic that was previously interspersed with HTML tags in the ASP page has been moved into a click handling routine in the code-behind class file. The Button control's click event is mapped to an event handler named QueryButton_Click. The code in the event handler makes several ADO.NET method calls to retrieve a DataReader object from the Northwind database and bind its content to the DataGrid control on the Web Form. Working with the Visual Studio .NET Editor makes this event mapping trivial, as you can double-click the button in the Web Form Designer view and it will automatically create an event-handling method that is wired to the click event. This is very similar to the paradigm introduced by Visual Basic to interact with the Editor and have it generate code stubs automatically while allowing the programmer to concentrate on the programming logic. We discuss delegates and event handlers, and how to add them to custom-developed server controls, in Chapter 5.

The `DataGrid` control handles the grunge work of translating the ADO.NET data into a nicely formatted HTML table display. The only action required of the programmer is to set the `DataSource` property of the `DataGrid` to the `DataReader` object and call the `DataBind` method implemented in the control. The `DataGrid` supports a template mechanism not shown in this demonstration that allows a graphic designer to customize its look by declaratively modifying the control's tag on the .aspx page without a corresponding need for the programmer to make any changes to the data-binding code.

Another improvement in this example is the "memory" that the `CustName TextBox` control demonstrates. The control remembers its contents between postback round-trips without requiring the programmer to resort to reading the form post or using hidden variables. All the programmer has to do is query the control for its `Text` property. This state-management capability is called *ViewState*. The controls in ASP.NET take advantage of this architecture and make life easier for developers. We cover how to add ViewState capabilities to custom server controls in Chapter 4.

Why Learn How to Build Server Controls?

Although the set of controls included in ASP.NET provides developers with a solid toolset for building capable web-based applications, there will undoubtedly be a need for custom-developed server controls from third parties and from within enterprise development teams for several reasons:

- Developers are not willing to give up functionality for ease of development, and their application end users are not willing to do so either. If an existing ASP.NET control falls short of what is available using earlier technology such as DHTML, someone will fill the need through custom controls. (Maybe that person will be you!)

- Once developers get a taste of the Visual Basic–like development environment that ASP.NET provides, they will demand that all types of UI functionality be provided in ASP.NET server control object.

- As legacy ASP applications are migrated to ASP.NET, architects will see an opportunity to rid their applications of ASP include files by enforcing standards through ASP.NET user and server controls.

- Third-party ActiveX control developers will be expected to move their controls to the ASP.NET platform as server controls. This provides opportunities for increased competition in the developer tools market, as controls can be offered that provide increased functionality, better design-time support, a richer UI, and so on.

Luckily, the ASP.NET platform provides all the necessary plumbing to build first-class custom controls either from scratch as a new control or through inheriting from an existing control such as the ASP.NET `DataGrid`. Custom-developed controls can fully integrate with the Visual Studio .NET IDE, including support for drag-and-drop layout and positioning as well as providing custom property editors.

To help fill part of the demand for ASP.NET control development, this book offers guidance on how to build controls smartly and efficiently. We cover the basics of building controls as well as the most advanced techniques that you can use to squeeze the most out of the ASP.NET framework. Along the way, we develop several controls with copious source code to give you a head start on your own projects.

Summary

In this chapter, we covered how the primitive nature of web development combined with the challenge to rapidly convert legacy applications to web-enabled applications provides for a challenging application development environment. This demand for web-enabled applications has exploded due to corporations' continued migration of business processes to the Internet. Development platforms such as ASP do not provide enough relief in meeting the ever-increasing requirements and severe time restrictions inherent in web application projects.

ASP has a linear, flat execution model that uses interpreted script along with IIS includes to generate HTML content. ASP does not provide support for modularity, componentization, and task separation between UI layout and business logic processing. On the other hand, tools such as Visual Basic with its RAD capabilities, along with the ActiveX control architecture, helped revolutionize and simplify Win32 development, setting the bar high for needed improvements in the web development model. ASP.NET goes a long way toward bringing the RAD model to web development through compiled code, server control objects, and code-behind.

Drag-and-drop UI design, ViewState, server-side event handling, and many other capabilities of the ASP.NET server control architecture are fully accessible to control developers from within the ASP.NET platform and the Visual Studio .NET IDE. These capabilities are the subject of this book.

Though this chapter is brief, the information we present in this chapter bolsters the argument that there are real benefits to migrating web coding efforts to server control–based development. Also, there is plenty of opportunity and need for ASP.NET control development, whether as part of corporate internal development efforts or as part of the third-party market.

CHAPTER 2

Server Control Basics

IN THIS CHAPTER, we examine the basics of working with server controls. In order to create server controls, it is important to understand how they work. We start by reviewing what a server control provides to clients and we take a look at some of the prebuilt controls supplied by ASP.NET. At the start of this journey, we study the controls' inheritance bloodlines, examining how the namespaces are organized to become familiar with what is available for immediate use in ASP.NET. Because inheritance and composition of existing controls are important timesaving control-building techniques available in ASP.NET, this rapid journey through the object model is well worth the effort.

The Heart and Soul of ASP.NET

Each piece of HTML delivered by an ASP.NET page, whether a `<SPAN>` tag without server-side side interactivity, a complex list control such as the `DataGrid` that supports templates, or the Web Form itself that hosts the HTML tags, is generated by an object that inherits from the `System.Web.UI.Control` base class. These objects, or server controls, are the engine that drives the ASP.NET page-rendering process. The fact that every snippet of rendered HTML exists as a server control allows for a consistent page parsing process that permits easy control configuration and manipulation to create dynamic and powerful content. The clean, consistent object model provided by ASP.NET also facilitates extension through custom server controls that share a common object model.

A "Hello, World" Web Form

The first stop on our journey through the ASP.NET server controls is construction of a simple "Hello, World" Web Form. The first thing we do is create a blank Web Form and drop a few controls from the control Toolbox in Visual Studio .NET onto the Designer surface. The resulting arrangement in the Designer is shown in Figure 2-1 with a `DropDownList` control, a `TextBox` control, two `Label` controls, and a `Button` control. The resulting source code generated by Visual Studio .NET is shown in Listings 2-1 and 2-2.

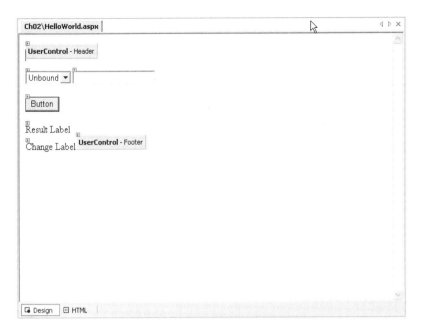

Figure 2-1. The HelloWorld *server control Web Form*

Listing 2-1. The HelloWorld *Server Control .aspx Page*

```
<%@ Register TagPrefix="apressUC" TagName="ControlsBookFooter"
Src="..\ControlsBookFooter.ascx" %>
<%@ Register TagPrefix="apressUC" TagName="ControlsBookHeader"
Src="..\ControlsBookHeader.ascx" %>
<%@ Page language="c#" Codebehind="HelloWorld.aspx.cs" AutoEventWireup="false"
Inherits="ControlsBookWeb.Ch02.HelloWorld" %>
<!DOCTYPE HTML PUBLIC "-//W3C//DTD HTML 4.0 Transitional//EN" >
<HTML>
  <HEAD>
    <title>Ch02 HelloWorld</title>
    <meta name="GENERATOR" Content="Microsoft Visual Studio 7.0">
    <meta name="CODE_LANGUAGE" Content="C#">
    <meta name="vs_defaultClientScript" content="JavaScript">
    <meta name="vs_targetSchema"
     content="http://schemas.microsoft.com/intellisense/ie5">
  </HEAD>
  <body>
    <form id="HelloWorld" runat="server">
      <apressUC:ControlsBookHeader id="Header" runat="server" ChapterNumber=2
      ChapterTitle="Server Control Basics" />
      <H3><%# GetTitle() %></H3>
      <asp:DropDownList id="DropDownList1" runat="server"></asp:DropDownList>
      <asp:TextBox id="TextBox1" runat="server" Font-Italic="True">
      </asp:TextBox><br>
      <br>
```

```
        <asp:Button id="Button1" runat="server" Text="Button"></asp:Button><br>
        <br>
        <asp:Label id="Label1" runat="server">Result Label</asp:Label>
        <br>
        <asp:Label id="Label2" runat="server">Change Label</asp:Label>
        <apressUC:ControlsBookFooter id="Footer" runat="server" />
    </form>
  </body>
</HTML>
```

Listing 2-2. The HelloWorld *Server Control Code-Behind Class File*

```
using System;
using System.Collections;
using System.ComponentModel;
using System.Data;
using System.Drawing;
using System.Web;
using System.Web.SessionState;
using System.Web.UI;
using System.Web.UI.WebControls;
using System.Web.UI.HtmlControls;

namespace ControlsBookWeb.Ch02
{
    public class HelloWorld : System.Web.UI.Page
    {
        protected System.Web.UI.WebControls.TextBox TextBox1;
        protected System.Web.UI.WebControls.Button Button1;
        protected System.Web.UI.WebControls.DropDownList DropDownList1;
        protected System.Web.UI.WebControls.Label Label2;
        protected System.Web.UI.WebControls.Label Label1;

        private void Page_Load(object sender, System.EventArgs e)
        {

            Label1.Text = "";

            if (!Page.IsPostBack)
                LoadDropDownList();

            DataBind();
        }

        private void LoadDropDownList()
        {
            ArrayList list = new ArrayList();
            list.Add("Hello");
            list.Add("Goodbye");
```

```
        DropDownList1.DataSource = list;
    }

    protected string GetTitle()
    {
        return "Ch02 Hello World!";
    }

    #region Web Form Designer generated code
    override protected void OnInit(EventArgs e)
    {
        //
        // CODEGEN: This call is required by the ASP.NET Web Form Designer.
        //
        InitializeComponent();
        base.OnInit(e);
    }

    /// <summary>
    /// Required method for Designer support - do not modify
    /// the contents of this method with the code editor.
    /// </summary>
    private void InitializeComponent()
    {
        this.TextBox1.TextChanged +=
                    new System.EventHandler(this.TextBox_TextChanged);
        this.Button1.Click += new System.EventHandler(this.Button1_Click);
        this.Load += new System.EventHandler(this.Page_Load);

    }
    #endregion

    private void Button1_Click(object sender, System.EventArgs e)
    {
        Label1.Text = DropDownList1.SelectedItem.Value + " " +
                        TextBox1.Text + "!";
    }

    private void TextBox_TextChanged(object sender, System.EventArgs e)
    {
        Label2.Text = "Changed to " + TextBox1.Text;
    }
  }
}
```

The server controls on our "Hello, World" Web Form (specifically, the Label, TextBox, and DropDownList objects) render as HTML and, for the TextBox control, remember what is typed in the control between postback cycles. What is rendered as HTML to the browser is backed by powerful objects that can be wired up to programming logic to perform useful work on the web server. During server-side processing, the object-oriented nature of server controls provides us with three main constructs to interact with controls as objects: properties, methods, and events. We discuss these constructs in the sections that follow.

Control Properties

The most common means of working with a server control is through the properties it exposes. *Properties* allow the control to take information from the Web Form to configure its output or modify its behavior in the HTML generation process.

 NOTE *Properties are different and more powerful than public data members. Properties provide an additional layer of abstraction through the use of "getter" and "setter" methods. Get and Set methods or function calls provide a convenient location for programming logic, such as displaying an error if a value is out of range or otherwise invalid, enforcing read-only access (implementing a Set function only), and so on. Properties can be declared as public, protected, or private.*

Properties are easily viewable in the Properties window available when you select a control in the Visual Studio .NET Design view of the .aspx page. Figure 2-2 shows the Properties window when the TextBox is selected. Notice that the Font property has been configured to show the TextBox's Text property text in italics.

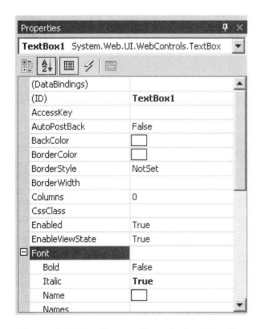

Figure 2-2. The Properties window for the TextBox

The Visual Studio .NET Designer translates the entries in the Properties window into attribute values on the HTML view of the .aspx page. To see this, set a property for a control and then switch to HTML view. Likewise, if you modify attribute values in the HTML view of the .aspx page, these changes will be reflected in the Designer, assuming you typed in the values correctly. This behavior can be very handy for quickly duplicating attributes between controls. Simply copy the HTML version of the attributes and then paste the HTML into the target control that you want to match the original. You can think of the Designer as a code generator that allows you to declaratively work with the look and feel of the ASP.NET application without having to write the code. As an example, the font settings set in the Properties window for the TextBox control described previously map directly to Font attributes:

```
<asp:TextBox id="TextBox1" runat="server" Font-Italic="True"></asp:TextBox>
```

The Label and TextBox controls work a little differently in that the content between the opening and closing tags is controlled by the Text property:

```
<asp:Label id="Label1" runat="server">Result Label</asp:Label>
```

You can also set a control's properties programmatically in the code-behind class file. The "Hello, World" demonstration sets the Text property for Label1 to a blank string each time the Web Form is loaded to overwrite the Label value that is declaratively set in the .aspx page. The activity happens in a method named Page_Load that is mapped to the Page object's Load event:

```
private void Page_Load(object sender, System.EventArgs e)
{
    Label1.Text = "";

    if (!Page.IsPostBack)
        LoadDropDownList();

    DataBind();
}
```

You can also use the properties exposed by the control to read input from the client browser during postback on the server side. The Button click event handling routine in the "Hello, World" Web Form reads the Text property of the TextBox control and the Value property of the SelectedItem property on the DropDownList control to display the greeting to the client of the web browser:

```
 private void Button1_Click(object sender, System.EventArgs e)
{
    Label1.Text = DropDownList1.SelectedItem.Value + " " + TextBox1.Text + "!";
}
```

Control Methods

The second feature exposed by a server control is a collection of object methods. *Methods* typically go beyond the features of a property's Set or Get method. Methods usually perform a more complex action against the control. One of the best examples in ASP.NET of using methods for a server control is the data binding process that links a control with a data source.

NOTE *Methods describe the actions that can be exercised by the object on its data. To put it another way, methods are actions or verbs that significantly manipulate object state. In addition, it is recommended that write-only properties be implemented as methods calls. Note that methods can have return values like a function call, or they can have a return value of void to behave like a procedure call. Like properties, methods can have modifiers of public, private, or protected.*

In the "Hello, World" Web Form example, the Page_Load event checks to see if the page is requested via a form postback or if it was called for the first time as an HTTP "Get" so that the page can generate the initial HTML for the browser, creating the option list. In the postback scenario, a load is not necessary for the DropDownList control via the LoadDropDownList method, because the server control DropDownList1 maintains its internal option list via the Web Form ViewState mechanism for subsequent postback operations to the server. We cover ViewState extensively in Chapter 4.

The page's LoadDropDownList method's first task is to create an ArrayList collection and load it with the string values "Hello" and "Goodbye". It also links the ArrayList to the DropDownList by setting the DataSource property to the ArrayList:

```
private void Page_Load(object sender, System.EventArgs e)
{
    Label1.Text = "";

    if (!Page.IsPostBack)
        LoadDropDownList();

    DataBind();
}

private void LoadDropDownList()
{
    ArrayList list = new ArrayList();
    list.Add("Hello");
    list.Add("Goodbye");

    DropDownList1.DataSource = list;
}
```

Note that we do not call the DataBind method directly for the DropDownList. Instead, we call the DataBind method on the Page class itself. The DataBind method of the Page class recursively calls the DataBind methods for all its child controls that have references to a data source. In this case, when the Page class's DataBind method is invoked, the DropDownList control data-binds to the ArrayList object as shown previously, and the following simple data binding expression for the title of the Web Form retrieves the data and prepares content for final output rendering:

```
<H3><%# GetTitle() %></H3>
```

The expression embedded in the .aspx page is configured to execute the GetTitle method on the Page class and insert the return value inside the contents of an <H3> HTML tag.

Control Events

The final construct used for interacting with controls that we discuss in this chapter is events. *Events* provide a mechanism to notify clients of state changes inside the control. In ASP.NET, such events always coincide with an HTTP POST submission back to the web server. Through the autopostback mechanism, events in ASP.NET appear to behave very much like their counterparts in Visual Basic.

 NOTE *Events provide an object-oriented mechanism for a control to communicate with other controls that care to know about state changes within that control. If events did not exist, then objects would have to resort to polling to know about state changes in other objects. The asynchronous nature of events provides an elegant means for communicating between objects. Event handler methods are generally private to the control class (the event subscriber), as it would not make sense to call event handlers outside the consuming class.*

The Page class in the "Hello, World" example consumes the Click event raised by the Button to read values and sets the first Label control. The Button Click event is easy to map in the Designer by simply double-clicking the button. Double-clicking a control in Visual Studio .NET automatically generates the default event handler for the control. In the case of the Button, it is the Click event. In addition, Visual Studio .NET performs other housekeeping tasks, such as wiring up the event delegate exposed by the Button control to the generated method (in this case, Button1_Click) in the Page class. Events in ASP.NET take advantage of delegates as the infrastructure for this communication between objects. In Chapter 5, we discuss how to work with events in detail.

The Properties window in the Design view of the Visual Studio .NET Designer can help map the events from a control that don't result from double-clicking the control.

NOTE *Use the yellow lightning-bolt icon as a filter at the top of the Properties window to view events exposed by a particular control.*

Each available event for a control is listed on a separate line, and creating a wired-up event handler is as simple as either double-clicking the blank area next to the event name to generate an event with the default naming scheme (*ControlName_EventName*) or typing in a name and pressing the Enter key for the TextBox control (see Figure 2-3).

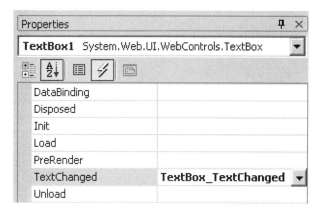

Figure 2-3. Adding an event handler to the TextChanged *event of the* TextBox *control*

The end result of using the Properties window to add the private event handler to the Page class is a method named TextBox_TextChanged that is wired to the TextChanged event of the TextBox control. You can add code to this handling routine to announce the state change of the TextBox control by setting the Text property of the Label2 control on the Web Form:

```
private void TextBox_TextChanged(object sender, System.EventArgs e)
{
   Label2.Text = "Changed to " + TextBox1.Text;
}
```

Visual Studio .NET performs specific actions to map events in the code-behind class files of a C# web application project. This code is located in a #region named "Web Form Designer generated code" that is not visible by default. The first thing the class does is override the OnInit protected method that the page calls when it is initializing itself. The override calls a private InitializeComponent method that performs the event mapping work:

```
#region Web Form Designer generated code
override protected void OnInit(EventArgs e)
{
    //
    // CODEGEN: This call is required by the ASP.NET Web Form Designer.
    //
    InitializeComponent();
    base.OnInit(e);
}

/// <summary>
/// Required method for Designer support - do not modify
/// the contents of this method with the code editor.
/// </summary>
private void InitializeComponent()
{
    this.TextBox1.TextChanged += new System.EventHandler(this.TextBox_TextChanged);
    this.Button1.Click += new System.EventHandler(this.Button1_Click);
    this.Load += new System.EventHandler(this.Page_Load);

}
#endregion
```

The InitializeComponent method has code to map page-level events such as the Page_Load event and events generated from the controls that are protected members of the Page class. It does the delegate registering for each event using the += operator while creating a new instance of the System.EventHandler delegate that wraps the desired event handler. You can clearly see how the TextBox_TextChanged method is wrapped in a delegate that is linked to the TextBox1 control's TextChanged event. This is normally hidden in a #region preprocessor directive that can be expanded or closed to hide the grunge work performed by Visual Studio .NET in the code-behind class file.

The result of all the hard work to this point is the browser view in Figure 2-4, which shows what happens when Dale enters his name and selects a polite greeting.

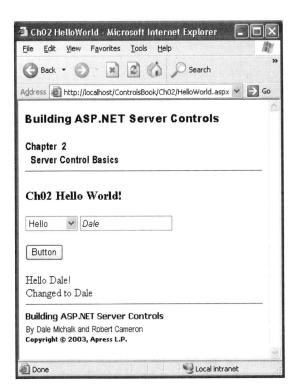

Figure 2-4. The result of the work done with the "Hello, World" demonstration

The Web Page As a Control Tree

In Chapter 1, we alluded to ASP.NET's capability to provide full programmatic access to the tags on an HTML page in an object-oriented way. The architecture in ASP.NET that provides this capability is the .aspx page control tree. In this section we discuss the control tree as it relates to the "Hello, World" example.

At first glance, the "Hello, World" Web Form would seem to contain only a few visible server controls that were explicitly placed on the form. As we alluded to at the beginning of this chapter, the reality is that the entire display surface of the .aspx page becomes a cornucopia of controls during processing. Any HTML content in the Web Form that is not part of the server controls laid out in the Visual Studio .NET Designer is packaged up into a server control that renders the HTML. The control structure of the Web Form can be seen by turning on the Trace features of ASP.NET through setting the Trace=True attribute on the Page directive:

```
<%@ Page language="c#" Trace="True" Codebehind="HelloWorld.aspx.cs"
   AutoEventWireup="false" Inherits="ControlsBookWeb.Ch02.HelloWorld" %>
```

For this feature to work, you need to make sure that tracing is enabled in the trace Extensible Markup Language (XML) element inside of the web.config configuration file for the web application:

```
<trace
enabled="true"
requestLimit="10"
pageOutput="false"
traceMode="SortByTime"
localOnly="true"
/>
```

Figure 2-5 shows the portion of the Trace output that displays the control tree for the Web Form.

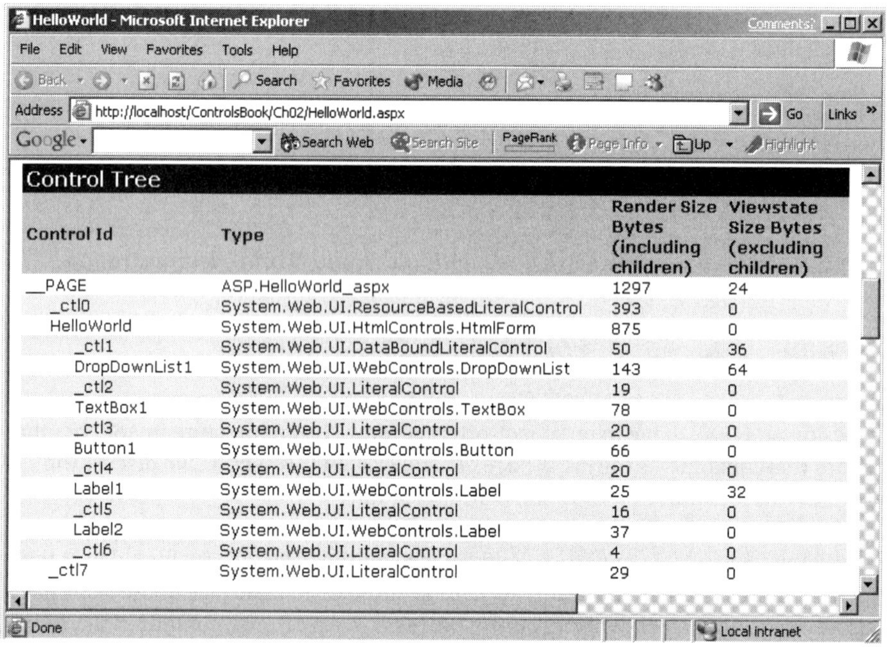

Control Id	Type	Render Size Bytes (including children)	Viewstate Size Bytes (excluding children)
__PAGE	ASP.HelloWorld_aspx	1297	24
_ctl0	System.Web.UI.ResourceBasedLiteralControl	393	0
HelloWorld	System.Web.UI.HtmlControls.HtmlForm	875	0
_ctl1	System.Web.UI.DataBoundLiteralControl	50	36
DropDownList1	System.Web.UI.WebControls.DropDownList	143	64
_ctl2	System.Web.UI.LiteralControl	19	0
TextBox1	System.Web.UI.WebControls.TextBox	78	0
_ctl3	System.Web.UI.LiteralControl	20	0
Button1	System.Web.UI.WebControls.Button	66	0
_ctl4	System.Web.UI.LiteralControl	20	0
Label1	System.Web.UI.WebControls.Label	25	32
_ctl5	System.Web.UI.LiteralControl	16	0
Label2	System.Web.UI.WebControls.Label	37	0
_ctl6	System.Web.UI.LiteralControl	4	0
_ctl7	System.Web.UI.LiteralControl	29	0

Figure 2-5. Tracing the controls on the "Hello, World" Web Form

The X-ray vision provided by the Trace feature dissects the Web Form in gory detail. At the top is the `Page` control that represents the Web Form of type ASP.HelloWorld_aspx. Below it are the server controls that you would expect to be there: `DropDownList`,

`TextBox`, `Button`, and `Label`. What you wouldn't expect to see in the trace is the `ResourceBasedLiteralControl`, `HtmlForm`, `DataBoundLiteralControl`, and `LiteralControl` objects in the control tree dump.

`HtmlForm` is responsible for representing the `<FORM>` tag on the .aspx page and providing the missing method and action properties to ensure the page is always sent back to the original URL via an HTTP POST. The server control form looks like the following in the .aspx page:

```
<form id="HelloWorld" runat="server">
```

The `HtmlForm` renders HTML with all the necessary information to post the page back to itself, as shown in the following code. This allows each control on the page to remember its previous state via the ViewState mechanism and raise the appropriate server control event.

```
<form name="HelloWorld" method="post" action="HelloWorld.aspx" id="HelloWorld">
```

The literal controls have the responsibility for rendering the generic text and HTML tags in the Web Form without much of a server-side presence. These are the "flyweight" classes of the ASP.NET server control framework. The literal controls pick up text or tags that do not have the `runat="server"` attribute identifying them as a server control. The `LiteralControl` class is the simplest of the three shown in the control dump because it is a pure text-in and text-out operation. Notice how the control tree picks up the `<BR>` tags between the other server controls as well as the closing `<BODY>` and `<HTML>` tags as `LiteralControl` objects. The `ResourceBasedLiteralControl` does the same thing but is geared toward the header section of the HTML document. It is an internally implemented class in the ASP.NET framework that is not creatable or accessible by the programmer.

The `DataBoundLiteralControl` is the most complex of the literal controls because it represents a data-binding expression like the one in the document that binds to the `GetTitle()` method of the `Page` object. It has a `DataBind` method that must be called by the `Page` class to resolve its value, just like the `DropDownList` control had to read from the `ArrayList` data source in its `DataBind` operations.

The Root Controls

The previous demonstration highlighted the server control–centric nature of the ASP.NET Web Form page execution process. We now shift gears to briefly discuss where the various controls exist inside the .NET Framework and what features they provide in rendering HTML. The controls are factored into three primary namespaces in the .NET Framework: `System.Web.UI`, `System.Web.UI.HtmlControls`, and `System.Web.UI.WebControls` (see Figure 2-6).

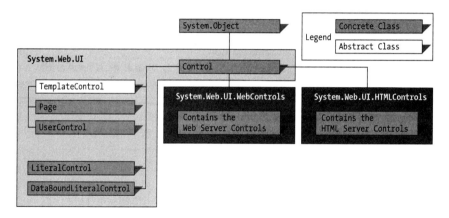

Figure 2-6. The major namespaces of ASP.NET under `System.Web.UI`

First up is the `System.Web.UI` namespace.

The System.Web.UI Namespace

At the top of the hierarchy, and our first destination, is the `System.Web.UI` namespace and its root controls. It contains the well-traveled `Control` class, which is the mandatory parent class for all objects that want to call themselves controls. Directly inheriting from the `Control` class in this namespace is a set of specialized classes that implement the Web Form through the `Page` class, the user control through the `UserControl` class, and the literal controls. The `Page` class and the literal controls are discussed in detail in the previous "Hello, World" Web Form demonstration. We focus in more detail on the `UserControl` class at the end of the chapter when we cover control creation. In the next section, we discuss the `System.Web.UI.HtmlControls` namespace.

System.Web.UI.HtmlControls

The controls under `System.Web.UI.HtmlControls` have the capability to take existing HTML content and make it available as a server control with the addition of a `runat="server"` attribute. The canonical example of this type of control is turning an HTML text box into a server control:

```
<input type="text" id="name" runat="server"/>
```

The ASP.NET parsing engine is responsible for mapping the HTML tag to the correct control type in `System.Web.UI.HtmlControls` when it sees this marker attribute. The preceding example adds an instance of the `HtmlInputText` control to the Web Form's control collection.

NOTE *If you want to modify or interact with any of the literal controls on the server side, you have two options. One option is to walk the page's control tree collection to find the desired control. The other option is declare the control in the code-behind class file. In the previous input example, the declaration would look like this:* `protected System.Web.UI.HtmlControls.HtmlInputText name;`

Although they may look like their HTML cousins, these controls set themselves apart by remembering state, raising events, allowing themselves to be programmatically manipulated, and providing other value-added services such as file upload when the form post has reached the Web. The full list of HTML controls available in the `System.Web.UI.HtmlControls` namespace is depicted in Figure 2-7.

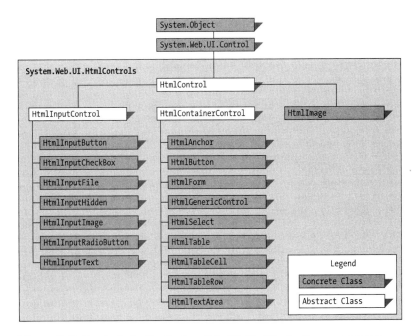

Figure 2-7. Controls in the `System.Web.UI.HtmlControls` *namespace*

Table 2-1 is useful for figuring out which of the HTML tags maps to a specific HTML control. Note that some of controls (such as the `HtmlInputText` control) map to multiple HTML tags on an .aspx page. For tags that do not have a specific control mapping, the `HtmlGeneric` control is used to represent them as a server-side control object when they have a `runat="server"` attribute.

Table 2-1. Mapping HTML Tags to Their HTML Server Control Counterparts

HTML TAG	HTML SERVER CONTROL
`<form>`	`HtmlForm`
`<input type="text">`	`HtmlInputText`
`<input type="password">`	`HtmlInputText`
`<input type="radio">`	`HtmlInputRadioButton`
`<input type="checkbox">`	`HtmlInputCheckBox`
`<input type="submit">`	`HtmlInputButton`
`<input type="hidden">`	`HtmlInputHidden`
`<input type="button">`	`HtmlInputButton`
`<input type="reset">`	`HtmlInputButton`
`<input type="image">`	`HtmlInputImage`
`<input type="file">`	`HtmlInputFile`
`<button>`	`HtmlButton`
`<select>`	`HtmlSelect`
`<textarea>`	`HtmlTextArea`
`<img>`	`HtmlImage`
`<a>`	`HtmlAnchor`
`<table>`	`HtmlTable`
`<tr>`	`HtmlTableRow`
`<td>`	`HtmlTableCell`
All other tags	`HtmlGenericControl`

HTML Controls Demonstration

To examine the `System.Web.UI.HtmlControls` namespace, we examine the execution of several demonstrations showing the controls in action. The first demonstration dynamically constructs an HTML table from X and Y coordinates that are present on the Web Form using the code shown in Listings 2-3 and 2-4. We discuss this code following the listings.

Listing 2-3. The `HTMLControls` *Web Form .aspx Page*

```
<%@ Register TagPrefix="apressUC" TagName="ControlsBookFooter"
Src="..\ControlsBookFooter.ascx" %>
<%@ Register TagPrefix="apressUC" TagName="ControlsBookHeader"
Src="..\ControlsBookHeader.ascx" %>
<%@ Page language="c#" Codebehind="HtmlControls.aspx.cs" AutoEventWireup="false"
Inherits="ControlsBookWeb.Ch02.HtmlControls" %>
<!DOCTYPE HTML PUBLIC "-//W3C//DTD HTML 4.0 Transitional//EN" >
<HTML>
  <HEAD>
    <title>Ch02 HtmlControls</title>
    <meta name="GENERATOR" Content="Microsoft Visual Studio 7.0">
```

```
    <meta name="CODE_LANGUAGE" Content="C#">
    <meta name="vs_defaultClientScript" content="JavaScript">
    <meta name="vs_targetSchema"
     content="http://schemas.microsoft.com/intellisense/ie5">
  </HEAD>
  <body>
    <form id="HtmlControls" method="post" runat="server">
      <apressUC:ControlsBookHeader id="Header" runat="server"
       ChapterNumber=2 ChapterTitle="Server Control Basics"/>
      <h3>Ch02 HTML Controls</h3>
      X <input type="text" id="XTextBox" runat="server"><br>
      <br>
      Y <input type="text" id="YTextBox" runat="server"><br>
      <br>
      <input type="submit" id="Button1" runat="server" Value="Build Table"><br>
      <br>
      <span id="Span1" runat="server"></span>
      <apressUC:ControlsBookFooter id="Footer" runat="server" />
    </form>
  </body>
</HTML>
```

Listing 2-4. The HTMLControls *Code-Behind Class File*

```
using System;
using System.Collections;
using System.ComponentModel;
using System.Data;
using System.Drawing;
using System.Web;
using System.Web.SessionState;
using System.Web.UI;
using System.Web.UI.WebControls;
using System.Web.UI.HtmlControls;

namespace ControlsBookWeb.Ch02
{
    public class HtmlControls : System.Web.UI.Page
    {
        protected System.Web.UI.HtmlControls.HtmlInputText XTextBox;
        protected System.Web.UI.HtmlControls.HtmlInputText YTextBox;
        protected System.Web.UI.HtmlControls.HtmlGenericControl Span1;
        protected System.Web.UI.HtmlControls.HtmlInputButton Button1;

        private void Page_Load(object sender, System.EventArgs e)
        {

        }
```

```
#region Web Form Designer generated code
override protected void OnInit(EventArgs e)
{
   //
   // CODEGEN: This call is required by the ASP.NET Web Form Designer.
   //
   InitializeComponent();
   base.OnInit(e);
}

/// <summary>
/// Required method for Designer support - do not modify
/// the contents of this method with the code editor.
/// </summary>
private void InitializeComponent()
{
   this.Button1.ServerClick +=
            new System.EventHandler(this.Button1_ServerClick);
   this.Load += new System.EventHandler(this.Page_Load);

}
#endregion

private void Button1_ServerClick(object sender, System.EventArgs e)
{
   int xDim = Convert.ToInt32(XTextBox.Value);
   int yDim = Convert.ToInt32(YTextBox.Value);
   BuildTable(xDim,yDim);
}

private void BuildTable(int xDim, int yDim)
{
   HtmlTable table;
   HtmlTableRow row;
   HtmlTableCell cell;
   HtmlGenericControl content;

   table = new HtmlTable();
   table.Border = 1;
   for (int y=0; y < yDim; y++)
   {
      row = new HtmlTableRow();
      for (int x=0; x < xDim; x++)
      {
         cell = new HtmlTableCell();
         cell.Style.Add("font","16pt verdana bold italic");
         cell.Style.Add("background-color","red");
         cell.Style.Add("color","yellow");

         content = new HtmlGenericControl("SPAN");
         content.InnerHtml = "X:" + x.ToString() +
            "Y:" + y.ToString();
```

```
            cell.Controls.Add(content);
            row.Cells.Add(cell);
        }
        table.Rows.Add(row);
    }

    Span1.Controls.Add(table);
  }
 }
}
```

Dynamically adding controls to an existing control structure is a common way to implement Web Forms that vary their content and structure according to the user's input. The BuildTable method encapsulates this dynamic functionality in the HTML Controls demonstration by rendering the table when passed X and Y parameters. The variables passed in to BuildTable are retrieved using the Value property of the HtmlInputText controls:

```
int xDim = Convert.ToInt32(XTextBox.Value);
int yDim = Convert.ToInt32(YTextBox.Value);
BuildTable(xDim,yDim);
```

The bulk of the work in the HTML Controls demonstration is located in the BuildTable method. This method starts out by creating an HtmlTable control representing the outer <TABLE> tag and then jumps into nested For loops to add HtmlTableRow controls representing the <TR> tags along with HtmlTableCell controls rendering <TD> tags.

One of the more interesting sections of this routine is the cell creation and CSS styling configuration code. Once the HtmlTableCell control is created, the CSS styles are set as strings and then added to the Style property representing the cell's CSS attributes. This is a manual, string-based process that is not helped by any type or enumeration from the System.Web.UI.HtmlControls namespace:

```
cell = new HtmlTableCell();
cell.Style.Add("font","16pt verdana bold italic");
cell.Style.Add("background-color","red");
cell.Style.Add("color","yellow");
```

After the styling is set, the cell adds an HtmlGenericControl representing a <SPAN> tag to its control collection. The HtmlGenericControl's InnerHtml, or content, is then set to the "X" and "Y" values for the cell. The result is that the <SPAN> tag is nested in the table cell's <TD> tag. The final step in the process is to add the cell to its parent row:

```
content = new HtmlGenericControl("SPAN");
content.InnerHtml = "X:" + x.ToString() +
   "Y:" + y.ToString();
cell.Controls.Add(content);
row.Cells.Add(cell);
```

The HTML rendered at the browser client shows the direct insertion of the CSS attributes into the `<TD>` tag and the `HtmlGenericControl` production of the `<SPAN>` content:

```
<td style="font:16pt verdana bold italic;
background-color:red;color:yellow;">
<SPAN>X:0Y:0</SPAN>
</td>
```

Figure 2-8 shows the output of all this work.

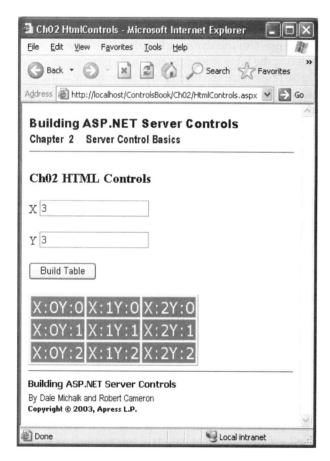

Figure 2-8. Output from the HTML Controls Web Form

File Upload Demonstration

This section's File Upload Web Form demonstration highlights the use of the
HtmlInputFile control and its capability to work in a file upload scenario. To get this
working properly, you need to set up the Web Form to instruct the browser that the file
upload features of HTTP should be used. The required addition to the <FORM> tag on the
.aspx page to make the file upload process happen is the enctype="multipart/form-data"
attribute. Your mileage may vary as to whether your web server has permissions to
write to the C:\temp directory to save the file. Please consult the ASP.NET documentation for information on the security permissions required so that the ASP.NET worker
process can write data to the local file system. Listings 2-5 and 2-6 show the code for
the File Upload demonstration.

Listing 2-5. The FileUpload *Web Form .aspx Page*

```
<%@ Register TagPrefix="apressUC" TagName="ControlsBookFooter"
Src="..\ControlsBookFooter.ascx" %>
<%@ Register TagPrefix="apressUC" TagName="ControlsBookHeader"
Src="..\ControlsBookHeader.ascx" %>
<%@ Page language="c#" Codebehind="FileUpload.aspx.cs"
AutoEventWireup="false"
Inherits="ControlsBookWeb.Ch02.FileUpload" %>
<!DOCTYPE HTML PUBLIC "-//W3C//DTD HTML 4.0 Transitional//EN" >
<HTML>
  <HEAD>
    <title>Ch02 File Upload</title>
    <meta name="GENERATOR" Content="Microsoft Visual Studio 7.0">
    <meta name="CODE_LANGUAGE" Content="C#">
    <meta name="vs_defaultClientScript" content="JavaScript">
    <meta name="vs_targetSchema"
        content="http://schemas.microsoft.com/intellisense/ie5">
  </HEAD>
  <body>
    <form id="FileUpload" enctype="multipart/form-data"
          method="post" runat="server">
      <apressUC:ControlsBookHeader id="Header" runat="server"
          ChapterNumber=2 ChapterTitle="Server Control Basics"/>
      <h3>Ch02 File Upload</h3>
      File: <input type="file" id="File" runat="server"><br>
      <br>
      Upload FileName: <INPUT type="text" id="Name" runat="server" NAME="Name"><br>
      <br>
      <input type="submit" value="Upload" runat="server"
        id="Submit1" name="Submit1"><br>
      <br>
      <div id="result" runat="server"></div>
      <apressUC:ControlsBookFooter id="Footer" runat="server" />
    </form>
  </body>
</HTML>
```

Listing 2-6. The FileUpload *Code-Behind Class File*

```
using System;
using System.Collections;
using System.ComponentModel;
using System.Data;
using System.Drawing;
using System.Web;
using System.Web.SessionState;
using System.Web.UI;
using System.Web.UI.WebControls;
using System.Web.UI.HtmlControls;

namespace ControlsBookWeb.Ch02
{
    public class FileUpload : System.Web.UI.Page
    {
        protected System.Web.UI.HtmlControls.HtmlInputFile File;
        protected System.Web.UI.HtmlControls.HtmlInputButton Submit1;
        protected System.Web.UI.HtmlControls.HtmlInputText Name;
        protected System.Web.UI.HtmlControls.HtmlGenericControl result;

        private void Page_Load(object sender, System.EventArgs e)
        {

        }

        #region Web Form Designer generated code
        override protected void OnInit(EventArgs e)
        {
            //
            // CODEGEN: This call is required by the ASP.NET Web Form Designer.
            //
            InitializeComponent();
            base.OnInit(e);
        }

        /// <summary>
        /// Required method for Designer support - do not modify
        /// the contents of this method with the code editor.
        /// </summary>
        private void InitializeComponent()
        {
            this.Submit1.ServerClick +=
                new System.EventHandler(this.Submit1_ServerClick);
            this.Load += new System.EventHandler(this.Page_Load);

        }
        #endregion

        private void Submit1_ServerClick(object sender, System.EventArgs e)
        {
```

```
        if (File.PostedFile != null)
        {
            HttpPostedFile file = File.PostedFile;
            string filename = @"C:\temp\" + Name.Value;
            file.SaveAs(filename);
            result.InnerHtml = "Source File: " + file.FileName + "<BR>" +
                "Saved File: " + filename + "." + "<BR>" +
                "Length: " + file.ContentLength + "<BR>" +
                "Type: " + file.ContentType + "<BR>";
        }
        else
            result.InnerHtml = "No file posted!";
    }
  }
}
```

The HtmlInputFile server control provides a very clean abstraction of what can be a cumbersome process. The PostedFile property exposes an HttpPostedFile object that allows the Web Form to save the file to disk or work with it as a stream through the InputStream property. Our example takes the first option, using the Save method to write it to the C:\temp directory on the web server. The example also uses an HtmlInputText control to save the new filename and an HtmlGenericControl named "result" that renders a <DIV> tag to display the results of the operation through its InnerHtml property. Figure 2-9 shows the output of the File Upload demonstration.

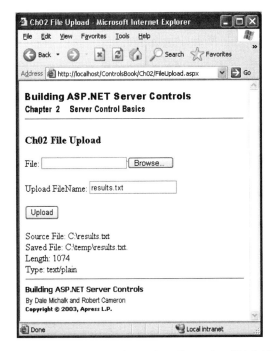

Figure 2-9. Output from the File Upload Web Form

The System.Web.UI.WebControls Namespace

Like the HTML controls in the previous section, the web controls occupy a separate namespace in the .NET Framework—namely, System.Web.UI.WebControls. Figure 2-10 shows the graphical breakdown of the namespace and the myriad server control objects available.

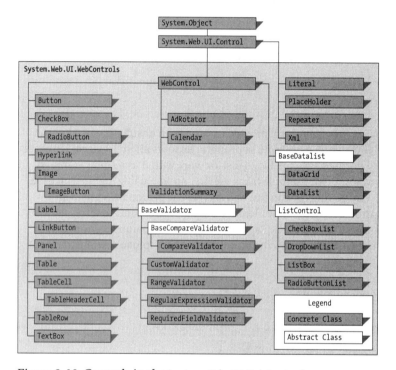

Figure 2-10. Controls in the System.Web.UI.WebControls *namespace*

The controls under the System.Web.UI.WebControls namespace are grouped into a few primary categories:

- Simple

- List

- Rich

- Validation

The following sections cover each category.

Simple Controls

The *simple* controls are the web control cousins to the HTML controls in that they generally map one-to-one to an HTML tag. A good example of this is the mapping of the Label control to the <SPAN> tag and the TextBox control to the <INPUT type="text"> tag.

Because simple controls map closely to a single HTML tag, we bring back the ever-popular tag-to-control mapping table in a manner similar to our discussion in the last section on HTML controls. Like the previous table, some controls in Table 2-2 handle more than one tag by property settings. The LiteralControl from the System.Web.UI namespace is used for tags that are not represented in System.Web.UI.WebControls as a control.

Table 2-2. Mapping HTML Tags to Their Web Control Counterparts

HTML TAG	SIMPLE WEB CONTROL
<input type="text">	TextBox w/TextMode=Single
<input type="password">	TextBox w/TextMode=Password
<textarea>	TextBox w/TextMode=MultiLine
<input type="checkbox">	CheckBox
<input type="radio">	RadioButton
<input type="submit">	Button
<input type="image">	ImageButton
<button>	Button
<select>	DropDownList
<select size=3>	SelectList w/Rows=4
<textarea>	HtmlTextArea
<img>	Image
<a>	HyperLink, LinkButton
<table>	Table
<tr>	TableRow
<td>	TableCell
<table>	Panel
<span>	Label

Simple Controls Demonstration

The following Simple Controls demonstration is a port of the original HTML Controls demonstration to show the same output using dynamically built controls from the System.Web.UI.WebControls namespace. Listings 2-7 and 2-8 contain the code.

Listing 2-7. The SimpleControls *Web Form .aspx Page*

```
<%@ Page language="c#" Codebehind="SimpleControls.aspx.cs"
AutoEventWireup="false" Inherits="ControlsBookWeb.Ch02.SimpleControls" %>
<%@ Register TagPrefix="apressUC" TagName="ControlsBookHeader"
Src="..\ControlsBookHeader.ascx" %>
<%@ Register TagPrefix="apressUC" TagName="ControlsBookFooter"
Src="..\ControlsBookFooter.ascx" %>
<!DOCTYPE HTML PUBLIC "-//W3C//DTD HTML 4.0 Transitional//EN" >
<HTML>
  <HEAD>
    <title>Ch02 Simple Controls</title>
    <meta content="Microsoft Visual Studio 7.0" name="GENERATOR">
    <meta content="C#" name="CODE_LANGUAGE">
    <meta content="JavaScript" name="vs_defaultClientScript">
    <meta content="http://schemas.microsoft.com/intellisense/ie5"
            name="vs_targetSchema">
  </HEAD>
  <body>
    <form id="SimpleControls" method="post" runat="server">
      <apressUC:ControlsBookHeader id="Header" runat="server" />
      <h3>Ch02 Simple Controls</h3>
      X
      <asp:textbox id="XTextBox" runat="server"></asp:textbox><br>
      <br>
      Y
      <asp:textbox id="YTextBox" runat="server"></asp:textbox><br>
      <br>
      <asp:button id="Button1" runat="server" Text="Build Table"></asp:button><br>
      <br>
      <asp:placeholder id="PlaceHolder1" runat="server"></asp:placeholder>
      <apressUC:ControlsBookFooter id="Footer" runat="server" />
    </form>
  </body>
</HTML>
```

Listing 2-8. The SimpleControls *Code-Behind Class File*

```
using System;
using System.Collections;
using System.ComponentModel;
using System.Data;
using System.Drawing;
using System.Web;
using System.Web.SessionState;
using System.Web.UI;
using System.Web.UI.WebControls;
using System.Web.UI.HtmlControls;
```

```csharp
namespace ControlsBookWeb.Ch02
{
    public class SimpleControls : System.Web.UI.Page
    {
        protected System.Web.UI.WebControls.TextBox XTextBox;
        protected System.Web.UI.WebControls.TextBox YTextBox;
        protected System.Web.UI.WebControls.PlaceHolder PlaceHolder1;
        protected System.Web.UI.WebControls.Button Button1;
        protected ControlsBookWeb.ControlsBookHeader Header ;

        private void Page_Load(object sender, System.EventArgs e)
        {
            Header.ChapterNumber = 2 ;
            Header.ChapterTitle = "Server Control Basics" ;
        }

        #region Web Form Designer generated code
        override protected void OnInit(EventArgs e)
        {
            //
            // CODEGEN: This call is required by the ASP.NET Web Form Designer.
            //
            InitializeComponent();
            base.OnInit(e);
        }

        /// <summary>
        /// Required method for Designer support - do not modify
        /// the contents of this method with the code editor.
        /// </summary>
        private void InitializeComponent()
        {
            this.Button1.Click += new System.EventHandler(this.Button1_Click);
            this.Load += new System.EventHandler(this.Page_Load);

        }
        #endregion

        private void Button1_Click(object sender, System.EventArgs e)
        {
            int xDim = Convert.ToInt32(XTextBox.Text);
            int yDim = Convert.ToInt32(YTextBox.Text);
            BuildTable(xDim,yDim);
        }

        private void BuildTable(int xDim, int yDim)
        {
            Table table;
            TableRow row;
            TableCell cell;
            Literal content;
```

```
table = new Table();
table.BorderWidth = 1;
table.BorderStyle = BorderStyle.Ridge;
for (int y=0; y < yDim; y++)
{
    row = new TableRow();
    for (int x=0; x < xDim; x++)
    {
        cell = new TableCell();
        cell.BackColor = Color.Blue;
        cell.BorderWidth = 1;
        cell.ForeColor = Color.Yellow;
        cell.Font.Name = "Verdana";
        cell.Font.Size = 16;
        cell.Font.Bold = true;
        cell.Font.Italic = true;

        content = new Literal();
        content.Text = "<SPAN>X:" + x.ToString() +
            "Y:" + y.ToString() + "</SPAN>";
        cell.Controls.Add(content);
        row.Cells.Add(cell);
    }
    table.Rows.Add(row);
}
PlaceHolder1.Controls.Add(table);
        }
    }
}
```

Comparing the Simple Controls demonstration to the HTML Controls demonstration shows little difference beyond changes to control names and namespaces. One minor difference is the fact that in the Simple Controls demonstration, a `PlaceHolder` control (yes, there really is a `PlaceHolder` class!) acts as the container for holding the cell content. The `PlaceHolder` control does not have a UI; instead, it renders only the UI of its child controls. This is contrast to the HTML Controls demonstration, which used `HtmlGenericControl` representing a `<SPAN>` tag for holding the cell content.

The bigger difference between the two examples is the CSS-style configuration. In the HTML Controls demonstration, we had to use a more explicit syntax without the benefit of help from the control object model or IntelliSense in Visual Studio .NET. However, in the Simple Controls demonstration, we have full access to the assistance provided by the Framework and Visual Studio .NET. The following code snippet shows how easy it is to set color and other font styling in the Simple Controls demonstration:

```
cell = new TableCell();
cell.BackColor = Color.Blue;
cell.BorderWidth = 1;
cell.ForeColor = Color.Yellow;
cell.Font.Name = "Verdana";
```

```
cell.Font.Size = 16;
cell.Font.Bold = true;
cell.Font.Italic = true;
```

The content rendered in the browser demonstrates the nice abstraction of CSS styling made available to controls by the System.Web.UI.WebControls namespace:

```
<td style="color:Yellow;background-color:Blue;border-width:1px;border-style:solid;

font-family:Verdana;font-size:16pt;font-weight:bold;font-style:italic;">
<SPAN>X:0Y:0</SPAN>
</td>
```

Figure 2-11 shows the output from the Simple Controls demonstration.

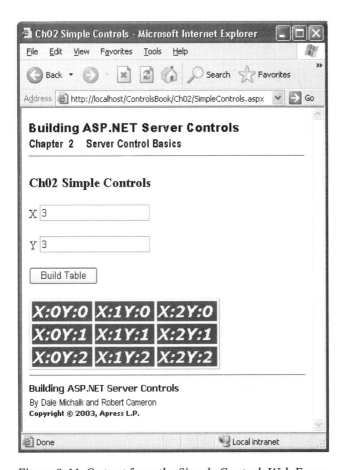

Figure 2-11. Output from the Simple Controls Web Form

List Controls

List controls provide enhanced capabilities beyond those of the simple controls by generating their content using an external data source. They range from the simple CheckBoxList and RadioButtonList controls, which build a group of simple HTML tags, to the more complex DataGrid, DataList, and Repeater controls, which support a highly customizable UI. List controls are a key instrument in the toolkit of the ASP.NET developer because they provide broad functionality when tasked with getting a data-oriented web site up and running quickly.

List Controls Demonstration

The following List Controls demonstration with source code provided in Listings 2-9 and 2-10 uses a Repeater control to build an HTML table representing data from the SQL Server Northwind sample database. The demonstration illustrates two key features of ASP.NET UI development: templates and data binding, which we cover in Chapter 7.

With templates and data binding, the programmer can focus on building the data access class library in the n-tier model and hooking up the control to a data source via data binding in the code-behind page, while the UI designer can tweak the HTML content and templates on the .aspx page to ensure that it is displayed according to the requirements of the web development project.

Listing 2-9. The ListControls *Web Form .aspx Page*

```
<%@ Register TagPrefix="apressUC" TagName="ControlsBookFooter"
Src="..\ControlsBookFooter.ascx" %>
<%@ Register TagPrefix="apressUC" TagName="ControlsBookHeader"
Src="..\ControlsBookHeader.ascx" %>
<%@ Page language="c#" Codebehind="ListControls.aspx.cs" AutoEventWireup="false"
Inherits="ControlsBookWeb.Ch02.ListControls" %>
<!DOCTYPE HTML PUBLIC "-//W3C//DTD HTML 4.0 Transitional//EN" >
<HTML>
  <HEAD>
    <title>Ch02 List Controls</title>
    <meta content="Microsoft Visual Studio 7.0" name="GENERATOR">
    <meta content="C#" name="CODE_LANGUAGE">
    <meta content="JavaScript" name="vs_defaultClientScript">
    <meta content=
      "http://schemas.microsoft.com/intellisense/ie5" name="vs_targetSchema">
  </HEAD>
  <body>
    <form id="ListControls" method="post" runat="server">
      <apressUC:ControlsBookHeader id="Header" runat="server"
ChapterNumber=2 ChapterTitle="Server Control Basics"/>
      <h3>Ch02 List Controls</h3>
      <asp:repeater id="Repeater1" runat="server">
        <HeaderTemplate>
```

```
            <table>
              <th>
                Customer ID</th><th>Contact Name</th>
         <th>Contact Title</th><th>Company Name</th>
        </HeaderTemplate>
        <ItemTemplate>
          <tr bgcolor="Silver">
            <td><%# DataBinder.Eval(Container.DataItem,"CustomerID") %></td>
            <td><%# DataBinder.Eval(Container.DataItem,"ContactName") %></td>
            <td><%# DataBinder.Eval(Container.DataItem,"ContactTitle") %></td>
            <td><%# DataBinder.Eval(Container.DataItem,"CompanyName") %></td>
          </tr>
        </ItemTemplate>
        <AlternatingItemTemplate>
          <tr bgcolor="White">
            <td><%# DataBinder.Eval(Container.DataItem,"CustomerID") %></td>
            <td><%# DataBinder.Eval(Container.DataItem,"ContactName") %></td>
            <td><%# DataBinder.Eval(Container.DataItem,"ContactTitle") %></td>
            <td><%# DataBinder.Eval(Container.DataItem,"CompanyName") %></td>
          </tr>
        </AlternatingItemTemplate>
        <FooterTemplate>
          </table>
        </FooterTemplate>
      </asp:repeater><br>
      <apressUC:ControlsBookFooter id="Footer" runat="server" />
    </form>
  </body>
</HTML>
```

Listing 2-10. The ListControls *Web Form Code-Behind Class File*

```
using System;
using System.Collections;
using System.ComponentModel;
using System.Data;
using System.Data.SqlClient;
using System.Drawing;
using System.Web;
using System.Web.SessionState;
using System.Web.UI;
using System.Web.UI.WebControls;
using System.Web.UI.HtmlControls;

namespace ControlsBookWeb.Ch02
{
    public class ListControls : System.Web.UI.Page
    {
        protected System.Web.UI.WebControls.Button Button1;
```

```
        protected System.Web.UI.WebControls.Repeater Repeater1;

        private void Page_Load(object sender, System.EventArgs e)
        {
           Repeater1.DataSource = GetCustomerData();
           Repeater1.DataBind();
        }

        private DataSet GetCustomerData()
        {
           SqlConnection conn =
              new SqlConnection(
"Server=(local);Database=Northwind;Integrated Security=true;");
           conn.Open();

           SqlDataAdapter da =
              new SqlDataAdapter (
"SELECT CustomerID, ContactName, ContactTitle, CompanyName
FROM Customers WHERE CustomerID LIKE '[AB]%'",
              conn);
           DataSet ds = new DataSet();
           da.Fill(ds,"Customers");

           return ds;
        }

        #region Web Form Designer generated code
        override protected void OnInit(EventArgs e)
        {
           //
           // CODEGEN: This call is required by the ASP.NET Web Form Designer.
           //
           InitializeComponent();
           base.OnInit(e);
        }

        /// <summary>
        /// Required method for Designer support - do not modify
        /// the contents of this method with the code editor.
        /// </summary>
        private void InitializeComponent()
        {
           this.Load += new System.EventHandler(this.Page_Load);

        }
        #endregion
     }
}
```

The data source in the List Controls example is a `DataSet` that contains rows from the Customers table in the Northwind database that have `CustomerID` column values starting with *A* or *B*. The `DataSet` is built using ADO.NET code in the `GetCustomerData` helper method.

The returned `DataSet` from the `GetCustomerData` helper method is bound to the `Repeater1` control via its `DataSource` property on each page request. We call the `DataBind` method on the `Repeater1` control to have it examine the contents of the data source and build up its control structure by evaluating each row of the data source with respect to its declared UI templates:

```
private void Page_Load(object sender, System.EventArgs e)
{
 Repeater1.DataSource = GetCustomerData();
 Repeater1.DataBind();
}
```

The `Repeater` control is templated to produce an HTML table with HTML rows representing each data row in the Customers `DataSet`. The `HeaderTemplate` and `FooterTemplate` give us the table opening and closing tags, and the `ItemTemplate` and `AlternatingItemTemplate` give us the structure for each row in the table:

```
<ItemTemplate>
    <tr bgcolor="Silver">
        <td><%# DataBinder.Eval(Container.DataItem,"CustomerID") %></td>
        <td><%# DataBinder.Eval(Container.DataItem,"ContactName") %></td>
        <td><%# DataBinder.Eval(Container.DataItem,"ContactTitle") %></td>
        <td><%# DataBinder.Eval(Container.DataItem,"CompanyName") %></td>
    </tr>
</ItemTemplate>
<AlternatingItemTemplate>
    <tr bgcolor="White">
        <td><%# DataBinder.Eval(Container.DataItem,"CustomerID") %></td>
        <td><%# DataBinder.Eval(Container.DataItem,"ContactName") %></td>
        <td><%# DataBinder.Eval(Container.DataItem,"ContactTitle") %></td>
        <td><%# DataBinder.Eval(Container.DataItem,"CompanyName") %></td>
    </tr>
</AlternatingItemTemplate>
```

The data in each row of the `DataSet` is available via the `Container.DataItem` reference available for use inside the template content. A string index name like "CustomerID" is used to grab a particular column for display. Although we do prefer to use code-behind over inline script as much as possible, `DataBinder.Eval` is a late-bound formatting method that we use to keep from having to do ugly casts to satisfy the strongly typed nature of C# and ASP.NET. Figure 2-12 shows the output from the List Controls demonstration.

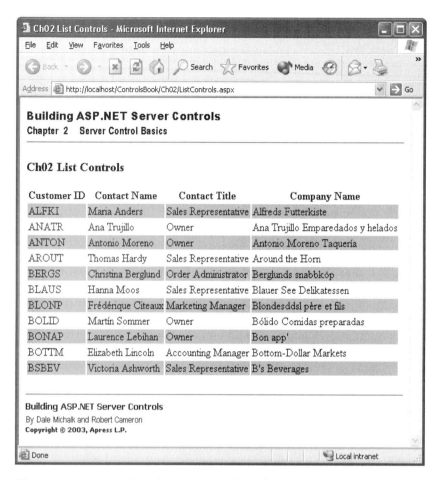

Figure 2-12. Output from the List Controls Web Form

Rich Controls

The list controls are nice for working with data sources and building templated user interfaces, but sometimes a web project needs more help from a control when building dauntingly complex pieces of HTML content. This is the domain of *rich* controls, such as the Calendar and AdRotator, in System.Web.UI.WebControls. They make the hard in terms of generated HTML appear easy, as they turn little in the way of required development into significant HTML output.

Rich Controls Demonstration

The Rich Controls Web Form demonstration shows the Calendar control in action. The source code is provided in Listings 2-11 and 2-12.

Listing 2-11. The RichControls *Web Form .aspx Page*

```
<%@ Register TagPrefix="apressUC" TagName="ControlsBookFooter"
Src="..\ControlsBookFooter.ascx" %>
<%@ Register TagPrefix="apressUC" TagName="ControlsBookHeader"
Src="..\ControlsBookHeader.ascx" %>
<%@ Page language="c#" Codebehind="RichControls.aspx.cs" AutoEventWireup="false"
Inherits="ControlsBookWeb.Ch02.RichControls" %>
<!DOCTYPE HTML PUBLIC "-//W3C//DTD HTML 4.0 Transitional//EN" >
<HTML>
  <HEAD>
    <title>Ch02 Rich Controls</title>
    <meta name="GENERATOR" Content="Microsoft Visual Studio 7.0">
    <meta name="CODE_LANGUAGE" Content="C#">
    <meta name="vs_defaultClientScript" content="JavaScript">
    <meta name="vs_targetSchema"
content="http://schemas.microsoft.com/intellisense/ie5">
  </HEAD>
  <body>
    <form id="RichControls" method="post" runat="server">
      <apressUC:ControlsBookHeader id="Header" runat="server" />
      <h3>Ch02 Rich Controls</h3>
      <P>
        <asp:Calendar id="Calendar1" runat="server" BackColor="White"
Width="220px" ForeColor="#003399" Height="200px" Font-Size="8pt"
Font-Names="Verdana" BorderColor="#3366CC" BorderWidth="1px"
DayNameFormat="FirstLetter" CellPadding="1">
          <TodayDayStyle ForeColor="White" BackColor="#99CCCC"></TodayDayStyle>
          <SelectorStyle ForeColor="#336666" BackColor="#99CCCC"></SelectorStyle>
          <NextPrevStyle Font-Size="8pt" ForeColor="#CCCCFF"></NextPrevStyle>
          <DayHeaderStyle Height="1px" ForeColor="#336666" BackColor="#99CCCC">
</DayHeaderStyle>
          <SelectedDayStyle Font-Bold="True" ForeColor="#CCFF99"
              BackColor="#009999">
</SelectedDayStyle>
          <TitleStyle Font-Size="10pt" Font-Bold="True" Height="25px"
BorderWidth="1px" ForeColor="#CCCCFF" BorderStyle="Solid" BorderColor="#3366CC"
BackColor="#003399"></TitleStyle>
          <WeekendDayStyle BackColor="#CCCCFF"></WeekendDayStyle>
          <OtherMonthDayStyle ForeColor="#999999"></OtherMonthDayStyle>
        </asp:Calendar></P>
      <P>
      <asp:Label id="Label1" runat="server"></asp:Label></P>
      <apressUC:ControlsBookFooter id="Footer" runat="server" />
    </form>
  </body>
</HTML>
```

Listing 2-12. The `RichControls` *Web Form Code-Behind Class File*

```
using System;
using System.Collections;
using System.ComponentModel;
using System.Data;
using System.Drawing;
using System.Web;
using System.Web.SessionState;
using System.Web.UI;
using System.Web.UI.WebControls;
using System.Web.UI.HtmlControls;

namespace ControlsBookWeb.Ch02
{
    public class RichControls : System.Web.UI.Page
    {
        protected System.Web.UI.WebControls.Label Label1;
        protected System.Web.UI.WebControls.Calendar Calendar1;
        protected ControlsBookWeb.ControlsBookHeader Header ;

        private void Page_Load(object sender, System.EventArgs e)
        {
            Header.ChapterNumber = 2 ;
            Header.ChapterTitle = "Server Control Basics" ;
        }

        #region Web Form Designer generated code
        override protected void OnInit(EventArgs e)
        {
            //
            // CODEGEN: This call is required by the ASP.NET Web Form Designer.
            //
            InitializeComponent();
            base.OnInit(e);
        }

        /// <summary>
        /// Required method for Designer support - do not modify
        /// the contents of this method with the code editor.
        /// </summary>
        private void InitializeComponent()
        {
            this.Calendar1.SelectionChanged +=
                    new System.EventHandler(this.Date_Selected);
            this.Load += new System.EventHandler(this.Page_Load);

        }
        #endregion
```

```
    private void Date_Selected(object sender, System.EventArgs e)
    {
        Label1.Text = "Selected: " + Calendar1.SelectedDate.ToLongDateString();
    }
  }
}
```

The Rich Controls demonstration has the least amount of code surface area of all the demonstrations we've shown in this chapter. The .aspx page contains the Calendar control and all the declarative settings to have the Calendar render in a manner pleasing to the eye along with a Label control to display the selected date. The code-behind has a Date_Selected method mapped to the SelectionChanged event of the Calendar control to set the value of the Label control when we click a date to select it. Figure 2-13 shows the output from the Rich Controls demonstration.

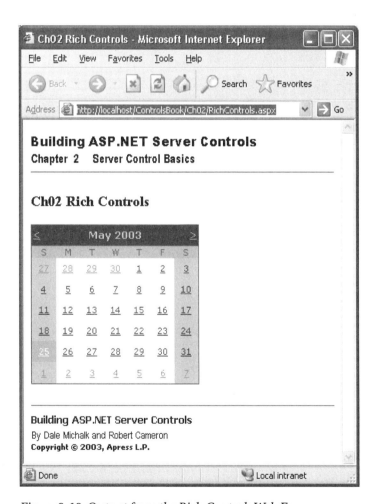

Figure 2-13. Output from the Rich Controls Web Form

Rich Controls and XSLT

Another interesting control from the rich controls portion of the System.Web.UI.Web-Controls namespace is the XML control. This control takes both an XML data source and an XML Stylesheet Language Transformations (XSLT) stylesheet in order to generate the final HTML output. An XSLT stylesheet can be brought to bear as an alternate UI generation paradigm that separates the display of data from its source in a similar fashion to what we accomplished with templates and data binding in the List Controls demonstration.

XML Control and XSLT Demonstration

The XML Control Web Form generates an HTML table similar to the List Controls demonstration, using the same data source and the native XML support available in ADO.NET. Listings 2-13 and 2-14 provide the source code for our demonstration. Listing 2-15 presents the XML Control Web Form's Customer.xslt file.

Listing 2-13. The XMLControl *Web Form .aspx Page*

```
<%@ Page language="c#" Codebehind="XMLControl.aspx.cs"
AutoEventWireup="false" Inherits="ControlsBookWeb.Ch02.XMLControl" %>
<%@ Register TagPrefix="apressUC" TagName="ControlsBookHeader"
Src="..\ControlsBookHeader.ascx" %>
<%@ Register TagPrefix="apressUC" TagName="ControlsBookFooter"
Src="..\ControlsBookFooter.ascx" %>
<!DOCTYPE HTML PUBLIC "-//W3C//DTD HTML 4.0 Transitional//EN" >
<HTML>
  <HEAD>
    <title>Ch02 XML Control</title>
    <meta name="GENERATOR" Content="Microsoft Visual Studio 7.0">
    <meta name="CODE_LANGUAGE" Content="C#">
    <meta name="vs_defaultClientScript" content="JavaScript">
    <meta name="vs_targetSchema"
        content="http://schemas.microsoft.com/intellisense/ie5">
  </HEAD>
  <body>
    <form id="XMLControl" method="post" runat="server">
      <apressUC:ControlsBookHeader id="Header" runat="server"
ChapterNumber=2 ChapterTitle="Server Control Basics" />
      <h3>Ch02 XML Control</h3>
      <asp:Xml id="Xml1" runat="server"></asp:Xml>
      <apressUC:ControlsBookFooter id="Footer" runat="server" />
    </form>
  </body>
</HTML>
```

Listing 2-14. The XMLControl *Web Form Code-Behind Class File*

```
using System;
using System.Collections;
using System.ComponentModel;
using System.Drawing;
using System.Web;
using System.Web.SessionState;
using System.Web.UI;
using System.Web.UI.WebControls;
using System.Web.UI.HtmlControls;
using System.Data;
using System.Data.SqlClient;
using System.Xml;
using System.Xml.Xsl;
using System.Xml.XPath;

namespace ControlsBookWeb.Ch02
{
    public class XMLControl : System.Web.UI.Page
    {
        protected System.Web.UI.WebControls.Xml Xml1;

        private void Page_Load(object sender, System.EventArgs e)
        {
            // load up the A/B data from DataSet
            DataSet ds = GetCustomerData();

            // create an XML source
            XmlDataDocument datadoc = new XmlDataDocument(ds);

            // load up the XSLT source
            XslTransform transform = new XslTransform();
            transform.Load(Server.MapPath("Customer.xslt"));

            // give the XML control the data it needs
            Xml1.Document = datadoc;
            Xml1.Transform = transform;

        }

        private DataSet GetCustomerData()
        {
            SqlConnection conn =
                new SqlConnection(
                    "Server=(local);Database=Northwind;Integrated Security=true;");
            conn.Open();
```

```
        SqlDataAdapter da =
            new SqlDataAdapter("SELECT CustomerID, ContactName, ContactTitle,
    CompanyName FROM Customers WHERE CustomerID LIKE '[AB]%'",
            conn);
        DataSet ds = new DataSet();
        da.Fill(ds,"Customers");

        return ds;
    }


    #region Web Form Designer generated code
    override protected void OnInit(EventArgs e)
    {
        //
        // CODEGEN: This call is required by the ASP.NET Web Form Designer.
        //
        InitializeComponent();
        base.OnInit(e);
    }

    /// <summary>
    /// Required method for Designer support - do not modify
    /// the contents of this method with the code editor.
    /// </summary>
    private void InitializeComponent()
    {
        this.Load += new System.EventHandler(this.Page_Load);

    }
    #endregion
    }
}
```

Listing 2-15. The XMLControl *Web Form Customer.xslt File*

```
<xsl:stylesheet version='1.0' xmlns:xsl='http://www.w3.org/1999/XSL/Transform'>
  <xsl:template match="/">
    <table>
        <th>Customer ID</th><th>Contact Name</th>
<th>Contact Title</th><th>Company Name</th>
        <xsl:for-each select='//Customers'>
        <xsl:choose>
        <xsl:when test="position() mod 2 = 1">
          <tr bgcolor="Silver">
            <td><xsl:value-of select='CustomerID' /></td>
            <td><xsl:value-of select='ContactName' /></td>
            <td><xsl:value-of select='ContactTitle' /></td>
            <td><xsl:value-of select='CompanyName' /></td>
          </tr>
```

```
      </xsl:when>
      <xsl:otherwise>
        <tr bgcolor="White">
          <td><xsl:value-of select='CustomerID' /></td>
          <td><xsl:value-of select='ContactName' /></td>
          <td><xsl:value-of select='ContactTitle' /></td>
          <td><xsl:value-of select='CompanyName' /></td>
        </tr>
      </xsl:otherwise>
      </xsl:choose>
      </xsl:for-each>
    </table>
  </xsl:template>
</xsl:stylesheet>
```

The code reuses the `GetCustomerData` method from the List Controls demonstration to generate the `DataSet`, and then passes it to the `XmlDataDocuments` class's constructor to create an XML view of the `DataSet` data:

```
DataSet ds = GetCustomerData();
XmlDataDocument datadoc = new XmlDataDocument(ds);
```

The code then creates a new `XslTransform` class to load the Customer.xslt XSLT document, which contains the instructions to transform the source XML into the final HTML table. It has the same HTML table styling to replicate the previous demonstration:

```
XslTransform transform = new XslTransform();
transform.Load(Server.MapPath("Customer.xslt"));
```

The final task is to configure the XML control by setting a reference to the `XmlData-Document` via its `Document` property and the `XslTransform` class via the `Transform` property, as follows. Once this is done, the code is ready to generate XML during the rendering process of the page.

```
Xml1.Document = datadoc;
Xml1.Transform = transform;
```

Figure 2-14 shows the output from the XML and XSLT demonstration.

Figure 2-14. Output from the XML Control Web Form

Although the XML control seems to be a great way to build UIs, we do not recommend the XSLT technique as a way to take advantage of ASP.NET and its server control mechanism for several reasons:

- All UI layout information must be specified declaratively inside of the XSLT document, which requires the programmer to take over the task of rendering the entire HTML document.

- It is not possible to leverage server controls, which have the capability to render conditional UI based on browser capabilities in this model, nor is it possible to capture events during postback on the server side that are connected to the HTML tags rendered by the XSLT.

- Extra steps are required to debug the XSLT stylesheet outside of Visual Studio .NET. The programmer must either manually look at the HTML output or buy a third-party XSLT debugger such as XML Spy to be able to step through the XSLT code. Contrast this with the ability to completely step through the page generation process with templates and data binding.

Validation Controls

Checking user input on a web page is one of the least favorite tasks on a web developer's to-do list. It falls somewhere between maintenance of old code and sitting in another project planning meeting. Fortunately, ASP.NET comes to the rescue with a set of controls that not only take care of validation of input when it reaches the web server, but also handle the task of generating JavaScript validation routines to check the validity of input on the client side, minimizing additional round-trips to the server. This is accomplished by setting the `EnableClientScript` property to true.

Table 2-3 shows the various validation controls that are available in the `System.Web.UI.WebControls` namespaces and the input-checking features they provide.

Table 2-3. Validation Controls Available in ASP.NET

VALIDATION CONTROL	DESCRIPTION
RequiredFieldValidator	Checks for a null or empty value in a server control
CompareValidator	Compares two server controls by various operators
RangeValidator	Ensures the values of a server control fall in a specific range
RegularExpressionValidator	Uses a regular expression to validate the input of a server control
CustomValidator	Allows the programmer to specify client-side and server-side validation routines to constrain a server control's input
ValidationSummary	Shows a summary of all the error messages generated by validator controls on a Web Form

Validation Controls Demonstration

The following Validation Controls Web Form demonstrates all of the validation controls in action on a Web Form. Full source code is provided in Listings 2-16 and 2-17. The Web Form has `TextBox` controls to test input and a `Label` to display the success or failure of the Web Form postback according to the validation process.

Listing 2-16. The ValidationControls *Web Form .aspx Page*

```
<%@ Page language="c#" Codebehind="ValidationControls.aspx.cs"
AutoEventWireup="false" Inherits="ControlsBookWeb.Ch02.ValidationControls" %>
<%@ Register TagPrefix="apressUC" TagName="ControlsBookHeader"
Src="..\ControlsBookHeader.ascx" %>
<%@ Register TagPrefix="apressUC" TagName="ControlsBookFooter"
Src="..\ControlsBookFooter.ascx" %>
<!DOCTYPE HTML PUBLIC "-//W3C//DTD HTML 4.0 Transitional//EN" >
<HTML>
  <HEAD>
    <title>Ch02 Validator Controls</title>
    <meta name="GENERATOR" Content="Microsoft Visual Studio 7.0">
```

```
    <meta name="CODE_LANGUAGE" Content="C#">
    <meta name="vs_defaultClientScript" content="JavaScript">
    <meta name="vs_targetSchema"
      content="http://schemas.microsoft.com/intellisense/ie5">
    <script language="javascript">
      function validateEven(oSrc, args){
        args.IsValid = ((args.Value % 2) == 0);
      }
    </script>
  </HEAD>
  <body>
    <form id="ValidationControls" method="post" runat="server">
      <apressUC:ControlsBookHeader id="Header" runat="server"
ChapterNumber=2 ChapterTitle = "Server Control Basics"/>
      <h3>Ch02 Validation Controls</h3>
      <asp:Label id="Label1" runat="server"> RequiredField</asp:Label><br>
      <asp:TextBox id="RequiredField" runat="server"></asp:TextBox>
      <asp:RequiredFieldValidator id="RequiredFieldValidator1"
runat="server" ErrorMessage="RequiredField needs an input value!"
        ControlToValidate="RequiredField"></asp:RequiredFieldValidator><br>
      <asp:Label id="Label2" runat="server"> ComparedField</asp:Label><br>
      <asp:TextBox id="ComparedField" runat="server"></asp:TextBox>
      <asp:CompareValidator id="CompareValidator1" runat="server"
ErrorMessage="RequiredField and ComparedField are not equal!"
        ControlToValidate="ComparedField"
ControlToCompare="RequiredField"></asp:CompareValidator><br>
      <asp:Label id="Label3" runat="server"> RangeField</asp:Label><br>
      <asp:TextBox id="RangeField" runat="server"></asp:TextBox>
      <asp:RangeValidator id="RangeValidator1" runat="server"
ErrorMessage="RangeField value must be between 1-10!"
        ControlToValidate="RangeField" MaximumValue="10" MinimumValue="1"
Type="Integer"></asp:RangeValidator><br>
      <asp:Label id="Label4" runat="server"> RegexField (Phone)</asp:Label><br>
      <asp:TextBox id="RegexField" runat="server"></asp:TextBox>
      <asp:RegularExpressionValidator id="RegularExpressionValidator1"
runat="server" ErrorMessage="RegexField must be a valid US phone number!"
        ControlToValidate="RegexField"
ValidationExpression="((\(\d{3}\) ?)|(\d{3}-))?\d{3}-\d{4}">
</asp:RegularExpressionValidator><br>
      <asp:Label id="Label5" runat="server">CustomField (Even Number)
</asp:Label><br>
      <asp:TextBox id="CustomField" runat="server"></asp:TextBox>
      <asp:CustomValidator id="CustomValidator1" runat="server"
ErrorMessage="CustomField must be an even number!"
        ControlToValidate="CustomField"
ClientValidationFunction="validateEven"></asp:CustomValidator><br>
      <br>
      <asp:Button id="Button1" runat="server" Text="Submit"></asp:Button><br>
      <asp:Label id="ResultsLabel" runat="server"></asp:Label><br>
      <br>
      <asp:ValidationSummary id="ValidationSummary1"
```

```
runat="server"></asp:ValidationSummary>
      <apressUC:ControlsBookFooter id="Footer" runat="server" />
    </form>
  </body>
</HTML>
```

Listing 2-17. The ValidationControls *Web Form Code-Behind Class File*

```
using System;
using System.Collections;
using System.ComponentModel;
using System.Data;
using System.Drawing;
using System.Web;
using System.Web.SessionState;
using System.Web.UI;
using System.Web.UI.WebControls;
using System.Web.UI.HtmlControls;

namespace ControlsBookWeb.Ch02
{
    public class ValidationControls : System.Web.UI.Page
    {
        protected System.Web.UI.WebControls.Label Label1;
        protected System.Web.UI.WebControls.Label Label2;
        protected System.Web.UI.WebControls.Label Label3;
        protected System.Web.UI.WebControls.Label Label4;
        protected System.Web.UI.WebControls.Label Label5;
        protected System.Web.UI.WebControls.ValidationSummary ValidationSummary1;
        protected System.Web.UI.WebControls.Button Button1;
        protected System.Web.UI.WebControls.RequiredFieldValidator
                    RequiredFieldValidator1;
        protected System.Web.UI.WebControls.CompareValidator CompareValidator1;
        protected System.Web.UI.WebControls.CustomValidator CustomValidator1;
        protected System.Web.UI.WebControls.RegularExpressionValidator
                    RegularExpressionValidator1;
        protected System.Web.UI.WebControls.RangeValidator RangeValidator1;
        protected System.Web.UI.WebControls.TextBox RequiredField;
        protected System.Web.UI.WebControls.TextBox ComparedField;
        protected System.Web.UI.WebControls.TextBox RangeField;
        protected System.Web.UI.WebControls.TextBox RegexField;
        protected System.Web.UI.WebControls.TextBox CustomField;
        protected System.Web.UI.WebControls.Label ResultsLabel;

        private void Page_Load(object sender, System.EventArgs e)
        {

        }
```

```
#region Web Form Designer generated code
override protected void OnInit(EventArgs e)
{
    //
    // CODEGEN: This call is required by the ASP.NET Web Form Designer.
    //
    InitializeComponent();
    base.OnInit(e);
}

/// <summary>
/// Required method for Designer support - do not modify
/// the contents of this method with the code editor.
/// </summary>
private void InitializeComponent()
{
    this.CustomValidator1.ServerValidate += new
    System.Web.UI.WebControls.ServerValidateEventHandler(this.ValidateEven);
    this.Button1.Click += new System.EventHandler(this.Button1_Click);
    this.Load += new System.EventHandler(this.Page_Load);

}
#endregion

private void Button1_Click(object sender, System.EventArgs e)
{
    ResultsLabel.Text = "Page submitted at " + DateTime.Now + "
IsValid:" + Page.IsValid;
}

private void ValidateEven(object source,
System.Web.UI.WebControls.ServerValidateEventArgs args)
{
    if ((Convert.ToInt32(args.Value) % 2) == 0)
        args.IsValid = true;
    else
        args.IsValid = false;
}
}
}
```

The Web Form button that submits the .aspx page uses the `IsValid` property of the Page class to determine if the form post was successful. It also displays the time.

```
private void Button1_Click(object sender, System.EventArgs e)
{
    ResultsLabel.Text = "Page submitted at " + DateTime.Now +
                        " IsValid:" + Page.IsValid;
}
```

Of course, this Label output won't be displayed on the browser window like in Figure 2-16 unless the form post has successfully passed through client-side validation that occurs when the demonstration is executed using a JavaScript-capable browser such as Internet Explorer 6.0. Figure 2-15 shows the result of erroneous client-side input with the JavaScript features enabled. You should also notice the display of the error messages by the input elements and the summary at the bottom generated by the ValidationSummary control.

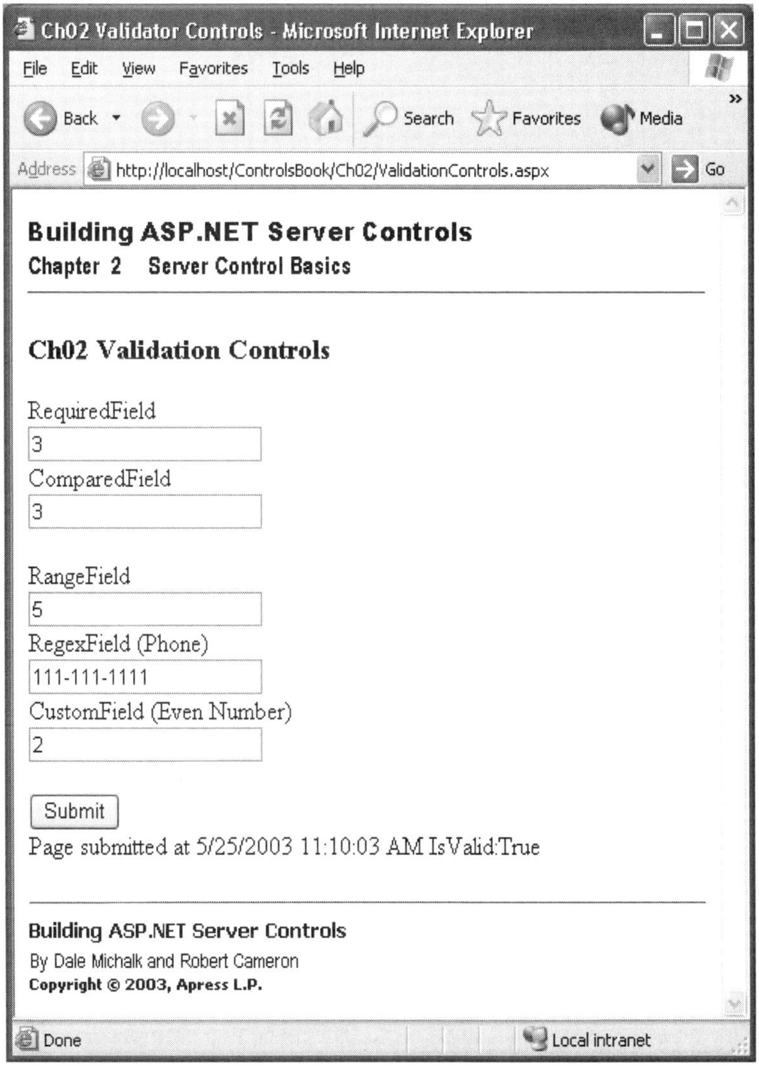

Figure 2-15. Output from the Validation Controls Web Form with successful input

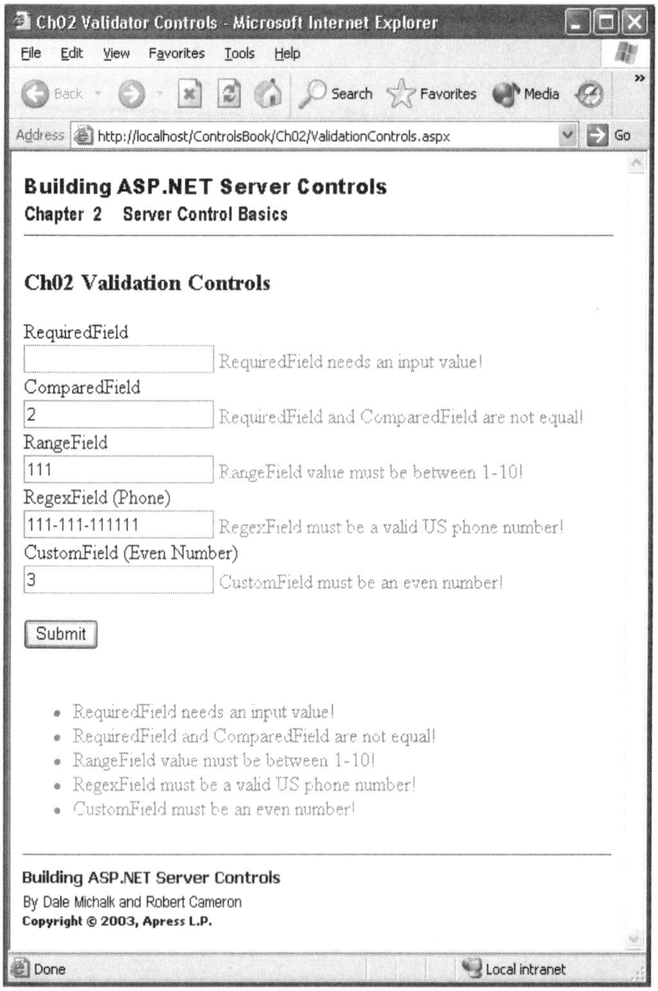

Figure 2-16. Output from the Validation Controls Web Form with validation errors

If the posted data makes its way past the guard of client-side validation, it has a second hurdle to overcome: validation on the server side. Each validation control is checked once again for correctness of values. This prevents spoofing or tampering with the HTTP post back to the web server in an attempt to get around the validation process.

The validation system in ASP.NET also provides the ability to customize the client-side and server-side routines that verify input. The preceding example demonstrates this with the CustomerValidator control that is linked to the CustomField TextBox control. The first step is to wire up custom client-side validation through the ClientValidationFunction property. We set the value of this property to "validateEven" and include a like-named JavaScript function in our .aspx page in the <HEAD> section of the HTML content:

```
<script language="javascript">
    function validateEven(oSrc, args){
        args.IsValid = ((args.Value % 2) == 0);
    }
</script>
```

The arguments passed to our routine provide us with the means to check the state of the validated HTML element and communicate the results of our validation work. The second argument is a structure with an `IsValid` property that is set to true or false to signal the results as well as a `Value` property representing the input value. The validateEven routine uses modulo arithmetic to detect if a number is even or odd.

Configuring the server-side validation for the same control is done by wiring up the `ValidateEven` method in the code-behind file with the `ServerValidate` event of the `CustomValidator` control. The parameters work in a similar fashion to their JavaScript counterparts with a `Value` and `IsValid` property.

```
private void ValidateEven(object source,
    System.Web.UI.WebControls.ServerValidateEventArgs args)
{
    if ((Convert.ToInt32(args.Value) % 2) == 0)
        args.IsValid = true;
    else
        args.IsValid = false;
}
```

Web Controls vs. HTML Controls

The controls discussed in this chapter spanned both the `System.Web.UI.WebControls` and `System.Web.UI.HtmlControls` namespaces. On the surface, the functionality in these two namespaces appears to overlap significantly. This is particularly true when generating content that maps to a single HTML tag such as `<INPUT type="text">` or `<TEXTAREA>`. Both the HTML control `HtmlInputText` and web control `TextBox` handle this with equal functionality when added to a Web Form as a server control. Deciding on which to use in this situation is a commonly asked question about ASP.NET.

The HTML controls have the advantage of looking similar to their HTML brethren, taking on attributes that are familiar to web developers. This eases the porting process and helps keep people comfortable with the changes to ASP.NET. This is both a blessing and a curse. It is easy to overlook the `runat="server"` attribute and assume that the control is raw HTML. This is especially a problem late at night when things on the monitor don't look as they should to tired eyes.

The web controls provide a more consistent attribute model for specifying properties on controls. The best example is the use of the more intuitive `Text` property on a `Label` and `TextBox` control contrasted with the `Value` or `Name` property that is used in the `HtmlControls` namespace. The CSS styling support is also much better with web controls, as the Web Controls example demonstrated the CSS-related types added to the `System.Web.UI.WebControls` namespace.

Also notice that web controls have the addition of an "asp:" tag prefix added to the HTML tag on the .aspx page that identifies the tag as a server control within a particular namespace. The classes in the `HtmlControls` namespace do not have a tag prefix and cannot be used as a base class for a custom server control class.

We would have been remiss to not include a detailed discussion of what is available in the `HtmlControls` namespace, as these controls can provide a potential interim step to help ease the migration challenges to ASP.NET. However, it is our opinion that outside the necessary `HtmlForm` control for Web Form construction and the file upload functionality of the `HtmlInputFile` control, programmers should stay away from using the HTML controls in ASP.NET applications. We recommend that developers strive to fully migrate toward the web control classes in application development to gain the benefits from the level of abstraction web controls provide as well as the rich programming model available. This is especially true if custom control development is planned or desired.

Summary

This chapter was devoted to the topic of server controls. Server controls are objects, and as such they provide the time-honored constructs of properties, methods, and events. The HTML content rendered to the browser client is generated in its entirety by a tree of server controls representing each item on the page.

Controls in ASP.NET are separated into three hierarchies: `System.Web.UI`, `System.Web.UI.HtmlControls`, and `System.Web.UI.WebControls`. `System.Web.UI` contains the `Page` class, which represents the Web Form, and the `Control` class, which is the root base class of all the other server controls in ASP.NET.

`System.Web.UI.HtmlControls` contains controls that directly map to HTML tags and make porting from HTML pages easier. `HtmlInputText`, `HtmlForm`, and `HtmlInputHidden` are examples of HTML controls.

`System.Web.UI.WebControls` contains a full-featured set of controls, including simple, list, rich, and validation controls. Simple controls are web controls that provide server-side mapping to HTML tags. `TextBox`, `Button`, and `DropDownList` are examples of simple controls. List controls support building HTML content through data binding and templates. The `DataList`, `DataGrid`, and `Repeater` controls are some examples of list controls. Rich controls generate complex UI from a minimal amount of input. The `Calendar` control is an example of a rich control.

Validation controls simplify the tedious nature of Web Form input validation. Validation can occur on the client side for JavaScript-capable browsers. It is also possible to write custom validation scripts using the `CustomValidator` control.

There is overlapping functionality between `WebControls` and `HtmlControls`. We recommend using the `System.Web.UI.WebControls` namespace over `System.Web.UI.HtmlControls` due to its rich control set, enhanced styling features, and powerful abstraction layer around HTML rendering. Also, it is not possible to create a custom server control that derives from an `HtmlControl` class.

CHAPTER 3

Developing Custom Server Controls

THE PREVIOUS CHAPTER provided a high-level overview of the large number of prebuilt controls available in ASP.NET. These battle-tested components serve admirably in a variety of scenarios that web application designers can dream up. In addition, control builders can extend and enhance the capabilities of the components delivered out of the box through inheritance and encapsulation.

Even though the built-in controls are flexible and provide strong feature sets, they sometimes fall short of the needs of demanding web applications. Sometimes, the requirements of a web application are such that you just have to have a cool drop-down DHTML menu system or a floating pop-up Calendar that allows the user to pick a range of dates via JavaScript. At other times, you want to bundle up portions of your UI for reuse in a web application with a higher level of abstraction than the "cut-and-paste" IIS include mechanism. For this kind of task, you will need to either buy or build your own set of ASP.NET controls.

In addition, there are invariably cases where gaps exist in the capabilities of any given framework, including ASP.NET. The creators of ASP.NET have to ship within deadlines, so any holes that do exist in the control hierarchy create an opportunity for either third-party developers or corporate in-house developers to create new server controls to meet requirements. In this chapter, we discuss the various methods available in ASP.NET to create controls that have the same amount of modularity and reuse potential as the built-in controls.

Packaging Content in ASP.NET

Fortunately, the rich, object-oriented framework that ASP.NET provides allows for a couple of control-building options. These options generally fall into two categories:

- User controls

- Custom server controls

User controls are a great option when you are packaging common-UI layout for reuse across a project or group of projects. Custom server controls are more akin to what is traditionally considered a control or widget. Before we discuss these two methods of creating controls in ASP.NET, we first cover a couple of key concepts: inheritance and encapsulation.

Inheritance

One way to package new functionality and take advantage of the rich, object-oriented framework in ASP.NET is to use *inheritance*. This elegant, tried-and-true technique is the central theme of this book and the topic on which we spend the most time.

Inheritance works because of the polymorphic behavior of objects. This capability permits you to override methods defined as *virtual* in the base object class so that you can add or customize the objects' behavior, with the option of still leveraging the functionality available in the original base class method. To put it another way, you don't have to reinvent the wheel to add new functionality. In terms of code, this will generally look something like the following:

```
//overide virtual method "Render"
protected override void Render(HtmlTextWriter output)
{
    //add some new style to output
    output.AddStyleAttribute("somestylename","somevalue");
    base.Render(output);  //render the output using the base class Render method
}
```

In this code snippet, we override the virtual method `Render`, which is defined in the base class `System.Web.UI.Control`. This syntax may look a little strange at first. For example, where is base defined? Like the `this` reference, the object that `base` actually references is context defined, made available by the framework. As its name suggests, `base` is a convenient way to reference the base class that the custom server control inherits from in its class definition. In our version of the `Render` method, we tack on some styling to the output class (of type `HtmlTextWriter`) and then call the base class's `Render` method to display the control's new styled output on the ASP.NET page.

In the preceding example, if `Render` was not defined as virtual in the base class, the ease with which we perform this task would not have been possible. Without the virtual modifier, the base class's `Render` method would have been "hidden" or redefined when we declared a method named `Render` in the derived server control class. We would not have been able to make use of the base object's `Render` method in our new `Render` method, and we would have been forced to re-create all of the base class's `Render` functionality.

 NOTE *Keep in mind the role that modifiers such as virtual play when you add new methods to your custom server controls and you would like to support polymorphic behavior.*

All custom server controls inherit from an ASP.NET server control class to ensure that the new control falls in line with the .NET Framework. There are several choices for a base class, including `System.Web.UI.Control`, `System.Web.UI.WebControl`, or one of the full-featured server controls such as `TextBox`. We discuss what factors affect this decision and we provide several introductory examples of custom server controls later in this chapter.

Encapsulation

Another construct available to package functionality within an object-oriented frame-work such as .NET is *encapsulation*. Encapsulation is also referred to as *composition* or *building composite controls*. Composite controls can inherit from any ASP.NET server control, but generally they are inherited from System.Web.UI.Control or System.Web.UI.WebControl. This inheritance is necessary to gain access to the necessary ASP.NET plumbing (rendering, state management, postback, and so on); however, composition does not rely on inheritance or polymorphism to achieve reuse.

Composite controls package functionality by combining server controls as children controls, but they are still treated as a single entity. This promotes information hiding and eases development by allowing the composite control developer/user to focus on the combined functionality of the parent control and to not worry about setting individual properties or calling methods on the children controls.

ASP.NET provides two different methods for building composite controls: composition through custom server controls and composition through user controls. We discuss what factors can go into choosing one method over the other and provide several introductory examples later on in this chapter.

Comparing the Control-Building Techniques

As described earlier in this chapter, there are primarily two methods of packing content in ASP.NET: user controls and custom server controls. We provide a high-level overview of these methods in the following sections. To assist with this discussion, we create user controls and custom server controls that implement the same functionality to help us compare and contrast the two construction methodologies.

User Controls

User controls are a form of composite control that you can use to package functionality within ASP.NET. Generally, the focus of user control development is to encapsulate application-specific business logic that can be shared within a single application or within a family of related applications.

Of the two primary means of building controls in ASP.NET, user controls are the simpler of the two control types to create. Constructing user controls is similar to building ASP.NET Web Forms, as they support a declarative style of development through dragging and dropping controls from the Toolbox in Visual Studio .NET onto the user control design surface.

A user control page has intermixed HTML tags and server controls like in an .aspx page, except they are stored in an .ascx file. Like Web Forms, user controls also support separation of the HTML tags and UI from the page logic through the code-behind mechanism. The Design view of a user control is almost identical to that of a Web Form, as shown in Figure 3-1.

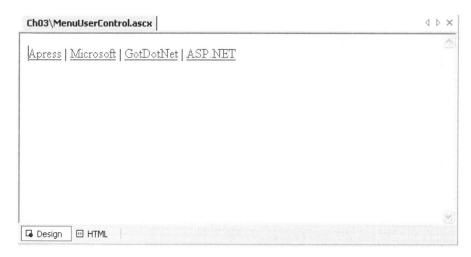

Figure 3-1. The Visual Studio .NET Design view of a user control

You will typically implement a user control when you want to build a control that requires a fair number of declarative HTML tags with the least amount of effort. This option makes it easier for the UI designer to go back in and modify the output of the control using the Visual Studio .NET web page designer interface when compared to custom server controls, which are programmatically designed in code. Here is a list of other important characteristics of user controls:

- User controls are a great way to package HTML and modularize web development. They are also a means of replacing the use of IIS include files.

- User controls support properties and methods that can be set either in the HTML as attributes or in the code-behind page of the hosting .ascx page.

- User controls can be cached in the ASP.NET cache based on a number of different parameters to speed web application performance (as detailed in the ASP.NET documentation).

- Certain tags are not permitted in a user control—specifically, the `<HTML>`, `<HEAD>`, `<BODY>`, and `<FORM>` tags. Using these tags would interfere with the functioning of the hosting .aspx page.

- User control tag declarations should appear between the hosting .aspx page's beginning and ending `FORM` tags to ensure proper operation.

The Header and Footer user controls present in all of the sample .aspx pages included in this book demonstrate how user controls can package common functionality and help modularize web application development. Listings 3-1 and 3-2 contain the source code for the Header user control. We don't list the source control for the Footer control because it is even simpler than that for the Header control.

Listing 3-1. The ControlsBookHeader *.ascx File*

```
<%@ Control Language="c#" AutoEventWireup="false"
Codebehind="ControlsBookHeader.ascx.cs"
Inherits="ControlsBookWeb.ControlsBookHeader"
TargetSchema="http://schemas.microsoft.com/intellisense/ie5"%>
<DIV id="HeaderPanel">
  <font face="Arial Black">
    <asp:label id="Label2" Height="16px" Width="360px" runat="server">
    Building ASP.NET Server Controls</asp:label></font>
  <br>
  <b><font face="Arial Narrow">
      <asp:label id="Label1" runat="server">Chapter</asp:label> 
      <asp:label id="Label3" Width="16px" runat="server">10</asp:label> 
      <asp:label id="Label4" Height="8px" Width="288px" runat="server">
      Chapter Title</asp:label></b></FONT>
  <HR color="#0033ff" SIZE="1">
</DIV>
```

Listing 3-2. The ControlsBookHeader *Code-Behind Class File*

```
using System;
using System.Data;
using System.Drawing;
using System.Web;
using System.Web.UI.WebControls;
using System.Web.UI.HtmlControls;

namespace ControlsBookWeb
{
    public class ControlsBookHeader : System.Web.UI.UserControl
    {
        private void Page_Load(object sender, System.EventArgs e)
        {
            Label3.Text = chapterNumber.ToString() ;
            Label4.Text = bookChapterTitle ;
        }

        protected System.Web.UI.WebControls.Label Label1;
        protected System.Web.UI.WebControls.Label Label2;
        protected System.Web.UI.WebControls.Label Label3;
        protected System.Web.UI.WebControls.Label Label4;
```

```
        //private members
        private string bookChapterTitle ;
        private int chapterNumber ;

        //properties
        public String ChapterTitle
        {
          get
          {
            return bookChapterTitle ;
          }
          set
          {
            bookChapterTitle = value;
          }
        }

        public int ChapterNumber
        {
          get
          {
            return chapterNumber ;
          }
          set
          {
            chapterNumber = value;
          }
        }

        #region Web Form Designer generated code
        override protected void OnInit(EventArgs e)
        {
          //
          // CODEGEN: This call is required by the ASP.NET Web Form Designer.
          //
          InitializeComponent();
          base.OnInit(e);
        }

        /// <summary>
        /// Required method for Designer support - do not modify
        /// the contents of this method with the code editor.
        /// </summary>
        private void InitializeComponent()
        {
          this.Load += new System.EventHandler(this.Page_Load);

        }
        #endregion
    }
}
```

For the Header user control, properties such as ChapterTitle and ChapterNumber are set in the HTML through attributes except in the Chapter 3 sample page named MenuCustomControlDemo.aspx. In this page, the attributes are set in the code-behind class page. To access the Header user control in the code-behind page, we had to first add a declaration for the user control to the code-behind class. The declaration looks like this:

```
protected ControlsBookWeb.ControlsBookHeader Header ;
```

 NOTE *In ASP.NET, to access any control declared in the .aspx page on the server during execution from within the code-behind page, the control must have the* runat="server" *attribute as well as a declaration for the control in the code-behind class. By default, user controls do not have this declaration automatically created for them, as is the case with server controls.*

When compared to building custom server controls, user controls are easier on the development staff in terms of the learning curve. As long as a developer is capable of building Web Forms, he or she can build user controls.

Custom Server Controls

The other option for control development in ASP.NET, *custom server controls,* package functionality through inheritance or composition, or both. Server controls do not support declarative, drag-and-drop–style UI development. Everything that is rendered by the control is specified within a code class. In Chapter 7, we examine templates, which allow UI designers to specify the UI of a custom control in a declarative fashion. This compensates to some degree for the lack of a tag page that is edited in the Designer during server control development. The requirement to put everything (UI layout, functionality, and so on) in code gives server controls a superior packaging and deployment story, as they compile into an assembly. The resulting assembly can be copied between web development projects and stored in the global assembly cache (GAC).

Custom controls are a fully programmatic way of packaging reusable content in ASP.NET. They allow developers to tap into the underlying ASP.NET plumbing, replacing or adding core functionality, such as how a control renders, in order to achieve the desired behavior. They tend to implement richer functionality and exhibit greater reuse from project to project as shown by advanced controls such as the TextBox, DataGrid, and Calendar controls that exist in the ASP.NET WebControls namespace.

A custom control also has better support in the Design view of the control when it is placed on a Web Form .aspx page by the developer/user. In the Design view, a custom control renders the HTML output that it normally would when generating for HTML browser consumption. In contrast, user controls placed on a Web Form display themselves as a gray box. Figures 3-2 and 3-3 highlight the differences between a user control and a custom control that render identical HTML output in the browser.

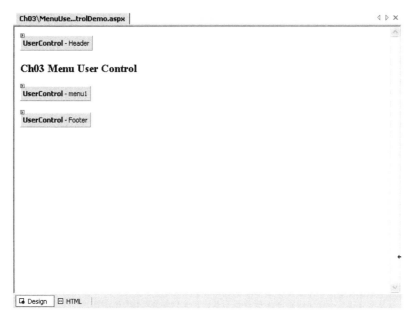

Figure 3-2. The Visual Studio .NET Design view of a user control placed on a Web Form

Figure 3-3. The Visual Studio .NET Design view of a custom control placed on a Web Form

Another major difference between user controls and custom controls is deployment. Reusing a user control requires copying its .ascx files along with code-behind assemblies, if necessary, in order to reuse it in different web applications.

In contrast to user controls, custom server controls compile down to an assembly. For independent software vendors, this is a requirement because it eases deployment and protects intellectual capital by not having an exposed .ascx file. Also, your typical enterprise developer/user benefits because he or she can easily deploy an assembly to the GAC on a machine that has a large number of web applications using a particular control.

Naturally, all the benefits of custom controls do not come for free. Generally, custom controls require a longer development cycle and a higher skill level from the development staff. The focus of this book is on custom server control development with the goal of easing the learning curve and developing some useful server control samples to help you get started.

Building a User Control

So far we've discussed user controls and custom server controls, and their benefits and differences. User controls and server controls have differing strengths and trade-offs that we highlight in this section by building two families of controls:

- A static hyperlink menu control

- A dynamically generated HTML table control

The example controls we present may seem simple and somewhat removed from real-world web projects, but we do this for a reason. We believe that you must start simple and build toward more complexity to achieve a deep understanding of the process. In upcoming chapters, we explore controls that leverage the complete functionality available to controls in ASP.NET as well as provide interesting capabilities.

ASP.NET developers typically look to the user control as the first option for creating controls due to its ease of construction and simplicity. Building a user control closely mirrors the construction techniques and technical details of a Web Form. User controls support drag-and-drop development with the Visual Studio .NET control Toolbox, a fully editable design surface in the IDE, and a code-behind class file structure to support a separation of UI and logic programming. User controls are built in two ways:

- From scratch

- By taking out reusable content from an existing Web Form

The first method is used when enough planning and design work is done ahead of time to figure out which portions of the UI are going to be reused on the web site. The second technique results from refactoring the content of a site after it has been built to make it modular and easier to maintain.

The MenuUserControl User Control

Our first example takes advantage of the declarative nature of the user control to encapsulate a simple hyperlink menu as a control that we build from scratch. The control is pure static HTML without a single embedded server control. It consists of nothing more than a list of fixed hyperlinks to a variety of web sites.

The simplicity is shown in the tags present in the .ascx file in Listing 3-3. The code-behind class in Listing 3-4 is left unchanged from the blank template Visual Studio .NET produces when you add a user control to a web application.

Listing 3-3. The MenuUserControl *.ascx Page File*

```
<%@ Control Language="c#" AutoEventWireup="false"
Codebehind="MenuUserControl.ascx.cs"
Inherits="ControlsBookWeb.Ch03.MenuUserControl"
TargetSchema="http://schemas.microsoft.com/intellisense/ie5"%>
<div>
  <span><a href="http://www.apress.com">Apress</a></span> |
  <span><a href="http://www.microsoft.com">Microsoft</a></span> |
  <span><a href="http://www.gotdotnet.com">GotDotNet</a></span> |
  <span><a href="http://www.aspnet.com">ASP.NET</a></span>
</div>
```

Listing 3-4. The MenuUserControl *Code-Behind Class File*

```
using System;
using System.Data;
using System.Drawing;
using System.Web;
using System.Web.UI.WebControls;
using System.Web.UI.HtmlControls;

namespace ControlsBookWeb.Ch03
{
    public abstract class MenuUserControl : System.Web.UI.UserControl
    {

        private void Page_Load(object sender, System.EventArgs e)
        {
            // Put user code to initialize the page here
        }

        #region Web Form Designer generated code
        override protected void OnInit(EventArgs e)
        {
```

```
        //
        // CODEGEN: This call is required by the ASP.NET Web Form Designer.
        //
        InitializeComponent();
        base.OnInit(e);
    }

    /// Required method for Designer support - do not modify
    /// the contents of this method with the code editor.
    /// </summary>
    private void InitializeComponent()
    {
        this.Load += new System.EventHandler(this.Page_Load);
    }
    #endregion
    }
}
```

The Control directive at the top of the user control .ascx file identifies it as a user control to the ASP.NET parsing engine. The format is similar to that of the Page directive in an .aspx page file:

```
<%@ Control Language="c#" AutoEventWireup="false"
Codebehind="MenuUserControl.ascx.cs"
Inherits="ControlsBookWeb.Ch03.MenuUserControl"
TargetSchema="http://schemas.microsoft.com/intellisense/ie5"%>
```

The Control directive helps set up the code-behind system through its Codebehind and Inherits properties. The Codebehind attribute points to the location of the class file, and the Inherits attribute specifies the class name the .ascx tag page inherits from. A keen observer will notice that the inheritance process in an .ascx file uses the System.Web.UI.UserControl class instead of the System.Web.UI.Page base class (as in an .aspx file).

Using the MenuUserControl User Control

To actually see the content of the user control, we must host the user control on a Web Form. Doing so requires a registration step to give the Web Form enough information to find the user control content and bring it into the scope of the page via a tag associated with the user control. The Menu User Control Demo Web Form accomplishes this task, as shown in the Design view in Figure 3-2. Figure 3-4 shows the final output of the Web Form in the browser.

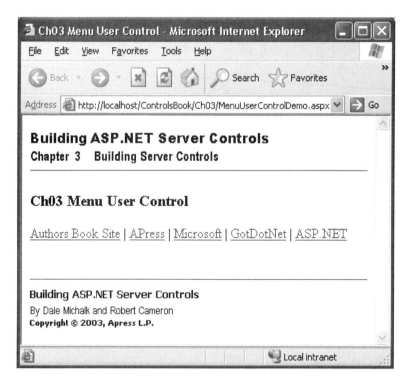

Figure 3-4. The browser view of the HTML output from the Menu User Control Demo Web Form

Listing 3-5 shows the source code for the MenuUserControlDemo .aspx file.

Listing 3-5. The MenuUserControlDemo *.aspx Page File*

```
<%@ Register TagPrefix="apressUC" TagName="MenuUserControl"
Src="MenuUserControl.ascx" %>
<%@ Page language="c#" Codebehind="MenuUserControlDemo.aspx.cs"
AutoEventWireup="false" Inherits="ControlsBookWeb.Ch03.MenuUserControlDemo" %>
<%@ Register TagPrefix="apressUC" TagName="ControlsBookFooter"
 Src="..\ControlsBookFooter.ascx" %>
<%@ Register TagPrefix="apressUC" TagName="ControlsBookHeader"
Src="..\ControlsBookHeader.ascx" %>
<!DOCTYPE HTML PUBLIC "-//W3C//DTD HTML 4.0 Transitional//EN" >
<HTML>
  <HEAD>
    <title>Ch03 Menu User Control</title>
    <meta name="GENERATOR" Content="Microsoft Visual Studio 7.0">
    <meta name="CODE_LANGUAGE" Content="C#">
    <meta name="vs_defaultClientScript" content="JavaScript">
    <meta name="vs_targetSchema"
      content="http://schemas.microsoft.com/intellisense/ie5">
```

```
  </HEAD>
  <body MS_POSITIONING="FlowLayout">
    <form id="MenuUserControlDemo" method="post" runat="server">
      <apressUC:ControlsBookHeader id="Header" runat="server"
       ChapterNumber=3 ChapterTitle="Building Server Controls" />
      <h3>Ch03 Menu User Control</h3>
      <apressUC:MenuUserControl id="menu1" runat="server" /><br>
      <br>
      <apressUC:ControlsBookFooter id="Footer" runat="server" />
    </form>
  </body>
</HTML>
```

The `Register` directive does its part by locating the .ascx file representing the user control with its `src` attribute and determining its look on the page with the `TagName` and `TagPrefix` attributes:

```
<%@ Register TagPrefix="apressuc" TagName="MenuUserControl"
Src="MenuUserControl.ascx" %>
```

As a common convention in the book we use "apressuc" as the tag prefix for our user controls and "apress" for custom controls. You are free to choose a prefix to suit your organizational or company standards. In the example, we use `MenuUserControl` as the name of the tag and identify our single instance with the `id` attribute "menu1". The `runat="server"` attribute is also present to signify that it is a server control and must be handled appropriately by the ASP.NET parsing system:

```
<apressuc:MenuUserControl id="menu1" runat="server" />
```

An interesting thing to note about this example is how the user control displays on the Web Form when you view the hosting Web Form in Design view. It is shown as a gray box that provides little feedback as to what the final output in the browser will be.

The `TableUserControl` User Control

Our second user control example raises the degree of difficulty by demonstrating how to use the dynamic control-building features of ASP.NET inside a user control. Because the `UserControl` class itself has an inheritance chain back to the root `System.Web.UI.Control` class and is a full-blown control in its own right, we can add controls to its `Controls` collection at runtime to build up its content structure. We can also manipulate the child controls on its surface programmatically.

This example has similar functionality to the examples in Chapter 2. Here the action is orchestrated according to the properties that the control exposes to the Web Form at runtime in its declaration, specifically the X and Y properties. Listing 3-6 shows the source code for the `TableUserControl` .ascx file. Listing 3-7 shows the source code for the `TableUserControl` code-behind class file.

Listing 3-6. The TableUserControl *.ascx Page File*

```
<%@ Control Language="c#" AutoEventWireup="false"
Codebehind="TableUserControl.ascx.cs"
Inherits="ControlsBookWeb.Ch03.TableUserControl"
TargetSchema="http://schemas.microsoft.com/intellisense/ie5"%>
<h3>TableUserControl<br>
  X:<asp:Label id="XLabel" Runat="server"></asp:label> 
  Y:<asp:label id="YLabel" Runat="server"></asp:label> 
</h3>
<table id="Table1" border="1" runat="server">
</table>
```

Listing 3-7. The TableUserControl *Code-Behind Class File*

```
namespace ControlsBookWeb.Ch03
{
    using System;
    using System.Data;
    using System.Drawing;
    using System.Web;
    using System.Web.UI.WebControls;
    using System.Web.UI.HtmlControls;

    public abstract class TableUserControl : System.Web.UI.UserControl
    {
        protected System.Web.UI.HtmlControls.HtmlTable Table1;
        protected System.Web.UI.WebControls.Label XLabel;
        protected System.Web.UI.WebControls.Label YLabel;

        // variables to hold dimensions of HTML table
        private int yDim = 1;
        private int xDim = 1;

        // properties to access dimensions of HTML table
        public int X
        {
            get{ return xDim; }
            set{ xDim = value; }
        }
        public int Y
        {
            get{ return yDim; }
            set{ yDim = value; }
        }


        // HTML table building routine
        private void BuildTable(int xDim, int yDim)
        {
            HtmlTableRow row;
            HtmlTableCell cell;
            HtmlGenericControl content;
```

```
        for (int y=0; y < yDim; y++)
        {
           // create <TR>
           row = new HtmlTableRow();

           for (int x=0; x < xDim; x++)
           {
              // create <TD cellspacing=1>
              cell = new HtmlTableCell();
              cell.Attributes.Add("border","1");

              // create a <SPAN>
              content = new HtmlGenericControl("SPAN");
              content.InnerHtml = "X:" + x.ToString() +
                 "Y:" + y.ToString();
              cell.Controls.Add(content);

              row.Cells.Add(cell);
           }
           Table1.Rows.Add(row);
        }
     }

     private void Page_Load(object sender, System.EventArgs e)
     {
        XLabel.Text = X.ToString();
        YLabel.Text = Y.ToString();

        BuildTable(X, Y);
     }

     #region Web Form Designer generated code
     override protected void OnInit(EventArgs e)
     {
        //
        // CODEGEN: This call is required by the ASP.NET Web Form Designer.
        //
        InitializeComponent();
        base.OnInit(e);
     }

     /// Required method for Designer support - do not modify
     /// the contents of this method with the code editor.
     /// </summary>
     private void InitializeComponent()
     {
        this.Load += new System.EventHandler(this.Page_Load);

     }
     #endregion
  }
}
```

In this example, the .ascx page is a mix of HTML content and server controls. The two `Label` controls come from the `System.Web.UI.WebControls` namespace. The labels display the `X` and `Y` property configuration of the user control:

```
X:<asp:label id="XLabel" Runat="server"></asp:label> 
Y:<asp:label id="YLabel" Runat="server"></asp:label> 
```

The `HtmlTable` control comes from the `System.Web.UI.HtmlControls` namespace and is declared as a table with a border size of 1 on the .ascx page:

```
<table id="Table1" border="1" runat="server">
```

The table control in the `HtmlControl` namespace was chosen over the table in the `WebControl` namespace because it does not automatically add styling information to the final output. This is desirable at this point in the book; we defer the control styling discussion to Chapter 6.

```
<table id="Table1" border="1" runat="server">
```

The code-behind class file of the user control is much more interesting in this example because it contains the content-building code. The `X` and `Y` properties exposed by the user control map to private variables in a demonstration of data encapsulation. These properties are exposed to the containing Web Forms in their .aspx page file via attributes on the user control tag or programmatically in the code-behind class file via a variable reference to an instance of the user control. We could have exposed public methods, fields, and events from the user control as well.

```
// variables to hold dimensions of HTML table
private int yDim = 1;
private int xDim = 1;

// properties to access dimensions of HTML table
public int X
{
    get{ return xDim; }
    set{ xDim = value; }
}
public int Y
{
    get{ return yDim; }
    set{ yDim = value; }
}
```

The `Page_Load` method that is mapped to the Web Form's `Page.Load` event is responsible for transferring the data from the dimension properties to build the table hierarchy via the `BuildTable` routine. It also configures the display of the `Label` controls on the user control to indicate what data was passed in to build the table. We pass on examining the BuildTable routine in more detail here because it is very similar to the HTML table building routine from Chapter 2.

```
private void Page_Load(object sender, System.EventArgs e)
{
    XLabel.Text = X.ToString();
    YLabel.Text = Y.ToString();

    BuildTable(X, Y);
}
```

Using the TableUserControl User Control

Like the menu demonstration, the Table User Control Demo Web Form hosts the user control in order for us to realize its output. The Table User Control Demo Web Form sets the X and Y properties of the TableUserControl control in both the .aspx tag page and the code-behind class file. This demonstrates how you can work with the user control in a declarative and a programmatic fashion on a Web Form. Figure 3-5 shows the Table User Control Demo Web Form at design time, and Figure 3-6 shows Table User Control Demo Web Form at runtime.

Figure 3-5. The Visual Studio .NET Design view of the Table User Control Demo Web Form

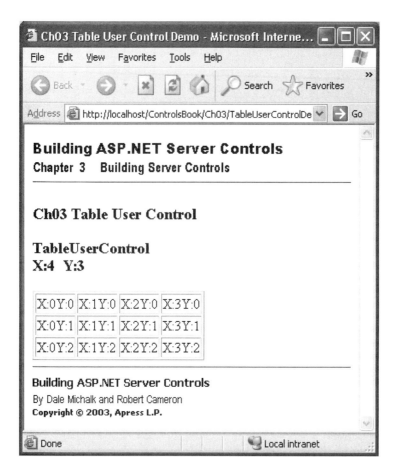

Figure 3-6. The browser view of the HTML output from the Table User Control Demo Web Form

Listings 3-8 and 3-9 show `TableUserControlDemo`'s .aspx page file and its code-behind class file, respectively.

Listing 3-8. The `TableUserControlDemo` *.aspx Page File*

```
<%@ Page language="c#" Codebehind="TableUserControlDemo.aspx.cs"
  AutoEventWireup="false" Inherits="ControlsBookWeb.Ch03.TableUserControlDemo" %>
<%@ Register TagPrefix="apressUC" TagName="TableUserControl"
Src="TableUserControl.ascx" %>
<%@ Register TagPrefix="apressUC" TagName="ControlsBookHeader"
Src="..\ControlsBookHeader.ascx" %>
<%@ Register TagPrefix="apressUC" TagName="ControlsBookFooter"
Src="..\ControlsBookFooter.ascx" %>
<!DOCTYPE HTML PUBLIC "-//W3C//DTD HTML 4.0 Transitional//EN" >
<HTML>
```

```
<HEAD>
  <title>Ch03 Table User Control Demo</title>
  <meta name="GENERATOR" Content="Microsoft Visual Studio 7.0">
  <meta name="CODE_LANGUAGE" Content="C#">
  <meta name="vs_defaultClientScript" content="JavaScript">
  <meta name="vs_targetSchema"
   content="http://schemas.microsoft.com/intellisense/ie5">
</HEAD>
<body MS_POSITIONING="FlowLayout">
  <form id="TableUserControlDemo" method="post" runat="server">
    <apressUC:ControlsBookHeader id="Header"
     runat="server" ChapterNumber="3" ChapterTitle="Building Server Controls" />
    <h3>Ch03 Table User Control</h3>
    <apressUC:tableusercontrol id="TableUserControl1"
     runat="server" Y="1" X="1" />
    <apressUC:ControlsBookFooter id="Footer" runat="server" />
  </form>
</body>
</HTML>
```

Listing 3-9. The TableUserControlDemo *Code-Behind Class File*

```csharp
using System;
using System.Collections;
using System.ComponentModel;
using System.Data;
using System.Drawing;
using System.Web;
using System.Web.SessionState;
using System.Web.UI;
using System.Web.UI.WebControls;
using System.Web.UI.HtmlControls;

namespace ControlsBookWeb.Ch03
{
    public class TableUserControlDemo : System.Web.UI.Page
    {
        protected ControlsBookWeb.Ch03.TableUserControl TableUserControl1;

        private void Page_Load(object sender, System.EventArgs e)
        {
            TableUserControl1.X = 4;
            TableUserControl1.Y = 3;
        }

        #region Web Form Designer generated code
        override protected void OnInit(EventArgs e)
        {
            //
```

```
        // CODEGEN: This call is required by the ASP.NET Web Form Designer.
        //
        InitializeComponent();
        base.OnInit(e);
    }

    /// <summary>
    /// Required method for Designer support - do not modify
    /// the contents of this method with the code editor.
    /// </summary>
    private void InitializeComponent()
    {
        this.Load += new System.EventHandler(this.Page_Load);

    }
    #endregion
    }
}
```

The user control is registered at the top of the .aspx page and declared via an apressuc tag prefix as before:

```
<apressuc:tableusercontrol id="TableUserControl1" runat="server" Y="1" X="1" />
```

Although we declare the HTML table structure to be a 1×1 grid declaratively in the .aspx page file, the code-behind class file changes it to 4×3 programmatically. The Page_Load method is executed after the ASP.NET system has set the value of the control declaratively, so it wins the contest over the value of the X and Y parameters.

```
private void Page_Load(object sender, System.EventArgs e)
{
    TableUserControl1.X = 4;
    TableUserControl1.Y = 3;
}
```

To gain access to the user control in the code-behind class file and set the parameters programmatically, we had to declare a member variable with the name and type of our user control:

```
protected ControlsBookWeb.Ch03.TableUserControl TableUserControl1;
```

The user control must be declared with at least a protected level of accessibility so that the Web Form .aspx tag page that inherits from the code-behind class has access to it.

After this chapter, we do not touch upon building user controls, as this book focuses on building custom server controls. For more information on building ASP.NET user controls, please refer to the ASP.NET documentation.

Building a Custom Control

We now turn our attention to creating custom server controls. The first decision that we must make when building a custom server control is what base class to inherit from, Control or WebControl?

Control or WebControl?

The discussion of the control hierarchy in Chapter 2 covered the various families of controls in the three main namespaces: System.Web.UI, System.Web.UI.WebControls, and System.Web.UI.HtmlControls. You have the option to inherit from any of the controls in these namespaces.

For those who prefer to start from a blank slate, which is the approach we take in this section, two control classes stand out as a potential starting point:

- System.Web.UI.Control

- System.Web.UI.WebControls.WebControl

System.Web.UI.Control is the base class that all controls directly or indirectly inherit from. It provides the bare minimum features required to call a class a server control. System.Web.UI.WebControls.WebControl adds CSS styling management to the rendering process, which makes it easier to build a styled custom control.

The examples in this chapter use the System.Web.UI.Control class to keep things as simple as possible and provide you with a foundation in the features of the root control class. In later chapters, we examine the extra features that make System.Web.UI.WebControls.WebControl the best starting point for most projects.

Another option for building controls is inheriting from existing controls that are available in the framework. An example would be to inherit from the TextBox control and add validation capabilities to ensure that only a phone number is entered into it. You could also take a more complex control such as the DataGrid and customize it to your needs. Though we do provide a simple example of inheriting from an existing control, this chapter concentrates on building custom controls from scratch or, more accurately, from the base System.Web.UI.Control class.

Rendered or Composite Control?

The second major decision in building a custom control concerns the construction technique. The two main options available relate to how a control generates its HTML:

- A server control that renders its own HTML

- A composite control that relies on its children controls to perform the HTML rendering

Figure 3-7 shows these two control options.

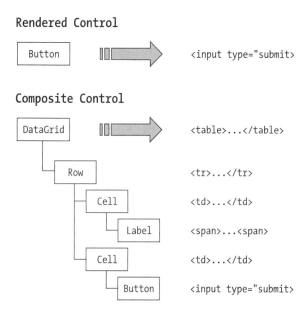

Figure 3-7. Rendered versus composite custom controls

Rendered controls tend to be simpler in nature and have a close relationship with individual HTML tags. Examples of this type of control are the TextBox and Button controls in the ASP.NET framework that emit the <INPUT> tag into the HTML stream. Nothing prevents a developer from putting more complex HTML rendering into these custom controls, but at some point maintaining large amounts of rendered HTML can present a code maintenance problem.

Composite controls are able to take on more complex UI rendering tasks because they follow good object-oriented principles of abstraction and encapsulation. Instead of trying to generate all the output through direct HTML emission, they break down the content generation process into a hierarchy of child controls that are responsible for rendering the portion of HTML that is their responsibility. A great example of this is the DataGrid control, which builds a fairly complex hierarchy of controls to generate its HTML table output.

Separating the Web Application and Control Library

The examples demonstrated so far in the book have all been built under the assumption that they are part of the same ASP.NET web application. Custom control development should deviate from this method and be constructed in a separate library project to generate an assembly independent of any web application code. The sample source code for the book follows this advice, as it has a web application project and a control library project holding the source code for all the custom controls.

The MenuCustomControl Server Control

The `MenuCustomControl` class is a clone of its user control cousin, rendering a simple HTML hyperlink menu. Because custom controls do not have the luxury of declaratively specifying the HTML output using drag and drop with the Visual Studio .NET Toolbox and the Designer surface, we must use the facilities of the `HtmlTextWriter` class to generate the HTML output programmatically.

`HtmlTextWriter` is passed as the only parameter to the all-important `Render` method of the `System.Web.UI.Control` base class. `Render` is overridden by a custom control to inject the appropriate HTML content into the output stream.

The `Render` method in Listing 3-10 calls on the services of a helper method named `RenderMenuItem` that does the work for each item in the menu. Using helper methods is a good habit, as it keeps the rendering code more manageable.

Listing 3-10. The MenuCustomControl *Class File*

```
using System;
using System.Web;
using System.Web.UI;

namespace ControlsBookLib.Ch03
{
    [ToolboxData("<{0}:MenuCustomControl runat=server></{0}:MenuCustomControl>")]
    public class MenuCustomControl : Control
    {
        protected override void Render(HtmlTextWriter writer)

{
    base.Render(writer);
     writer.WriteLine("<div>");
        writer.WriteLine("<div>");
        RenderMenuItem(writer,"Apress","http://www.apress.com");
        writer.Write(" | ");
        RenderMenuItem(writer,"Microsoft","http://www.microsoft.com");
        writer.Write(" | ");
        RenderMenuItem(writer,"GotDotNet","http://www.gotdotnet.com");
        writer.Write(" | ");
        RenderMenuItem(writer,"ASP.NET","http://www.aspnet.com");
        writer.WriteLine("</div>");
    }

    private void RenderMenuItem(HtmlTextWriter writer, string title, string url)
    {
        writer.Write("<span><a href=\"");
        writer.Write(url);
        writer.Write("\">");
        writer.Write(title);
        writer.WriteLine("</a><span>");
    }
  }
}
```

`HtmlTextWriter` in this example is used in its more basic mode by sticking to its `Write` and `WriteLine` methods. These methods should be familiar to the ASP developer, as they are analogous to the `Response.Write` and `Response.WriteLine` methods that take string input and pass it directly to the output stream.

Using the MenuCustomControl Server Control

Like the user control, custom controls cannot stand alone without the hosting support of a Web Form .aspx page. The registration process with custom controls is similar to that of user controls except for describing the location of the control content. Instead of providing a path to an .ascx file, we are looking for an assembly and namespace that contains the code of the custom control:

```
<%@ Register TagPrefix="apress" Namespace="ControlsBookLib.Ch03"
Assembly="ControlsBookLib" %>
```

You have to remember to make the control assembly, like `ControlsBookLib` in this example, available to the web application either through the GAC or the web application's bin directory. If things are set up properly, the `MenuCustomControl` provides an accurate representation in the Design view of its HTML output, as shown in Figure 3-8.

Figure 3-8. The Visual Studio .NET Design view of the MenuCustomControl *on a Web Form*

Figure 3-9 confirms that the HTML output from our `MenuCustomControl` custom server control is the same as that of the user control in a browser. Listing 3-11 presents `MenuCustomControlDemo`'s .aspx file.

Figure 3-9. Output from the Menu Custom Control Demo Web Form

Listing 3-11. The `MenuCustomControlDemo` *.aspx Page File*

```
<%@ Register TagPrefix="apressUC" TagName="ControlsBookHeader"
Src="..\ControlsBookHeader.ascx" %>
<%@ Register TagPrefix="apressUC" TagName="ControlsBookFooter"
Src="..\ControlsBookFooter.ascx" %>
<%@ Register TagPrefix="apress" Namespace="ControlsBookLib.Ch03"
Assembly="ControlsBookLib" %>
<%@ Page language="c#" Codebehind="MenuCustomControlDemo.aspx.cs"
AutoEventWireup="false" Inherits="ControlsBookWeb.Ch03.MenuCustomControlDemo" %>
<!DOCTYPE HTML PUBLIC "-//W3C//DTD HTML 4.0 Transitional//EN" >
<HTML>
  <HEAD>
    <title>Ch03 Menu Custom Control Demo</title>
    <meta name="GENERATOR" Content="Microsoft Visual Studio 7.0">
    <meta name="CODE_LANGUAGE" Content="C#">
    <meta name="vs_defaultClientScript" content="JavaScript">
    <meta name="vs_targetSchema"
```

```
      content="http://schemas.microsoft.com/intellisense/ie5">
  </HEAD>
  <body MS_POSITIONING="FlowLayout">
    <form id="MenuCustomControlDemo" method="post" runat="server">
      <apressUC:ControlsBookHeader id="Header" runat="server" />
      <h3>Ch03 Menu Custom Control</h3>
      <apress:MenuCustomControl id="menu1" runat="server" /><br>
      <br>
      <apressUC:ControlsBookFooter id="Footer" runat="server" />
    </form>
  </body>
</HTML>
```

The `TableCustomControl` Server Control via Rendering

We continue our task of duplicating the user control examples via custom controls by implementing the dynamic HTML table. To make things more interesting, we demonstrate some of the more advanced techniques of the `HtmlTextWriter` class and we use control composition to build the HTML table content. The rendering version is on deck first. Listing 3-12 shows the `TableCustomControl` class file.

Listing 3-12. The `TableCustomControl` Class File

```
using System;
using System.Web;
using System.Web.UI;

namespace ControlsBookLib.Ch03
{
    [ToolboxData("<{0}:TableCustomControl runat=server></{0}:TableCustomControl>")]
    public class TableCustomControl : Control
    {
        // variables to hold dimensions of HTML table
        private int yDim = 1;
        private int xDim = 1;

        // properties to access dimensions of HTML table
        public int X
        {
            get
            {
                return xDim;
            }
            set
            {
                xDim = value;
            }
        }
        public int Y
```

```
      {
         get
         {
            return yDim;
         }
         set
         {
            yDim = value;
         }
      }

      protected override void Render(HtmlTextWriter writer)
{
   base.Render(writer);

         RenderHeader(writer);
         RenderTable(writer,X,Y);
      }

      private void RenderHeader(HtmlTextWriter writer)
      {
         // write just <H3
         writer.WriteBeginTag("h3");
         // write >
         writer.Write(HtmlTextWriter.TagRightChar);
         writer.Write("TableCustomControl");
         // write <br>
         writer.WriteFullBeginTag("br");
         writer.Write("X:" + X.ToString() + " ");
         writer.WriteLine("Y:" + Y.ToString() + " ");
         // write </h3>
         writer.WriteEndTag("h3");
      }

      private void RenderTable(HtmlTextWriter writer, int xDim, int yDim)
      {
         // write <TABLE border="1">
         writer.AddAttribute(HtmlTextWriterAttribute.Border,"1");
         writer.RenderBeginTag(HtmlTextWriterTag.Table);

         for (int y=0; y < yDim; y++)
         {
            // write <TR>
            writer.RenderBeginTag(HtmlTextWriterTag.Tr);

            for (int x=0; x < xDim; x++)
            {
               // write <TD cellspacing="1">
               writer.AddAttribute(HtmlTextWriterAttribute.Cellspacing,"1");
               writer.RenderBeginTag(HtmlTextWriterTag.Td);

               // write <SPAN>
               writer.RenderBeginTag(HtmlTextWriterTag.Span);
```

```
            writer.Write("X:" + x.ToString());
            writer.Write("Y:" + y.ToString());
            // write </SPAN>
            writer.RenderEndTag();

            // write </TD>
            writer.RenderEndTag();
        }
        // write </TR>
        writer.RenderEndTag();
    }
    // write </TABLE>
    writer.RenderEndTag();
    }
  }
}
```

The top portion of the custom control class contains the fields representing the X and Y dimensions of the HTML table. It also provides access to the fields through public properties as in the user control. More interestingly, the Render method drives the process of rendering the control output:

```
protected override void Render(HtmlTextWriter writer)
{
    base.Render(writer);
    RnderHeader(writer);
    RenderTable(writer,X,Y);
}
```

Rendering the Table Header

The RenderHeader method is responsible for displaying information about the X and Y properties inside of an <H3> section. The code to build the <H3> tag demonstrates the ability to use the special Write methods of the HtmlTextWriter class.

WriteBeginTag writes the starting portion of a tag, including the opening bracket and the name of the tag, without closing it out:

```
// write just <H3
writer.WriteBeginTag("h3");
```

At this point, you can manually add HTML attributes such as border and style using the Write method of HtmlTextWriter if necessary. You also have the responsibility of explicitly closing out the tag.

A handy way to write out special characters is to use the helper fields exposed by HtmlTextWriter to produce the correct strings, which sure beats the escaping that has to occur inside the C# string for special characters if you do all the work on your own. Table 3-1 shows what fields are available.

Table 3-1. String Fields Exposed by `HtmlTextWriter`

HTMLTEXTWRITER FIELD	STRING OUTPUT
DefaultTabString	(Single tab character)
DoubleQuoteChar	"
EndTagLeftChars	</
EqualsChar	=
EqualsDoubleQuoteString	="
SelfClosingChars	/
SelfClosingTagEnd	/>
SemicolonChar	;
SingleQuoteChar	'
SlashChar	/
SpaceChar	(Space)
StyleEqualsChar	:
TagLeftChar	<
TagRightChar	>

The `RenderHeader` code uses `TagRightChar` to generate the closing bracket for the `<H3>` tag:

```
// write >
writer.Write(HtmlTextWriter.TagRightChar);
```

An easier method to write a fully formed tag is to use the `WriteFullBegin` tag method. This is useful for HTML tags such as `<BR>` that are commonly used without attributes:

```
// write <br>
writer.WriteFullBeginTag("br");
```

Closing out the `<H3>` tag requires a tag that contains a closing slash before the name (e.g., `</H3>`). `WriteEndTag` can be used to generate this content in one atomic action:

```
// write </h3>
writer.WriteEndTag("h3");
```

Rendering the Table

Once the control header content is rendered, we move on to building the HTML table in the `RenderTable` method. This portion of the control demonstrates a nifty feature of the `HtmlTextWriter` in working with HTML attributes. The `AddAttribute` method takes a key/value string pair for each attribute you wish to render on an HTML tag. You can call this method multiple times to build up as many attributes as necessary to the follow-on tag. Once you've finished adding attributes, the next step is to use the `RenderBeginTag` method. This method is smart enough to look at the attributes that were added previously and render them into the final output stream along with the tag name and brackets. The `RenderTable` method uses this functionality to build the `<TABLE>` tag and add a `Border` attribute to it:

```
// write <TABLE border="1">
writer.AddAttribute(HtmlTextWriterAttribute.Border,"1");
writer.RenderBeginTag(HtmlTextWriterTag.Table);
```

The `HtmlTextWriterTag` enumeration is used for the `<TABLE>` tag and the `Border` attribute strings as a simplified means of specifying the correct HTML name. Many of the `HtmlTextWriter` methods are overloaded to accept this enumeration and return the appropriate string value. See the ASP.NET documentation for full details on what names are supported.

If you use the `RenderBeginTag` to build your opening tag, you must remember to pair it with a `RenderEndTag` call to generate the closing tag. Fortunately, the `HtmlTextWriter` class is smart enough to remember the nesting and the order of the two routines to match them up and generate the correct closing tags. Closing out our table is a direct call to `RenderEndTag` with no parameters:

```
// write </TABLE>
writer.RenderEndTag();
```

The rest of the `RenderTable` routine uses `RenderBeginTag` and `RenderEndTag` in a two-loop scenario to build the `<TR>` and `<TD>` tags along with their content according to the size specified in the X and Y dimension fields of the control.

The TableCustomControl Server Control via Control Composition

The second table custom control example accomplishes the same task as the first but does not bother with getting its hands dirty with HTML rendering. It follows the lead of the table user control and builds up its control content programmatically by adding child controls such as the table and its cells.

 NOTE *Because we are building a composite control, we implement the* `INamingContainer` *interface. We discuss why this is necessary in Chapter 5.*

Listing 3-13 shows `TableCompCustomControl`'s class file.

Listing 3-13. The TableCompCustomControl *Class File*

```
using System;
using System.ComponentModel;
using System.Web;
using System.Web.UI;
using System.Web.UI.HtmlControls;
using System.Text;
using ControlsBookLib.Ch12.Design;

namespace ControlsBookLib.Ch03
{
   [ToolboxData("<{0}:TableCompCustomControl runat=server>
     </{0}:TableCompCustomControl>"),
   Designer(typeof(CompCntrlDesigner))]
   public class TableCompCustomControl : Control, INamingContainer
   {
      private HtmlTable table;

      // properties to access dimensions of HTML table
      int xDim;
      public int X
      {
         get
         {
            return xDim;
         }
         set
         {
            xDim =  value;
         }
      }

      int yDim;
      public int Y
      {
         get
         {
            return yDim;
         }
         set
         {
            yDim  = value;
         }
      }

      public override ControlCollection Controls
      {
         get
         {
            EnsureChildControls();
            return base.Controls;
         }
```

```
      }

      protected override void CreateChildControls()
      {
         Controls.Clear();
         BuildHeader();
         BuildTable(X,Y);
      }

      private void BuildHeader()
      {
         StringBuilder sb = new StringBuilder();
         sb.Append("TableCompCustomControl<br>");
         sb.Append("X:");
         sb.Append(X.ToString());
         sb.Append(" ");
         sb.Append("Y:");
         sb.Append(Y.ToString());
         sb.Append(" ");

         HtmlGenericControl header = new HtmlGenericControl("h3");
         header.InnerHtml = sb.ToString();
         Controls.Add(header);
      }

      private void BuildTable(int xDim, int yDim)
      {
         HtmlTableRow row;
         HtmlTableCell cell;
         HtmlGenericControl content;

         // create <TABLE border=1>
         table = new HtmlTable();
         table.Border = 1;

         for (int y=0; y < Y; y++)
         {
            // create <TR>
            row = new HtmlTableRow();

            for (int x=0; x < X; x++)
            {
               // create <TD cellspacing=1>
               cell = new HtmlTableCell();
               cell.Attributes.Add("border","1");

               // create a <SPAN>
               content = new HtmlGenericControl("SPAN");
               content.InnerHtml = "X:" + x.ToString() +
                  "Y:" + y.ToString();
               cell.Controls.Add(content);

               row.Cells.Add(cell);
            }
```

```
            table.Rows.Add(row);
        }
        Controls.Add(table);
    }
  }
}
```

Composite custom controls typically do not override the Render method. They rely on the base class implementation of Render provided by the System.Web.UI.Control class that locates the Controls collection and calls Render for each child control. This in turn causes the child controls to either render or do the same with their children, recursively walking through the render tree. In the end, we have a nice HTML output.

At design time, composite controls can sometimes have trouble rendering themselves in the Visual Studio .NET Designer. What can happen is Render gets called on a composite control at design time before the Controls collection has been created, causing the default UI of the control type and ID to be displayed as text in brackets. To assist composite controls with building out their UI at design time, we apply a custom Designer class with this attribute:

```
Designer(typeof(CompCntrlDesigner))
```

We provide an overview of attributes in Chapter 4 and discuss how to implement design time functionality for server controls in Chapter 12.

Although the composite control doesn't override the Render method, it needs to override the CreateChildControls method that is called by the ASP.NET framework. This method is called to give the custom server control the opportunity to create its Controls collection, populating it with the appropriate child controls for rendering the desired output:

```
protected override void CreateChildControls()
{
    Controls.Clear();
    BuildHeader();
    BuildTable(X,Y);
}
```

One extra task we need to perform is override the Controls property exposed by the base Control class, as follows. This ensures that when an outside client attempts to access our composite control, the child control content will always be created and ready for access.

```
public override ControlCollection Controls
{
    get
    {
        EnsureChildControls();
        return base.Controls;
    }
}
```

The EnsureChildControls method does the work for us. Calling it will call CreateChildControls if the child controls have not been initialized. Overriding Controls is always recommended in composite controls.

It is also recommended to call EnsureChildControls for properties in a composite control right at the beginning of the Get and Set methods. This prevents any chance of accessing a child control before it is created. We deviate from this practice for the TableCompCustomControl control because the X and Y properties must be set and available before we can create the control hierarchy. Otherwise, we wouldn't know what dimensions to use for the table.

Our implementation of CreateChildControls calls into routines responsible for adding the child controls representing the header and the HTML table of the control, which are named BuildHeader and BuildTable, respectively. It is also the linkage point for evaluating the X and Y dimensions of the table.

BuildHeader demonstrates the use of an HtmlGenericControl control from the System.Web.UI.HtmlControls namespace to render the <H3> content. This control was chosen due to its lack of built-in styling capabilities to keep the example simple. We build up the string content of the control by using the StringBuilder class. This class is a more efficient way of building up strings in .NET than concatenating literals as Strings, because StringBuilder uses a buffer. Variables of type String are immutable, and a concatenation operation actually builds a third string from the two strings brought together, literal or otherwise. For those who were worried about the HtmlTextWriter class and its efficiencies, the Render and Write methods write to a buffer so there aren't any performance concerns about calling these methods multiple times.

```
private void BuildHeader()
{
    StringBuilder sb = new StringBuilder();
    sb.Append("TableCompCustomControl<br>");
    sb.Append("X:");
    sb.Append(X.ToString());
    sb.Append(" ");
    sb.Append("Y:");
    sb.Append(Y.ToString());
    sb.Append(" ");

    HtmlGenericControl header = new HtmlGenericControl("h3");
    header.InnerHtml = sb.ToString();
    Controls.Add(header);
}
```

Once we have built up the string content, we next use the InnerHtml property to easily load the HTML information inside the <H3> control. The final step is to add the HtmlGenericControl to the Controls collection of our new custom server control.

Building the HTML table in the BuildTable method follows the well-worn process of programmatically building up the HtmlTable control's child content. The result is almost an exact image of the user control version of the table. This is a good indication of the strength of custom controls when it comes to dynamic generation. The declarative advantages of the user control are not as powerful when content is built "on the fly."

Using the Custom Table Controls

To verify that both custom controls provide identical HTML output, we use a Web Form that hosts them side-by-side in an HTML table. Figure 3-10 shows that they have the same Designer capability, though `TableCompCustomControl` requires the additional `Designer` attribute on its class to render correctly at design time as discussed previously. Figure 3-11 shows that the final output is identical in the browser.

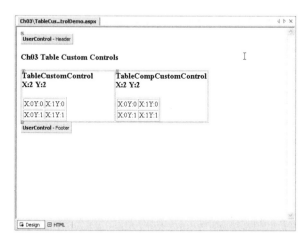

Figure 3-10. The Visual Studio .NET Design view of custom table controls on a Web Form

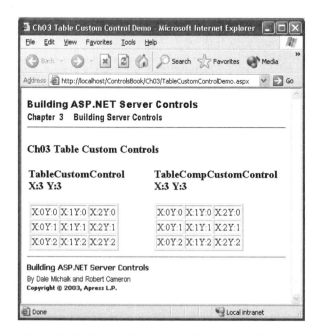

Figure 3-11. Output from the Table Custom Control Demo Web Form

Listings 3-14 and 3-15 show TableCustomControlDemo's .aspx and class files.

Listing 3-14. The TableCustomControlDemo *.aspx Page File*

```
<%@ Register TagPrefix="apressUC" TagName="ControlsBookFooter"
    Src="..\ControlsBookFooter.ascx" %>
<%@ Register TagPrefix="apressUC" TagName="ControlsBookHeader"
    Src="..\ControlsBookHeader.ascx" %>
<%@ Page language="c#" Codebehind="TableCustomControlDemo.aspx.cs"
    AutoEventWireup="false"
Inherits="ControlsBookWeb.Ch03.TableCustomControlDemo" %>
<%@ Register TagPrefix="apress" Namespace="ControlsBookLib.Ch03"
Assembly="ControlsBookLib" %>
<!DOCTYPE HTML PUBLIC "-//W3C//DTD HTML 4.0 Transitional//EN" >
<HTML>
  <HEAD>
    <title>Ch03 Table Custom Control Demo</title>
    <meta content="Microsoft Visual Studio 7.0" name="GENERATOR">
    <meta content="C#" name="CODE_LANGUAGE">
    <meta content="JavaScript" name="vs_defaultClientScript">
    <meta content="http://schemas.microsoft.com/intellisense/ie5"
name="vs_targetSchema">
  </HEAD>
  <body MS_POSITIONING="FlowLayout">
    <form id="TableCustomControlDemo" method="post" runat="server">
      <apressUC:ControlsBookHeader id="Header" runat="server"
ChapterNumber="3" ChapterTitle="Building Server Controls" />
      <h3>Ch03 Table Custom Controls</h3>
      <table>
        <tr>
          <td width="50%"><apress:TableCustomControl id="TableCust1"
           runat="server" X="2" Y="2" /></td>
          <td><apress:TableCompCustomControl id="TableCompCust1"
                   runat="server" X="2" Y="2" /></td>
        </tr>
      </table>
      <apressUC:ControlsBookFooter id="Footer" runat="server" />
    </form>
  </body>
</HTML>
```

Listing 3-15. The TableCustomControlDemo *Code-Behind Class File*

```
using System;
using System.Collections;
using System.ComponentModel;
using System.Data;
using System.Drawing;
using System.Web;
using System.Web.SessionState;
```

```
using System.Web.UI;
using System.Web.UI.WebControls;
using System.Web.UI.HtmlControls;

namespace ControlsBookWeb.Ch03
{
   public class TableCustomControlDemo : System.Web.UI.Page
   {
      protected ControlsBookLib.Ch03.TableCustomControl TableCust1;
      protected ControlsBookLib.Ch03.TableCompCustomControl TableCompCust1;

      private void Page_Load(object sender, System.EventArgs e)
      {
         TableCust1.X = 3;
         TableCust1.Y = 3;
         TableCompCust1.X = 3;
         TableCompCust1.Y = 3;
      }

      #region Web Form Designer generated code
      override protected void OnInit(EventArgs e)
      {
         //
         // CODEGEN: This call is required by the ASP.NET Web Form Designer.
         //
         InitializeComponent();
         base.OnInit(e);
      }

      /// <summary>
      /// Required method for Designer support - do not modify
      /// the contents of this method with the code editor.
      /// </summary>
      private void InitializeComponent()
      {
         this.Load += new System.EventHandler(this.Page_Load);

      }
      #endregion
   }
}
```

Inheriting from an Existing Server Control

The previous examples are very simple controls in concept. This was by design; we
focused on the details required to build the simplest of controls in order to give you a
taste of the control-building process. In this section, we demonstrate how with just a
little bit of code it is possible to add pleasing functionality through inheritance to one
of the existing ASP.NET controls.

In our simple inheritance example, we add a three-dimensional (3D) look to the `WebControl TextBox` class. To add this UI behavior, we take advantage of the DHTML features of Internet Explorer when rendering our new server control. Listing 3-16 contains `TextBox3d`'s class file.

Listing 3-16. The `TextBox3d` *Class File*

```
using System;
using System.Web.UI;
using System.Web.UI.WebControls;
using System.ComponentModel;
using System.Drawing;

namespace ControlsBookLib.Ch03
{
    [ToolboxData("<{0}:TextBox3d runat=server></{0}:TextBox3d>"),
ToolboxBitmap(typeof(ControlsBookLib.Ch03.TextBox3d),
"ControlsBookLib.Ch03.TextBox3d.bmp")]
    public class TextBox3d : TextBox// Inherit from rich control
    {
        // Private member to store value
        private bool _threeD;

        public TextBox3d()
        {
            _threeD = true ;
        }

        // Custom property to set 3D appearance
        [DescriptionAttribute("Set to true for 3d appearance"),DefaultValue("True")]
        public bool Enable3D
        {
            get
            {
                return _threeD;
            }
            set
            {
                _threeD = value;
            }
        }

        protected override void Render(HtmlTextWriter output)
        {
            // Add DHTML style attribute
            if (_threeD)
                output.AddStyleAttribute("FILTER",
"progid:DXImageTransform.Microsoft.dropshadow(OffX=2, OffY=2, Color='gray',
Positive='true'");
```

```
        base.Render(output);
    }
}
```

In our inheritance example, we have two main features: a property and an overridden Render method. The property is used to determine whether or not to render with a 3D look. Providing a Boolean property that allows the developer to revert to the default behavior of the base class server control is a good design guideline to follow when inheriting from rich server controls in ASP.NET.

```
public bool Enable3D
{
    get
    {
        return _threeD;
    }
    set
    {
        _threeD = value;
    }
}
```

We make this property available so that it is possible to revert to the TextBox base class look and feel without having to swap out the control. The property uses a private member _threeD to store the value, with a default value of true set in the control's constructor:

```
public TextBox3d()
{
    _threeD = true ;
}
```

The only other interesting code in this simple control is the Render method. Here we add a style attribute to the output variable to provide the 3D look to the base TextBox control. We round out this method with a call to the base class's Render method to finish off all the work:

```
protected override void Render(HtmlTextWriter output)
{
    //Add DHTML style attribute
    if (_threeD)
        output.AddStyleAttribute("FILTER",
        "progid:DXImageTransform.Microsoft.dropshadow(OffX=2, OffY=2, Color='gray',
        Positive='true'");

        base.Render(output);
}
```

As in previous examples, we need an .aspx page to host our custom control and show off our new 3D look. Figure 3-12 shows the 3D TextBox at runtime.

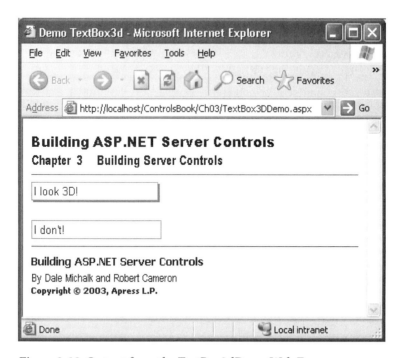

Figure 3-12. Output from the TextBox3dDemo Web Form

Listings 3-17 and 3-18 contain TextBox3dDemo's .aspx and class files, respectively.

Listing 3-17. The TextBox3dDemo .aspx Page File

```
<%@ Register TagPrefix="apressUC" TagName="ControlsBookFooter"
Src="..\ControlsBookFooter.ascx" %>
<%@ Register TagPrefix="apressUC" TagName="ControlsBookHeader"
Src="..\ControlsBookHeader.ascx" %>
<%@ Register TagPrefix="apress" Namespace="ControlsBookLib.Ch03"
Assembly="ControlsBookLib" %>
<%@ Page language="c#" Codebehind="TextBox3DDemo.aspx.cs" AutoEventWireup="false"
Inherits="TestTextBox3d.WebForm1" %>
<!DOCTYPE HTML PUBLIC "-//W3C//DTD HTML 4.0 Transitional//EN" >
<HTML>
  <HEAD>
    <title>Demo TextBox3d</title>
    <meta name="GENERATOR" Content="Microsoft Visual Studio 7.0">
    <meta name="CODE_LANGUAGE" Content="C#">
    <meta name="vs_defaultClientScript" content="JavaScript">
    <meta name="vs_targetSchema"
     content="http://schemas.microsoft.com/intellisense/ie5">
```

```
    </HEAD>
    <body MS_POSITIONING="FlowLayout">
      <form id="Form1" method="post" runat="server">
        <apressUC:ControlsBookHeader id="Header" runat="server" ChapterNumber="3"
ChapterTitle="Building Server Controls" />
        <apress:TextBox3d id="TextBox3d1" runat="server"
          Width="159px" Height="22px">I look 3D!</apress:TextBox3d>
        <br>
        <br>
        <apress:TextBox3d id="Textbox3d2" runat="server" Width="159px" Height="22px"
                  Enable3D="false">I don't!</apress:TextBox3d>
        <br>
        <apressUC:ControlsBookFooter id="Footer" runat="server" />
      </form>
    </body>
</HTML>
```

Listing 3-18. The TextBox3dDemo *Code-Behind Class File*

```csharp
using System;
using System.Collections;
using System.ComponentModel;
using System.Data;
using System.Drawing;
using System.Web;
using System.Web.SessionState;
using System.Web.UI;
using System.Web.UI.WebControls;
using System.Web.UI.HtmlControls;

namespace ControlsBookWeb.Ch03
{
    public class TextBox3dDemo : System.Web.UI.Page
    {
        protected ControlsBookLib.Ch03.TextBox3d Textbox3d2;
        protected ControlsBookLib.Ch03.TextBox3d TextBox3d1;

        private void Page_Load(object sender, System.EventArgs e)
        {

        }

        #region Web Form Designer generated code
        override protected void OnInit(EventArgs e)
        {
            //
            // CODEGEN: This call is required by the ASP.NET Web Form Designer.
            //
            InitializeComponent();
            base.OnInit(e);
        }
```

107

```
/// <summary>
/// Required method for Designer support - do not modify
/// the contents of this method with the code editor.
/// </summary>
private void InitializeComponent()
{
    this.Load += new System.EventHandler(this.Page_Load);

}
#endregion
    }
}
```

Having a rich server control as the base class is a powerful means of packaging functionality that takes advantage of browser DHTML capabilities to generate pleasing output, as this example demonstrates.

In the preceding examples we do not provide persistent state for control properties to keep the example code simple. This requires that the control's value be set in the page's Load event if the desired value is different than what is set declaratively in the page. In the next chapter we discuss how to take advantage of state management in server controls, but first we provide a quick introduction to design-time attributes.

Using Design-Time Attributes

Visual Studio .NET provides a rich, powerful development environment with autocomplete, default properties, as well as custom property editors to speed developers' coding efforts. There are a few different technologies available to integrate and extend the Visual Studio environment. Attributes provide one means to extend Visual Studio .NET and are used to integrate custom server controls into the environment. Before we present a quick overview of the most important design-time attributes, we provide a short background on attributes.

What's an Attribute?

An *attribute* is essentially a class that contains properties and methods used to modify other classes, class methods, or class properties. Attribute information is stored with the metadata of the element and can be retrieved at runtime through reflection.

Attributes can be applied to an entire class or to a specific class method or property. Attribute classes are defined as public classes. All attributes derive directly or indirectly from the System.Attribute class, and attribute classes generally end in the word "Attribute" to enhance readability. Here is a sample attribute declaration:

```
public class SampleAttribute : Attribute
{
}
```

An attribute is declared within brackets just before the element to which it is applied. The syntax consists of calling a constructor on the attribute. Here is how an attribute is applied to a class method:

```
public class SampleClass
{
    [SampleAttribute]
    public virtual void SampleMethod()
    {
        //...
    }
}
```

Attributes provide an object-oriented way to extend the declarative syntax of the .NET Framework without having to resort to macros or some other outside mechanism to store configuration information such as the registry.

Common Design-Time Attributes

Now that you have a bit of background on attributes, let's move on to design-time attributes for server controls. Design-time attributes exist in the System.ComponentModel namespace. Table 3-2 provides a brief description of the most common design-time attributes.

Table 3-2. Common Design-Time Attributes

ATTRIBUTE	DESCRIPTION
BindableAttribute	Indicates whether or not a property supports two-way data binding
BrowsableAttribute	Indicates whether or not a property or event should be listed in a property browser
CategoryAttribute	Specifies in which category a property or event should be listed in the property browser
DefaultEvent	Specifies the name of the default event for a class
DefaultProperty	Specifies the name of the default property for a class
DefaultValue	Sets the default value for a property
DescriptionAttribute	Allows the property browser to display a brief description of a property
DesignOnlyAttribute	Specifies that a property can be set only at design time
EditorAttribute	Associates a UI type editor with a property
TagPrefix	Assembly-level attribute that indicates the tag prefix for a control or set of controls within an assembly
ToolboxData	Specifies default values for control attributes and customizes the initial HTML content
TypeConverterAttribute	Defines a custom type converter for a property

You can apply multiple attributes to a particular class, method, or property. There are two ways to do this. One syntax is to separate attributes by a comma within a set of brackets:

```
[DefaultProperty("Text"),
    ToolboxData("<{0}:SuperLabel runat=server></{0}:MyLabel>")]
  public class SuperLabel : Label
  {...}
```

The other syntax is to put each attribute in its own set of brackets:

```
[DefaultProperty("Text")]
[ToolboxData("<{0}:SuperLabel runat=server></{0}:MyLabel>")]
  public class SuperLabel : Label
  {...}
```

This completes our whirlwind tour of attributes and of the most common design-time attributes available for use on custom controls. Here we provided a short overview of basic Designer attributes that we use in the code samples in this book. We cover design-time support in more detail in Chapter 12.

Summary

The ASP.NET object model fully supports inheritance as a method of providing additional functionality to existing controls. Given the object-oriented nature of the framework, it is quite easy to add powerful functionality with just a few lines of code.

ASP.NET provides two primary means of building controls: user controls and custom controls. Encapsulation or composition is another method available in ASP.NET to package functionality. Server control encapsulation is more applicable when focused on generic logic. User control encapsulation is more applicable when packaging application-specific logic.

User controls have the benefit of declarative UI development and require less skill from the development staff. Custom controls provide bare-bones access to the ASP.NET plumbing, myriad design options, a superior deployment mechanism as an assembly, and better Designer support for the developer/user.

Custom controls typically inherit from either System.Web.UI.Control or System.Web.UI.WebControls.WebControl and are built using one of two primary techniques: direct rendering or control composition. The HtmlTextWriter class provides a significant amount of assistance with rendering HTML content from a custom control through its Write and Render methods. Custom controls that use control composition speed development time by letting child controls handle their own HTML generation through the application of good object-oriented design principles.

CHAPTER 4

State Management

THE NEED TO MAINTAIN STATE in a web application has driven vendors and those who participate in the evolution of web protocols to provide additional tools and standards to make life easier on web developers. Through these clever techniques, it is possible to make it appear to the user as if the browser is intimately linked to the web application and maintains an ongoing, connected relationship as experienced when using a thick-client application running locally on the user's desktop. In this chapter, we cover the various techniques available in ASP.NET to maintain state and demonstrate how these techniques relate to building server controls.

Maintaining User State

Hypertext Transfer Protocol (HTTP), the protocol that provides the underlying foundation for the Web, is inherently stateless. The typical interaction of a client browser with a web server starts with opening a connection to port 80 via Transmission Control Protocol (TCP), continues with fetching the HTML document along with its graphical images, and ends with the connection closing, as shown in Figure 4-1. Once the web server has delivered the goods, both parties are free to go their separate ways. This enhances scalability because connection- and memory-consuming sockets are not continuously maintained during the session between a web browser and web server.

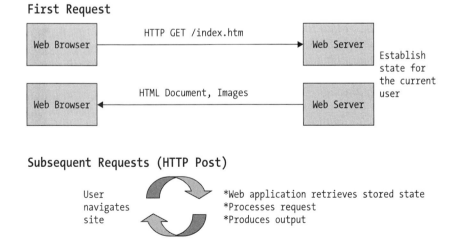

Figure 4-1. HTTP and the stateless nature of the Web

Unfortunately, the statelessness and scalability of HTTP are in direct conflict with the requirement to build interactive, useful web applications. Users want a web application to remember their preferences, keep track of what they've accomplished, and guide them on what steps to take based on contextual information maintained on their behalf by the application. Users won't stay around very long on a web site that requires them to reenter data to use the application upon each request.

There are two locations where web developers can choose to maintain application state in a web application: on the client side or on the web server. In ASP, client-side state management techniques include cookies and hidden form fields. Also in ASP, server-side state management techniques include Session and Application variables. ASP.NET includes these options and provides additional options that we discuss later in this chapter. Before diving into a state-management discussion, we provide additional background detail on the ASP.NET architecture as it relates to state management and request processing.

The ASP.NET Request-Processing Architecture

When you develop web-based applications, managing user state and implementing a secure robust application are high on the list of requirements. On the Internet, ensuring state and application integrity (i.e., authorization, authentication, and auditing) is even more important due to the wild nature of the Web. Although it is possible to implement these features within ASP, many web development teams choose to implement these important functions using ISAPI libraries.

ISAPI libraries provide tight integration with IIS and put the full power of the C or C++ language at the developer's disposal. To some degree, this architecture also promotes application modularity. Though ISAPI extensions and filters are very useful, the ASP Session and Application state constructs are not directly accessible to these libraries. Some other means of communication, such as cookies or URL parameters, is required to pass state between an ISAPI library and ASP, which generally limits the degree of interaction to a Boolean (valid or invalid) decision.

In ASP.NET, ISAPI libraries can still be put to task in the same manner, but ASP.NET implements a highly pluggable architecture with a simple object model that allows for much greater interaction using HttpModules and HttpHandlers. HttpModules and HttpHandlers are easier to write than ISAPI extensions, because developers are not limited to the C/C++ language and the raw API.

TIP *As in ASP, ASP.NET resides inside of an ISAPI library in IIS that is configured to process files through IIS application mappings with the extensions .aspx, .asax, .ascx, .ashx, and .asmx. The name of the ISAPI library is aspnet_isapi.dll, and it is located in the directory where the .NET Framework is installed. For the .NET Framework 1.0, the default install location is C:\Windows\Microsoft.NET\Framework\v1.0.3705\. When more than one version of the .NET Framework is installed, the ISAPI .dll name is the same, but the location is different according the Framework version number. This makes it possible to have multiple versions of the Framework installed on a single server and the version used can be configured at the IIS virtual directory level in the web.config file.*

Processing Requests

When a browser client makes a request to IIS for a resource such as an .aspx file, ASP.NET initiates and then maintains user state for the duration of the session, which can include multiple request/response HTTP sessions. Figure 4-2 shows the logical data flow for a typical ASP.NET request. The request is made to IIS, which checks the file extension mappings to determine how to handle the request. If it is an ASP.NET request, IIS hands the request off to the ASP.NET ISAPI library, aspnet_isapi.dll. The library aspnet_isapi.dll next funnels the request into the ASP.NET pluggable architecture, handing the request off to the ASP.NET worker process, aspnet_wp.exe.

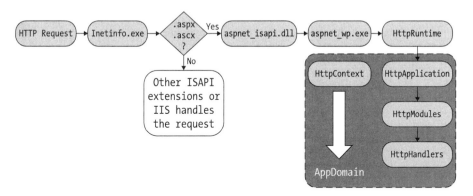

Figure 4-2. ASP.NET request data flow

The worker process implements the HttpRuntime, which handles ASP.NET requests within the same process space and achieves isolation using AppDomains. You can think of AppDomains as featherweight subprocesses. In ASP.NET, a web application can have only one IIS virtual directory. Each virtual directory represents a separate AppDomain. The HttpRuntime object uses an HttpApplicationFactory object to locate the correct AppDomain and create an HttpApplication to process the request. The global.asax file can be used to subscribe to events available on the HttpApplication object.

User state information for the current user session within the application is made available through the Context property of the HttpApplication-derived object. We cover Context in more detail in the section "ASP.NET and Server-Side State Management." At this point in the processing pipeline, any objects that implement the HttpModule class and are registered in the application will have their events fired. For example, Session_Start and Session_End are implemented in an HttpModule named SessionStateModule. HttpModules can be used to implement a variety of sitewide functionality such as a custom authentication architecture that authenticates requests based on custom HTTP header information.

After all registered HttpModules have a chance to process events, the request is shepherded to the appropriate HttpHandler by calling its ProcessRequest method. The ProcessRequest method takes one parameter of type HttpContext containing the user state of the current request. The HttpHandler is responsible for generating a response to the request using the Context.Response.Write method. This entire process is illustrated in Figure 4-2.

As you can see, request processing flows through a series of ASP.NET objects that have full access to ASP.NET state. The ASP.NET classes in Figure 4-3 can examine the state of user request to implement authentication, authorization, and auditing in a web application. These objects also implement numerous useful events and can be extended. The ASP.NET classes that manage user state flow and request processing are shown in the figure. Note that the familiar Request, Response, Application, and Session objects are implemented via classes in this section of the ASP.NET class hierarchy.

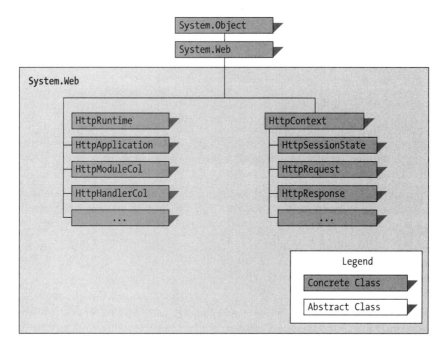

Figure 4-3. ASP.NET request processing classes

The ASP.NET request processing architecture permits developers to plug into the architecture by authoring custom objects that implement the `HttpHandler` or `HttpModule` class. As a point of reference, the `HttpHandler` class has similar behavior to ISAPI extensions. Likewise, the `HttpModule` class provides similar functionality to ISAPI filters. These two .NET classes take the ISAPI library concept much further, as the classes are fully integrated into the ASP.NET architecture.

HttpHandlers

`HttpHandlers` deserve special attention because ASP.NET uses this same architecture to process requests for .aspx and .asmx pages. `HttpHandlers` enable processing of individual HTTP URLs or groups of URL extensions within an application. Table 4-1 shows examples of the `HttpHandlers` provided in ASP.NET by default.

Table 4-1. Built-in ASP.NET Handlers

HANDLER	DESCRIPTION
ASP.NET Service Handler	Default `HttpHandler` for all ASP.NET service (.asmx) pages
ASP.NET Page Handler	Default `HttpHandler` for all ASP.NET (.aspx) pages

The ASP.NET Page Handler `PageHandlerFactory` performs the important task of receiving the user request and creating the `Page` object for manipulation by the developer. The `Page` object makes user state easily accessible, including application and session state, and data stored in ViewState.

In general, an `HttpHandler` can be either synchronous or asynchronous. As you would guess, a *synchronous handler* does not return until it finishes processing the HTTP request for which it is called. An *asynchronous handler* returns immediately and is usually tasked with launching a process that can be lengthy. As mentioned previously, `HttpHandlers` have a simple implementation compared to writing an ISAPI extension library. After writing and compiling code to implement an `HttpHandler`, deployment is a matter of registering the handler in the application's web.config file.

The single drawback when you compare `HttpHandlers` to ISAPI extensions is that on web servers where both ASP.NET and ASP applications need to share the same application infrastructure (e.g., a common security model), you cannot use `HttpModules` and `HttpHandlers` outside of ASP.NET in this manner. For ASP web sites, the developer must revert to ISAPI extensions and filters.

ASP.NET and Server-Side State Management

Server-side state in ASP consists of the `Application` and `Session` objects. A similar construct exists in ASP.NET as well. `Application` and `Session` objects store application and user state in a collection. Variables can be stored in these collections using a familiar syntax:

```
Application["SessionTimeOut"] = 15 ;
Session["FirstName"] = "John" ;
```

In general, data stored in `Application` variables tends to be like constants, shared by application users and unchanging. `Application` variables are usually set in the global.asax file. `Session` variables are user connection–specific and quite convenient for maintaining state throughout an application. To gain access to these server-side state mechanisms, you use the `Context` object.

The Context Object

We mentioned in the previous section that the `HttpApplication` class makes user state available to the developer in the `Context` property of type `HttpContext`. The `HttpContext` class implements `HttpSessionState` and `HttpApplicationState` to provide server-side state management. In this section, we cover these classes in more detail because they are important features of the ASP.NET request-processing engine, as they provide server-side state mechanisms to web applications.

The `System.Web.HttpContext` class unifies what was once a scattered object model in ASP into a one-stop shop for gaining access to the request-processing engine internals. The .NET Framework maintains a collection of important references that model request information, server-side state, security information, utility functions, error handling, and access to the response output stream in a nice, compact package. `Context` is an important component of this collection.

Table 4-2 contains a partial description of some of the important properties attached to the `HttpContext` class and what capabilities they provide. Refer to the .NET Framework documentation for more detailed information on the `HttpContext` class.

Table 4-2. Properties of the `HttpContext` Class

PROPERTY	DESCRIPTION
Application	Provides sever-side state management for all clients of the web application
ApplicationInstance	Reference-controls the execution process of the ASP.NET web request
Cache	Provides access to the server-side cache in ASP.NET
Error	Provides access to the error exceptions that occur during ASP.NET execution
Items	Key/value pair collection used to pass information between the components in a request
Request	Contains information from the client request including browser type, cookies, and values encoded in form and URL query string collections
Response	Key/value pair collection used to pass information between the requesting components
Server	Provides utilities including `Server.Transfer`, `Server.HtmlEncode`, and `Server.MapPath`
Session	State collection maintained on behalf of a web application user
Trace	Debugging utility for writing to the trace output of the Web Form
User	Makes security information available when a user is authenticated

Web Forms and controls have different methods to obtain a reference to the `HttpContext` instance. A static property, `HttpContext.Current`, returns an instance of the current `HttpContext` to any class that is interested, even if it is not inside an ASP.NET page. For example, the `Current` static property can be referenced in helper classes used within the Web Form page server-side code to gain access to any of the properties in Table 4-2, such as `Cache`. This ease of access allows for more modular code that's easier to read.

Controls inherit a `Context` property from `System.Web.UI.Control` that is mapped to the current instance of `HttpContext` as a convenient reference for use in server control development. The `Page` class has a `Context` property as well, but it goes one step further by providing properties that are mapped to their `Context` counterparts such as `Request` and `Response`. This shortens the syntactic space required to work with `Context` on a Web Form and is more familiar to ASP developers.

Server-Side State Considerations

In ASP, server-side state management techniques are problematic in a web farm environment for many reasons we won't rehash here. In an Internet scenario, the problem is worse because users can have cookies disabled on the client or users can be located behind reverse proxies, making it more difficult to track server-side state.

In ASP.NET, server-side state can be stored in a database to help get around the web farm issue. Application Center 2000 can also help get around server-side state issues in an Internet environment through request forwarding. Please refer to the Application Center 2000 documentation for more information. For intranet applications, use of Sticky IP can usually help developers get around server-side limitations. In situations where it is feasible and the limitations acceptable, server-side state can be a convenient method to store state for custom controls. For more information on server-side state mechanisms, please review the .NET Framework documentation. ASP.NET also provides client-side state management techniques that can help alleviate these issues. We investigate these in the next section.

ASP.NET and Client-Side State Management

ASP.NET provides access to a variety of client-side state management techniques to give you a helping hand in building useful, interactive web sites. Control developers can leverage these state management features to provide extra value in their controls by making it look as if the controls can remember their previous values or obviate the need to go back to a data source to display information for tabular controls. What makes this capability wonderful is that these options do not require any special-purpose mechanism on the web server; instead, they use the everyday features of a web browser to make this magic happen. In this section, we provide an overview of the client-side state options that are available:

- URL strings

- Cookies

- HTML hidden variables

- ViewState

URL Strings

Encoding information in the URL string passed to the web server is one of the simplest and most widely used techniques for storing client state. A great example is your favorite e-commerce store that puts the category and product-identifying information in a list of hyperlinks for the rows of products that fit a category. The embedded information in the URL allows the web site to remember what category the user came from when choosing to follow a link for a particular product. Developers can also add non-navigational information at the end of the URL string by just appending another variable to track such information as the customer's buying history with the web site in order to provide a discount. For example:

```
http://acme.com/product.aspx?
categoryid=1&productid=1&custtype=preferred
```

ASP.NET parses the URL string that it receives as part of the page request and provides easy access to the key/value pairs through two properties of the `HttpRequest` class: `QueryString` and `Params`. `HttpRequest` is available through the `Request` property of the `Context` object. The following code snippet shows how either the `QueryString` or `Params` collection can read the incoming product.aspx URL string for category and custom information:

```
string categoryID = Request.QueryString["categoryid"];
string productID = Request.Params["productid"];
string custType = Request.Querystring["custtype"];
```

Adding extra variables or removing variables from the URL string in maintaining an application is something that the programmer must do manually. Forgetting to add variables or neglecting to modify all hyperlinks on a Web Form is a common mistake. Finally, URL strings have size limitations that vary among browser devices, so developers must take a one-size-fits-all approach when attempting to store state in the URL string.

Cookies

The second client-side state feature of ASP.NET we discuss here is the *client-side cookie*, a mechanism familiar to most web developers, which is added to the HTTP protocol that allows the web server and web browser to collaborate in storing information on the user's machine. A cookie can store site-specific data for a defined period of time, after which the cookie expires. The cookie time limit is put to use by server-side state mechanisms in ASP.NET such as session state and security mechanisms such as ASP.NET forms authentication. Both emit cookies to identify the user and track information related to storing data on the web server or authenticating the user browsing the web site.

The cookie information passed between browser and server is delivered via HTTP headers. The web server will send down to the browser client an HTTP header named Set-Cookie with the information it wants the browser to persist on the user's local machine. The next time the user visits that site (and only that site), the browser responds with a Cookie HTTP header containing the locally stored site-specific data, as long as the cookie hasn't expired.

ASP.NET provides access to outgoing cookies via the Cookies property of the HttpResponse class. HttpResponse represents the output of the Web Form and is reached through the Response property of the Context object, which is available to server controls via the System.Web.UI.Control class. The Cookies collection is serialized to a set of string values attached to HTTP headers.

The following code adds two differently named cookies representing the first and last name of one of the authors to the Cookies collection:

```
Response.Cookies["firstname"] = "Dale";
Response.Cookies["lastname"] = "Michalk";
```

The Cookies collection serialization process generates two Set-Cookie headers, one for each cookie being sent down to the browser:

```
Set-Cookie: firstname=Dale; path=/
Set-Cookie: lastname=Michalk; path=/
```

The HttpRequest class has a Cookies collection that allows the developer to read incoming cookies in a manner identical to the outgoing collection. In our example, when the browser comes back to the same Web Form, it will send the cookie information for both cookies in a single HTTP header named Cookie:

```
Cookie: firstname=Dale; lastname=Michalk
```

The following code shows you how to read the two cookies via the Cookies collection on a Web Form:

```
string firstname = Request.Cookies["firstname"];
string lastname = Request.Cookies["lastname"];
```

Common sense dictates not storing a large value because the information stored in a cookie is transmitted as part of the web page automatically, unlike a URL string parameter, which must be continuously refreshed by the programmer, or an HTML hidden variable, which must be sent via an HTTP POST request for a specific page. The cookie technique also presents challenges when the user either disables cookies or has problems with maintaining or deleting them from the local cookie store. Some browsing devices don't support cookies at all, so you may have to avoid them entirely as an option for storing state in your controls.

HTML Hidden Variables

Hidden input variables inside of an HTML form are the third method of client-side state management available in ASP.NET that we discuss in this section. This technique is familiar to many developers who created web applications with technologies such as Common Gateway Interface (CGI) and ASP. Unlike the URL string and cookie options, size limitations and device support issues are not pressing concerns, so hidden input variables as part of an HTML form are a heavily used technique for client-side state management.

For data stored in an HTML form to be available, the use of the HTTP POST mechanism is required to transmit the state information back to the web server. ASP.NET helps ensure this through the `System.Web.UI.HtmlControls.HtmlInputForm` server control. `HtmlInputForm` is smart enough to render a `method="post"` attribute, along with an `action` attribute that directs the page back to the original URL. The following tag on a hypothetical Web Form named first.aspx is rendered as a server control because of the `runat="server "` attribute:

```
<form id="first" method="post" runat="server">
```

The server control representing the form tag emits the following HTML output:

```
<form id="first" method="post" action="first.aspx">
```

Notice how the tag is tied to the HTTP POST protocol and has an `action` attribute to submit the page back to the original URL of the web page. This round-tripping of form submissions is referred to as *postback* because it performs an HTTP POST back to the original page. It's a key requirement to ensure that all emitted form variables, hidden or not, can be read upon form submission. Here's the complete form output for our simple example:

```
<form id="first" method="post" action="first.aspx">
   <input id="names" type="text" value="Dale Michalk Rob Cameron">
   <input id="task" type="text" value="write book">
</form>
```

Once the Web Form is submitted via a button click or through a JavaScript submission of the form, ASP.NET parses the input values to allow Web Form and control code to extract the values and drive the logic of the web application. The variables in an HTTP POST are encoded using HTML encoding rules and are separated in the body of the request via ampersand characters:

```
names=dale+michalk+rob+cameron&task=writebook
```

ASP.NET provides the `Form` or `Params` collections attached to the `HttpRequest` class in the current `HttpContext` to read the values:

```
string names = Request.Form["names"];
string task = Request.Params["task"];
```

As you can see, form data is made available on the server through the construct of the ASP.NET postback mechanism and the `HttpContext`. Figure 4-4 shows the ASP.NET postback mechanism.

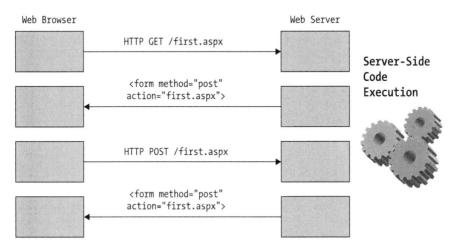

Figure 4-4. The ASP.NET postback mechanism

Most of the time, when building web applications, developers need to store state information that shouldn't be exposed to the user, such as application-specific logic to aid in processing a request. Hidden input fields give developers the ability to store additional information as part of the Web Form without making the data directly visible to the user. The `<INPUT type="hidden">` tag can carry the additional state information as part of the `<FORM>` tag inside an HTML document:

```
<form id="writing" method="post" action="writing.aspx">
    <input id="names" value="Dale Michalk Rob Cameron">
    <input id="task" value="write book">
    <input id="SessionNumber" type="hidden" value="234234222">
    <input id="progress" type="hidden" value="50%">
</form>
```

Naturally, the hidden form fields can be accessed in server-side code in the same way as the text form fields were previously, by using either the `Request.Form` or `Request. Params` collection. Hidden form variables do have some potential drawbacks:

- As with URL query string variables, programmers must manually track changes to hidden variables and emit values each time a page is rendered in order to maintain the user's state within the application.

- Although hidden fields are not immediately visible to the user, selecting View ➤ Source in the browser enables the user to see what information is available in hidden fields. In most cases, this may not be an issue, but it is important to be cognizant of this and either refrain from storing sensitive data or manually add an additional processing layer of encryption to prevent exposure.

- Storing a large amount of data in hidden variables can become a performance issue depending on the amount of network bandwidth and processing available. Like the previous drawback, developers can manually add an additional processing layer that implements compression to minimize data size.

Despite these limitations, hidden form fields remain a popular method for developers to maintain application state. ASP.NET takes its cue from this and adds a layer of abstraction called ViewState on top of the HTML form hidden variable mechanism to make life easier on web developers wishing to take advantage of client-side state with a minimal amount of fuss and effort.

ViewState

As mentioned in the previous section, the ViewState server control state management technique builds upon the hidden form field client-side method, taking advantage of its well-documented benefits while minimizing its potential drawbacks. ViewState addresses hidden form variable limitations by providing built-in data management, compression, encoding and tamper-resistance so that web developers and control builders can focus on the application requirements and business logic.

The StateBag Class and the IStateManager Interface

The client-side state management technique ViewState exists in the .NET Framework class hierarchy as a member property of the `System.Web.UI.Control` class. `ViewState` is of type `StateBag`, which implements a dictionary data structure to store name/value pairs. The `StateBag` class implements the interfaces in Table 4-3.

Table 4-3. Interfaces Implemented by the StateBag *Class*

INTERFACE	DESCRIPTION
ICollection	Defines enumerators, synchronization methods, and size for collections
IDictionary	Specialized collection interface that implements a collection of name/value pairs
IEnumerable	Provides the enumerator for iteration over a collection
IStateManager	Defines the properties and methods required to support ViewState management in server controls

The interfaces `ICollection` and `IEnumerable` are standard interfaces used to give collection functionality to a class. `IDictionary` provides the name/value storage mechanism familiar when working with ViewState. `IStateManager` is the interface that handles all the tedious state maintenance functions during server-side processing and greatly contributes to the Visual Basic–like ease of programming model for ASP.NET web developers.

As you can see, the `IStateManager` interface is the most interesting interface implemented by the `StateBag` class, as it includes methods to load and save a control's data or state. Because all server controls descend from `System.Web.UI.Control`, the .NET Framework uses the methods and properties implemented by `IStateManager` to dehydrate controls before serialization into the hidden `__VIEWSTATE` field. Likewise, ASP.NET calls upon `IStateManager` during postback to rehydrate server control objects for server-side processing.

State Data Management

Because both custom controls and the `Page` class inherit from `Control`, `ViewState` is easily accessible to the ASP.NET developer from either the Web Form or from within a custom control class. As described in the previous section, the type of the `ViewState` collection is `System.Web.UI.StateBag`, a strongly typed dictionary data structure that stores name/value pairs with the value having a type that is either serializable or has a `TypeConverter` defined.

Native data types such as `int`, `String`, and so forth have default `TypeConverters` that provide string-to-value conversions so no additional work is required on the part of the developer. In situations where a developer creates a custom type for use in a server control, it is recommended that the developer create a `TypeConverter` class for the custom type in place of implementing `ISerializable`. The reason is that types that are only defined as serializable are slower and generate much larger `ViewState` than types that have a `TypeConverter` implemented. We discuss how to create a `TypeConverter` in Chapter 12.

An alternative to implementing a `TypeConverter` is to customize how property data is stored in `ViewState`. The `System.Web.UI.Control` class provides two methods for this purpose: `SaveViewState` and `LoadViewState`. As you would guess, these methods must be implemented in tandem.

Compression and Integrity

State information placed inside of the `ViewState` collection is kept separate for each control as well as from the Web Form itself. During page processing, `ViewState` data is converted into a hashed, compressed, and encoded blob that is streamed to the client as a hidden form field named `__VIEWSTATE`.

TIP *To see what* `ViewState` *looks like on the client side, simply load one of the book's sample Web Forms (you can find them in the Downloads section of the Apress web site at* `http://www.apress.com`*) and select View* ➤ *Source in your web browser. You will find a hidden form field named* `__VIEWSTATE` *and its value.*

The output that is sent to the browser by ViewState overcomes one of the big weaknesses of other client-side state systems whose values can be mimicked in an attempt to spoof the server. Any attempts to manipulate ViewState outside of the page life cycle process will be detected by the ASP.NET, minimizing the possibility of tampering.

Ease of Use

Having a tamper-resistant, efficient state management technology is one thing, but what truly makes ViewState successful is how easy it is to put to work. Using ViewState is like using any of the collection types available in .NET. The following code snippet adds the value "writebook" with a key value of "task":

```
ViewState["task"] = "writebook";
```

Accessing ViewState in this way results in a hidden form variable like the following that contains not only the values loaded by all controls with ViewState enabled, but also the data loaded in our example:

```
<input type="hidden" name="__VIEWSTATE" value="dDw2MDQ5NjY2NDk7dDxw... " />
```

Reading the value back is a simple process of accessing the ViewState collection when the form is posted back to the web server. ASP.NET checks the ViewState data for its hash value and ensures no unscheduled modifications have taken place prior to populating the collection:

```
string name = ViewState["task"] = "writebook";
```

As described previously, ViewState uses the well-known <INPUT type=hidden name="__VIEWSTATE"> HTML tag to hold the page's state data. No special browser techniques or proprietary mechanisms are required to work with ViewState.

The primary consideration with ViewState is the serialization process used to dehydrate and rehydrate state for each server control in the page's control tree. On a Web Form with either numerous server controls or controls with a large amount of data, the size of the __VIEWSTATE hidden variable can be large. Because ViewState data is transported over the wire for each round-trip, it's recommended that developers turn off ViewState for controls that don't need to retain state. This can greatly decrease the size of the generated ViewState transported with the HTML document. Managing ViewState emissions is handled through the EnableViewState property that all controls inherit from System.Web.UI.Control. Developers need to be cognizant of this ability to disable ViewState when building server controls.

A Client State Workshop

The ClientState.aspx Web Form example (you can find this example in the Downloads section of the Apress web site at http://www.apress.com) demonstrates the process of working with the client side. It is a rather contrived but sufficient example with a single TextBox that provides the input device for storing a name on the client using a cookie, URL query string, hidden fields, and ViewState.

The Web Form has two buttons that can submit the page back to the web server using the HTTP POST mechanism. One button, labeled "Set State," causes the page to post back to the web server and change the name that is persisted to the client. The other button, labeled "Submit Page," posts the page back to the server without changing any state information. This button simply causes a round-trip to test the holding power of each of the state mechanisms. There is also a hyperlink on the page to test the use of the URL query string as a state persistence device.

Figure 4-5 shows the web page generated from ClientState.aspx after an initial HTTP GET request from the browser. Listings 4-1 and 4-2 contain the .aspx file and code-behind class, respectively. One of the author's names is entered into the TextBox control in order to set the page up for saving that name via client-side state. The bottom portion of the Web Form has readouts for all the client-state mechanisms: URL strings, cookies, hidden variables, and ViewState. It shows the result of an attempt to read the state mechanism, which is initially blank because no state has been set just yet.

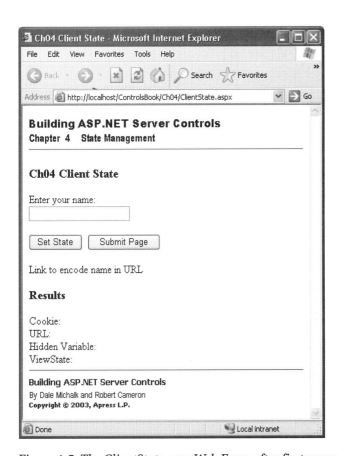

Figure 4-5. The ClientState.aspx Web Form after first request

Listing 4-1. The `ClientState` *.aspx Page File*

```
<%@ Page language="c#" Codebehind="ClientState.aspx.cs"
AutoEventWireup="false" Inherits="ControlsBookWeb.Ch04.ClientState" %>
<%@ Register TagPrefix="apressUC"
TagName="ControlsBookHeader" Src="..\ControlsBookHeader.ascx" %>
<%@ Register TagPrefix="apressUC"
TagName="ControlsBookFooter" Src="..\ControlsBookFooter.ascx" %>
<!DOCTYPE HTML PUBLIC "-//W3C//DTD HTML 4.0 Transitional//EN" >
<HTML>
  <HEAD>
    <title>Ch04 Client State</title>
    <meta content="Microsoft Visual Studio 7.0" name="GENERATOR">
    <meta content="C#" name="CODE_LANGUAGE">
    <meta content="JavaScript" name="vs_defaultClientScript">
    <meta content="http://schemas.microsoft.com/intellisense/ie5"
          name="vs_targetSchema">
  </HEAD>
  <body MS_POSITIONING="FlowLayout">
    <form id="ClientState" method="post" runat="server">
      <apressUC:ControlsBookHeader id="Header" runat="server"
        ChapterNumber="4" ChapterTitle="State Management" />
      <h3>Ch04 Client State</h3>
      Enter your name:<br>
      <asp:textbox id="NameTextBox" runat="server"></asp:textbox><br>
      <br>
      <asp:button id="SetStateButton" runat="server"
       Text="Set State"></asp:button> 
      <asp:button id="SubmitPageButton" runat="server"
       Text="Submit Page"></asp:button><br>
      <input id="HiddenName" type="hidden" runat="server">
      <br>
      <asp:hyperlink id="URLEncodeLink" runat="server">
       Link to encode name in URL</asp:hyperlink><br>
      <br>
      <h3>Results</h3>
      Cookie:<asp:label id="CookieLabel" runat="server"></asp:label><br>
      URL:<asp:label id="URLLabel" runat="server"></asp:label><br>
      Hidden Variable:<asp:label id="HiddenLabel" runat="server"></asp:label><br>
      ViewState:<asp:label id="ViewStateLabel" runat="server"></asp:label><br>
      <apressUC:ControlsBookFooter id="Footer" runat="server" />
    </form>
  </body>
</HTML>
```

Listing 4-2. The ClientState *Code-Behind Class File*

```
using System;
using System.Collections;
using System.ComponentModel;
using System.Data;
using System.Drawing;
using System.Web;
using System.Web.SessionState;
using System.Web.UI;
using System.Web.UI.WebControls;
using System.Web.UI.HtmlControls;

namespace ControlsBookWeb.Ch04
{
    public class ClientState : System.Web.UI.Page
    {
        protected System.Web.UI.HtmlControls.HtmlInputHidden HiddenName;
        protected System.Web.UI.WebControls.TextBox NameTextBox;
        protected System.Web.UI.WebControls.HyperLink URLEncodeLink;
        protected System.Web.UI.WebControls.Label CookieLabel;
        protected System.Web.UI.WebControls.Label URLLabel;
        protected System.Web.UI.WebControls.Label HiddenLabel;
        protected System.Web.UI.WebControls.Button SetStateButton;
        protected System.Web.UI.WebControls.Button SubmitPageButton;
        protected System.Web.UI.WebControls.Label ViewStateLabel;

        private void Page_Load(object sender, System.EventArgs e)
        {
            GetClientState();
        }

        #region Web Form Designer generated code
        override protected void OnInit(EventArgs e)
        {
            //
            // CODEGEN: This call is required by the ASP.NET Web Form Designer.
            //
            InitializeComponent();
            base.OnInit(e);
        }

        /// <summary>
        /// Required method for Designer support - do not modify
        /// the contents of this method with the code editor.
        /// </summary>
        private void InitializeComponent()
        {
            this.SetStateButton.Click +=
                new System.EventHandler(this.SetStateButton_Click);
            this.Load += new System.EventHandler(this.Page_Load);
```

```
        }
        #endregion

        private void SetStateButton_Click(object sender, System.EventArgs e)
        {
            SetClientState();
        }

        private void SetClientState()
        {
            string name = NameTextBox.Text;

            // set the name Cookie value
            Response.Cookies["cookiename"].Value = name;

            // encode the name in the redirect URL
            URLEncodeLink.NavigateUrl = "ClientState.aspx?urlname=" + name;

            // put the name in the hidden variable
            HiddenName.Value = name;

            // put the name in ViewState
            ViewState["viewstatename"] = name;
        }

        private void GetClientState()
        {
            // check the cookiename Cookie
            CookieLabel.Text = "";
            if (Request.Cookies["cookiename"] != null)
                CookieLabel.Text = Request.Cookies["cookiename"].Value;

            // check the URL for urlname variable
            URLLabel.Text = "";
            if (Request.QueryString["urlname"] != null)
                URLLabel.Text = Request.Params["urlname"];

            // check the form data for hiddenname variable
            HiddenLabel.Text = "";
            if (Context.Request.Form["hiddenname"] != null)
                HiddenLabel.Text = Request.Params["hiddenname"];

            // check the Viewstate for the viewstatename variable
            ViewStateLabel.Text = "";
            if (ViewState["viewstatename"] != null)
                ViewStateLabel.Text = ViewState["viewstatename"].ToString();
        }
    }
}
```

Setting the Client State

To move to the next step in the demonstration, click the Set State button. This button submits the page via postback to ASP.NET, which executes the click-handling routine named SetStateButton_Click for the SetStateButton control. This simple event-handling routine hands off its work to a helper method named SetClientState. SetClientState retrieves the name gathered from the NameTextBox control on the ClientState.aspx Web Form and pushes it out to the client-state mechanisms we are interested in testing.

The first task SetClientState accomplishes is working with cookies. The code manipulates a cookie named cookiename to store the name entered into the TextBox control:

```
Page.Response.Cookies["cookiename"].Value = name;
```

After the cookie is configured, we set the NavigateURL value of a Hyperlink control by encoding the urlname variable:

```
URLEncodeLink.NavigateUrl = "ClientState.aspx?urlname=" + name;
```

The HtmlHidden control from System.Web.UI.HtmlControls represents the hidden variable mechanism for storing client-side state. Using this control saves us from having to build a LiteralControl to manually emit <INPUT type="hidden">:

```
HiddenName.Value = name;
```

The final task is to put the name in ViewState via a key named viewstatename:

```
ViewState["viewstatename"] = name;
```

The page that renders after the server-side execution of Set State is complete contains the client state for the name entered into the NameTextBox control. The URL has the name embedded as part of the query string. If you click the link, it will force a "read" of the query string state, which allows the URL field at the bottom of the page a chance to show the value through this state mechanism. The Web Form has two hidden variables: one populated with ViewState and another hidden variable used to hold the name, as a developer would code using just hidden input tags. To see this, select View ▶ Source in the browser. Finally, the Cookie value is included in the HTTP response.

Interestingly, the URL fields at the bottom of the page are blank. It is not until the next round-trip to the server that ASP.NET has a chance to access the current state and populate the fields at the bottom of the page. The reason for this is that when you click Set State, the Page_Load event fires first, which executes the GetClientState helper method. GetClientState loads the current values from the various state storage mechanisms into the labels on the bottom portion of the Web Form. Because the server-side click event SetStateButton_Click has not had a chance to fire just yet, the state loaded into the fields at the bottom of the Web Form by GetClientState in Page_Load is the previous state, as shown in Figure 4-5. After the Page_Load event completes,

SetStateButton_Click executes next, calling SetClientState, which loads the value from the TextBox control into all the client-state mechanisms. The resulting page that displays shows that all the state mechanisms are storing the value.

Now that the state has been set, clicking the Submit button one more time forces a round-trip to the server, executing the Page_Load event. This time around, the fields at the bottom of the page have a chance to pick up the current state in GetClientState and display the expected values. The only difference between Figure 4-5 and Figure 4-6 is the fact the browser notices our hyperlink has a nonblank URL and displays the link text in blue underlined font.

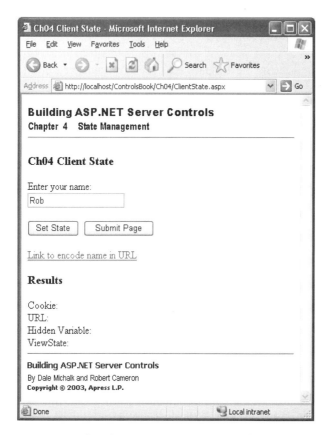

Figure 4-6. The ClientState.aspx Web Form during the Set State button postback

Reading the Client State

Click the Submit Page button to submit the Web Form back to the server one more time. There is no button-handling routine for this button on the server, so the only logic that executes is the Page_Load method. All this simple routine does is call Get-ClientState. The GetClientState routine pulls back values for all systems except the URL-encoding scheme, as shown in Figure 4-7.

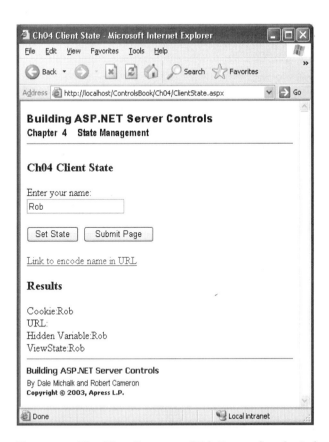

Figure 4-7. The ClientState.aspx Web Form after the Submit Page button postback

GetClientState is careful when accessing the state collections by checking for null values and setting the name to a blank string where appropriate. This provides more reliable code that is capable of operating under failure conditions. The following is an excerpt of the code that reads values from ViewState. See Listing 4-2 for the details on the code for the other state mechanisms.

```
// check the Viewstate for the viewstatename variable
ViewStateLabel.Text = "";
if (ViewState["viewstatename"] != null)
ViewStateLabel.Text = ViewState["viewstatename"].ToString();
```

Getting the URL State

The URL string did not display in the previous attempts because we navigated to the same page through the postback mechanism enforced by the HtmlInputForm control and its <FORM> tag generation, which uses an HTTP POST. The URL string state mechanism is activated in our demonstration only through clicking the hyperlink on the Web Form.

Figure 4-8 displays the values from the URL string, but loses the information that was available for our HTML hidden variable and ViewState. The reason for the change in behavior is a switch from an HTTP POST request using the postback mechanism to an HTTP GET request by clicking through the hyperlink. Because we bypassed the form postback with an HTTP GET, all values based on HTML form information such as hidden variables and ViewState are lost. ViewState must go though the postback cycle to the original page it was produced from for it to work and give our controls the capability to remember state.

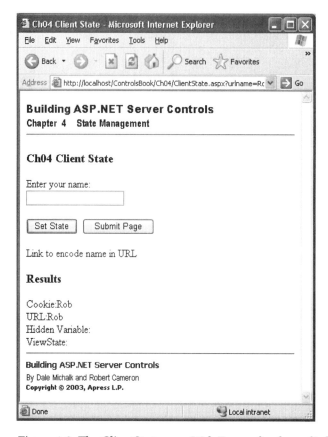

Figure 4-8. The ClientState.aspx Web Form after hyperlink navigation

ASP.NET Server Controls and State

Now that we have demonstrated a Web Form taking advantage of the various client-side state management techniques, we transition to using it inside server controls. Of all the client-side state facilities available, it is strongly recommended that you follow the lead of the prebuilt controls in ASP.NET and use ViewState within your server controls. With its extensive support in the ASP.NET framework, using ViewState in custom control development will greatly reduce development time and ensure consistent behavior.

The StatelessLabel Server Control

The first label control we build here does not take advantage of any of the state mechanisms in ASP.NET as an example of working without state. StatelessLabel inherits from System.Web.UI.Control and provides a string Text property that it uses to render its content inside a <SPAN>. The Text property is mapped to a private field named text that is not persisted and is only available when the control is in memory on the web server. Listing 4-3 shows the code for the StatelessLabel server control.

Listing 4-3. The StatelessLabel *Class File*

```
using System;
using System.Web.UI;
using System.ComponentModel;

namespace ControlsBookLib.Ch04
{
    [ToolboxData("<{0}:StatelessLabel runat=server></{0}:StatelessLabel>"),
    DefaultProperty("Text")]
    public class StatelessLabel : Control
    {
        private string text;
        public string Text
        {
            get
            {
                return text;
            }
            set
            {
                text = value;
            }
        }

        override protected void Render(HtmlTextWriter writer)
{
    base.Render(writer);
        writer.RenderBeginTag(HtmlTextWriterTag.Span);
        writer.Write(Text);
        writer.RenderEndTag();
        }
    }
}
```

The StatefulLabel Server Control

To spiff things up and take advantage of ViewState, the second label control, StatefulLabel, has a different mechanism for storing the information passed to the Text property. It uses the ViewState collection to read/write the property information in its get and set methods. Listing 4-4 contains the source code for the StatefulLabel class file.

Listing 4-4. The StatefulLabel *Class File*

```
using System;
using System.Web.UI;
using System.ComponentModel;

namespace ControlsBookLib.Ch04
{
    [ToolboxData("<{0}:StatefulLabel runat=server></{0}:StatefulLabel>"),
    DefaultProperty("Text")]
    public class StatefulLabel : Control
    {
        public virtual string Text
        {
            get
            {
                object text = ViewState["Text"];
                if (text == null)
                    return string.Empty;
                else
                    return (string) text;
            }
            set
            {
                ViewState["Text"] = value;
            }
        }

    override protected void Render(HtmlTextWriter writer)
{
    base.Render(writer);

            writer.RenderBeginTag(HtmlTextWriterTag.Span);
            writer.Write(Text);
            writer.RenderEndTag();
        }
    }
}
```

The get method for the Text property uses some guard code to correctly deal with the ViewState collection if the key we are looking for is not available. If the return value is null, it returns an empty string:

```
if (text == null)
    return string.Empty;
else
    return (string) text;
```

This is a good habit to get into, especially for control properties that are more complex than a primitive, such as a string or integer.

Comparing the Labels

Label Controls is a Web Form example that directly compares both the stateless and stateful controls in their lack of/use of client-side state. The GUI layout uses a setup similar to the one we used for ClientState.aspx in the previous demonstration but changes the bottom portion of the Web Form layout to display the two label controls. Navigating to the Web Form URL directly renders the output shown in Figure 4-9. Listings 4-5 and 4-6 contain the .aspx page and code-behind class file for the Label Controls demonstration.

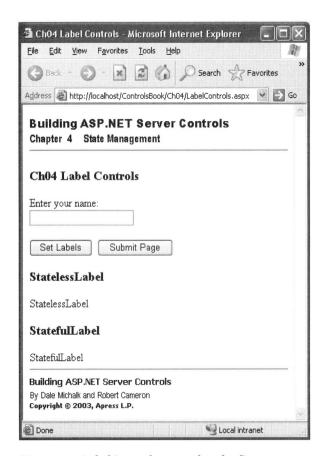

Figure 4-9. LabelControls.aspx after the first request

Listing 4-5. The LabelControls *.aspx Page File*

```
<%@ Register TagPrefix="apress" Namespace="ControlsBookLib.Ch04"
Assembly="ControlsBookLib" %>
<%@ Page language="c#" Codebehind="LabelControls.aspx.cs"
AutoEventWireup="false" Inherits="ControlsBookWeb.Ch04.LabelControls" %>
<%@ Register TagPrefix="apressUC" TagName="ControlsBookHeader"
```

```
Src="..\ControlsBookHeader.ascx" %>
<%@ Register TagPrefix="apressUC" TagName="ControlsBookFooter"
Src="..\ControlsBookFooter.ascx" %>
<!DOCTYPE HTML PUBLIC "-//W3C//DTD HTML 4.0 Transitional//EN" >
<HTML>
    <HEAD>
        <title>Ch04 Label Controls</title>
        <meta name="GENERATOR" Content="Microsoft Visual Studio 7.0">
        <meta name="CODE_LANGUAGE" Content="C#">
        <meta name="vs_defaultClientScript" content="JavaScript">
        <meta name="vs_targetSchema"
content="http://schemas.microsoft.com/intellisense/ie5">
    </HEAD>
    <body MS_POSITIONING="FlowLayout">
        <form id="Labels" method="post" runat="server">
            <apressUC:ControlsBookHeader id="Header" runat="server"
ChapterNumber=4 ChapterTitle="State Management" />
            <h3>Ch04 Label Controls</h3>
            Enter your name:<br>
            <asp:textbox id="NameTextBox" runat="server"></asp:textbox><br>
            <br>
            <asp:button id="SetLabelButton" runat="server"
                            Text="Set Labels"></asp:button> 
            <asp:button id="SubmitPageButton" runat="server" \
                            Text="Submit Page"></asp:button><br>
            <br>
            <h3>StatelessLabel</h3>
            <apress:StatelessLabel id="StatelessLabel1"
                        Text="StatelessLabel" runat="server" />
            <br>
            <h3>StatefulLabel</h3>
            <apress:StatefulLabel id="StatefulLabel1"
                                    Text="StatefulLabel" runat="server" />
            <apressUC:ControlsBookFooter id="Footer" runat="server" />
        </form>
    </body>
</HTML>
```

Listing 4-6. The LabelControls *Code-Behind Class File*

```
using System;
using System.Collections;
using System.ComponentModel;
using System.Data;
using System.Drawing;
using System.Web;
using System.Web.SessionState;
using System.Web.UI;
using System.Web.UI.WebControls;
using System.Web.UI.HtmlControls;
```

```
namespace ControlsBookWeb.Ch04
{
    public class LabelControls : System.Web.UI.Page
    {
        protected System.Web.UI.WebControls.Button SetLabelButton;
        protected System.Web.UI.WebControls.Button SubmitPageButton;
        protected ControlsBookLib.Ch04.StatelessLabel StatelessLabel1;
        protected ControlsBookLib.Ch04.StatefulLabel StatefulLabel1;
        protected System.Web.UI.WebControls.TextBox NameTextBox;

        private void Page_Load(object sender, System.EventArgs e)
        {

        }

        #region Web Form Designer generated code
        override protected void OnInit(EventArgs e)
        {
            //
            // CODEGEN: This call is required by the ASP.NET Web Form Designer.
            //
            InitializeComponent();
            base.OnInit(e);
        }

        /// <summary>
        /// Required method for Designer support - do not modify
        /// the contents of this method with the code editor.
        /// </summary>
        private void InitializeComponent()
        {
            this.SetLabelButton.Click +=
                new System.EventHandler(this.SetLabelButton_Click);
            this.Load += new System.EventHandler(this.Page_Load);

        }
        #endregion

        private void SetLabelButton_Click(object sender, System.EventArgs e)
        {
            string name = NameTextBox.Text;

            StatelessLabel1.Text = "Set by " + name;
            StatefulLabel1.Text = "Set by " + name;
        }
    }
}
```

Setting the Label Control State

Click the Set Labels button to post the web page back to the server. The
SetLabelButton_Click routine is executed by ASP.NET when the SetLabelButton
button is notified that the HTML button it represents caused the postback.

SetLabelButton_Click has the simple job of setting the Text property of the
StatelessLabel and StatefulLabel controls:

```
private void SetLabelButton_Click(object sender, System.EventArgs e)
{
    string name = NameTextBox.Text;

    StatelessLabel1.Text = "Set by " + name;
    StatefulLabel1.Text = "Set by " + name;
}
```

The output of the Web Form for these controls is identical because they both render their contents into HTML based on the recently set Text property, as shown in
Figure 4-10.

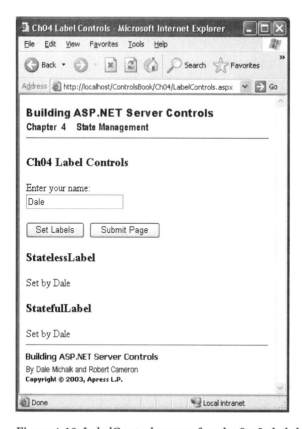

Figure 4-10. LabelControls.aspx after the Set Labels button postback

Testing Control ViewState

To test the state-saving features of ViewState and its impact on controls, click the Submit Page button. The `SubmitPageButton` control has no event-handling routines defined, and our `Page_Load` method is blank, so the net result of clicking the button is a recycling of the Web Form without any explicit Web Form code.

In this sample page, the only action in the controls is getting and setting properties during the page life cycle through postback. The controls are involved in regenerating their HTML content and the possibility of taking advantage of the `ViewState` that was posted back from the client. In Figure 4-11, you can see that the `StatefulLabel` control was able to remember its previous `Text` property value while the `StatelessLabel` control reverted to the initial value set in its `Text` attribute as part of the .aspx page markup.

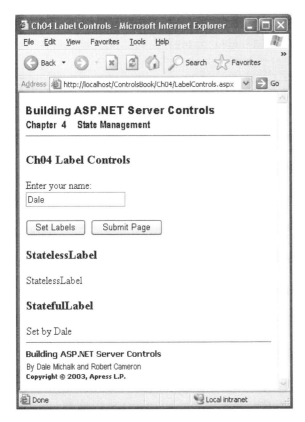

Figure 4-11. LabelControls.aspx after the Submit Page button postback

Form Post Data and ASP.NET Controls

The postback mechanism in ASP.NET provides a means of generating client-side state as well as the opportunity to receive input from the user. The first part of this chapter concentrated on client-side state. Now we focus on interacting with the normal HTML form input elements.

Many controls model themselves after <INPUT> tags and provide value-added features such as remembering state and raising events to their clients when internal state changes occur. To work with the HTTP POST mechanism to retrieve data, one implementation would be for the client to simply read all of the form variables directly. Fortunately, ASP.NET provides a more organized mechanism to server controls that implement the IPostBackDataHandler interface.

The IPostBackDataHandler Interface

The IPostBackDataHandler interface is the recommended method to read form post data from a control in ASP.NET without having to use the Page class and its Request object.

> **NOTE** *In general, it is not recommended that you directly access the* Request *or* Response *object provided by the* Page *class (*HttpContext*), as this would interfere with normal page processing. If you need to write to the output stream, use the* HtmlTextWriter *class for this purpose.*

IPostBackDataHandler also provides a framework to allow the control to raise change events at a later point in time if the state of the control has changed sufficiently to warrant such an action. Listing 4-7 shows the interface definition for IPostBackDataHandler. LoadPostData is the interface method we concentrate on in this section, as it provides the means to retrieve data posted to the web server.

Listing 4-7. The IPostBackDataHandler *Interface Definition*

```
public interface IPostBackDataHandler{
    public bool LoadPostData(string postDataKey,
                        NameValueCollection postCollection);
    public void RaisePostDataChangedEvent();
}
```

On a postback of a Web Form to the web server, the ASP.NET framework searches the posted form values for matches between the corresponding id of the form element and the UniqueID property of the matching control. It then calls the LoadPostData method for each control where there is a match to give the control a chance to retrieve its posted data. The UniqueID property of a control is the same as the ID value.

The ID value is determined by its value in the .aspx page for a control. As an example, the following StatefulLabel control tag would have an ID and UniqueID property value equal to "StatefulLabel1":

```
<apress:StatefulLabel id="StatefulLabel1" Text="StatelessLabel" runat="server" />
```

The two id properties only need to differ when working with composite controls that may contain multiple versions of the same control definition via templates. They are still required, however, to have a way to uniquely identify themselves to ASP.NET. We examine how the INamingContainer interface solves this problem in Chapter 5.

The return value from LoadPostData provides a means for a control to raise a state change event at a later point in time. If you return true in your implementation of LoadPostData in your server control, the ASP.NET framework will call your RaisePost-DataChangedEvent method further down in the page processing life cycle. If you return false, ASP.NET will skip the callback notification for your control.

The Textbox Control

A commonly used HTML form input element is the <INPUT type="text"> tag. The ASP.NET framework provides controls that render this type of tag, including System.Web.UI.HtmlControls.HtmlInputText and System.Web.UI.WebControls.TextBox. We reinvent the wheel here (see Listing 4-8) to show you how these controls use ViewState and work with the postback data submitted from a Web Form.

Listing 4-8. The Textbox *Class File*

```
using System;
using System.Web;
using System.Web.UI;
using System.Collections.Specialized;
using System.ComponentModel;

namespace ControlsBookLib.Ch04
{
    [ToolboxData("<{0}:Textbox runat=server></{0}:Textbox>"),
    DefaultProperty("Text")]
    public class Textbox : Control, IPostBackDataHandler
    {
        public virtual string Text
        {
            get
            {
                object text = ViewState["Text"];
                if (text == null)
                    return string.Empty;
                else
                    return (string) text;
            }
```

```
        set
        {
            ViewState["Text"] = value;
        }
    }

    public bool LoadPostData(string postDataKey,
        NameValueCollection postCollection)
    {
        string postedValue = postCollection[postDataKey];
        Text = postedValue;
        return false;
    }

    public virtual void RaisePostDataChangedEvent()
    {

    }

    override protected void Render(HtmlTextWriter writer)
{

Page.VerifyRenderingInServerForm(this);

    base.Render(writer);

        writer.Write("<INPUT type=\"text\" name=\"");
        writer.Write(this.UniqueID);
        writer.Write("\" value=\"" + this.Text + "\" />");
    }
  }
}
```

The Textbox control in Listing 4-8 inherits from System.Web.UI.Control and reuses the same Text property ViewState handling from our previous StatefulLabel control class. This provides the control all the memory it needs to rehydrate itself completely.

The Render method override has to do a little more work by inserting the UniqueID and Text properties of our control into the output, along with some quote character escapes in the string. The UniqueID property is used by ASP.NET to identify our control and retrieve its data from the postback:

```
override protected void Render(HtmlTextWriter writer)
{

Page.VerifyRenderingInServerForm(this);

    base.Render(writer);

    writer.Write("<INPUT type=\"text\" name=\"");
    writer.Write(this.UniqueID);
    writer.Write("\" value=\"" +  this.Text + "\" />");
}
```

Notice the call to `VerifyRenderingInServerForm` in the `Render` method. Developers should call this method when building a server control that requires rendering inside a `<FORM runat="server">` tag. ASP.NET will throw an exception if a developer/user attempts to put such a control outside an HTML `<FORM>` tag.

The `IPostBackDataHandler` interface is implemented by our `LoadPostData` and `RaisePostDataChangedEvent` methods. `RaisePostDataChangedEvent` is blank because we are not emitting events from our control based on state changes, but it still must be present to satisfy the terms of the interface. In the next chapter, we go further into raising our own events and examine what kind of code you would normally put into the `RaisePostDataChangedEvent`.

```
public bool LoadPostData(string postDataKey, NameValueCollection postCollection)
{
    string postedValue = postCollection[postDataKey];
    Text = postedValue;
    return false;
}

public virtual void RaisePostDataChangedEvent()
{
}
```

`LoadPostData` has the necessary logic to read the information posted by our `<INPUT type="text">` tag rendered in the HTML document. `LoadPostData` uses the passed-in key to read from the `postCollection` collection passed into the routine. The type of the collection is `NameValueCollection`, so you can expect a string value to be passed back when you access the data with your key.

Once we pull out the data, we store it immediately in `ViewState` via the `Text` property so the control can remember what was sent to it as well as render the correct HTML for the `<INPUT>` tag with the value filled in upon return to the browser. The `LoadPostData` routine closes by returning false because it does not need to have `RaisePostDataChangedEvent` called as no events are implemented.

Using the Textbox Control

The Postback Data Web Form is identical to the previous Label Controls demonstration except for removal of the ASP.NET TextBox control and substitution of the one we just created. It has the button setup you have become familiar with: one button sets the value of the labels and the other button recycles the form to exercise ViewState. Because the Textbox control receives its own postback data, we do not need to set its value in the code-behind class explicitly or worry about maintaining its state.

The initial page in Figure 4-12 looks identical to the previous Web Form that demonstrated our labels. Our `Textbox` control performs admirably well as a substitute for the ASP.NET built-in version of the control. Listings 4-9 and 4-10 contain the source code for this demonstration.

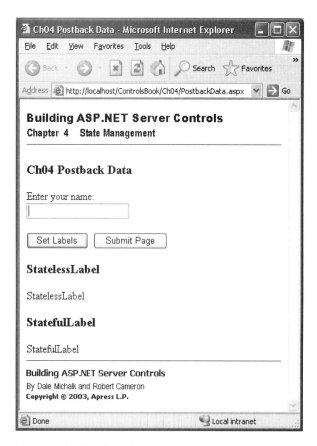

Figure 4-12. PostbackData.aspx after the first request

Listing 4-9. The PostbackData *.aspx Page File*

```
<%@ Register TagPrefix="apress" Namespace="ControlsBookLib.Ch04"
Assembly="ControlsBookLib" %>
<%@ Page language="c#" Codebehind="PostbackData.aspx.cs"
 AutoEventWireup="false" Inherits="ControlsBookWeb.Ch04.PostbackData" %>
<%@ Register TagPrefix="apressUC" TagName="ControlsBookHeader"
Src="..\ControlsBookHeader.ascx" %>
<%@ Register TagPrefix="apressUC" TagName="ControlsBookFooter"
Src="..\ControlsBookFooter.ascx" %>
<!DOCTYPE HTML PUBLIC "-//W3C//DTD HTML 4.0 Transitional//EN" >
<HTML>
  <HEAD>
    <title>Ch04 Postback Data</title>
    <meta content="Microsoft Visual Studio 7.0" name="GENERATOR">
    <meta content="C#" name="CODE_LANGUAGE">
    <meta content="JavaScript" name="vs_defaultClientScript">
    <meta content=http://schemas.microsoft.com/intellisense/ie5
      name="vs_targetSchema">
```

```
  </HEAD>
  <body MS_POSITIONING="FlowLayout">
    <form id="PostbackData" method="post" runat="server">
      <apressUC:ControlsBookHeader id="Header" runat="server"
       ChapterNumber="4" ChapterTitle="State Management" />
      <h3>Ch04 Postback Data</h3>
      Enter your name:<br>
      <apress:textbox id="NameTextBox" runat="server"></apress:textbox><br>
      <br>
      <asp:button id="SetLabelButton" runat="server" Text="Set Labels">
      </asp:button> 
      <asp:button id="SubmitPageButton" runat="server"
        Text="Submit Page"></asp:button><br>
      <br>
      <h3>StatelessLabel</h3>
      <apress:statelesslabel id="StatelessLabel1" runat="server"
          Text="StatelessLabel"></apress:statelesslabel><br>
      <h3>StatefulLabel</h3>
      <apress:statefullabel id="StatefulLabel1" runat="server"
          Text="StatefulLabel"></apress:statefullabel>
      <apressUC:ControlsBookFooter id="Footer" runat="server" />
    </form>
  </body>
</HTML>
```

Listing 4-10. The PostbackData *Code-Behind Class File*

```
using System;
using System.Collections;
using System.ComponentModel;
using System.Data;
using System.Drawing;
using System.Web;
using System.Web.SessionState;
using System.Web.UI;
using System.Web.UI.WebControls;
using System.Web.UI.HtmlControls;

namespace ControlsBookWeb.Ch04
{
   public class PostbackData : System.Web.UI.Page
   {
      protected System.Web.UI.WebControls.Button SetLabelButton;
      protected ControlsBookLib.Ch04.StatefulLabel StatefulLabel1;
      protected ControlsBookLib.Ch04.Textbox NameTextBox;
      protected ControlsBookLib.Ch04.StatelessLabel StatelessLabel1;
      protected System.Web.UI.WebControls.Button SubmitPageButton;

      private void Page_Load(object sender, System.EventArgs e)
      {
```

```
        }

        #region Web Form Designer generated code
        override protected void OnInit(EventArgs e)
        {
            //
            // CODEGEN: This call is required by the ASP.NET Web Form Designer.
            //
            InitializeComponent();
            base.OnInit(e);
        }

        /// <summary>
        /// Required method for Designer support - do not modify
        /// the contents of this method with the code editor.
        /// </summary>
        private void InitializeComponent()
        {
            this.SetLabelButton.Click +=
                new System.EventHandler(this.SetLabelButton_Click);
            this.Load += new System.EventHandler(this.Page_Load);

        }
        #endregion

        private void SetLabelButton_Click(object sender, System.EventArgs e)
        {
            string name = NameTextBox.Text;

            StatelessLabel1.Text = "Set by " + name;
            StatefulLabel1.Text = "Set by " + name;
        }
    }
}
```

To exercise the page, click the Set Labels button on the Web Form to generate a postback to the web server. The button click code in the code-behind class file sets the two label controls' Text properties. The postback itself gives our Textbox control the opportunity to receive data from the HTML form and set its Text property in its LoadPostData implementation without any additional work needed in the test .aspx page. The emitted HTML control from the Textbox Render method also sets the value of the <INPUT type="text"> tag, as shown in Figure 4-13.

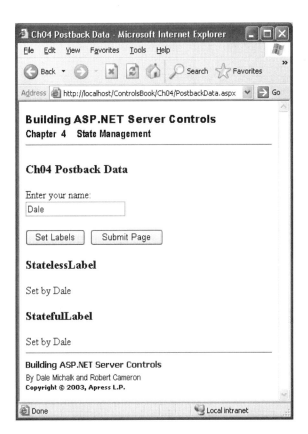

Figure 4-13. PostbackData.aspx after the first postback via the SetLabelButton *control*

Next, click the Submit Page button to test the ViewState capabilities of the label controls and submit the Textbox data to the Textbox control yet again via another postback. The net result is that one label control can read from ViewState, and the other control reverts to its initial value, as shown in Figure 4-14.

The use of ViewState for our Textbox control was not really necessary. A control based on an <INPUT> tag has built-in state management within the ASP.NET framework. The posted data of the tag is always returned to the control via LoadPostData. However, we put the extra work here with ViewState to good use in the next chapter, which covers server control events. The control will be extended to take the value persisted in ViewState and check it against the postback data in order to raise a state change event.

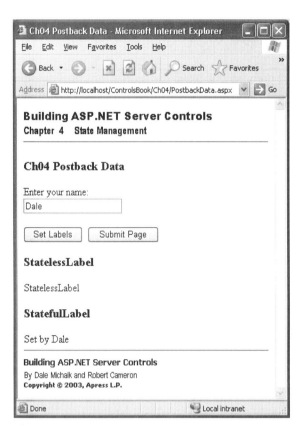

Figure 4-14. PostbackData.aspx after the second postback via the SubmitPageButton *control*

Summary

Client-side state takes on four forms in ASP.NET: URL strings, cookies, HTML hidden form variables, and ViewState. HttpContext bundles together the important classes in ASP.NET for working with the request/response cycle of a Web Form in ASP.NET, including Session and Application server-side state mechanisms. Controls access the HttpContext class through the Context property they inherit from System.Web.UI.Control.

Variables in URL strings can be accessed through the QueryString or Params collection properties attached to the HttpRequest class. Cookies can be manipulated via the Request.Cookies or Response.Cookies collections attached to the Page class. HTML form hidden variables are accessible through the Form and QueryString properties attached to the HttpRequest class.

ViewState is a client-side state management technology built on top of the HTML hidden form variable state management technique. It abstracts out the details of managing state for Web Form and server control programmers. ViewState is manipulated through the ViewState property available to all controls through inheritance from

System.Web.UI.Control. ViewState requires the postback system where a Web Form always executes an HTTP POST back to the same page. This allows all controls to read their previous states and provide memory in the application for server-side page processing.

IPostBackDataHandler is the interface a control implements to receive HTML form's post data from a postback. The control must emit an <INPUT> tag with its UniqueID property to be called by the framework. LoadPostData is the method in IPostBackDataHandler that allows a control to read its post data.

CHAPTER 5

Event-Based Programming

IN THIS CHAPTER, we explore the intricacies of working with server control events. The first part of this chapter is a general discussion of the .NET event architecture. We discuss how to add events to a control, bringing back our favorite `Textbox` control as part of the demonstration. Then we illustrate how to define custom events and add them to yet another version of our famous `Textbox`. We also examine `System.Web.UI.Control`'s support for maintaining events. Next, we show how to initiate and capture a postback using a `Button` control that we create named `SuperButton`. This section examines `Command` events and event bubbling with an example composite control to demonstrate these concepts. In the final portion of the chapter, we bring it all together with a discussion of the page life cycle, focusing on events. The next section provides an overview of events and ASP.NET controls.

Events and ASP.NET Controls

The event-based development paradigm is a well-traveled path on the Windows platform with Visual Basic 6.0 and Visual C++ Microsoft Foundation Classes (MFC) development tools. In this model, developers need not be concerned with the details of how to gather input from hardware or render output to the video card; instead, they can focus on business logic coded in event handlers attached to UI widgets that receive events from the operating system. In ASP.NET, this development model is brought to the Web in much the same way through server controls.

The key technology that sets ASP.NET apart from previous web development paradigms is the use of server-side controls as first-class objects in a similar fashion to Visual Basic or MFC. Server controls provide a rich, object-oriented method of building web content in an environment that is normally spartan in its feature set and procedural in its execution model. A critical aspect of working with objects such as ASP.NET server controls is event-based programming, which we cover in this chapter.

The Need for Events in ASP.NET

In any object-oriented development framework, events are a necessary means of decoupling reusable functionality from the specifics of any given application. This is true in ASP.NET as well. Events allow the encapsulated functionality of a server control, such as a `Button`, to be hooked into the logic of an application without requiring any changes, such as recompilation, to the UI object.

Events simplify the work of the programmer by providing a consistent protocol for development. Client applications can register their interest in a control via an event and be notified later by the control when some activity has taken place in the same way regardless of the control. The only thing that changes from control to control is the number or type of events that are available as well as possibly the arguments that a particular event makes available in its method signature. Figure 5-1 presents a comparison between traditional programming and event-based programming.

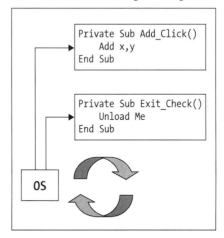

Figure 5-1. Traditional programming versus event-based programming

ASP.NET turns on its head the traditional assumption that UI controls are only appropriate for thick-client applications. Through clever use of client-side state and the HTTP POST protocol, ASP.NET server controls appear as if they maintain memory on the client and react to user interaction by raising events. Server controls do this without having to resort to a bunch of client-side tricks such as applets or ActiveX controls. Even browsing devices that don't support JavaScript on the client can raise events through HTML form actions.

Figure 5-2 illustrates how a control can raise events and make it look like ASP.NET has turned the browser into an interactive thick-client application. The TextBox exposes the TextChanged event, while the Button notifies interested clients through a Click event. All event-handling code for the TextChanged and Click events is located on the server where the ASP.NET processing occurs.

For the event code to react to changes the user makes with the TextBox on the Web Form in the browser, the control must shift execution from the browser back to the web server. The Button control is responsible for handling this by generating a form postback when it is clicked.

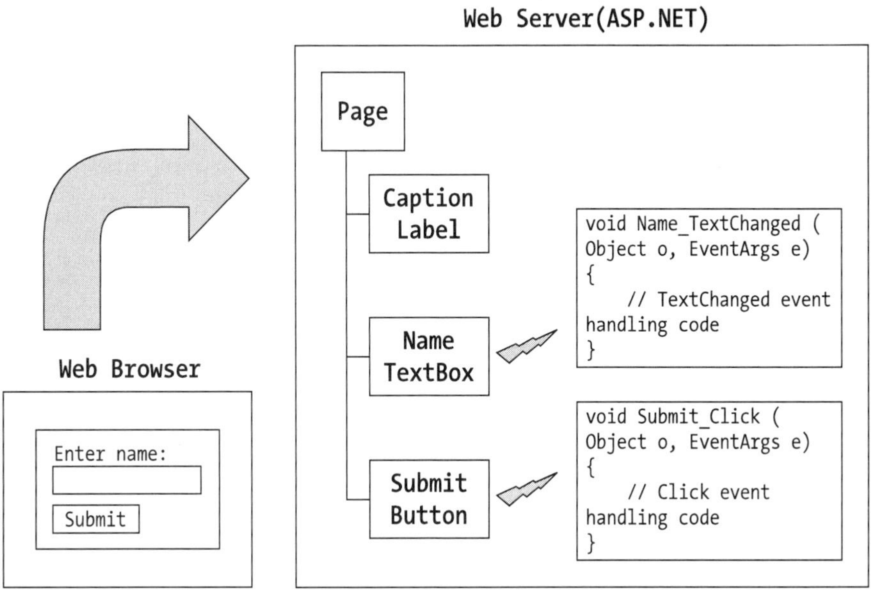

Figure 5-2. Server-side control events in ASP.NET

`Buttons` automatically generate a form postback, but other server controls can also generate a postback using JavaScript. Changing the `AutoPostBack` property for a control from the default value of `false` to `true` will cause the control to emit the appropriate JavaScript, taking advantage of client-side events to cause postback.

When a user clicks a `Button` in a Web Form and the browser performs an HTTP POST back to the web server, ASP.NET builds the page control tree on the server to dynamically handle the postback request. As discussed in Chapter 4, ASP.NET gives each control in the control tree that has ViewState enabled a chance to examine posted data through its `LoadPostData` method. In this method, the control can examine the user input on the server via the posted data and compare it to what was previously stored in ViewState. If the data has indeed changed, and if the control has an event that can be fired in response to the data change, the control should return true to ASP.NET in `LoadPostData`. Later on in the page life cycle, ASP.NET will call the `RaisePostDataChangedEvent` member for each server control that returned true in `LoadPostData` so that the control can in turn raise the appropriate event and execute any business logic implemented via an event handler written by the developer. This is the ASP.NET page life cycle that repeats during each postback for state (data) changes and event firing. Before we dive into writing events for ASP.NET, we first provide a high-level overview of events in the .NET Framework in the next section.

The .NET Framework Event Model

Events are generally used in UI development to notify the appropriate object that the user has made a selection, but events can be used for any asynchronous communication need. Whether you're developing desktop Windows applications using Windows Forms or web applications using ASP.NET, classes as objects need a mechanism to communicate with each other. The .NET Framework provides a first-class event model based on delegates, which we discuss in this section.

Delegates

Delegates are similar to interfaces—they specify a contract between the publisher and the subscriber. Although an interface is generally used to specify a set of member functions, a delegate specifies the signature of a single function. To create an instance of a delegate, you must create a function that matches the delegate signature in terms of parameters and data types.

Delegates are often described as safe function pointers; however, unlike function pointers, delegates call more than one function at a time and can represent both static and instance methods. Also unlike function pointers, delegates provide a type-safe callback implementation and can be secured through code access permissions as part of the .NET Framework security model.

Delegates have two parts in the relationship: the delegate declaration and the delegate instance or static method. The *delegate declaration* defines the function signature as a reference type. Here is how a delegate is declared:

```
public delegate int PrintStatusNotify (object printer, object document) ;
```

Delegates can be declared either outside a class definition or as part of a class through the use of the `delegate` keyword. The .NET Framework `Delegate` class and the .NET Framework `MulticastDelegate` class serve as the base classes for delegates, but neither of these classes is creatable by developers; instead, developers use the `delegate` keyword. As background, the `MulticastDelegate` base class maintains a linked list of delegates that are invoked in order of declaration when the delegate is fired, as you will see in our example in the next section.

One question that arises with delegates is what happens if an invoked method throws an exception. Does the delegate continue processing the methods in the invocation list? Actually, if an exception is thrown, the delegate stops processing methods in the invocation list. It does not matter whether or not an exception handler is present. This makes sense because odds are that if an invoked method throws an exception, methods that follow may throw an exception as well, but it is something to keep in mind.

Working with Delegates

In this section we create a console-based application to demonstrate how delegates work. In our example, we declare a very simple delegate that takes one parameter:

```
delegate void SimpleMulticastDelegate(int i);
```

We next declare a class that contains two class instance methods and one static method. These methods match the signature of the previous delegate declaration:

```
public class DelegateImplementorClass
{
    public void ClassMethod(int i)
    {
        Console.WriteLine("You passed in " + i.ToString() +"
                        to the class method");
    }

    static public void StaticClassMethod(int j)
    {
        Console.WriteLine("You passed in "+ j.ToString() +"
         to the static class method");
    }

    public void YetAnotherClassMethod(int k)
    {
        Console.WriteLine("You passed in " + k.ToString() +"
        to yet another class method");
    }
}
```

In method Main, the entry point of any console application in .NET, we put the delegate to work. Here we declare an instance of DelegateImplementorClass, as we will add instance methods from this class as subscribers to our delegate:

```
DelegateImplementorClass ImpClass = new DelegateImplementorClass();
```

We next declare an instance of our delegate, adding an instance method to the delegate invocation list that will be called when the delegate instance executes:

```
SimpleMulticastDelegate d = new SimpleMulticastDelegate(ImpClass.ClassMethod);
```

Firing the delegate is simply a matter of calling the delegate instance function:

```
d(5);
```

The rest of method Main adds additional methods to the delegate's invocation list. Listing 5-1 is the full code listing. Figure 5-3 shows the output. Notice how each subsequent call to the delegate reflects this in the output. Each time the delegate fires, it passes the parameter value to each subscriber in its invocation list, taking advantage of multicasting behavior.

Listing 5-1. Delegates in Action

```
using System;

namespace ControlsBookWeb.Ch05
{
    delegate void SimpleMulticastDelegate(int i);

    public class DelegateImplementorClass
    {
        public void ClassMethod(int i)
        {
            Console.WriteLine("You passed in " + i.ToString() +"
            to the class method");
        }

        static public void StaticClassMethod(int j)
        {
            Console.WriteLine("You passed in "+ j.ToString() +"
             to the static class method");
        }

        public void YetAnotherClassMethod(int k)
        {
            Console.WriteLine("You passed in " + k.ToString() +"
             to yet another class method");
        }
    }

    class main
    {
        [STAThread]
        static void Main(string[] args)
        {
            DelegateImplementorClass ImpClass = new DelegateImplementorClass();

            SimpleMulticastDelegate d =
                new SimpleMulticastDelegate(ImpClass.ClassMethod);
            d(5);
            Console.WriteLine("");

            d +=
            new SimpleMulticastDelegate(DelegateImplementorClass.StaticClassMethod);
            d(10);
            Console.WriteLine("");

            d += new SimpleMulticastDelegate(ImpClass.YetAnotherClassMethod);
            d(15);
        }
    }
}
```

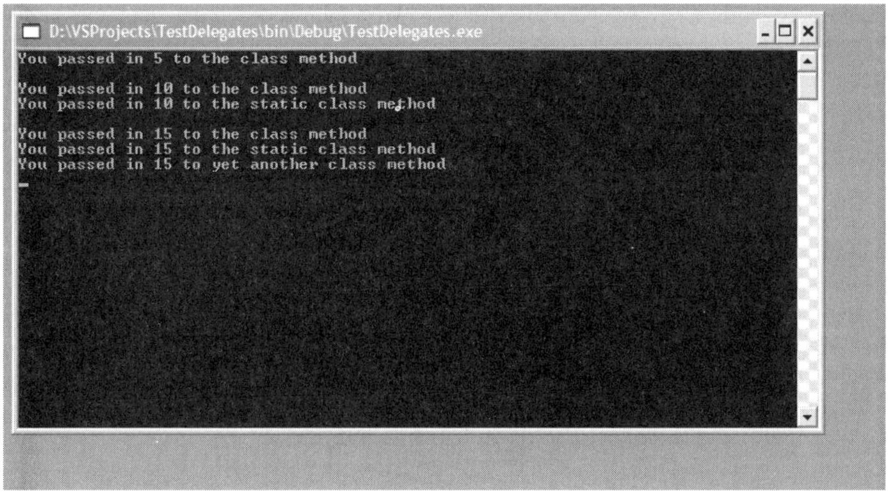

Figure 5-3. Output from our work with delegates

Stepping back for a minute, you can see how delegates quite successfully fulfill the requirements of the publisher/subscriber model. Here we have the member function `Main` using an instance of the delegate to send messages to subscribing methods in the `DelegateImplementorClass` class. As long as the subscribing methods match the delegate signature, the delegate is happy to add those methods to its invocation list, and it promptly processes this list each time it is invoked with a call to `d()`.

If you step through this code with the debugger, you will notice that methods on the delegate's invocation list are synchronously called in the order that they are added to the invocation list. The syntax for adding a delegate to the invocation list may seem strange at first, because what we are really adding is something more akin to function pointers than, say, an integer. The magic behind this is the keyword `delegate` and the .NET infrastructure provided by the `System.Delegate` and `System.Delegate.MulticastDelegate` classes. The result is that the language compiler simplifies things by providing a keyword that developers use to plug into the delegate infrastructure.

Events

As you may have guessed by now, delegates are the heart and soul of event handling in .NET. They provide the underlying infrastructure for asynchronous callbacks and UI events in web applications under ASP.NET. In addition to the `delegate` keyword, there is also the `event` keyword in C#. The `event` keyword lets you specify a delegate that will fire upon the occurrence of some event in your code. The delegate associated with an event can have one or more client methods in its invocation list that will be called when the object indicates that an event has occurred, as is the case with a `MulticastDelegate`.

We can declare an event using the event keyword followed by a delegate type and the name of the event. The following event declaration creates a Click event with public accessibility that would be right at home on a Button control:

```
public event EventHandler Click;
```

The name of the event should be a verb signifying that some action has taken place. Init, Click, Load, Unload, and TextChanged are all good examples of such verbs used in the ASP.NET framework.

The event declaration causes the C# compiler to emit code that adds a private field to the class named Click, along with add and remove methods for working with the delegates passed in from clients. The nice thing about the event declaration and the code it generates is that it happens under the covers without your having to worry about it. Later on in this chapter, we discuss how to optimize event registration with respect to storage for controls that publish a large number of events, but only a small fraction of them are likely to be subscribed to for a given control instance.

System.EventHandler Delegate

The common denominator of the event declarations with .NET controls is the delegate class System.EventHandler. All the built-in controls in ASP.NET use its signature or some derivative of it to notify their clients when events occur. We recommend that you leverage this infrastructure because it reduces the amount of custom event development required. In addition, the signature of EventHandler permits server controls in the .NET Framework and their clients to interoperate:

```
delegate void EventHandler(Object o, EventArgs e);
```

The first parameter to EventHandler is an object reference to the control that raised the event. The second parameter to the delegate, EventArgs, contains data pertinent to the event. The base EventArgs class doesn't actually hold any data; it's more of an extensibility point for custom events to override. The EventArgs class does have a read-only static field named Empty that returns an instance of the class that's syntactically convenient to use when raising an event that doesn't require any special arguments or customization.

Invoking an Event in a Control

After you add an event to a control, you need to raise the event in some manner. Instead of calling the event directly, a good design pattern followed by all the prebuilt server controls in ASP.NET is to add a virtual protected method that invokes the event with a prefix of On attached to the name of the method. This provides an additional level of abstraction that allows controls that derive from a base control to easily override the event-raising mechanism to run additional business logic or suppress event invocation altogether. The following code shows an OnClick protected method used to provide access to the Click event of class:

```
protected virtual void OnClick(EventArgs e)
{
   if (Click != null)
      Click(this, e);
}
```

The first thing the protected method does is check to see if any client methods have registered themselves with the Click event instance. The event field will have a null value if no clients have registered a method onto the delegate's invocation list. If clients have subscribed to the Click event with a method having a matching signature, the event field will contain an object reference to a delegate that maintains the invocation list of all registered delegates. The OnClick routine next invokes the event using the function call syntax along with the name of the event. The parameters passed in are a reference to the control raising the event and the event arguments passed into the routine.

Adding an Event to the Textbox Control

The Textbox control that we started in Chapter 4 had the beginnings of a nice clone of the ASP.NET System.Web.UI.WebControls.TextBox control. It saves its values to View-State, emits the correct HTML to create a text box in the browser, and handles postback data correctly. The control is well on its way to becoming a respectable member of the family.

We next enhance our Textbox control by adding the capability to raise an event when the Text property of the control has changed, as detected by comparing the value currently stored in ViewState with postback data.

Enhancing the Textbox Control with a TextChanged Event

The next step in our Textbox journey is to add a TextChanged event to help bring its functionality more in line with that of the built-in ASP.NET text controls. This necessitates adding an event declaration and enhancing the implementation of the IPostBackDataHandler interface in our control. The most important upgrade is the addition of the TextChanged event field and a protected OnTextChanged method to invoke it:

```
protected virtual void OnTextChanged(EventArgs e)
{
   if (TextChanged != null)
      TextChanged(this, e);
}
public event EventHandler TextChanged;
```

The second upgrade is the logic enhancement to the LoadPostData and RaisePostDataChanged methods. In LoadPostData, the ViewState value of the Text property is checked against the incoming value from postback for any differences.

If there is a difference, the Text property is changed to the new value in ViewState and true is returned from the routine. This guarantees that the event is raised when RaisePostDataChangedEvent is called by ASP.NET further on in the page life cycle.

```
public bool LoadPostData(string postDataKey, NameValueCollection postCollection)
{
    string postedValue = postCollection[postDataKey];
    if (!Text.Equals(postedValue))
    {
        Text = postedValue;
        return true;
    }
    else
        return false;
}
```

The upgrade to the RaisePostDataChangedEvent method is the addition of a single line. Instead of being blank, it calls on our newly created OnTextChanged method to invoke the TextChanged event. We use the static field Empty of the EventArgs class to create an instance of EventArgs for us, as we don't need to customize EventArgs in this case:

```
public void RaisePostDataChangedEvent()
{
    OnTextChanged(EventArgs.Empty);
}
```

The code in Listing 5-2 is full text of the control after the modifications required to add the TextChanged event.

Listing 5-2. Event-Based Programming

```
using System;
using System.Web;
using System.Web.UI;
using System.Collections.Specialized;
using System.ComponentModel;

namespace ControlsBookLib.Ch05
{
    [ToolboxData("<{0}:Textbox runat=server></{0}:Textbox>"),
    DefaultProperty("Text")]
    public class Textbox : Control, IPostBackDataHandler
    {
        public virtual string Text
        {
            get
            {
                object text = ViewState["Text"];
```

```
        if (text == null)
            return string.Empty;
        else
            return (string) text;
    }
    set
    {
        ViewState["Text"] = value;
    }
}

public bool LoadPostData(string postDataKey,
    NameValueCollection postCollection)
{
    string postedValue = postCollection[postDataKey];
    if (!Text.Equals(postedValue))
    {
        Text = postedValue;
        return true;
    }
    else
        return false;
}

public void RaisePostDataChangedEvent()
{
    OnTextChanged(EventArgs.Empty);
}

protected virtual void OnTextChanged(EventArgs e)
{
    if (TextChanged != null)
        TextChanged(this, e);
}

public event EventHandler TextChanged;

override protected void Render(HtmlTextWriter writer)
{
    base.Render(writer);
    Page.VerifyRenderingInServerForm(this);
    // write out the <INPUT type="text"> tag
    writer.Write("<INPUT type=\"text\" name=\"");
    writer.Write(this.UniqueID);
    writer.Write("\" value=\"" + this.Text + "\" />");
    }
  }
}
```

Using the Textbox Control on a Web Form

The Textbox Web Form shown in the Design view in Figure 5-4 hosts the newly minted Textbox control with its TextChanged event capabilities.

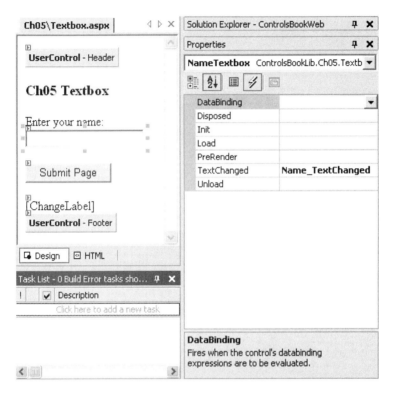

Figure 5-4. Server-side control events in ASP.NET

The Web Form contains an instance of our Textbox control named NameTextbox, along with a Label control named ChangeLabel that is used to indicate the raising of TextChanged event. The label is programmatically set to a value of "No change!" along with the current time by default during the loading of the Web Form. Raising the TextChanged event causes the event-handling code to set the label's value to "Changed." along with the current time. This allows you to recycle the control several times to verify that the event is working properly.

The TextChanged event of the NameTextbox control is visible when you select the control in the Design view of Visual Studio .NET and look at it in the Properties window, as shown in Figure 5-5. Click the lightning bolt icon to categorize the properties by events and you will see TextChanged. We used an event handler called Name_TextChanged as a client subscriber to the TextChanged event. The full extent of our code work is shown in Listings 5-3 and 5-4.

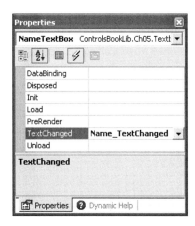

Figure 5-5. The Server-side events tab of the Properties window

Listing 5-3. The Textbox Web Form .aspx Page File

```
<%@ Page language="c#" Codebehind="Textbox.aspx.cs" AutoEventWireup="false"
Inherits="ControlsBookWeb.Ch05.Textbox" %>
<%@ Register TagPrefix="apress" Namespace="ControlsBookLib.Ch05"
Assembly="ControlsBookLib" %>
<%@ Register TagPrefix="apressUC" TagName="ControlsBookHeader"
Src="..\ControlsBookHeader.ascx" %>
<%@ Register TagPrefix="apressUC" TagName="ControlsBookFooter"
Src="..\ControlsBookFooter.ascx" %>
<!DOCTYPE HTML PUBLIC "-//W3C//DTD HTML 4.0 Transitional//EN" >
<HTML>
  <HEAD>
    <title>Ch05 Textbox</title>
    <meta name="GENERATOR" Content="Microsoft Visual Studio 7.0">
    <meta name="CODE_LANGUAGE" Content="C#">
    <meta name="vs_defaultClientScript" content="JavaScript">
    <meta name="vs_targetSchema"
     content="http://schemas.microsoft.com/intellisense/ie5">
  </HEAD>
  <body MS_POSITIONING="FlowLayout">
    <form id="Textbox" method="post" runat="server">
      <apressUC:ControlsBookHeader id="Header" runat="server"
       ChapterNumber="5" ChapterTitle="Event-based Programming" />
      <h3>Ch05 TextBox</h3>
      Enter your name:<br>
      <apress:textbox id="NameTextbox" runat="server"></apress:textbox><br>
      <br>
      <asp:button id="SubmitPageButton" runat="server" Text=
         "Submit Page"></asp:button><br>
      <br>
      <asp:label id="ChangeLabel" runat="server" Text=""></asp:label><br>
      <apressUC:ControlsBookFooter id="Footer" runat="server" />
    </form>
  </body>
</HTML>
```

Listing 5-4. The Textbox Web Form Code-Behind Class File

```
using System;
using System.Collections;
using System.ComponentModel;
using System.Data;
using System.Drawing;
using System.Web;
using System.Web.SessionState;
using System.Web.UI;
using System.Web.UI.WebControls;
using System.Web.UI.HtmlControls;

namespace ControlsBookWeb.Ch05
{
    public class Textbox : System.Web.UI.Page
    {
        protected System.Web.UI.WebControls.Button SubmitPageButton;
        protected ControlsBookLib.Ch05.Textbox NameTextbox;
        protected System.Web.UI.WebControls.Label ChangeLabel;

        private void Page_Load(object sender, System.EventArgs e)
        {
            ChangeLabel.Text = DateTime.Now.ToLongTimeString() + ": No change.";
        }

        #region Web Form Designer generated code
        override protected void OnInit(EventArgs e)
        {
            //
            // CODEGEN: This call is required by the ASP.NET Web Form Designer.
            //
            InitializeComponent();
            base.OnInit(e);
        }

        /// <summary>
        /// Required method for Designer support - do not modify
        /// the contents of this method with the code editor.
        /// </summary>
        private void InitializeComponent()
        {
            this.NameTextbox.TextChanged += new
            System.EventHandler(this.Name_TextChanged);
            this.Load += new System.EventHandler(this.Page_Load);

        }
        #endregion

        private void Name_TextChanged(object sender, System.EventArgs e)
        {
            ChangeLabel.Text = DateTime.Now.ToLongTimeString() + ": Changed!";
        }
    }
}
```

The event wiring is conducted inside the `InitializeComponent` routine:

```
private void InitializeComponent()
{
   this.NameTextbox.TextChanged += new System.EventHandler(this.Name_TextChanged);
   this.Load += new System.EventHandler(this.Page_Load);
}
```

The `Name_TextChanged` method is wrapped by a `System.EventHandler` delegate and then passed to the `TextChanged` event of our custom `Textbox` control to add it to its delegate invocation list. Notice also the wiring up of the `Page_Load` method to the `Load` event that the `Page` class will raise during request processing.

The execution of the Web Form during the initial page request results in the UI output of Figure 5-6. The ViewState rendered by the control into this Web Form shows the `Text` property as a blank value. We entered a name into the `Textbox` as well, but we haven't clicked the button to submit the Web Form via postback.

Figure 5-6. Initial rendering of the Textbox *control*

Upon clicking the button to execute a postback to the web server, the `Textbox` control will read the blank value from ViewState and find the name value "Dale Michalk" when the ASP.NET invokes `LoadPostData`. Because the posted data is different from the current ViewState value, it calls its internal `OnTextChanged` method to raise events to all registered delegate subscribers. This results in the Name_TextChanged event handler method firing, and the code that changes the label to reflect the new value executes:

```
private void Name_TextChanged(object sender, System.EventArgs e)
{
    ChangeLabel.Text = DateTime.Now.ToLongTimeString() + ": Changed!";
}
```

The result is that ChangeLabel displays the text containing the current time and the word "Changed!" as shown in Figure 5-7.

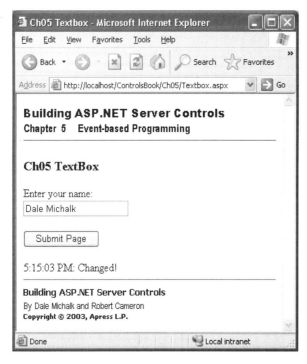

Figure 5-7. The firing of the TextChanged *event by the* Textbox *control*

The next step in this demonstration is to recycle the page without changing the value in the Textbox control by simply clicking the Submit Page button. Because the ViewState and the control's text post data contain the same value of "Dale Michalk," no event is raised. The increment of the timestamp in the label in Figure 5-8 confirms that the page was processed successfully. Our control is able to react appropriately to changes of its Text property.

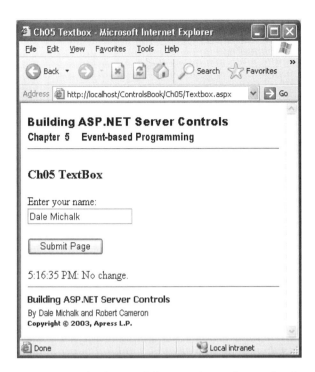

Figure 5-8. The firing of the TextChanged *event by the* Textbox *control*

Creating a Custom Event

If an event does not provide data but is merely a signal that something has happened, you can take advantage of the EventHandler delegate class and its empty EventArgs implementation. However, we want to provide additional information in the TextChanged event raised by our Textbox control. The newly minted event will track both before and after values of the Text property between postback submissions. The control loads the oldValue from data saved in ViewState; the newValue value loads from the data received in the <INPUT type="text"> HTML element through postback. We now move on to create our custom EventArgs class to support our custom event.

Creating a TextChangedEventArgs Class

The first requirement is to create an enhanced EventArgs-based class that holds the event data. We create a new class derived from EventArgs that exposes two read-only properties to clients, OldValue and NewValue, as shown in the following code:

```
public class TextChangedEventArgs : EventArgs
{
    private string oldValue;
    private string newValue;
```

```
    public TextChangedEventArgs(string oldValue, string newValue)
    {
       this.oldValue = oldValue;
       this.newValue = newValue;
    }

    public string OldValue
    {
       get
       {
          return oldValue;
       }
    }

    public string NewValue
    {
       get
       {
          return newValue;
       }
    }
}
```

The class created is fairly straightforward. The two properties have only get accessors to make them read-only, making the constructor the only way to populate the internal fields with their values.

Creating a TextChangedEventHandler Delegate

Delegate creation is the next step in defining our custom event. There is not an inheritance chain that must be followed with delegates, as all delegate types are created using the keyword delegate. Instead, we choose to follow the method signature used by other controls in ASP.NET to build upon a successful design pattern.

The signature of the delegate has two parameters and a void return value. The first parameter remains of type object, and the second parameter must be of type EventArgs or derived from it. Because we already created the TextChangedEventArgs class, we use that as our second parameter to take advantage of its OldValue and NewValue properties.

The name used in the declaration of the following delegate is also important. The pattern for ASP.NET controls is to add the word "EventHandler" to the end of the event of the delegate. In this case, we add "TextChanged" to "EventHandler" to get TextChangedEventHandler as our name.

Both the TextChangedEventArgs class and the TextChangedEventHandler delegate are put into a file named TextChanged.cs that is part of the ControlsBookLib library project for reference by our new control, as shown in Listing 5-5.

Listing 5-5. The TextChanged *Class File for the* TextChangedEventArgs *Class and* TextChangedEventHandler *Delegate Definitions*

```
using System;

namespace ControlsBookLib.Ch05
{
    public delegate void
            TextChangedEventHandler(object o, TextChangedEventArgs tce);

    public class TextChangedEventArgs : EventArgs
    {
        private string oldValue;
        private string newValue;

        public TextChangedEventArgs(string oldValue, string newValue)
        {
            this.oldValue = oldValue;
            this.newValue = newValue;
        }

        public string OldValue
        {
            get
            {
                return oldValue;
            }
        }

        public string NewValue
        {
            get
            {
                return newValue;
            }
        }
    }
}
```

Adding an Event to the CustomEventTextbox Control

To demonstrate the newly minted TextChangedEventHandler delegate, we take our Textbox control and copy its contents into a class named CustomEventTextbox. Another option would be to customize the behavior in an object-oriented manner by overriding the necessary methods in a derived class. However, in this chapter, we choose the route of separate classes so that we can more clearly isolate the two Textbox control examples and highlight the different design decisions embodied in them.

Replacing the event declaration is the easiest part. The control starts with an EventHandler delegate but is changed to take a TextChangedEventHandler delegate:

```
public event TextChangedEventHandler TextChanged;
```

The second change is the replacement of the OnTextChanged event invocation method to take TextChangedEventArgs as the single parameter to the method, as shown in the following code. This is one of the reasons for having the On-prefixed methods in controls as an abstraction layer. It makes it a simpler code change to augment or replace the event mechanism.

```
protected virtual void OnTextChanged(TextChangedEventArgs tce)
{
    if (TextChanged != null)
      TextChanged(this, tce);
}
```

The next step is to add logic to track the before and after values. A private string field named oldText is added to the class and is given its value inside LoadPostData. This gives us a chance to load TextChangedEventArgs properly when we raise the event. Here is a snippet of the code change from LoadPostData that does the work:

```
if (!Text.Equals(postedValue))
{
    oldText = Text;
    Text = postedValue;
    return true;
}
```

The last step is to replace all routines that call OnTextChanged. We have only one: RaisePostDataChanged. It takes the before and after values from the oldText field and the Text property in LoadPostData and creates a new TextChangedEventArgs class instance:

```
public void RaisePostDataChangedEvent()
{
    OnTextChanged(new TextChangedEventArgs(oldText, Text));
}
```

Our control is now ready for testing on a Web Form to display its dazzling event capabilities. Listing 5-6 contains the full source code.

Listing 5-6. The CustomEventTextbox *Control Class File*

```csharp
using System;
using System.Web;
using System.Web.UI;
using System.Collections.Specialized;
using System.ComponentModel;

namespace ControlsBookLib.Ch05
{
    [ToolboxData("<{0}:CustomEventTextbox runat=server></{0}:CustomEventTextbox>"),
    DefaultProperty("Text")]
    public class CustomEventTextbox : Control, IPostBackDataHandler
    {
        private string oldText;

        public virtual string Text
        {
            get
            {
                object text = ViewState["Text"];
                if (text == null)
                    return string.Empty;
                else
                    return (string) text;
            }
            set
            {
                ViewState["Text"] = value;
            }
        }

        public bool LoadPostData(string postDataKey,
            NameValueCollection postCollection)
        {
            string postedValue = postCollection[postDataKey];
            if (!Text.Equals(postedValue))
            {
                oldText = Text;
                Text = postedValue;
                return true;
            }
            else
                return false;
        }
```

```
      public void RaisePostDataChangedEvent()
      {
         OnTextChanged(new TextChangedEventArgs(oldText, Text));
      }

      protected void OnTextChanged(TextChangedEventArgs tce)
      {
         if (TextChanged != null)
            TextChanged(this, tce);
      }
      public event TextChangedEventHandler TextChanged;

      override protected void Render(HtmlTextWriter writer)
      {
         base.Render(writer);
         Page.VerifyRenderingInServerForm(this);
         // write out the <INPUT type="text"> tag
         writer.Write("<INPUT type=\"text\" name=\"");
         writer.Write(this.UniqueID);
         writer.Write("\" value=\"" + this.Text + "\" />");
      }
   }
}
```

Using the CustomEventTextbox Control on a Web Form

After building our new control, we are ready to put it to use in the CustomEventTextbox Web Form. This Web Form has the CustomEventTextbox control plus a button and two labels named BeforeLabel and AfterLabel that are used to track the before and after values of the control when the custom TextChanged event is raised.

Creating the event mapping in Visual Studio .NET is performed in the same manner as the previous TextChanged event in the preceding Textbox demonstration. We use the Properties window as shown in Figure 5-9 to wire up the event to the NameCustom_TextChanged handling method in the code-behind class.

The Web Form starts out with the labels displaying blank values, as shown in Figure 5-10. We enter Dale's name to cause the next form submit to raise the event. Listings 5-7 and 5-8 contain the source code for the CustomEventTextbox Web Form.

Figure 5-9. The Properties window view of our custom TextChanged *event*

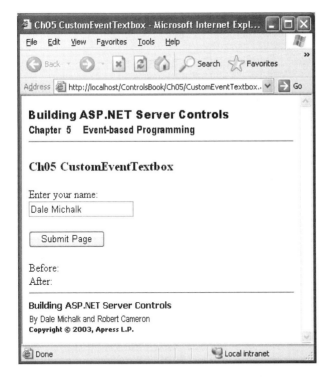

Figure 5-10. Initial page request with the CustomEventTextbox Web Form

Listing 5-7. The CustomEventTextbox Web Form .aspx Page File

```
<%@ Register TagPrefix="apress" Namespace="ControlsBookLib.Ch05"
Assembly="ControlsBookLib" %>
<%@ Page language="c#" Codebehind="CustomEventTextbox.aspx.cs" AutoEventWireup="false"
Inherits="ControlsBookWeb.Ch05.CustomEventTextbox" %>
<%@ Register TagPrefix="apressUC" TagName="ControlsBookHeader"
Src="..\ControlsBookHeader.ascx" %>
<%@ Register TagPrefix="apressUC" TagName="ControlsBookFooter"
Src="..\ControlsBookFooter.ascx" %>
<!DOCTYPE HTML PUBLIC "-//W3C//DTD HTML 4.0 Transitional//EN" >
<HTML>
  <HEAD>
    <title>Ch05 CustomEventTextbox</title>
    <meta name="GENERATOR" Content="Microsoft Visual Studio 7.0">
    <meta name="CODE_LANGUAGE" Content="C#">
    <meta name="vs_defaultClientScript" content="JavaScript">
    <meta name="vs_targetSchema" c
          ontent="http://schemas.microsoft.com/intellisense/ie5">
  </HEAD>
  <body MS_POSITIONING="FlowLayout">
    <form id="Textbox" method="post" runat="server">
      <apressUC:ControlsBookHeader id="Header"
          runat="server" ChapterNumber="5"
          ChapterTitle="Event-based Programming" />
      <h3>Ch05 CustomEventTextbox</h3>
      Enter your name:<br>
      <apress:customeventtextbox id="NameTextbox"
 runat="server"></apress:customeventtextbox><br>
      <br>
      <asp:button id="SubmitPageButton" runat="server"
            Text="Submit Page"></asp:button><br>
      <br>
      Before:<asp:label id="BeforeLabel" runat="server" Text=""></asp:label><br>
      After:<asp:label id="AfterLabel" runat="server" Text=""></asp:label><br>
      <apressUC:ControlsBookFooter id="Footer" runat="server" />
    </form>
  </body>
</HTML>
```

Listing 5-8. The CustomEventTextbox Web Form Code-Behind Class File

```
using System;
using System.Collections;
using System.ComponentModel;
using System.Data;
using System.Drawing;
using System.Web;
using System.Web.SessionState;
using System.Web.UI;
```

```
using System.Web.UI.WebControls;
using System.Web.UI.HtmlControls;

namespace ControlsBookWeb.Ch05
{
    public class CustomEventTextbox : System.Web.UI.Page
    {
        protected System.Web.UI.WebControls.Button SubmitPageButton;
        protected System.Web.UI.WebControls.Label BeforeLabel;
        protected System.Web.UI.WebControls.Label AfterLabel;
        protected ControlsBookLib.Ch05.CustomEventTextbox NameTextbox;

        private void Page_Load(object sender, System.EventArgs e)
        {
            BeforeLabel.Text = NameTextbox.Text;
            AfterLabel.Text = NameTextbox.Text;
        }

        #region Web Form Designer generated code
        override protected void OnInit(EventArgs e)
        {
            //
            // CODEGEN: This call is required by the ASP.NET Web Form Designer.
            //
            InitializeComponent();
            base.OnInit(e);
        }

        /// <summary>
        /// Required method for Designer support - do not modify
        /// the contents of this method with the code editor.
        /// </summary>
        private void InitializeComponent()
        {
            this.NameTextbox.TextChanged += new
           ControlsBookLib.Ch05.TextChangedEventHandler(this.NameCustom_TextChanged);
            this.Load += new System.EventHandler(this.Page_Load);

        }
        #endregion

        private void NameCustom_TextChanged(object o,
                    ControlsBookLib.Ch05.TextChangedEventArgs tce)
        {
            BeforeLabel.Text = tce.OldValue;
            AfterLabel.Text = tce.NewValue;
        }
    }
}
```

We exercise the custom event by submitting the page by clicking the Submit Page button. This causes the AfterLabel control to change to "Dale Michalk," whereas the BeforeLabel keeps the old blank value, as shown in Figure 5-11.

Figure 5-11. The page after submitting the CustomEventTextbox Web Form

The Visual Studio .NET Properties window did its job in wiring up to the custom event. It was smart enough to realize we had to use TextChangedEventHandler as a delegate to wrap the NameCustom_TextChanged event-handling method. This behavior by the Designer is one more reason we recommend sticking to the event model design pattern implemented in .NET. Here is the code that performs this work:

```
private void InitializeComponent()
{
    this.NameTextbox.TextChanged += new
        ControlsBookLib.Ch05.TextChangedEventHandler(this.NameCustom_TextChanged);
    this.Load += new System.EventHandler(this.Page_Load);
}
```

The following definition of NameCustom_TextChanged shows it is connected to TextChanged correctly, taking TextChangedEventArgs as its second parameter. The parameter named tce is the conduit to the information added to the BeforeLabel and AfterLabel Text values:

```
private void NameCustom_TextChanged(object o,
                     ControlsBookLib.Ch05.TextChangedEventArgs tce)
{
   BeforeLabel.Text = tce.OldValue;
   AfterLabel.Text = tce.NewValue;
}
```

Figure 5-12 shows what happens if we type a second name in the CustomEventTextbox control input box and click the Submit Page button to generate another postback. The control successfully remembers what the previous input was.

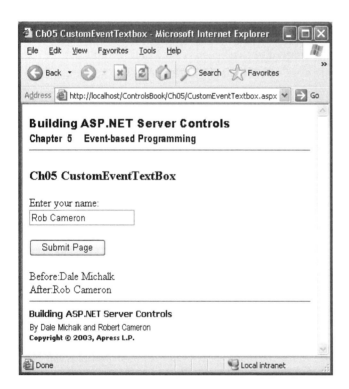

Figure 5-12. The second request with a new name on the CustomEventTextbox Web Form

Capturing Postback with the Button Control

The Textbox control does a great job in gathering input and raising state change events to their clients, but sometimes we need controls that provide action and post data back to the server. A perfect example of this type of control in the ASP.NET framework is the System.Web.UI.WebControls.Button control. The Button control exists for one reason: to post the page back to the server and raise events.

We would be remiss if we only reverse-engineered the ASP.NET TextBox control and left out the Button control, so our next task is to build our own version of the Button control. We add some bells and whistles along the way, such as the capability for the control to display itself as a Button or as a hyperlink similar to the LinkButton control in ASP.NET. This new, amazing Button server control will be named SuperButton for all its rich functionality.

Rendering the Button

The first decision we have to make when building our button relates to how it will render. Because we decided to render either as an <INPUT type="submit"> or an <A> tag, we choose to use a strongly-typed enumeration as a means to configure its display output. We call this enumeration ButtonDisplay and give it values that reflect how our button can appear in a Web Form:

```
public enum ButtonDisplay
{
   Button = 0,
   Hyperlink = 1
}
```

The ButtonDisplay enumeration is exposed from our control through a Display property. It defaults to a Button value if nothing is passed into the control:

```
public virtual ButtonDisplay Display
{
   get
   {
      object display = ViewState["Display"];
      if (display == null)
         return ButtonDisplay.Button;
      else
         return (ButtonDisplay) display;
   }
   set
   {
      ViewState["Display"] = value;
   }
}
```

We also have a Text property that has an identical representation in the code to our previous examples. It will appear as text on the surface of the button or as the text of the hyperlink.

The button-rendering code needs to have an if/then construct to switch the display based on the enumeration value set by the developer/user. It also needs a way to submit the page back to the web server when using the hyperlink display mode. The hyperlink is normally used for navigation and is not wired into the postback mechanism that buttons get for free.

The Page class comes to the rescue in this instance. It has a static method named GetPostBackClientHyperlink that registers the JavaScript necessary to submit the Web Form via an HTTP POST. In the Web Form example that hosts our SuperButton control, we examine the HTML output to see how it is integrated into the postback process. Here is the code that hooks into the postback mechanism:

```
override protected void Render(HtmlTextWriter writer)
{
   base.Render(writer);
   Page.VerifyRenderingInServerForm(this);

   if (Display == ButtonDisplay.Button)
   {
      writer.Write("<INPUT type=\"submit\"");
      writer.Write(" name=\"" + this.UniqueID + "\"");
      writer.Write(" id=\"" + this.UniqueID + "\"");
      writer.Write(" value=\"" + Text + "\"");
        writer.Write(" />");
   }
   else if (Display == ButtonDisplay.Hyperlink)
   {
      writer.Write("<A href=\"");
      writer.Write(Page.GetPostBackClientHyperlink(this,""));
      writer.Write("\">" + Text + "</A>");
   }
}
```

Exposing a Click Event and the Events Collection

The first event we add to our SuperButton control is a Click event. This is your garden-variety System.EventHandler delegate type event, but our actual event implementation will be different this time around. Instead of adding an event field to the control class, we reuse a mechanism given to all controls from the System.Web.UI.Control base class.

The Events read-only property inherited from the Control class provides access to an event collection of type System.ComponentModel.EventHandlerList. EventHandlerList provides access to delegates that represent the invocation list for each event the control exposes. This means that the only memory taken up to handle event delegates is by those events that have a client event handler method registered, unlike the previous technique, which takes a hit for each event, regardless of any clients using it. This can potentially save a fair amount of memory on a control that exposes many events. Figure 5-13 graphically depicts the benefits of using the Events collection.

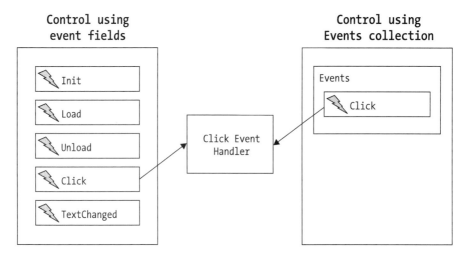

Figure 5-13. The difference between using an event field and using the Events *collection*

The first thing we need to do for an event using this new model is provide a key for the delegate that is used to store it inside the Events collection. We add this at the top of our class by creating a generic static, read-only object to represent the key for our click-related delegate:

```
private static readonly object ClickEvent = new object();
```

The second step is to use the syntax C# provides for custom delegate registration with our Click event. It is an expansion of the event declaration used previously that includes add and remove code blocks. It is similar to the get and set code blocks that programmers can use to define properties in C#. The result is the following Click event:

```
public event EventHandler Click
{
    add
    {
        Events.AddHandler(ClickEvent, value);
    }
    remove
    {
        Events.RemoveHandler(ClickEvent, value);
    }
}
```

The first thing to notice is the event declaration itself. It is declared with an event keyword, delegate type, name, and accessibility modifier as before. The new functionally is added via code blocks below the declaration. The add and remove code blocks handle the delegate registration process in whatever manner they see fit to do so. In this case, these code blocks are passed the delegate reference via the value keyword to accomplish their assigned tasks.

The code in our Click event uses the Events collection to add the delegate via AddHandler or to remove the delegate via RemoveHandler. ClickEvent is the access key used to identify the Click delegates in our Events collection, keeping like event handlers in separate buckets.

After we declare our event with its event subscription code, we need to define our OnClick method to raise the event. The code uses the Events collection and our defined key object to get the Click delegate and raise the event to subscribers:

```
protected virtual void OnClick(EventArgs e)
{
    EventHandler clickEventDelegate = (EventHandler)Events[ClickEvent];
    if (clickEventDelegate != null)
    {
        clickEventDelegate(this, e);
    }
}
```

The first step is to pull the delegate of type EventHandler from the Events collection. Our second step as before is to check it for a null value to ensure that we actually need to invoke it. The invocation code on the delegate is the same as we used previously with our event in the Textbox demonstrations. We invoke the delegate using function call syntax with the name of the delegate. At this point, our Click event is ready to go—all we need to do is raise it when a postback occurs.

Command Events and Event Bubbling

The second event exposed by our SuperButton control is a *command* event. The command event is a design pattern borrowed from the controls in the System.Web.UI.WebControls namespace that makes event handling in list controls easier.

The primary example of this scenario is the DataGrid control, which can have buttons embedded in a column for edit and delete operations. The buttons activate edit or delete functionality respectively in the DataGrid control as long as the command events exposed by these buttons have the correct CommandName property in the CommandEventArgs class as part of the event. If the button is set with a CommandName of "Delete", it kicks off delete activity. If the button is set with a CommandName of "Edit", it starts edit functions in the DataGrid control. Controls that raise command events that are not in those expected by the DataGrid control are wrapped into an ItemCommand event exposed by the control.

The capabilities provided by a command event are an implementation of event bubbling. *Event bubbling* is a technique that allows a child control to propagate command events up its control hierarchy, allowing the event to be handled in a more convenient location. Figure 5-14 provides a graphical depiction of event bubbling. This technique allows the DataGrid control to take a crack at handling the button events despite the fact that the buttons are several layers deep inside of its control hierarchy.

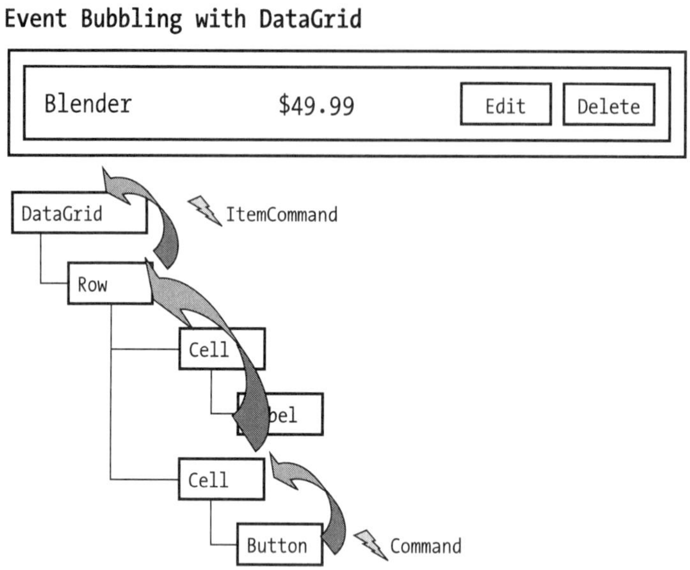

Event Bubbling with DataGrid

Figure 5-14. Event bubbling

Exposing the Command Event

The techniques used to expose a command event on our control are similar to those used with the Click event. As before, an important preliminary task to creating the event declaration is the need for an object to provide a "key" that gives access to the event in the Events collection. The CommandEvent field handles this chore:

```
private static readonly object CommandEvent = new object();
```

The event declaration for the Command event is almost identical to the Click event except for the delegate type used. It exposes the CommandEventHandler delegate, which provides data through the CommandEventArgs parameter to clients registered to process the event:

```
public event CommandEventHandler Command
{
   add
   {
      Events.AddHandler(CommandEvent, value);
   }
   remove
   {
      Events.RemoveHandler(CommandEvent, value);
   }
}
```

The CommandEventArgs class provides two properties: CommandName and CommandArgument. A control is expected to maintain these values as part of a command event bubbling protocol. These values are copied directly into the CommandEventArgs class when the command event is raised. Command controls expose these values through the CommandName and CommandArgument public properties, respectively:

```
public virtual string CommandName
{
   get
   {
      object name = ViewState["CommandName"];
      if (name == null)
         return string.Empty;
      else
         return (string) name;
   }
   set
   {
      ViewState["CommandName"] = value;
   }
}

public virtual string CommandArgument
{
   get
   {
      object arg = ViewState["CommandArgument"];
      if (arg == null)
         return string.Empty;
      else
         return (string) arg;
   }
   set
   {
      ViewState["CommandArgument"] = value;
   }
}
```

The final step in working with a command event is to raise the event. The OnCommand method in our class holds this important code. It pulls back the appropriate delegate type from the Events collection and invokes it in a similar manner to the OnClick method we reviewed earlier:

```
protected virtual void OnCommand(CommandEventArgs ce)
{
   CommandEventHandler commandEventDelegate =
     (CommandEventHandler) Events[CommandKey];
   if (commandEventDelegate != null)
   {
      commandEventDelegate(this, ce);
   }

   RaiseBubbleEvent(this, ce);
}
```

The new code that stands out is the RaiseBubbleEvent method call at the end of the OnCommand method. This code takes advantage of the internal event-bubbling plumbing that all controls receive just by inheriting from System.Web.UI.Control.

RaiseBubbleEvent takes an object reference and a System.EventArgs reference for its two parameters. This permits all events, even those not related to command event functionality, to take advantage of event bubbling. Naturally, the primary concern of event bubbling in ASP.NET is with command events.

At this point in our design, we have successfully exposed both the Click event and the command event for our control using the Events collection. One of the limitations of the Events collection is its implementation as a linked list. Given the nature of the linked list data structure, it can cause a performance problem in certain scenarios when many delegate nodes are traversed in order to find the correct event delegate. As background, you are free to use other collection types to hold event delegates. One alternative to using a linked list is to implement the events collection as a Hashtable, which can speed access.

Capturing the Postback via IPostBackEventHandler

As part of our design, we had the requirement of rendering the button as either a normal button or as a specially configured hyperlink to submit the Web Form. With events in hand, we now move on to hooking the button click into the postback process through implementation of the IPostBackEventHandler interface. To achieve this, we next implement the single method of the postback interface, RaisePostBackEvent:

```
public void RaisePostBackEvent(string argument);
```

RaisePostBackEvent takes a single argument as a means to retrieve a value from the form submission. When a Button submits a Web Form, it always passes a blank value for this argument to RaisePostBackEvent. Our hyperlink-rendering code has a choice of what information to pass via the Page.GetPostBackClientHyperlink method call. The following code snippet submits a blank value to keep things in line with our button rendering:

```
writer.Write("<A href=\"");
writer.Write(Page.GetPostBackClientHyperlink(this,""));
writer.Write("\">" + Text + "</A>");
```

The RaisePostBackEvent implementation in our SuperButton control has very little work to do, as we encapsulated the bulk of our event-generating code in the OnClick and OnCommand methods:

```
public void RaisePostBackEvent(string argument)
{
   OnCommand(new CommandEventArgs(CommandName, CommandArgument));
   OnClick(EventArgs.Empty);
}
```

Completing the RaisePostBackEvent method brings our SuperButton control to fruition. Listing 5-9 is the class file for the control and its related enumeration. The control needs a "using" import for the System.Web.UI.WebControls namespace because it takes advantage of Command events.

Listing 5-9. The SuperButton *Control Class File*

```
using System;
using System.Web.UI;
using System.Web.UI.WebControls;

namespace ControlsBookLib.Ch05
{
   public enum ButtonDisplay
   {
      Button = 0,
      Hyperlink = 1
   }

   [ToolboxData("<{0}:SuperButton runat=server></{0}:SuperButton>")]
   public class SuperButton : Control, IPostBackEventHandler
   {
      public virtual ButtonDisplay Display
      {
         get
         {
            object display = ViewState["Display"];
```

```csharp
      if (display == null)
          return ButtonDisplay.Button;
      else
          return (ButtonDisplay) display;
   }
   set
   {
      ViewState["Display"] = value;
   }
}

public virtual string Text
{
   get
   {
      object text = ViewState["Text"];
      if (text == null)
          return string.Empty;
      else
          return (string) text;
   }
   set
   {
      ViewState["Text"] = value;
   }
}

private static readonly object ClickKey = new object();

public event EventHandler Click
{
   add
   {
      Events.AddHandler(ClickKey, value);
   }
   remove
   {
      Events.RemoveHandler(ClickKey, value);
   }
}

protected virtual void OnClick(EventArgs e)
{
   EventHandler clickEventDelegate =
      (EventHandler)Events[ClickKey];
   if (clickEventDelegate != null)
   {
      clickEventDelegate(this, e);
   }
}
```

```csharp
private static readonly object CommandKey = new object();

public event CommandEventHandler Command
{
    add
    {
        Events.AddHandler(CommandKey, value);
    }
    remove
    {
        Events.RemoveHandler(CommandKey, value);
    }
}

public virtual string CommandName
{
    get
    {
        object name = ViewState["CommandName"];
        if (name == null)
            return string.Empty;
        else
            return (string) name;
    }
    set
    {
        ViewState["CommandName"] = value;
    }
}

public virtual string CommandArgument
{
    get
    {
        object arg = ViewState["CommandArgument"];
        if (arg == null)
            return string.Empty;
        else
            return (string) arg;
    }
    set
    {
        ViewState["CommandArgument"] = value;
    }
}

protected virtual void OnCommand(CommandEventArgs ce)
{
    CommandEventHandler commandEventDelegate =
        (CommandEventHandler) Events[CommandKey];
    if (commandEventDelegate != null)
```

```
        {
            commandEventDelegate(this, ce);
        }

        RaiseBubbleEvent(this, ce);
    }

    public void RaisePostBackEvent(string argument)
    {
        OnCommand(new CommandEventArgs(CommandName, CommandArgument));
        OnClick(EventArgs.Empty);
    }

    override protected void Render(HtmlTextWriter writer)
    {
        base.Render(writer);
        Page.VerifyRenderingInServerForm(this);

        if (Display == ButtonDisplay.Button)
        {
            writer.Write("<INPUT type=\"submit\"");
            writer.Write(" name=\"" + this.UniqueID + "\"");
            writer.Write(" id=\"" + this.UniqueID + "\"");
            writer.Write(" value=\"" + Text + "\"");
            writer.Write(" />");
        }
        else if (Display == ButtonDisplay.Hyperlink)
        {
            writer.Write("<A href=\"");
            writer.Write(Page.GetPostBackClientHyperlink(this,""));
            writer.Write("\">" + Text + "</A>");
        }
    }
  }
}
```

Using the SuperButton Control on a Web Form

The SuperButton Web Form hosts two SuperButton controls: one of the button variety and the other of the hyperlink persuasion. It also has a label that is set according to event handlers for each button. The first request to the Web Form generates Figure 5-15. Listings 5-10 and 5-11 provide the source code for this Web Form.

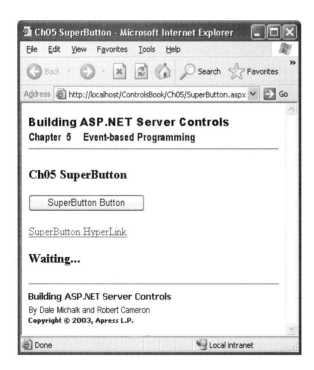

Figure 5-15. The SuperButton Web Form rendering its first request

Listing 5-10. The SuperButton Web Form .aspx Page File

```
<%@ Page language="c#" Codebehind="SuperButton.aspx.cs" AutoEventWireup="false"
Inherits="ControlsBookWeb.Ch05.SuperButton" %>
<%@ Register TagPrefix="apress" Namespace="ControlsBookLib.Ch05"
Assembly="ControlsBookLib" %>
<%@ Register TagPrefix="apressUC" TagName="ControlsBookHeader"
Src="..\ControlsBookHeader.ascx" %>
<%@ Register TagPrefix="apressUC" TagName="ControlsBookFooter"
Src="..\ControlsBookFooter.ascx" %>
<!DOCTYPE HTML PUBLIC "-//W3C//DTD HTML 4.0 Transitional//EN" >
<HTML>
  <HEAD>
    <title>Ch05 SuperButton</title>
    <meta name="GENERATOR" Content="Microsoft Visual Studio 7.0">
    <meta name="CODE_LANGUAGE" Content="C#">
    <meta name="vs_defaultClientScript" content="JavaScript">
    <meta name="vs_targetSchema"
    content="http://schemas.microsoft.com/intellisense/ie5">
  </HEAD>
  <body MS_POSITIONING="FlowLayout">
    <form id="SuperButton" method="post" runat="server">
      <apressUC:ControlsBookHeader id="Header" runat="server" ChapterNumber="5"
```

```
ChapterTitle="Event-based Programming" />
    <h3>Ch05 SuperButton</h3>
    <apress:superbutton id="superbtn" runat="server" Text="SuperButton
Button"></apress:superbutton><br>
    <br>
    <apress:superbutton display="hyperlink" id="superlink" runat="server"
Text="SuperButton HyperLink"></apress:superbutton><br>
    <br>
    <h3><asp:Label id="ClickLabel" runat="server">Waiting...</asp:Label></h3>
    <apressUC:ControlsBookFooter id="Footer" runat="server" />
  </form>
 </body>
</HTML>
```

Listing 5-11. The SuperButton Web Form Code-Behind Class File

```csharp
using System;
using System.Collections;
using System.ComponentModel;
using System.Data;
using System.Drawing;
using System.Web;
using System.Web.SessionState;
using System.Web.UI;
using System.Web.UI.WebControls;
using System.Web.UI.HtmlControls;

namespace ControlsBookWeb.Ch05
{
    public class SuperButton : System.Web.UI.Page
    {
        protected ControlsBookLib.Ch05.SuperButton superlink;
        protected System.Web.UI.WebControls.Label ClickLabel;
        protected ControlsBookLib.Ch05.SuperButton superbtn;

        private void Page_Load(object sender, System.EventArgs e)
        {
            ClickLabel.Text = "Waiting...";
        }

        #region Web Form Designer generated code
        override protected void OnInit(EventArgs e)
        {
            //
            // CODEGEN: This call is required by the ASP.NET Web Form Designer.
            //
            InitializeComponent();
            base.OnInit(e);
        }

        /// <summary>
        /// Required method for Designer support - do not modify
        /// the contents of this method with the code editor.
```

```
    /// </summary>
    private void InitializeComponent()
    {
        this.superbtn.Click += new System.EventHandler(this.superbtn_Click);
        this.superlink.Click += new System.EventHandler(this.superlink_Click);
        this.Load += new System.EventHandler(this.Page_Load);

    }
    #endregion

    private void superbtn_Click(object sender, System.EventArgs e)
    {
        ClickLabel.Text = "superbtn was clicked!";
    }

    private void superlink_Click(object sender, System.EventArgs e)
    {
        ClickLabel.Text = "superlink was clicked!";
    }
  }
}
```

Clicking the button generates the output in Figure 5-16. Clicking the hyperlink generates the output in Figure 5-17.

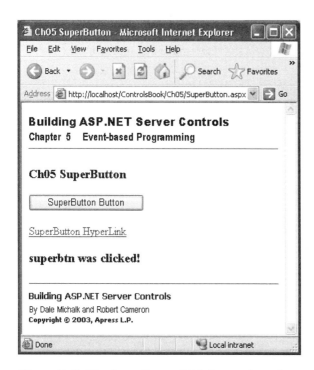

Figure 5-16. The SuperButton Web Form after a button click

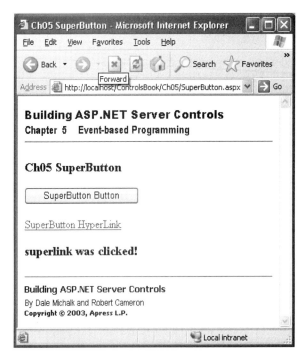

Figure 5-17. The SuperButton Web Form after a hyperlink click

Of more interest is what is rendered on the HTML page that represents the Web Form. Listing 5-12 shows the HTML.

Listing 5-12. The SuperButton Web Form Rendered HTML

```
<!DOCTYPE HTML PUBLIC "-//W3C//DTD HTML 4.0 Transitional//EN" >
<HTML>
<HEAD>
    <title>Ch05 Super Button</title>
    <meta name="GENERATOR" Content="Microsoft Visual Studio 7.0">
    <meta name="CODE_LANGUAGE" Content="C#">
    <meta name="vs_defaultClientScript" content="JavaScript">
    <meta name="vs_targetSchema"
    content="http://schemas.microsoft.com/intellisense/ie5">
</HEAD>
<body MS_POSITIONING="FlowLayout">
<form name="SuperButton" method="post" action="SuperButton.aspx" id="SuperButton">
<input type="hidden" name="__VIEWSTATE"
value="dDwtMTgOMzczNjQyMztOPDtsPGk8MT47PjtsPHQ8O2w8aTw1Pjs+O2w8dDxwPHA8bDxUZXh0O00z4
7bDxzdXBlcmxpbmsgd2FzIGNsaWNrZWQhOz4+Oz470z47
Pj47Pj47PiynDcUVBayIzW4ijbIz/Ks9mMxm" />
    <h3>Ch05 SuperButton</h3>
    <INPUT type="submit" name="superbtn" id="superbtn"
    value="SuperButton Button" /><br>
    <br>
```

```
    <A href="javascript:__doPostBack('superlink','')">SuperButton HyperLink</A><br>
    <br>
    <h3><span id="ClickLabel">superlink was clicked!</span></h3>

<input type="hidden" name="__EVENTTARGET" value="" />
<input type="hidden" name="__EVENTARGUMENT" value="" />
<script language="javascript">
<!--
      function __doPostBack(eventTarget, eventArgument) {
          var theform = document.SuperButton;
          theform.__EVENTTARGET.value = eventTarget;
          theform.__EVENTARGUMENT.value = eventArgument;
          theform.submit();
      }
// -->
</script>
</form>
</body>
</HTML>
```

The first thing to examine is how our hyperlink generates a postback:

```
<A href="javascript:__doPostBack('superlink','')">SuperButton HyperLink</A><br>
```

It uses a JavaScript function named __doPostBack, which actually sends the page back to the server. This JavaScript invocation is added by our Page.GetPostBackClientHyperlink call in the Render method of SuperButton. The __doPostBack JavaScript routine is emitted into the HTML by the ASP.NET framework as a result of this method call:

```
<input type="hidden" name="__EVENTTARGET" value="" />
<input type="hidden" name="__EVENTARGUMENT" value="" />
<script language="javascript">
<!--
      function __doPostBack(eventTarget, eventArgument) {
          var theform = document.SuperButton;
          theform.__EVENTTARGET.value = eventTarget;
          theform.__EVENTARGUMENT.value = eventArgument;
          theform.submit();
      }
// -->
</script>
```

The JavaScript code programmatically submits the form and sets two hidden variables to give ASP.NET enough information about what control was responsible for causing the postback. It doesn't need this extra step when rendering the <INPUT type="submit"> button, but it is mandatory for hyperlinks. You can also see that the purpose of the second parameter in Page.GetPostBackClientHyperlink is to pass an eventArgument, which makes its way back to the RaisePostBack method invocation on the server-side control implementation as the string parameter named argument.

Composing the SuperButton Control into a Composite Pager Control

Our SuperButton control is capable of raising command events through the event-bubbling mechanism. To capture these bubbled events, we use a composite control named Pager. Pager recognizes bubbled command events from its children and raises a PageCommand event to its event clients. This is similar to the event bubbling performed by the DataGrid list control when it grabs all command events from child controls and exposes them via a single ItemCommand event. We next describe the design of the Pager control, starting with how the control is constructed.

Building the Pager Child Control Hierarchy

Composite control development begins with creating a child control hierarchy. The Pager control uses a private method named CreateChildControlHierarchy that is called from the overridden protected CreateChildControls method. Listing 5-13 provides the source code for CreateChildControlHierarchy. CreateChildControls is called by the ASP.NET framework to allow composite controls to build up their structure prior to rendering.

Listing 5-13. The Pager *Implementation of* CreateChildControlHierarchy

```
private SuperButton buttonLeft ;
private SuperButton buttonRight;
private void CreateChildControlHierarchy()
{
   LiteralControl tableStart = new
      LiteralControl("<table border=1><tr><td>");
   Controls.Add(tableStart);

   buttonLeft = new SuperButton();
   buttonLeft.ID = "buttonLeft";
   if (Context != null)
   {
      buttonLeft.Text = Context.Server.HtmlEncode("<") + " Left";
   }
   else
   {
      buttonLeft.Text = "< Left";
   }
   buttonLeft.CommandName = "Page";
   buttonLeft.CommandArgument = "Left";
   Controls.Add(buttonLeft);

   LiteralControl spacer = new LiteralControl("  ");
   Controls.Add(spacer);

   buttonRight = new SuperButton();
```

```
   buttonRight.ID = "buttonRight";
   buttonRight.Display = Display;
   if (Context != null)
   {
      buttonRight.Text = "Right " + Context.Server.HtmlEncode(">");
   }
   else
   {
      buttonRight.Text = "Right  >";
   }
   buttonRight.CommandName = "Page";
   buttonRight.CommandArgument = "Right";
   Controls.Add(buttonRight);

   LiteralControl tableEnd = new
      LiteralControl("</td></tr></table>");
   Controls.Add(tableEnd);
}
```

The child control collection created by the Pager control includes a set of SuperButtons representing left and right direction arrows that are wrapped inside an HTML table. The Left direction SuperButton includes the text < Left, and the Right direction SuperButton uses Right >. The Text property uses HtmlEncode to properly render the special characters. Otherwise, CreateChildControlHierarchy renders straight text when Context is not available at design time.

```
if (Context != null)
{
   buttonLeft.Text = Context.Server.HtmlEncode("<") + " Left";
}
else
{
   buttonLeft.Text = "< Left";
}
```

The most important settings in CreateChildControlHierarchy are the Command properties. The CommandName value chosen for the SuperButton controls is Page. This lets the Pager know that it is receiving Command events from its specially configured SuperButton controls. CommandArgument tells the Pager whether it is the left or right control emitting the event:

```
buttonLeft.CommandName = "Page";
buttonLeft.CommandArgument = "Left";
...
buttonRight.CommandName = "Page";
buttonRight.CommandArgument = "Right";
```

The final rendering feature is the `Display` property passed on to the `SuperButton` controls. Our `Pager` can display its left and right UI elements as either buttons or hyperlinks. The implementation of the `Display` property in `Pager` is as follows. It calls `EnsureChildControls` and then gets or sets the `Display` property on the child controls. The `SuperButton` server control defaults to a `Display` value of `Button`, which becomes the default for `Pager` as well if the value is not set.

```
public virtual ButtonDisplay Display
{
   get
   {
      EnsureChildControls();
      return buttonLeft.Display ;
   }
   set
   {
      EnsureChildControls();
      buttonLeft.Display  = value;
      buttonRight.Display = value;
   }
}
```

Defining the PageCommand Event

The `Pager` control exposes a custom `PageCommand` event to let its client know whether it is moving in the left or right direction. The `PageDirection` enumeration provides a finite way to specify this in code:

```
public enum PageDirection
{
   Left = 0,
   Right = 1
}
```

The `PageCommandEventArgs` class uses this enumeration as the data type for its `Direction` property exposed as part of an `EventArgs` replacement for the `PageCommand` delegate. The complete `PageCommand` event–related code is grouped in the `PageCommand` class file shown in Listing 5-14.

Listing 5-14. The `PageCommand` *Class File*

```
using System;

namespace ControlsBookLib.Ch05
{
   public enum PageDirection
   {
      Left = 0,
      Right = 1
   }
```

```
public delegate void PageCommandEventHandler(object o,
                                    PageCommandEventArgs pce);

public class PageCommandEventArgs
{
   public PageCommandEventArgs(PageDirection direction)
   {
      this.direction = direction;
   }

   PageDirection direction;
   public PageDirection Direction
   {
      get{ return direction; }
   }
}
}
```

Exposing the PageCommand Event from the Pager Control

The Pager control uses the PageCommandEventHandler delegate to declare its event-handling code. As with the SuperButton, we use the Events property technique for handling delegate registration:

```
private static readonly object PageCommandKey = new object();
public event PageCommandEventHandler PageCommand
{
   add
   {
      Events.AddHandler(PageCommandKey, value);
   }
   remove
   {
      Events.RemoveHandler(PageCommandKey, value);
   }
}
```

We also add an OnPageCommand method to raise the event. This method uses the custom PageCommandEventArgs class we defined earlier to invoke the PageCommandEventHandler delegate:

```
protected virtual void OnPageCommand(PageCommandEventArgs pce)
{
   PageCommandEventHandler pageCommandEventDelegate =
               (PageCommandEventHandler) Events[PageCommandEvent];
   if (pageCommandEventDelegate != null)
   {
      pageCommandEventDelegate(this, pce);
   }
}
```

OnPageCommand is the last bit of code required to raise events associated with the PageCommand event type. The next task is to capture the bubbled Command events and turn them into PageCommand events.

Capturing the Bubbles via OnBubbleEvent

The OnBubbleEvent method inherited from System.Web.UI.Control is the counterpart to the RaiseBubbleEvent method used inside the SuperButton control. It allows a control to hook into the stream of bubbled events from child controls and process them accordingly:

```
protected override bool OnBubbleEvent(object source, EventArgs e);
```

The method definition for OnBubbleEvent specifies the ubiquitous System.EventHandler method signature, with one difference. It takes an object reference and an EventArgs reference, but returns a bool. The bool return value indicates whether or not the control has processed the bubble event. A value of false indicates that the bubble event should continue bubbling up the control hierarchy; a value of true indicates a desire to stop the event in its tracks because it has been handled. If a control does not implement OnBubbleEvent, the default implementation passes the event on up to parent controls.

The Pager control implements its OnBubbleEvent as shown in Listing 5-15.

Listing 5-15. The Pager *Implementation of* OnBubbleEvent

```
protected override bool OnBubbleEvent(object source, EventArgs e)
{
   bool result = false;
   CommandEventArgs ce = e as CommandEventArgs;

   if (ce != null)
   {
      if (ce.CommandName.Equals("Page"))
      {
         PageDirection direction;
         if (ce.CommandArgument.Equals("Right"))
            direction = PageDirection.Right;
         else
            direction = PageDirection.Left;

         PageCommandEventArgs pce =
            new PageCommandEventArgs(direction);

         OnPageCommand(pce);
         result = true;
      }
   }
   return result;
}
```

The `result` variable holds the return value of `OnBubbleEvent` for the `Pager` control. It is set to `false`, assuming failure until success. The first check is to cast the `EventArgs` reference to ensure we receive a `Command` event of the proper type. The code performs this check using the as keyword in C# to cast the reference to the desired type, which returns `null` if the cast fails.

If the type cast succeeds, the next check is to ensure the proper `CommandName` is set to "Page". After the checks pass, the `OnBubbleEvent` code can create a `PageCommandEventArgs` class and set the `Direction` property according to the `CommandArgument` value. The final task is to raise the `PageCommand` event by calling `OnPageCommand`. Finally, the function returns the value of result to tell the ASP.NET framework whether or not the event was handled.

The `INamingContainer` Interface

When a composite control builds up its child control tree, it sets each control's identification via the `ID` property. For example, the `Pager` control sets the left `SuperButton` child control `ID` property value in the following single line of code:

```
buttonLeft.ID = "buttonLeft";
```

The problem with using just the `ID` value to uniquely identify child controls is that multiple `Pager` controls could be used on a Web Form, and the emitted button or hyperlink `ID` values would conflict. To protect against name collisions, each composite control creates a unique namespace that prefixes the ID of a control with the parent control's ID and a colon. The `INamingContainer` interface tells ASP.NET to do this. `INamingContainer` is a marker interface (i.e., an interface without any defined methods) used by ASP.NET to identify the parent in a composite control to ensure unique names or IDs for child controls as they are dynamically created during the page-rendering process.

Implementing the `INamingContainer` interface in the `Pager` server control activates this mechanism, causing ASP.NET to prefix the ID of a control with the parent control's ID and a colon. The previous left button in a `Pager` control named "pagerbtn" would therefore have an `ID` value of "buttonLeft" but a `UniqueID` value of "pagerbtn:buttonLeft". Listing 5-16 contains the full code listing for the `Pager` control.

Listing 5-16. The `Pager` *Control Class File*

```
using System;
using System.ComponentModel;
using System.Web.UI;
using System.Web.UI.WebControls;
using ControlsBookLib.Ch12.Design;

namespace ControlsBookLib.Ch05
{
    [ToolboxData("<{0}:Pager
runat=server></{0}:Pager>"),Designer(typeof(CompCntrlDesigner))]
    public class Pager : Control, INamingContainer
```

```csharp
{
    private static readonly object PageCommandKey = new object();
    public event PageCommandEventHandler PageCommand
    {
        add
        {
            Events.AddHandler(PageCommandKey, value);
        }
        remove
        {
            Events.RemoveHandler(PageCommandKey, value);
        }
    }

    protected virtual void OnPageCommand(PageCommandEventArgs pce)
    {
        PageCommandEventHandler pageCommandEventDelegate =
            (PageCommandEventHandler) Events[PageCommandKey];
        if (pageCommandEventDelegate != null)
        {
            pageCommandEventDelegate(this, pce);
        }
    }

    protected override bool OnBubbleEvent(object source, EventArgs e)
    {
        bool result = false;
        CommandEventArgs ce = e as CommandEventArgs;

        if (ce != null)
        {
            if (ce.CommandName.Equals("Page"))
            {
                PageDirection direction;
                if (ce.CommandArgument.Equals("Right"))
                    direction = PageDirection.Right;
                else
                    direction = PageDirection.Left;

                PageCommandEventArgs pce =
                    new PageCommandEventArgs(direction);

                OnPageCommand(pce);
                result = true;
            }
        }
        return result;
    }

    public virtual ButtonDisplay Display
    {
        get
        {
            EnsureChildControls();
            return buttonLeft.Display ;
        }
```

```
      set
      {
         EnsureChildControls();
         buttonLeft.Display  = value;
         buttonRight.Display = value;
      }
   }

   protected override void CreateChildControls()
   {
      Controls.Clear();
      CreateChildControlHierarchy();
   }

   public override ControlCollection Controls
   {
      get
      {
         EnsureChildControls();
         return base.Controls;
      }
   }

   private SuperButton buttonLeft ;
   private SuperButton buttonRight;
   private void CreateChildControlHierarchy()
   {
      LiteralControl tableStart = new
         LiteralControl("<table border=1><tr><td>");
      Controls.Add(tableStart);

       buttonLeft = new SuperButton();
      buttonLeft.ID = "buttonLeft";
      if (Context != null)
      {
         buttonLeft.Text = Context.Server.HtmlEncode("<") + " Left";
      }
      else
      {
         buttonLeft.Text = "< Left";
      }
      buttonLeft.CommandName = "Page";
      buttonLeft.CommandArgument = "Left";
      Controls.Add(buttonLeft);

      LiteralControl spacer = new LiteralControl("  ");
      Controls.Add(spacer);

      buttonRight = new SuperButton();
      buttonRight.ID = "buttonRight";
      buttonRight.Display = Display;
      if (Context != null)
      {
         buttonRight.Text = "Right " + Context.Server.HtmlEncode(">");
      }
      else
      {
```

```
            buttonRight.Text = "Right  >";
        }
        buttonRight.CommandName = "Page";
        buttonRight.CommandArgument = "Right";
        Controls.Add(buttonRight);

        LiteralControl tableEnd = new
            LiteralControl("</td></tr></table>");
        Controls.Add(tableEnd);
    }
  }
}
```

Using the Pager Control on a Web Form

The Pager Event Bubbling Web Form demonstrates the Pager control in both its button and hyperlink display motifs. A single label represents the PageCommand activity generated by the two controls. The first request for the page appears in the browser, as shown in Figure 5-18. Listings 5-17 and 5-18 provide the .aspx and code-behind files for this Web Form.

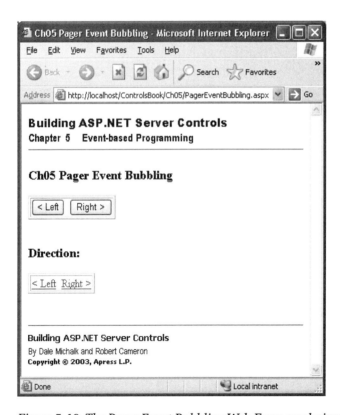

Figure 5-18. The Pager Event Bubbling Web Form rendering its first request

Listing 5-17. The Pager Event Bubbling Web Form .aspx Page File

```
<%@ Register TagPrefix="apress" Namespace="ControlsBookLib.Ch05"
Assembly="ControlsBookLib" %>
<%@ Page language="c#" Codebehind="PagerEventBubbling.aspx.cs"
AutoEventWireup="false"
Inherits="ControlsBookWeb.Ch05.PagerEventBubbling" %>
<%@ Register TagPrefix="apressUC" TagName="ControlsBookHeader"
Src="..\ControlsBookHeader.ascx" %>
<%@ Register TagPrefix="apressUC" TagName="ControlsBookFooter"
Src="..\ControlsBookFooter.ascx" %>
<!DOCTYPE HTML PUBLIC "-//W3C//DTD HTML 4.0 Transitional//EN" >
<HTML>
  <HEAD>
    <title>Ch05 Pager Event Bubbling</title>
    <meta name="GENERATOR" Content="Microsoft Visual Studio 7.0">
    <meta name="CODE_LANGUAGE" Content="C#">
    <meta name="vs_defaultClientScript" content="JavaScript">
    <meta name="vs_targetSchema"
            content="http://schemas.microsoft.com/intellisense/ie5">
  </HEAD>
  <body MS_POSITIONING="FlowLayout">
    <form id="PagerEventBubbling" method="post" runat="server">
      <apressUC:ControlsBookHeader id="Header" runat="server" ChapterNumber="5"
            ChapterTitle="Event-based Programming" />
      <h3>Ch05 Pager Event Bubbling</h3>
      <apress:pager id="pager1" display="button" runat="server"></apress:pager><br>
      <br>
      <h3>Direction: <asp:Label ID="DirectionLabel"
                Runat="server"></asp:Label></h3>
      <apress:pager id="pager2" display="hyperlink"
                runat="server"></apress:pager><br>
      <br>
      <apressUC:ControlsBookFooter id="Footer" runat="server" />
    </form>
  </body>
</HTML>
```

Listing 5-18. The Pager Event Bubbling Web Form Code-Behind Class File

```
using System;
using System.Collections;
using System.ComponentModel;
using System.Data;
using System.Drawing;
using System.Web;
using System.Web.SessionState;
using System.Web.UI;
using System.Web.UI.WebControls;
using System.Web.UI.HtmlControls;

namespace ControlsBookWeb.Ch05
{
    public class PagerEventBubbling : System.Web.UI.Page
    {
        protected System.Web.UI.WebControls.Label DirectionLabel;
```

```
        protected ControlsBookLib.Ch05.Pager pager1;
        protected ControlsBookLib.Ch05.Pager pager2;

        private void Page_Load(object sender, System.EventArgs e)
        {
            DirectionLabel.Text = "<none>";
        }

        #region Web Form Designer generated code
        override protected void OnInit(EventArgs e)
        {
            //
            // CODEGEN: This call is required by the ASP.NET Web Form Designer.
            //
            InitializeComponent();
            base.OnInit(e);
        }

        /// <summary>
        /// Required method for Designer support - do not modify
        /// the contents of this method with the code editor.
        /// </summary>
        private void InitializeComponent()
        {
            this.pager1.PageCommand +=
          new ControlsBookLib.Ch05.PageCommandEventHandler(this.Pagers_PageCommand);
            this.pager2.PageCommand +=
          new ControlsBookLib.Ch05.PageCommandEventHandler(this.Pagers_PageCommand);
            this.Load += new System.EventHandler(this.Page_Load);

        }
        #endregion

        private void Pagers_PageCommand(object o,
                                    ControlsBookLib.Ch05.PageCommandEventArgs pce)
        {
            DirectionLabel.Text =
                Enum.GetName(typeof(ControlsBookLib.Ch05.PageDirection),
                pce.Direction);
        }
    }
}
```

The Pager controls are wired to the same event handler in the code-behind class named Pagers_PageCommand in the InitializeComponent method of the Web Form:

```
private void InitializeComponent()
{
    this.pager1.PageCommand += new
        ControlsBookLib.Ch05.PageCommandEventHandler(this.Pagers_PageCommand);
    this.pager2.PageCommand += new
        ControlsBookLib.Ch05.PageCommandEventHandler(this.Pagers_PageCommand);
    this.Load += new System.EventHandler(this.Page_Load);
}
```

Pagers_PageCommand has an all-important second parameter of type PageCommandEventArgs. We use it along with the System.Enum class's static GetName method to produce a textual representation of the PageDirection enumeration value for display in the DirectionLabel Text property:

```
private void Pagers_PageCommand(object o, C
                         ontrolsBookLib.Ch05.PageCommandEventArgs pce)
{
   DirectionLabel.Text =
      Enum.GetName(typeof(ControlsBookLib.Ch05.PageDirection),
            pce.Direction);
}
```

Click the Left button of the top Pager control to verify that it is working. The result should look something like Figure 5-19.

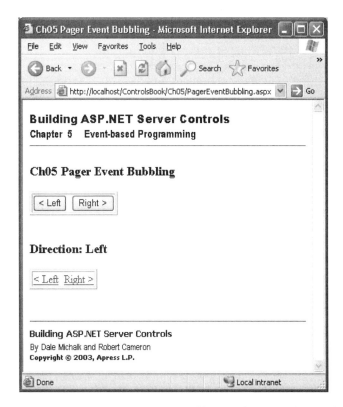

Figure 5-19. The Page Event Bubbling Web Form after clicking the Left hyperlink button

Try the Right button with the bottom Pager that is in a hyperlink form and you should get output similar to Figure 5-20.

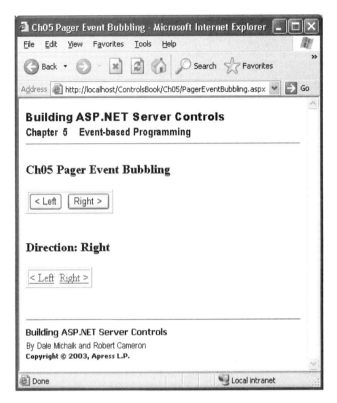

Figure 5-20. The Page Event Bubbling Web Form after clicking the Right hyperlink button

A snippet from the rendered HTML shows that the pager1 and pager2 Pager controls from the Pager Event Bubbling Web Form have their child controls identified in a nested fashion due to the INamingContainer interface with ASP.NET generating the UniqueID property:

```
<INPUT type="submit" name="pager1:buttonLeft" id="pager1:buttonLeft"
        value="&lt; Left"/>  
<INPUT type="submit" name="pager1:buttonRight" id="pager1:buttonRight"
        value="Right &gt;"
<A href="javascript:__doPostBack('pager2:buttonLeft','')">&lt; Left
</A>  <A href="javascript:__doPostBack('pager2:buttonRight','')">
Right &gt;</A></td></tr></table><br>
```

In the final section of this chapter, we review the control life cycle, which provides orderly processing to the busy life of server controls.

Control Life Cycle

The examples so far have demonstrated the use of server-side events to coordinate the activities of an ASP.NET application as part of an .aspx page. Each HTTP request/response cycle that the page executes follows a well-defined process known as the *control execution life cycle*. The Page server control orchestrates these activities on behalf of all the server controls in the Page's control tree. Control developers need to understand the flow of execution to ensure that their custom controls perform as expected as part of an ASP.NET Web Form. Figure 5-21 provides a high-level view of the page life cycle process.

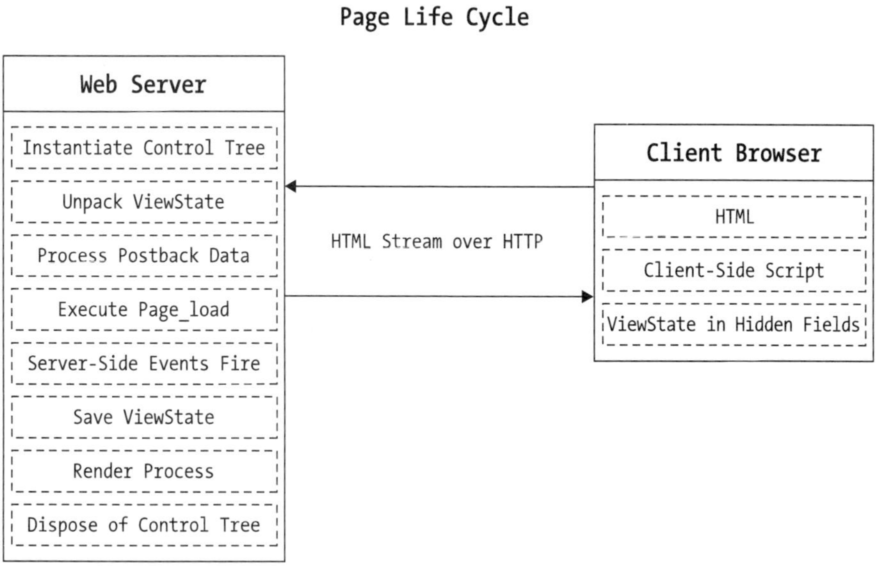

Page Life Cycle

```
        Web Server                                          Client Browser

 ┌────────────────────────┐                          ┌────────────────────────┐
 │ Instantiate Control Tree│                         │          HTML          │
 ├────────────────────────┤                          ├────────────────────────┤
 │    Unpack ViewState    │ ◄───                      │    Client-Side Script  │
 ├────────────────────────┤     HTML Stream over HTTP ├────────────────────────┤
 │  Process Postback Data │                           │ ViewState in Hidden Fields│
 ├────────────────────────┤ ───►                      └────────────────────────┘
 │    Execute Page_load   │
 ├────────────────────────┤
 │  Server-Side Events Fire│
 ├────────────────────────┤
 │     Save ViewState     │
 ├────────────────────────┤
 │     Render Process     │
 ├────────────────────────┤
 │  Dispose of Control Tree│
 └────────────────────────┘
```

Figure 5-21. An overview of the page life cycle

After the initial page request as an HTTP GET, each subsequent HTTP POST page request/response cycle generally consists of the following steps:

1. Instantiate the control tree, creating each server control object.

2. Unpack ViewState for each server control object.

3. Set the state from the previous server-side processing cycle for each object in the tree.

4. Process postback data.

5. Handle the Page_Load event.

6. Let controls know that data changed through postback, updating control state as necessary.

7. Execute server-side events based on data changes from postback.

8. Persist state back to ViewState.

9. Execute the render process for each server control.

10. Unload the page and its control tree.

This process is what provides the illusion of a stateful application to the end user. During each request/response round-trip, state is unpacked, changes are processed, the UI is updated, and the page is sent back to the user's browser with its new state values embedded in a hidden form field as ViewState, ready for the next request/response cycle. We next examine what events are available to controls as the page life cycle executes on the server side.

Plugging Into the Life Cycle

Server controls have a well-defined behavior pattern that coincides with the overall page life cycle. The ASP.NET framework provides a series of events that server controls can override to customize behavior during each phase of the life cycle. Table 5-1 provides an overview of each of these events.

Table 5-1. Server Control Events Related to the Control Execution Life Cycle

SERVER CONTROL EVENT	PAGE LIFE CYCLE PHASE	DESCRIPTION
Init	Initialization	Initializes settings for the control.
LoadViewState	Unpack ViewState	Populates the state values of the control from ViewState.
LoadPostData	Handle form postback data	Updates control's state values from posted data.
Load	Page_Load event	Executes code common to every page request/response cycle.
RaisePostDataChangedEvent	Initialization for server-side events	Notifies control that newly posted data changed its state.
RaisePostBackEvent	Execute server-side events	Goes hand-in-hand with previous event. Server-side events fire as a result of changes found in posted data for a particular control.
PreRender	Render process	Allows each control a chance to update state values before rendering.
SaveViewState	Save ViewState	Persists a control's updated state through the ViewState mechanism.
Render	Render process	Generates HTML reflecting the control's state and settings.
Dispose	Dispose of control tree	Releases any resources held by the control before teardown.

As you can see in Table 5-1, ASP.NET provides each server control the capability to finely tune each phase in the life cycle. You can choose to accept default behavior, or you can customize a particular phase by overriding the appropriate event.

The Lifecycle Server Control

Now that we have covered the basics of the control execution life cycle, we are going to examine this process in more detail by overriding all available events in a server control named Lifecycle. The overridden methods fall into two camps: those that raise defined events exposed by a control and those that are not events but perform a necessary action for the control.

OnInit, OnLoad, OnPreRender, and OnUnload are events defined in System.Web.UI.Control that a control developer can override as required for a particular control. LoadViewState, LoadPostData, RaisePostDataChangedEvent, RaisePostBackEvent, TrackViewState, SaveViewState, and Render are all events that perform necessary actions for the control to maintain its state and event processing.

 CAUTION *As with most object-oriented class hierarchies, it is usually (though not always) necessary to call the base class's version of an overridden method in the descendent class to ensure consistent behavior. If the base method is not called in the descendent class, instances of that class will most likely fail to behave as expected—or worse, they could cause instability.*

The implementation of Dispose deviates from the previous description for overridden methods. The Control class does expose a Dispose event, but it does not have an OnDispose method to raise it. Instead, providing a Dispose method follows the design pattern for objects that work with scarce resources, implementing the IDisposable interface.

Life Cycle and the HTTP Protocols GET and POST

The page life cycle differs based on whether the Web Form is requested for the first time via an HTTP GET or instead is initiated as part of a postback resulting from an HTTP POST generated by a control element on the page submitting the Web Form back to the server. The HTTP POST generally causes more life cycle activities because of the requirement to process data posted by the client back to the web server, raising events associated with state changes.

Figure 5-22 shows the two variants (initial GET versus POST) of the Web Form life cycle and the names of the phases we discuss in detail shortly.

HTTP GET

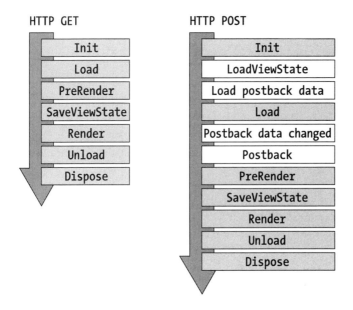

HTTP POST

Figure 5-22. The control life cycle

In order to discuss the control life cycle, we use a control that overrides the methods necessary to track the execution of each of the life cycle events as they occur. Listing 5-19 provides the class file for the Lifecycle control that handles this task. The implementation of each overridden method is quite simple, with a call to the trace function notifying us that the method is executing.

Listing 5-19. The Lifecycle *Control Class File*

```
using System;
using System.Web.UI;
using System.Collections.Specialized;
using System.Diagnostics;

namespace ControlsBookLib.Ch05
{
    [ToolboxData("<{0}:Lifecycle runat=server></{0}:Lifecycle>")]
    public class Lifecycle : Control, IPostBackEventHandler, IPostBackDataHandler
    {
        // Init Event
        override protected void OnInit(System.EventArgs e)
        {
            Trace("Lifecycle: Init Event.");
            base.OnInit(e);
        }

        override protected void TrackViewState()
        {
            Trace("Lifecycle: Track ViewState.");
            base.TrackViewState();
```

```
}

// Load ViewState Event
override protected void LoadViewState(object savedState)
{
    Trace("Lifecycle: Load ViewState Event.");
    base.LoadViewState(savedState);
}

// Load Postback Data Event
public bool LoadPostData(string postDataKey,
    NameValueCollection postCollection)
{
    Trace("Lifecycle: Load PostBack Data Event.");

    Page.RegisterRequiresRaiseEvent(this);
    return true;
}

// Load Event
override protected void OnLoad(System.EventArgs e)
{
    Trace("Lifecycle: Load Event.");
    base.OnLoad(e);
}

// Post Data Changed Event
public void RaisePostDataChangedEvent()
{
    Trace("Lifecycle: Post Data Changed Event.");
}

// Postback Event
public void RaisePostBackEvent(string argument)
{
    Trace("Lifecycle: PostBack Event.");
}

// PreRender Event
override protected void OnPreRender(System.EventArgs e)
{
    Trace("Lifecycle: PreRender Event.");
    Page.RegisterRequiresPostBack(this);
    base.OnPreRender(e);
}

// Save ViewState
override protected object SaveViewState()
{
    Trace("Lifecycle: Save ViewState.");
    return base.SaveViewState();
}

// Render Event
override protected void Render(HtmlTextWriter writer)
{
```

```
        base.Render(writer);
        Trace("Lifecycle: Render Event.");
        writer.Write("<h3>LifeCycle Control</h3>");

    }

    // Unload Event
    override protected void OnUnload(System.EventArgs e)
    {
        Trace("Lifecycle: Unload Event.");
        base.OnUnload(e);
    }

    // Dispose Event
    public override void Dispose()
    {
        Trace("Lifecycle: Dispose Event.");
        base.Dispose();
    }

    private void Trace(string info)
    {
        Context.Trace.Warn(info);
        Debug.WriteLine(info);
    }
    }
}
```

Listings 5-20 and 5-21 outline the Web Form that hosts the control, with the ASP.NET tracing mechanism turned on. The UI appearance is a single button on the Web Form with trace output turned on.

Listing 5-20. The Life Cycle Web Form .aspx Page File

```
<%@ Register TagPrefix="apressUC" TagName="ControlsBookFooter"
Src="..\ControlsBookFooter.ascx" %>
<%@ Register TagPrefix="apressUC" TagName="ControlsBookHeader"
Src="..\ControlsBookHeader.ascx" %>
<%@ Register TagPrefix="apress" Namespace="ControlsBookLib.Ch05"
Assembly="ControlsBookLib" %>
<%@ Page Trace="true" language="c#" Codebehind="LifeCycle.aspx.cs"
        AutoEventWireup="false" Inherits="ControlsBookWeb.Ch05.LifeCycle" %>
<!DOCTYPE HTML PUBLIC "-//W3C//DTD HTML 4.0 Transitional//EN" >
<HTML>
  <HEAD>
    <title>Ch05 Lifecycle</title>
    <meta name="GENERATOR" Content="Microsoft Visual Studio 7.0">
    <meta name="CODE_LANGUAGE" Content="C#">
    <meta name="vs_defaultClientScript" content="JavaScript">
    <meta name="vs_targetSchema"
        content="http://schemas.microsoft.com/intellisense/ie5">
  </HEAD>
  <body MS_POSITIONING="FlowLayout">
    <form id="LifeCycle" method="post" runat="server">
```

```
        <apressUC:ControlsBookHeader id="Header" runat="server" ChapterNumber="5"
                        ChapterTitle="Event-based Programming" />
        <h3>Ch05 Lifecycle</h3>
        <apress:Lifecycle id="life1" runat="server" />
        <asp:Button id="Button1" runat="server" Text="Button"></asp:Button>
        <apressUC:ControlsBookFooter id="Footer" runat="server" />
     </form>
   </body>
</HTML>
```

Listing 5-21. The Life Cycle Web Form Code-Behind Class File

```csharp
using System;
using System.Web;
using System.Web.SessionState;
using System.Web.UI;
using System.Web.UI.WebControls;
using System.Web.UI.HtmlControls;

namespace ControlsBookWeb.Ch05
{

   public class LifeCycle : System.Web.UI.Page
   {
      protected System.Web.UI.WebControls.Button Button1;
      protected ControlsBookLib.Ch05.Lifecycle life1;

      private void Page_Load(object sender, System.EventArgs e)
      {

      }

      #region Web Form Designer generated code
      override protected void OnInit(EventArgs e)
      {
         //
         // CODEGEN: This call is required by the ASP.NET Web Form Designer.
         //
         InitializeComponent();
         base.OnInit(e);
      }

      /// <summary>
      /// Required method for Designer support - do not modify
      /// the contents of this method with the code editor.
      /// </summary>
      private void InitializeComponent()
      {
         this.Load += new System.EventHandler(this.Page_Load);

      }
      #endregion
   }
}
```

The first execution of the Life Cycle Web Form results in an HTTP GET protocol request and generates the life cycle events shown in the ASP.NET Trace output of Figure 5-23.

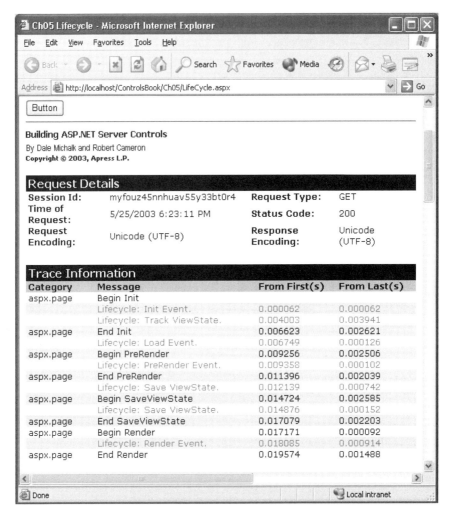

Figure 5-23. The Lifecycle.aspx trace output from an HTTP GET request

We next cover the life cycle events that occur when an HTTP GET request occurs, starting with the Init event.

Init Event

The first phase processed by the control is the Init event. We are notified of this phase by overriding the protected OnInit method inherited from the base class System.Web.UI.Control:

```
override protected void OnInit(System.EventArgs e)
{
   base.OnInit();
   Trace("Lifecycle:  Init Event.");
}
```

The code in the OnInit method uses a private utility method called Trace that sends status information to the Trace class via the control's Context property available to ASP.NET server controls:

```
private void Trace(string info)
{
   Page.Trace.Warn(info);
   Debug.WriteLine(info);
}
```

This class method also sends output to the debug stream via the System.Diagnostics.Debug class and its WriteLine method. The reason for this extra step is to view Unload and Dispose event execution, which occurs after the Web Form is finished writing out its content via the Render method and the ASP.NET trace tables have been generated. You can view debug stream information in the Output window of Visual Studio .NET when debugging.

The Init event is an opportunity for the control to initialize any resources it needs to service the page request. A control can access any child controls in this method if necessary; however, peer- and parent-level controls are not guaranteed to be accessible at this point in the life cycle.

Overriding methods such as OnInit from the base class System.Web.UI.Control requires that we call the base version of this method to ensure proper functioning of the event. The base class implementation of OnInit actually raises the Init event exposed by the root Control class to clients.

If you override OnInit but do not call the base class version of this event, the event will not be raised to clients that are registered to receive it. This applies to the other On-prefixed methods such as OnLoad, OnPreRender, and OnUnload, which are part of the life cycle process, as well as other non-life-cycle-specific event methods such as OnDataBinding and OnBubbleEvent.

TrackViewState Method

The TrackViewState method executes immediately after initialization and marks the beginning of ViewState processing, and state tracking, in the control life cycle. If you have attribute values that you do not want to save in ViewState across page round-trips for efficiency purposes, you should set these values in the OnInit method. Otherwise, all control property value modifications performed after this method executes will persist to ViewState.

If desired, you can make modifications to state values in this method that won't be marked as dirty as long as you do so before executing the inherited base.TrackViewState method or before calling the encapsulated StateBag.TrackViewState method.

Load Event

The Load event should be quite familiar to you because we have leveraged this convenient location for common page code in our Web Forms in previous examples. It is a handy place to put page initialization logic because you are guaranteed that all controls in the Page's control tree are created and all state-loading mechanisms have restored each control's state back to where it was at the end of the previous request/ response page round-trip. This event also occurs before any controls in the Page's control tree fire their specific events resulting from value changes in postback data. To customize control behavior in this phase, override the OnLoad method.

PreRender Event

The PreRender event is a phase in the control life cycle that represents the last-ditch chance for a control to do something before it is rendered. This is the location to put code that must execute before rendering but after the Load event, state management methods, and postback events have occurred. Controls can override the OnPreRender method for this special situation. Note that changes made to a control's state at this point in the life cycle will persist to ViewState.

SaveViewState Method

The SaveViewState method saves the ViewState dictionary by default without any additional action by you. Overriding this method is only necessary when a control needs to customize state persistence in ViewState. This method is called only when the EnableViewState property inherited from Control is set to true. The object instance that is returned from this method is serialized by ASP.NET into the final ViewState string that is emitted into the page's __VIEWSTATE hidden field. Be aware that SaveViewState is called twice in our sample code as a result of enabling page tracing, which makes a call to SaveViewState to gather information for tracing purposes. With tracing disabled during normal page execution, SaveViewState is called only once.

Render Method

You are by now very familiar with overriding the Render method in a custom control to generate a control's UI. The HtmlTextWriter class does the bulk of the work here, writing out the control as HTML and script where applicable to the HTTP response stream. Note that any changes to a control's state made within this method will render into the UI but will not be saved as part of ViewState.

Unload Event

The Page class implements this method to perform cleanup. Overriding the OnUnload method from the base control class allows the control to hook into this event. Although the Unload event is an opportunity for a control to release any resources that it has obtained in earlier control events such as Init or Load, it is recommended that you release resources in its Dispose method.

The trace output from the ASP.NET page does not display any information pertaining to this event because it fires after Render executes, but we can use the debug stream output from the Output window when debugging the Web Form in Visual Studio .NET to see the result:

```
Lifecycle: Init Event.
Lifecycle: Track ViewState.
Lifecycle: Load Event.
Lifecycle: PreRender Event.
Lifecycle: Save ViewState.
Lifecycle: Save ViewState.
Lifecycle: Render Event.
Lifecycle: Unload Event.
Lifecycle: Dispose Event.
```

Dispose Method

Dispose is the recommended location for cleaning up resources. Implementing a Dispose method is recommended in .NET Framework programming when unmanaged resources (such as a connection to SQL Server) are acquired by a control and need to be safely released within the garbage collection architecture. The pattern is based on the IDispose interface that gives a way for clients to tell an object to clean up its unmanaged resources:

```
Interface IDispose
{
   void Dispose();
}
```

Once a client is finished working with an object, the client notifies the object it is finished by calling the object's `Dispose` method. This gives the object immediate confirmation that it can clean up its resources instead of waiting for its `Finalize` method to be called during garbage collection. Because `Dispose` is the design pattern common in .NET, it is recommended that you implement cleanup in `Dispose` instead of `Unload` to release unmanaged resources.

HTTP POST Request via Postback

Additional events and methods of the control life cycle are exercised once we execute a postback of the Life Cycle Web Form by clicking the button. The output of the trace is much larger, so the screen shot in Figure 5-24 is filled by that table.

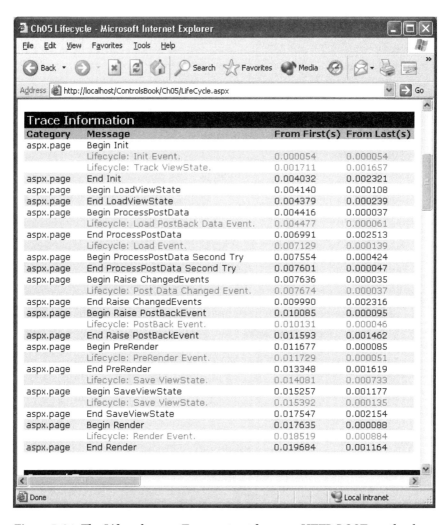

Figure 5-24. The Lifecycle.aspx Trace output from an HTTP POST postback

The output from the Visual Studio .NET Debug window confirms the sequence of events as well:

```
Lifecycle: Init Event.
Lifecycle: Track ViewState.
Lifecycle: Load PostBack Data Event.
Lifecycle: Load Event.
Lifecycle: Post Data Changed Event.
Lifecycle: PostBack Event.
Lifecycle: PreRender Event.
Lifecycle: Save ViewState.
Lifecycle: Save ViewState.
Lifecycle: Render Event.
Lifecycle: Unload Event.
Lifecycle: Dispose Event.
```

LoadViewState Method

Overriding the LoadViewState method is necessary if a control has previously overridden SaveViewState to customize ViewState serialization. Customization of the ViewState persistence mechanism is commonly performed by developers in more complex controls that have complex properties such as a reference type or a collection of objects. The decision to customize ViewState really comes down to whether or not a control's state can be easily or efficiently reduced to a string representation.

LoadPostBackData Method

In the previous chapter, we discussed how to retrieve client form post data via implementation of the IPostBackDataHandler interface. The LoadPostData routine is given the opportunity to process the postback data and to update the control's state. It also allows the control to notify ASP.NET that it wishes to raise an event at a later time in order to permit clients a chance to process the state change. For our purposes, the Lifecycle control always returns true, so the change event is always raised.

Keen observers will notice that we really should not be receiving the form post information, because we did not emit an HTML tag such as <INPUT>. However, we greased the wheels in the ASP.NET framework by calling Page.RegisterRequiresPostBack in OnPreRender:

```
override protected void OnPreRender(System.EventArgs e)
{
    base.OnPreRender(e);
    Trace("Lifecycle: PreRender Event.");
    Page.RegisterRequiresPostBack(this);
}
```

This makes it possible to receive a call to our `LoadPostData` method by ASP.NET. We perform a similar task in `LoadPostData` to ensure we receive the `PostBack` event by calling `Page.RegisterRequiresRaiseEvent`:

```
public bool LoadPostData(string postDataKey, NameValueCollection postCollection)
{
    Trace("Lifecycle: Load PostBack Data Event.");
    Page.RegisterRequiresRaiseEvent(this);
    return true;
}
```

RaisePostDataChangedEvent Method

For controls that have state changes reflected in postback data, these controls most likely need to raise server-side events. These events are raised from within the `RaisePostDataChangedEvent` method of each respective control. Following this design guideline ensures that control state is restored from ViewState and updated from postback data before the various events begin to fire. Raising server-side events from within any other control method can cause hard-to-debug side effects for event consumers. This routine is called only if the `LoadPostData` returns true.

RaisePostBackEvent Method

Implementing `RaisePostBackEvent` ensures that the server control notifies ASP.NET that the state of the control has changed. To participate in postback processing, a control must implement the `IPostBackEventHandler` interface. Controls implement this interface and emit some sort of HTML to submit the Web Form back to the server, whether via a button or an HTML element with JavaScript code to submit the form programmatically.

In our sample `Lifecycle` control, we rigged the system by calling `Page.RegisterRequiresRaiseEvent` in the `LoadPostData` method. Our `SuperButton` control sample in this chapter demonstrates how to execute this properly. We use this shortcut to hook into this event for purposes discussing the control life cycle.

Summary

In this chapter, we discussed how to implement events in the ASP.NET framework. Event-based programming is a critical aspect of ASP.NET development, making web development more like developing with Visual Basic on the Windows desktop. We also discussed how to bubble events up the control hierarchy and we explored the control life cycle.

`System.EventHandler` is the default delegate type for events in ASP.NET. Inherit from this type when you create custom event handlers so that your controls behave in a similar manner to the built-in controls.

Events are generally invoked in a control through a `virtual protected` method that prefixes the word "On" to the event name to create a method name such as `OnClick` and `OnTextChanged`. Custom events implement their own delegate type with the name suffixed by "EventHandler". Custom events can also implement a custom `EventArgs`-derived class to provide event data tailored to the particular situation. The simplest way for a control to expose an event is to declare one as a public field of a custom control class.

Controls can use the `Events` collection inherited from `System.Web.UI.Control` to efficiently manage events in a sparse collection instead of the one-field-per-event model. Using the `Events` collection along with custom event registration code can potentially save a large amount of memory for a control with many events that are not all normally implemented.

`Command` events are a special event type used by list controls in ASP.NET to simplify handling buttons as child controls. `Command` events expose `CommandName` and `CommandArgument` properties to communicate their intentions to the parent control.

Event bubbling is a concept in ASP.NET whereby a control can raise an event through its parent control hierarchy. `RaiseBubbleEvent` starts the event in motion. Parent controls can catch the event by overriding `OnBubbleEvent`. `RaisePostBackEvent` is the method in `IPostBackEventHandler` that allows a control to capture a postback generated by a change in data.

`INamingContainer` is used by a composite control to ensure that its child controls have a unique name on the page even if the composite control is used several times on the page via the `UniqueID` property.

Controls follow a well-defined life cycle execution process to help coordinate events and activities. Understanding the control life cycle will ensure your custom controls behave as expected. The complete control life cycle for an HTTP GET request includes these events in order: `Init`, `TrackViewState`, `Load`, `PreRender`, `SaveViewState`, `Render`, `Unload`, and `Dispose`. The complete control life cycle for an HTTP POST request includes these events in order: `Init`, `TrackViewState`, `LoadViewState`, `LoadPostData`, `Load`, `RaisePostDataChangedEvent`, `PostBack`, `PreRender`, `SaveViewState`, `Render`, `Unload`, and `Dispose`.

CHAPTER 6

Control Styles

THE ABILITY TO CONFIGURE how a web page renders its HTML elements is an essential requirement of any web development model. As you would expect, the .NET Framework and ASP.NET provide a rich architecture to support styling of web page elements through server controls on the Web Form.

In this chapter, we introduce a new server control construction model and build several custom server controls that inherit from WebControl (instead of Control) as a means to examine how to customize control styling using the System.Web.UI.WebControls.Style class, as well as a means to introduce the more powerful rendering model provided by the WebControl class.

In the final portion of the chapter, we discuss how to customize ViewState storage to preserve any applied styling and we show how to override the Style property to support your own customized style class for further customization of appearance. This section also highlights the benefits the strongly-typed styling mechanism provided by ASP.NET.

Customizing the Appearance of Controls

Controls have a tough crowd to please. Programmers want them to be powerful, easy to use, robust, high performing, and fully customizable in their look and feel. Not a short list by any means. The last item, look and feel, garners most of the attention. After all, who cares what the control does on the inside if the HTML it produces is a pain to configure or is rigidly fixed to a certain output? Because many controls will be distributed to their consumer as an assembly, without source code, a customizable look and feel is a requirement.

Controls based on System.Web.UI.WebControls.WebControl benefit from a wonderful amount of prebuilt functionality to customize themselves with Cascading Style Sheet (CSS) styling. Controls of type WebControl are also smart enough to appropriately render HTML tags for browsers that support HTML 3.2 so that many of the style features are not lost in down-level browsers.

HTML: Content and Appearance

The HTML document that renders in your favorite browser has two core aspects to its makeup. The first is the textual content placed in the document—the information that users seek. The second is the appearance and layout of the content on the page. The style of the document determines whether the text is a certain font, is italicized, or has a particular color. Style also involves how information is laid out on the page, which determines the position and flow of text and other content such as images.

Styling Using Tags

HTML was invented to provide access to textual information that can be easily navigated and cross-referenced via hyperlinks. Commercialization of the Internet drove the need for rich HTML content, and the ensuing browser competition generated strong demand for styling capability. The initial wave of style support came in the form of tags that would modify the output of text or attributes such as color. The `<FONT>`, `<B>`, and `<I>` tags are a perfect example of the style tags added to HTML.

The following piece of HTML displays text using an Arial font with bold and italic styling:

```
<font face="Arial" color="blue"><b><i>This text is Bold,
                                Italic Blue Text</i></b></font>
```

Layout tags such as `<CENTER>` and `<TABLE>` can also be considered part of the style of the document. Originally designed to display data in a tabular format, these tags have been co-opted for layout purposes by web designers. Most of the HMTL sites you see on the Web use the `<TABLE>` tag to lay out content. Unfortunately, tables render differently in different browsers and much tweaking is required to get them "just right." Having a more precise layout mechanism would go a long way toward reducing the amount of work needed.

Another unfortunate side effect of using style tags to manage the appearance of an HTML document is tag maintenance. Modifying `<FONT>` tags scattered throughout a complex HTML document, let alone an entire site, is an error-prone and time-consuming undertaking. Luckily, as the Internet has evolved, so have the technologies used to present content to web surfers. One such technological advancement is the topic of the next section: CSS, which permits separation of content from styling and layout.

Styling Using Cascading Style Sheets

CSS technology permits web developers to separate the concerns of HTML content from its appearance by defining a system for applying styling rules to informational content. The heart of CSS is a set of style properties that are defined separately from the content.

The syntax for a CSS style property is simple. It consists of a property name followed by a colon (:) and then the value of that property. Multiple properties are separated by semicolons (;). The following style properties specify that the textual content be displayed in blue Arial font with bold and italic effects:

```
<span style="font-family: Arial; color: Blue;  font-weight:bold;
font-style:italic;">This text is Bold, Italic Blue Text</span>
```

Contrast this with the use of the `<FONT>`, `<B>`, and `<I>` tags in the previous section to describe the same textual styling. If the style properties are not defined inline with the HTML element, they take on a slightly different appearance. A mechanism called a *selector* is needed to join style rules to HTML elements. The following stylesheet snippet defines a rule for `<SPAN>` elements where the textual content should be displayed in blue Arial font with bold and italic effects:

```
span
{ font-family: Arial; color: Blue;  font-weight:bold;  font-style:italic; }
```

The `span` keyword is an HTML element selector in CSS because it uses HTML element names to modify the selection process. HTML element selectors are good for setting up default styles for specific tags that a web site uses for its content.

Sometimes you want to target a specific group of HTML elements with CSS styles instead of all instances of an element type. Putting a period in front of the CSS style class name defines a class selector, as you can see in the following code snippet. The class selector applies to all HTML tags with a class attribute equal to the selector name. The period in front of the class name makes it a class selector.

```
.second
{ font-family: Arial; color: Blue;  font-weight:bold;  font-style:italic; }
```

The second class style rule would apply to the following `<SPAN>` because of its class attribute:

```
<span id="class_style" class="second ">Bold, Italic Blue Text</span>
```

A selector with a hash (#) character in front of it signals the use of an `id` selector. It applies to HTML elements that have the same `id` attribute value as the selector name. Because `id` attributes for HTML elements on a page need to be unique, this specifies a style setting for a specific tag. If we changed the selector from the previous style definition to

```
#third
{ font-family: Arial; color: Blue;  font-weight:bold;  font-style:italic; }
```

then to use it we need a `<SPAN>` with an `id` attribute equal to `third`:

```
<span id="third">Bold, Italic Blue Text</span>
```

You can combine the id or class technique along with tag selector to separate the CSS classes from the tags they mark up. The following CSS definition shows the SPAN and DIV HTML element selector names combined with the same class selector:

```
SPAN.first
{ font-family: Arial; color: Blue;  font-weight:bold; font-style:italic; }
DIV.first
{ font-family: Arial; color: Red;  font-weight:bold;  font-style:italic; }
```

This produces different text layout depending on whether the class attribute first is used with a <SPAN> or <DIV> tag:

```
<span class="first">Bold, Italic Blue Text</span>
<div class="first">Bold,  Italic Red Text</span>
```

There are additional selectors that do more specialized selection of HTML elements, such as the ability to group several selectors via commas. Please refer to a good text on CSS styling for more information on CSS selectors.

CSS provides several ways to formulate the style rules. You can place styles in their own separate CSS file and bring them in via a <LINK> tag:

```
<LINK href="WebControlStyle.css" type="text/css" rel="stylesheet">
```

You can also place CSS styles in a <STYLE> block in the <HEAD> section of the document:

```
<style type="text/css">
   .bluetext
   {
     color: blue;
     background-color: yellow;
   }
</style>
```

Or you can place CSS styles inline with the style attribute:

```
<span class="bluetext" style=" color: red;">Yellow background, red text</span>
```

This begs the question, what happens when style attributes that are defined in several different locations come together on the same document? CSS is built to handle this situation and this is where the "cascading" part of the CSS acronym comes in to play. The process can be summarized this way: If the styles do not conflict, the attributes are combined in an additive process. Also, style settings in the parent container apply to the parent's child elements.

When conflicts do arise because of the flow of style attributes, there is a pecking order as to which style takes precedence. The rule is simple: Definitions closer to the tag take precedence over the more remote definitions in terms of location on the page. The following order is taken into consideration, with the last bullet taking precedence over the first bullet:

- Browser defaults

- External stylesheet

- Internal stylesheet (inside the <HEAD> tag)

- Inline style (style attribute on HTML element)

The previous SPAN example displays with a yellow background that it inherits from the class selector, and its inline style color displays the text in red.

Style Properties and Visual Studio .NET

Trying to remember what the various CSS properties are and how to use them can be a daunting task. You either need to have a thick reference close at hand or use the CSS editing features bundled with Visual Studio .NET. Figure 6-1 shows a CSS stylesheet in the main window and the Explorer view of its rules on the left side.

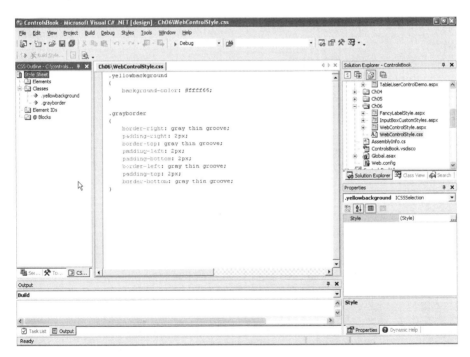

Figure 6-1. The Visual Studio .NET CSS file designer

Right-click the design surface to add new styles or build on existing styles. The Add Style Rule dialog box shown in Figure 6-2 helps build the selector and outlines how the cascading style rules are applied.

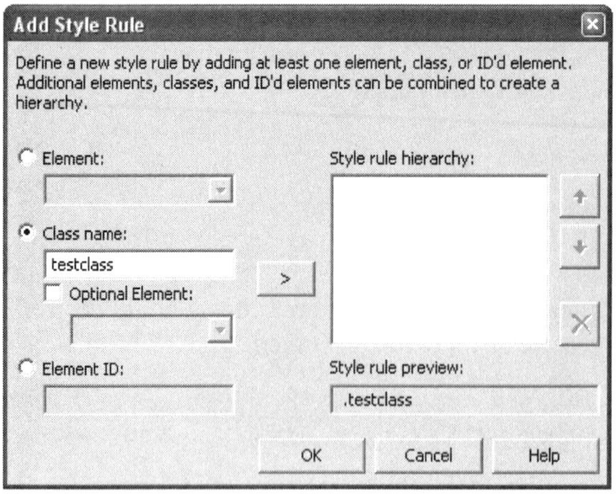

Figure 6-2. The Visual Studio .NET CSS designer Add Style Rule dialog box

Once you've added a new style selector to a CSS file, you can right-click the selector in the outline view to get the Style Builder dialog box, as shown in Figure 6-3. This is an excellent way to configure CSS classes, as it previews the style in the dialog box as it is created.

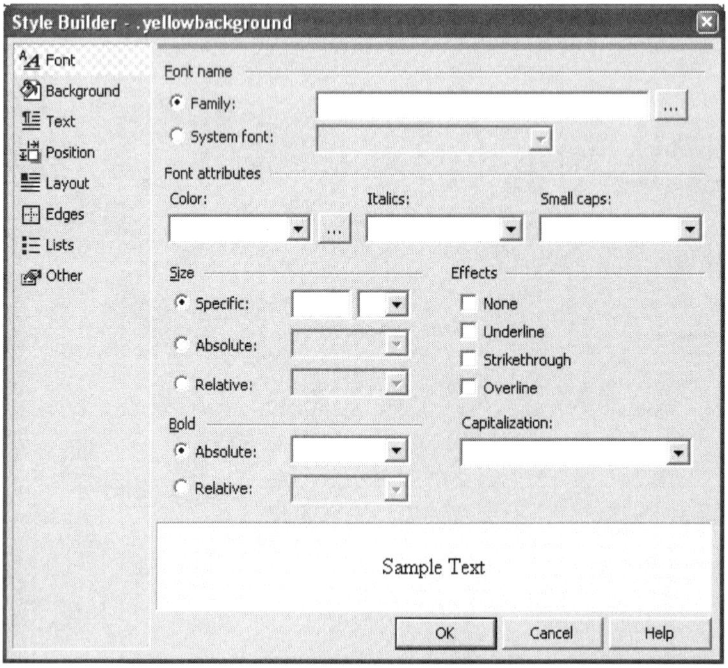

Figure 6-3. The Visual Studio .NET CSS designer Style Builder dialog box

Visual Studio .NET takes advantage of the layout features of CSS in the Web Form Designer, which enables precise positioning of server controls when the page layout is set to GridLayout. Figure 6-4 shows the Property Pages dialog box that displays when you right-click the Web Form Designer view and select Properties from the context menu.

Figure 6-4. The Visual Studio .NET Designer dialog box for setting the Web Form layout to GridLayout

GridLayout uses the features of CSS absolute positioning, specifying pixel locations for server control objects as shown in Figure 6-5. Visual Studio .NET translates the developer's drag-and-drop movements of controls on the Designer surface into CSS style attributes.

The following server control style attributes position a button 133 pixels from the top of the document and 252 pixels from the left edge.

```
<asp:Button id="Button1" style="Z-INDEX: 101; LEFT: 252px; POSITION: absolute;
TOP: 133px" runat="server" Text="Button"></asp:Button>
```

CSS absolute positioning is enabled with the position property having an absolute value. The z-index provides a way to position the HTML elements in a third dimension: depth. This allows for overlapping content and some interesting visual effects.

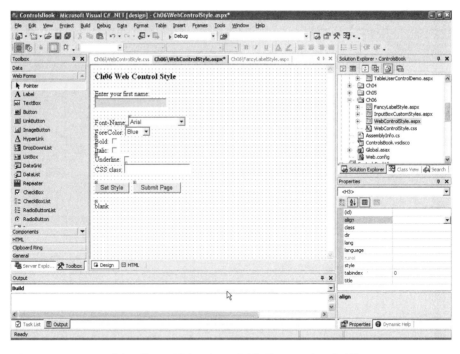

Figure 6-5. A Visual Studio .NET Designer Web Form using GridLayout

WebControl and Control Styling

Up to this point in the book, we built our server controls by inheriting from
System.Web.UI.Control as the base class. We did this to keep things simple, concentrating on the basics of control development. However, Control as a base class starts to
show its inherent limitations when we start working with styling and cross-browser
support. When inheriting from Control, developers are responsible for manually building up the HTML tags, providing a style property, and manually emitting the style
property into the HTML output stream. To avoid this work, a better choice is inheriting
from the WebControl class, as you will see in the ensuing discussion.

NOTE *There will be times when inheriting from* Control *is desired in order to have
full control over the rendering process and the capabilities built into* WebControl
are not required. When this is not the case, we recommend inheriting from
WebControl *whenever possible.*

In this section we discuss how to add styling capabilities to server controls. We also introduce a new method of building server controls that inherit from the WebControl class. The WebControl class provides an abstraction layer over the rendering process to support strong styling capabilities and rendering in down-level browsers.

The WebControl class from the System.Web.UI.WebControls namespace provides a wealth of style support in the form of style properties and automatic style rendering. Not only does it take care of rendering CSS style properties, but it also goes the extra mile to support HTML 3.2 with explicit style tags for down-level browsers.

Control styling and rendering are closely coupled because, at the end of the day, raw HTML is the output from a server control. In the next section, we dive into the styling capabilities available in WebControl. Along the way, we discuss the new rendering model in WebControl that provides the necessary support for styling and down-level browsers without requiring too much effort on the developer's part to make it happen.

WebControl's ControlStyle Property

ControlStyle is the property of interest in the WebControl class for manipulating styling. It is a read-only property that provides access to an instance of the System.Web.UI.WebControls.Style class. The Style class captures most of the commonly used style attributes that a web developer needs to use with a control, focusing on text, font, color, and borders. Table 6-1 shows the properties that hang from the Style class and the CSS property that is rendered in conjunction with the property.

Table 6-1. Properties of the System.Web.UI.WebControls.Style *Class*

STYLE PROPERTY	CSS PROPERTY
BackColor	background-color
BorderColor	border-color
BorderStyle	border-style
BorderWidth	border-width
CssClass	CSS class name
Font	Font weight, style, family, and so on
ForeColor	color
Height	height
Width	width

CssClass is a string property that translates directly to rendering a class attribute on the control tag. Setting the CssClass property in the .aspx page for the ASP.NET Label WebControl

```
<asp:label id="myspan" runat="server" CssClass="mycssclass" Text="blank" />
```

translates into the following HTML:

```
<span id=myspan class=mycssclass>blank</span>
```

The Font property exposes a set of subproperties, so we continue our property examination with Table 6-2 for the System.Web.UI.FontInfo class.

Table 6-2. Properties of the System.Web.UI.WebControls.FontInfo *Class*

FONT PROPERTY	CSS PROPERTY
Bold	font-weight: bold
Italic	font-style: italic
Name	font-family
Names	font-family
Overline	text-decoration: overline
Size	font-size
Strikeout	text-decoration: line-through
Underline	text-decoration: underline

WebControl Top-Level Style Properties

Going through the ControlStyle property to access these attributes would require a lot of extra typing when setting style properties in either the .aspx control tag or the code-behind class file. The WebControl class makes life easier by exposing all of the properties listed in Tables 6-1 and 6-2 directly as properties (see Figure 6-6), which saves a lot of typing.

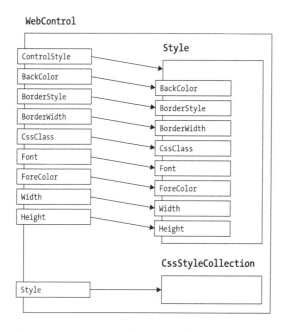

Figure 6-6. WebControl *and top-level style properties*

The top-level property exposure as shown in Figure 6-6 shortens the syntax from

```
Mycontrol.ControlStyle.ForeColor = red;
```

to the more pleasant

```
MyControl.ForeColor = red;
```

The style properties are also available for configuration of the control tag via attributes in the .aspx page as well:

```
<apress:textbox id="MyControl" runat="server" forecolor="red" font-bold="true"  />
```

These top-level properties are convenient to use, but there are other styling attributes available too numerous to hang off of the WebControl class. Instead, you can access these styling capabilities through the Style property.

The Style Property

The ControlStyle property and top-level properties of WebControl do not expose the complete spectrum of CSS styling capabilities. The most notable omissions are the placement attributes that allow you to do CSS absolute positioning.

To handle these "other" style attributes, WebControl exposes a collection via the Style property. The Style property is an instance of type CssStyleCollection. CssStyleCollection is a string-based collection that uses string names as indexers into the values. This is similar to the Hashtable class, except it mandates strings for both keys and values.

You can set the Style property programmatically, but it is more commonly set by adding style attributes to the .aspx page. The WYSIWYG designers, such as the ASP.NET Designer in Visual Studio .NET in GridLayout mode, are the best examples of this. The ASP.NET Designer uses the style attribute on the .aspx page to control the layout of the controls when it is set to a GridLayout:

```
<asp:Button id="Button1" style="Z-INDEX: 101; LEFT: 252px; POSITION: absolute;
b
```

Parsing an .aspx page creates start-up code that initializes a control's Style property collection with declarative style attributes. You can modify the Style property programmatically as well. The following line of code changes the button's text color from its declarative red value to a programmatically set blue value:

```
Button1.Style[color] = blue;
```

The primary drawback to adding style properties via the Style property collection is that it isn't browser-aware. Although ControlStyle properties render HTML tags for down-level browsers, the Style properties are streamed to the browser verbatim as CSS properties. If the browser doesn't understand the CSS properties, it simply ignores them.

We next move on to discuss how to provide cross-browser compatible styling capabilities by taking advantage of the rendering system provided by the WebControl class.

A New Rendering System

As we stated earlier, the custom controls we have developed so far inherit from Control and require that we override the Render method of the base Control class to emit HTML output. Going forward in this chapter, we will inherit from the WebControl class, which overrides Render by default to save us from having to emit raw HTML tags and style content into the output stream. Instead, we override RenderContents, which is a new method in the WebControl class.

RenderContents provides a method signature identical to that of Render with an HtmlTextWriter reference as its sole parameter. The difference is that you are tasked with emitting what is inside the outermost HTML tag for the control. For this reason, you need to let WebControl know what kind of HTML tag formulates your control's outer shell. You can do this in one of two ways: by passing the tag via the HtmlTextWriterTag enumeration to the base WebControl constructor or by setting either the TagKey or TagName property of WebControl. The more common way is to use the base constructor:

```
public Label() : base(HtmlTextWriterTag.Span)
{
}
```

In the next section, we dive into WebControl-based control building and create a simple Label control.

A Styled Label Control

Label controls are probably the simplest controls in the ASP.NET server control arsenal. They have a single mission: to render a piece of content within a <SPAN> tag. To demonstrate the styling powers of the WebControl class, we will build our own version of the Label control. Listing 6-1 shows how easy this truly is.

Listing 6-1. The Label *Control*

```
using System;
using System.Web;
using System.Web.UI;
using System.Web.UI.WebControls;
using System.ComponentModel;
```

```
namespace ControlsBookLib.Ch06
{
   [ToolboxData("<{0}:Label runat=server></{0}:Label>"),
   DefaultProperty("Text")]
   public class Label : WebControl
   {
      public Label() : base(HtmlTextWriterTag.Span)
      {
      }

      public virtual string Text
      {
         get
         {
            object text = ViewState["Text"];
            if (text == null)
               return string.Empty;
            else
               return (string) text;
         }
         set
         {
            ViewState["Text"] = value;
         }
      }

      override protected void RenderContents(HtmlTextWriter writer)
      {
         writer.Write(Text);
      }
   }
}
```

The constructor of the Label control calls the base constructor of WebControl to have it emit the content inside of <SPAN> tags via the HtmlTextWriterTag.Span enumeration value. This sets up the control to call our overridden RenderContents method. Note that we do not emit a single HTML tag directly. The RenderContents method simply has to write out the Text property to complete the control functionality. We next create a Textbox control to demonstrate further how to work with WebControl, laying the groundwork for building stylized server controls that take full advantage of the capabilities built into ASP.NET and the WebControl class.

The AddAttributesToRender Method

The Label was an easy enough control to build, but its limited functionality did not require the use of attributes on the <SPAN> tag. What happens when you have an <INPUT> tag like our various Textbox controls from previous chapters? It needs to output type and value attributes inside the <INPUT> tag.

For those who need to render attributes on the outer tag, the AddAttributesToRender method is a method override available when inheriting from WebControl that fits the bill. It is part of the customized Render process that WebControl orchestrates, and it is called by the RenderBeginTag method of WebControl. The WebControl version of Render executes the following routines in order, with RenderBeginTag calling AddAttributesToRender:

- RenderBeginTag

- RenderContents

- RenderEndTag

Figure 6-7 shows the relationship graphically.

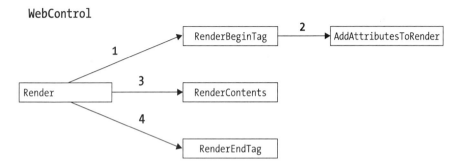

Figure 6-7. The rendering process in the WebControl *class*

Depending on the level of control required, you can overload each step of the process as necessary. The RenderBeginTag/RenderEndTag method pairs are less commonly overloaded because they do the outer tag rendering by looking up the TagKey or TagName property values and emitting the content via HtmlTextWriter.

The key point to remember is that when you override AddAttributesToRender, you must also call the base WebControl version of the method to ensure that the style attributes managed by WebControl are emitted properly:

```
base.AddAttributesToRender(writer);
```

Also, you can use HtmlTextWriter and its AddAttribute method to add other attributes as necessary:

```
writer.AddAttribute("value",Text);
```

Now that we have covered the basics of inheriting from WebControl, we can move on to add style capabilities to our Textbox control.

A Styled Textbox Control

In this section, we bring back our favorite Textbox control from chapters past and update it with WebControl capabilities. As you would guess, most of the implementation remains the same. The biggest changes relate to how we handle the rendering process.

The first step in updating Textbox is to inherit from WebControl and set the constructor to create the tag for the outer shell of the control. The following code snippet sets up our WebControl version of the Textbox to render an <INPUT> tag:

```
public class Textbox : WebControl, IPostBackDataHandler
{
   public Textbox() : base(HtmlTextWriterTag.Input)
   {
   }
}
```

The rendering code in this version of Textbox is dramatically smaller than the previous version that inherited from Control. All we have to implement is the AddAttributesToRender method to set the <INPUT> tag with the appropriate attributes, and we need to call the base class version to add the style attributes:

```
override protected void AddAttributesToRender(HtmlTextWriter writer)
{
   writer.AddAttribute("type","text");
   writer.AddAttribute("name",UniqueID);
   writer.AddAttribute("value",Text);

   base.AddAttributesToRender(writer);
}
```

Listing 6-2 shows the full code for the Textbox control.

Listing 6-2. The Textbox *Control*

```
using System;
using System.Web;
using System.Web.UI;
using System.Web.UI.WebControls;
using System.Collections.Specialized;
using System.ComponentModel;

namespace ControlsBookLib.Ch06
{
   [ToolboxData("<{0}:Textbox runat=server></{0}:Textbox>"),
   DefaultProperty("Text")]
   public class Textbox : WebControl, IPostBackDataHandler
   {
      public Textbox() : base(HtmlTextWriterTag.Input)
      {
      }
```

```
public virtual string Text
{
   get
   {
      object text = ViewState["Text"];
      if (text == null)
         return string.Empty;
      else
         return (string) text;
   }
   set
   {
      ViewState["Text"] = value;
   }
}

public bool LoadPostData(string postDataKey,
   NameValueCollection postCollection)
{
   string postedValue = postCollection[postDataKey];
   if (!Text.Equals(postedValue))
   {
      Text = postedValue;
      return true;
   }
   else
      return false;
}

public void RaisePostDataChangedEvent()
{
   OnTextChanged(EventArgs.Empty);
}

private static readonly object TextChangedKey = new object();
public event EventHandler TextChanged
{
   add
   {
      Events.AddHandler(TextChangedKey, value);
   }
   remove
   {
      Events.RemoveHandler(TextChangedKey, value);
   }
}

protected virtual void OnTextChanged(EventArgs e)
{
   EventHandler textChangedEventDelegate =
      (EventHandler) Events[TextChangedKey];
   if (textChangedEventDelegate != null)
   {
      textChangedEventDelegate(this, e);
   }
}

override protected void AddAttributesToRender(HtmlTextWriter writer)
```

```
    {
        writer.AddAttribute("type","text");
        writer.AddAttribute("name",UniqueID);
        writer.AddAttribute("value",Text);

        base.AddAttributesToRender(writer);
    }
  }
}
```

The Web Control Style Web Form

The Web Control Style Web Form is a workbench for testing both the Label and the
Textbox controls we have created so far in this chapter. It has a set of controls to allow
the user to interactively change style properties, rendering the control with its new
styles on the Web Form. Figure 6-8 displays what the Web Form looks like when displayed in a browser.

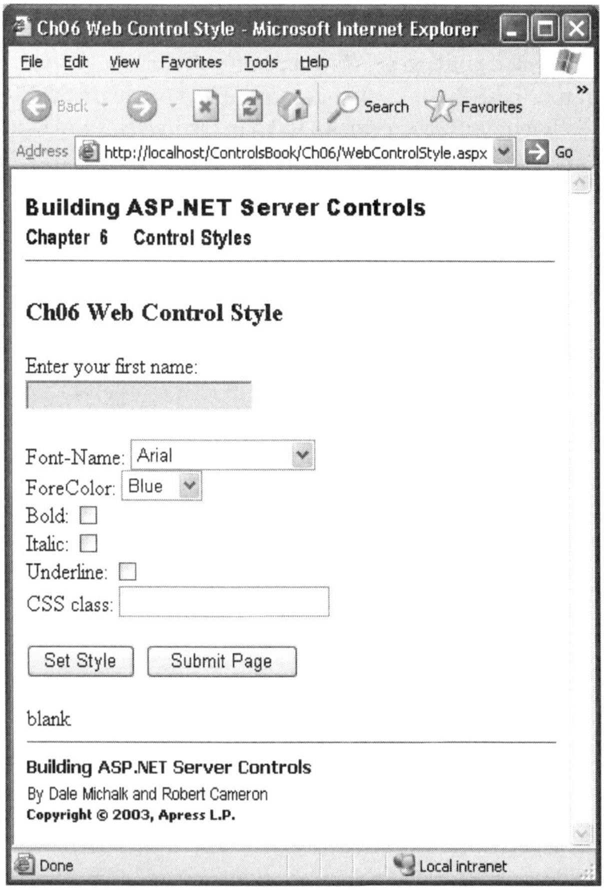

Figure 6-8. The Web Control Style Web Form

The top of the form is the `Textbox` control with properties that are set in the .aspx tag page to make the `Textbox` background gray and set its text to Tahoma font with bold and italic features:

```
<apress:textbox id="NameTextbox" runat="server" Font-Bold="True"
BackColor="#E0E0E0" Font-Italic="True" Font-Names="Tahoma"></apress:textbox>
```

Below the Web Form is a set of server controls that provide a control panel for styling a `Label` control at the very bottom of the .aspx page, just before the footer:

```
<apress:label id="NameLabel" runat="server" Text="blank"></apress:label><br>
```

The user can set the following properties: Font-Name, ForeColor, Bold, Italic, and Underline, along with CssClass. Also, the .aspx page has a link to an external style sheet called WebControlStyle. This is useful for exercising the CssClass property, as all the style rules have class selectors:

```
<LINK href="WebControlStyle.css" type="text/css" rel="stylesheet">
```

To try this, type either **yellowbackground** or **grayborder** in the CSS class text box and click the Set Style button. You can see the style changes take effect based on the class name you typed. The full listing of the Web Form is shown in Listings 6-3 and 6-4, and the stylesheet is shown in Listing 6-5.

Listing 6-3. The Web Control Style Web Form .aspx Page File

```
<%@ Register TagPrefix="apressUC" TagName="ControlsBookFooter"
Src="..\ControlsBookFooter.ascx" %>
<%@ Register TagPrefix="apressUC" TagName="ControlsBookHeader"
Src="..\ControlsBookHeader.ascx" %>
<%@ Page language="c#" Codebehind="WebControlStyle.aspx.cs" AutoEventWireup="false"
Inherits="ControlsBookWeb.Ch06.WebControlStyle" %>
<%@ Register TagPrefix="apress" Namespace="ControlsBookLib.Ch06"
Assembly="ControlsBookLib" %>
<!DOCTYPE HTML PUBLIC "-//W3C//DTD HTML 4.0 Transitional//EN" >
<HTML>
  <HEAD>
    <title>Ch06 Web Control Style</title>
    <meta content="Microsoft Visual Studio 7.0" name="GENERATOR">
    <meta content="C#" name="CODE_LANGUAGE">
    <meta content="JavaScript" name="vs_defaultClientScript">
    <meta content="http://schemas.microsoft.com/intellisense/ie5"
                                    name="vs_targetSchema">
    <LINK href="WebControlStyle.css" type="text/css" rel="stylesheet">
  </HEAD>
  <body>
    <form id="WebControlStyle" method="post" runat="server">
      <apressUC:ControlsBookHeader id="Header" runat="server" ChapterNumber="6"
```

```
ChapterTitle="Control Styles" />
      <h3>Ch06 Web Control Style</h3>
      <span id="Prompt">Enter your first name:</span><br>
      <apress:textbox id="NameTextbox" runat="server" Font-Bold="True"
BackColor="#E0E0E0" Font-Italic="True"
        Font-Names="Tahoma"></apress:textbox><br>
      <br>
      Font-Name:
      <asp:dropdownlist id="FontDropDownList" Runat="server">
        <asp:ListItem Value="Arial">Arial</asp:ListItem>
        <asp:ListItem Value="Courier New">Courier New</asp:ListItem>
        <asp:ListItem Value="Times New Roman">Times New Roman</asp:ListItem>
        <asp:ListItem Value="Monotype Corsiva">Monotype Corsiva</asp:ListItem>
      </asp:dropdownlist><br>
      ForeColor:
      <asp:dropdownlist id="ForeColorDropDownList" Runat="server">
        <asp:ListItem Value="Blue">Blue</asp:ListItem>
        <asp:ListItem Value="Red">Red</asp:ListItem>
        <asp:ListItem Value="Black">Black</asp:ListItem>
      </asp:dropdownlist><br>
      <asp:checkbox id="BoldCheckbox" runat="server" Text="Bold: "
TextAlign="Left"></asp:checkbox><br>
      <asp:checkbox id="ItalicCheckbox" runat="server" Text="Italic: "
TextAlign="Left"></asp:checkbox><br>
      <asp:checkbox id="UnderlineCheckbox" runat="server" Text="Underline: "
TextAlign="Left"></asp:checkbox><br>
      CSS class:
      <asp:textbox id="CssClassTextBox" Runat="server" Text=""></asp:textbox><br>
      <br>
      <asp:button id="SetStyleButton" runat="server" Text="Set Style">
</asp:button> 
      <asp:button id="SubmitPageButton" runat="server"
Text="Submit Page"></asp:button><br>
      <br>
      <apress:label id="NameLabel" runat="server" Text="blank"></apress:label><br>
      <apressUC:ControlsBookFooter id="Footer" runat="server" />
    </form>
  </body>
</HTML>
```

Listing 6-4. The Web Control Style Web Form Code-Behind Class File

```
using System;
using System.Collections;
using System.ComponentModel;
using System.Data;
using System.Drawing;
using System.Web;
using System.Web.SessionState;
using System.Web.UI;
using System.Web.UI.WebControls;
```

```
using System.Web.UI.HtmlControls;

namespace ControlsBookWeb.Ch06
{
    public class WebControlStyle : System.Web.UI.Page
    {
        protected ControlsBookLib.Ch06.Textbox NameTextbox;
        protected ControlsBookLib.Ch06.Label NameLabel;
        protected System.Web.UI.WebControls.CheckBox BoldCheckbox;
        protected System.Web.UI.WebControls.CheckBox ItalicCheckBox;
        protected System.Web.UI.WebControls.DropDownList FontDropDownList;
        protected System.Web.UI.WebControls.CheckBox ItalicCheckbox;
        protected System.Web.UI.WebControls.CheckBox UnderlineCheckbox;
        protected System.Web.UI.WebControls.DropDownList ForeColorDropDownList;
        protected System.Web.UI.WebControls.Button SetStyleButton;
        protected System.Web.UI.WebControls.TextBox CssClassTextBox;
        protected System.Web.UI.WebControls.Label StylePropsLabel;
        protected System.Web.UI.WebControls.Label ControlStylePropsLabel;
        protected System.Web.UI.WebControls.Button SubmitPageButton;

        private void Page_Load(object sender, System.EventArgs e)
        {

        }

        #region Web Form Designer generated code
        override protected void OnInit(EventArgs e)
        {
            //
            // CODEGEN: This call is required by the ASP.NET Web Form Designer.
            //
            InitializeComponent();
            base.OnInit(e);
        }

        /// <summary>
        /// Required method for Designer support - do not modify
        /// the contents of this method with the code editor.
        /// </summary>
        private void InitializeComponent()
        {
            this.SetStyleButton.Click +=
                       new System.EventHandler(this.SetStyleButton_Click);
            this.Load += new System.EventHandler(this.Page_Load);

        }
        #endregion

        private void SetStyleButton_Click(object sender, System.EventArgs e)
        {
            NameLabel.Text = NameTextbox.Text;

            NameLabel.CssClass = CssClassTextBox.Text;

            NameLabel.Font.Name = FontDropDownList.SelectedItem.Value;
            NameLabel.Font.Bold = (BoldCheckbox.Checked == true);
            NameLabel.Font.Italic = (ItalicCheckbox.Checked == true);
```

```
            // Use the TypeConverter for the System.Drawing.Color class
            // to get the typed Color value from the string value
            Color c =
                (Color)TypeDescriptor.GetConverter(typeof(Color)).ConvertFromString(
                ForeColorDropDownList.SelectedItem.Value);
            NameLabel.ForeColor = c;

            // set the text-decoration CSS style attribute
            // using manual manipulation of the Style property
            string textdecoration = "none";
            if (UnderlineCheckbox.Checked == true)
                textdecoration = "underline";
            NameLabel.Style["text-decoration"] = textdecoration;
        }
    }
}
```

Listing 6-5. The WebControlStyle.css File

```
.yellowbackground
{
  background-color: #ffff66;
}

.grayborder
{
  border-right: gray thin groove;
  padding-right: 2px;
  border-top: gray thin groove;
  padding-left: 2px;
  padding-bottom: 2px;
  border-left: gray thin groove;
  padding-top: 2px;
  border-bottom: gray thin groove;
}
```

The Set Style button on the Web Control Style Web Form is used to programmatically change the style properties of the Label control in the code-behind file. The SetStyleButton_Click routine performs the heavy lifting. The attributes set are fairly easy ones that include the Text- and Font-related properties, along with the CssClass of the control:

```
NameLabel.Text = NameTextbox.Text;
NameLabel.CssClass = CssClassTextBox.Text;
NameLabel.Font.Name = FontDropDownList.SelectedItem.Value;
NameLabel.Font.Bold = (BoldCheckbox.Checked == true);
NameLabel.Font.Italic = (ItalicCheckbox.Checked == true);
```

A more complicated effort is required to set up the ForeColor property of the control to a value of type System.Drawing.Color. We use the TypeConverter class that is available to perform this conversion from our string value to the exact Color type necessary to set the ForeColor property:

```
// Use the TypeConverter for the System.Drawing.Color class
// to get the typed Color value from the string value
Color c =
    (Color)TypeDescriptor.GetConverter(typeof(Color)).ConvertFromString(
    ForeColorDropDownList.SelectedItem.Value);
NameLabel.ForeColor = c;
```

In Chapter 12, in which we discuss designer support, we show how to build and work with TypeConverter classes.

The final part of the Set Style button click handler is code that uses the Style property to set the underline styling of the Label control. This step is not necessary, as there is an Underline property exposed by the Font object. We do it here to demonstrate the longer version:

```
// set the text-decoration CSS style attribute
// using manual manipulation of the Style property
string textdecoration = "none";
if (UnderlineCheckbox.Checked == true)
    textdecoration = "underline";
NameLabel.Style["text-decoration"] = textdecoration;
```

The other button on the Web Form with a Submit Page caption is there to execute a postback without any server-side code executing. We use it to cycle the values from ViewState to demonstrate that the controls are working with client state properly.

Navigate to the WebControlStyle.aspx page to display the Web Form in your browser. Enter your first name in the Textbox at the top and click the Set Style button. The display should look similar to Figure 6-9, with the Label control picking up the Textbox Text property value.

The HTML emitted by the Textbox control shows the translation from top-level server control properties to the style attribute on the HTML input element:

```
<input type="text" name="NameTextbox" value="" id="NameTextbox"
style="background-color:#E0E0E0;font-family:Tahoma;font-weight:bold;
font-style:italic;" />
```

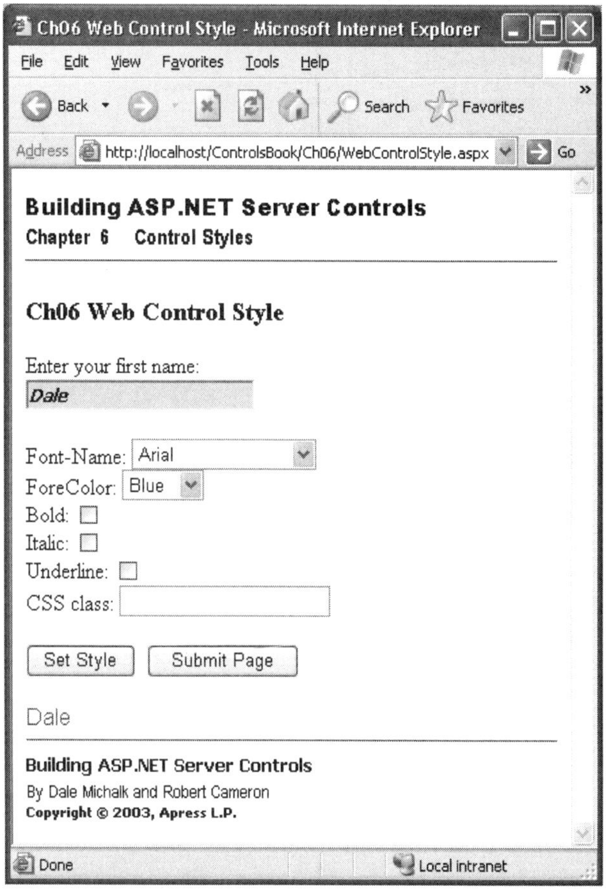

Figure 6-9. Setting the name and style in the Web Control Style Web Form

The same process occurs at the bottom of the Web Form with the Label control. It picks up the style attributes we set in HTML:

```
<span id="NameLabel" style="color:Blue;font-family:Arial;
text-decoration:none;">Dale</span>
```

For the next demonstration, we change the Font-Name to Monotype Corsiva; select the italic, bold, and underline options; and enter **grayborder** in the CssClass TextBox control.

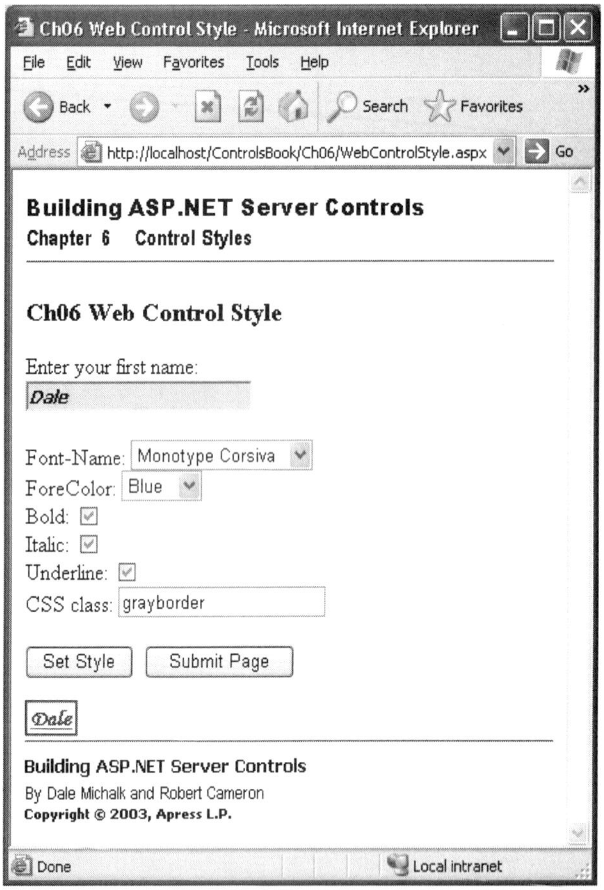

Figure 6-10. Grayborder CSS class, Monotype Corsiva font, and italic, bold, and underline styles in the Web Control Style Web Form

This renders the Label in quite a different manner, as shown in Figure 6-10, picking up the color and the font textual settings such as italic, bold, and underline. The most prominent feature is the gray border styling picked up by using the CssClass attribute in conjunction with the external stylesheet, WebControlStyle.css. The HTML for the Label control is as follows:

```
<span id="NameLabel" class="grayborder" style="color:Blue;font-family:Monotype
Corsiva;font-weight:bold;font-style:italic;text-decoration:underline;">Dale</span>
```

The same settings rendered in Netscape 7.02 shown in Figure 6-11 demonstrate that it displays the style settings with aplomb.

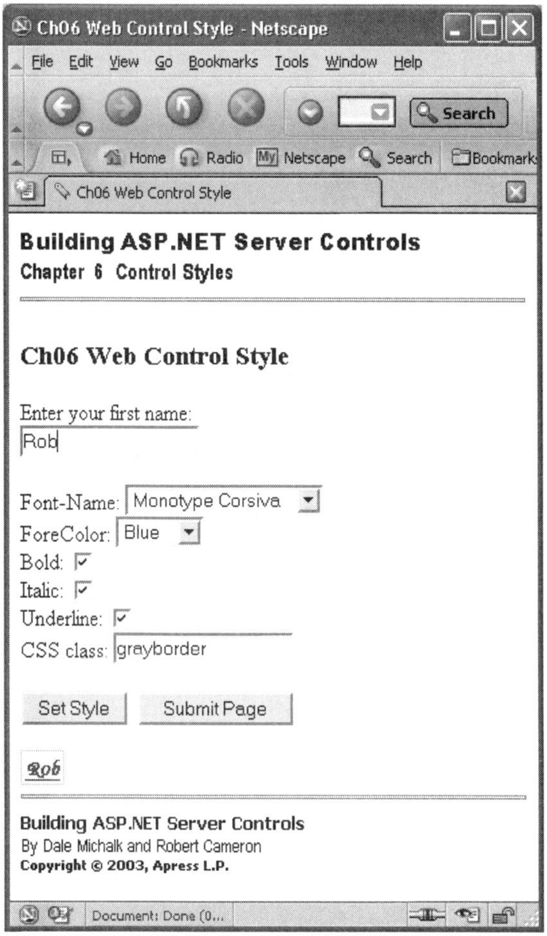

Figure 6-11. Styles in Netscape 7.02

Styles, HTML 3.2, and Down-Level Browsers

The styling in ASP.NET is thankfully smart enough to help a browser that only supports HTML 3.2 display the page properly as well. You have two options for testing this: adding the `ClientTarget="downlevel"` attribute to the `@Page` directive at the top of the Web Form .aspx page or finding a browser client that only supports HTML 3.2. The 3.2 browser is a better test because Internet Explorer (IE) or Netscape will still render styles that are present that don't translate into HTML 3.2 tags.

In order to test this, we dusted off our floppies and dragged out an old version of Netscape 3.03 just to see how good down-level support really is in ASP.NET. Running the same Web Form test with the `Font-Name` set to Monotype Corsiva, `CssClass` set to grayborder, and the italic, bold, and underline options selected results in the screen-shot shown in Figure 6-12.

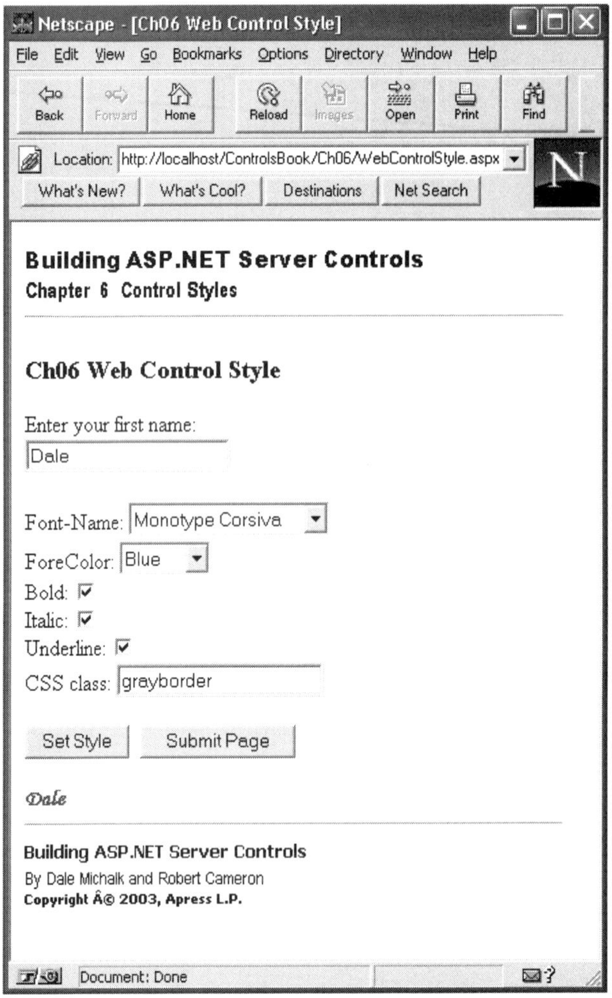

Figure 6-12. Down-level browser rendering

The Web Form does its best to translate the desired CSS style attributes to HTML 3.2 tags for the old Netscape browser. For the most part, it does a good job, especially with text. Viewing the HTML source shows how this compatibility was achieved:

```
<span id="NameLabel" class="grayborder" style="text-decoration:underline;"><b><i>
<font face="Monotype Corsiva" color="Blue">Dale</font></i></b></span>
```

The style tag is still present because we used the Style collection for setting the text-decoration attribute in the code-behind class. Setting the font to have an underline style using this method is the reason why the underline attribute does not display in HTML 3.2, and why you should be careful when using the Style property unless you are only targeting an up-level browser. The CLASS tag is present as well, but it is ignored by the down-level browser, so we won't see a border either. As you can see, building controls that inherit from WebControl provides cross-browser support without your having to worry about the details of browser detection and raw HTML output. We next discuss what goes on under the covers with respect to down-level browser support.

Down-Level Browser Style Rendering Behind the Scenes

The style conversion that occurs automatically when the Web Control Style Web Form is viewed in the down-level Netscape browser is a clever technology built into the ASP.NET framework. When a request is made for an .aspx page, ASP.NET parses the header information to determine the capability of the browser. An instance of the System.Web.HttpBrowserCapabilities class is attached to the HttpRequest class via its Browser property.

The HttpBrowserCapabilities class has a TagWriter property pointing to an instance of the HtmlTextWriter class, or a type inherited from it, to inject HTML into the output stream. Up-level browsers such as Internet Explorer 6.0 and Netscape 7.02 are rendered with an instance of HtmlTextWriter, whereas HTML 3.2 and down-level browsers are rendered with an instance of Html32TextWriter.

Html32TextWriter has a special implementation for handling style information added through AddStyleAttribute. When you call RenderBeginTag, it converts the style attributes into necessary HTML tags such as <FONT>, <B>, and <I>. Because the interfaces are identical between HtmlTextWriter and Html32TextWriter, controls are none the wiser and do not need to worry about the differences, which makes developing cross-browser–friendly web pages as well as server controls much easier to develop when inheriting from WebControl.

We examine the HttpBrowserCapabilities class in more detail in Chapter 8, which is dedicated to integrating client script with control development.

Custom Styling

The WebControl base class provides a great start in implementing styling in your control. It offers a base set of style properties that affect the look and feel of the rendered HTML. With that said, sometimes your controls will be more complex than a single HTML tag. Think of how the composite control renders a whole host of child controls by recursively calling Render on each control. Because the child controls are not directly accessible to outside clients, how can you make the individual controls accessible without breaking the composite control object?

The Style class that backs the ControlStyle property on a WebControl-based control can easily be used by the composite control to provide custom style properties for its child controls. Many of the more advanced list controls, such as the DataGrid in ASP.NET, provide the ability to stylize different settings—for example, how alternating items or edited items appear through the ItemStyle, AlternateItemStyle, and EditItemStyle properties. The DataGrid exposes the Style classes through these properties, applying the styles prior to the start of the rendering process. We demonstrate how to manage styles in a composite control in the next section.

The Styled InputBox Control

To demonstrate custom styling, we develop a composite control called InputBox that aggregates the controls built so far in this chapter (see Figure 6-13). It consists of a Label control and a Textbox control placed near each other, as a web developer normally would place them when laying out a Web Form. To set the styles on each of the child controls, InputBox exposes LabelStyle and TextBoxStyle properties. It also merges the child control styles with the parent styles set via the ControlStyle property to provide a consistent appearance.

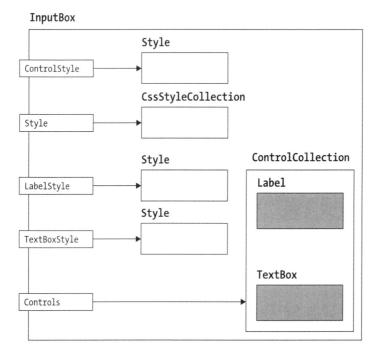

Figure 6-13. The InputBox *control and its multiple styles*

The first step in building our control is to select the tag that represents the outer shell of our custom control. For the InputBox we use a <DIV> tag. We pass the tag enumeration value to the base constructor of WebControl so that it knows how to render itself:

```
public InputBox() : base(HtmlTextWriterTag.Div)
{
}
```

Because we are building a composite control, we need to override the CreateChildControls method so we can populate the internal Controls collection with our child controls. InputBox adds the Label and Textbox controls, in that order:

```
override protected void CreateChildControls()
{
    ControlsBookLib.Ch06.Label label = new ControlsBookLib.Ch06.Label();
    Controls.Add(label);

    ControlsBookLib.Ch06.Textbox textbox = new ControlsBookLib.Ch06.Textbox();
    Controls.Add(textbox);
}
```

The text properties of the child `Label` and `Textbox` controls are wired up to top-level properties of our new `InputBox` control as `LabelText` and `TextboxText`, respectively. The bulk of the code is spent looking up the child controls by position in the `Controls` collection to set or get the `Text` property value by casting to the appropriate type:

```
public string LabelText
{
    get
    {
        EnsureChildControls();
        ControlsBookLib.Ch06.Label label =
            (ControlsBookLib.Ch06.Label) Controls[0];
        return label.Text;
    }
    set
    {
        EnsureChildControls();
        ControlsBookLib.Ch06.Label label =
            (ControlsBookLib.Ch06.Label) Controls[0];
        label.Text = value;
    }
}

public string TextboxText
{
    get
    {
        EnsureChildControls();
        ControlsBookLib.Ch06.Textbox textbox =
            (ControlsBookLib.Ch06.Textbox) Controls[1];
        return textbox.Text;
    }
    set
    {
        EnsureChildControls();
        ControlsBookLib.Ch06.Textbox textbox =
            (ControlsBookLib.Ch06.Textbox) Controls[1];
        textbox.Text = value;
    }
}
```

One item to highlight for our new composite control is the EnsureChildControls method of System.Web.UI.Control, which prevents us from trying to work with a null pointer. EnsureChildControls checks to see if the child control collection is populated and will cause the CreateChildControls method to be called if necessary. We do this in our Text routines to ensure that we find the appropriate child control and can safely manipulate its Text property. This is an important step to take before accessing the control hierarchy when working with composite controls.

LabelStyle and TextboxStyle

Now that we have code to create the child Label and Textbox controls, as well as code to get and set their Text properties, we can move on to demonstrating how to implement custom styles.

Both LabelStyle and TextboxStyle rely on private instances of the Style class to hold style properties. The private instance is exposed via a read-only property. One of the tasks for this read-only property is to make an instance copy of the configured Style class for each child control available. The other task of the property is to manage ViewState tracking for style settings:

```
Style labelStyle;
public virtual Style LabelStyle
{
   get
   {
      if (labelStyle == null)
      {
         labelStyle = new Style();
         if (IsTrackingViewState)
            ((IStateManager)labelStyle).TrackViewState();
      }
      return labelStyle;
   }
}

Style textboxStyle;
public virtual Style TextboxStyle
{
   get
   {
      if (textboxStyle == null)
      {
         textboxStyle = new Style();
         if (IsTrackingViewState)
            ((IStateManager)textboxStyle).TrackViewState();
      }
      return textboxStyle;
   }
}
```

As discussed in Chapter 4, ViewState is implemented via a StateBag collection that tracks modifications to its collection. Both the Style class and the Control class support ViewState, providing access through implementing the IStateManager interface:

```
interface IStateManager
{
   bool IsTrackingViewState() {  get; }
   void TrackViewState();
   void LoadViewState(object state);
   object SaveViewState();
}
```

The TextboxStyle and LabelStyle properties' get accessor methods call the IsTrackingViewState method of the InputBox control to determine if the control is tracking ViewState changes. If it is, the code ensures that state is maintained for the style properties as well.

Customizing ViewState

The WebControl class has facilities to manage ViewState serialization for styles maintained in WebControl's ControlStyle property instance of the Style class. Because we are providing our own style management implementation, we need to customize ViewState persistence mechanisms to include our new styling information, as shown in the following code:

```
override protected object SaveViewState()
{
   object baseState = base.SaveViewState();
   object labelStyleState = (labelStyle != null) ?
((IStateManager)labelStyle).SaveViewState() : null;
   object textboxStyleState = (textboxStyle != null) ?
((IStateManager)textboxStyle).SaveViewState() : null;

   object[] state = new object[3];
   state[0] = baseState;
   state[1] = labelStyleState;
   state[2] = textboxStyleState;

   return state;
}
```

The first thing we do in the code is call WebControl's version of SaveViewState to ensure we don't break any behavior implemented in the base class. Calling base.SaveViewState persists state information, including the values in the ControlStyle property. Next, we persist the styling information for the label and text box into ViewState. This is accomplished by casting the Style instances to the IStateManager interface on the Style class so that we gain access to the SaveViewState method. Finally, we package the three object state binary large objects (BLOBs) into an object array that the ASP.NET framework persists into ViewState.

Retrieving style information from ViewState performs these steps in reverse. Our
LoadViewState method is as follows:

```
override protected void LoadViewState(object savedState)
{
    if (savedState != null)
    {
        object[] state = (object[])savedState;

        if (state[0] != null)
            base.LoadViewState(state[0]);
        if (state[1] != null)
            ((IStateManager)LabelStyle).LoadViewState(state[1]);
        if (state[2] != null)
            ((IStateManager)TextboxStyle).LoadViewState(state[2]);
    }
}
```

LoadViewState casts the incoming parameter to an object array identical to what
we used to persist style information in SaveViewSate. We next call LoadViewSate for
each Style class, checking to ensure that we don't have a null reference before loading
state from ViewState. Order matters, so WebControl LoadViewState goes first followed
by the Label and Textbox controls' LoadViewState routines. At the end of the InputBox
LoadViewState routine, we can be assured that the saved ViewState is retrieved from the
postback and is ready to go for rendering.

Rendering the Output

Normally, a composite control leaves the rendering to the base class implementation
of Control or WebControl. Because we are doing our own custom style work, we override Render for the maximum amount of control. In our Render method override
(shown in the following code snippet), we need to call RenderBigTag to emit the starting <DIV> tag and the base style attributes, we need to call RenderChildren to have the
child controls render their content, and finally we need to call RenderEndTag to emit the
closing </DIV> tag. We skip calling RenderContents because we took full responsibility
for rendering the control, including the inner HTML.

```
override protected void Render(HtmlTextWriter writer)
{
    PrepareControlHierarchy();
    RenderBeginTag(writer);
    RenderChildren(writer);
    RenderEndTag(writer);
}
```

Our implementation of Render performs some extra work to massage the style
information in a helper method named PrepareControlHierarchy prior to rendering.
PrepareControlHierarchy obtains a reference to each of our child controls so that it can
apply style attributes:

```
private void PrepareControlHierarchy()
{
    ControlsBookLib.Ch06.Label label = (ControlsBookLib.Ch06.Label) Controls[0];
    label.ApplyStyle(LabelStyle);
    label.MergeStyle(ControlStyle);

    ControlsBookLib.Ch06.Textbox textbox =
                        (ControlsBookLib.Ch06.Textbox) Controls[1];
    textbox.ApplyStyle(TextboxStyle);
    textbox.MergeStyle(ControlStyle);
}
```

The ApplyStyle class method overwrites any existing style properties that are in effect for a control. You can use this to wipe the slate clean as it replaces all style properties.

The MergeStyle class method is used to add style properties that are not already set in the Style instance. You have to be careful with what MergeStyle considers to be "set." For a Style attribute such as Font.Italic, it does not consider a false value to be a "set" value. So, if the existing Style instance has Font.Italic explicitly set to false, MergeStyle will set Font.Italic to true if the style to be copied has it set to true as a value of true is considered to be "set."

PrepareControlHierachy uses ApplyStyle for the custom style properties to load all their attributes. This ensures that the Textbox is decorated with its TextboxStyle properties and the Label is decorated with its LabelStyle properties. The parent InputBox ControlStyle style is then merged using MergeStyle to fill in any style attributes that are not set by the custom styles. If there aren't any custom style attributes selected, the ControlStyle properties will be the default for the two custom controls. Listing 6-6 shows the full listing for InputBox.

Listing 6-6. The InputBox *Custom Control Class File*

```
using System;
using System.Web;
using System.Web.UI;
using System.Web.UI.WebControls;
using System.Collections.Specialized;

namespace ControlsBookLib.Ch06
{
    [ToolboxData("<{0}:InputBox runat=server></{0}:InputBox>")]
    public class InputBox : WebControl
    {
        public InputBox() : base(HtmlTextWriterTag.Div)
        {
        }

        public string LabelText
        {
            get
```

```
      {
         EnsureChildControls();
         ControlsBookLib.Ch06.Label label =
            (ControlsBookLib.Ch06.Label) Controls[0];
         return label.Text;
      }
      set
      {
         EnsureChildControls();
         ControlsBookLib.Ch06.Label label =
            (ControlsBookLib.Ch06.Label) Controls[0];
         label.Text = value;
      }
   }

   public string TextboxText
   {
      get
      {
         EnsureChildControls();
         ControlsBookLib.Ch06.Textbox textbox =
            (ControlsBookLib.Ch06.Textbox) Controls[1];
         return textbox.Text;
      }
      set
      {
         EnsureChildControls();
         ControlsBookLib.Ch06.Textbox textbox =
            (ControlsBookLib.Ch06.Textbox) Controls[1];
         textbox.Text = value;
      }
   }

   Style labelStyle;
   public virtual Style LabelStyle
   {
      get
      {
         if (labelStyle == null)
         {
            labelStyle = new Style();
            if (IsTrackingViewState)
               ((IStateManager)labelStyle).TrackViewState();
         }
         return labelStyle;
      }
   }

   Style textboxStyle;
   public virtual Style TextboxStyle
   {
```

```csharp
        get
        {
           if (textboxStyle == null)
           {
              textboxStyle = new Style();
              if (IsTrackingViewState)
                 ((IStateManager)textboxStyle).TrackViewState();
           }
           return textboxStyle;
        }
     }

     override protected void LoadViewState(object savedState)
     {
        if (savedState != null)
        {
           object[] state = (object[])savedState;

           if (state[0] != null)
              base.LoadViewState(state[0]);
           if (state[1] != null)
              ((IStateManager)LabelStyle).LoadViewState(state[1]);
           if (state[2] != null)
              ((IStateManager)TextboxStyle).LoadViewState(state[2]);
        }
     }

     override protected object SaveViewState()
     {
        object baseState = base.SaveViewState();
        object labelStyleState = (labelStyle != null) ?
((IStateManager)labelStyle).SaveViewState() : null;
        object textboxStyleState = (textboxStyle != null) ?
((IStateManager)textboxStyle).SaveViewState() : null;

        object[] state = new object[3];
        state[0] = baseState;
        state[1] = labelStyleState;
        state[2] = textboxStyleState;

        return state;
     }

     override protected void CreateChildControls()
     {

        ControlsBookLib.Ch06.Label label = new ControlsBookLib.Ch06.Label();
        Controls.Add(label);

        ControlsBookLib.Ch06.Textbox textbox = new ControlsBookLib.Ch06.Textbox();
        Controls.Add(textbox);
```

```
      }

      public override ControlCollection Controls
      {
         get
         {
            EnsureChildControls();
            return base.Controls;
         }
      }

      private void PrepareControlHierarchy()
      {
         ControlsBookLib.Ch06.Label label =
                     (ControlsBookLib.Ch06.Label) Controls[0];
         label.ApplyStyle(LabelStyle);
         label.MergeStyle(ControlStyle);

         ControlsBookLib.Ch06.Textbox textbox =
                     (ControlsBookLib.Ch06.Textbox) Controls[1];
         textbox.ApplyStyle(TextboxStyle);
         textbox.MergeStyle(ControlStyle);
      }

      override protected void Render(HtmlTextWriter writer)
      {
         PrepareControlHierarchy();
         RenderBeginTag(writer);
         RenderChildren(writer);
         RenderEndTag(writer);
      }
   }
}
```

The InputBox Style Web Form

We now put our new server control to the test with an updated version of the styling
workbench from the previous example. The Web Form example for the InputBox control takes the previous style setting workbench and adds the ability to set styles for the
Label and the Textbox as well. Figure 6-14 provides a snapshot of the updated workbench with a panel for styling both child controls.

The control panel for each child control's Style has the same feature set as our
previous Web Control Style Web Form, minus the ability to set the CssClass style attribute. It does add a radio button group at the top of the control boxes that allows you to
either set or not set the styling for the Label or Textbox control. The full code listings
for the Web Form and the code-behind class file are shown in Listings 6-7 and 6-8,
respectively.

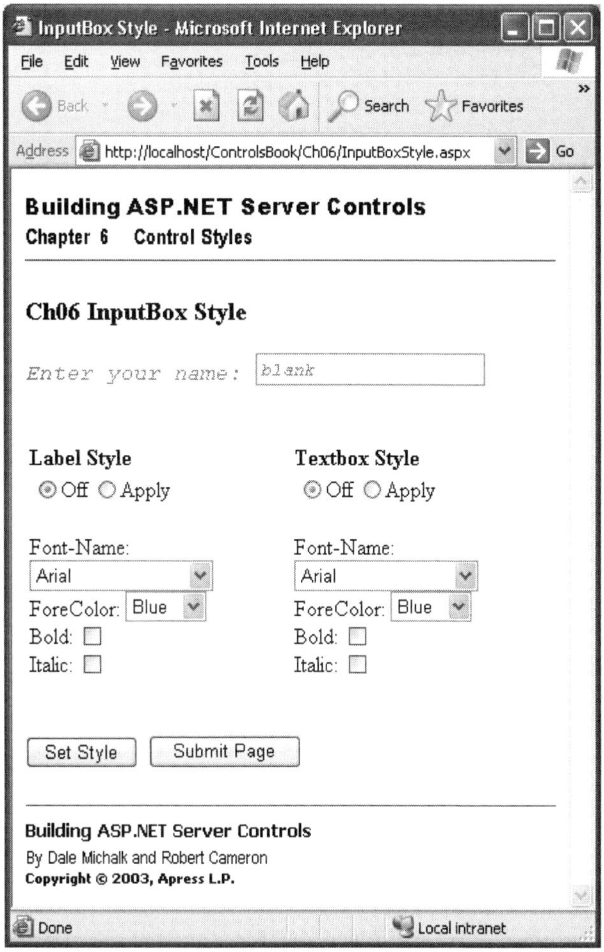

Figure 6-14. The InputBox Style Web Form

Listing 6-7. The InputBox Style Web Form .aspx Page File

```
<%@ Register TagPrefix="apress" Namespace="ControlsBookLib.Ch06"
 Assembly="ControlsBookLib" %>
<%@ Page language="c#" Codebehind="InputBoxStyle.aspx.cs" AutoEventWireup="false"
Inherits="ControlsBookWeb.Ch06.InputBoxStyle" %>
<%@ Register TagPrefix="apressUC" TagName="ControlsBookHeader"
Src="..\ControlsBookHeader.ascx" %>
<%@ Register TagPrefix="apressUC" TagName="ControlsBookFooter"
Src="..\ControlsBookFooter.ascx" %>
<!DOCTYPE HTML PUBLIC "-//W3C//DTD HTML 4.0 Transitional//EN" >
<HTML>
  <HEAD>
    <title>InputBox Style</title>
    <meta name="GENERATOR" Content="Microsoft Visual Studio 7.0">
```

```
      <meta name="CODE_LANGUAGE" Content="C#">
      <meta name="vs_defaultClientScript" content="JavaScript">
      <meta name="vs_targetSchema"
        content="http://schemas.microsoft.com/intellisense/ie5">
</HEAD>
<body MS_POSITIONING="FlowLayout">
  <form id="InputBoxStyle" method="post" runat="server">
    <apressUC:ControlsBookHeader id="Header" runat="server"
                 ChapterNumber="6" ChapterTitle="Control Styles" />
    <h3>Ch06 InputBox Style</h3>
    <apress:inputbox id="NameInputBox" runat="server"
             LabelText="Enter your name: " TextboxText="blank"
       Font-Names="Courier New" ForeColor="Red" Font-Italic="True">
     </apress:inputbox><br>
    <br>
    <table>
      <tr>
        <td><span style="FONT-WEIGHT: bold">Label Style</span><br>
          <asp:radiobuttonlist id="LabelActionList" RepeatColumns="3"
            Runat="server">
            <asp:ListItem Value="Off" Selected="True">Off</asp:ListItem>
            <asp:ListItem Value="Apply">Apply</asp:ListItem>
          </asp:radiobuttonlist><br>
          Font-Name:
          <asp:dropdownlist id="LabelFontDropDownList" Runat="server">
            <asp:ListItem Value="Arial">Arial</asp:ListItem>
            <asp:ListItem Value="Courier New">Courier New</asp:ListItem>
            <asp:ListItem Value="Times New Roman">Times New Roman</asp:ListItem>
            <asp:ListItem Value="Monotype Corsiva">Monotype Corsiva
            </asp:ListItem>
          </asp:dropdownlist><br>
          ForeColor:
          <asp:dropdownlist id="LabelForeColorDropDownList" Runat="server">
            <asp:ListItem Value="Blue">Blue</asp:ListItem>
            <asp:ListItem Value="Red">Red</asp:ListItem>
            <asp:ListItem Value="Black">Black</asp:ListItem>
          </asp:dropdownlist><br>
          <asp:checkbox id="LabelBoldCheckbox" runat="server"
           Text="Bold: " TextAlign="Left"></asp:checkbox><br>
          <asp:checkbox id="LabelItalicCheckbox" runat="server"
           Text="Italic: " TextAlign="Left"></asp:checkbox><br>
        </td>
        <td><span style="FONT-WEIGHT: bold">Textbox Style</span><br>
          <asp:radiobuttonlist id="TextboxActionList" RepeatColumns="3"
           Runat="server">
            <asp:ListItem Value="Off" Selected="True">Off</asp:ListItem>
            <asp:ListItem Value="Apply">Apply</asp:ListItem>
          </asp:radiobuttonlist><br>
          Font-Name:
          <asp:dropdownlist id="TextboxFontDropDownList" Runat="server">
            <asp:ListItem Value="Arial">Arial</asp:ListItem>
```

```
            <asp:ListItem Value="Courier New">Courier New</asp:ListItem>
            <asp:ListItem Value="Times New Roman">Times New Roman</asp:ListItem>
            <asp:ListItem Value="Monotype Corsiva">Monotype Corsiva
            </asp:ListItem>
          </asp:dropdownlist><br>
          ForeColor:
          <asp:dropdownlist id="TextboxForeColorDropDownList" Runat="server">
            <asp:ListItem Value="Blue">Blue</asp:ListItem>
            <asp:ListItem Value="Red">Red</asp:ListItem>
            <asp:ListItem Value="Black">Black</asp:ListItem>
          </asp:dropdownlist><br>
          <asp:checkbox id="TextboxBoldCheckbox" runat="server" Text="Bold: "
           TextAlign="Left"></asp:checkbox><br>
          <asp:checkbox id="TextboxItalicCheckbox" runat="server" Text="Italic: "
           TextAlign="Left"></asp:checkbox><br>
        </td>
      </tr>
    </table>
    <br>
    <br>
    <asp:button id="SetStyleButton" runat="server" Text="Set Style"
     Height="23px" Width="83px"></asp:button> 
    <asp:button id="SubmitPageButton" runat="server" Text="Submit Page">
    </asp:button><br>
    <br>
    <apressUC:ControlsBookFooter id="Footer" runat="server" />
  </form>
 </body>
</HTML>
```

Listing 6-8. The InputBox Style Web Form Code-Behind Class File

```
using System;
using System.Collections;
using System.ComponentModel;
using System.Data;
using System.Drawing;
using System.Web;
using System.Web.SessionState;
using System.Web.UI;
using System.Web.UI.WebControls;
using System.Web.UI.HtmlControls;

namespace ControlsBookWeb.Ch06
{
    public class InputBoxStyle : System.Web.UI.Page
    {
        protected ControlsBookLib.Ch06.InputBox NameInputBox;
        protected System.Web.UI.WebControls.RadioButtonList LabelActionList;
        protected System.Web.UI.WebControls.DropDownList LabelFontDropDownList;
```

261

```
protected System.Web.UI.WebControls.DropDownList LabelForeColorDropDownList;
protected System.Web.UI.WebControls.CheckBox LabelBoldCheckbox;
protected System.Web.UI.WebControls.CheckBox LabelItalicCheckbox;
protected System.Web.UI.WebControls.RadioButtonList TextboxActionList;
protected System.Web.UI.WebControls.DropDownList TextboxFontDropDownList;
protected System.Web.UI.WebControls.
                    DropDownList TextboxForeColorDropDownList;
protected System.Web.UI.WebControls.CheckBox TextboxBoldCheckbox;
protected System.Web.UI.WebControls.CheckBox TextboxItalicCheckbox;
protected System.Web.UI.WebControls.Button SetStyleButton;
protected System.Web.UI.WebControls.Button SubmitPageButton;

private void Page_Load(object sender, System.EventArgs e)
{

}

#region Web Form Designer generated code
override protected void OnInit(EventArgs e)
{
   //
   // CODEGEN: This call is required by the ASP.NET Web Form Designer.
   //
   InitializeComponent();
   base.OnInit(e);
}

/// <summary>
/// Required method for Designer support - do not modify
/// the contents of this method with the code editor.
/// </summary>
private void InitializeComponent()
{
   this.SetStyleButton.Click +=
      new System.EventHandler(this.SetStyleButton_Click);
   this.Load += new System.EventHandler(this.Page_Load);

}
#endregion

private void SetLabelStyle()
{
   NameInputBox.LabelStyle.Font.Name =
         LabelFontDropDownList.SelectedItem.Value;
   NameInputBox.LabelStyle.Font.Bold = (LabelBoldCheckbox.Checked == true);
   NameInputBox.LabelStyle.Font.Italic =
         (LabelItalicCheckbox.Checked == true);
   Color labelColor =
      (Color)TypeDescriptor.GetConverter(typeof(Color)).ConvertFromString(
      LabelForeColorDropDownList.SelectedItem.Value);
   NameInputBox.LabelStyle.ForeColor = labelColor;
}
```

```
        private void SetTextboxStyle()
        {
           NameInputBox.TextboxStyle.Font.Name =
                    TextboxFontDropDownList.SelectedItem.Value;
           NameInputBox.TextboxStyle.Font.Bold =
                    (TextboxBoldCheckbox.Checked == true);
           NameInputBox.TextboxStyle.Font.Italic =
                    (TextboxItalicCheckbox.Checked == true);

           // Use the TypeConverter for the System.Drawing.Color class
           // to get the typed Color value from the string value
           Color textboxColor =
               (Color)TypeDescriptor.GetConverter(typeof(Color)).ConvertFromString(
               TextboxForeColorDropDownList.SelectedItem.Value);
           NameInputBox.TextboxStyle.ForeColor = textboxColor;
        }

        private void SetStyleButton_Click(object sender, System.EventArgs e)
        {
           if (LabelActionList.SelectedIndex > 0)
               SetLabelStyle();

           if (TextboxActionList.SelectedIndex > 0)
               SetTextboxStyle();
        }
    }
}
```

The default rendering style of the Web Form displays our InputBox in a red Courier New font with italic enabled. Both the Label and Textbox controls inside the InputBox pick up the parent-level settings in the .aspx page:

```
<apress:inputbox id="NameInputBox" runat="server" LabelText="Enter your name: "
TextboxText="blank"
Font-Names="Courier New" ForeColor="Red" Font-Italic="True">
</apress:inputbox>
```

The style attributes from the .aspx page render the following HTML tags for the InputBox control:

```
<div id="NameInputBox" style="color:Red;font-family:
                         Courier New;font-style:italic;">
   <span style="color:Red;font-family:Courier New;font-style:italic;">
Enter your name: </span>
   <input type="text" name="_ctl1" value="blank"
    style="color:Red;font-family:Courier New;font-style:italic;" />
</div>
```

The HTML snippet shows that the <DIV>, <SPAN>, and <INPUT> tags all have identical style attribute strings.

Applying the LabelStyle and TextboxStyle Settings

Now it is time to mix things up a little. Go to the Label Style panel and select the Apply radio button. Check the Bold check box, leaving the rest of the settings for the Label style as they are. Click the Set Style button to post the Web Form back to the web server and apply the style changes to the Label child control of the InputBox control:

```
private void SetStyleButton_Click(object sender, System.EventArgs e)
{
    if (LabelActionList.SelectedIndex > 0)
        SetLabelStyle();

    if (TextboxActionList.SelectedIndex > 0)
        SetTextboxStyle();
}
```

The SetStyleButton_Click routine handles the button click activity and is responsible for checking the radio button group for each control to determine whether or not to update the custom styles for the embedded Label and Textbox Style controls to the current settings on the Web Form. In this iteration, only the SetLabelStyle routine is executed because we set the radio button group to Apply. The code in SetLabelStyle is almost identical to what we discussed in the previous Web Control Style Web Form example. The Web Form renders as shown in Figure 6-15.

The HTML for our InputBox control reveals the presence of a different style attribute for the <SPAN> tag representing the Label control:

```
<div id="NameInputBox" style="color:Red;font-family:Courier New;
  font-style:italic;">
    <span style="color:Blue;font-family:Arial;font-weight:bold;
font-style:italic;">Enter your name:     </span>
    <input type="text" name="_ctl1" value="Dale"
    style="color:Red;font-family:Courier New;font-style:italic;" />
</div>
```

The <SPAN> tag has a style attribute that reflects the Arial font and bold font weight settings. What is interesting is that the <SPAN> tag still inherits the italic font style from the parent InputBox ControlStyle property settings. This shows how the control method MergeStyle will overwrite a Font.Italic = false style setting. The code-behind class sets it every time in the following line of code, so it is not an issue of us not accessing the LabelStyle property. It is a behavior to be aware of in the current implementation of the ASP.NET style system.

```
NameInputBox.LabelStyle.Font.Italic = (LabelItalicCheckbox.Checked == true);
```

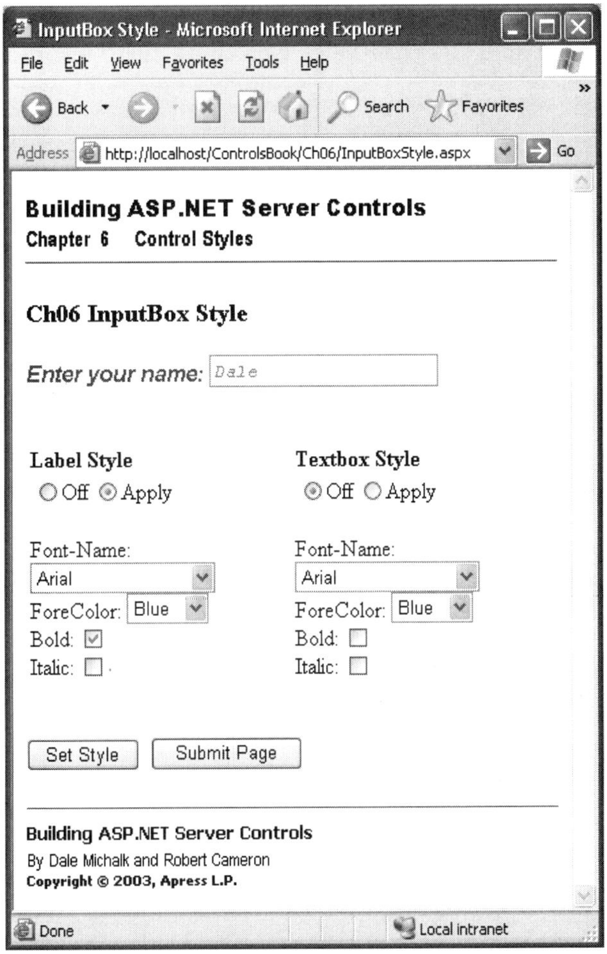

Figure 6-15. The InputBox Style Web Form with the Label *style applied*

The next step in our demonstration is to exercise the Textbox Style settings. Check the Apply radio button for the TextboxStyle box and then select a different font, such as bold Monotype Corsiva, with a ForeColor of black. Click the Set Style button again to post the Web Form. The result in Figure 6-16 shows that the two child controls have separate styles but are both inheriting the italic setting from their parent control via MergeStyle.

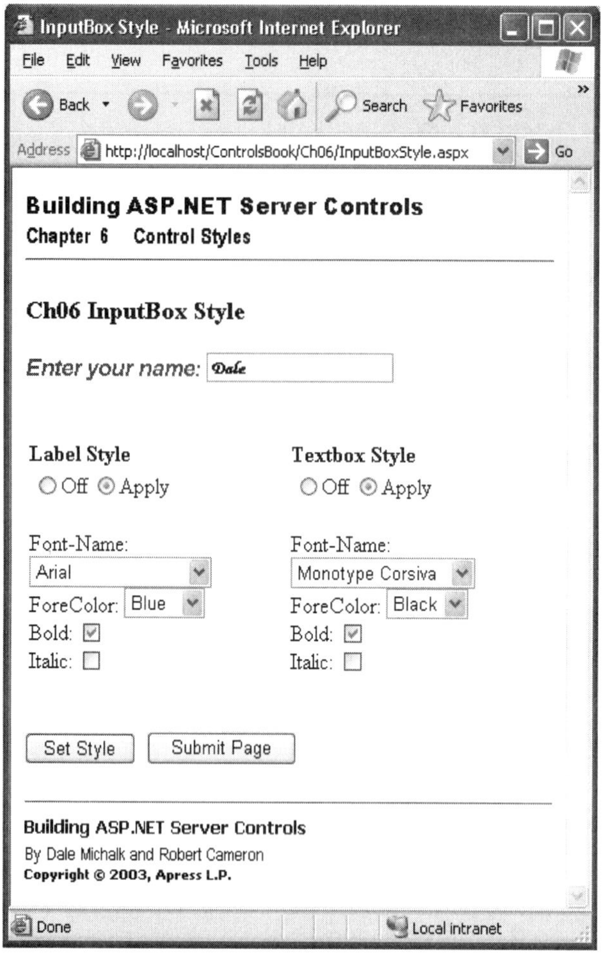

Figure 6-16. The InputBox Style Web Form with both Label *and* TextBox *styles applied*

The HTML source confirms the screenshot style view in the browser:

```
<div id="NameInputBox" style="color:Red;font-family:Courier New;
font-style:italic;">
   <span style="color:Blue;font-family:Arial;font-weight:bold;
                     font-style:italic;">Enter your name:   </span>
   <input type="text" name="_ctl1" value="Dale"
   style="color:Black;font-family:Monotype Corsiva;
                            font-weight:bold;font-style:italic;" />
</div>
```

Now that we have covered the basics on styling when inheriting from WebControl, we will now move on to cover how to create a custom style class that integrates into the framework while providing additional capabilities.

Creating a Custom Style Class

The Style class that we have worked with so far in this chapter is geared toward a small set of CSS style features. However, IE supports a much larger range of CSS capabilities that allow for some very nice features in your web application. One such attribute is the CSS property named cursor. As you would guess, the CSS cursor property changes the mouse cursor when the mouse passes over HTML elements configured with this attribute.

One method available to add styles not directly supported by the Style class is to use the Styles collection provided by WebControl and add additional styling using name/value pairs. This option is geared more toward control users. Server control developers should instead provide access to additional styles through custom Style classes, which provide strongly-typed access to styling and better designer support with drop-down boxes containing enumeration types or perhaps made available to control users via a custom designer. This is the approach taken by the DataGrid control, which exposes the TableItemStyle via its HeaderStyle, FooterStyle, ItemStyle, AlternatingItemStyle, EditItemStyle, and SelectedItemStyle properties.

Following our own recommendation, we next create a FancyLabelStyle class for our FancyLabel server control that provides a new styling capability that configures how the cursor renders. This takes advantage of the CSS cursor attribute supported by IE.

The CursorStyle Enumeration

To add our new custom style to the FancyLabel server control, the first task is to create an enumeration that represents the various settings available to the CSS cursor attribute:

```
public enum CursorStyle
{
    auto,
    hand,
    crosshair,
    help,
    move,
    text,
    wait
}
```

This makes it convenient for us to emit the appropriate text value in the output string using the Enum.Format method. The next step is to create the FancyLabelStyle class, overriding the constructors from the base Style class:

```
public class FancyLabelStyle : Style
{
    public FancyLabelStyle() : base()
    {
    }

    public FancyLabelStyle(StateBag ViewState) : base(ViewState)
    {
    }
}
```

In the preceding declaration are two constructors. We can either create a Style object that maintains its own ViewState or integrate into the ViewState of the control by calling base(ViewState). For a noncomposite server control, we recommend passing in the control's ViewState and not creating a separate StateBag for a custom Style class in order to maximize performance. We maintain the value of the Cursor's style in View-State, as shown in the following code:

```
public CursorStyle Cursor
{
    get
    {
        if (ViewState["cursor"]!= null)
        {
            return (CursorStyle)ViewState["cursor"] ;
        }
        else
        {
            return CursorStyle.auto ;
        }
    }
    set
    {
        ViewState["cursor"] = value;
    }
}
```

Style classes add their attributes to a control's output stream by implementing the AddAttributesToRender method. It takes a reference to the HtmlTextWriter instance the control is using, along with a direct reference to the control itself. Our version of AddAttributesToRender checks to make sure the Cursor property has been set by checking for the value in ViewState before it adds style attributes to HtmlTextWriter:

```
override public void AddAttributesToRender(HtmlTextWriter writer, WebControl owner)
{
   base.AddAttributesToRender(writer, owner); // Ensure base Style class adds its
   // attributes to the output stream
   if (ViewState["cursor"] != null)
   {
      string cursor =
         Enum.Format(typeof(CursorStyle), (CursorStyle)ViewState["cursor"], "G");
      writer.AddStyleAttribute("cursor", cursor);
   }
}
```

The CursorStyle enumeration is formatted into a string value and added to HtmlTextWriter through its AddStyleAttribute method. Before we do this, we call the base version of AddAttributesToRender at the beginning of the method to ensure that the rest of the Style class attributes make it into the final output along with our custom property extension.

The Style class also has two overrides available, CopyFrom and MergeWith, that allow a control developer to extend the copying and merging of style information. WebControl uses these methods in its ApplyStyle and MergeStyle methods. WebControl.MergeStyle calls Style.MergeWith, and WebControl.ApplyStyle calls Style.CopyFrom.

The first method we implement to enhance our custom style class is CopyFrom:

```
override public void CopyFrom(Style style)
{
   base.CopyFrom(style);

   FancyLabelStyle flstyle = style as FancyLabelStyle;
   if (flstyle != null)
      Cursor = flstyle.Cursor;
}
```

CopyFrom calls the base class version to copy all the standard style properties. It then casts the Style reference passed in to make sure it is of type FancyLabelStyle before it copies the Cursor property. CopyFrom overwrites Cursor regardless of its current setting.

MergeWith is similar to CopyFrom, except it should copy a property only if the value in the Style object has not already been set. Our implementation uses our custom IsEmpty property to determine whether it needs to perform the copy operation. If our current style is "set," then IsEmpty returns false and prevents us from overwriting the current setting. It also does a cast to ensure that we are dealing with the correct Style type before copying:

```
override public void MergeWith(Style style)
{
   base.MergeWith(style);

   FancyLabelStyle flstyle = style as FancyLabelStyle;
```

```
    //Only merge if inbound style is set and current style is not set
    if ((flstyle != null) && (!flstyle.IsEmpty) && (IsEmpty))
        Cursor = flstyle.Cursor;
}
```

The IsEmpty property follows the pattern of the base Style class. Here is the signature of our version:

```
protected internal new bool IsEmpty
{
    get
    {   //Call base class version to get default behavior
        return base.IsEmpty && (ViewState["cursor"] == null);
    }
}
```

Note that we don't use the override keyword. The base class Style implements this property with the internal keyword, which prevents us from overriding this property. Instead, we use the keyword new to provide our custom replacement. We still call the base version of this method internally, but we also implement custom logic to handle our additional style setting.

The final method we implement is Reset. This method simply calls the base class version of Reset and removes the cursor value from ViewState:

```
override public void Reset()
{
    base.Reset();

    if (ViewState["cursor"] != null)
    {
        ViewState.Remove("cursor");
    }
}
```

Listing 6-9 presents the complete FancyLabelStyle class.

Listing 6-9. The FancyLabelStyle *Class File*

```
using System;
using System.Web.UI;
using System.Web.UI.WebControls;

namespace ControlsBookLib.Ch06
{
    public enum CursorStyle
    {
        auto,
        hand,
        crosshair,
```

```
    help,
    move,
    text,
    wait
}

public class FancyLabelStyle : Style
{
    public FancyLabelStyle() : base()
    {
    }

    public FancyLabelStyle(StateBag ViewState) : base(ViewState)
    {
    }

    public CursorStyle Cursor
    {
        get
        {
            if (ViewState["cursor"]!= null)
            {
                return (CursorStyle)ViewState["cursor"] ;
            }
            else
            {
                return CursorStyle.auto ;
            }
        }
        set
        {
            ViewState["cursor"] = value;
        }
    }

    override public void CopyFrom(Style style)
    {
        base.CopyFrom(style);

        FancyLabelStyle flstyle = style as FancyLabelStyle;
        if (flstyle != null)
            Cursor = flstyle.Cursor;
    }

    override public void MergeWith(Style style)
    {
        base.MergeWith(style);

        FancyLabelStyle flstyle = style as FancyLabelStyle;

        //Only merge if inbound style is set and current style is not set
```

```
         if ((flstyle != null) && (!flstyle.IsEmpty) && (IsEmpty))
            Cursor = flstyle.Cursor;
      }

      override public void Reset()
      {
         base.Reset();

         if (ViewState["cursor"] != null)
         {
            ViewState.Remove("cursor");
         }
      }


      // Hide base class version of IsEmpty using the keyword "new"
      // and provide our own
      // The keyword "internal" limits access to within the assembly only,
      // following the pattern
      // established by the base Style class
      protected internal new bool IsEmpty
      {
         get
         { // Call base class version to get default behavior
            return base.IsEmpty && (ViewState["cursor"] == null);
         }
      }

      override public void AddAttributesToRender(
                  HtmlTextWriter writer, WebControl owner)
      {
         // Ensure base Style class adds its
         base.AddAttributesToRender(writer, owner);
         // attributes to the output stream
         if (ViewState["cursor"] != null)
         {
            string cursor =
               Enum.Format(typeof(CursorStyle),
                 (CursorStyle)ViewState["cursor"], "G");
            writer.AddStyleAttribute("cursor", cursor);
         }
      }
   }
}
```

The FancyLabel Control

The FancyLabel control is our choice for implementing the wonderful cursor capability of the FancyLabelStyle style class. It inherits the code from our Label example earlier in the chapter. We take it into the garage for an overhaul to gain the new style capabilities.

The first upgrade for FancyLabel is overriding the ControlStyle property creation logic. The CreateControlStyle method override is the recommended way to replace the Style class that is normally associated with ControlStyle to one of your own. We substitute in FancyLabelStyle for the FancyLabel control:

```
protected override Style CreateControlStyle()
{
   FancyLabelStyle style = new FancyLabelStyle(ViewState);
   return style;
}
```

One of the nice features about WebControl is the top-level support it gives to style properties. We mimic this feature set by adding a new top-level property to make it easy to set the cursor styling. It is linked directly to our LabelStyle class instance operating under the ControlStyle property:

```
public CursorStyle Cursor
{
   get
   {
      return ((FancyLabelStyle)ControlStyle).Cursor;
   }
   set
   {
      ((FancyLabelStyle)ControlStyle).Cursor = value;
   }
}
```

The Cursor property accessor must cast ControlStyle to the FancyLabelStyle class via an explicit cast because ControlStyle is defined to be of type of Style. Once this is complete, the Cursor property of the style class is available.

Rendering the FancyLabel Control

The final step is to provide the correct rendering of the new style class in our FancyLabel control. Unfortunately, this step is not the automatic process you might think it would be. The culprit causing the implementation challenge is the design of the Style base class and how WebControl interacts with it.

Both WebControl and the Style class have an implementation of the AddAttributesToRender method, as Figure 6-17 illustrates. The WebControl version does things such as add utility attributes to the HTML start tag for the control for settings such as Enabled, AccessKey, ToolTip, and TabIndex via the HtmlTextWriter AddAttribute method. It also walks through the Attributes collection of WebControl, adding those through HtmlTextWriter as well.

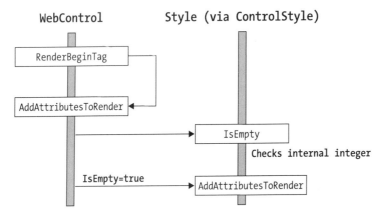

Figure 6-17. WebControl *and* Style AddAttributesToRender

The Style class instance that is linked to the ControlStyle property is called by WebControl to add its style attributes through its version of AddAttributesToRender. There is one caveat with this call. It is executed only if the Style object signals that its internal state has been modified via the return value of the Style IsEmpty property. In the base Style class, IsEmpty is declared as internal. Because we want our new version of IsEmpty to be called, we hide the base class version by declaring our version of IsEmpty with the new modifier:

```
protected internal new bool IsEmpty
{
   get
   { // Call base class version to get default behavior
      return base.IsEmpty && (ViewState["cursor"] == null);
   }
}
```

Listing 6-10 shows the full control class.

Listing 6-10. The FancyLabel *Control Class File*

```
using System;
using System.Web;
using System.Web.UI;
using System.Web.UI.WebControls;
using System.ComponentModel;

namespace ControlsBookLib.Ch06
{
   [ToolboxData("<{0}:FancyLabel runat=server></{0}:FancyLabel>"),
   DefaultProperty("Text")]
   public class FancyLabel : WebControl
   {
      public FancyLabel() : base(HtmlTextWriterTag.Span)
      {
      }

      public CursorStyle Cursor
      {
         get
         {
            return ((FancyLabelStyle)ControlStyle).Cursor;
         }
         set
         {
            ((FancyLabelStyle)ControlStyle).Cursor = value;
         }
      }

      public virtual string Text
      {
         get
         {
            object text = ViewState["Text"];
            if (text == null)
               return string.Empty;
            else
               return (string) text;
         }
         set
         {
            ViewState["Text"] = value;
         }
```

```
        }

        protected override Style CreateControlStyle()
        {
            FancyLabelStyle style = new FancyLabelStyle(ViewState);
            return style;
        }

        override protected void RenderContents(HtmlTextWriter writer)
        {
            writer.Write(Text);
        }
    }
}
```

The FancyLabel Style Web Form

FancyLabel Style is a Web Form that provides an opportunity to demonstrate our newly minted FancyLabel Style class and the containing control, FancyLabel. The Web Form contains eight different FancyLabel controls with different Cursor properties and one FancyLabel without any cursor set to test default behavior. The Web Form code is provided in full in Listings 6-11 and 6-12.

Listing 6-11. The FancyLabel Style Web Form .aspx Page File

```
<%@ Register TagPrefix="apress" Namespace="ControlsBookLib.Ch06"
Assembly="ControlsBookLib" %>
<%@ Page language="c#" Codebehind="FancyLabelStyle.aspx.cs" AutoEventWireup="false"
Inherits="ControlsBookWeb.Ch06.FancyLabelStyle" %>
<%@ Register TagPrefix="apressUC" TagName="ControlsBookHeader"
Src="..\ControlsBookHeader.ascx" %>
<%@ Register TagPrefix="apressUC" TagName="ControlsBookFooter"
Src="..\ControlsBookFooter.ascx" %>
<!DOCTYPE HTML PUBLIC "-//W3C//DTD HTML 4.0 Transitional//EN" >
<HTML>
  <HEAD>
    <title>Ch06 FancyLabelStyle</title>
    <meta content="Microsoft Visual Studio 7.0" name="GENERATOR">
    <meta content="C#" name="CODE_LANGUAGE">
    <meta content="JavaScript" name="vs_defaultClientScript">
    <meta content="http://schemas.microsoft.com/intellisense/ie5"
     name="vs_targetSchema">
    <LINK href="WebControlStyle.css" type="text/css" rel="stylesheet">
  </HEAD>
  <body MS_POSITIONING="FlowLayout">
    <form id="FancyLabelStyle" method="post" runat="server">
      <apressuc:controlsbookheader id="Header" runat="server"
        ChapterTitle="Control Styles" ChapterNumber="6">
      </apressuc:controlsbookheader>
```

```
    <H3>Ch06 FancyLabelStyle</H3>
    <apress:fancylabel id="DefaultLabel" runat="server" CssClass="grayborder"
      Text="No cursor set"></apress:fancylabel><br>
    <br>
    <apress:fancylabel id="AutoLabel" runat="server" CssClass="grayborder"
       Text="Auto cursor set"></apress:fancylabel><br>
    <br>
    <apress:fancylabel id="CrosshairLabel" runat="server" CssClass="grayborder"
        Text="Crosshair cursor set"></apress:fancylabel><br>
    <br>
    <apress:fancylabel id="HandLabel" runat="server" CssClass="grayborder"
         Text="Hand cursor set"></apress:fancylabel><br>
    <br>
    <apress:fancylabel id="HelpLabel" runat="server" CssClass="grayborder"
         Text="Help cursor set"></apress:fancylabel><br>
    <br>
    <apress:fancylabel id="MoveLabel" runat="server" CssClass="grayborder"
          Text="Move cursor set"></apress:fancylabel><br>
    <br>
    <apress:fancylabel id="TextLabel" runat="server" CssClass="grayborder"
           Text="Text cursort set"></apress:fancylabel><br>
    <br>
    <apress:fancylabel id="WaitLabel" runat="server" CssClass="grayborder"
           Text="Wait cursor set"></apress:fancylabel>
    <P><asp:button id="Button1" runat="server" Text="Submit"></asp:button></P>
    <apressuc:controlsbookfooter id="Footer" runat="server">
                                      </apressuc:controlsbookfooter></form>
  </body>
</HTML>
```

Listing 6-12. The FancyLabel Style Web Form Code-Behind Class File

```
using System;
using System.Collections;
using System.ComponentModel;
using System.Data;
using System.Drawing;
using System.Web;
using System.Web.SessionState;
using System.Web.UI;
using System.Web.UI.WebControls;
using System.Web.UI.HtmlControls;

namespace ControlsBookWeb.Ch06
{
    public class FancyLabelStyle : System.Web.UI.Page
    {
        protected ControlsBookLib.Ch06.FancyLabel AutoLabel;
        protected ControlsBookLib.Ch06.FancyLabel CrosshairLabel;
        protected ControlsBookLib.Ch06.FancyLabel HandLabel;
```

```
      protected ControlsBookLib.Ch06.FancyLabel MoveLabel;
      protected ControlsBookLib.Ch06.FancyLabel TextLabel;
      protected ControlsBookLib.Ch06.FancyLabel WaitLabel;
      protected System.Web.UI.WebControls.Button Button1;
      protected ControlsBookLib.Ch06.FancyLabel DefaultLabel;
      protected ControlsBookLib.Ch06.FancyLabel HelpLabel;

      private void Page_Load(object sender, System.EventArgs e)
      {
         if (!Page.IsPostBack)
         {
            AutoLabel.Cursor = ControlsBookLib.Ch06.CursorStyle.auto;
            CrosshairLabel.Cursor = ControlsBookLib.Ch06.CursorStyle.crosshair;
            HandLabel.Cursor = ControlsBookLib.Ch06.CursorStyle.hand;
            HelpLabel.Cursor = ControlsBookLib.Ch06.CursorStyle.help;
            MoveLabel.Cursor = ControlsBookLib.Ch06.CursorStyle.move;
            TextLabel.Cursor = ControlsBookLib.Ch06.CursorStyle.text;
            WaitLabel.Cursor = ControlsBookLib.Ch06.CursorStyle.wait;
         }
      }

      #region Web Form Designer generated code
      override protected void OnInit(EventArgs e)
      {
         //
         // CODEGEN: This call is required by the ASP.NET Web Form Designer.
         //
         InitializeComponent();
         base.OnInit(e);
      }

      /// <summary>
      /// Required method for Designer support - do not modify
      /// the contents of this method with the code editor.
      /// </summary>
      private void InitializeComponent()
      {
         this.Load += new System.EventHandler(this.Page_Load);

      }
      #endregion
   }
}
```

Figure 6-18 shows what the Web Form looks like when it's rendered.

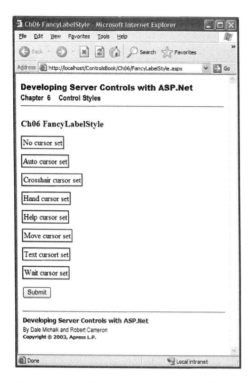

Figure 6-18. The FancyLabel Style Web Form

The following HTML fragment shows the rendered <SPAN> tags and their style attributes for the CSS cursor property:

```
<span id="AutoLabel" class="grayborder" style="cursor:auto;">
        Auto cursor set</span><br>
        <br>
        <span id="CrosshairLabel" class="grayborder" style="cursor:crosshair;">
        Crosshair cursor set</span><br>
        <br>
        <span id="HandLabel" class="grayborder" style="cursor:hand;">
                                        Hand cursor set</span><br>
        <br>
        <span id="HelpLabel" class="grayborder" style="cursor:help;">
                                        Help cursor set</span><br>
        <br>
        <span id="MoveLabel" class="grayborder" style="cursor:move;">
                                        Move cursor set</span><br>
        <br>
        <span id="TextLabel" class="grayborder" style="cursor:text;">
                                        Text cursor set</span><br>
        <br>
        <span id="WaitLabel" class="grayborder" style="cursor:wait;">
                                        Wait cursor set</span>
        <P><input type="submit" name="Button1" value="Submit" id="Button1" />
```

Summary

In this chapter, we started off with a discussion of how HTML documents have two aspects to them: content and appearance. HTML initially promoted tags such as `<FONT>`, `<B>`, and `<TABLE>` to enhance document appearance. This mixed content with the appearance, increasing code maintenance challenges. We next covered Cascading Style Sheets (CSS). CSS specifies a language to modify the appearance of an HTML document that permits separation of content from appearance. CSS style rules can be declared inline via the `style` attribute, in the document in the `<HEAD>` section via a `<STYLE>` block, or externally via the `<LINK>` tag.

Then we covered the new rendering model provided by `WebControl`. When you develop your own custom controls, we recommend starting with `WebControl` to leverage the capabilities it brings to the table such as styling and down-level browser support.

`WebControl` offers explicit support for CSS styling via the `ControlStyle` class, which exposes the `System.Web.UI.WebControls.Style` class, and the `Style` properties, which expose the `CssStyleCollection` class. `WebControl` provides top-level style properties that are directly linked to the properties of the `Style` class exposed by the `ControlStyle` property for easier access by web developers.

As part of the down-level browser support built into `WebControl`, ASP.NET is smart enough to choose `HtmlTextWriter` to emit CSS styles for up-level browsers or to choose `Html32TextWriter` to use HTML 3.2 style tags for down-level browsers.

Developers can expose multiple `Style` class instances via custom properties, but they must explicitly manage instance creation, ViewState persistence, and rendering. To implement a custom style class, start with the base `Style` class and then add additional custom style properties as necessary to meet requirements.

CHAPTER 7

Templates and Data Binding

THE VAST MAJORITY of web sites that provide dynamic content do so by rendering HTML that represents a data source to a database back-end system. A common task for web developers is to retrieve data and manually format it for output. To simplify this process, ASP.NET borrows the data-binding concept from the Visual Basic desktop world. *Data binding* dynamically merges a collection of data with a server control at runtime to produce HTML content representing the data source, as shown in Figure 7-1.

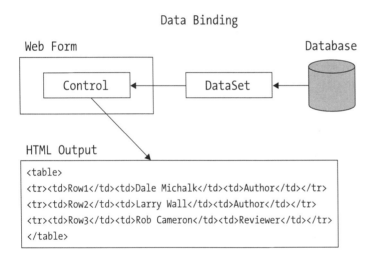

Figure 7-1. Data binding with server controls

Templates and data binding are naturally complementary. Data binding efficiently brings data into the control, and templates allow customization of how server controls or HTML elements display the data. Templates and data binding generally are brought together in more advanced controls, such as the ASP.NET DataGrid or Repeater server controls, making database-driven web development quick and easy. Pull a piece of data from the database via ADO.NET, bind it to a server control, configure its style properties and templates, and web developers can build a very appealing HTML display that appears to act like a Visual Basic form with data paging, alternate colors, and so on. The server control handles all the heavy lifting that would normally require a large amount of hand coding in plain old ASP.

In this chapter, we start off the examples with a template control named `Menu` that shows how to build a server control that lets you apply templates to hyperlinks. The next example control builds on the template work of the `Menu` control and adds data binding to the mix. This control is a clone of the ASP.NET `Repeater` control that puts templates and data binding in action together. We close the chapter by examining how to interact with the rich features of our `Repeater` control and demonstrating how to load templates dynamically from disk and create them programmatically.

Customized Control Content

HTML is a combination of content and appearance. The previous chapter showed how server controls customize the appearance of content through the use of style attributes that modify features such as font, color, size, or even placement of the HTML. In this chapter, we discuss how to modify the core content of the Web Form through two incredibly useful techniques: templates and data binding.

Templates allow web developers to specify the HTML elements and server controls that render as part of the main server control's output. The server control provides templates that are placeholders for content insertion, as illustrated in Figure 7-2. Templates allow customization of how a control renders simply by editing the .aspx page, without requiring a recompile of the Web Form. This flexibility permits web developers to customize look and feel without involving development. Otherwise, the Web Form developer would have to recompile the page every time the page needed a change, minor or not. Server control developers should look to add template functionality to custom controls to provide this level of flexibility when it makes sense.

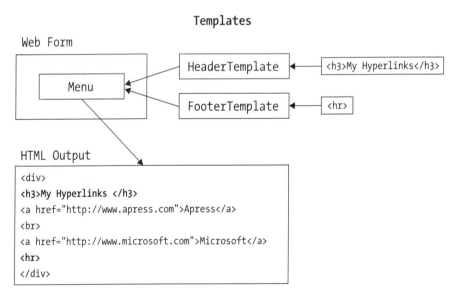

Figure 7-2. Templates with server controls

Using Control Templates

An ASP.NET template is a mix of HTML elements and ASP.NET controls that make up the layout for a particular area of a control. Templates increase the level of flexibility in a control and allow the developer/user to customize the graphical presentation of control content. The following code snippet is a hypothetical MyTemplate template:

```
<MyTemplate>
    <span>Raw HTML</span>
    <asp:Label id="Label1" runat="server" Text="My Server Control Label" />
</MyTemplate>
```

The template has begin and end tags with some content consisting of raw HTML intermixed with ASP.NET server controls. You normally specify the content declaratively, but you can load it from a file or instantiate it from a prebuilt template class at runtime for dynamic template use as we show later in this chapter when we test our version of the Repeater control.

In some ways, ASP.NET's support for templates partially removes the look-and-feel burden from the control developer. The control developer can focus on plumbing while the control user, or the graphic designer working in concert with the control user, can build pleasing templates that lay inside the control. Of course, the control developer can provide custom designers that can help with template creation, but this is not required. (We cover design-time functionality in Chapter 12.) The ability to customize a server control's template, whether manually or through a designer that data binds at runtime, is a welcomed advancement.

The ParseChildren Attribute

A control that provides support for templates must indicate to the ASP.NET page parser that it wishes to manage its child content by adding the ParseChildren attribute to its class declaration. This attribute instructs the page parser to handle child elements as control properties. For controls that inherit from System.Web.UI.WebControls.WebControl, this functionality comes for free via inheritance. You must add the attribute manually to controls based on System.Web.UI.Control.

The ParseChildren attribute has a property named ChildrenAsProperties that configures the parsing behavior. WebControl sets the ChildrenAsProperties property of the ParseChildren attribute to true by default, as shown in the following line of code. If you need to use a different value for a server control based on WebControl, remember to set the attribute explicitly to override the default behavior.

```
ParseChildrenAttribute(ChildrenAsProperties = true)
```

ParseChildrenAttribute also takes a shortened version to set the ChildrenAsProperties property:

```
ParseChildren(true)
```

The presence of the `ParseChildren` attribute set to true for `ChildrenAsProperties` causes the ASP.NET page parser to map top-level XML elements or tags under the server control directly to its exposed properties. The server control is responsible for providing the appropriate mapping, as illustrated in Figure 7-3.

[ParseChildren(ChildrenAsProperties=true)]

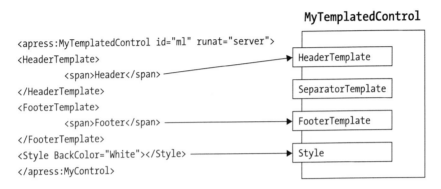

Figure 7-3. The ParseChildren *attribute with* ChildrenAsProperties=true

If the `ChildrenAsProperties` property value is set to false instead of true, ASP.NET attempts to process the child content of the outer control tags as embedded server controls, as shown in Figure 7-4. The default implementation of a control's `IParserAccessor` interface and its single `AddParsedSubObject` method adds those child server controls to the parent control's `Controls` collection. Literal text in between the tags becomes a `LiteralControl` server control instance.

[ParseChildren(ChildrenAsProperties=false)]

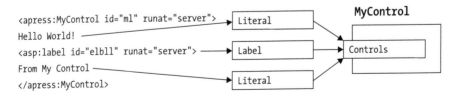

Figure 7-4. The ParseChildren *attribute with* ChildrenAsProperties=false

A Menu Control with Templates

The menu control implemented back in Chapter 3 displayed a simple list of HTML hyperlinks. We revisit its design to illustrate the use of UI templates. The hyperlinks will be retained while we provide several custom templates to render the output.

We build the `TemplateMenu` control as a composite `WebControl` with three templates: `HeaderTemplate`, `FooterTemplate`, and `SeparatorTemplate` (see Figure 7-5). As you would guess, `HeaderTemplate` and `FooterTemplate` allow developers to customize the top and bottom portions of the menu control. `SeparatorTemplate` provides customization of the content between hyperlinks. To keep things simple, the control uses an internal data source to provide content for rendering each hyperlink in the menu.

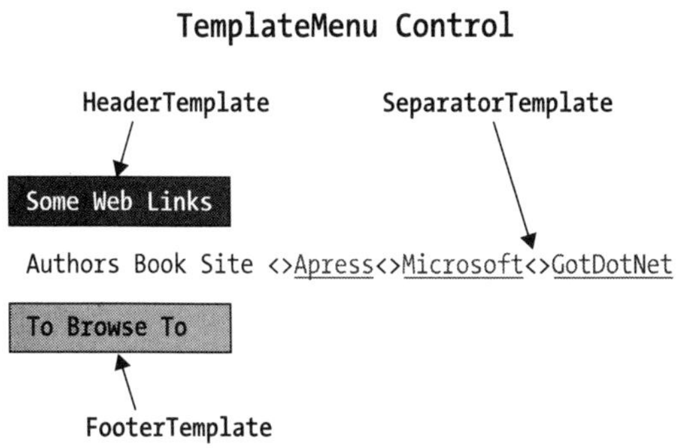

Figure 7-5. The TemplateMenu *control templates*

The first step in building `System.Web.UI.WebControls.WebControl`-based controls is deciding on the outer tag to contain all the control content. We chose the `<DIV>` tag as an enclosing tag for the menu control's hyperlinks and templates. The use of the `INamingContainer` interface is recommended for templated composite controls, because you will embed controls in templates that may conflict in their ID values. The following code shows our server control declaration:

```
[ToolboxData("<{0}:TemplateMenu
runat=server></{0}:TemplateMenu>"),Designer(typeof(TemplateMenuDesigner))]
public class TemplateMenu : WebControl, INamingContainer
{
    private ArrayList menuData;
    public TemplateMenu() : base(HtmlTextWriterTag.Div)
    {
        menuData = new ArrayList();
        menuData.Add(new MenuItemData("Authors Book Site","","",""));
        menuData.Add(new MenuItemData("Apress","http://www.apress.com","",""));
        menuData.Add(new MenuItemData("Microsoft","http://www.microsoft.com","",""));
        menuData.Add(new MenuItemData("GotDotNet","http://www.gotdotnet.com","",""));
    }
...
}
```

Notice the attributes applied to the TemplateMenu class. The ToolBoxData attribute provides a means to customize the initial HTML, such as initial or default values, when the control is dragged from the Visual Studio .NET Toolbox and placed on the design surface.

The Designer attribute specifies a custom designer that provides visual template editing in the Visual Studio design-time environment. We cover how to create custom designer classes in Chapter 12, but we use it here to demonstrate its functionality.

The constructor for our control fills a private ArrayList collection that holds the title and URL of each of the hyperlinks in the menu. Hard-coding the data in the control is replaced in later examples where data from a database is provided to the child tags.

MenuItemData is the type held in the private ArrayList. It has properties for the title of the hyperlink, the URL it directs the browser to, the URL to display it as an image instead of text, and the Target property to direct a particular frame to load the address from the hyperlink. We use it to store hyperlink data in all our menu examples.

The Template Properties

Because WebControl parses the child content into properties, we need to give the ASP.NET page parser a target that matches up with properties on our control when it encounters the child HeaderTemplate, FooterTemplate, and SeparatorTemplate tags in the .aspx page. The control does this by exposing ITemplate type properties of those exact names:

```
private ITemplate headerTemplate;
[Browsable(false),Description("The header template"),
PersistenceMode(PersistenceMode.InnerProperty),
TemplateContainer(typeof(BasicTemplateContainer))]
public ITemplate HeaderTemplate
{
    get
    {
        return headerTemplate;
    }
    set
    {
        headerTemplate = value;
    }
}
```

The preceding snippet is the portion of the control that implements the HeaderTemplate property and its storage. The HeaderTemplate property does a set and get on the private ITemplate type field named headerTemplate. ASP.NET is smart enough to query the type of the property and realize that it is working with ITemplate. It then follows a set of steps to instantiate a Template class and assign it to the property. The code for the FooterTemplate and SeparatorTemplate properties is identical to that of the HeaderTemplate property.

The final item that a template property needs is a TemplateContainer attribute to tell ASP.NET what type of control will contain the template. This wires up the control content inside the template to its outside container and allows value-added features such as data binding to occur.

The HeaderTemplate property uses the BasicTemplateContainer type to do this. BasicTemplateContainer is nothing more than a WebControl shell that renders a <SPAN> tag. The full class definition is as follows:

```
public class BasicTemplateContainer : WebControl, INamingContainer
{
   public BasicTemplateContainer() : base(HtmlTextWriterTag.Span)
   {
   }
}
```

Creating the Header Section

The TemplateMenu control is a composite control, so it needs to override the CreateChildControls method to add child controls to its Controls collection. The control abstracts this process by using a CreateControlHierarchy helper method to do the child creation work. CreateControlHierarchy contains code to add the templates and the hyperlinks as child controls:

```
override protected void CreateChildControls()
{
   Controls.Clear();
   CreateControlHierarchy();
}
```

CreateControlHierarchy starts out by working with the HeaderTemplate template. The first item that must always be checked is whether the template property has a value. This is detected by examining the template property for a null value:

```
if (HeaderTemplate != null)
{
   BasicTemplateContainer header = new BasicTemplateContainer();
   HeaderTemplate.InstantiateIn(header);
   Controls.Add(header);
   Controls.Add(new LiteralControl("<br>"));
}
```

If the template property is null, a common feature of server controls is to render a generic default HTML template so the output is consistent. The ASP.NET DataGrid control does this by rendering a simple, plain HTML table when it is bound to a data source without templates. For the HeaderTemplate template, we ignore the template and display nothing if it is null.

After it checks for a null value of the template property, the code next instantiates the container that will serve as the host for the template content. The TemplateMenu control wraps all templates into a <SPAN> HTML element via the use of a custom BasicTemplateContainer control based on System.Web.UI.WebControls.WebControl. To load the template content into the BasicTemplateContainer control, the ITemplate interface provides an InstantiateIn method that takes the container as a parameter, as shown in Figure 7-6.

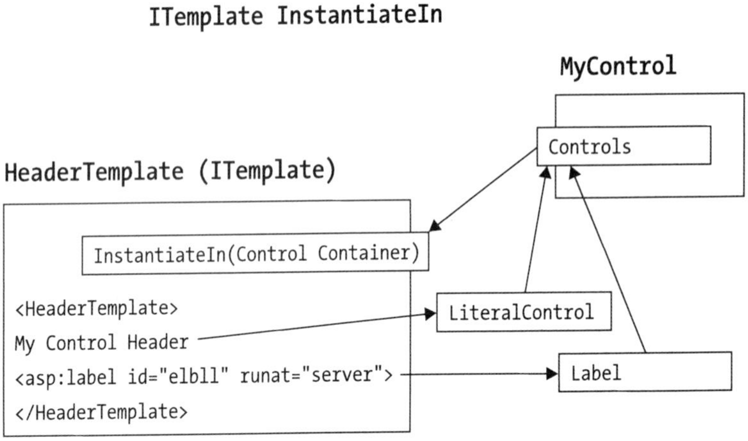

Figure 7-6. ITemplate *and* InstantiateIn

The use of InstantiateIn completes the work required for the header control container. The control code next adds the header to its child Controls collection. We also add a LiteralControl object that renders a <BR> tag to make the separation of the header from the hyperlinks a mandatory feature of the UI rendering of the TemplateMenu control.

Creating the Footer Section

The code for the FooterTemplate at the end of CreateControlHierarchy is almost identical to that of the HeaderTemplate. The only real difference besides a different template property is that it adds the <BR> tag before it adds the template content:

```
if (FooterTemplate != null)
{
    Controls.Add(new LiteralControl("<br>"));
    BasicTemplateContainer footer = new BasicTemplateContainer();
    FooterTemplate.InstantiateIn(footer);
    Controls.Add(footer);
}
```

Creating the Hyperlink Section

The middle of the code for the CreateControlHierarchy method adds the items in the menu using the ASP.NET HyperLink control. The data for the process is provided by the ArrayList collection exposed by the private menuData field that we instantiated in the constructor for our control.

The first task in building each hyperlink is iterating through the menuData ArrayList. We use a loop and a counter to help us track when we need to apply the MenuSeparatorTemplate template to separate the hyperlinks. The loop drives retrieval of the instances of the MenuItemData class from the collection and the execution of the CreateMenuItem helper method:

```
int count = menuData.Count;
for (int index = 0; index < count; index++)
{
    MenuItemData itemdata = (MenuItemData) menuData[index];
    CreateMenuItem(itemdata.Title, itemdata.Url,itemdata.ImageUrl, itemdata.Target);

    if (index != count-1)
    {
        if (SeparatorTemplate != null)
        {
            BasicTemplateContainer separator = new BasicTemplateContainer();
            SeparatorTemplate.InstantiateIn(separator);
            Controls.Add(separator);
        }
        else
        {
            Controls.Add(new LiteralControl(" | "));
        }
    }
}
```

CreateMenuItem creates an ASP.NET HyperLink control and adds it to the TemplateMenu control child controls:

```
private void CreateMenuItem(string title, string url,
                                    string target, string imageurl)
{
    HyperLink link = new HyperLink();
    link.Text = title;
    link.NavigateUrl = url;
    link.ImageUrl = imageurl;
    link.Target = target;
    Controls.Add(link);
}
```

The `SeparatorTemplate` code follows the lead of the `FooterTemplate` and `HeaderTemplate` templates, adding a control based on `BasicTemplateMenuContainer` to host the content of the template. What is unique in this piece of code is the addition of code to render a sensible separator via `LiteralControl` should the user decide not to wire in a `SeparatorTemplate` value in the .aspx page.

When you build a server control that supports templates, it is recommended that you ensure the control functions properly or at least degrades gracefully if templates are not specified.

The full version of the `TemplateMenu` control is shown in Listing 7-1. The container for the templates, `BasicTemplateMenuContainer`, is shown in Listing 7-2. Listing 7-3 contains the `MenuItemData` data class used to populate the menu hyperlinks.

Listing 7-1. The `TemplateMenu` *Control*

```
using System;
using System.Web;
using System.Web.UI;
using System.Web.UI.WebControls;
using System.Collections;
using System.ComponentModel;
using ControlsBookLib.Ch12.Design;

namespace ControlsBookLib.Ch07
{
    [ToolboxData("<{0}:TemplateMenu runat=server></{0}:TemplateMenu>"),
Designer(typeof(TemplateMenuDesigner))]
    public class TemplateMenu : WebControl, INamingContainer
    {
        private ArrayList menuData;
        public TemplateMenu() : base(HtmlTextWriterTag.Div)
        {
            menuData = new ArrayList();
            menuData.Add(new MenuItemData(
            "Author's Book Site","http://www.apress.com","",""));
            menuData.Add(new MenuItemData("Apress","http://www.apress.com","",""));
            menuData.Add(new MenuItemData("Microsoft",
                                "http://www.microsoft.com","",""));
            menuData.Add(new MenuItemData("GotDotNet",
                                "http://www.gotdotnet.com","",""));
        }

        private ITemplate headerTemplate;
        [Browsable(false),Description("The header template"),
                    PersistenceMode(PersistenceMode.InnerProperty),
        TemplateContainer(typeof(BasicTemplateContainer))]
        public ITemplate HeaderTemplate
        {
          get
          {
```

```
            return headerTemplate;
        }
        set
        {
            headerTemplate = value;
        }
    }

    private ITemplate footerTemplate;
    [Browsable(false),Description("The footer template"),
                    PersistenceMode(PersistenceMode.InnerProperty),
    TemplateContainer(typeof(BasicTemplateContainer))]
    public ITemplate FooterTemplate
    {
        get
        {
            return footerTemplate;
        }
        set
        {
            footerTemplate = value;
        }
    }

    private ITemplate separatorTemplate;
    [Browsable(false),Description("The separator template"),
                    PersistenceMode(PersistenceMode.InnerProperty),
    TemplateContainer(typeof(BasicTemplateContainer))]
    public ITemplate SeparatorTemplate
    {
        get
        {
            return separatorTemplate;
        }
        set
        {
            separatorTemplate = value;
        }
    }

    private void CreateMenuItem(string title, string url,
                                string target, string imageUrl)
    {
        HyperLink link = new HyperLink();
        link.Text = title;
        link.NavigateUrl = url;
        link.ImageUrl = imageUrl;
        link.Target = target;
        Controls.Add(link);
    }
```

```
private void CreateControlHierarchy()
{
   if (HeaderTemplate != null)
   {
      BasicTemplateContainer header = new BasicTemplateContainer();
      HeaderTemplate.InstantiateIn(header);
      Controls.Add(header);
      Controls.Add(new LiteralControl("<br>"));
   }

   int count = menuData.Count;
   for (int index = 0; index < count; index++)
   {
      MenuItemData itemdata = (MenuItemData) menuData[index];
      CreateMenuItem(itemdata.Title, itemdata.Url,
                           itemdata.ImageUrl, itemdata.Target);

      if (index != count-1)
      {
         if (SeparatorTemplate != null)
         {
            BasicTemplateContainer separator = new BasicTemplateContainer();
            SeparatorTemplate.InstantiateIn(separator);
            Controls.Add(separator);
         }
         else
         {
            Controls.Add(new LiteralControl(" | "));
         }
      }
   }

   if (FooterTemplate != null)
   {
      Controls.Add(new LiteralControl("<br>"));
      BasicTemplateContainer footer = new BasicTemplateContainer();
      FooterTemplate.InstantiateIn(footer);
      Controls.Add(footer);
   }
}

override protected void CreateChildControls()
{
   Controls.Clear();
   CreateControlHierarchy();
}

public override ControlCollection Controls
{
   get
   {
```

```
                EnsureChildControls();
                return base.Controls;
            }
        }

        public override void DataBind()
        {
            CreateChildControls();
            ChildControlsCreated = true;

            base.DataBind();
        }
    }
}
```

Listing 7-2. The BasicTemplateContainer *Control*

```
using System;
using System.Web;
using System.Web.UI;
using System.Web.UI.WebControls;

namespace ControlsBookLib.Ch07
{
    public class BasicTemplateContainer : WebControl, INamingContainer
    {
        public BasicTemplateContainer() : base(HtmlTextWriterTag.Span)
        {
        }
    }
}
```

Listing 7-3. The MenuItemData *Data Class*

```
using System;
using System.ComponentModel;

namespace ControlsBookLib.Ch07
{
    [TypeConverter(typeof(ExpandableObjectConverter))]
    public class MenuItemData
    {
        public MenuItemData()
        {
            this.Title = "";
            this.Url = "";
            this.ImageUrl = "";
            this.Target = "";
        }
```

```
public MenuItemData(string title, string url, string imageUrl, string target)
{
   this.Title = title;
   this.Url = url;
   this.ImageUrl = imageUrl;
   this.Target = target;
}

//Override this method to display just MenuItemData
//instead of fully qualified type
//in the custom collection editor
public override string ToString()
{
   return "MenuItemData";
}

private string title;
[NotifyParentProperty(true)]
public string Title
{
   get
   {
      return title;
   }
   set
   {
      title = value;
   }
}

private string url;
[NotifyParentProperty(true)]
public string Url
{
   get
   {
      return url;
   }
   set
   {
      url = value;
   }
}

public string imageUrl;
[NotifyParentProperty(true)]
public string ImageUrl
{
   get
   {
      return imageUrl;
```

```
        }
        set
        {
            imageUrl = value;
        }
    }

    public string target;
    [NotifyParentProperty(true)]
    public string Target
    {
        get
        {
            return target;
        }
        set
        {
            target = value;
        }
    }
  }
}
```

Viewing the TemplateMenu Control

The Web Form created for viewing the TemplateMenu control could not be simpler. It consists of a single control on the form—that's it. The following templates exercise the UI customization features of the control:

```
<apress:templatemenu id="menu1" runat="server" Width="378px" Height="43px" >
    <HeaderTemplate>
        <SPAN style="FONT-WEIGHT: bold; COLOR: white;
                    BACKGROUND-COLOR: blue">Some web links.</SPAN>
    </HeaderTemplate>
    <SeparatorTemplate>
        &lt;&gt;
    </SeparatorTemplate>
    <FooterTemplate>
        <SPAN style="FONT-WEIGHT: bold; COLOR: white;
                    BACKGROUND-COLOR: red">To browse to</SPAN>
    </FooterTemplate>
</apress:templatemenu>
```

We can edit the templates for the Web Form by clicking the HTML tab in Visual Studio. The .NET Framework also provides the ability to visually edit templates, and the Designer(typeof(TemplateMenuDesigner))] attribute applied to the TemplateMenu class provides this support for the TemplateMenu server control.

This custom designer, which we cover in detail in Chapter 12, adds a menu item to the context menu for the control. Right-click the TemplateMenu control, select Edit Template, and then choose the template you want to edit. This brings up a visual UI for the template where you can drag and drop other ASP.NET controls, such as an image control for the separator template, and edit the style for the template in the Properties tool window. Figure 7-7 shows the results of our control after customizing its templates. Listings 7-4 and 7-5 contain the .aspx file and code-behind class for the TemplateMenu Web Form, respectively.

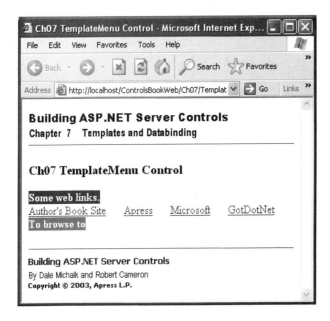

Figure 7-7. The TemplateMenu *Web Form displayed in a browser*

Listing 7-4. The TemplateMenu *Web Form .aspx Page File*

```
<%@ Register TagPrefix="apress" Namespace="ControlsBookLib.Ch07"
Assembly="ControlsBookLib" %>
<%@ Page language="c#" Codebehind="TemplateMenu.aspx.cs"
AutoEventWireup="false" Inherits="ControlsBookWeb.Ch07.TemplateMenu" %>
<%@ Register TagPrefix="apressUC" TagName="ControlsBookHeader"
Src="..\ControlsBookHeader.ascx" %>
<%@ Register TagPrefix="apressUC" TagName="ControlsBookFooter"
Src="..\ControlsBookFooter.ascx" %>
<!DOCTYPE HTML PUBLIC "-//W3C//DTD HTML 4.0 Transitional//EN" >
<HTML>
    <HEAD>
        <title>Ch07 TemplateMenu Control</title>
        <meta content="Microsoft Visual Studio 7.0" name="GENERATOR">
        <meta content="C#" name="CODE_LANGUAGE">
        <meta content="JavaScript" name="vs_defaultClientScript">
```

```
        <meta content=http://schemas.microsoft.com/intellisense/ie5
                name="vs_targetSchema">
    </HEAD>
    <body MS_POSITIONING="FlowLayout">
        <form id="TemplateMenu" method="post" runat="server">
            <apressUC:ControlsBookHeader id="Header" runat="server" ChapterNumber="7"
                    ChapterTitle="Templates and Data Binding" />
            <h3>Ch07 TemplateMenu Control</h3>
            <apress:templatemenu id="menu1" runat="server" Width="378px"
                    Height="43px" >
                <HeaderTemplate>
                    <SPAN style="FONT-WEIGHT: bold; COLOR: white;
                      BACKGROUND-COLOR: blue">Some web links.</SPAN>
                </HeaderTemplate>
                <SeparatorTemplate>
                    &lt;&gt;
                </SeparatorTemplate>
                <FooterTemplate>
                    <SPAN style="FONT-WEIGHT: bold; COLOR: white;
                            BACKGROUND-COLOR: red">To browse to</SPAN>
                </FooterTemplate>
            </apress:templatemenu>
            <br>
            <apressUC:ControlsBookFooter id="Footer" runat="server" />
        </form>
    </body>
</HTML>
```

Listing 7-5. The TemplateMenu *Code-Behind Class File*

```csharp
using System;

namespace ControlsBookWeb.Ch07
{
    public class TemplateMenu : System.Web.UI.Page
    {
        protected ControlsBookLib.Ch07.TemplateMenu menu1;

        private void Page_Load(object sender, System.EventArgs e)
        {

        }

        #region Web Form Designer generated code
        override protected void OnInit(EventArgs e)
        {
            //
            // CODEGEN: This call is required by the ASP.NET Web Form Designer.
            //
            InitializeComponent();
```

```
        base.OnInit(e);
    }


    /// <summary>
    /// Required method for Designer support - do not modify
    /// the contents of this method with the code editor.
    /// </summary>
    private void InitializeComponent()
    {
        this.Load += new System.EventHandler(this.Page_Load);


    }
    #endregion
}
}
```

Checking the Rendered HTML

The HTML rendered by the `TemplateMenu` control verifies that the control has successfully included the templates in its output:

```
<div id="menu1">
<span><span style="COLOR: white; BACKGROUND-COLOR: blue;
              FONT-WEIGHT:BOLD">Some web links.</span></span><br>
<a>Authors Book Site</a><span> <> </span>
<a href="http://www.apress.com">Apress</a><span> <> </span>
<a href="http://www.microsoft.com">Microsoft</a><span> <> </span>
<a href="http://www.gotdotnet.com">GotDotNet</a><span> <> </span><br>
<span><span style="COLOR: white; BACKGROUND-COLOR: red; FONT-WEIGHT:BOLD">
                     To browse to</span></span>
</div>
```

The `HeaderTemplate` and `FooterTemplate` templates go into the final HTML verbatim. The code that builds the hyperlinks correctly inserts the `SeparatorTemplate` template with the `<>` characters as well. The next section discusses how to store data as child tags that are part of a server control.

Parsing Data from the Control Tags

The `TemplateMenu` control has one major limitation. The data it uses to display the hyperlinks is hard-coded in its constructor. A user of this control must have the source code to modify what is displayed. This is not the best way to go about building controls that are flexible and adaptable. Giving web developers a way to pass in the necessary data is a much better approach and is what we cover in the sections that follow.

The approach that we take to add customizable data to the control is to use child tags that pass in the data to the control. This is similar to the method used by the ASP.NET list controls, such as `DropDownList` and `CheckBoxList`, which support the use of the `asp:listitem` tag to pass in data declaratively. The server control we build in the next section uses the ParseChildren attribute. In the following section, we build a server control that shows how to customize this process further using a ControlBuilder class.

The TagDataMenu Control

The TagDataMenu control is an example control we create in this section that reads its child tag values to build its collection of data for hyperlinks. It does this by taking advantage of a feature of the ParseChildren attribute that tells the ASP.NET page parser to treat child content as items to be added to a collection.

The following attribute shows the ChildrenAsProperties property being set on the ParseChildren attribute, along with a DefaultProperty property:

```
[ParseChildren(ChildrenAsProperties=true, DefaultProperty="MenuItems")]
```

The following shorthand code does the same thing:

```
[ParseChildren(true, "MenuItems")]
```

Setting the DefaultProperty property in the ParseChildren attribute causes the ASP.NET page parser to look at all the child XML content of the server control as items in a collection. The items are created by the page parser and added to the collection specified by the MenuItems property. The type of the item in the collection is determined by the name of the child tag. ASP.NET looks for that type name in the project and creates an object for it, filling in its properties according to the tag attributes.

Notice the other attribute on TagDataMenu:

```
Designer(typeof(CompCntrlDesigner))
```

This attribute enables design-time display of the UI in the Visual Studio .NET Designer by forcing child control creation on the control that has this attribute applied. We discuss design-time behavior in Chapter 12.

TagDataMenu configures itself for using a MenuItems collection by setting up its ParseChildren attribute accordingly:

```
[ParseChildren(true, "MenuItems"),Designer(typeof(CompCntrlDesigner))]
[ToolboxData("<{0}:TagDataMenu runat=server></{0}:TagDataMenu>")]
public class TagDataMenu : WebControl, INamingContainer
{
    public TagDataMenu() : base(HtmlTextWriterTag.Div)
    {
    }
    …
}
```

Figure 7-8 illustrates the relationship between the `TagDataMenu` control and its `MenuItems` collection.

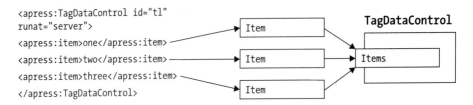

Figure 7-8. The `ParseChildren` *attribute with the* `Default` *property*

The read-only `MenuItems` property exposed by the control is an instance of a custom collection type named `MenuItemDataCollection`. This collection is populated by ASP.NET based on the control's child tag data:

```
private MenuItemDataCollection menuData;
[DesignerSerializationVisibility(DesignerSerializationVisibility.Content),
PersistenceMode(PersistenceMode.InnerDefaultProperty),NotifyParentProperty(true)]
public MenuItemDataCollection MenuItems
    {
      get
      {
        if (menuData == null)
        {
            menuData = new MenuItemDataCollection();
        }
        return menuData;
      }
    }
```

Permitting data entry in child tags has one trade-off: a lack of template support. ASP.NET assumes that all the child tags go into the `DefaultProperty` collection, and it will not parse if it sees templates. For controls as simple as `TagDataMenu`, this is a reasonable trade-off. More advanced controls, such as the `Repeater` control we build later in the chapter, will expose a property that allows web developers to set the data source programmatically.

The slimmed-down `CreateControlHierarchy` method doesn't have to worry about template building. We're able to reuse `CreateMenuItem` from the `TemplateMenu` control. For menu link separation, we use the pipe character (|) as the separator this time around:

```
override protected void CreateChildControls()
{
   Controls.Clear();
   CreateControlHierarchy();
}

private void CreateControlHierarchy()
{
   int count = menuData.Count;
   for (int index = 0; index < count; index++)
   {
      MenuItemData itemdata = (MenuItemData) menuData[index];
      CreateMenuItem(itemdata.Title, itemdata.Url,
         itemdata.ImageUrl, itemdata.Target);

      if ((count > 1) && (index < count -1))
      {
         Controls.Add(new LiteralControl(" | "));
      }
   }
}
```

Listing 7-6 presents the full code for the TagDataMenu control.

Listing 7-6. The TagDataMenu *Control Class File*

```
using System;
using System.Web;
using System.Web.UI;
using System.Web.UI.WebControls;
using System.Collections;
using System.ComponentModel;
using ControlsBookLib.Ch12.Design;

namespace ControlsBookLib.Ch07
{
   // ParseChildren attribute tells the ASP.NET page parser to treat
   // child content as items to be added to a collection.
   [ParseChildren(true, "MenuItems"),Designer(typeof(CompCntrlDesigner))]
   [ToolboxData("<{0}:TagDataMenu runat=server></{0}:TagDataMenu>")]
   public class TagDataMenu : WebControl, INamingContainer
   {
      public TagDataMenu() : base(HtmlTextWriterTag.Div)
      {
      }

      private MenuItemDataCollection menuData;

      // This collection is automatically populated by ASP.NET because of the
      // ParseChildren attribute on the class
```

```
[DesignerSerializationVisibility(DesignerSerializationVisibility.Content),
Description("Collection of MenuItemData objects for display"),
PersistenceMode(PersistenceMode.InnerDefaultProperty),
                                     NotifyParentProperty(true)]
public MenuItemDataCollection MenuItems
{
   get
   {
      if (menuData == null)
      {
         menuData = new MenuItemDataCollection();
      }
      return menuData;
   }
}

private void CreateMenuItem(string title, string url,
                                     string target, string imageUrl)
{
   HyperLink link = new HyperLink();
   link.Text = title;
   link.NavigateUrl = url;
   link.ImageUrl = imageUrl;
   link.Target = target;
   Controls.Add(link);
}

override protected void CreateChildControls()
{
   Controls.Clear();
   CreateControlHierarchy();
}

private void CreateControlHierarchy()
{
   int count = MenuItems.Count;
   for (int index = 0; index < count; index++)
   {
      MenuItemData itemdata = (MenuItemData) MenuItems[index];
      CreateMenuItem(itemdata.Title, itemdata.Url,
                        itemdata.ImageUrl, itemdata.Target);

      if ((count > 1) && (index < count -1))
      {
         Controls.Add(new LiteralControl(" | "));
      }
   }
}

public override ControlCollection Controls
{
```

```
      get
      {
        EnsureChildControls();
        return base.Controls;
      }
    }
  }
}
}
```

We mentioned previously that the MenuItems property has a custom collection named MenuItemDataCollection as its type. This type provides us with the ability to add a collection editor at design time to permit editing of menu item data via a dialog box in much the same way as the built-in ASP.NET server controls that have InnerDefaultProperty persistence. Listing 7-7 has the full code for MenuItemDataCollection.

Listing 7-7. The MenuItemDataCollection *Class File*

```
using System;
using System.Collections;
using System.ComponentModel;
using System.Drawing.Design;
using ControlsBookLib.Ch12.Design;

namespace ControlsBookLib.Ch07
{
    [Editor(typeof(ControlsBookLib.Ch12.Design.MenuItemDataCollectionEditor),
            typeof(UITypeEditor))]
    public sealed class MenuItemDataCollection : IList
    {
        private ArrayList menuItems;
        internal MenuItemDataCollection()
        {
            menuItems = new ArrayList();
        }

        public MenuItemData this[int index]
        {
            get
            {
                return (MenuItemData)menuItems[index];
            }
        }

        object IList.this[int index]
        {
            get
            {
                return menuItems[index];
            }
```

```
      set
      {
         menuItems[index] = (MenuItemData)value;
      }
   }

   public int Add(MenuItemData item)
   {
      if (item == null)
      {
         throw new ArgumentNullException("item");
      }

      menuItems.Add(item);
      return menuItems.Count - 1;
   }

   public void Clear()
   {
      menuItems.Clear();
   }

   public bool Contains(MenuItemData item)
   {
      if (item == null)
      {
         return false;
      }
      return menuItems.Contains(item);
   }

   public int IndexOf(MenuItemData item)
   {
      if (item == null)
      {
         throw new ArgumentNullException("item");
      }
      return menuItems.IndexOf(item);
   }

   public void Insert(int index, MenuItemData item)
   {
      if (item == null)
      {
         throw new ArgumentNullException("item");
      }

      menuItems.Insert(index,item);
   }

   public void RemoveAt(int index)
```

```
{
   menuItems.RemoveAt(index);
}

public void Remove(MenuItemData item)
{
   if (item == null)
   {
      throw new ArgumentNullException("item");
   }

   int index = IndexOf(item);
   if (index >= 0)
   {
      RemoveAt(index);
   }
}

public IEnumerator GetEnumerator()
{
   return menuItems.GetEnumerator();
}

[DesignerSerializationVisibility(DesignerSerializationVisibility.Hidden),
    Browsable(false) ]
public int Count
{
   get
   {
      return menuItems.Count;
   }
}

public void CopyTo(Array array, int index)
{
   menuItems.CopyTo(array,index);
}

[DesignerSerializationVisibility(DesignerSerializationVisibility.Hidden),
 Browsable(false)]
public bool IsSynchronized
{
   get
   {
      return false;
   }
}

[DesignerSerializationVisibility(DesignerSerializationVisibility.Hidden),
 Browsable(false) ]
public object SyncRoot
```

```
        {
          get
          {
            return this;
          }
        }

        bool IList.IsReadOnly
        {
          get
          {
            return false;
          }
        }

        bool IList.IsFixedSize
        {
          get
          {
            return false;
          }
        }

        int IList.Add(object item)
        {
          if (item == null)
          {
            throw new ArgumentNullException("item");
          }
          if (!(item is MenuItemData))
          {
            throw new ArgumentException("item must be a MenuItemData");
          }

          return Add((MenuItemData)item);
        }

        bool IList.Contains(object item)
        {
          return Contains(item as MenuItemData);
        }

        void IList.Clear()
        {
          Clear();
        }

        int IList.IndexOf(object item)
        {
          if (item == null)
          {
```

```
                throw new ArgumentNullException("item");
            }
            if (!(item is MenuItemData))
            {
                throw new ArgumentException("item must be a MenuItemData");
            }

            return IndexOf((MenuItemData)item);
        }

        void IList.RemoveAt(int index)
        {
            RemoveAt(index);
        }

        void IList.Remove(object item)
        {
            if (item == null)
            {
                throw new ArgumentNullException("item");
            }
            if (!(item is MenuItemData))
            {
                throw new ArgumentException("item must be a MenuItemData");
            }

            Remove((MenuItemData)item);
        }

        void IList.Insert(int index, object item)
        {
            if (item == null)
            {
                throw new ArgumentNullException("item");
            }
            if (!(item is MenuItemData))
            {
                throw new ArgumentException("item must be a MenuItemData");
            }

            Insert(index, (MenuItemData)item);
        }
    }
}
```

Notice the attribute applied to our custom collection type:

```
[Editor(typeof(ControlsBookLib.Ch12.Design.MenuItemDataCollectionEditor),
 typeof(UITypeEditor))]
```

This attribute makes the custom UI type editor available at design time. For collection properties that we do not want to be visible in the Visual Studio .NET Properties tool window, we add this attribute:

```
[Browsable(false)]
```

For collection properties that we do not want to be serialized as data, we add this attribute:

```
[DesignerSerializationVisibility(DesignerSerializationVisibility.Hidden)]
```

The DesignerSerializationVisibility attribute indicates whether the value for a property is Visible and should be persisted in initialization code; or whether it is Hidden and should not be persisted in initialization code; or whether it consists of Content, which should have initialization code generated for each public, not hidden property of the object assigned to the property. The default value if the attribute is not present is Visible, and the Visual Studio .NET Designer at design time will attempt to serialize the property based on the property's type. The MenuItems property on the TagDataMenu class is an example of a property with visibility set to Content:

```
[DesignerSerializationVisibility(DesignerSerializationVisibility.Content),
PersistenceMode(PersistenceMode.InnerDefaultProperty),NotifyParentProperty(true)]
public MenuItemDataCollection MenuItems
    {

    }
...
}
```

We now move on to discuss how to customize the parsing process using a ControlBuilder class. This option provides for complete customization of the parsing process, as you will see in the next section.

The MenuBuilder Control

The MenuBuilder control demonstrates a second technique for reading the child tags and creating the menu data. It uses a feature of ASP.NET that allows for complete customization of the control parsing process by implementing a custom ControlBuilder class. The implementation of the MenuBuilder control will be identical to that of the TagDataMenu control, except for the ability to manage the tag parsing process.

The normal default ControlBuilder that is linked to classes that derive from the base System.Web.UI.Control class performs the following tasks:

- Parses the child XML content into control types

- Creates the child control

- Calls on the `IParserAccessor` interface method `AddParsedSubObject` to add the child control to the server control's `Controls` collection, as shown in Figure 7-9

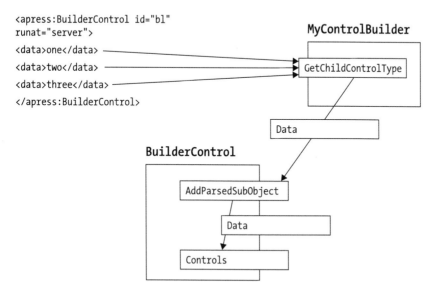

Figure 7-9. `ControlBuilder` *and the* `IParserAccessor.AddParsedSubObject` *default*

A custom `ControlBuilder` gets the opportunity to completely customize the way the ASP.NET page parser parses the child content. This is configured by adding the `ControlBuilder` attribute. The class declaration portion of the `BuilderMenu` control looks like this:

```
[ParseChildren(false)]
[ControlBuilder(typeof(MenuControlBuilder))]
[ToolboxData("<{0}:BuilderMenu runat=server></{0}:BuilderMenu>")]
public class BuilderMenu : WebControl, INamingContainer
{
    public BuilderMenu() : base(HtmlTextWriterTag.Div)
    {

    }
…
}
```

The first thing to note is that the ParseChildren attribute is set to false. This means that we want the ControlBuilder to make the decisions on how the child XML tags are handled. The attribute of interest is the ControlBuilder attribute, which is passed the System.Type reference of the MenuControlBuilder class.

MenuControlBuilder derives from the System.Web.UI.ControlBuilder class and overrides two methods to customize the parsing process. The most common reason to create your own ControlBuilder is to override the GetChildControlType method so that the control to which the builder is applied can determine how to map between a child tag and the class that needs to be created to represent the child tag during server-side processing:

```
public class MenuControlBuilder : ControlBuilder
{
public override Type GetChildControlType(String tagName,          Dictionary attributes)
{
    if (String.Compare(tagName, "data", true) == 0)
    {
      return typeof(MenuItemData);
    }

    return null;
}
```

MenuControlBuilder looks for child tags with a name of "data". If it finds a match, it returns the MenuItemData type back to the BuilderMenu control to which it is linked. This assumes that the data tag has the appropriate attributes that map to the MenuItemData type's properties.

The other method that the MenuControlBuilder class overrides is AppendLiteralString. We give this method an empty implementation to ignore the literal content that is between the tags that hold the data.

```
public override void AppendLiteralString(string s)
{
    // Ignores literals between tags
}
```

There are other features of ControlBuilder parsing that we left out in this demonstration. For example, ControlBuilders can parse the raw string content between the server control's parent tags and provide support for nested ControlBuilders to process child control content. Please refer to the .NET Framework documentation for more information.

Going back to the MenuBuilder control, let's look at the implementation of IParserAccessor and the AddParsedSubObject method. The following code simply adds the data object passed into its internal ArrayList collection exposed by the menuData field. The only check it performs is a type check to ensure the right type instance is being passed from the ControlBuilder associated with the control.

```
protected override void AddParsedSubObject(Object obj)
{
    if (obj is MenuItemData)
    {
        menuData.Add(obj);
    }
}
```

Listings 7-8 and 7-9 show the final listing of BuilderMenu and its helper MenuControlBuilder.

Listing 7-8. The BuilderMenu *Control Class File*

```
using System;
using System.Web;
using System.Web.UI;
using System.Web.UI.WebControls;
using System.Collections;

namespace ControlsBookLib.Ch07
{
    [ParseChildren(false)]
    [ControlBuilder(typeof(MenuControlBuilder))]
    [ToolboxData("<{0}:BuilderMenu runat=server></{0}:BuilderMenu>")]
    public class BuilderMenu : WebControl, INamingContainer
    {
        public BuilderMenu() : base(HtmlTextWriterTag.Div)
        {
        }

        private ArrayList menuData = new ArrayList();
        public ArrayList MenuItems
        {
            get
            {
                return menuData;
            }
        }

        protected override void AddParsedSubObject(Object obj)
        {
            if (obj is MenuItemData)
            {
                menuData.Add(obj);
            }
        }

        private void CreateMenuItem(string title, string url, string target,
                                   string imageUrl)
        {
```

```
        HyperLink link = new HyperLink();
        link.Text = title;
        link.NavigateUrl = url;
        link.ImageUrl = imageUrl;
        link.Target = target;
        Controls.Add(link);
    }

    private void CreateControlHierarchy()
    {
        int count = menuData.Count;
        for (int index = 0; index < count; index++)
        {
            MenuItemData itemdata = (MenuItemData) menuData[index];
            CreateMenuItem(itemdata.Title, itemdata.Url,
                itemdata.ImageUrl, itemdata.Target);

            if ((count > 1) && (index < count -1))
            {
                Controls.Add(new LiteralControl(" | "));
            }
        }
    }

    override protected void CreateChildControls()
    {
        CreateControlHierarchy();
    }

    public override ControlCollection Controls
    {
        get
        {
            EnsureChildControls();
            return base.Controls;
        }
    }
  }
}
```

Listing 7-9. The MenuControlBuilder *Control Builder Class File*

```
using System;
using System.Web;
using System.Web.UI;
using System.Collections;

namespace ControlsBookLib.Ch07
{
    public class MenuControlBuilder : ControlBuilder
```

```
{
    public override Type GetChildControlType(String tagName,
        IDictionary attributes)
    {
        if (String.Compare(tagName, "data", true) == 0)
        {
            return typeof(MenuItemData);
        }

        return null;
    }

    public override void AppendLiteralString(string s)
    {
        s.Trim();
        // Ignores literals between tags.
    }
}
}
```

Viewing the Tag Parsing Menu Controls

The Tag Parsing Menu Web Form demonstrates both of our declaratively loaded menu controls in action. In Visual Studio .NET, if you click the TagDataMenu control and select the MenuItems property, you will see a button that if clicked will bring up a UI collection editor for the MenuItemData collection. For the TagDataMenu control, the child tags take the name of the MenuItemData hyperlink data class:

```
<apress:tagdatamenu id="menu1" runat="server">
  <apress:MenuItemData title="Apress" url="http://www.apress.com" imageurl=""
            target="" />
  <apress:MenuItemData title="Microsoft" url="http://www.microsoft.com"
            imageurl="" target="" />
  <apress:MenuItemData title="GotDotNet" url="http://www.gotdotnet.com"
            imageurl="" target="" />
</apress:tagdatamenu>
```

The BuilderMenu control needs tags with the "data" name so that the MenuControlBuilder grabs each item and passes it into the control:

```
<apress:buildermenu id="menu2" runat="server">
  <data title="Apress" url="http://www.apress.com" imageurl="" target="" />
  <data title="Microsoft" url="http://www.microsoft.com" imageurl="" target="" />
  <data title="GotDotNet" url="http://www.gotdotnet.com" imageurl="" target="" />
</apress:buildermenu>
```

Figure 7-10 shows that the final result for the two controls in the browser after they are rendered is identical.

Figure 7-10. The Tag Parsing Menu Web Form displayed in a browser

Listings 7-10 and 7-11 contain the full code for the Web Form.

Listing 7-10. The TemplateMenu *Web Form .aspx Page File*

```
<%@ Register TagPrefix="apress" Namespace="ControlsBookLib.Ch07"
Assembly="ControlsBookLib" %>
<%@ Page language="c#" Codebehind="TagParsingMenus.aspx.cs" AutoEventWireup="false"
Inherits="ControlsBookWeb.Ch07.TagParsingMenuControls" %>
<%@ Register TagPrefix="apressUC" TagName="ControlsBookHeader"
Src="..\ControlsBookHeader.ascx" %>
<%@ Register TagPrefix="apressUC" TagName="ControlsBookFooter"
Src="..\ControlsBookFooter.ascx" %>
<!DOCTYPE HTML PUBLIC "-//W3C//DTD HTML 4.0 Transitional//EN" >
<HTML>
  <HEAD>
    <title>Ch07 Tag-Parsing Menu Controls</title>
    <meta content="Microsoft Visual Studio 7.0" name="GENERATOR">
    <meta content="C#" name="CODE_LANGUAGE">
    <meta content="JavaScript" name="vs_defaultClientScript">
    <meta content="http://schemas.microsoft.com/intellisense/ie5"
                  name="vs_targetSchema">
  </HEAD>
  <body MS_POSITIONING="FlowLayout">
    <form id="TagParsingMenuControls" method="post" runat="server">
      <apressuc:controlsbookheader id="Header" runat="server"
      ChapterTitle="Templates and Data Binding"
```

```
        ChapterNumber="7"></apressuc:controlsbookheader>
        <h3>Ch07 Tag-Parsing Menu Controls</h3>
        <apress:tagdatamenu id="menu1" runat="server">
          <apress:MenuItemData title="Apress" url="http://www.apress.com"
            imageurl="" target="" />
          <apress:MenuItemData title="Microsoft" url="http://www.microsoft.com"
            imageurl="" target="" />
          <apress:MenuItemData title="GotDotNet" url="http://www.gotdotnet.com"
            imageurl="" target="" />
        </apress:tagdatamenu>
        <apress:buildermenu id="menu2" runat="server">
          <data title="Apress" url="http://www.apress.com" imageurl="" target="" />
          <data title="Microsoft" url="http://www.microsoft.com" imageurl=""
            target="" />
          <data title="GotDotNet" url="http://www.gotdotnet.com" imageurl=""
            target="" />
        </apress:buildermenu>
        <apressuc:controlsbookfooter id="Footer"
         runat="server"></apressuc:controlsbookfooter></form>
  </body>
</HTML>
```

Listing 7-11. The Tag Parsing Menu Web Form Code-Behind Class File

```
using System;

namespace ControlsBookWeb.Ch07
{
    public class TagParsingMenuControls : System.Web.UI.Page
    {
        protected ControlsBookLib.Ch07.BuilderMenu menu2;
        protected ControlsBookLib.Ch07.TagDataMenu menu1;

        private void Page_Load(object sender, System.EventArgs e)
        {

        }

        #region Web Form Designer generated code
        override protected void OnInit(EventArgs e)
        {
            //
            // CODEGEN: This call is required by the ASP.NET Web Form Designer.
            //
            InitializeComponent();
            base.OnInit(e);
        }

        /// <summary>
        /// Required method for Designer support - do not modify
```

```
/// the contents of this method with the code editor.
/// </summary>
private void InitializeComponent()
{
    this.Load += new System.EventHandler(this.Page_Load);

}
#endregion
    }
}
```

Control Data Binding

Using server control tags is a convenient way to declaratively configure simple server controls such as the menu controls we developed. For complex, dynamically loaded data, we need to take a more sophisticated path. The tried-and-true approach to passing data into a server control is through data binding, which we cover in this section. This is a complex topic, but we present plenty of code in the following subsections to help you get started with adding data binding capabilities to your own controls.

Data binding comes in several different forms. *Simple* data binding occurs when a data-binding expression is evaluated to a single value and that value is used to set the property of a server control. The following code snippet binds the result of a method named MyDataBoundMethod on a Web Form to the Text property of an ASP.NET server control:

```
<asp:Label id="MyLabel" runat="server" Text="<%= MyDataBoundMethod() %> />
```

Repeated or *complex* data binding occurs when a collection of multirow data is bound to a list control that iterates through its contents to generate HTML output. The classic example of this is binding a DataSet to an ASP.NET DataGrid control to generate an HTML table representing the data. This is also the case when we take a simple collection such as an ArrayList full of strings and bind it to a DropDownList control.

The Repeater Control

The case study we present to help explain data binding creates a replica of the Repeater control built into ASP.NET. The Repeater control is a data-bound server control that takes advantage of templates to generate the display for the data source. It is a complex control that requires a fair amount of source code, but this effort is worth the ease of use data binding provides to the user of a data-bindable server control.

The Repeater control includes five templates: HeaderTemplate, FooterTemplate, SeparatorTemplate, ItemTemplate, and AlternatingItemTemplate. We provided the first three templates types in our TemplateMenu control. Those three templates do not take advantage of data binding to keep things simple. We are adding data binding capabilities to the ItemTemplate and AlternatingItemTemplate templates.

The `ItemTemplate` and `AlternatingItemTemplate` templates are applied to each row of data retrieved from the data source based on an alternating pattern. The `SeparatorTemplate` template is placed between the item templates to keep things looking nice. The diagram in Figure 7-11 shows how the templates determine the output of the control rendering process.

Repeater Control

Name	Title	Company	
			← HeaderTemplate
Maria Anders	Sales Representative	Alfreds Futterkiste	
Ana Trujillo	Owner	Ana Trujillo Emparedados y helados	
Antonio Moreno	Owner	Antonio Moreno Taqueria	← ItemTemplate
Thomas Hardy	Sales Representative	Around the Horn	
Christina Berglund	Order Administrator	Berglunds snabbköp	
Hanna Moos	Sales Representative	Blauer See Delikatessen	← AlternatingItemTemplate
Frédérique Citeaux	Marketing Manager	Blondesddsl pére et fils	
Martin Sommer	Owner	Bólido Comidas preparadas	
Laurence Lebihan	Owner	Bon app'	
Elizabeth Lincoln	Accounting Manager	Bottom-Dollar Markets	
Victoria Ashworth	Sales Representative	B's Beverages	
			← FooterTemplate

Figure 7-11. The Repeater *control and its templates*

Our `Repeater` control implements a fairly sophisticated system of events that provide rich functionality: `ItemCommand`, `ItemCreated`, and `ItemDataBound`. `ItemCommand` is an event raised by our `Repeater` control that aggregates bubbled command events raised by subordinate command controls such as an ASP.NET `Button` control. We discuss these events in detail in the section titled "Repeater Control Event Management" later in this chapter.

The `ItemCreated` event is raised each time a `RepeaterItem` control is created. This gives the client of the event an opportunity to modify or change the final control output in the template dynamically. `ItemDataBound` gives the same opportunity, except it is raised *after* any data binding has been performed on a template. This event is limited to the `ItemTemplate` and `AlternatingItemTemplate` templates because the header and footer templates do not support data binding.

The RepeaterItem Container Control

`RepeaterItem` is a building block used by the `Repeater` control to create its content. It is based on the `System.Web.UI.Control` base class and serves as the primary container for instantiating templates and working with events.

The following code snippet shows how the `RepeaterItem` control is declared, inheriting from `Control` and implementing the `INamingContainer` interface to prevent name collisions on child controls:

```
public class RepeaterItem : Control, INamingContainer
{
    public RepeaterItem(int itemIndex, ListItemType itemType, object dataItem)
    {
        this.itemIndex = itemIndex;
        this.itemType = itemType;
        this.dataItem = dataItem;
    }
...
}
```

The private data members are instantiated by the constructor. These fields are exposed as public properties as well:

```
private object dataItem;
public object DataItem
{
    get
    {
        return dataItem;
    }
    set
    {
        dataItem = value;
    }
}

private int itemIndex;
public int ItemIndex
{
    get
    {
        return itemIndex;
    }
}

private ListItemType itemType;
public ListItemType ItemType
{
    get
    {
        return itemType;
    }
}
```

ItemIndex exposes the relative position of the RepeaterItem control with respect to its siblings underneath the parent Repeater control. ItemType borrows the ListItemType enumeration from the System.Web.UI.WebControl namespace to identify the purpose of the RepeaterItem control. The following code shows a reproduction of the enumeration definition in the System.Web.UI.WebControls namespace:

```
enum ListItemType
{
    Header,
    Footer,
    Item,
    AlternatingItem,
    SelectedItem,
    EditItem,
    Separator,
    Pager
}
```

The last property exposed by the RepeaterItem class is DataItem. For RepeaterItem child controls that are bound to a data source (i.e., ItemTemplate or AlternatingItemTemplate RepeaterItems), DataItem will reference a particular row in the collection that makes up the data source. This permits us to use the Container.DataItem syntax in a data-binding expression:

```
<ItemTemplate>
    <% Container.DataItem[Name] %>
</ItemTemplate>
```

Command Events and the RepeaterItem Control

The RepeaterItem control plays a key role in ensuring that Command events are bubbled up to the parent Repeater control so that it can raise an ItemCommand event to the outside world. The following code takes Command events that are bubbled and wraps the events in a custom RepeaterCommandEventArgs object to provide additional information on the event's source:

```
protected override bool OnBubbleEvent(object source, EventArgs e)
{
    CommandEventArgs ce = e as CommandEventArgs;

    if (ce != null)
    {
        RepeaterCommandEventArgs rce = new
                            RepeaterCommandEventArgs(this, source, ce);
        RaiseBubbleEvent(this, rce);

        return true;
    }
    else
        return false;
}
```

The OnBubbleEvent member function performs a typecast to validate that it is indeed a Command event, instantiates a RepeaterCommandEventArgs class, and then sends it on up to the Repeater control through the RaiseBubbleEvent method. The return value of true indicates to ASP.NET that the event was handled. Later on, we show the code in Repeater that handles the bubbled event and raises its own Command event.

We create a custom EventArgs class to make working with the Repeater control easier, as shown in Listing 7-12. Instead of having to search through all the controls that are in the Repeater's Control collection, we can narrow it down to just the RepeaterItem control of interest.

Listing 7-12. The RepeaterCommand *Event Class File*

```
using System;
using System.Web.UI.WebControls;

namespace ControlsBookLib.Ch07
{
    public delegate void RepeaterCommandEventHandler(object o,
                                    RepeaterCommandEventArgs rce);

    public class RepeaterCommandEventArgs : CommandEventArgs
    {
        public RepeaterCommandEventArgs(RepeaterItem item, object commandSource,
            CommandEventArgs originalArgs) : base(originalArgs)
        {
            this.item = item;
            this.commandSource = commandSource;
        }

        private RepeaterItem item;
        public RepeaterItem Item
        {
            get
            {
                return item;
            }
        }

        private object commandSource;
        public object CommandSource
        {
            get
            {
                return commandSource;
            }
        }
    }
}
```

The source of the event is available in the `RepeaterCommandEventArgs` class via the `CommandSource` property. The `RepeaterItem` container control that houses the `CommandSource` property is reachable through the `Item` property. It allows us to identify and programmatically manipulate the exact block of content that was the source of the event. Our code for this control also defines a delegate named `RepeaterCommandEventHandler` to work with the custom `EventArgs` class. Listing 7-13 shows the full listing for the `RepeaterItem` control.

Listing 7-13. The `RepeaterItem` *Control Class File*

```
using System;
using System.Web;
using System.Web.UI;
using System.Web.UI.WebControls;

namespace ControlsBookLib.Ch07
{
    public class RepeaterItem : Control, INamingContainer
    {
        public RepeaterItem(int itemIndex, ListItemType itemType, object dataItem)
        {
            this.itemIndex = itemIndex;
            this.itemType = itemType;
            this.dataItem = dataItem;
        }

        private object dataItem;
        public object DataItem
        {
            get
            {
                return dataItem;
            }
            set
            {
                dataItem = value;
            }
        }

        private int itemIndex;
        public int ItemIndex
        {
            get
            {
                return itemIndex;
            }
        }

        private ListItemType itemType;
        public ListItemType ItemType
```

```
        {
          get
          {
            return itemType;
          }
        }

        protected override bool OnBubbleEvent(object source, EventArgs e)
        {
          CommandEventArgs ce = e as CommandEventArgs;

          if (ce != null)
          {
            RepeaterCommandEventArgs rce = new
                        RepeaterCommandEventArgs(this, source, ce);
            RaiseBubbleEvent(this, rce);

            return true;
          }
          else
            return false;
        }
      }

      public delegate void RepeaterItemEventHandler(object o,
                                    RepeaterItemEventArgs rie);

      public class RepeaterItemEventArgs : EventArgs
      {
        public RepeaterItemEventArgs(RepeaterItem item)
        {
          this.item = item;
        }

        private RepeaterItem item;
        public RepeaterItem Item
        {
          get
          {
            return item;
          }
        }
      }
    }
  }
```

In the next section, we discuss the implementation details of our version of the Repeater server control.

The Repeater Control Architecture

Now that we have the main building block of our Repeater control ready for action, we can move on to the core logic of our control. As shown in the following code, Repeater inherits from System.Web.UI.Control and implements INamingContainer to prevent control ID conflicts like its RepeaterItem sibling. The ParseChildren attribute set to true on the Repeater class enables the use of template properties. PersistChildren is set to false to prevent child controls from being persisted as nested inner controls; they are instead persisted as nested elements. The Designer attribute associates a custom designer named RepeaterDesigner that permits the Repeater control to see any design-time data sources available on the Visual Studio .NET Designer surface for the Web Form at design time. We discuss RepeaterDesigner further in Chapter 12.

```
[ToolboxData("<{0}:Repeater
runat=server></{0}:Repeater>"),ParseChildren(true),PersistChildren(false),
Designer(typeof(RepeaterDesigner))]
public class Repeater : Control, INamingContainer
{
```

The heart of the architecture behind Repeater is two methods: CreateChildControls and DataBind. Both of these member functions create the control hierarchy for Repeater, but each does so as a result of two fundamentally different scenarios. Here is the code for the DataBind method:

```
public override void DataBind()
{
   OnDataBinding(System.EventArgs.Empty);
   Controls.Clear();
   ClearChildViewState();
   TrackViewState();

   CreateControlHierarchy(true);
   ChildControlsCreated = true;
}
```

As you would guess, DataBind takes precedence as a control loading mechanism when binding to a data source. It is called on the Web Form after the data source has been linked to the control.

The first task of DataBind is to fire the data-binding event OnDataBinding. If the Repeater control is binding to a design-time data source, firing this event in DataBind is required for the control to see the selected design-time data source at runtime.

Next, DataBind starts with a clean slate, clearing the current set of controls and any ViewState values that are lingering, after which the control is ready to track ViewState. As shown in the preceding code, once the table has been set, DataBind builds the child control hierarchy based on the data source through the CreateControlHierarchy method. It then sets the ChildControlsCreated property to true to let ASP.NET know that the control is populated. This prevents the framework from calling CreateChildControls after DataBind.

We next discuss how CreateChildControls handles control creation. Here is the code for CreateChildControls:

```
override protected void CreateChildControls()
{
   Controls.Clear();
   if (ViewState["ItemCount"] != null)
   {
      CreateControlHierarchy(false);
   }
    ClearChildViewState();
}
```

You have already encountered CreateChildControls in all the composite controls samples so far in the book. It is called whenever the control needs to render itself outside of a DataBind. The code implementation uses the CreateControlHierarchy helper method to do the dirty work as in the DataBind method. The single difference is that the code in CreateChildControls checks the ViewState ItemCount property. If ItemCount is not null, this indicates that we need to re-create the control hierarchy using postback control ViewState values. Figure 7-12 illustrates the difference between DataBind and CreateChildControls.

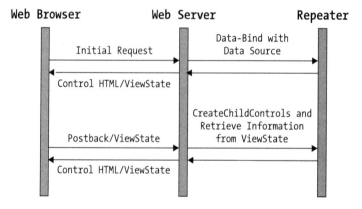

Figure 7-12. DataBind *versus* CreateChildControls

We pass a Boolean value to CreateControlHierarchy to indicate whether it needs to use the data source to build up the control hierarchy or it should try to rebuild the control hierarchy from ViewState at the beginning of a postback cycle. For CreateChildControls, we pass in false to CreateChildHierarchy if ItemCount is present in ViewState.

The data-binding process is controlled by two properties: DataSource and DataMember. DataSource is a public property that is tied to a private object field, as shown in the following code. We have code in the property's set function to validate whether or not the data source supports the IList or IEnumerable interface. This allows us to work with simple collection classes such as Arrays and ArrayLists, all the way up to the more complicated DataSet.

```
private object dataSource;
[Category("Data"),Description(
        "The data source with which to populate the control's list."),
DesignerSerializationVisibility(DesignerSerializationVisibility.Hidden),
DefaultValue(null),Bindable(true)]
public object DataSource
{
   get
   {
      return dataSource;
   }
   set
   {
      if ((value is IEnumerable) || (value is IListSource) || (value == null))
         dataSource = value;
      else
         throw new Exception("Invalid DataSource type");
   }
}
```

The DataMember property specifies the child content of the DataSource property when dealing with more complex data sources such as a DataSet that can have multiple DataTables present:

```
[Category("Data"),Description(
"The table used for binding when a DataSet is used as a data source.")]
public virtual string DataMember
{
   get
   {
      object member = ViewState["DataMember"];
      if (member == null)
         return string.Empty;
      else
         return (string) member;
   }
   set
   {
      ViewState["DataMember"] = value;
   }
}
```

In the next section, we dissect CreateControlHierarchy by breaking the code into bite-sized chunks as part of the discussion.

The CreateControlHierarchy Method

CreateControlHierarchy contains the most complicated logic in the Repeater control. It has logic that covers creating the header and footer section of the control, along with the data-bound item content. The first part of CreateControlHierarchy creates the header section of the control:

```
private void CreateControlHierarchy(bool useDataSource)
{
    items = new ArrayList();

    if (HeaderTemplate != null)
    {
        RepeaterItem header = CreateItem(-1, ListItemType.Header, false, null);
    }
```

The preceding code checks for the presence of a HeaderTemplate template and, if it exists, it creates a header RepeaterItem via CreateItem. CreateItem is the code that handles the actual RepeaterItem creation and adds it to the Repeater's Controls collection.

The items field is an ArrayList containing the RepeaterItem collection for the RepeaterControl. It is declared as a private field under the Repeater class:

```
private ArrayList items = null;
```

You can think of this as a secondary collection of child controls like the Controls collection but that is filtered to include just the RepeaterItem containers that represent data from the data source.

After the header is created, CreateControlHierarchy creates the core data-oriented RepeaterItem child controls. The first step in the process is resolving the DataSource. If CreateControlHierarchy is called from the DataBind method, the useDataSource Boolean parameter will be set to true. Otherwise, if CreateControlHierarchy is called from CreateChildControls, it will be set to false:

```
int count = 0;
if (useDataSource)
{
    DataSource = (IEnumerable) DataSourceHelper.ResolveDataSource(DataSource,
        DataMember);
}
else
{
    count = (int)ViewState["ItemCount"];
    if (count != -1)
    {
```

```
      DataSource = new DummyDataSource(count);
   }
}
```

We now move on to discuss how the Repeater control resolves its data source and builds up its control hierarchy as it data binds.

The DataSourceHelper Class and Data Binding

When building the control hierarchy as a result of data binding, we use a helper class named DataSourceHelper to resolve the DataSource to something that supports the IEnumerable interface. You can use this code directly to perform the same task in your data-bound custom server controls.

The ResolveDataSource method of the DataSourceHelper class detects the interfaces supported by the data source and will walk into the DataMember field of the DataSource if necessary. For collections such as arrays based on System.Array, ArrayList, and the DataReader classes of ADO.NET, ResolveDataSource performs a simple cast to IEnumerable.

Complex IListSource data collections such as the DataSet account for the bulk of the work in ResolveDataSource. For a DataSet, we need to drill down into its child collections based on the DataMember passed into the control. Here is how DataSet is declared:

```
public class DataSet : MarshalByValueComponent, IListSource,
                       ISupportInitialize, ISerializable
```

The IListSource interface implemented by the DataSet provides a way to determine if there are multiple DataTable child collections by checking the value of the Boolean ContainsListCollection property. If the class implementing IListSource supports a bindable list, we need to use the ITypedList interface to bind to it at runtime. The DataViewManager class provides just such a bindable list for the DataTables that make up a DataSet. DataViewManager has the following declaration:

```
public class DataViewManager : MarshalByValueComponent,
   IBindingList, IList, ICollection, IEnumerable, ITypedList
```

The GetList method of the IListSource interface implemented by the DataSet class returns an instance of the ITypedList interface implemented by the DataViewManager class through casting to the appropriate interface. We use the ITypedList interface to dynamically bind to the correct data source. Figure 7-13 provides a diagram of the process required to handle an ITypedList data source such as a DataSet.

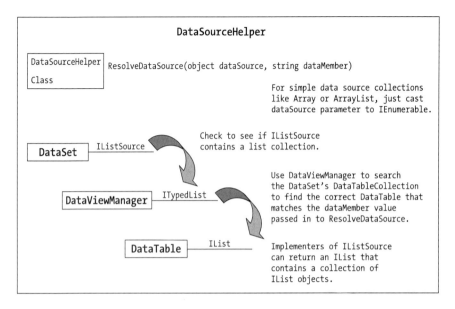

Figure 7-13. Resolving `IListSource` *data sources*

`ITypedList` gives us the ability to dynamically find properties exposed by a class. `DataViewManager`, as part of its `ITypedList` implementation, exposes the `DataTables` as properties in its `DataViewSettingCollection`. The code checks the dynamic properties of `DataViewManager` to see if it can retrieve the `DataViewSetting` property that matches the `DataMember` passed into the `Repeater` control. If the `DataMember` is blank, we choose the first `DataTable` in the `DataSet`. Listing 7-14 presents the full source code for the `DataSourceHelper` class.

Listing 7-14. The `DataSourceHelper` *Class File*

```
using System;
using System.Collections;
using System.ComponentModel;

namespace ControlsBookLib.Ch07
{
    public class DataSourceHelper
    {
        public static object ResolveDataSource(object dataSource, string dataMember)
        {
            if (dataSource == null)
                return null;
```

```
        if (dataSource is IEnumerable)
        {
            return (IEnumerable) dataSource;
        }
        else if (dataSource is IListSource)
        {
            IList list = null;
            IListSource listSource = (IListSource) dataSource;
            list = listSource.GetList();
            if (listSource.ContainsListCollection)
            {
                ITypedList typedList = (ITypedList) list;
                PropertyDescriptorCollection propDescCol =
                    typedList.GetItemProperties(null);

                if (propDescCol.Count == 0)
                    throw new Exception("ListSource without DataMembers");

                PropertyDescriptor propDesc = null;
                //Check to see if dataMember has a value, if not, default to first
                //property (DataTable) in the property collection
                                                    (DataTableCollection)
                if ((dataMember == null) || (dataMember.Length < 1))
                {
                    propDesc = propDescCol[0];
                }
                else  //If dataMember is set, try to find
                        //it in the property collection
                    propDesc = propDescCol.Find(dataMember,true);

                if (propDesc == null)
                    throw new Exception("ListSource missing DataMember");

                object listitem = list[0];

                //Get the value of the property (DataTable) of interest
                object member = propDesc.GetValue(listitem);

                if ((member == null) || !(member is IEnumerable))
                    throw new Exception("ListSource missing DataMember");

                return (IEnumerable) member;
            }
            else
                return list;
        }
        return null;
    }
  }
}
```

The end result is a `PropertyDescriptor` that allows us to dynamically retrieve the appropriate data for binding. For the `DataSet`, this gives us a reference to a `DataTable`. We cast the result to `IEnumerable` and return it to the control so that we can continue the data-binding process.

`PropertyDescriptor`, `PropertyDescriptorCollection`, and `IListSource` are all members of the `System.ComponentModel` namespace. This namespace plays a critical role in performing dynamic lookups and enhancing the design-time experience of controls. We focus on the design time support, including data binding design time support, in Chapter 12.

The DummyDataSource Class and Postback

If `CreateControlHierarchy` is not in the midst of a `DataBind`, it needs to determine whether or not it is in a postback environment. We can check this by looking for the `ItemCount` variable in ViewState. If it is present, we create a `DummyDataSource` object that is appropriately named because it serves as a placeholder to rehydrate the control state that was originally rendered and sent back to the web server via postback. Listing 7-15 provides the class source code for `DummyDataSource`.

Listing 7-15. The `DummyDataSource` Class File

```
internal sealed class DummyDataSource : ICollection
    {
        private int dataItemCount;

        public DummyDataSource(int dataItemCount)
        {
            this.dataItemCount = dataItemCount;
        }

        public int Count
        {
            get
            {
                return dataItemCount;
            }
        }

        public bool IsReadOnly
        {
            get
            {
                return false;
            }
        }

        public bool IsSynchronized
        {
```

```csharp
      get
      {
        return false;
      }
}

public object SyncRoot
{
   get
   {
     return this;
   }
}

public void CopyTo(Array array, int index)
{
   for (IEnumerator e = this.GetEnumerator(); e.MoveNext();)
     array.SetValue(e.Current, index++);
}

public IEnumerator GetEnumerator()
{
   return new DummyDataSourceEnumerator(dataItemCount);
}

private class DummyDataSourceEnumerator : IEnumerator
{
   private int count;
   private int index;

   public DummyDataSourceEnumerator(int count)
   {
     this.count = count;
     this.index = -1;
   }

   public object Current
   {
     get
     {
       return null;
     }
   }

   public bool MoveNext()
   {
     index++;
     return index < count;
   }

   public void Reset()
```

```
        {
            this.index = -1;
        }
    }
  }
}
```

DummyDataSource implements the necessary collection interfaces to be compatible with the rendering logic in Repeater. The key ingredients are implementation of the IEnumerable and IEnumeration interfaces. As an example of how this works, this code snippet enumerates a string array:

```
string[] numbers = new string[] { one,two,three };
foreach (string number in numbers)
{
    // action
}
```

IEnumerable signifies that the collection supports enumeration via constructs such as the foreach statement in C#. The method to get the enumerator from an IEnumerable collection is GetEnumerator. It returns an IEnumerator interface.

Client code uses the IEnumerator interface to move around the collection. MoveNext advances the cursor, and the Current property allows the client to grab the item pointed to by the cursor in the collection. The following code shows what really goes on when you use foreach in C#:

```
IEnumerator enum = numbers.GetEnumerator();
string number = null;
while (enum.MoveNext())
{
    number = enum.Current;
    // action
}
```

DummyDataSource implements its enumerator as a private nested class named DummyDataSourceEnumerator. It returns an instance of this class from its GetEnumerator method. Figure 7-14 illustrates the role that the DummyDataSource class plays during postback.

The dummy collection source is initialized by passing in the count of items to the DummyDataSource constructor. When a client retrieves the enumerator, it will iterate through that count of items, returning a null value. This may seem pointless, but it is enough to prime the pump inside CreateControlHierarchy to rehydrate the RepeaterItem controls from ViewState during postback. Once the controls are added, each RepeaterItem control can retrieve its former contents using ViewState and postback data. We now move on to how the Repeater control creates its content when data binding to a data source.

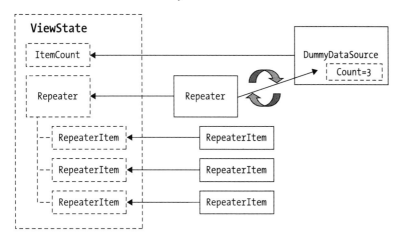

Figure 7-14. Using DummyDataSource

Creating the Middle Content

Once we have a valid object in the DataSource property, we can continue the task of creating the RepeaterItem controls in CreateControlHierarchy, as shown in the following code. If the previous step failed, the DataSource will be null, and no content gets rendered. However, if the call to ResolveDataSource is successful, the code loops through the DataSource using a foreach construct to create RepeaterItem controls. Like the header section of the Repeater control, the CreateItem method does the bulk of work in configuring each RepeaterItem.

```
if (DataSource != null)
{
    int index = 0;
    count = 0;
    RepeaterItem item;
    ListItemType itemType = ListItemType.Item;

    foreach (object dataItem in (IEnumerable) DataSource)
    {
        if (index != 0)
        {
            RepeaterItem separator = CreateItem(-1, ListItemType.Separator,
                                    false, null);
        }

        item = CreateItem(index, itemType, useDataSource, dataItem);
        items.Add(item);
        index++;
```

```
        count++;

        if (itemType == ListItemType.Item)
            itemType = ListItemType.AlternatingItem;
        else
            itemType = ListItemType.Item;
    }
}
```

The looping code also keeps track of the index of the RepeaterItem and the total count of controls added to the Controls collection. It meets our specification of having an item, an alternating item, and a separator by alternating between ItemTemplate and AlternatingItemTemplate, as well as including a RepeaterItem control implementing SeparatorTemplate between each data item.

The final section of CreateControlHierarchy is the portion that creates the footer for our Repeater implementation:

```
if (FooterTemplate != null)
{
    RepeaterItem footer = CreateItem(-1, ListItemType.Footer, false, null);
}

if (useDataSource)
{
    ViewState["ItemCount"] = ((DataSource != null) ? count : -1);
}
```

The last if-then construct stores the count of RepeaterItem controls in ViewState so we can rehydrate DummyDataSource on postback. We drill into the CreateItem method in the next section.

Creating the RepeaterItem Control in CreateItem

Much of the previous code in CreateControlHierarchy offloaded work to CreateItem. CreateItem is tasked with doing quite a few things beyond just creating a RepeaterItem control: it handles template instantiation and raises the ItemDataBound and ItemCreated events.

The first portion of CreateItem checks the ListItemType so that it can determine the right enumeration to use with the RepeaterItem control:

```
private RepeaterItem CreateItem(int itemIndex, ListItemType itemType,
                                bool dataBind, object dataItem)
{
    ITemplate selectedTemplate;

    switch (itemType)
    {
        case ListItemType.Header :
```

```
            selectedTemplate = headerTemplate;
            break;
        case ListItemType.Item :
            selectedTemplate = itemTemplate;
            break;
        case ListItemType.AlternatingItem :
            selectedTemplate = alternatingItemTemplate;
            break;
        case ListItemType.Separator :
            selectedTemplate = separatorTemplate;
            break;
        case ListItemType.Footer :
            selectedTemplate = footerTemplate;
            break;
        default:
            selectedTemplate = null;
            break;
    }

    if ((itemType == ListItemType.AlternatingItem) &&
        (alternatingItemTemplate == null))
    {
        selectedTemplate = itemTemplate;
        itemType = ListItemType.Item;
    }
```

The code next instantiates a RepeaterItem control with the index of the object, the ListItemType, and a reference to the data source. For RepeaterItem instances that are based on the HeaderTemplate, FooterTemplate, and SeparatorTemplate templates, the dataItem parameter will be null. Only the ItemTemplate- and AlternatingItemTemplate-based RepeaterItem controls are linked to a row in the data source:

```
RepeaterItem item = new RepeaterItem(itemIndex, itemType, dataItem);

if (selectedTemplate != null)
{
    selectedTemplate.InstantiateIn(item);
}

OnItemCreated(new RepeaterItemEventArgs(item));

Controls.Add(item);
```

At this point in CreateItem, the RepeaterItem control is fully populated, and we raise the ItemCreated event through the OnItemCreated method to allow interested clients to react to the creation process. They can then add additional controls to our RepeaterItem to customize its content if necessary. After this event is raised, we add the RepeaterItem control to the Controls collection of the Repeater class.

If we are data binding, the code calls DataBind on the RepeaterItem to resolve its data-binding expressions to the piece of data attached to its DataItem property. We also raise an event via OnItemDataBound, as shown in the following code. This causes any data-binding expressions in the templates to resolve to the particular row in the data source and get needed data for the final render process.

```
if (dataBind)
{
    item.DataBind();
    OnItemDataBound(new RepeaterItemEventArgs(item));
}
return item;
}
```

The last step is to return the RepeaterItem so that the calling code can add it to the items ArrayList maintained by Repeater.

Accessing RepeaterItem Instances After Creation

CreateControlHierarchy, along with CreateItem, does a great job of creating RepeaterItem instances and adding them to the Controls collection and the items ArrayList. The control is easy enough to access, but what about the items ArrayList? Our code provides a read-only collection type called RepeaterItemCollection to give access to the RepeaterInfo instances, as shown in Listing 7-16.

Listing 7-16. The RepeaterItemCollection *Class File*

```
using System;
using System.Collections;

namespace ControlsBookLib.Ch07
{
    public class RepeaterItemCollection : CollectionBase
    {
        public RepeaterItemCollection(ArrayList list)
        {
            foreach (object item in list)
            {
                if (item is RepeaterItem)
                    List.Add(item);
            }
        }

        public RepeaterItem this[int index]
        {
            get
            {
                return (RepeaterItem) List[index];
            }
        }
    }
}
```

RepeaterItemCollection inherits from the CollectBase base class and only implements a get indexer to read from the collection. The constructor is designed to populate instances of RepeaterItem from an ArrayList:

```
[Browsable(false)]
public RepeaterItemCollection Items
{
    get
    {
        EnsureChildControls();
        RepeaterItemCollection col = new RepeaterItemCollection(items);
        return col;
    }
}
```

The Items property on Repeater uses this custom collection type to allow easy access to the RepeaterItems. Note that items is a private field of the Repeater class that we use in CreateControlHierarchy. We now move on to discuss the various events that the Repeater control implements.

Repeater Control Event Management

Repeater exposes an ItemCommand event, an ItemCreated event, and an ItemDataBound event. We use the Events collection provided by System.Web.UI.Control to track registered client delegates. The following code for the ItemCommand event is reproduced in a similar manner for the ItemCreated and ItemDataBound events:

```
private static readonly object ItemCommandKey = new object();
public event RepeaterCommandEventHandler ItemCommand
{
    add
    {
        Events.AddHandler(ItemCommandKey, value);
    }
    remove
    {
        Events.RemoveHandler(ItemCommandKey, value);
    }
}
```

The On-prefixed protected methods use standard event techniques to notify the delegates that subscribe to the event when it is fired. The following OnItemCommand is mirrored by OnItemDataBound and OnItemCreated:

```
protected virtual void OnItemCommand(RepeaterCommandEventArgs rce)
{
    RepeaterCommandEventHandler repeaterCommandEventDelegate =
        (RepeaterCommandEventHandler) Events[ItemCommandKey];
    if (repeaterCommandEventDelegate != null)
    {
        repeaterCommandEventDelegate(this, rce);
    }
}
```

ItemCommand requires an extra step to handle the RepeaterCommand events bubbled up from child RepeaterItem controls. To wire into the event bubbling, it implements OnBubbleEvent:

```
protected override bool OnBubbleEvent(object source, EventArgs e)
{
   RepeaterCommandEventArgs rce = e as RepeaterCommandEventArgs;

   if (rce != null)
   {
      OnItemCommand(rce);
      return true;
   }
   else
      return false;
}
```

OnBubble traps the RepeaterCommand events and raises them as ItemCommand events to event subscribers. Listing 7-17 shows the final source code for the Repeater control class.

Listing 7-17. The Repeater *Control Class File*

```
using System;
using System.Web;
using System.Web.UI;
using System.Web.UI.WebControls;
using System.Collections;
using System.ComponentModel;
using ControlsBookLib.Ch12.Design;

namespace ControlsBookLib.Ch07
{
   [ToolboxData("<{0}:Repeater runat=server></{0}:Repeater>"),ParseChildren(true),
    PersistChildren(false),
   Designer(typeof(RepeaterDesigner))]
   public class Repeater : Control, INamingContainer
   {
      private ITemplate headerTemplate;
      [Browsable(false),TemplateContainer(typeof(RepeaterItem)),
      PersistenceMode(PersistenceMode.InnerProperty)]
      public ITemplate HeaderTemplate
      {
         get
         {
            return headerTemplate;
         }

         set
```

```
      {
         headerTemplate = value;
      }
   }

   private ITemplate footerTemplate;
   [Browsable(false),TemplateContainer(typeof(RepeaterItem)),
   PersistenceMode(PersistenceMode.InnerProperty)]
   public ITemplate FooterTemplate
   {
      get
      {
         return footerTemplate;
      }

      set
      {
         footerTemplate = value;
      }
   }

   private ITemplate itemTemplate;
   [Browsable(false),TemplateContainer(typeof(RepeaterItem)),
   PersistenceMode(PersistenceMode.InnerProperty)]
   public ITemplate ItemTemplate
   {
      get
      {
         return itemTemplate;
      }

      set
      {
         itemTemplate = value;
      }
   }

   private ITemplate alternatingItemTemplate;
   [Browsable(false),TemplateContainer(typeof(RepeaterItem)),
   PersistenceMode(PersistenceMode.InnerProperty)]
   public ITemplate AlternatingItemTemplate
   {
      get
      {
         return alternatingItemTemplate;
      }

      set
      {
         alternatingItemTemplate = value;
      }
   }
```

```csharp
        private ITemplate separatorTemplate;
        [Browsable(false),TemplateContainer(typeof(RepeaterItem)),
        PersistenceMode(PersistenceMode.InnerProperty)]
        public ITemplate SeparatorTemplate
        {
          get
          {
            return separatorTemplate;
          }

          set
          {
            separatorTemplate = value;
          }
        }

        [Browsable(false)]
        public RepeaterItemCollection Items
        {
          get
          {
            EnsureChildControls();
            RepeaterItemCollection col = new RepeaterItemCollection(items);
            return col;
          }
        }

        private object dataSource;
        [Category("Data"),
    Description("The data source with which to populate the control's list."),
        DesignerSerializationVisibility(DesignerSerializationVisibility.Hidden),
        DefaultValue(null),Bindable(true)]
        public object DataSource
        {
          get
          {
            return dataSource;
          }
          set
          {
            if ((value is IEnumerable) || (value is IListSource)
                                    || (value == null))
              dataSource = value;
            else
              throw new Exception("Invalid DataSource type");
          }
        }

        [Category("Data"),Description(
    "The table used for binding when a DataSet is used as a data source.")]
        public virtual string DataMember
```

```
{
  get
  {
    object member = ViewState["DataMember"];
    if (member == null)
      return string.Empty;
    else
      return (string) member;
  }
  set
  {
    ViewState["DataMember"] = value;
  }
}

private RepeaterItem CreateItem(int itemIndex, ListItemType itemType,
                               bool dataBind, object dataItem)
{
  ITemplate selectedTemplate;

  switch (itemType)
  {
    case ListItemType.Header :
      selectedTemplate = headerTemplate;
      break;
    case ListItemType.Item :
      selectedTemplate = itemTemplate;
      break;
    case ListItemType.AlternatingItem :
      selectedTemplate = alternatingItemTemplate;
      break;
    case ListItemType.Separator :
      selectedTemplate = separatorTemplate;
      break;
    case ListItemType.Footer :
      selectedTemplate = footerTemplate;
      break;
    default:
      selectedTemplate = null;
      break;
  }

  if ((itemType == ListItemType.AlternatingItem) &&
      (alternatingItemTemplate == null))
  {
    selectedTemplate = itemTemplate;
    itemType = ListItemType.Item;
  }

  RepeaterItem item = new RepeaterItem(itemIndex, itemType, dataItem);
```

```
      if (selectedTemplate != null)
      {
         selectedTemplate.InstantiateIn(item);
      }

      OnItemCreated(new RepeaterItemEventArgs(item));

      Controls.Add(item);

      if (dataBind)
      {
         item.DataBind();
         OnItemDataBound(new RepeaterItemEventArgs(item));
      }
      return item;
   }

   private ArrayList items = null;
   private void CreateControlHierarchy(bool useDataSource)
   {
      items = new ArrayList();
      IEnumerable ds = null;

      if (HeaderTemplate != null)
      {
         RepeaterItem header = CreateItem(-1, ListItemType.Header, false, null);
      }

      int count = -1 ;
      if (useDataSource)
      {
         ds = (IEnumerable) DataSourceHelper.ResolveDataSource(DataSource,
            DataMember);
      }
      else
      {
         count = (int)ViewState["ItemCount"];
         if (count != -1)
         {
            ds = new DummyDataSource(count);
         }
      }

      if (ds != null)
      {
         int index = 0;
         count = 0;
         RepeaterItem item;
         ListItemType itemType = ListItemType.Item;

         foreach (object dataItem in (IEnumerable) ds)
```

```
    {
       if (index != 0)
       {
          RepeaterItem separator = CreateItem(-1, ListItemType.Separator,
                                              false, null);
       }

       item = CreateItem(index, itemType, useDataSource, dataItem);
       items.Add(item);
       index++;
       count++;

       if (itemType == ListItemType.Item)
          itemType = ListItemType.AlternatingItem;
       else
          itemType = ListItemType.Item;
    }
  }

  if (FooterTemplate != null)
  {
     RepeaterItem footer = CreateItem(-1, ListItemType.Footer, false, null);
  }

  if (useDataSource)
  {
     ViewState["ItemCount"] = ((ds != null) ? count : -1);
  }
}

override protected void CreateChildControls()
{
   Controls.Clear();
   if (ViewState["ItemCount"] != null)
   {
      CreateControlHierarchy(false);
   }
   ClearChildViewState();
}

public override ControlCollection Controls
{
   get
   {
      EnsureChildControls();
      return base.Controls;
   }
}

public override void DataBind()
{
```

```
        //Must call either this.OnDataBinding or
        //base.OnDataBinding for the control to be able to
        //access or "see" design-time data sources at runtime.
        OnDataBinding(System.EventArgs.Empty);
        Controls.Clear();
        ClearChildViewState();
        TrackViewState();

        CreateControlHierarchy(true);
        ChildControlsCreated = true;
    }

    protected override void OnDataBinding(EventArgs e)
    {
        base.OnDataBinding(e);
    }

    private static readonly object ItemCommandKey = new object();
    public event RepeaterCommandEventHandler ItemCommand
    {
        add
        {
            Events.AddHandler(ItemCommandKey, value);
        }
        remove
        {
            Events.RemoveHandler(ItemCommandKey, value);
        }
    }

    private static readonly object ItemCreatedKey = new object();
    public event RepeaterItemEventHandler ItemCreated
    {
        add
        {
            Events.AddHandler(ItemCreatedKey, value);
        }
        remove
        {
            Events.RemoveHandler(ItemCreatedKey, value);
        }
    }

    private static readonly object ItemDataBoundKey = new object();
    public event RepeaterItemEventHandler ItemDataBound
    {
        add
        {
            Events.AddHandler(ItemDataBoundKey, value);
        }
        remove
```

```
        {
            Events.RemoveHandler(ItemDataBoundKey, value);
        }
    }

    protected override bool OnBubbleEvent(object source, EventArgs e)
    {
        RepeaterCommandEventArgs rce = e as RepeaterCommandEventArgs;

        if (rce != null)
        {
            OnItemCommand(rce);
            return true;
        }
        else
            return false;
    }

    protected virtual void OnItemCommand(RepeaterCommandEventArgs rce)
    {
        RepeaterCommandEventHandler repeaterCommandEventDelegate =
            (RepeaterCommandEventHandler) Events[ItemCommandKey];
        if (repeaterCommandEventDelegate != null)
        {
            repeaterCommandEventDelegate(this, rce);
        }
    }

    protected virtual void OnItemCreated(RepeaterItemEventArgs rie)
    {
        RepeaterItemEventHandler repeaterItemEventDelegate =
            (RepeaterItemEventHandler) Events[ItemCreatedKey];
        if (repeaterItemEventDelegate != null)
        {
            repeaterItemEventDelegate(this, rie);
        }
    }

    protected virtual void OnItemDataBound(RepeaterItemEventArgs rie)
    {
        RepeaterItemEventHandler repeaterItemEventDelegate =
            (RepeaterItemEventHandler) Events[ItemDataBoundKey];
        if (repeaterItemEventDelegate != null)
        {
            repeaterItemEventDelegate(this, rie);
        }
    }
    }
}
```

Now that we have covered the construction of our version of the `Repeater` control, in the next section we put it to the test to see if it behaves like the built-in ASP.NET `Repeater` server control.

Data Binding with the Repeater Control

Our long journey to build a `Repeater` control replica is complete. Now we need to take it for a test drive with a variety of .NET collection types and a design-time `DataSet` to prove that the core feature set works as advertised.

The Databound Repeater Web Form has five `Repeater` controls that are attached to four different collection types: `Array`, `ArrayList`, `SqlDataReader`, and two `DataSets` (runtime and design time). The form also has a button on it to exercise the postback capabilities of the `Repeater` control to show how the control remembers its previous content without having to perform an additional data bind. The UI for the Web Form is shown in Figure 7-15.

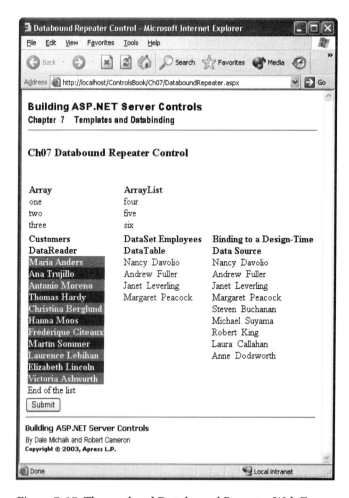

Figure 7-15. The rendered Databound Repeater Web Form

Listings 7-18 and 7-19 show the full code for the Web Form.

Listing 7-18. The DataboundRepeater *.aspx Page File*

```
<%@ Register TagPrefix="apressUC" TagName="ControlsBookFooter"
Src="..\ControlsBookFooter.ascx" %>
<%@ Register TagPrefix="apressUC" TagName="ControlsBookHeader"
Src="..\ControlsBookHeader.ascx" %>
<%@ Page language="c#" Codebehind="DataboundRepeater.aspx.cs" AutoEventWireup="false"
Inherits="ControlsBookWeb.Ch07.DataboundRepeater" %>
<%@ Register TagPrefix="apress" Namespace="ControlsBookLib.Ch07"
Assembly="ControlsBookLib" %>
<!DOCTYPE HTML PUBLIC "-//W3C//DTD HTML 4.0 Transitional//EN" >
<HTML>
    <HEAD>
        <title>Databound Repeater Control</title>
        <meta content="Microsoft Visual Studio 7.0" name="GENERATOR">
        <meta content="C#" name="CODE_LANGUAGE">
        <meta content="JavaScript" name="vs_defaultClientScript">
        <meta content="http://schemas.microsoft.com/intellisense/ie5"
                    name="vs_targetSchema">
    </HEAD>
    <body MS_POSITIONING="FlowLayout">
        <form id="DataboundRepeater" method="post" runat="server">
            <apressuc:controlsbookheader id="Header" runat="server" ChapterNumber="7"
              ChapterTitle="Templates and Data Binding"></apressuc:controlsbookheader>
            <h3>Ch07 Databound Repeater Control</h3>
            <br>
            <table>
               <TBODY>
                   <tr vAlign="top">
                       <td><apress:repeater id="repeaterA"
runat="server"><HEADERTEMPLATE><B>Array</B><BR>
                           </HEADERTEMPLATE>
                           <ITEMTEMPLATE>
                               <%# Container.DataItem %>
                           </ITEMTEMPLATE>
                           <SEPARATORTEMPLATE>
                               <BR>
                           </SEPARATORTEMPLATE>
                         </apress:repeater><br>
                       </td>
                       <td>  </td>
                       <td><apress:repeater id="repeaterAl"
runat="server"><HEADERTEMPLATE><B>ArrayList</B><BR>
                           </HEADERTEMPLATE>
                           <ITEMTEMPLATE>
                               <%# Container.DataItem %>
                           </ITEMTEMPLATE>
                           <SEPARATORTEMPLATE>
                               <BR>
                           </SEPARATORTEMPLATE>
```

```
                        </apress:repeater><br>
                 </td>
           </tr>
           <tr vAlign="top">
               <td><apress:repeater id="repeaterRdrCust"
runat="server"><HEADERTEMPLATE><B>Customers
                           DataReader</B><BR>
                   </HEADERTEMPLATE>
                   <ITEMTEMPLATE>
                       <DIV style="DISPLAY:
                        inline; FONT-WEIGHT: bold; WIDTH: 130px;
COLOR: yellow; HEIGHT: 15px; BACKGROUND-COLOR: red"
                           ms_positioning="FlowLayout">
            <%# DataBinder.Eval(Container.DataItem,"ContactName") %></DIV>
                   </ITEMTEMPLATE>
                   <ALTERNATINGITEMTEMPLATE>
<DIV style="DISPLAY: inline; FONT-WEIGHT: bold; WIDTH: 130px; COLOR: yellow;
                           HEIGHT: 15px; BACKGROUND-COLOR: blue"
                           ms_positioning="FlowLayout">
                   <%# DataBinder.Eval(Container.DataItem,"ContactName")
%></DIV></SPAN></ALTERNATINGITEMTEMPLATE>
                   <SEPARATORTEMPLATE>
                       <BR>
                   </SEPARATORTEMPLATE>
                   <FOOTERTEMPLATE><BR>End
of the list </FOOTERTEMPLATE>
                   </apress:repeater></td>
               <td>  </td>
               <td><apress:repeater id="repeaterDtEmp"
runat="server"><HEADERTEMPLATE><B>DataSet Employees
                           DataTable</B><BR>
                   </HEADERTEMPLATE>
                   <ITEMTEMPLATE><%# DataBinder.Eval(Container.DataItem,
                   "FirstName") %> 
<%# DataBinder.Eval(Container.DataItem,"LastName") %></ITEMTEMPLATE>
                   <SEPARATORTEMPLATE>
                       <BR>
                   </SEPARATORTEMPLATE>
                   </apress:repeater></td>
           <td>
               <apress:repeater id=RepeaterDesignTime runat="server"
               DataSource="<%# dataSetEmp %>" DataMember="Employees">
                   <HEADERTEMPLATE>
                       <B>Binding to a Design-Time Data Source</B><BR>
                   </HEADERTEMPLATE>
                   <ITEMTEMPLATE><%# DataBinder.Eval(Container.DataItem,
                   "FirstName") %> 
<%# DataBinder.Eval(Container.DataItem,"LastName") %></ITEMTEMPLATE>
                   <SEPARATORTEMPLATE>
                       <BR>
                   </SEPARATORTEMPLATE>
```

```
                        </apress:repeater></td>
                </tr>
            </TBODY>
        </table>
        <asp:button id="Button1" runat="server"
Text="Submit"></asp:button><apressuc:controlsbookfooter id="Footer"
runat="server"></apressuc:controlsbookfooter></form>
    </body>
</HTML>
```

Listing 7-19. The DataboundRepeater *Code-Behind Class File*

```
using System;
using System.Collections;
using System.ComponentModel;
using System.Data;
using System.Web.UI;
using System.Web.UI.WebControls;
using System.Data.SqlClient;

namespace ControlsBookWeb.Ch07
{
    public class DataboundRepeater : System.Web.UI.Page
    {
        protected ControlsBookLib.Ch07.Repeater RepeaterDesignTime;
        protected System.Data.SqlClient.SqlDataAdapter dataAdapterEmp;
        protected System.Data.SqlClient.SqlCommand sqlSelectCommand1;
        protected System.Data.SqlClient.SqlConnection connEmp;
        protected ControlsBookWeb.Ch07.dataSetEmp dataSetEmp;
        protected ControlsBookLib.Ch07.Repeater repeaterA;
        protected ControlsBookLib.Ch07.Repeater repeaterAl;
        protected ControlsBookLib.Ch07.Repeater repeaterDtEmp;
        protected ControlsBookLib.Ch07.Repeater repeaterRdrCust;
        protected System.Web.UI.WebControls.Button Button1;

        private void Page_Load(object sender, System.EventArgs e)
        {
            if (!Page.IsPostBack)
            {
                string[] array = new String[] { "one", "two", "three" };
                repeaterA.DataSource = array;
                repeaterA.DataBind();

                ArrayList list = new ArrayList();
                list.Add("four");
                list.Add("five");
                list.Add("six");
                repeaterAl.DataSource = list;
                repeaterAl.DataBind();
```

```
        SqlDataReader dr = GetCustomerDataReader();
        repeaterRdrCust.DataSource = dr;
        repeaterRdrCust.DataBind();
        dr.Close();

        DataSet ds = new DataSet();
        FillEmployeesDataSet(ds);

        repeaterDtEmp.DataSource = ds;
        repeaterDtEmp.DataMember = "Employees";
        repeaterDtEmp.DataBind();

        connEmp.Open();
        dataAdapterEmp.Fill(dataSetEmp);
        RepeaterDesignTime.DataBind();
        connEmp.Close();
    }
}

private SqlDataReader GetCustomerDataReader()
{
    SqlConnection conn =
        new SqlConnection("Server=(local);Database=Northwind;
                            Integrated Security=true;");
    conn.Open();

    SqlCommand cmd =
        new SqlCommand(
"SELECT CustomerID, ContactName, ContactTitle, CompanyName FROM Customers"+
" WHERE CustomerID LIKE '[AB]%'",
        conn);
    SqlDataReader dr = cmd.ExecuteReader(CommandBehavior.CloseConnection);
    return dr;
}

private void FillEmployeesDataSet(DataSet ds)
{
    SqlConnection conn =
        new SqlConnection("Server=(local);Database=Northwind;
            Integrated Security=true;");
    conn.Open();

    SqlDataAdapter da =
        new SqlDataAdapter("SELECT EmployeeID, FirstName, LastName,
        Title FROM Employees WHERE EmployeeID < 5",
        conn);
    da.Fill(ds,"Employees");

    conn.Close();
}
```

```
        #region Web Form Designer generated code
        override protected void OnInit(EventArgs e)
        {
           //
           // CODEGEN: This call is required by the ASP.NET Web Form Designer.
           //
           InitializeComponent();
           base.OnInit(e);
        }


        /// <summary>
        /// Required method for Designer support - do not modify
        /// the contents of this method with the code editor.
        /// </summary>
        private void InitializeComponent()
        {
           System.Configuration.AppSettingsReader configurationAppSettings =
           new System.Configuration.AppSettingsReader();
           this.dataAdapterEmp = new System.Data.SqlClient.SqlDataAdapter();
           this.connEmp = new System.Data.SqlClient.SqlConnection();
           this.sqlSelectCommand1 = new System.Data.SqlClient.SqlCommand();
           this.dataSetEmp = new ControlsBookWeb.Ch07.dataSetEmp();
           ((System.ComponentModel.ISupportInitialize)(this.dataSetEmp)).BeginInit();
           //
           // dataAdapterEmp
           //
           this.dataAdapterEmp.SelectCommand = this.sqlSelectCommand1;
           this.dataAdapterEmp.TableMappings.AddRange(new
           System.Data.Common.DataTableMapping[] {

new System.Data.Common.DataTableMapping("Table", "Employees",
new System.Data.Common.DataColumnMapping[] {

new System.Data.Common.DataColumnMapping("EmployeeID", "EmployeeID"),

new System.Data.Common.DataColumnMapping("LastName", "LastName"),

new System.Data.Common.DataColumnMapping("FirstName", "FirstName"),

new System.Data.Common.DataColumnMapping("Title", "Title"),
/

new System.Data.Common.DataColumnMapping("TitleOfCourtesy",
"TitleOfCourtesy"),

new System.Data.Common.DataColumnMapping("BirthDate", "BirthDate"),

new System.Data.Common.DataColumnMapping("HireDate", "HireDate"),

new System.Data.Common.DataColumnMapping("Address", "Address"),
```

```
new System.Data.Common.DataColumnMapping("City", "City"),

new System.Data.Common.DataColumnMapping("Region", "Region"),

new System.Data.Common.DataColumnMapping("PostalCode", "PostalCode"),

new System.Data.Common.DataColumnMapping("Country", "Country"),

new System.Data.Common.DataColumnMapping("HomePhone", "HomePhone"),

new System.Data.Common.DataColumnMapping("Extension", "Extension"),

new System.Data.Common.DataColumnMapping("Photo", "Photo"),

new System.Data.Common.DataColumnMapping("Notes", "Notes"),

new System.Data.Common.DataColumnMapping("ReportsTo", "ReportsTo"),

new System.Data.Common.DataColumnMapping("PhotoPath", "PhotoPath")})});
        //
        // connEmp
        //
        this.connEmp.ConnectionString =
((string)(configurationAppSettings.GetValue("connEmp.ConnectionString",
typeof(string))));
        //
        // sqlSelectCommand1
        //
            "FirstName, Title, TitleOfCourtesy, BirthDate, HireDa" +
            "te, Address, City, Region, PostalCode, Country, HomePhone,"+
            "Extension, Photo, Not" +
            "es, ReportsTo, PhotoPath FROM Employees";
        this.sqlSelectCommand1.Connection = this.connEmp;
        //
        // dataSetEmp
        //
        this.dataSetEmp.DataSetName = "dataSetEmp";
        this.dataSetEmp.Locale = new System.Globalization.CultureInfo("en-US");
        this.Load += new System.EventHandler(this.Page_Load);
        ((System.ComponentModel.ISupportInitialize)(this.dataSetEmp)).EndInit();

    }
    #endregion
  }
}
```

In the next section we test the events published by our Replica Repeater server control created in this chapter.

Advanced Interaction with the Repeater Control

The previous Web Form demonstrates that our Repeater control is capable of binding to a variety of data sources. The Advanced Repeater Web Form takes this a few steps further. Instead of just binding a SqlDataReader to a Repeater control, the Advanced Repeater Web Form hooks into the ItemCreated and ItemDataBound events of our Repeater control to dynamically alter its output.

The Advanced Repeater Web Form dynamically adds an ASP.NET Label control to each RepeaterItem row in its ItemCreated handler:

```
private void RepeaterItemCreated(object o,
          ControlsBookLib.Ch07.RepeaterItemEventArgs rie)
{
   ControlsBookLib.Ch07.RepeaterItem item = rie.Item;
   if (item.ItemType == ListItemType.Item)
   {
      Label lblID = new Label();
      lblID.ID = "lblID";
      item.Controls.Add(lblID);
      item.Controls.Add(new LiteralControl(" "));
   }
}
```

Once the control data binds, it changes the value of the added Label control to the CustomerID value of the current row in the SqlDataReader:

```
    private void RepeaterItemDataBound(object o,
ControlsBookLib.Ch07.RepeaterItemEventArgs rie)
    {
        ControlsBookLib.Ch07.RepeaterItem item = rie.Item;
        DbDataRecord row = (DbDataRecord) item.DataItem;
        string ID = (string) row["CustomerID"];
        Label lblID = (Label) item.FindControl("lblID");
        lblID.Text = ID;
    }
```

The result of the event handling during creation and data binding is the browser output shown in Figure 7-16.

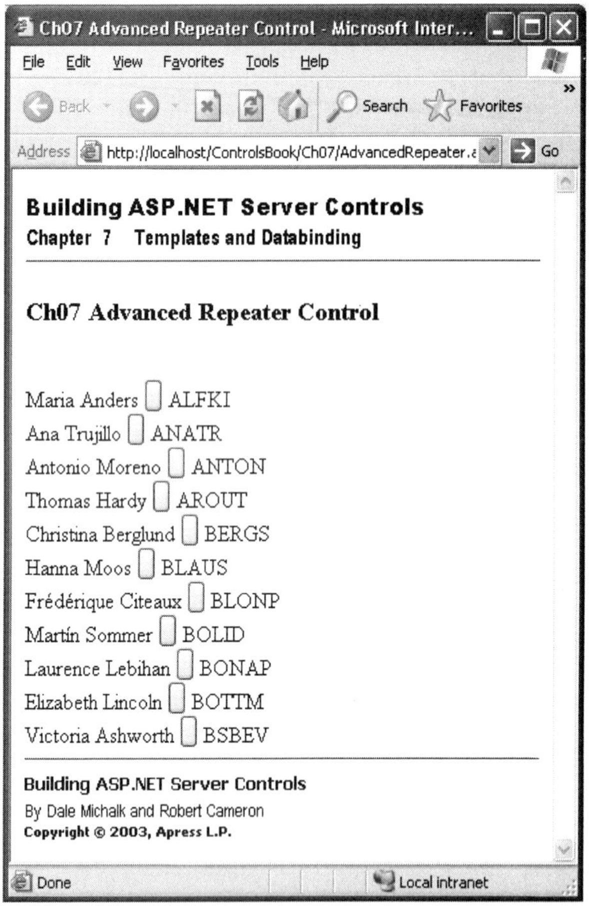

Figure 7-16. The rendered Advanced Repeater Web Form

Listings 7-20 and 7-21 present the full code for the Web Form.

Listing 7-20. The AdvancedRepeater *.aspx Page File*

```
<%@ Register TagPrefix="apressUC" TagName="ControlsBookFooter"
Src="..\ControlsBookFooter.ascx" %>
<%@ Register TagPrefix="apressUC" TagName="ControlsBookHeader"
Src="..\ControlsBookHeader.ascx" %>
<%@ Register TagPrefix="apress" Namespace="ControlsBookLib.Ch07"
Assembly="ControlsBookLib" %>
<%@ Page language="c#" Codebehind="AdvancedRepeater.aspx.cs"
AutoEventWireup="false"
Inherits="ControlsBookWeb.Ch07.AdvancedRepeater" %>
<!DOCTYPE HTML PUBLIC "-//W3C//DTD HTML 4.0 Transitional//EN" >
<HTML>
```

```
<HEAD>
  <title>Ch07 Advanced Repeater Control</title>
  <meta content="Microsoft Visual Studio 7.0" name="GENERATOR">
  <meta content="C#" name="CODE_LANGUAGE">
  <meta content="JavaScript" name="vs_defaultClientScript">
  <meta content="http://schemas.microsoft.com/intellisense/ie5"
    name="vs_targetSchema">
</HEAD>
<body MS_POSITIONING="FlowLayout">
  <form id="AdvancedRepeater" method="post" runat="server">
    <apressUC:ControlsBookHeader id="Header" runat="server" ChapterNumber="7"
ChapterTitle="Templates and Data Binding" />
    <h3>Ch07 Advanced Repeater Control</h3>
    <b>
      <asp:label id="status" runat="server"></asp:label></b><br>
    <apress:repeater id="repeaterRdrCust" runat="server">
      <ITEMTEMPLATE>
        <%# DataBinder.Eval(Container.DataItem,"ContactName") %>
        <asp:button id="contact1" runat="server"></asp:button>
      </ITEMTEMPLATE>
      <SEPARATORTEMPLATE>
        <BR>
      </SEPARATORTEMPLATE>
    </apress:repeater>
    <apressUC:ControlsBookFooter id="Footer" runat="server" />
  </form>
</body>
</HTML>
```

Listing 7-21. The AdvancedRepeater *Code-Behind Class File*

```csharp
using System;
using System.Collections;
using System.ComponentModel;
using System.Data;
using System.Data.Common;
using System.Data.SqlClient;
using System.Drawing;
using System.Web;
using System.Web.SessionState;
using System.Web.UI;
using System.Web.UI.WebControls;
using System.Web.UI.HtmlControls;

namespace ControlsBookWeb.Ch07
{
    public class AdvancedRepeater : System.Web.UI.Page
    {
        protected System.Web.UI.WebControls.Label status;
        protected System.Web.UI.WebControls.Button contact1;
        protected ControlsBookLib.Ch07.Repeater repeaterRdrCust;
```

```
        private void Page_Load(object sender, System.EventArgs e)
        {
            status.Text = "";

            if (!Page.IsPostBack)
            {
                SqlDataReader dr = GetCustomerDataReader();
                repeaterRdrCust.DataSource = dr;
                repeaterRdrCust.DataBind();
                dr.Close();

            }
        }

        private SqlDataReader GetCustomerDataReader()
        {
            SqlConnection conn =
                new SqlConnection("Server=(local);Database=Northwind;
                                   Integrated Security=true;");
            conn.Open();

            SqlCommand cmd =
                new SqlCommand(
"SELECT CustomerID, ContactName, ContactTitle, CompanyName FROM Customers WHERE " +
"CustomerID LIKE '[AB]%'",
                conn);
            SqlDataReader dr = cmd.ExecuteReader(CommandBehavior.CloseConnection);
            return dr;
        }

        #region Web Form Designer generated code
        override protected void OnInit(EventArgs e)
        {
            //
            // CODEGEN: This call is required by the ASP.NET Web Form Designer.
            //
            InitializeComponent();
            base.OnInit(e);
        }

        /// <summary>
        /// Required method for Designer support - do not modify
        /// the contents of this method with the code editor.
        /// </summary>
        private void InitializeComponent()
        {
            this.repeaterRdrCust.ItemCreated += new
ControlsBookLib.Ch07.RepeaterItemEventHandler(this.RepeaterItemCreated);
            this.repeaterRdrCust.ItemDataBound += new
ControlsBookLib.Ch07.RepeaterItemEventHandler(this.RepeaterItemDataBound);
            this.repeaterRdrCust.ItemCommand += new
```

```
ControlsBookLib.Ch07.RepeaterCommandEventHandler(this.RepeaterCommand);
        this.Load += new System.EventHandler(this.Page_Load);


    }
    #endregion

    private void RepeaterCommand(object o,
                ControlsBookLib.Ch07.RepeaterCommandEventArgs tce)
    {
        ControlsBookLib.Ch07.RepeaterItem item = tce.Item;
        Label lblID = (Label) item.FindControl("lblID");
        status.Text = lblID.Text + " was clicked!";
    }

    private void RepeaterItemCreated(object o,
ControlsBookLib.Ch07.RepeaterItemEventArgs rie)
    {
        ControlsBookLib.Ch07.RepeaterItem item = rie.Item;
        if (item.ItemType == ListItemType.Item)
        {
            Label lblID = new Label();
            lblID.ID = "lblID";
            item.Controls.Add(lblID);
            item.Controls.Add(new LiteralControl(" "));
        }
    }

    private void RepeaterItemDataBound(object o,
ControlsBookLib.Ch07.RepeaterItemEventArgs rie)
    {
        ControlsBookLib.Ch07.RepeaterItem item = rie.Item;
        DbDataRecord row = (DbDataRecord) item.DataItem;
        string ID = (string) row["CustomerID"];
        Label lblID = (Label) item.FindControl("lblID");
        lblID.Text = ID;
    }
  }
}
```

More work remains for the AdvancedDataRepeater after rendering—specifically, firing events. The Web Form is wired into the ItemCommand event raised by the Repeater control. This is triggered by the ASP.NET Button control that is a part of each row rendered in conjunction with the data from the Customers table in the Northwind database:

```
private void RepeaterCommand(object o,
        ControlsBookLib.Ch07.RepeaterCommandEventArgs tce)
{
    ControlsBookLib.Ch07.RepeaterItem item = tce.Item;
    Label lblID = (Label) item.FindControl("lblID");
    status.Text = lblID.Text + " was clicked!";
}
```

The RepeaterCommand method that handles the ItemCommand event uses RepeaterCommandEventArgs and its Item property to retrieve the RepeaterItem control that contains the row where the button was clicked. It uses this control reference along with the FindControl method to locate the dynamically added Label control. The Text property value of the Label control is the same as the CustomerID value from the database. RepeaterCommand displays this information in the status Label control at the top the Web Form. Figure 7-17 shows what happens when we click the first row's button.

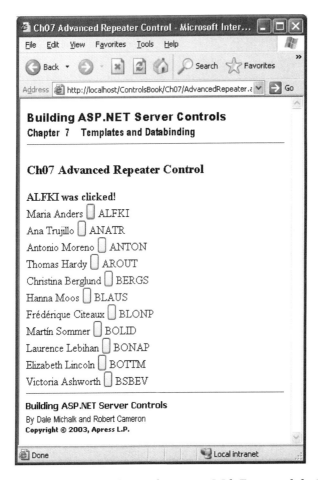

Figure 7-17. The Advanced Repeater Web Form and the ItemCommand *event*

Using Dynamic Templates

The templates used in the Menu and Repeater demonstrations to this point were statically declared in an .aspx page. Sometimes web developers must generate the templates on the fly to modify the output of the templated control. ASP.NET lends a helping hand with two techniques: loading from file via the LoadTemplate method of the Page class and creating a prebuilt class that implements the ITemplate interface. We discuss these techniques in the following sections.

The Dynamic Templates Web Form

The Dynamic Templates Web Form demonstrates how to dynamically load templates into an instance of the `Repeater` control built in this chapter. The `Repeater` control on the Web Form looks like the typical `Repeater` bound to a `SqlDataReader`. The difference is the `DropDownList` control that is used to select which template to apply to the `Repeater` control when it is loaded:

```
<asp:DropDownList id="templateList" Runat="server" AutoPostBack="True">
  <asp:ListItem>FileTemplate.ascx</asp:ListItem>
  <asp:ListItem>CustCodeTemplate</asp:ListItem>
  <asp:ListItem>CustFileTemplate.ascx</asp:ListItem>
</asp:DropDownList>
```

The first two selections load the template from .ascx files that are present in the same virtual directory as the Web Form. The default template is FileTemplate.ascx, as shown in Figure 7-18.

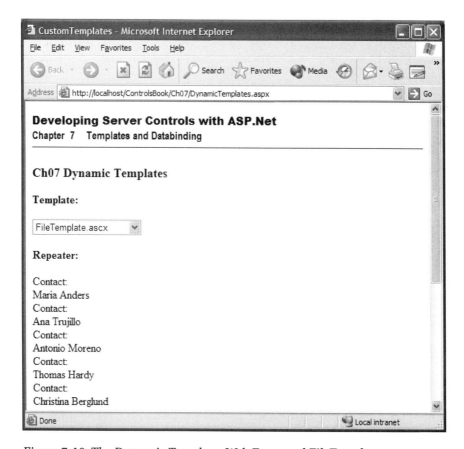

Figure 7-18. The Dynamic Templates Web Form and FileTemplate.ascx

The actual code for the .ascx file is shown in Listing 7-22. Notice that we did not have to include the `<ITEMTEMPLATE>` container tags.

Listing 7-22. The `FileTemplate.ascx` *Template File*

```
<%@ Control Language="c#" AutoEventWireup="false" Codebehind="FileTemplate.ascx.cs"
Inherits="ControlsBookWeb.Ch07.FileTemplate"
TargetSchema="http://schemas.microsoft.com/intellisense/ie5"%>
Contact:<br>
<span> <%# DataBinder.Eval(Container, "DataItem.ContactName") %> </span>
<br>
```

Because the `DropDownList` control has the `AutoPostBack` property set to `true`, changing the template used by the `Repeater` control is as easy as selecting a different template in the `DropDownList` control. This causes a postback to occur and executes the code in `LoadRepeater` that is responsible for finding the right template and binding it to the `Repeater` control:

```
string templateName = templateList.SelectedItem.Text;
if (templateName.IndexOf(".ascx") > 0)
{
    repeaterRdrCust.ItemTemplate = Page.LoadTemplate(templateName);
}
```

The first thing the code does is check for the .ascx file extension to determine whether this is a file-based template. Next, the code calls `Page.LoadTemplate` to load the template from disk. At that point it can assign the `ITemplate` reference to the `ItemTemplate` property of the `Repeater` server control and continue with the rest of the data-binding process. Figure 7-19 demonstrates a different layout with the template CustFileTemplate.ascx.

Selecting the `CustCodeTemplate` option from the `DropDownList` control executes a different code path that programmatically instantiates templates and assigns them to the `Repeater` control:

```
else
{
    repeaterRdrCust.HeaderTemplate = new CustCodeHeaderTemplate();

    repeaterRdrCust.ItemTemplate = new CustCodeItemTemplate(true);

    repeaterRdrCust.AlternatingItemTemplate = new CustCodeItemTemplate(false);

    repeaterRdrCust.FooterTemplate = new CustCodeFooterTemplate();
}
```

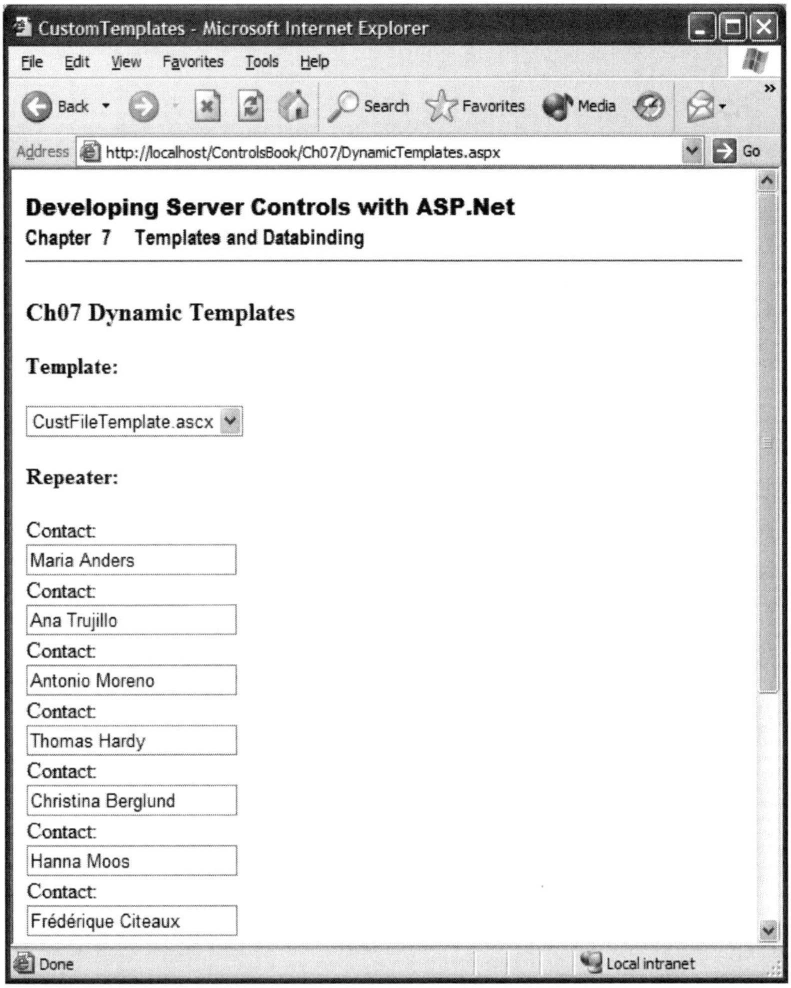

Figure 7-19. The Dynamic Templates Web Form and CustFileTemplate.ascx

Three custom template classes are used to affect the output of `Repeater`: `CustCodeHeaderTemplate`, `CustCodeItemTemplate`, and `CustCodeFooterTemplate`. The `CustCodeItemTemplate` class does double duty by implementing both the `ItemTemplate` and `AlternatingItemTemplate` templates for the `Repeater` control. The Boolean value passed to the templates' class ensures they have unique colors to make the output easy to read, as shown in Figure 7-20.

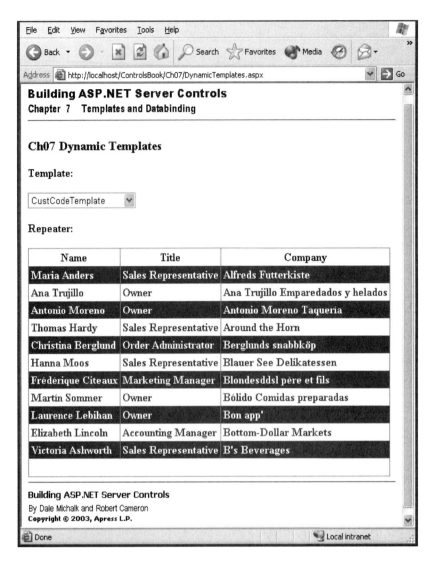

Figure 7-20. The Dynamic Templates Web Form and CustCodeTemplates.cs

Listings 7-23 and 7-24 show the full code for the Web Form.

Listing 7-23. The DynamicTemplates *.aspx Page File*

```
<%@ Register TagPrefix="apressUC" TagName="ControlsBookFooter"
Src="..\ControlsBookFooter.ascx" %>
<%@ Register TagPrefix="apressUC" TagName="ControlsBookHeader"
Src="..\ControlsBookHeader.ascx" %>
<%@ Page language="c#" Codebehind="DynamicTemplates.aspx.cs"
AutoEventWireup="false"
```

```
Inherits="ControlsBookWeb.Ch07.DynamicTemplates" %>
<%@ Register TagPrefix="apress" Namespace="ControlsBookLib.Ch07"
Assembly="ControlsBookLib" %>
<!DOCTYPE HTML PUBLIC "-//W3C//DTD HTML 4.0 Transitional//EN" >
<HTML>
  <HEAD>
    <title>CustomTemplates</title>
    <meta name="GENERATOR" Content="Microsoft Visual Studio 7.0">
    <meta name="CODE_LANGUAGE" Content="C#">
    <meta name="vs_defaultClientScript" content="JavaScript">
    <meta name="vs_targetSchema"
     content="http://schemas.microsoft.com/intellisense/ie5">
  </HEAD>
  <body MS_POSITIONING="FlowLayout">
    <form id="CustomTemplates" method="post" runat="server">
      <apressUC:ControlsBookHeader id="Header" runat="server" ChapterNumber="7"
       ChapterTitle="Templates and Data Binding" />
      <h3>Ch07 Dynamic Templates</h3>
      <b>Template: </b>
      <br>
      <br>
      <asp:DropDownList id="templateList" Runat="server" AutoPostBack="True">
        <asp:ListItem>FileTemplate.ascx</asp:ListItem>
        <asp:ListItem>CustCodeTemplate</asp:ListItem>
        <asp:ListItem>CustFileTemplate.ascx</asp:ListItem>
      </asp:DropDownList>
      <br>
      <br>
      <b>Repeater:</b><br>
      <br>
      <apress:repeater id="repeaterRdrCust" runat="server"></apress:repeater>
      <apressUC:ControlsBookFooter id="Footer" runat="server" />
    </form>
  </body>
</HTML>
```

Listing 7-24. The DynamicTemplates *Web Form Code-Behind Class File*

```
using System;
using System.Collections;
using System.ComponentModel;
using System.Data;
using System.Data.SqlClient;
using System.Drawing;
using System.Web;
using System.Web.SessionState;
using System.Web.UI;
using System.Web.UI.WebControls;
using System.Web.UI.HtmlControls;
using ControlsBookLib.Ch07;
```

```
namespace ControlsBookWeb.Ch07
{
    public class DynamicTemplates : System.Web.UI.Page
    {
        protected System.Web.UI.WebControls.DropDownList templateList;
        protected ControlsBookLib.Ch07.Repeater repeaterRdrCust;

        private void Page_Load(object sender, System.EventArgs e)
        {
            LoadRepeater();
        }

        private void LoadRepeater()
        {
            string templateName = templateList.SelectedItem.Text;
            if (templateName.IndexOf(".ascx") > 0)
            {
                repeaterRdrCust.ItemTemplate = Page.LoadTemplate(templateName);
            }
            else
            {
                repeaterRdrCust.HeaderTemplate = new CustCodeHeaderTemplate();

                repeaterRdrCust.ItemTemplate = new CustCodeItemTemplate(true);

                repeaterRdrCust.AlternatingItemTemplate =
                        new CustCodeItemTemplate(false);

                repeaterRdrCust.FooterTemplate = new CustCodeFooterTemplate();
            }

            SqlDataReader dr = GetCustomerDataReader();
            repeaterRdrCust.DataSource = dr;
            repeaterRdrCust.DataBind();
            dr.Close();
        }

        private SqlDataReader GetCustomerDataReader()
        {
            SqlConnection conn =
                new SqlConnection("Server=(local);Database=Northwind;
                Integrated Security=true;");
            conn.Open();

            SqlCommand cmd =
                new SqlCommand(
"SELECT CustomerID, ContactName, ContactTitle, CompanyName FROM Customers WHERE"+
"CustomerID LIKE '[AB]%'",
                conn);
            SqlDataReader dr = cmd.ExecuteReader(CommandBehavior.CloseConnection);
```

```
      return dr;
  }

  #region Web Form Designer generated code
  override protected void OnInit(EventArgs e)
  {
      //
      // CODEGEN: This call is required by the ASP.NET Web Form Designer.
      //
      InitializeComponent();
      base.OnInit(e);
  }

  /// <summary>
  /// Required method for Designer support - do not modify
  /// the contents of this method with the code editor.
  /// </summary>
  private void InitializeComponent()
  {
      this.Load += new System.EventHandler(this.Page_Load);

  }
  #endregion
  }
}
```

Now that we have covered the basics with respect to templates, in the next section we dig a bit deeper with a discussion of the template implementation in the TemplateMenu server control.

Implementing the ITemplate Interface

We now move on to the TemplateMenu sample as an example to demonstrate the nuts and bolts of implementing templates. The ITemplate interface requires that only a single method named InstantiateIn be implemented by a control. The template code gets a reference to its container as the sole parameter and is free to add control content to the container.

The TemplateMenu sample shares its templates with the Dynamic Templates sample implemented in the CustomCodeTemplates class. The following implementation of InstantiateIn in the CustCodeHeaderTemplate template shows that its job is to set up the Literal control that emits an HTML table header. CustCodeFooterTemplate does much the same for closing out the HTML table.

```
public void InstantiateIn(Control container)
{
    LiteralControl table =
        new LiteralControl(
        "<table cellspacing=\"0\" cellpadding=\"3\" " +
        "rules=\"cols\" bordercolor=\"#999999\" border=\"1\" " +
```

```
            "style=\"background-color:White;border-color:#999999;" +
            "border-width:1px;border-style:None;" +
            "border-collapse:collapse;\">" +
            "<th>Name</th><th>Title</th><th>Company</th>"
            );
    container.Controls.Add(table);
}
```

CustCodeItemTemplate is a bit more complex because it adds Label controls representing the ContactName, ContactTitle, and CompanyName columns into the mix. These tags go hand in hand with the necessary <TR> and <TD> tags to build the rows in the HTML table.

We also wire in the capability for this template class to serve as an ItemTemplate or AlternatingItemTemplate template via a Boolean parameter that is passed to its constructor:

```
public class CustCodeItemTemplate : ITemplate
{
   bool isItem = false;

   public CustCodeItemTemplate(bool IsItem)
   {
      isItem = IsItem;
}
```

CustCodeItemTemplate also has a Color property and a BackgroundColor property that generate a blue and white color string depending on the Boolean value of isItem:

```
public string BackgroundColor
{
   get
   {
      if (isItem)
         return "blue";
      else
         return "white";
   }
}

public string Color
{
   get
   {
      if (isItem)
         return "white";
      else
         return "blue";
   }
}
```

This customization provides a nice alternating blue and white color scheme in the table output for the control using the templates. `InstantiateIn` makes use of the property to set the `<TR>` tag up with the right CSS style properties. It also adds the necessary `LiteralControl` controls that will data-bind to the data source:

```
public void InstantiateIn(Control container)
{
    LiteralControl row =
        new LiteralControl("<tr style=\"color:" + Color +
        ";background-color:" + BackgroundColor +
        ";font-weight:bold;\">");
    container.Controls.Add(row);

    LiteralControl contactName = new LiteralControl();
    contactName.DataBinding += new EventHandler(BindContactName);
    container.Controls.Add(contactName);

    LiteralControl contactTitle = new LiteralControl();
    contactTitle.DataBinding += new EventHandler(BindContactTitle);
    container.Controls.Add(contactTitle);

    LiteralControl companyName = new LiteralControl();
    companyName.DataBinding += new EventHandler(BindCompanyName);
    container.Controls.Add(companyName);

    row = new LiteralControl("</tr>");
    container.Controls.Add(row);
}
```

To make the data-binding process work properly, the template has built-in data-binding event handlers wired to each `LiteralControl` instance representing a column in the data source. During data binding, each template data binds and the `LiteralControls` inside of the template data bind as well, firing events that the template handles by casting to the `RepeaterItem` container and accessing the current data source row to fill in the `Text` property of the `LiteralControl` controls. The code for `ContactName` is as follows:

```
private void BindContactName(object source, EventArgs e)
{
    LiteralControl contactName = (LiteralControl) source;
    RepeaterItem item = (RepeaterItem) contactName.NamingContainer;
    contactName.Text = "<td>" +
        DataBinder.Eval(item.DataItem, "ContactName")
        + "</td>";
}
```

Listing 7-25 contains the full code for all the custom-coded templates.

Listing 7-25. The CustCodeTemplates.cs *Template Class File*

```
using System;
using System.Web.UI;
using ControlsBookLib.Ch07 ;

namespace ControlsBookLib.Ch07
{
    public class CustCodeHeaderTemplate : ITemplate
    {
        public void InstantiateIn(Control container)
        {
            LiteralControl table =
                new LiteralControl(
                "<table cellspacing=\"0\" cellpadding=\"3\" " +
                "rules=\"cols\" bordercolor=\"#999999\" border=\"1\" " +
                "style=\"background-color:White;border-color:#999999;" +
                "border-width:1px;border-style:None;" +
                "border-collapse:collapse;\">" +
                "<th>Name</th><th>Title</th><th>Company</th>"
                );
            container.Controls.Add(table);
        }
    }

    public class CustCodeItemTemplate : ITemplate
    {
        bool isItem = false;

        public CustCodeItemTemplate(bool IsItem)
        {
            isItem = IsItem;

        }

        public string BackgroundColor
        {
            get
            {
                if (isItem)
                    return "blue";
                else
                    return "white";
            }
        }

        public string Color
        {
            get
            {
                if (isItem)
```

```
            return "white";
        else
            return "blue";
    }
}

public void InstantiateIn(Control container)
{
    LiteralControl row =
        new LiteralControl("<tr style=\"color:" + Color +
        ";background-color:" + BackgroundColor +
        ";font-weight:bold;\">");
    container.Controls.Add(row);

    LiteralControl contactName = new LiteralControl();
    contactName.DataBinding += new EventHandler(BindContactName);
    container.Controls.Add(contactName);

    LiteralControl contactTitle = new LiteralControl();
    contactTitle.DataBinding += new EventHandler(BindContactTitle);
    container.Controls.Add(contactTitle);

    LiteralControl companyName = new LiteralControl();
    companyName.DataBinding += new EventHandler(BindCompanyName);
    container.Controls.Add(companyName);

    row = new LiteralControl("</tr>");
    container.Controls.Add(row);
}

private void BindContactName(object source, EventArgs e)
{
    LiteralControl contactName = (LiteralControl) source;
    RepeaterItem item = (RepeaterItem) contactName.NamingContainer;
    contactName.Text = "<td>" +
        DataBinder.Eval(item.DataItem, "ContactName")
        + "</td>";
}

private void BindContactTitle(object source, EventArgs e)
{
    LiteralControl contactTitle = (LiteralControl) source;
    RepeaterItem item = (RepeaterItem) contactTitle.NamingContainer;
    contactTitle.Text = "<td>" +
        DataBinder.Eval(item.DataItem, "ContactTitle")
        + "</td>";
}

private void BindCompanyName(object source, EventArgs e)
{
    LiteralControl companyName = (LiteralControl) source;
```

```
        RepeaterItem item = (RepeaterItem) companyName.NamingContainer;
        companyName.Text = "<td>" +
           DataBinder.Eval(item.DataItem, "CompanyName")
           + "</td>";
      }
    }

    public class CustCodeFooterTemplate : ITemplate
    {
       public void InstantiateIn(Control container)
       {
          LiteralControl table = new
LiteralControl("<tr><td colspan=3> </td></tr></table>");
          container.Controls.Add(table);
       }
    }
}
```

Summary

Templates and data binding are the two primary ways to modify the graphical content of an ASP.NET Web Form. Templates provide a way for developers to declaratively insert raw HTML through server controls into the output of a prebuilt control. Templates can be loaded dynamically through Page.LoadTemplate or instantiated by classes that implement the ITemplate interface.

Data binding simplifies the task of rendering data intermixed with HTML for web developers by rendering a control according to the information in the data source that is bound to the control. Data-bound controls should strive to support a variety of data sources by implementing both IEnumerable and IListSource.

The ParseChildren attribute determines if ASP.NET parses a server control's inner tag content in an .aspx page as child controls or child properties. The ControlBuilder attribute allows a control to redirect the tag parsing process to a custom ControlBuilder class.

CHAPTER 8

Integrating Client-Side Script

SOFTWARE DEVELOPMENT, like any other engineering discipline, progresses toward an architecture resulting from a set of design decisions. There are trade-offs between competing issues such as browser compatibility versus display richness and the number of round-trips versus client-side computation, to name a couple. This chapter focuses on how these trade-offs come into play with respect to integrating client-side script into your ASP.NET server control development efforts.

Using client-side script can significantly enhance the usability and scalability of a web application at the cost of additional time in development and most likely a reduction in cross-browser support. However, due to the fact that the browser market is dominated by recent browsers produced by Microsoft and Netscape (with the majority of users currently using Microsoft's Internet Explorer), most developers have opted to make web applications more appealing and interactive like their desktop application cousins, despite the additional costs in terms of development effort. This means the addition of JavaScript and DHTML to an already complex web development effort in ASP or any other server-side development environment.

Although the .NET Framework provides top-notch support for server-side development through its rich object model, ASP.NET server controls are an excellent way to facilitate development of web applications with a rich client-side UI. ASP.NET provides the means to encapsulate client-side script complexity within the confines of a server control. Instead of the entire development team having to know the ins and outs of client-side script, the team can factor the code into custom server controls as part of a reusable UI widget library.

To start the chapter off, we describe the various features that client-side script can provide to a web application, after which we dive into the details of how to integrate those client-side features into custom server controls.

Client-Side Script Server Control Scenarios

In this chapter we cover the gamut of client-side features. Here are the highlights of the topics we cover:

- *Handling client-side events:* This script executes when a client activity occurs, such as when the user clicks with the mouse, moves the mouse, or presses a key. You handle these events by adding script code to HTML tag attributes on the page.

- *Detecting browser capabilities:* The detection process includes analyzing the user agent string from the browser device to check its suitability for more advanced features such as JavaScript and DHTML.

- *Handling the* Page_Load *event in the browser:* You add this script code to the bottom of an HTML page that executes on page load in the browser. It usually performs initialization tasks.

- *Running script when a page form is submitted:* This consists of adding script to handle verification or validation tasks before postback to the web server. You accomplish this through JavaScript form submit code or by handling the onsubmit event of the <FORM> tag.

- *Integrating client- and server-side events:* This script ensures client-side events and data are appropriately mapped to server-side code operations when the form is posted back to the web server.

We feel the best way to cover these client-side script scenarios is to develop a set of server controls that demonstrates the listed capabilities. The controls we build in this chapter include an image control that performs client-side image mouse rollovers, a browser capabilities control that lets you troubleshoot what features a browser supports and how your code handles content generation, a control that sets the focus of the web page on loading the HTML document, a control that confirms the user's action when clicking a link button, and finally an up/down numeric control similar to its desktop cousin that can work with or without JavaScript support. We move on to discuss how to handle client-side events in the next section.

Handling Client-Side Events

The web browser has its own object model representing the HTML tags and events that occur when the user is interacting with them. This event system within the browser has been around for a while and is completely different from the server-side event mechanism we discussed in detail in Chapter 5.

Client-side events fired in the browser window are added to HTML tags via attributes with names such as onclick, onblur, onmouseover, onmouseout, and so on. The value of the event-handling attribute contains the script that you want to execute when the event is raised. The following HTML snippet shows a <SPAN> tag with an inline onclick event handler that pops up an alert message box:

```
<span id="TopLabel" tabindex="1" onclick=
"alert('TopLabel clicked!');">TopLabel</span>
```

The browser is perfectly happy to execute this JavaScript when the `<SPAN>` tag is clicked. The first server control example demonstrates how to add script code to an ASP.NET server control to handle a client-side click event like the previous one. As an ASP.NET developer, you have two options available to add the `onclick` event code to the server control:

- You can add it declaratively via an attribute on the control's tag in the .aspx page.

- You can add it programmatically to the `Attributes` collection of the server control in the code-behind class.

Adding the code to the .aspx page is the simpler of the two options. Another way to add a client-side click event handler is to encapsulate the script into a server control. The following code shows how to generate the `<SPAN>` content with an `onclick` event handler using an ASP.NET `Label` server control and adding an `onclick` attribute. The page parser is responsible for ensuring this becomes part of the control's final output.

```
<asp:Label ID="TopLabel" Runat="server" Text="TopLabel"
tabIndex=1 onclick="alert('TopLabel clicked!');">TopLabel</asp:Label>
```

The following code shows the second option: adding the attribute to the HTML element via the `Attributes` collection of the server control in the code-behind class. The recommended place to put this type of code is in the `Page_Load` event because the control is fully initialized.

```
BottomLabel.Attributes.Add("onclick", "alert('BottomLabel clicked!');");
```

The two preceding techniques add the client-side script code via external manipulation of the server control. You can add the same attribute-handling code internally to a server control just as easily. Listing 8-1 shows a server control that inherits from the ASP.NET `Label` control and adds code to an override of the `OnPreRender` method that generates an `onclick` attribute to the final output of our new custom `Label` control, `ClickLabel`.

Listing 8-1. The `ClickLabel` *Server Control*

```
using System;
using System.Web.UI;
using System.Web.UI.WebControls;

namespace ControlsBookLib.Ch08
{
    [ToolboxData("<{0}:ClickLabel runat=server></{0}:ClickLabel>"),
    DefaultProperty("ClickText")]
    public class ClickLabel : Label
    {
```

```
        private string clickText = "";
        public virtual string ClickText
        {
            get{ return clickText; }
            set{ clickText = value; }
        }

        protected override void OnPreRender(EventArgs e)
        {
            base.OnPreRender(e);

            // Add the onclick client-side event handler to
            // display a JavaScript alert box
            Attributes.Add("onclick","alert('" + clickText + "');");
        }
    }
}
```

This ensures that the control's `Attributes` collection is loaded before the `Render` method is called. A `ClickText` property is provided to make the control easily configurable as to what text message displays in the JavaScript alert pop-up. Though this is a trivial example, it does demonstrate one way to make client-side script capabilities available through a server control to the developer/user without the developer having to know how to write the JavaScript. In the next section, we present a Web Form that demonstrates these three options.

The Click Web Form

The following Click Web Form example demonstrates all three techniques for emitting client-side event handlers. The Web Form renders with three `Label` controls that all generate the same JavaScript alert pop-up when clicked. The following HTML code shows the `<SPAN>` tags and their inline client-side JavaScript:

```
<span id="TopLabel" onclick="alert('TopLabel clicked!');">Click the TopLabel</span>
<br>
<span id="MiddleLabel" onclick="alert('MiddleLabel clicked!');">
Click the MiddleLabel</span>
<br>
<span id="BottomLabel" onclick="alert('BottomLabel clicked!');">
Click the BottomLabel</span>
```

Figure 8-1 shows what happens when the middle `ClickLabel` text output is clicked.

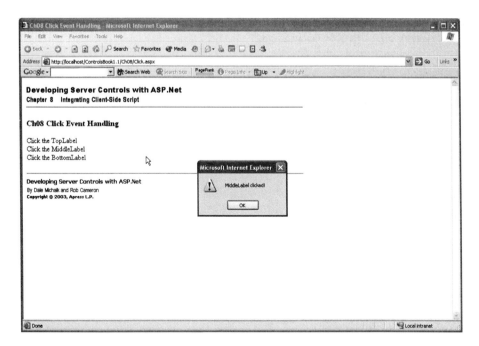

Figure 8-1. The Click Web Form after the middle label is clicked

The full listing for the Web Form is shown in Listings 8-2 and 8-3.

Listing 8-2. The Click Web Form .aspx Page File

```
<%@ Register TagPrefix="apressUC" TagName="ControlsBookFooter"
 Src="..\ControlsBookFooter.ascx" %>
<%@ Register TagPrefix="apressUC" TagName="ControlsBookHeader"
Src="..\ControlsBookHeader.ascx" %>
<%@ Page language="c#" Codebehind="Click.aspx.cs" AutoEventWireup="false"
Inherits="ControlsBookWeb.Ch08.Click" %>
<%@ Register TagPrefix="apress" Namespace="ControlsBookLib.Ch08"
Assembly="ControlsBookLib" %>
<!DOCTYPE HTML PUBLIC "-//W3C//DTD HTML 4.0 Transitional//EN" >
<HTML>
  <HEAD>
    <title>Ch08 Click Event Handling</title>
    <meta name="GENERATOR" Content="Microsoft Visual Studio 7.0">
    <meta name="CODE_LANGUAGE" Content="C#">
    <meta name="vs_defaultClientScript" content="JavaScript">
    <meta name="vs_targetSchema"
content="http://schemas.microsoft.com/intellisense/ie5">
  </HEAD>
  <body MS_POSITIONING="FlowLayout">
    <form id="Click" method="post" runat="server">
```

```
            <apressUC:ControlsBookHeader id="Header" chapternumber="8"
chaptertitle="Integrating Client-Side Script" runat="server" />
            <h3>Ch08 Click Event Handling</h3>
            <asp:Label ID="TopLabel" Runat="server" Text="Click the TopLabel"
onclick="alert('TopLabel clicked!');" />
            <br>
            <apress:ClickLabel ID="MiddleLabel" Runat="server" Text=
"Click the MiddleLabel" ClickText="MiddleLabel clicked!" />
            <br>
            <asp:Label ID="BottomLabel" Runat="server" Text="Click the BottomLabel" />
            <apressUC:ControlsBookFooter id="Footer" runat="server" />
        </form>
    </body>
</HTML>
```

Listing 8-3. The Click Web Form Code-Behind Class File

```
using System;
using System.Collections;
using System.ComponentModel;
using System.Data;
using System.Drawing;
using System.Web;
using System.Web.SessionState;
using System.Web.UI;
using System.Web.UI.WebControls;
using System.Web.UI.HtmlControls;

namespace ControlsBookWeb.Ch08
{
    public class Click : System.Web.UI.Page
    {
        protected System.Web.UI.WebControls.Label TopLabel;
        protected ControlsBookLib.Ch08.ClickLabel MiddleLabel;
        protected System.Web.UI.WebControls.Label BottomLabel;
        protected ControlsBookWeb.ControlsBookHeader Header ;

        private void Page_Load(object sender, System.EventArgs e)
        {
            BottomLabel.Attributes.Add("onclick",
                "alert('BottomLabel clicked!');");
        }

        #region Web Form Designer generated code
        override protected void OnInit(EventArgs e)
        {
            //
            // CODEGEN: This call is required by the ASP.NET Web Form Designer.
            //
            InitializeComponent();
```

```
        base.OnInit(e);
    }

    /// <summary>
    /// Required method for Designer support - do not modify
    /// the contents of this method with the code editor.
    /// </summary>
    private void InitializeComponent()
    {
        this.Load += new System.EventHandler(this.Page_Load);

    }
    #endregion
    }
}
```

Now that we have introduced how to add client-side script to a server control, we move on to a more interesting example of providing image rollovers within a server control by integrating client-side script.

Handling Mouse Events for Image Rollovers

Although the ASP.NET Image control makes it easy to assign image URL information through its Designer property support, its distinct lack of rich functionality provides ample room for improvement. A nice extension to this control would be the capability to perform client-side image mouse rollovers. As we demonstrate in Chapter 3 with the TextBox3d control, the object-oriented nature of ASP.NET makes it easy to take existing controls and inherit from them to add additional features. RolloverImageLink is a server control that we build next that inherits the full feature-set of the ASP.NET Image server control while adding client-side rollover capability and hyperlink navigation.

As shown in the following code, RolloverImageLink adds an OverImageUrl property that stores the location of the rollover image file and a NavigationalUrl property that stores the hyperlink location. The EnableClientScript property allows the user to turn on or off the client JavaScript functionality on demand.

```
[ToolboxData("<{0}:RolloverImageLink runat=server></{0}:RolloverImageLink>"),
DefaultProperty("NavigateUrl")]
public class RolloverImageLink : Image
{
    public virtual bool EnableClientScript
    {
        get
        {
            object script = ViewState["EnableClientScript"];
            return (script == null) ? true : (bool) script;
        }
        set
        {
            ViewState["EnableClientScript"] = value;
```

```
            }
        }

    public string NavigateUrl
    {
        get
        {
            object url = ViewState["NavigateUrl"];
            return (url == null) ? "" : (string) url;
        }
        set
        {
            ViewState["NavigateUrl"] = value;
        }
    }

    public string OverImageUrl
    {
        get
        {
            object url = ViewState["OverImageUrl"];
            return (url == null) ? "" : (string) url;
        }
        set
        {
            ViewState["OverImageUrl"] = value;
        }
    }

    public bool PreLoadImages
    {
        get
        {
            object pre = ViewState["PreLoadImages"];
            return (pre == null) ? true : (bool) pre;
        }
        set
        {
            ViewState["PreLoadImages"] = value;
        }
    }
```

RolloverImageLink also supports preloading the images pointed to by the ImageUrl and OverImageUrl properties so you don't have to write the time-consuming JavaScript that makes the rollover effect much more responsive in the browser. If the user sets the PreLoadImages property of the control to true, this generates extra JavaScript that loads the images when the page is loaded into the browser.

JavaScript Detection

The RolloverImageLink control is a good citizen in that it detects the browser support
for JavaScript before it generates the client script to render the rollover images. The
DetermineRenderClientScript method encapsulates the verification logic and sets a
private bool named renderClientScript, depending on the outcome:

```
private bool renderClientScript = false;
protected void DetermineRenderClientScript()
{
   if (EnableClientScript &&
      Context.Request.Browser.JavaScript)
      renderClientScript = true;
}
```

The JavaScript capability is checked by examining an instance of the
HttpBrowserCapabilities class that is taken from the Browser property of the current
request. For now, all we use is the JavaScript property. In a moment, we will implement a control that displays all of the browser capability properties.

Rendering Client Script Code

RolloverImageLink takes advantage of most of the features built into ASP.NET for
emitting JavaScript into the HTML output in a modular manner. This capability
includes a registration system that ensures only a single instance of a block of script
code is emitted in the final HTML output despite the presence of multiple instances
of a server control on a Web Form that need it. This helps to keep page size to a minimum. Table 8-1 summarizes the feature set.

Table 8-1. ASP.NET Page *Class Script Registration Methods*

METHOD	DESCRIPTION
RegisterClientScriptBlock	Emits the specified JavaScript code at the top of the HTML form to allow all of the controls on the page rendered after it to reference it.
IsClientScriptBlockRegistered	Checks to see if a previous control has registered a JavaScript block at the top of the HTML form.
RegisterStartupScript	Emits the specified JavaScript code at the bottom of the HTML form to be able to access any of the controls on the Web Form from the script block.
IsStartupScriptRegistered	Checks to see if a previous control has registered a start-up JavaScript block at the bottom of the HTML form.
RegisterArrayDeclaration	Emits an array value to the specified JavaScript array name at the bottom of the HTML form. This method can be called repeatedly from multiple controls. The values are aggregated in the same array.
RegisterOnSubmitStatement	Emits JavaScript code that is executed in the context of an onsubmit event handler on the HTML <FORM> element.

The bulk of the JavaScript creation occurs in the OnPreRender method of the RolloverImageLink control:

```
protected override void OnPreRender(EventArgs e)
{
   base.OnPreRender(e);

   // use type of control to uniquely id the
   // registered JavaScript code (only one
   // copy is needed per web form)
   string typename =
       typeof(RolloverImageLink).ToString().Replace(".","_");

   DetermineRenderClientScript();

   if (renderClientScript)
   {
      // register the image-swapping JavaScript
      // if it is not already registered
      if (!Page.IsClientScriptBlockRegistered(typename))
      {
         Page.RegisterClientScriptBlock(
            typename,
            SWAP_SCRIPT_BLOCK);
      }

      if (this.PreLoadImages)
      {
         // add image names to the
         // array of rollover images to be preloaded
         Page.RegisterArrayDeclaration(typename,
            "'" + ResolveUrl(this.ImageUrl) + "'," +
            "'" + ResolveUrl(this.OverImageUrl) + "'");

         // register the image, preloading JavaScript
         // if it is not already registered
         if (!Page.IsStartupScriptRegistered(typename))
         {
            Page.RegisterStartupScript(
               typename,
               PRELOAD_SCRIPT_BLOCK.Replace("{arrayname}",typename));
         }
      }
   }
}
```

The first client script feature we use in RolloverImageLink is the capability to render a swap script function that swaps the images for rollover effect at the top of the HTML document. The server control code uses the Page method RegisterClientScript in conjunction with the constant string named SWAP_SCRIPT_BLOCK, as shown in the following code. This string constant uses the at symbol (@) to enable verbatim strings that allow for easy formatting and maintenance inside the server control. Before we register the client script, we check to see if the script block has already been registered by another instance of the control on the page with a call to `IsClientScriptBlockRegistered`. Note that if we were to call `RegisterClientScript` twice, the content of the second invocation replaces the script generated by the first call.

```
protected const string SWAP_SCRIPT_BLOCK = @"
<script language='JavaScript'>
function __Image_Swap(sName, sSrc)
{
document.images[sName].src = sSrc;
}
</script>
";
```

`RegisterClientScriptBlock` takes two parameters: the ID of the script block and the script to be emitted. Because we want only a single version of the script block emitted for all our controls on a given page, we pass in the fully scoped assembly type name of the control. It is formatted to change the period (.) characters to underscore (_) characters to be more JavaScript-friendly.

If we are preloading the images, we register the necessary information using a data-oriented approach to the script processing. We can easily do this—ASP.NET makes it simple to emit JavaScript arrays. The `RegisterArrayDeclaration` method of the `Page` object allows us to add all the image names to the HTML document as an array that our `PRELOAD_SCRIPT_BLOCK` script block can iterate over when loading images. Unlike the swap script function, this script is emitted near the end of the document.

The image preloading script comes from a constant string like the one for swapping images. It is a little different because it has a placeholder {arrayname} for the array that is emitted into the output:

```
protected const string PRELOAD_SCRIPT_BLOCK = @"
<script language='JavaScript'>
for (index = 0; index < {arrayname}; index++)
{
loadimg = new Image();
loadimg.src = {arrayname}[index];
}
</script>
";
```

The `OnPreRender` code replaces the array name correctly from the script template and passes it to the `RegisterStartupScript` method of the `Page` class. This will emit it at the very bottom of the HTML form, after any registered JavaScript arrays. Of course, we also check to see if the script was registered by a previous control with a call to `IsStartupScriptRegistered` provided by the `Page` class.

Rendering the HTML Code

The RolloverImageLink control overrides the rendering process of the inherited image control so that it can add the hyperlink and JavaScript code. The main task is to wrap the <IMG> tag generation process of the base Image control with an enclosing <A> tag.

NOTE *Because generating the link (<A> tag) is an HTML operation, it is not affected by the value of the* EnableClientScript *property on the server control. This functionality is present on the server regardless of JavaScript capabilities.*

Before we do this, we call the Page method named VerifyRenderingInServerForm, as shown in the following code. This method raises an exception if the control is not rendering within the confines of a <FORM runat="server"> tag required for the Web Form environment. It is a good habit to put this call into the Render phase of a control, especially if the control is emitting client-side script that performs a postback to the web server.

```
protected override void Render(HtmlTextWriter writer)
{
    // ensure the control is used inside <form runat="server">
    Page.VerifyRenderingInServerForm(this);

    // set up attributes for the enclosing hyperlink
    // <a href></a> tag pair that go around the <img> tag
    writer.AddAttribute("href",this.NavigateUrl);

    // we have to create an ID for the <a> tag so that it
    // doesn't conflict with the <img> tag generated by
    // the base Image control
    writer.AddAttribute("name",this.UniqueID + "_href");

    // emit onmouseover/onmouseout attributes that handle
    // client events and invoke our image-swapping JavaScript
    // code if client supports it
    if (renderClientScript)
    {
        writer.AddAttribute("onmouseover",
            IMAGE_SWAP_FUNC + "('" + this.UniqueID + "','" +
            ResolveUrl(this.OverImageUrl) + "');");
        writer.AddAttribute("onmouseout",
            IMAGE_SWAP_FUNC + "('" + this.UniqueID + "','" +
            ResolveUrl(this.ImageUrl) + "');");

    }
    writer.RenderBeginTag(HtmlTextWriterTag.A);
```

```
        // use name attribute to identify HTML <img> element
        // for older browsers
        writer.AddAttribute("name",this.UniqueID);

        base.Render(writer);

        writer.RenderEndTag();
}
```

The first section of our Render override adds attributes to help generate the <A> hyperlink, including the href attribute that is linked to NavigateUrl. Notice that we create a unique name attribute for the <A> tag to prevent any naming conflicts with other tags on the page, including a potential conflict with the <IMG> tag of the inherited Image control.

The next step in working with the <A> tag is to add the onmouseover and onmouseout event-handling attributes. Render puts values in the attributes to call the image-swapping JavaScript function. This is done using the IMAGE_SWAP_FUNC constant that points to the actual JavaScript function name. After the <A> tag attributes are added to the HtmlTextWriter stream, we render the <A> begin tag.

The next step is to prepare for the base Image class to render the <IMG> tag. To make the script friendlier to browsers that favor the name attribute in JavaScript, we add a name attribute to the HtmlTextWriter stream before we call on the base Image class's Render method. The RolloverImageLink override of Render ends by emitting the closing </A> tag.

At this point, the control is fully implemented, as shown in Listing 8-4.

Listing 8-4. The RolloverImageLink *Server Control*

```
using System;
using System.Web;
using System.Web.UI;
using System.Web.UI.WebControls;
using System.Text;

namespace ControlsBookLib.Ch08
{
   [ToolboxData("<{0}:RolloverImageLink runat=server></{0}:RolloverImageLink>"),
   DefaultProperty("NavigateUrl")]
   public class RolloverImageLink : Image
   {
      public virtual bool EnableClientScript
      {
         get
         {
            object script = ViewState["EnableClientScript"];
            return (script == null) ? true : (bool) script;
         }
         set
         {
```

```
            ViewState["EnableClientScript"] = value;
      }
}

public string NavigateUrl
{
   get
   {
      object url = ViewState["NavigateUrl"];
      return (url == null) ? "" : (string) url;
   }
   set
   {
      ViewState["NavigateUrl"] = value;
   }
}

public string OverImageUrl
{
   get
   {
      object url = ViewState["OverImageUrl"];
      return (url == null) ? "" : (string) url;
   }
   set
   {
      ViewState["OverImageUrl"] = value;
   }
}

public bool PreLoadImages
{
   get
   {
      object pre = ViewState["PreLoadImages"];
      return (pre == null) ? true : (bool) pre;
   }
   set
   {
      ViewState["PreLoadImages"] = value;
   }
}

protected const string IMAGE_SWAP_FUNC = "__Image_Swap";

//@ symbol in front of the string preserves the layout of the string content
protected const string SWAP_SCRIPT_BLOCK = @"
<script language='JavaScript'>
function __Image_Swap(sName, sSrc)
{
document.images[sName].src = sSrc;
}
```

```
</script>
";

protected const string PRELOAD_SCRIPT_BLOCK = @"
<script language='JavaScript'>
for (index = 0; index < {arrayname}; index++)
{
loadimg = new Image();
loadimg.src = {arrayname}[index];
}
</script>
";

private bool renderClientScript = false;
protected void DetermineRenderClientScript()
{
   if (EnableClientScript &&
      Context.Request.Browser.JavaScript)
      renderClientScript = true;
}

protected override void OnPreRender(EventArgs e)
{
   base.OnPreRender(e);

   // use type of control to uniquely id the
   // register JavaScript code (only one
   // copy is needed per web form)
   string typename =
      typeof(RolloverImageLink).ToString().Replace(".","_");

   DetermineRenderClientScript();

   if (renderClientScript)
   {
      // register the image-swapping JavaScript
      // if it is not already registered
      if (!Page.IsClientScriptBlockRegistered(typename))
      {
         Page.RegisterClientScriptBlock(
            typename,
            SWAP_SCRIPT_BLOCK);
      }

      if (this.PreLoadImages)
      {
         // add image names to the
         // array of rollover images to be preloaded
         Page.RegisterArrayDeclaration(typename,
            "'" + ResolveUrl(this.ImageUrl) + "'," +
            "'" + ResolveUrl(this.OverImageUrl) + "'");
```

```
                    // register the image, preloading JavaScript
                    // if it is not already registered
                    if (!Page.IsStartupScriptRegistered(typename))
                    {
                        Page.RegisterStartupScript(
                            typename,
                            PRELOAD_SCRIPT_BLOCK.Replace("{arrayname}",typename));
                    }
                }
            }
        }
    }

    protected override void Render(HtmlTextWriter writer)
    {
        // ensure the control is used inside <form runat="server">
        Page.VerifyRenderingInServerForm(this);

        // set up attributes for the enclosing hyperlink
        // <a href></a> tag pair that go around the <img> tag
        writer.AddAttribute("href",this.NavigateUrl);

        // we have to create an ID for the <a> tag so that it
        // doesn't conflict with the <img> tag generated by
        // the base Image control
        writer.AddAttribute("name",this.UniqueID + "_href");

        // emit onmouseover/onmouseout attributes that handle
        // client events and invoke our image-swapping JavaScript
        // code if client supports it
        if (renderClientScript)
        {
            writer.AddAttribute("onmouseover",
                IMAGE_SWAP_FUNC + "('" + this.UniqueID + "','" +
                ResolveUrl(this.OverImageUrl) + "');");
            writer.AddAttribute("onmouseout",
                IMAGE_SWAP_FUNC + "('" + this.UniqueID + "','" +
                ResolveUrl(this.ImageUrl) + "');");

        }
        writer.RenderBeginTag(HtmlTextWriterTag.A);

        // use name attribute to identify HTML <img> element
        // for older browsers
        writer.AddAttribute("name",this.UniqueID);

        base.Render(writer);

        writer.RenderEndTag();
    }
  }
}
```

As we alluded to earlier in the chapter, generating client-side script in a server control is a browser-specific task requiring additional care on the part of the developer. In the next section, we cover how to determine the capabilities of a browser device to help us make better decisions when rendering script.

Detecting Browser Capabilities

To properly render script in the browser, we need to determine the supported capabilities of the current browsing device. We don't want to render script if it isn't supported. In this section, we cover how to determine browser capabilities. We build a server control that provides feedback on what the capabilities are of a browsing device directly on the web page. We can use this as a tool when troubleshooting client-side script generation within custom server controls.

In the RolloverImageLink server control, we check for JavaScript capabilities by accessing an instance of the HttpBrowserCapabilities class reachable via the Context.Request.Browser property chain of the root System.Web.UI.Control class. We discuss Context in Chapter 4.

The information stored in the properties of the HttpBrowserCapabilities object is gathered by parsing the HTTP_USER_AGENT header sent from the browsing device currently requesting a page in the web application. The configuration for ASP.NET client capability parsing is located in the machine.config configuration file for the .NET Framework.

 NOTE *The browser-detection process for version 1.0 of the .NET Framework has been extended in version 1.1 in a backward-compatible manner. In Chapter 10, we discuss what is going on with mobile controls in ASP.NET and how ASP.NET has enhanced the device capability checking process.*

For a machine running Windows XP with the .NET Framework version 1.1 installed on the C: drive with default settings, the machine.config file is located here:

```
C:\WINDOWS\Microsoft.NET\Framework\ v1.1.4322\CONFIG\machine.config
```

The section of machine.config related to browser detection is <browserCaps>. Inside the <browserCaps> XML tag is a set of XML tags and name/value pairs that guide the parsing process when ASP.NET handles a client request:

- <use> element

- <result> element

- <filter> element

- <case> element

- Name/value pairs

The `<use>` and `<result>` Elements

The `<use>` element points to the HTTP header that contains the information sent from the client to detect its feature set via the var attribute. This is set to HTTP_USER_AGENT, as shown here:

```
<use var="HTTP_USER_AGENT"/>
```

The `<result>` element has a type attribute that points to the class that will store the browser capability information. For version 1.0 of the .NET Framework, the class used is HttpBrowserCapabilities, as shown in the following code. Version 1.1 has an enhanced version class named MobileCapabilities that inherits from HttpBrowserCapabilities, so it is completely backward compatible.

```
<browserCaps>
    <result type="System.Web.HttpBrowserCapabilities"/>
```

The `<filter>` and `<case>` Elements

The `<filter>` element is used to whittle down the matching process from the user agent string. It has optional with and match attributes that contain regular expressions for pattern matching.

If there is not a with attribute on the `<filter>` element, the HTTP header specified by the `<use>` element becomes the source for pattern matching. A common use of the with attribute is to refer to a previously captured group via the substitution construct, such as the following example with sourcename:

```
<filter match="^matchname" with="${sourcename}">
```

The match attribute is used to test against the patterns provided that have made it to the `<filter>` tag, possibly guided by the with attribute. Once the match attribute is reached and evaluated, any of the patterns that successfully match against it will cause execution of assignment to the name/value pairs underneath `<filter>` to HttpBrowserCapabilities and kick off evaluation of child `<case>` elements.

The following small filter block receives its pattern from the group capture named extra and attempts to match on the Crawler string. Success in the match sets the crawler name/value pair to a true value.

```
<filter with="${extra}" match="Crawler">
   crawler=true
</filter>
```

The `<case>` element operates a little differently than `<filter>`. Instead of evaluating all patterns that are matched, this element stops on the first match that it finds. Otherwise, it operates in an identical manner to the `<filter>` element, having optional with and match attributes, along with the capability to have child name/value pairs for assignment operations. In the next section, we provide a high-level overview of regular expressions in the .NET Framework. Regular expressions help facilitate browser capabilities detection through efficient parsing of information passed from the browser to ASP.NET.

Regular Expressions Review

The XML tags in the <browserCaps> configuration section make heavy use of regular expressions, so a quick review of regular expression syntax and constructs is in order. This will be a short introduction—feel free to consult the .NET Framework documentation for more extensive information on regular expressions.

Regular expressions are designed to match patterns in a text stream with a terse, compact, yet extremely powerful pattern language. The pattern-matching expressions that process source text consist of two main elements: literal text and metacharacters.

The *literal text* is obviously the text in your regular expression that you wish to explicitly match against the source. You can use all of the typical American National Standards Institute (ANSI) characters except the following group of *metacharacters:* $ ^ { [(|) * + ? \ .

To use those metacharacters as literal text, you must escape them with a preceding back slash (\) character. For example, \$ represents the literal string $. The normal escape sequences that you would expect in C programming APIs, such as \t for tab, \n for newline, and so on, are also available with regular expressions.

Our examination of the useful metacharacters begins with the character classes. The character classes allow you to specify a range or a value space of characters instead of your having to explicitly list a group of literals that match. Think of the character classes as convenient shorthand or as an alias for more verbose literal expressions. Table 8-2 shows some of the commonly used character classes with the default set of regular expression options.

Table 8-2. Regular Expression Character Classes

CHARACTER CLASS	DESCRIPTION
.	Matches any single character except \n
[abc]	Matches any character in the set {a,b,c}
[^abc]	Matches any character not in the set {a,b,c}
[d-f1-3]	Matches any character in range from d to f or 1 to 3
\w	Matches any word character equivalent to [a-zA-Z_0-9]
\W	Matches any nonword character equivalent to [^a-zA-Z_0-9]
\s	Matches white space character equivalent to [\f\n\r\t\v]
\s	Matches non-white-space character equivalent to [^ \f\n\r\t\v]
\d	Matches any decimal digit equivalent to [0-9]
\D	Matches any nondecimal digit equivalent to [^0-9]

Zero-width assertions cause the pattern-matching process to succeed or fail based on the current location of the parsing process within the input string. Table 8-3 presents commonly used assertions. Most patterns will use assertions to match things that are at the beginning or the end of an input string.

Table 8-3. Regular Expression Zero-Width Assertions

ASSERTION	DESCRIPTION
^	Match must occur at the beginning of the string
$	Match must occur at the end of the string
\b	Match must occur between a \w (word) and \W (nonword) boundary
\B	Match must not occur between a \w (word) and \W (nonword) boundary

Regular expressions provide the ability to repeat the matching process through a construct known as a *quantifier*. Some of the quantifiers should look familiar to those who have worked with XML Document Type Definitions (DTDs). Table 8-4 contains a list of commonly used quantifiers.

Table 8-4. Regular Expression Quantifiers

QUANTIFIER	DESCRIPTION
*	Zero or more matches
+	One or more matches
?	Zero or one match
{n}	Specifies n number of matches
{n,m}	Specifies n to m number of matches
{n,}	Specifies at least n number of matches (note the comma)

Quantifier matching is greedy, as it will match all possible occurrences from the input string if the quantifier allows it. To make only one at a time, add a trailing ? to the quantifier to obtain "lazy" evaluation.

Regular expressions also have alternating constructs for picking between two options in pattern matching. The familiar pipe (|) character is used for alternation.

The preceding features are nice for selecting characters, but usually the source text has groups of content that must be checked, possibly in a repeated fashion. The ( ) group construct is used to capture an input pattern and have quantifiers apply to it repeatedly.

The group can also be captured by name in a different syntax using (!'name') to associate the matched pattern for later substitution. ASP.NET uses the ${name} substitution construct to reuse captured parts of the user agent string. In the next section, we examine Internet Explorer (IE) 6.0 as an example of how regular expressions are put to work in browser capabilities detection.

Internet Explorer 6.0 Example

The XML content in Listing 8-5 shows the <filter> and <case> elements for IE version 5.0 and higher detection snipped from a .NET Framework version 1.0 machine.config file.

Listing 8-5. Machine.config <browserCaps> for IE 5.0 and Higher

```
<filter>
  <case match="^Mozilla[^(]*\(compatible; MSIE
(?'version'(?'major'\d+)(?'minor'\.\d+)(?'letters'\w*))(?'extra'.*)">

                browser=IE
                version=${version}
                majorversion=${major}
                minorversion=${minor}

                <case match="[5-9]\." with="${version}">
                    frames=true
                    tables=true
                    cookies=true
                    backgroundsounds=true
                    vbscript=true
                    javascript=true
                    javaapplets=true
                    activexcontrols=true
                    tagwriter=System.Web.UI.HtmlTextWriter
                    ecmascriptversion=1.2
                    msdomversion=${major}${minor}
                    w3cdomversion=1.0
                    css1=true
                    css2=true
                    xml=true

                    <filter with="${letters}" match="^b">
                        beta=true
                    </filter>
                    <filter with="${extra}" match="Crawler">
                        crawler=true
                    </filter>
                </case>
</filter>
```

To see this configuration in action, consider the following user agent header value for IE 6.0:

```
Mozilla/4.0 (compatible; MSIE 6.0; Windows NT 5.1; .NET CLR 1.0.3705)
```

The top-level `<filter>` element has neither a with nor a match attribute, so the top-level `<case>` element receives the full user agent string. The `<case>` regular expression will then match on the Mozilla and MSIE strings to know that it is dealing with IE:

```
match="^Mozilla[^(]*\(compatible; MSIE
(?'version'(?'major'\d+)(?'minor'\.\d+)(?'letters'\w*))(?'extra'.*)"
```

The match string starts off by ensuring that Mozilla is at the very beginning of the user agent string:

```
^Mozilla
```

Then it looks for zero or more instances of any characters that are not opening parentheses (using this regular expression:

```
[^(]*
```

The next part of the match string is literal text with an escape for the open parentheses:

```
\(compatible; MSIE
```

After the literal text is a series of nested groups that capture for later substitution:

```
(?'version'(?'major'\d+)(?'minor'\.\d+)(?'letters'\w*))
```

The "version" group concatenates the entire match of its child groups. The "major" group matches on at least one decimal digit but can handle more in case the version number is greater than 9. In our user agent string, major is set to 6. The "minor" group escapes the . character that separates major and minor, adding its match on the next set of digits. Its final value is .0. The "letters" group picks up the remaining word characters, becoming a single ; character.

"Extra" is the next group. It picks up any remaining characters in the user agent string:

```
(?'extra'.*)"
```

In this case, it will be the following characters:

```
Windows NT 5.1; .NET CLR 1.0.3705)
```

The next step is to drill down into the version group capture with a child `<case>` element. Notice here that we use the match attribute set to pattern match against version, looking for a major version of 5 to 9:

```
<case match="[5-9]\." with="${version}">
```

Because our version group capture was 6.0, all the child name/value pairs are applied to the HttpBrowserCapabilities class. After this step, two child <filter> elements look to see if the request was made by a beta browser with a b character in the letters group or the string Crawler in the extras group. Neither one matches in this case. Table 8-5 shows the results of the matching process for IE 6.0 and the full set of properties for HttpBrowserCapabilities.

Table 8-5. IE 6.0 and HttpBrowserCapabilities *Properties*

PROPERTY	IE 6.0	FEATURE
ActiveXControls	True	Browser support for ActiveX controls.
AOL	False	Is the browser an AOL version?
Beta	False	Is the browser a beta version?
BackgroundSounds	True	Browser support for playing sounds.
Browser	IE	Full browser string from the request headers.
CDF	False	Browser support for Channel Definition Format (CDF).
ClrVersion	1.0.3705	Version of .NET common language runtime (CLR) supported by the browser.
Cookies	True	Browser support for cookies.
Crawler	False	Is the browser a web site crawler for search engines?
EcmaScriptVersion	1.2	Version of ECMAScript (JavaScript) supported by the browser.
Frames	True	Browser support for frames.
JavaApplets	True	Browser support for Java applets.
JavaScript	True	Browser support for JavaScript.
MajorVersion	6	Major version of browser.
MinorVersion	0	Minor version of browser.
MSDomVersion	6.0	Microsoft version of the Document Object Model (DOM) supported by the browser.
Platform	WinNT	Operating system platform the browser is running on.
Tables	True	Browser support for tables.
TagWriter	HtmlTextWriter	Class used to emit HTML content from the control.
Type	IE6	Browser name and major version in a single string.
VBScript	True	Browser support for VBScript.
Version	6.0	Major.minor version of browser in single string.
W3CDomVersion	1.0	W3C version of the DOM supported by the browser.
Win16	False	Is the operating system the browser running on Win16 based?
Win32	True	Is the operating system the browser is running on Win32 based?

An interesting item to note regarding Table 8-5 is that there are properties in the machine.config `<browserCaps>` that are not exposed by `HttpBrowserCapabilties`. The reason this does not cause a problem is that `HttpBrowserCapabilities` supports an index syntax for adding properties. You can refer to it in two ways:

```
Caps.Javascript
Caps["JavaScript"].
```

The `Css1`, `Css2`, and `Xml` properties are Boolean values available that are not exposed through a typed property. In the next section, we build a server control that provides a nice report on browser capabilities on a Web Form.

Browser Detection via the BrowserCaps Control

To display the information from `HttpBrowserCapabilities`, in this section we examine a simple server control named `BrowserCaps` that does the job for us. It displays the `HttpBrowserCapabilities` properties in a compact, tabular format, as shown in Listing 8-6. You can use this control to help debug why a certain browser is not working with your server controls or to help you debug changes to the `<browserCaps>` section of the machine.config file.

Listing 8-6. The BrowserCaps *Server Control*

```
using System;
using System.Web;
using System.Web.UI;
using System.Web.UI.WebControls;

namespace ControlsBookLib.Ch08
{
    [ToolboxData("<{0}:BrowserCaps runat=server></{0}:BrowserCaps>")]
    public class BrowserCaps : WebControl
    {
        public BrowserCaps() : base(HtmlTextWriterTag.Div)
        {
        }

        private void AddCapsRow(Table table, string lname, object lresult,
            string rname, object rresult)
        {
            TableRow row = new TableRow();
            row.Cells.Add(new TableCell());
            row.Cells.Add(new TableCell());
            row.Cells.Add(new TableCell());
            row.Cells.Add(new TableCell());

            row.Cells[0].Text = lname;
            row.Cells[0].Font.Bold = true;
            row.Cells[1].Text = lresult.ToString();
```

```
        row.Cells[2].Text = rname;
        row.Cells[2].Font.Bold = true;
        row.Cells[3].Text = rresult.ToString();

        table.Rows.Add(row);
    }

    protected override void CreateChildControls()
    {
        HttpBrowserCapabilities caps = Context.Request.Browser;

        Controls.Add(new LiteralControl("<b>HTTP_USER_AGENT:</b> " +
            Context.Request.UserAgent));

        Table table = new Table();

        AddCapsRow(table, "ActiveXControls", caps.ActiveXControls,
            "MajorVersion", caps.MajorVersion);

        AddCapsRow(table, "AOL", caps.AOL,
            "MinorVersion", caps.MinorVersion);

        AddCapsRow(table, "BackgroundSounds", caps.BackgroundSounds,
            "MSDomVersion", caps.MSDomVersion);

        AddCapsRow(table, "Beta", caps.Beta,
            "Platform", caps.Platform);

        AddCapsRow(table, "Browser", caps.Browser,
            "Tables", caps.Tables);

        AddCapsRow(table, "CDF", caps.CDF,
            "TagWriter",caps.TagWriter);

        AddCapsRow(table, "ClrVersion", caps.ClrVersion,
            "Type",caps.Type);

        AddCapsRow(table, "Cookies", caps.Cookies,
            "VBScript",caps.VBScript);

        AddCapsRow(table, "Crawler", caps.Crawler,
            "Version",caps.Version);

        AddCapsRow(table, "EcmaScriptVersion", caps.EcmaScriptVersion,
            "W3CDomVersion",caps.W3CDomVersion);

        AddCapsRow(table, "Frames", caps.Frames,
            "Win16",caps.Win16);

        AddCapsRow(table, "JavaApplets", caps.JavaApplets,
            "Win32",caps.Win32);
```

```
        AddCapsRow(table, "JavaScript", caps.JavaScript,
            "","");

        table.ApplyStyle(ControlStyle);

        Controls.Add(table);
    }
  }
}
```

In the next section, we put this handy server control to work and we test the
RolloverImageLink server control.

The RolloverImage Web Form

While demonstrating the RolloverImageLink server control on the RolloverImage Web
Form, we also work with the BrowserCaps control to demonstrate the browser detection
using multiple browsers. Notice on the Web Form that two RolloverImageLink controls
are added with large numeral symbols (1 and 2), as shown in Figure 8-2.

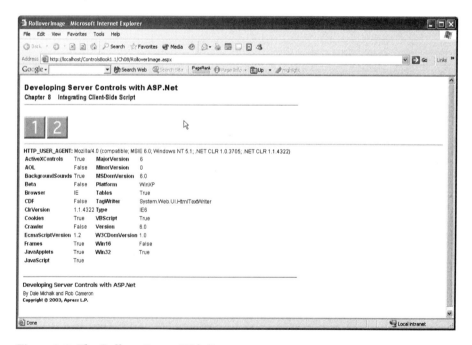

Figure 8-2. The RolloverImage Web Form

When you hover the mouse over a button, the image changes to a pushed-down
version, providing a nice effect, as shown in Figure 8-3.

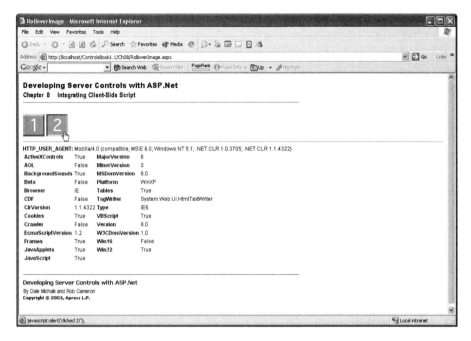

Figure 8-3. The RolloverImage Web Form on rollover

If you click an image, the page will navigate either to the publisher's site or to the ASP.NET web site. The full listing for the Web Form is shown in Listings 8-7 and 8-8.

Listing 8-7. The RolloverImage Web Form .aspx Page File

```
<%@ Page language="c#" Codebehind="RolloverImage.aspx.cs"
AutoEventWireup="false" Inherits="ControlsBookWeb.Ch08.RolloverImage" %>
<%@ Register TagPrefix="apress" Namespace="ControlsBookLib.Ch08"
Assembly="ControlsBookLib" %>
<%@ Register TagPrefix="apressUC" TagName="ControlsBookHeader"
Src="..\ControlsBookHeader.ascx" %>
<%@ Register TagPrefix="apressUC" TagName="ControlsBookFooter"
Src="..\ControlsBookFooter.ascx" %>
<!DOCTYPE HTML PUBLIC "-//W3C//DTD HTML 4.0 Transitional//EN" >
<HTML>
  <HEAD>
    <title>RolloverImage</title>
    <meta name="GENERATOR" Content="Microsoft Visual Studio 7.0">
    <meta name="CODE_LANGUAGE" Content="C#">
    <meta name="vs_defaultClientScript" content="JavaScript">
    <meta name="vs_targetSchema"
content="http://schemas.microsoft.com/intellisense/ie5">
  </HEAD>
  <body MS_POSITIONING="FlowLayout">
    <form id="RolloverImage" method="post" runat="server">
      <apressUC:ControlsBookHeader id="Header" chapternumber="8"
```

397

```
chaptertitle="Integrating Client-Side Script" runat="server" />
      <apress:RolloverImageLink id="image1" runat="server" ImageURL="ex1.gif"
OverImageURL="ex1_selected.gif" NavigateUrl="http://www.apress.com" />
      <apress:RolloverImageLink id="image2" runat="server" ImageURL="ex2.gif"
OverImageURL="ex2_selected.gif" NavigateUrl="http://asp.net"
        EnableClientScript="True" /><br>
      <hr>
      <apress:BrowserCaps Font-Name="Arial" Font-Size="12px" id="caps1"
runat="server" />
      <apressUC:ControlsBookFooter id="Footer" runat="server" />
    </form>
  </body>
</HTML>
```

Listing 8-8. The RolloverImage Web Form Code-Behind Class File

```
using System;
using System.Collections;
using System.ComponentModel;
using System.Data;
using System.Drawing;
using System.Web;
using System.Web.SessionState;
using System.Web.UI;
using System.Web.UI.WebControls;
using System.Web.UI.HtmlControls;

namespace ControlsBookWeb.Ch08
{
   public class RolloverImage : System.Web.UI.Page
   {
      protected ControlsBookLib.Ch08.RolloverImageLink image2;
      protected ControlsBookLib.Ch08.BrowserCaps caps1;
      protected ControlsBookLib.Ch08.RolloverImageLink image1;
      protected ControlsBookWeb.ControlsBookHeader Header ;

      private void Page_Load(object sender, System.EventArgs e)
      {

      }

      #region Web Form Designer generated code
      override protected void OnInit(EventArgs e)
      {
        //
        // CODEGEN: This call is required by the ASP.NET Web Form Designer.
        //
        InitializeComponent();
        base.OnInit(e);
      }
```

```
    /// <summary>
    /// Required method for Designer support - do not modify
    /// the contents of this method with the code editor.
    /// </summary>
    private void InitializeComponent()
    {
        this.Load += new System.EventHandler(this.Page_Load);

    }
    #endregion
  }
}
```

Now that we have verified the functionality of both the RolloverImageLink and BrowserCaps server controls, in the next section we move on to examine the HTML and script that is outputted when the RolloverImage Web Form renders in the browser.

Analyzing the Rollover HTML Output

The rollover functionality lives in the emitted hyperlink tags in the HTML output. The top of the HTML form also contains the image-swapping function called by the onmouseover and onmouseout client event handlers attached to the hyperlinks, as shown here:

```
<form name="RolloverImage" method="post" action="RolloverImage.aspx"
id="RolloverImage">
<input type="hidden" name="__VIEWSTATE"
value="dDwxNDQzMTA0MDt0PDtsPGk8MT47PjtsPHQ8O2w8aTwxPjs+O2w8dDw7bDxpPDU+O2k8Nz47P
jtsPHQ8cDxwPGw8VGV4dDs+O2w8ODs+Pjs+Ozs+O3Q8cDxwPGw8VGV4dDs+O2w8SW50ZWdyYXRpbmcgQ
2xpZW5OLVNpZGUgU2NyaXB0O3o+Oz470z47Pj47Pj47PjFpMsnVYgee1xGSgg1BNclKBkoR" />
```

```
        <script language='JavaScript'>
            function __Image_Swap(sName, sSrc)
            {
                document.images[sName].src = sSrc;
            }
        </script>
```

The Image control output shows the <IMG> tags wrapped by an <A> tag and the client-script event mappings for onmouseover and onmouseout:

```
  <a href="javascript:alert('clicked 1!');" name="image1_href"
onmouseover="__Image_Swap('image1','ex1_selected.gif');"
onmouseout="__Image_Swap('image1','ex1.gif');"><img name="image1" id="image1"
src="ex1.gif" border="0" /></a>
        <a href="javascript:alert('clicked 2!');" name="image2_href"
onmouseover="__Image_Swap('image2','ex2_selected.gif');"
onmouseout="__Image_Swap('image2','ex2.gif');"><img name="image2" id="image2"
src="ex2.gif" border="0" /></a><br>
```

At the bottom of the HTML document is the code to preload the images. It creates the Image JavaScript object and sets the `src` attribute to complete its task. One script block is emitted for each control to initialize its images:

```
<script language="javascript">
<!--
   var ControlsBookLib_Ch08_RolloverImageLink =  new
Array('ex1.gif','ex1_selected.gif', 'ex2.gif','ex2_selected.gif');
     // -->
</script>
<script language='JavaScript'>
          for (index = 0; index < ControlsBookLib_Ch08_RolloverImageLink;
index++)
             {
                 loadimg = new Image();
                 loadimg.src = ControlsBookLib_Ch08_RolloverImageLink[index];
             }
         </script>
```

The RolloverImage Web Form in the Netscape Browser

The previous demonstration showed the rollover working under IE 6.0. Figure 8-4 shows what happens when we run it under Netscape 7.0.

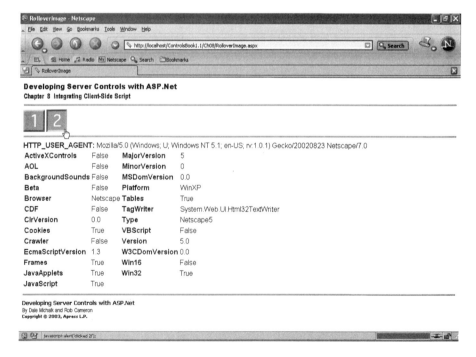

Figure 8-4. The RolloverImage Web Form in Netscape 7.0

You will notice that some of the features are not what you might expect. Although later browsers such as Netscape 7.0 can handle DHTML, the `tagwriter` attribute is set to `Html32TextWriter`. This makes the output only HTML 3.2 compliant. In examining the HTML source for Netscape 7.0, you will see the following:

```
<font face="Arial"><b>ActiveXControls</b>
```

Contrast this with IE 6.0, which used `HtmlTextWriter` and CSS properties in its HTML output:

```
<td style="font-weight:bold;">ActiveXControls</td>
```

The problem that we are seeing has to do with the `<browserCaps>` match pattern. The current pattern identifies Netscape browsers through version 6.0:

```
<case match="^Mozilla/5\.0 \(([^)]*\) (Gecko/[-\d]+
)?Netscape6/(?'version'(?'major'\d+)(?'minor'\.\d+)(?'letters'\w*)).*">
```

To see how this matches, Netscape 6.2.3 comes into the web server with the following user agent string that appears to repeat its version twice:

```
Mozilla/5.0 (Windows; U; Windows NT 5.1; en-US; rv:0.9.4.1) Gecko/20020508
Netscape6/6.2.3
```

It identifies itself at the end as `Netscape6` before giving its major and minor versions. Netscape 7.0 changes the URL string slightly by identifying itself as `Netscape`. This is what causes the issue. To fix the problem, edit the machine.config file and add a ? character immediately after `Netscape6` in the match string like this:

```
<case match="^Mozilla/5\.0 \(([^)]*\) (Gecko/[-\d]+
)?Netscape6?/(?'version'(?'major'\d+)(?'minor'\.\d+)(?'letters'\w*)).*">
```

The ? quantifier makes the 6 optional so that the Netscape 7.0 user string is matched while still working with Netscape 6.0 browsers. Unfortunately, our work is not yet done, although Netscape 7.0 matches and gets tag attributes such as `w3cdomversion`. The name/value pairs under the Netscape match section do not include a `tagwriter` pair. They are not configured to use `HtmlTextWriter` to output, but instead receive `Html32TextWriter` from the default attribute value for `tagwriter`.

You can easily fix this by adding the following name/value pair to a browser you feel comfortable supporting with the full range of up-level browser features:

```
Tagwriter=System.Web.UI.HtmlTextWriter
```

After you add the match string and `tagwriter` attributes for Netscape 7.0, the HTML and script renders in the precise manner you would expect from CSS, as shown in Figure 8-5.

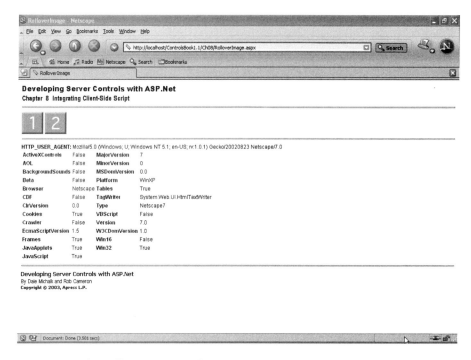

Figure 8-5. The RolloverImage Web Form in Netscape 7.0 after editing machine.config

We now move on to a discussion of how to integrate into a custom server control the capability to run client-side script when a page loads in the browser.

Running Client Script When a Page Loads

A common requirement in a web application is to have some action execute when the Web Form loads in the client browser. Executing client-side script at page load can be done two ways: wire up script code to the `<BODY>` tag, or emit the raw JavaScript at the end of the HTML document. ASP.NET provides support for the latter with the `Page.RegisterStartup` method call. We have already used this technique to load the images in the `RolloverImageLink` control. In this section, we examine this technique further by creating a custom server control, `Focus`, whose sole mission is to run script at start-up that sets what HTML element receives focus when a page loads in the browser.

Setting Focus on a Web Form

The Focus server control derives from System.Web.UI.Control because it generates no UI that is rendered in its final output. It is pure JavaScript. This nonvisual control calls VerifyRenderingInServerForm to ensure the script is created within a Web Form. Listing 8-9 provides the source code for the Focus server control.

Listing 8-9. The Focus *Server Control*

```
using System;
using System.Web;
using System.Web.UI;
using System.Text;

namespace ControlsBookLib.Ch08
{
    [ToolboxData("<{0}:Focus runat=server></{0}:Focus>"),
    DefaultProperty("TargetControl")]
    public class Focus : Control
    {
        public virtual string TargetControl
        {
            get
            {
                String targetControl = (String)ViewState["Target"];
                return !(targetControl == null) ? targetControl : "" ;
            }
            set
            {
                ViewState["Target"] = value;
            }
        }

        private string GetDOMScript(string targetID)
        {
            // build custom script to set the focus
            // to the passed-in element ID
            StringBuilder script = new StringBuilder();
            script.Append("<script language='javascript'>");
            script.Append("document.getElementById('");
            script.Append(targetID);
            script.Append("').focus();");
            script.Append("</script>");

            return script.ToString();
        }

        protected override void Render(HtmlTextWriter writer)
        {
            // only render inside <form runat="server"> tags
```

```
        Page.VerifyRenderingInServerForm(this);

        HttpBrowserCapabilities caps = Context.Request.Browser;

        // require JavaScript and DOM Level 1 and up
        // (uses DOM level 1 getElementById)
        // this works for IE5+ and Netscape 6+
        if (this.TargetControl != "" &&
           caps.JavaScript &&
           caps.W3CDomVersion.Major >= 1)
        {
           // register script at the bottom
           // of the form
           Page.RegisterStartupScript("Focus",
              GetDOMScript(this.TargetControl));
        }
      }
   }
  }
}
```

The Focus control publishes a property named TargetControl that stores the ID of the control or HTML element ID that you want to have focus upon browser page load. This functionality relies on browsers that support the World Wide Web Consortium (W3C) DOM Level 1 specification. The DOM Level 1 API exposes a document.getElementById method and a focus method on each element of the HTML document. The mainstream browsers that support this are IE 5.0 and higher and Netscape 6.0 and higher. In the next section, we discuss a Web Form that puts the Focus server control to work.

The Focus Web Form

For large Web Forms that have quite a bit of content, such as a page that incorporates data binding, the Focus control is an easy way to automatically move the browser viewpoint for the user and avoid having the user scroll manually. The demonstration Focus Web Form holds a DataGrid that is bound to the entire contents of the Northwind Customers table, creating a long page of tabular content that requires a decent amount of scrolling to get from top to bottom. We added a button that simply cycles the page through postback to demonstrate that the Web Form remembers what control should have focus. Figure 8-6 shows the top of the DataGrid on the Web Form.

At the top and the bottom of the Web Form are the TopLabel and BottomLabel controls. Two DropDownList web controls, one for each label, are placed in similar locations to allow us to set which label control will receive the focus of the browser using our handy Focus control. Each DropDownList control has its autopostback property set to true, so that when you change the selection to the BottomLabel from the default TopLabel, the page posts back to the server and immediately snaps focus to the very bottom of the page, where the BottomLabel renders as shown in Figure 8-7.

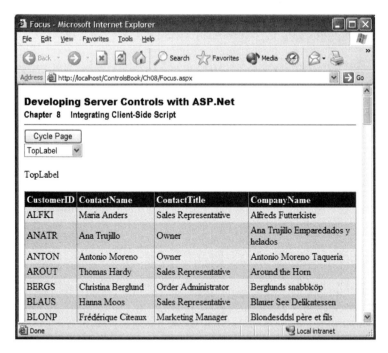

Figure 8-6. The Focus Web Form

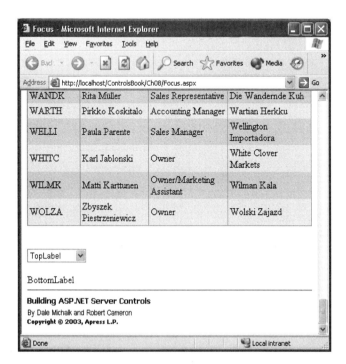

Figure 8-7. The view of the BottomLabel *control in the Focus Web Form*

After you select the BottomLabel control in the DropDownList control, the JavaScript code in the document sets the focus in the browser on the BottomLabel's emitted <SPAN> tag:

```
<span id="BottomLabel" tabindex="2">BottomLabel</span>
<script language='javascript'>
document.getElementById('BottomLabel').focus();
</script>
```

An additional step we required in the example is to add a tabindex attribute to the <SPAN> tag in the .aspx page in order for the <SPAN> tag to receive focus in IE. This is required, as a <SPAN> tag is not normally part of the tab order. Adding the tabindex permits tabbing to the control, and therefore permits the control to receive the focus. The Web Form that generates the focus content is shown in Listings 8-10 and 8-11.

Listing 8-10. The Focus Web Form .aspx Page File

```
<%@ Register TagPrefix="apress" Namespace="ControlsBookLib.Ch08"
Assembly="ControlsBookLib" %>
<%@ Page language="c#" Codebehind="Focus.aspx.cs" AutoEventWireup="false"
Inherits="ControlsBookWeb.Ch08.Focus" %>
<%@ Register TagPrefix="apressUC" TagName="ControlsBookHeader"
Src="..\ControlsBookHeader.ascx" %>
<%@ Register TagPrefix="apressUC" TagName="ControlsBookFooter"
Src="..\ControlsBookFooter.ascx" %>
<!DOCTYPE HTML PUBLIC "-//W3C//DTD HTML 4.0 Transitional//EN" >
<HTML>
  <HEAD>
    <title>Focus</title>
    <meta content="Microsoft Visual Studio 7.0" name="GENERATOR">
    <meta content="C#" name="CODE_LANGUAGE">
    <meta content="JavaScript" name="vs_defaultClientScript">
    <meta content="http://schemas.microsoft.com/intellisense/ie5"
name="vs_targetSchema">
  </HEAD>
  <body MS_POSITIONING="FlowLayout">
    <form id="Focus" method="post" runat="server">
      <apressuc:controlsbookheader id="Header" runat="server"
chaptertitle="Integrating Client-Side Script"
chapternumber="8"></apressuc:controlsbookheader><apress:focus id="focus1"
runat="server"></apress:focus><asp:button id="Button1" runat="server"
Text="Cycle Page"></asp:button><br>
      <asp:dropdownlist id="DropDownList1" runat="server" AutoPostBack="True">
        <asp:ListItem Value="TopLabel">TopLabel</asp:ListItem>
        <asp:ListItem Value="BottomLabel">BottomLabel</asp:ListItem>
      </asp:dropdownlist><br>
      <br>
      <asp:label id="TopLabel" tabIndex="1" Text="TopLabel"
Runat="server"></asp:label><br>
      <br>
      <asp:datagrid id="dataGrid1" Runat="server" GridLines="Vertical"
```

```
CellPadding="3" BackColor="White"
        BorderWidth="1px" BorderStyle="None" BorderColor="#999999">
        <SelectedItemStyle Font-Bold="True" ForeColor="White"
BackColor="#008A8C"></SelectedItemStyle>
        <AlternatingItemStyle BackColor="#DCDCDC"></AlternatingItemStyle>
        <ItemStyle ForeColor="Black" BackColor="#EEEEEE"></ItemStyle>
        <HeaderStyle Font-Bold="True" ForeColor="White"
BackColor="#000084"></HeaderStyle>
        <FooterStyle ForeColor="Black" BackColor="#CCCCCC"></FooterStyle>
        <PagerStyle HorizontalAlign="Center" ForeColor="Black"
BackColor="#999999" Mode="NumericPages"></PagerStyle>
     </asp:datagrid><br>
     <br>
     <asp:dropdownlist id="DropDownList2" runat="server" AutoPostBack="True">
       <asp:ListItem Value="TopLabel">TopLabel</asp:ListItem>
       <asp:ListItem Value="BottomLabel">BottomLabel</asp:ListItem>
     </asp:dropdownlist><br>
     <br>
     <asp:label id="BottomLabel" tabIndex="2" Text="BottomLabel"
Runat="server">BottomLabel</asp:label><apressuc:controlsbookfooter id="Footer"
runat="server"></apressuc:controlsbookfooter></form>
  </body>
</HTML>
```

Listing 8-11. The Focus Web Form Code-Behind Class File

```
using System;
using System.Collections;
using System.ComponentModel;
using System.Data;
using System.Drawing;
using System.Web;
using System.Web.SessionState;
using System.Web.UI;
using System.Web.UI.WebControls;
using System.Web.UI.HtmlControls;
using System.Data.SqlClient;

namespace ControlsBookWeb.Ch08
{
    [ToolboxData("<{0}:Focus runat=server></{0}:Focus>"),
    DefaultProperty("TargetControl")]
    public class Focus : System.Web.UI.Page
    {
        protected System.Web.UI.WebControls.DropDownList DropDownList1;
        protected ControlsBookLib.Ch08.Focus focus1;
        protected System.Web.UI.WebControls.Label TopLabel;
        protected System.Web.UI.WebControls.Label BottomLabel;
        protected System.Web.UI.WebControls.DropDownList DropDownlist2;
        protected System.Web.UI.WebControls.DropDownList DropDownList2;
```

407

```
        protected System.Web.UI.WebControls.DataGrid dataGrid1;
        protected System.Web.UI.WebControls.Button Button1;
        protected ControlsBookWeb.ControlsBookHeader Header ;

        private void Page_Load(object sender, System.EventArgs e)
        {
           if (!Page.IsPostBack)
           {
              dataGrid1.DataSource = GetCustomerData();
              dataGrid1.DataBind();
           }
        }

        private DataSet GetCustomerData()
        {
           SqlConnection conn =
              new SqlConnection(
   "Server=(local);Database=Northwind;Integrated Security=true;");
           conn.Open();

           SqlDataAdapter da =
              new SqlDataAdapter(
   "SELECT CustomerID, ContactName, ContactTitle, CompanyName FROM Customers",
              conn);
           DataSet ds = new DataSet();
           da.Fill(ds,"Customers");

           return ds;
        }

        #region Web Form Designer generated code
        override protected void OnInit(EventArgs e)
        {
           //
           // CODEGEN: This call is required by the ASP.NET Web Form Designer.
           //
           InitializeComponent();
           base.OnInit(e);
        }

        /// <summary>
        /// Required method for Designer support - do not modify
        /// the contents of this method with the code editor.
        /// </summary>
        private void InitializeComponent()
        {
           this.DropDownList1.SelectedIndexChanged += new
   System.EventHandler(this.DropDownList1_SelectedIndexChanged);
           this.DropDownList2.SelectedIndexChanged += new
```

```
System.EventHandler(this.DropDownList2_SelectedIndexChanged);
        this.Load += new System.EventHandler(this.Page_Load);
    }
    #endregion

    private void DropDownList1_SelectedIndexChanged(object sender,
System.EventArgs e)
    {
        focus1.TargetControl = DropDownList1.SelectedItem.Value;
        ResetLists();
    }

    private void DropDownList2_SelectedIndexChanged(object sender,
System.EventArgs e)
    {
        focus1.TargetControl = DropDownList2.SelectedItem.Value;
        ResetLists();
    }

    private void ResetLists()
    {
        DropDownList1.SelectedIndex = 0;
        DropDownList2.SelectedIndex = 1;
    }
  }
}
```

Now that we have covered how to integrate into a server control how to execute client-side script when a page loads, we now move on to discuss how to integrate client-side script that executes when an HTML form is submitted in the browser. We describe a couple of methods you can use to accomplish this task.

Running a Client Script When a Form Is Submitted

In this section, we discuss how to execute client script just after postback is initiated by the end user, whether through a button click or through a JavaScript-based method. We create two custom server controls to assist in presenting the concepts required to execute client script when a form is submitted. The first server control we discuss is the FormConfirmation control.

The FormConfirmation Control

FormConfirmation is a server control designed to display a message when the browser is ready to submit the HTML document back to the web server. We inherit from System.Web.UI.Control because we do not have a UI to display and, as such, we do not need the styling and device-rendering features of System.Web.UI.WebControls.WebControl.

Listing 8-12 provides the source code for the FormConfirmation server control. ASP.NET allows you to add code to the onsubmit event attribute of the <FORM> tag generated by the Web Form via the Page.RegisterOnSubmitStatement method. This hooks into the normal HTTP posting mechanism, as we describe in Chapter 5.

Listing 8-12. The FormConfirmation *Server Control*

```
using System;
using System.Web;
using System.Web.UI;

namespace ControlsBookLib.Ch08
{
    [ToolboxData("<{0}:FormConfirmation runat=server></{0}:FormConfirmation>"),
    DefaultProperty("Message")]
    public class FormConfirmation : Control
    {
        private string message = "";
        public virtual string Message
        {
            get
            {
                return message;
            }
            set
            {
                message = value;
            }
        }

        protected override void OnPreRender(EventArgs e)
        {
            if (HttpContext.Current.Request.Browser.JavaScript)
            {
                string script = "return (confirm('" + this.Message + "'));";

                // register JavaScript code for onsubmit event
                // of the HTML <form> element
                Page.RegisterOnSubmitStatement("FormConfirmation",script);
            }
        }

        protected override void Render(HtmlTextWriter writer)
        {
            // make sure the control is rendered inside
            // <form runat=server> tags
            Page.VerifyRenderingInServerForm(this);

            base.Render(writer);
        }
    }
}
```

FormConfirmation exposes a Message property to allow web developers to customize the JavaScript confirmation prompt to the end user. This simple control takes advantage of Page's RegisterOnSubmitStatement method we described previously to properly inject the script into the HTML stream loaded in the browser. Just drop it on a Web Form, and voila! You can confirm that the user is ready to proceed with submitting the form back to the server. If the user does not affirm the form submit, the script cancels the action by returning false. The other item to highlight for this control is the Render override for the purposes of ensuring the control is located inside a Web Form via Page's VerifyRenderingInServerForm method.

In the next section, we discuss an interesting variation on this theme of confirming navigation away from a page by adding the capability of checking whether a user wants to move on to a new page or stay on the current Web Form.

The ConfirmedLinkButton Control

The ConfirmedLinkButton button prompts with a custom message that will not navigate if the user cancels the action. ConfirmedLinkButton does not use the RegisterOnSubmitStatement of the Page class; rather, it uses the client-side postback system of ASP.NET. We use this control on a Web Form in conjunction with the previously created FormConfirmation control to show how the two mechanisms interact.

The source code for the ConfirmedLinkButton server control is provided in Listing 8-13. ConfirmedLinkButton exposes a Message property like FormConfirmation, but it differs in that it inherits from the LinkButton control. LinkButton renders as a hyperlink but submits the Web Form via JavaScript.

Listing 8-13. The ConfirmedLinkButton *Server Control*

```
using System;
using System.Web;
using System.Web.UI;
using System.Web.UI.WebControls;
using System.Text;

namespace ControlsBookLib.Ch08
{
    [ToolboxData("<{0}:ConfirmedLinkButton
runat=server></{0}:ConfirmedLinkButton>"),
    DefaultProperty("ClickText")]
    public class ConfirmedLinkButton : LinkButton
    {
        private string message = "";
        public virtual string Message
        {
            get{ return message; }
            set{ message = value; }
        }

        protected override void AddAttributesToRender(HtmlTextWriter writer)
        {
```

```
// enhance the LinkButton by replacing its
// href attribute while leaving the rest of the
// rendering process to the base class
if (HttpContext.Current.Request.Browser.JavaScript &&
    this.Message != "")
{
    StringBuilder script = new StringBuilder();
    script.Append("javascript: if (confirm('");
    script.Append(this.Message);
    script.Append("')) {");
    // get the ASP.NET JavaScript that does a form
    // postback and have this control submit it
    script.Append(Page.GetPostBackEventReference(this));
    script.Append("}");
    writer.AddAttribute(HtmlTextWriterAttribute.Href,
        script.ToString());
}
            }
        }
    }
}
```

We override the AddAttributesToRender method so that we can change the normal href attribute content to add a call to the JavaScript confirm method instead. Because we override the href attribute, we use the GetPostBackEventReference method to set up postback; otherwise, the form submission mechanism will not happen. GetPostBackEventReference obtains a reference to a client-side script function that causes the server to post back to the page. Because this control is inheriting from an existing WebControl, we do not need to call Page.VerifyRenderingInServerForm because it is already performed by the base class implementation of LinkButton. In the next section, we test the behavior of the ConfirmedLinkButton and FormConfirmation server controls in the Confirm Web Form demonstration .aspx page.

The Confirm Web Form

The interaction between the client form submit event and the code emitted by controls to perform JavaScript postbacks for ASP.NET is not as integrated as we would like. The core problem is that the onsubmit client event is not fired if the HTML form is submitted programmatically via JavaScript. To demonstrate the differences, the Confirm Web Form hosts a set of form posting controls.

On the Confirm Web Form is a regular ASP.NET Button that does a traditional HTML form post and an ASP.NET LinkButton that uses JavaScript from ASP.NET to cause postback. We also have our FormConfirmation and ConfirmedLinkButton server controls to show how they provide confirmation on form submit in their own unique manner. Figure 8-8 shows the static Web Form display output.

Figure 8-8. The Confirm Web Form

The code-behind Web Form class has logic to announce which control was responsible for the postback to help us see what is going on. The first control we exercise is the regular ASP.NET `Button` on the form. This `Button` causes the form to post, but we plugged into this mechanism with the `FormConfirmation` server control. When this `Button` is clicked, it kicks off the `FormConfirmation` server control's JavaScript code according to the setting on its `Message` property, as shown in Figure 8-9.

Figure 8-9. Using the ASP.NET `Button` control on the Web Form

The HTML generated by the Web Form shows the emission of the `onsubmit` JavaScript handler on the `<FORM>` tag:

```
<form name="Confirm" method="post" action="Confirm.aspx" language="javascript"
onsubmit="return (
confirm('formconfirmation: Are you sure you want to submit?'));" id="Confirm">
```

The next iteration with the Confirm Web Form in Figure 8-10 shows what happens when the ASP.NET `LinkButton` is clicked.

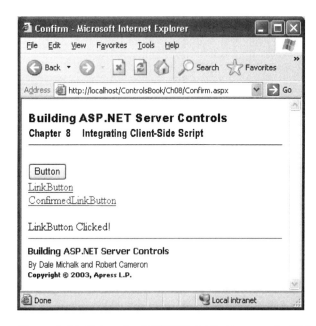

Figure 8-10. Using the ASP.NET `LinkButton` *on the Web Form*

This control executes the `__doPostback` JavaScript method emitted by ASP.NET to programmatically submit the Web Form:

```
<a id="linkbutton1" href="javascript:__doPostBack('linkbutton1','')">LinkButton</a>
```

`__doPostBack` is emitted by the core ASP.NET Framework when a control registers to initiate a client-side postback via JavaScript. If you select View ➤ Source in the browser, you can see how the script works. It locates the HTML `<FORM>` tag and calls its `Submit` method:

```
<script language="javascript">
<!--
    function __doPostBack(eventTarget, eventArgument) {
```

```
      var theform = document.forms["Confirm"];
      theform.__EVENTTARGET.value = eventTarget.replace(/\$/g, ":");
      theform.__EVENTARGUMENT.value = eventArgument;
      theform.submit();
   }
// -->
</script>
```

This results in the Web Form submitting without a JavaScript alert box popping up, frustrating our efforts to hook into the form submission process with the FormConfirmation control.

The use of the ConfirmedLinkButton control gives us yet a different, though similar outcome. It executes its own JavaScript pop-up before submitting the Web Form. This pop-up is different from the one emitted by the FormConfirmation control, however, as shown in Figure 8-11.

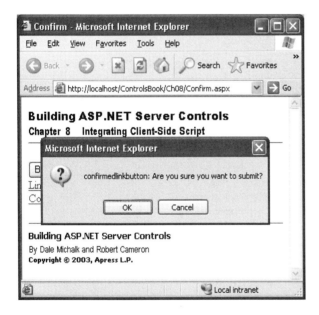

Figure 8-11. Using the ConfirmedLinkButton *control on the Web Form*

ConfirmedLinkButton emits a hyperlink that is similar to the LinkButton hyperlink, but it tacks on extra JavaScript to confirm the form submission before calling __doPostBack:

```
<a href="javascript: if (confirm(
'confirmedlinkbutton: Are you sure you want to submit?'))
{__doPostBack('confirmlink1','')}">ConfirmedLinkButton</a><br>
```

The point of this discussion is to show you what mechanisms are available to server controls to cause postback and how to plug into the architecture. It gets even more interesting when we talk about linking into the client-side validation process in Chapter 9, which covers validation server controls. The full Confirm Web Form is shown in Listings 8-14 and 8-15.

Listing 8-14. The Confirm Web Form .aspx Page File

```
<%@ Register TagPrefix="apress" Namespace="ControlsBookLib.Ch08"
Assembly="ControlsBookLib" %>
<%@ Page language="c#" Codebehind="Confirm.aspx.cs" AutoEventWireup="false"
Inherits="ControlsBookWeb.Ch08.Confirm" %>
<%@ Register TagPrefix="apressUC" TagName="ControlsBookHeader"
Src="..\ControlsBookHeader.ascx" %>
<%@ Register TagPrefix="apressUC" TagName="ControlsBookFooter"
Src="..\ControlsBookFooter.ascx" %>
<!DOCTYPE HTML PUBLIC "-//W3C//DTD HTML 4.0 Transitional//EN" >
<HTML>
  <HEAD>
    <title>Confirm</title>
    <meta content="Microsoft Visual Studio 7.0" name="GENERATOR">
    <meta content="C#" name="CODE_LANGUAGE">
    <meta content="JavaScript" name="vs_defaultClientScript">
    <meta content="http://schemas.microsoft.com/intellisense/ie5"
name="vs_targetSchema">
  </HEAD>
  <body MS_POSITIONING="FlowLayout">
    <form id="Confirm" method="post" runat="server">
      <apressUC:ControlsBookHeader id="Header" chapternumber="8"
chaptertitle="Integrating Client-Side Script" runat="server" />
      <apress:formconfirmation id="confirm1" runat="server"
Message=
"formconfirmation: Are you sure you want to submit?"></apress:formconfirmation>
      <br>
      <asp:Button ID="button1" Runat="server" Text="Button"></asp:Button><br>
      <asp:LinkButton ID="linkbutton1" Runat="server"
Text="LinkButton"></asp:LinkButton><br>
      <apress:confirmedlinkbutton id="confirmlink1" runat="server"
Message=
"confirmedlinkbutton: Are you sure you want to submit?">
ConfirmedLinkButton</apress:confirmedlinkbutton><br>
      <br>
      <asp:Label ID="status" Runat="server" />
      <apressUC:ControlsBookFooter id="Footer" runat="server" />
    </form>
  </body>
</HTML>
```

Listing 8-15. The Confirm Web Form Code-Behind Class File

```
using System;
using System.Collections;
using System.ComponentModel;
using System.Data;
using System.Drawing;
using System.Web;
using System.Web.SessionState;
using System.Web.UI;
using System.Web.UI.WebControls;
using System.Web.UI.HtmlControls;

namespace ControlsBookWeb.Ch08
{
    public class Confirm : System.Web.UI.Page
    {
        protected ControlsBookLib.Ch08.ConfirmedLinkButton confirmlink1;
        protected System.Web.UI.WebControls.Button submitbtn;
        protected System.Web.UI.WebControls.Label status;
        protected System.Web.UI.WebControls.LinkButton linkbutton1;
        protected ControlsBookLib.Ch08.FormConfirmation confirm1;
        protected System.Web.UI.WebControls.Button button1;
        protected ControlsBookWeb.ControlsBookHeader Header ;

        private void Page_Load(object sender, System.EventArgs e)
        {
            status.Text = "";
        }

        #region Web Form Designer generated code
        override protected void OnInit(EventArgs e)
        {
            //
            // CODEGEN: This call is required by the ASP.NET Web Form Designer.
            //
            InitializeComponent();
            base.OnInit(e);
        }

        /// <summary>
        /// Required method for Designer support - do not modify
        /// the contents of this method with the code editor.
        /// </summary>
        private void InitializeComponent()
        {
            this.button1.Click += new System.EventHandler(this.Button_Click);
            this.linkbutton1.Click += new System.EventHandler(this.LinkButton_Click);
            this.confirmlink1.Click += new
System.EventHandler(this.ConfirmLinkButton_ClickClick);
            this.Load += new System.EventHandler(this.Page_Load);
```

```
    }
    #endregion

    private void Button_Click(object sender, System.EventArgs e)
    {
        status.Text = "Regular Button Clicked!";
    }

    private void LinkButton_Click(object sender, System.EventArgs e)
    {
        status.Text = "LinkButton Clicked!";
    }

    private void ConfirmLinkButton_ClickClick(object sender, System.EventArgs e)
    {
        status.Text = "ConfirmLinkButton Clicked!";
    }
  }
}
```

So far in this chapter we have covered how to integrate client-side script in general, how to execute client script on page load, and how to execute client script during form submission or as part of navigation. In the next section, we explore how to integrate client-side events with server-side events to provide graceful degradation in the event that client-side script support is not available.

Integrating Client-Side and Server-Side Events

The event processing that occurs in the client browser is separate from the ASP.NET activity that occurs on the server to generate HTML output and respond to server-side events. In this section, we build an example server control that provides seamless integration of the two event models in a similar manner to how the built in ASP.NET Validator controls have both client-side and server-side functionality. We discuss Validator controls and their construction in the next chapter. The control we build in this chapter is similar in functionality to the NumericUpDown Windows Forms control.

Control developers who extend or create a server control that uses client-side features need to ensure that the client activities are smoothly integrated with the feature set of ASP.NET and do not contradict or interfere with mechanisms such as ViewState or postback. It is also recommended that developers build controls that integrate client-side script to degrade gracefully when the client viewing the generated HTML content does not support more advanced features. A good example of this is the Validator class of controls that only emit client-side JavaScript validation routines if the browser supports JavaScript. Let's now dive into creating the UpDown custom server control.

The UpDown Server Control

To demonstrate integration between client-side programming and server controls along with graceful down-level client rendering, we construct a server control that mimics the NumericUpDown control from the Windows Forms desktop .NET development environment, as shown in Figure 8-12.

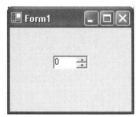

Figure 8-12. The UpDown *Windows Forms desktop control*

The UpDown server control takes the form of a composite control with a TextBox to hold the value and two Buttons with the captions + and – to represent up and down incrementing clicks. Although the UI is not spectacular, it permits us to show how to wire up client script with server events.

If the browser supports it, the UpDown server control emits JavaScript that increments or decrements the value in the TextBox in the local environment of the browser without having to make a round-trip to the web server to perform these operations. Client-side operations include the same functionality available in the server-side events, such as range checking, though we simply display a message notifying the user of the input error while in the server-side events we throw an ArgumentOutOfRangeException. The UpDown server control has a number of important properties that we discuss in the next section.

Key Properties: MinValue, MaxValue, Increment, and Value

The UpDown server control exposes four properties that allow developers to configure its behavior in the Visual Studio Designer: MinValue, MaxValue, Increment, and Value. The property handlers perform data validation tasks to ensure the number set for the Value property falls between the MinValue and MaxValue property range. We default to System.Int.MaxRange for the MaxValue property to prevent an exception if the value is too large. Here's how these properties are declared within the UpDown server control:

```
public virtual int MinValue
{
    get
    {
        EnsureChildControls();
        object min = ViewState["MinValue"];
        return (min == null) ? 0 : (int) min;
```

```
        }
     set
     {
        EnsureChildControls();
        if (value < MaxValue)
           ViewState["MinValue"] = value;
        else
           throw new ArgumentException(
"MinValue must be less than MaxValue.","MinValue");
     }
  }

  public virtual int MaxValue
  {
     get
     {
        EnsureChildControls();
        object max = ViewState["MaxValue"];
        return (max == null) ? System.Int32.MaxValue : (int) max;
     }
     set
     {
        EnsureChildControls();
        if (value > MinValue)
           ViewState["MaxValue"] = value;
        else
           throw new ArgumentException(
"MaxValue must be greater than MinValue.","MaxValue");
     }
  }

  public int Value
  {
     get
     {
        EnsureChildControls();
        object value = (int)ViewState["value"];
        return (value != null) ? (int)value : 0;
     }
     set
     {
        EnsureChildControls();
        if ((value <= MaxValue) &&
           (value >= MinValue))
        {
           valueTextBox.Text = value.ToString();
           ViewState["value"] = value ;
        }
        else
        {
           throw new ArgumentOutOfRangeException("Value",
```

```
                "Value must be between MinValue and MaxValue.");
        }
    }
}

public int Increment
{
    get
    {
        EnsureChildControls();
        object inc = ViewState["Increment"];
        return (inc == null) ? 1 : (int) inc;
    }
    set
    {
        EnsureChildControls();
        if (value > 0)
            ViewState["Increment"] = value;
    }
}
```

When you view the UpDown.aspx file in the Visual Studio Designer, if you select the updown1 control and try to give it a value that is either above MaxValue or below MinValue, you will get a message dialog box reporting the error. Likewise, if you set MaxValue to a number that is less than MinValue, or vice versa, you will get an error dialog box. This design-time behavior is a good way to help developers understand how your control works and what errors to catch in exception handler blocks when working with the control at runtime.

In the next section, we move on to describe how the control is constructed.

Accessing UpDown Child Controls

UpDown is a composite server control that declares private controls of type TextBox to render an <INPUT type="text"> tag and two Button controls to render <INPUT type="button"> tags. It adds these controls by overriding the CreateChildControls method from WebControl, and it wires up their events to the parent control's events.

Because our control will emit JavaScript that needs to know the fully qualified name of each child control in order to work properly on the client, we implement the INamingContainer interface to ensure generation of unique names and use the UniqueID property from each of our private control declarations. In the following code, we access the UniqueID of the valueTextBox that holds the value of the UpDown control:

```
scriptInvoke = DOWN_SCRIPT_FUNCTION + "('" + valueTextBox.UniqueID
```

Now that we have presented an overview of how the control is constructed, we can jump into a discussion in the next section on how the control renders itself to support client-side and server-side event integration.

Preparing the Script for Rendering

Like any good client-side script-rendering server control, UpDown checks to see if the
browser can support client-side script prior to rendering. DetermineRenderClientScript
is similar to what we looked at for the Focus control—it checks for DOM Level 1 compliance and JavaScript features. Our client script is not very demanding, as we use only
the document.getElementById method, but this method could be extended to perform
additional checking if you want to support other browsers:

```
protected void DetermineRenderClientScript()
{
    if (EnableClientScript)
    {
        if ((Page != null) && (Page.Request != null))
        {
            HttpBrowserCapabilities caps = Page.Request.Browser;

            // require JavaScript and DOM Level 1
            // support to render client-side code
            // (IE 5+ and Netscape 6+)
            if (caps.JavaScript &&
                caps.W3CDomVersion.Major >= 1)
            {
                renderClientScript = true;
            }
        }
    }
}
```

The OnPreRender method calls DetermineRenderClientScript to guide its JavaScript
emissions. In UpDown, we take a different approach from previous server controls in the
chapter if we get the green light that we can take advantage of client script.

The call to Page.RegisterClientScriptBlock uses a helper method named
GetClientScriptInclude to render a script block that uses the src attribute to specify
an external JavaScript file.

TIP *Using an external file is recommended to separate client-side code development and maintenance. Also, it precludes the need to recompile a server control if
its script changes. If the script was encapsulated as strings within the server control, recompilation would be required to update the client-side script.*

Once we determine whether client script is supported, we proceed to add script
blocks to each of our controls to perform various client-side tasks:

```csharp
protected override void OnPreRender(EventArgs e)
{
    base.OnPreRender(e);

    DetermineRenderClientScript();

    // textbox script that validates the textbox when it
    // loses focus after input
    string scriptInvoke = "";
    if (renderClientScript)
    {
        scriptInvoke = this.CHECK_SCRIPT_FUNCTION + "('" + valueTextBox.UniqueID +
            "'," + this.MinValue + "," + this.MaxValue + ")";
        valueTextBox.Attributes.Add("onblur",scriptInvoke);
    }

    // add the '+' button client script function that
    // manipulates the textbox on the client side
    if (renderClientScript)
    {
        scriptInvoke = UP_SCRIPT_FUNCTION + "('" + valueTextBox.UniqueID +
            "'," + this.MinValue + "," + this.MaxValue + "," +
            this.Increment + "); return false;";
        upButton.Attributes.Add("onclick",scriptInvoke);
    }

    // add the '-' button client script function that
    // manipulates the textbox on the client side
    if (renderClientScript)
    {
        scriptInvoke = DOWN_SCRIPT_FUNCTION + "('" + valueTextBox.UniqueID +
            "'," + this.MinValue + "," + this.MaxValue + "," +
            this.Increment + "); return false;";
        downButton.Attributes.Add("onclick",scriptInvoke);
    }

    // register to ensure we receive postback handling
    // to properly handle child input controls
    Page.RegisterRequiresPostBack(this);

    if (renderClientScript)
    {
        // register the <script> block that does the
        // client-side handling
        Page.RegisterClientScriptBlock(
            typeof(UpDown).ToString(),
            GetClientScriptInclude(UPDOWN_SCRIPT_FILE) );
    }
}
```

First, we add script to the `valueTextBox` TextBox to check its value upon tabbing out or otherwise exiting the control. The `onblur` client-side event is triggered anytime a user enters a value in the text box and switches the focus from that element on the web page to some other element. The `CHECK_SCRIPT_FUNTION` constant points to `__UpDown_Check` in UpDown.js. Here is the code for `__UpDown_Check`:

```
function __UpDown_Check(boxid, min, max)
{
   var box = document.getElementById(boxid);

   if (isNaN(parseInt(box.value)))
      box.value = min;
   if (box.value > max)
      box.value = max;
   if (box.value < min)
      box.value = min;
}
```

We have to pass in the exact ID of the control on the client side, as well as our minimum and maximum values for validation purposes. The client script checks for non-numeric values and resets to the minimum value if they are found. The next part of `OnPreRender` configures client-side script for the plus and minus buttons:

```
// add the '+' button client script function that
// manipulates the textbox on the client side
if (renderClientScript)
{
   scriptInvoke = UP_SCRIPT_FUNCTION + "('" + valueTextBox.UniqueID +
      "'," + this.MinValue + "," + this.MaxValue + "," +
      this.Increment + "); return false;";
   upButton.Attributes.Add("onclick",scriptInvoke);
}

// add the '-' button client script function that
// manipulates the textbox on the client side
if (renderClientScript)
{
   scriptInvoke = DOWN_SCRIPT_FUNCTION + "('" + valueTextBox.UniqueID +
      "'," + this.MinValue + "," + this.MaxValue + "," +
      this.Increment + "); return false;";
   downButton.Attributes.Add("onclick",scriptInvoke);
}
```

The client-side script for the up and down buttons is virtually identical. The script function for the up button is as follows:

```
function __UpDown_Up(boxid, min, max, howmuch)
{
   var box = document.getElementById(boxid);
```

```
    var newvalue = parseInt(box.value) + howmuch;
    if ((newvalue <= max) && (newvalue >= min))
        box.value = newvalue;
}
```

It takes the ID of the text box and the minimum, maximum, and increment values from the server control's properties. We check for valid numbers and staying within the range of the minimum and maximum values on the client. We display an alert message box if a constraint is violated. This makes sure client-side operations are validated as they are on the server.

Finally, we register to ensure that we receive postback handling and processing, and we register the `<SCRIPT>` block for our client-side code so that we are ready to go:

```
Page.RegisterRequiresPostBack(this);

if (renderClientScript)
{
    Page.RegisterClientScriptBlock(
        typeof(UpDown).ToString(),
        GetClientScriptInclude(UPDOWN_SCRIPT_FILE) );
}
```

In the next section, we demonstrate how to encapsulate the script in an external file and build the appropriate references for rendering the server control.

Rendering the Script Block with the src Attribute

The GetClientScriptInclude method handles the task of generating the script block to pull in external JavaScript. We do this because we recommend following the convention outlined in the ASP.NET Framework documentation for placing client-side script in external files for custom server controls.

The recommended location for scripts on a web server with ASP.NET installed is under the default web site in the aspnet_client directory. For a typical machine, this puts it in the path C:\inetpub\wwwroot\aspnet_client. This directory is mapped into the virtual folder namespace within IIS.

If you search underneath aspnet_client, you will find subfolders representing assemblies that have placed their client script in this location. ASP.NET installs a system_web folder underneath aspnet_client. It also installs yet another subfolder to hold the JavaScript files. The subfolder is the version number of the assembly: *major.minor.build.revision.* Both the assembly name and version folder replace periods with underscores to make things friendly for referencing via URL. The full path for scripts installed by ASP.NET for version 1.0 of the .NET Framework is as follows:

```
C:\Inetpub\wwwroot\aspnet_client\system_web\1_0_3705_0
```

You will see additional subdirectories if you installed updates to the .NET Framework. This is a nice system because it keeps script files separate for each assembly and facilitates versioning script files for controls. In Chapter 13, we discuss deployment issues when shipping custom server controls.

Directly beneath the assembly and version folder are the files for ASP.NET. It installs SmartNav.js, SmartNavIE.js, and WebUIValidation.ja. The first two files enable the SmartNavigation feature of ASP.NET, which uses a windowless <IFRAME> to make it look as if the page is not posting back to the web server, so as to avoid the normal flashing that occurs with rerendering content. The last script implements the client-side validation features in ASP.NET.

Returning to GetClientScriptInclude, we can examine the code necessary to emit the script block:

```
private string GetClientScriptInclude(string scriptFile)
{
    // get the location of the client script folder
    // on the web server
    string scriptLocation = CLIENT_SCRIPT_LOCATION;

    // the format of the location is
    // /aspnet_client/{0}/{1}
    // 0 becomes the assembly version number
    // 1 becomes the name of the script

    if (scriptLocation.IndexOf("{0}") >= 0)
    {
        AssemblyName assemblyInfo = GetType().Assembly.GetName();

        // replace dots in assembly name and version
        // to make it URL safe
        string assemblyName = assemblyInfo.Name.Replace('.', '_');
        string assemblyVersion = assemblyInfo.Version.ToString().Replace('.', '_');

        scriptLocation = String.Format(scriptLocation,
        assemblyName, assemblyVersion);
    }

    // emit the <script> tag to reference an external javascript file
    return String.Format("<script language=\"javascript\" src=\"{0}{1}\"></script>",
        scriptLocation, scriptFile);
}
```

The scriptLocation string is initialized with the aspnet_client location from a string constant in the control and is modified throughout the function to get a final value of

```
\aspnet_client\controlsbooklib\1_0_0_0
```

The tricky part is where to use reflection with the System.Type class to obtain the name of the assembly. The filename referenced from the script block src attribute is already passed in as UpDown.js. After everything is said and done, we use the String.Format method to output:

```
<script language="javascript"
src="\aspnet_client\controlsbooklib\1_0_0_0\UpDown.js"></script>
```

In the next section, we get into the nitty-gritty of how the control is constructed, starting with an examination of the CreateChildControls method.

Creating the ChildControls

We covered the supporting methods and prerendering steps. Now we can dive into CreateChildControls and see how it sets things up. At the top of the class file, we declare our child controls:

```
private TextBox valueTextBox ;
private Button upButton ;
private Button downButton ;
```

We use these references in CreateChildControls when building up the control hierarchy in our composite control:

```
protected override void CreateChildControls()
{
    Controls.Clear();

    // add the textbox that holds the value
    valueTextBox = new TextBox();
    valueTextBox.ID = "InputText";
    valueTextBox.Width = 40;
    valueTextBox.Text = "0";
    Controls.Add(valueTextBox);

    // add the '+' button
    upButton = new Button();
    upButton.ID = "UpButton";
    upButton.Text = " + ";
    upButton.Click += new System.EventHandler(this.UpButtonClick);
    Controls.Add(upButton);

    // add the '-' button
    downButton = new Button();
    downButton.ID = "DownButton";
    downButton.Text = " - ";
    downButton.Click += new System.EventHandler(this.DownButtonClick);
    Controls.Add(downButton);
}
```

The first thing we do is clear out the control tree so we start with a clean slate. We set the downButton Button to the same size as the upButton Button to improve our UI just a bit. We add server-side event handlers to both upButton and downButton in case we need them because either the client-side script is not enabled or the browser does not support the level of DOM access required. In the next section, we discuss how the UpDown control provides a smooth experience to the end user with a discussion of how the server control monitors for value changes.

The ValueChanged Event

Our server control makes it easy to monitor the UpDown control and only be notified when it changes value through a server-side event named ValueChanged. The ValueChanged event is raised when it detects a difference between the Value property of the control from ViewState and what is received from the client after a postback:

```
public event EventHandler ValueChanged
{
    add
    {
        Events.AddHandler(ValueChangedKey, value);
    }
    remove
    {
        Events.RemoveHandler(ValueChangedKey, value);
    }
}

protected virtual void OnValueChanged(EventArgs e)
{
    EventHandler valueChangedEventDelegate =
        (EventHandler) Events[ValueChangedKey];
    if (valueChangedEventDelegate != null)
    {
        valueChangedEventDelegate(this, e);
    }
}
```

ValueChanged follows the basic pattern of the System.EventHandler delegate for its event declaration, so we can reuse the System.EventArgs class that goes with it. We also leverage the built-in Events property from System.Web.Control to efficiently store our subscribing delegates. We covered event-handling mechanisms in Chapter 5.

Now we have a way to generate events based on the value being changed. In the next section, we discuss how to retrieve the old and new value to enforce the UI logic.

Retrieving the Data

The ValueChanged event does us little good if we cannot retrieve the value of the form at postback. Instead of relying on the default value and event handling of the TextBox control, we take matters into our own hands for our composite control to ensure that we are notified during the form postback processing. We set things up by calling Page.RegisterRequiresPostback in OnPreRender. We finish the task by implementing the methods of IPostBackDataHandler.

In the following code, LoadPostData uses knowledge of the TextBox control's UniqueID property to index into the posted data collection. Once we retrieve the value, we can validate that it is a number with the Parse function of the System.Int32 type. We include a try/catch so we can handle problems with parsing if it is not an integer:

```
bool IPostBackDataHandler.LoadPostData(string postDataKey,
   NameValueCollection postCollection)
{
   bool changed = false;

   // grab the value posted by the textbox
   string postedValue = postCollection[valueTextBox.UniqueID];
   int postedNumber = 0;

   try
   {
      postedNumber = System.Int32.Parse(postedValue);

      if (!Value.Equals(postedNumber))
         changed = true;

      Value = postedNumber;
   }
   catch (FormatException fe)
   {
      changed = false;
   }
   return changed;
}
```

If the value is an integer, we can assign it to the Value property. We perform range checking in the property declaration. Before we do assign the value, we first check the Value property's ViewState value to see if there was indeed a change. If this is the case, we return true from the function. Returning true causes RaisePostChangedEvent to be invoked and in turn raise our ValueChanged event via the OnValueChanged helper method, as shown in the following code:

```
void IPostBackDataHandler.RaisePostDataChangedEvent()
{
   OnValueChanged(EventArgs.Empty);
}
```

Because our control publishes just a single event, the corresponding RaisePostDataChangedEvent is also simple. In the next section we drill down into how child button clicks that change the value are handled by the composite control and how the control dynamically determines whether or not to fire server-side events.

Handling Child Control Events

We glossed over the fact that we mapped the button click events to server-side handlers in our composite UpDown control. They are not necessary if we assume the browser can handle the client-side script. The client-side onclick event fully handles the clicking of the up and down buttons and never needs to post back to the web server. Of course, this is not a good situation if you have a down-level client. If this is the case, you can fall back on the natural capability of the buttons to execute a postback by virtue of being located on a Web Form. We assign the server-side events to our buttons in CreateChildControls in case they are required.

The UpDown control can make several assumptions when the server reaches its handlers for the buttons. The first is that the Value property is loaded with the number in the TextBox. We discussed the LoadPostData handling that did this in the previous section. The second is that all other events have fired. Remember that buttons and other controls initiating postback always let other events fire before getting their turn.

The implementation of UpButtonClick takes the Increment property, applies it to the Value property, and makes sure its stays in bounds, as shown in the following code. Because it knows that a change has occurred, it raises the OnValueChanged event. DownButtonClick is identical except for subtracting the Increment.

```
protected void UpButtonClick(object source, EventArgs e)
{
    int newValue = Value + Increment;
    if ((newValue <= MaxValue) && (newValue >= MinValue))
    {
        Value = newValue;
        OnValueChanged(EventArgs.Empty);
    }
}
```

At this point, our data loading and event raising tasks are complete. Our control is prepared to render in the browser. Listing 8-16 presents the full source code for the UpDown control. Listing 8-17 contains the UpDown.js JavaScript file.

Listing 8-16. The UpDown *Server Control*

```
using System;
using System.Collections;
using System.Collections.Specialized;
using System.ComponentModel;
using System.Text;
using System.Web;
```

```csharp
using System.Reflection;
using System.Web.UI;
using System.Web.UI.HtmlControls;
using System.Web.UI.WebControls;
using ControlsBookLib.Ch12.Design;

namespace ControlsBookLib.Ch08
{


    [ToolboxData("<{0}:UpDown runat=server></{0}:UpDown>"),
DefaultProperty("Value"),
    Designer(typeof(CompCntrlDesigner))]
    public class UpDown : WebControl, IPostBackDataHandler, INamingContainer
    {
        protected const string CLIENT_SCRIPT_LOCATION = "/aspnet_client/{0}/{1}/";
        protected const string UPDOWN_SCRIPT_FILE = "UpDown.js";
        protected const string UP_SCRIPT_FUNCTION = "__UpDown_Up";
        protected const string DOWN_SCRIPT_FUNCTION = "__UpDown_Down";
        protected string CHECK_SCRIPT_FUNCTION = "__UpDown_Check";

        private TextBox valueTextBox ;
        private Button upButton ;
        private Button downButton ;
        private bool renderClientScript;
        private static readonly object ValueChangedKey = new object();

        public UpDown() : base(HtmlTextWriterTag.Div)
        {
            renderClientScript = false;
        }

        public virtual bool EnableClientScript
        {
            get
            {
                EnsureChildControls();
                object script = ViewState["EnableClientScript"];
                if (script == null)
                    return true;
                else
                    return (bool) script;
            }
            set
            {
                EnsureChildControls();
                ViewState["EnableClientScript"] = value;
            }
        }

        public virtual int MinValue
```

```
{
   get
   {
      EnsureChildControls();
      object min = ViewState["MinValue"];
      return (min == null) ? 0 : (int) min;
   }
   set
   {
      EnsureChildControls();
      if (value < MaxValue)
         ViewState["MinValue"] = value;
      else
         throw new ArgumentException(
         "MinValue must be less than MaxValue.","MinValue");
   }
}

public virtual int MaxValue
{
   get
   {
      EnsureChildControls();
      object max = ViewState["MaxValue"];
      return (max == null) ? System.Int32.MaxValue : (int) max;
   }
   set
   {
      EnsureChildControls();
      if (value > MinValue)
         ViewState["MaxValue"] = value;
      else
         throw new ArgumentException(
         "MaxValue must be greater than MinValue.","MaxValue");
   }
}

public int Value
{
   get
   {
      EnsureChildControls();
      object value = (int)ViewState["value"];
      return (value != null) ? (int)value : 0;
   }
   set
   {
      EnsureChildControls();
      if ((value <= MaxValue) &&
         (value >= MinValue))
      {
```

```
            valueTextBox.Text = value.ToString();
            ViewState["value"] = value ;
        }
        else
        {
            throw new ArgumentOutOfRangeException("Value",
            "Value must be between MinValue and MaxValue.");
        }
    }
}

public int Increment
{
    get
    {
        EnsureChildControls();
        object inc = ViewState["Increment"];
        return (inc == null) ? 1 : (int) inc;
    }
    set
    {
        EnsureChildControls();
        if (value > 0)
            ViewState["Increment"] = value;
    }
}

// LoadPostData is overridden to get the data
// back from the textbox and set up the
// ValueChanged event if necessary
bool IPostBackDataHandler.LoadPostData(string postDataKey,
    NameValueCollection postCollection)
{
    bool changed = false;

    // grab the value posted by the textbox
    string postedValue = postCollection[valueTextBox.UniqueID];
    int postedNumber = 0;

    try
    {
        postedNumber = System.Int32.Parse(postedValue);

        if (!Value.Equals(postedNumber))
          changed = true;

        Value = postedNumber;
    }
    catch (FormatException fe)
    {
        changed = false;
    }
```

```
      return changed;
}

void IPostBackDataHandler.RaisePostDataChangedEvent()
{
   OnValueChanged(EventArgs.Empty);
}

public event EventHandler ValueChanged
{
   add
   {
      Events.AddHandler(ValueChangedKey, value);
   }
   remove
   {
      Events.RemoveHandler(ValueChangedKey, value);
   }
}

protected virtual void OnValueChanged(EventArgs e)
{
   EventHandler valueChangedEventDelegate =
      (EventHandler) Events[ValueChangedKey];
   if (valueChangedEventDelegate != null)
   {
      valueChangedEventDelegate(this, e);
   }
}

// up/down button click handling when client-side
// script functionality is not enabled
protected void UpButtonClick(object source, EventArgs e)
{
   int newValue = Value + Increment;
   if ((newValue <= MaxValue) && (newValue >= MinValue))
   {
      Value = newValue;
      OnValueChanged(EventArgs.Empty);
   }
}

protected void DownButtonClick(object source, EventArgs e)
{
   int newValue = Value - Increment;
   if ((newValue <= MaxValue) && (newValue >= MinValue))
   {
         Value = newValue;
      OnValueChanged(EventArgs.Empty);
   }
}
```

```
protected void DetermineRenderClientScript()
{
   if (EnableClientScript)
   {
      if ((Page != null) && (Page.Request != null))
      {
         HttpBrowserCapabilities caps = Page.Request.Browser;

         // require JavaScript and DOM Level 1
         // support to render client-side code
         // (IE 5+ and Netscape 6+)
         if (caps.JavaScript &&
            caps.W3CDomVersion.Major >= 1)
         {
            renderClientScript = true;
         }
      }
   }
}

private string GetClientScriptInclude(string scriptFile)
{
   // get the location of the client script folder
   // on the web server
   string scriptLocation = CLIENT_SCRIPT_LOCATION;

   // the format of the location is
   // /aspnet_client/{0}/{1}
   // 0 becomes the assembly version number
   // 1 becomes the name of the script

   if (scriptLocation.IndexOf("{0}") >= 0)
   {
      AssemblyName assemblyInfo = GetType().Assembly.GetName();

      // replace dots in assembly name and version
      // to make it URL safe
      string assemblyName = assemblyInfo.Name.Replace('.', '_');
      string assemblyVersion =
      assemblyInfo.Version.ToString().Replace('.', '_');

      scriptLocation = String.Format(scriptLocation, assemblyName,
                     assemblyVersion);
   }

   // emit the <script> tag to reference an external javascript file
   return String.Format("<script language=\"javascript\"
                     src=\"{0}{1}\"></script>",
      scriptLocation, scriptFile);
}
```

```
protected override void OnPreRender(EventArgs e)
{
    base.OnPreRender(e);

    DetermineRenderClientScript();

    // textbox script that validates the textbox when it
    // loses focus after input
    string scriptInvoke = "";
    if (renderClientScript)
    {
        scriptInvoke = this.CHECK_SCRIPT_FUNCTION + "('" +
        valueTextBox.UniqueID +
            "'," + this.MinValue + "," + this.MaxValue + ")";
        valueTextBox.Attributes.Add("onblur",scriptInvoke);
    }

    // add the '+' button client script function that
    // manipulates the textbox on the client side
    if (renderClientScript)
    {
        scriptInvoke = UP_SCRIPT_FUNCTION + "('" + valueTextBox.UniqueID +
            "'," + this.MinValue + "," + this.MaxValue + "," + this.Increment
            + "); return false;";
        upButton.Attributes.Add("onclick",scriptInvoke);
    }

    // add the '-' button client script function that
    // manipulates the textbox on the client side
    if (renderClientScript)
    {
        scriptInvoke = DOWN_SCRIPT_FUNCTION + "('" + valueTextBox.UniqueID +
            "'," + this.MinValue + "," + this.MaxValue + "," + this.Increment
            + "); return false;";
        downButton.Attributes.Add("onclick",scriptInvoke);
    }

    // register to ensure we receive postback handling
    // to properly handle child input controls
    Page.RegisterRequiresPostBack(this);

    if (renderClientScript)
    {
        // register the <script> block that does the
        // client-side handling
        Page.RegisterClientScriptBlock(
            typeof(UpDown).ToString(),
            GetClientScriptInclude(UPDOWN_SCRIPT_FILE) );
    }
}
```

```
    public override ControlCollection Controls
    {
      get
      {
        EnsureChildControls();
        return base.Controls;
      }
    }

    protected override void CreateChildControls()
    {
      Controls.Clear();

      // add the textbox that holds the value
      valueTextBox = new TextBox();
      valueTextBox.ID = "InputText";
      valueTextBox.Width = 40;
      valueTextBox.Text = "0";
    Controls.Add(valueTextBox);

      // add the '+' button
      upButton = new Button();
      upButton.ID = "UpButton";
      upButton.Text = " + ";
      upButton.Click += new System.EventHandler(this.UpButtonClick);
      Controls.Add(upButton);

      // add the '-' button
      downButton = new Button();
      downButton.ID = "DownButton";
      downButton.Text = " - ";
      downButton.Click += new System.EventHandler(this.DownButtonClick);
    Controls.Add(downButton);
    }
  }
}
```

Listing 8-17. The UpDown *JavaScript File*

```
function __UpDown_Check(boxid, min, max)
{
  var box = document.getElementById(boxid);

  if (isNaN(parseInt(box.value)))
    box.value = min;
  if (box.value > max)
  {
    alert('Value cannot be greater than the Maximum allowed.');
    box.value = max;
  }
```

```
      if (box.value < min)
      {
        alert('Value cannot be less than the Minimum.');
        box.value = min;
      }
    }

    function __UpDown_Up(boxid, min, max, howmuch)
    {
      var box = document.getElementById(boxid);

      var newvalue = parseInt(box.value) + howmuch;
      if ((newvalue <= max) && (newvalue >= min))
        box.value = newvalue;
    }

    function __UpDown_Down(boxid, min, max, howmuch)
    {
      var box = document.getElementById(boxid);

      var newvalue = parseInt(box.value) - howmuch;
      if ((newvalue <= max) && (newvalue >= min))
        box.value = newvalue;
    }
```

In the next section, we move on to the Web Form demonstration of our newly minted UpDown custom server control, testing that it correctly implements the expected UI logic.

The UpDown Web Form

To test the UpDown control, we place it on a Web Form named UpDown. We also create the directory structure on the machine to handle the JavaScript source include file. If you rely on the default C: drive installation of the root web site with IIS, the full path to UpDown.js should look like the following:

```
C:\Inetpub\wwwroot\aspnet_client\ControlsBookLib\1_0_0_0\UpDown.js
```

Once you've done this, you can take UpDown for a test drive as shown in Figure 8-13. Clicking the buttons shows the time label isn't advancing.

If you add the following name/value pair to the @Page directive of the Web Form, it will force the control to stop emitting JavaScript:

```
ClientTarget="downlevel"
```

The result in Figure 8-14 shows the time label changing on each button click because a server postback occurs.

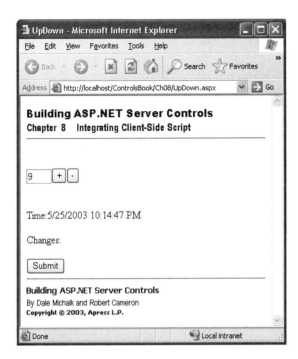

Figure 8-13. The UpDown *control in action on a Web Form*

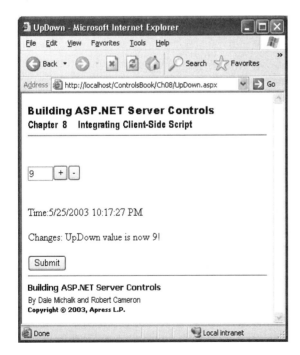

Figure 8-14. The UpDown *control with* EnableClientScript = "False"

As you can see, both client-side and server-side code works with aplomb. The full source code for the Web Form and code-behind class is shown in Listings 8-18 and 8-19.

Listing 8-18. The UpDown Web Form .aspx Page File

```
<%@ Page language="c#" Codebehind="UpDown.aspx.cs" AutoEventWireup="false"
Inherits="ControlsBookWeb.Ch08.UpDown" %>
<%@ Register TagPrefix="apressUC" TagName="ControlsBookFooter"
Src="..\ControlsBookFooter.ascx" %>
<%@ Register TagPrefix="apressUC" TagName="ControlsBookHeader"
Src="..\ControlsBookHeader.ascx" %>
<%@ Register TagPrefix="apress" Namespace="ControlsBookLib.Ch08"
Assembly="ControlsBookLib" %>
<!DOCTYPE HTML PUBLIC "-//W3C//DTD HTML 4.0 Transitional//EN" >
<HTML>
  <HEAD>
    <title>UpDown</title>
    <meta content="Microsoft Visual Studio 7.0" name="GENERATOR">
    <meta content="C#" name="CODE_LANGUAGE">
    <meta content="JavaScript" name="vs_defaultClientScript">
    <meta content="http://schemas.microsoft.com/intellisense/ie5"
name="vs_targetSchema">
  </HEAD>
  <body MS_POSITIONING="FlowLayout">
    <form id="UpDown" method="post" runat="server">
      <apressuc:controlsbookheader id="Header" runat="server" chapternumber="8"
chaptertitle="Integrating Client-Side Script"></apressuc:controlsbookheader><br>
      <br>
      <apress:updown id="updown1" runat="server" MinValue="1" MaxValue="15"
Increment="3" Value="6" EnableClientScript="False"></apress:updown><br>
      <br>
      Time:<asp:label id="timelabel" Runat="server"></asp:label><br>
      <br>
      Changes:<asp:label id="changelabel" Runat="server"></asp:label><br>
      <br>
      <asp:button id="submitbtn" Runat="server"
Text="Submit"></asp:button><apressuc:controlsbookfooter id="Footer"
runat="server"></apressuc:controlsbookfooter></form>
  </body>
</HTML>
```

Listing 8-19. UpDown Web Form Code-Behind Class File

```
using System;
using System.Collections;
using System.ComponentModel;
using System.Data;
using System.Drawing;
```

```csharp
using System.Web;
using System.Web.SessionState;
using System.Web.UI;
using System.Web.UI.WebControls;
using System.Web.UI.HtmlControls;

namespace ControlsBookWeb.Ch08
{
    public class UpDown : System.Web.UI.Page
    {
        protected System.Web.UI.WebControls.Label timelabel;
        protected System.Web.UI.WebControls.Button submitbtn;
        protected System.Web.UI.WebControls.Label changelabel;
        protected ControlsBookWeb.ControlsBookHeader Header ;
        protected ControlsBookLib.Ch08.UpDown updown1;

        private void Page_Load(object sender, System.EventArgs e)
        {

            timelabel.Text = DateTime.Now.ToString();
            changelabel.Text = "";
        }

        #region Web Form Designer generated code
        override protected void OnInit(EventArgs e)
        {
            //
            // CODEGEN: This call is required by the ASP.NET Web Form Designer.
            //
            InitializeComponent();
            base.OnInit(e);
        }

        /// <summary>
        /// Required method for Designer support - do not modify
        /// the contents of this method with the code editor.
        /// </summary>
        private void InitializeComponent()
        {
            this.updown1.ValueChanged += new
            System.EventHandler(this.updown1_ValueChanged);
            this.Load += new System.EventHandler(this.Page_Load);
        }
        #endregion

        private void updown1_ValueChanged(object sender, System.EventArgs e)
        {
            changelabel.Text = " UpDown value is now " + updown1.Value + "!";
        }
    }
}
```

In the next and final section of this chapter, we provide a list of good practices to follow when you integrate client-side script into your custom server controls.

Tips for Working with Client-Side Script

We round off this chapter with some general tips for building server controls that take advantage of client-side script:

- Create your script in an HTML file first. Once you are confident the script is correct, move it into the server control. This approach is much faster than trying to directly integrate the script creation and control creation processes, as you can change the code and test it without going through the process of compiling an ASP.NET web application.

- Install the Microsoft Script Debugger, which you can download from `http://www.microsoft.com/scripting/`. It enables you to single-step through your client-side script, and it provides much more valuable feedback than the errors from the web browser.

- While you are debugging, consider the client side and the server side separately. Your server-side code is generating HTML and client-side script, but once it is generated, the browser is effectively processing a bunch of text. If you want to debug fast, select View ➤ Source in the browser and debug your client script away from ASP.NET.

- Make sure you know what browsers your web site must support and install them on your machine. Test your script on all the browsers your users are likely to use. Even if you do not need the script to work 100 percent of the time, it should degrade gracefully.

- Arm yourself with some good resources on JavaScript, including MSDN (`http://msdn.microsoft.com`), W3 Schools (`http://www.w3schools.com/js`), and IRT (`http://tech.irt.org/articles/script.htm`).

- Make script embedded in your server control class file (.cs) more easily readable by using the @ prefix on strings so that you can spread the script across several lines.

- If you need to build a long script string from variables and pieces of script, use the `StringBuilder` class—it is faster than concatenating strings. Remember that your control may be used several times on a page or placed in a repeating control such as the `DataGrid` and instantiated multiple times. Cases like these make the `StringBuilder` class worth using, as the speed benefits add up.

- Before you build your own control to create a UI element, check to see if there is one out there already. Using third-party controls may well be more efficient than rolling your own, especially now that reuse is so much easier in ASP.NET. You should expect the market for ASP.NET server controls (free and commercial) to expand as rapidly as it did for custom controls in Visual Basic during the 1990s. A good starting point is the Control Gallery at the ASP.NET web site (`http://www.asp.net`).

- When you do decide to build your own control, we recommend leveraging client script wherever possible. ASP.NET provides a nice set of supporting methods to facilitate this, and the developers who use your custom server controls will appreciate the extra effort, as will their end users.

Summary

Client-side script can make a web application more appealing, interactive, and scalable. ASP.NET allows encapsulation of the client-side script code to reduce some of the inherent complexity client script can bring to web development projects. Controls support adding client-side event attributes to the .aspx page declaratively and programmatically via the `Attributes` collection. Also, the `Page` class supports several options for registering client-side script: `RegisterClientScriptBlock` for the top of the form, `RegisterStartupScript` for the bottom of the form, `RegisterArrayDeclaration` for adding an array, and `RegisterOnSubmitStatement` for hooking into the `onsubmit` event of the form.

Client-side detection is done through an instance of the `HttpBrowserCapabilities` class. An instance is provided by the `Page.Request.Browser` class. Machine.config has a `<browserCaps>` section that controls how client device detection occurs and can be modified to support the latest devices. Controls should provide graceful degradation wherever possible in the event a client doesn't support client-side functionality to the level required.

Be careful when you map to the `onsubmit` event of an HTML form. It will fire when a control such as `LinkButton` uses the client-side JavaScript form submission code provided by ASP.NET.

CHAPTER 9

Validation Controls

VALIDATION CONTROLS IN ASP.NET are very popular with web developers. These controls are great time-savers because they eliminate the need to write repetitive code that checks user input. This is especially true when developers want to validate a user's input on the client as well as on the server. Embedding validation JavaScript into the script code of an ASP page environment is not a task most folks volunteer for, so having built-in validation controls is a big step forward.

NOTE *Server-side validation always occurs in ASP.NET for security reasons. If the .NET Framework performed just client-side validation, it would be possible for a hacker to bypass client-side validation and inject invalid input en route to the web server that would be processed as posted data by ASP.NET.*

Fortunately for those developing in ASP.NET, there is a family of prebuilt validation controls that can handle probably 90 percent of the client-side and server-side validation requirements encountered in web development projects. Here is a brief description of each control's capabilities:

- RequiredFieldValidator notifies the user if a required field is left blank.

- CompareValidator handles the task of ensuring two input controls contain the same value.

- RangeValidator ensures input falls within a range of values, whether the type of input is text, numeric, currency, or date based.

- RegularExpressionValidator checks whether input matches a regular expression. This control provides great flexibility with respect to checking input, though regular expressions can be tedious to create.

- CustomValidator provides the most flexibility of all the built-in controls by allowing developers to supply both client-side and server-side user-defined validation routines to check input on a control.

- ValidationSummary is not a validation control per se, but it does provide a nice way to organize and display error messages in a tabular form.

In this chapter we examine how the Page class implements the validation framework and how validation controls interact with the framework to accomplish their tasks. We drill down into the ASP.NET client-side validation library and the feature set provided by the abstract base class BaseValidator. Along the way, we implement custom validation controls and controls that inherit from the BaseValidator abstract class to help demonstrate these concepts.

Extending the Validation System

There are situations in which you may want to extend the built-in validation system to encapsulate specific behavior for ease of use or to help minimize repetitive tasks. Fortunately, validation in ASP.NET is not a closed black-box environment that you cannot extend. The validation architecture is extendable primarily through three techniques:

- Using the CustomValidator control by attaching custom validation routines for client-side and server-side validation processing

- Creating a custom control that inherits from the BaseValidator abstract class

- Creating a custom control that implements the IValidator interface

Generally, web developers take the first option with the CustomValidator control to override validation logic. This option allows web developers to provide a server-side validation routine and specify a client-side JavaScript function to be called if the browser supports those features.

The second option, building a control that inherits from the abstract base class BaseValidator, is useful when web developers need to create a validation control that requires the least amount of configuration for the end user of the control. This option hides the custom client-side and server-side validation routines from public view. All developers need to do is drop it onto a Web Form, set its properties, and it's ready to go.

The final option, building a custom validation control from scratch that implements IValidator, is typically the last resort because of the amount of work involved. Developers will choose this route in those rare cases when they want to have absolute control over the validation process. If you choose this option, you are responsible for all of the implementation details.

Before we get into the details of extending the validation system in the sections that follow, we discuss the requisite knowledge necessary to work with validation controls in the next section by examining how they interact with the ASP.NET Web Form.

The Page Class and Validation

The validation controls leverage the framework built into the Web Form embodied by the System.Web.UI.Page class. The Page class not only houses the validation controls in a special collection exposed by the Validators property but also provides a means to execute the validation logic explicitly via its Validate method. Calling this method causes the Page class to iterate through the Validators collection, checking each validation control's status. You can check on the final result of this activity using the IsValid Boolean property. Table 9-1 summarizes the exposed features of the Page class relating to validation.

Table 9-1. Page *Class Validation Properties/Methods*

PROPERTY/METHOD	DESCRIPTION
Validators	Property linked to collection housing all validation controls on a Web Form
Validate	Method to initiate manual execution of validation logic on all validation controls on a Web Form
IsValid	Boolean property used to check on the validation results

Validation controls enter into a contract with the Page class via the IValidator interface when they add themselves to the Page class's Validators collection. IValidator has the methods/properties listed in Table 9-2 to complete all validation tasks as instructed by the Page class in the validation activity.

Table 9-2. IValidator *Properties/Methods*

PROPERTY/METHOD	DESCRIPTION
ErrorMessage	String property of message to display for invalid input
IsValid	Boolean property to check on the input check result
Validate	Method to initiate validation control input check

For each Validator in its Validators collection, Page calls the Validate method to fire validation logic. Page checks the IsValid property to retrieve the status of the validation operation. As you would guess, ErrorMessage is the property that publishes an error message when there is a validation problem that causes the validation control to return false in its IsValid property. The ValidationSummary control uses ErrorMessage as the source for its tabular summary display of error messages. ErrorMessage is separate from the inline display of an error message that validation controls support.

The Validation Life Cycle

The server-side validation process described previously normally kicks off in two different scenarios:

- Implicitly during the postback process before the postback event is raised by the control that started the postback (i.e., before a button click event)

- Explicitly by custom code that directly invokes the Page class's Validate method

We examined the page life cycle in depth in Chapter 5, and we use it to point out when the validation step occurs. The first request to a Web Form is an HTTP GET, which does not kick off the validation process, as this is the user's first opportunity to provide values. When the user causes a postback via either a button click or an auto-postback configured control, the following sequence of events occurs:

1. `Init` event
2. `LoadViewState` event
3. `LoadPostData` event
4. `Load` event
5. `RaisePostDataChanged` event
6. `Validate`
7. `RaisePostBack` event
8. `PreRender` event
9. `SaveViewState` event
10. `Render` event
11. `Unload` event
12. `Dispose` event

Control initialization, data loading, and the data change handling from the postback process all occur prior to validation happening. This allows the controls to fully react to the input of the user before validation occurs. Note that validation occurs before the control that initiated postback handles the `PostBack` event itself. This execution order checks input before navigation or other events fire as result of the postback event. As background, you do not have to follow this sequence. You can modify this behavior by inserting a call to the `Page` class's `Validate` method in the `Page` class's `Load` event if you need to check input earlier in the postback cycle.

Regardless of which scenario initiates the call to `Page.Validate`, `Validate` executes code that enumerates all the controls in `Page` class's `Validators ValidatorCollection` object, casting them to the `IValidator` interface and calling their `Validate` method. The code inside the ASP.NET framework probably looks similar to the following snippet:

```
void Validate()
{
   foreach(IValidator val in Page.Validators)
   {
      val.Validate();
   }
}
```

The Page class does not keep track of validation results in a private variable. To set the IsValid property, another foreach loop iterates through the Validators collection to check each validation control's IsValid property with something similar to the following IsValid routine:

```
bool IsValid()
{
   foreach(IValidator val in Page.Validators)
   {
     if (!val.IsValid)
        return false;
   }
   return true;
}
```

Knowledge of how Page.IsValid is calculated could be used by a savvy control developer to set/override the IsValid property of the validation controls after the normal validation cycle occurs in order to change the outcome. The control developer could disable the validation process on the fly if the context of the Web Form is known to be in an incomplete state and not ready for validation.

Armed with information on how the Page framework interacts with validation controls, we can now move on to looking at how web developers can extend the functionality of validation controls.

The CustomValidator Control for Phone Number Validation

The easiest way to customize the validation process starts with the CustomValidator control. It leaves implementation of the business logic that validates input on the client and the server to the developer, providing a simple framework to wire things up. We use its built-in functionality to validate input, ensuring that a properly formatted phone number for the United States is entered.

TIP *You could easily match this functionality by using the* RegularExpressionValidator *control. We use this method to demonstrate the features of the validation framework built into ASP.NET with a fairly simple example.*

`CustomValidator` provides two important properties/events to support custom validation:

- `ClientValidationFunction` is a control property that points to the client-side routine to call if the browser supports client-side validation.

- `ServerValidate` is an event exposed by the `CustomValidator` class that points to a server-side routine wrapped in a type-safe delegate in ASP.NET to hook into the server-side validation process, checking the validity of entered data once the information has been posted to the web server.

Our example uses both client-side and server-side validation to demonstrate the full power of the `CustomValidator` control. This means that we need to identify how we validate phone numbers in both JavaScript and ASP.NET. Because regular expressions are the easiest way to check the validity of complex inputs, we turn to the regular expression support in both environments. The following regular expression is geared to match a U.S.-style phone number with an area code:

`^\(?\d{3}\)?\s|-\d{3}\-\d{4}$`

In Chapter 8 we provide a brief discussion on the regular expression syntax required to describe a pattern for a U.S. phone number. The pattern matches only a phone number string that has three numeric digits in optional parentheses followed by a space or dash, three more numeric digits, a dash, and the final four numeric digits. This expression would match on strings similar to the following:

```
(555) 555-5555
555-555-5555
```

Now that you know how to validate the input using regular expressions, we move on to implement the client-side behavior in the next section.

Client-Side Validation Routine

In this section, we discuss how to implement the client-side validation behavior. The client-side validation API expects our client-side routine to match the following signature:

```
function FuncName(source, args)
```

It is able to call the routine dynamically through the `eval` function in JavaScript. The key parameter is the second one, `args`, which has two properties:

- `Value`: The current value of the input control undergoing validation

- `IsValid`: A property used by the validation routine to signal success or failure

Our client-side phone number validation routine uses the passed-in value and the RegExp object support in JavaScript to check for a properly formatted phone number. JavaScript provides a special syntax of forward slashes around the regular expression to automatically create a RegExp object behind the scenes. In Listing 9-1 you can see the syntax that assigns an instance of the RegExp object to the regex variable.

Listing 9-1. Client-Side Phone Validation Routine

```
function ClientPhoneValidate(source, args)
{
   var regex = /^\(?\d{3}\)?\s|-\d{3}\-\d{4}$/;
   var matches = regex.exec(args.Value);
   args.IsValid = (matches != null && args.Value == matches[0]);
}
```

We use the exec method of the RegExp JavaScript object to create a collection of string matches based on the pattern and the input value. If the string match collection is not null and the first match is our value passed in from the input control, we return true for the IsValid property.

Server-Side Validation Routine

The server-side validation features of CustomValidator are exposed through an event named ServerValidate. ServerValidate has a custom delegate type that inherits from System.EventHandler to add an overridden EventArgs class as its second parameter. The declaration of the delegate looks like the following:

```
Public delegate ServerValidateEventHandler(Object o, ServerValidateEventArgs e);
```

The ServerValidateEventArgs class holds key information for the validation process and is similar to the args parameter in the client-side validation function we discussed earlier. The definition for the class that is part of the ASP.NET probably looks something like this:

```
public class ServerValidateEventArgs : EventArgs
{
   private bool isValid;
   private string value;
   public ServerValidateEventArgs(string value, bool isValid)
   {
      this.isValid = isValid;
      this.value = value;
   }
   public string Value
   {
      get { return value; }
   }
   public bool IsValid
```

```
   {
     get { return isValid; }
     set { isValid = value; }
   }
 }
}
```

Using ServerValidateEventArgs is similar to the client-side validation routine defined by the client validation library in JavaScript with respect to its parameter syntax for obtaining the validated control's value and returning a status from the validation routine. What we do differently is use the .NET library for regular expressions available in the System.Text.RegularExpressions namespace.

The .NET Framework Regex class makes working with regular expressions very convenient. As shown in Listing 9-2, we pass the regular expression to the Regex constructor and then use either its IsMatch or Matches method to check if an input string fits the regular expression. We use the Matches method to mimic client-side behavior. If the input value of the validated control matches the first value in the Matches MatchCollection, we return true for the IsValid property of the ServerValidateEventArgs class that was passed into the routine.

Listing 9-2. Server-Side Phone Validation Routine

```
private void ServerPhoneValidate(object source,
      System.Web.UI.WebControls.ServerValidateEventArgs args)
{
   Regex expr = new Regex(@"^\(?\d{3}\)?\s|-\d{3}\-\d{4}$");
   MatchCollection matches = expr.Matches(args.Value, 0);
   args.IsValid = (matches != null && matches[0].Value == args.Value);
}
```

In the next section, we put our client-side and server-side validation routines to use in the Phone Validation Using CustomValidator Web Form.

The Phone Validation Using CustomValidator Web Form

Now that we have developed the client and server-side validation routines, it is trivial to link them up to a CustomValidator on a Web Form. Figure 9-1 shows a Web Form with a tabular design that gathers some contrived registration information from the user.

The Web Form contains a hodgepodge of input controls, including the TextBox, RadioButtonList, and DropDownList controls. The validators demonstrated include our CustomValidator phone number control, RequiredFieldValidator, RangeValidator, CompareValidator, and ValidationSummary for displaying error messages. The wide range of HTML elements allows us to examine just about every facet of the client-side validation library, which we do later in this chapter.

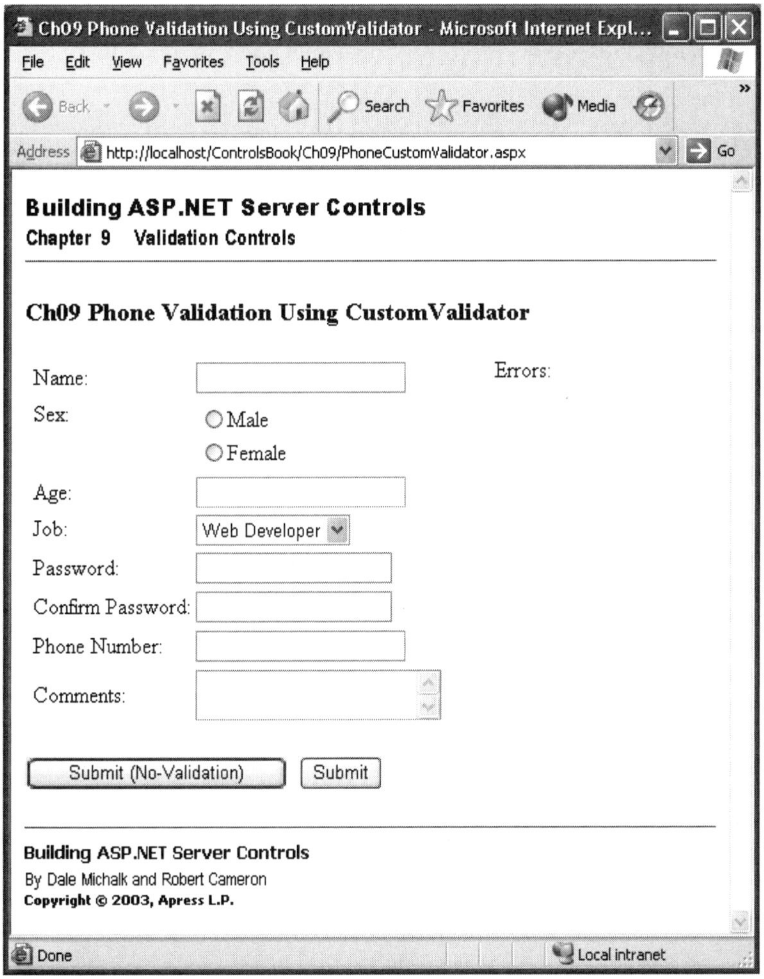

Figure 9-1. The Phone Validation Using CustomValidator Web Form

The buttons that submit the Web Form have two different roles. The `Button` titled Submit is configured without any special features. The other `Button` has its `CausesValidation` property set to false. The `Button` titled Submit causes the normal Web Form validation on the client side and then the server side if you satisfy the correct inputs in the browser. Figure 9-2 shows the error messages with an incomplete Web Form displayed.

If you click the other `Button` titled Submit (No-Validation), the Web Form is posted back to the web server without client or server validation occurring because the property `CausesValidation` is set to false. It displays a message from the code-behind event handling method that indicates this occurred, as shown in Figure 9-3.

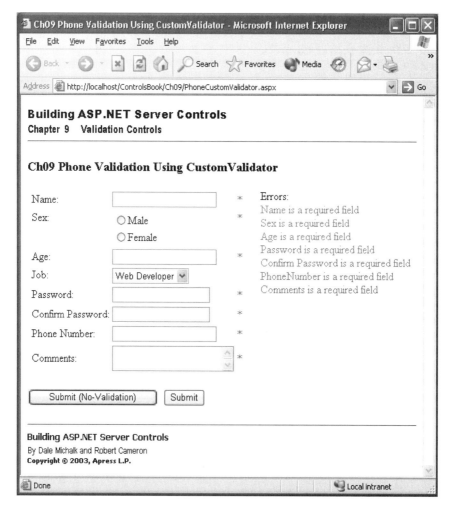

Figure 9-2. Validation error messages on the Phone Validation Using CustomValidator Web Form

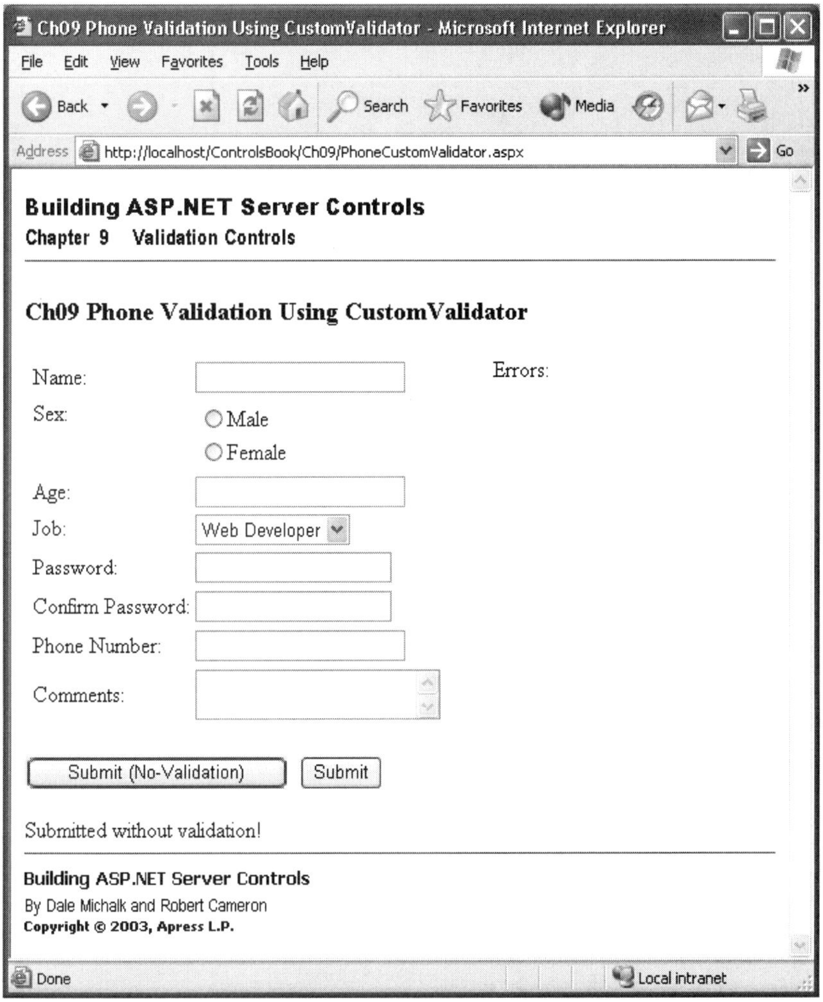

Figure 9-3. Clicking the Submit (No-Validation) button on the Phone Validation Using CustomValidator Web Form

If you click the Submit button and pass inspection with your data, the ASP.NET `Label` control at the bottom of the Web Form will confirm your entered phone number via server-side code, as depicted in Figure 9-4.

Figure 9-4. A successful phone number on the Phone Validation Using CustomValidator Web Form

Listings 9-3 and 9-4 show the full code for the Web Form.

Listing 9-3. The Phone Validation Using CustomValidator Web Form .aspx Page File

```
<%@ Register TagPrefix="apress" Namespace="ControlsBookLib.Ch09"
Assembly="ControlsBookLib" %>
<%@ Register TagPrefix="apressUC" TagName="ControlsBookHeader"
Src="..\ControlsBookHeader.ascx" %>
<%@ Register TagPrefix="apressUC" TagName="ControlsBookFooter"
Src="..\ControlsBookFooter.ascx" %>
<%@ Page language="c#" Codebehind="PhoneCustomValidator.aspx.cs"
```

```
AutoEventWireup="false" Inherits="ControlsBookWeb.Ch09.PhoneCustomValidator" %>
<!DOCTYPE HTML PUBLIC "-//W3C//DTD HTML 4.0 Transitional//EN" >
<HTML>
  <HEAD>
    <title>Ch09 Phone Validation Using CustomValidator</title>
    <meta content="Microsoft Visual Studio .NET 7.1" name="GENERATOR">
    <meta content="C#" name="CODE_LANGUAGE">
    <meta content="JavaScript" name="vs_defaultClientScript">
    <meta content="http://schemas.microsoft.com/intellisense/ie5"
     name="vs_targetSchema">
    <script language="javascript">
function ClientPhoneValidate(source, args)
{
var regex = /^\(?\d{3}\)?(\s|-)\d{3}\-\d{4}$/;
var matches = regex.exec(args.Value);
args.IsValid = (matches != null &&
args.Value == matches[0]);
}
    </script>
  </HEAD>
  <body MS_POSITIONING="FlowLayout">
    <form id="Form1" method="post" runat="server">
      <apressuc:controlsbookheader id="Header" runat="server"
       chaptertitle="Validation Controls"
chapternumber="9"></apressuc:controlsbookheader>
      <h3>Ch09 Phone Validation Using CustomValidator</h3>
      <table id="inputtable">
        <tr vAlign="top">
          <td>
            <table>
              <TBODY>
                <tr>
                  <td>Name:</td>
                  <td><asp:textbox id="Name" runat="server"></asp:textbox></td>
                  <td><asp:requiredfieldvalidator id="NameReqValidator"
                  runat="server" ControlToValidate="Name" ErrorMessage=
                  "Name is a required field">*</asp:requiredfieldvalidator></td>
                </tr>
                <tr vAlign="top">
                  <td>Sex:</td>
                  <td><asp:radiobuttonlist id="Sex" Runat="server">
                      <asp:ListItem>Male</asp:ListItem>
                      <asp:ListItem>Female</asp:ListItem>
                    </asp:radiobuttonlist></td>
                  <td><asp:requiredfieldvalidator id="SexReqValidator"
                  runat="server" Display="Dynamic" ControlToValidate="Sex"
ErrorMessage="Sex is a required field">*</asp:requiredfieldvalidator></td>
                </tr>
                <tr>
                  <td>Age:</td>
                  <td><asp:textbox id="Age" runat="server"></asp:textbox></td>
                  <td><asp:requiredfieldvalidator id="AgeReqValidator"
```

```
runat="server" Display="Dynamic" ControlToValidate="Age" ErrorMessage=
"Age is a required field">*</asp:requiredfieldvalidator>
<asp:rangevalidator id="AgeRangeValidator" Display="Dynamic"
ControlToValidate="Age" ErrorMessage="Age must be in range 1-100"
  Runat="server" MinimumValue="1" MaximumValue="100"
  Type="Integer">*</asp:rangevalidator></td>
                </tr>
                <tr vAlign="top">
                  <td>Job:</td>
                  <td><asp:dropdownlist id="Job" Runat="server">
                      <asp:ListItem>Web Developer</asp:ListItem>
                      <asp:ListItem>Manager</asp:ListItem>
                    </asp:dropdownlist></td>
                  <td><asp:requiredfieldvalidator id="Requiredfieldvalidator3"
runat="server" Display="Dynamic" ControlToValidate="Job"
                       ErrorMessage=
"Job is a required field">*</asp:requiredfieldvalidator></td>
                </tr>
                <tr>
                  <td>Password:</td>
                  <td><asp:textbox id="Password1" Runat="server"
TextMode="Password"></asp:textbox></td>
                  <td><asp:requiredfieldvalidator id="Requiredfieldvalidator4"
runat="server" Display="Dynamic" ControlToValidate="Password1"
                       ErrorMessage=
"Password is a required field">
*</asp:requiredfieldvalidator><asp:comparevalidator id="CompareValidator1"
Display="Dynamic" ControlToValidate="Password1" ErrorMessage=
"Passwords must match for confirmation" Runat="server"
ControlToCompare="Password2">*</asp:comparevalidator></td>
                </tr>
                <tr>
                  <td>Confirm Password:</td>
                  <td><asp:textbox id="Password2" Runat="server"
TextMode="Password"></asp:textbox></td>
                  <td><asp:requiredfieldvalidator id="Requiredfieldvalidator5"
runat="server" Display="Dynamic" ControlToValidate="Password2"
                       ErrorMessage=
"Confirm Password is a required field">*</asp:requiredfieldvalidator></td>
                </tr>
                <tr>
                  <td>Phone Number:</td>
                  <td><asp:textbox id="PhoneNumber"
Runat="server"></asp:textbox></td>
                  <td><asp:requiredfieldvalidator id="RequiredFieldValidator6"
runat="server" Display="Dynamic" ControlToValidate="PhoneNumber"
                       ErrorMessage=
"PhoneNumber is a required field">*</asp:requiredfieldvalidator>
                     <asp:customvalidator id="CustomValidator" Display="Dynamic"
```

```
ControlToValidate="PhoneNumber" ErrorMessage=
"PhoneNumber must be in format (xxx) xxx-xxxx or xxx-xxx-xxxx"
                      Runat="server"
ClientValidationFunction="ClientPhoneValidate">*</asp:customvalidator>
                  </td>
              </tr>
              <tr>
                <td>Comments:</td>
                <td><asp:textbox id="Comments" Runat="server"
TextMode="MultiLine" Rows="2"></asp:textbox></td>
                    <td><asp:requiredfieldvalidator id="Requiredfieldvalidator7"
runat="server" Display="Dynamic" ControlToValidate="Comments"
                      ErrorMessage=
"Comments is a required field">*</asp:requiredfieldvalidator></td>
              </tr>
            </TBODY>
          </table>
        </td>
        <td>    
        </td>
        <td>Errors:<br>
          <asp:validationsummary id="Summary" Runat="server"
DisplayMode="List"></asp:validationsummary><BR>
        </td>
      </tr>
    </table>
     <br>
    <asp:button id="NoValidationSubmit" runat="server" Text=
"Submit (No-Validation)" CausesValidation="False"></asp:button> 
    <asp:button id="Submit" Runat="server" Text="Submit"></asp:button><br>
    <BR>
    <asp:label id="Status" Runat="server"
Text=""></asp:label><apressuc:controlsbookfooter id="Footer"
runat="server"></apressuc:controlsbookfooter></form>
    </FORM>
  </body>
</HTML>
```

Listing 9-4. The Phone Validation Using CustomValidator Web Form Code-Behind Class File

```
using System;
using System.Collections;
using System.ComponentModel;
using System.Data;
using System.Drawing;
using System.Web;
using System.Web.SessionState;
using System.Web.UI;
using System.Web.UI.WebControls;
using System.Web.UI.HtmlControls;
using System.Text.RegularExpressions;

namespace ControlsBookWeb.Ch09
{

    public class PhoneCustomValidator : System.Web.UI.Page
    {
        protected System.Web.UI.WebControls.Button Submit;
        protected System.Web.UI.WebControls.TextBox PhoneNumber;
        protected System.Web.UI.WebControls.CustomValidator CustomValidator;
        protected System.Web.UI.WebControls.Label Status;
        protected System.Web.UI.WebControls.TextBox Name;
        protected System.Web.UI.WebControls.RadioButtonList Sex;
        protected System.Web.UI.WebControls.TextBox Comments;
        protected System.Web.UI.WebControls.TextBox Password1;
        protected System.Web.UI.WebControls.TextBox Password2;
        protected System.Web.UI.WebControls.RequiredFieldValidator
RequiredFieldValidator5;
        protected System.Web.UI.WebControls.RequiredFieldValidator
Requiredfieldvalidator3;
        protected System.Web.UI.WebControls.RequiredFieldValidator
Requiredfieldvalidator4;
        protected System.Web.UI.WebControls.CompareValidator CompareValidator1;
        protected System.Web.UI.WebControls.RequiredFieldValidator
Requiredfieldvalidator7;
        protected System.Web.UI.WebControls.DropDownList Job;
        protected System.Web.UI.WebControls.RequiredFieldValidator
RequiredFieldValidator6;
        protected System.Web.UI.WebControls.RequiredFieldValidator
NameReqValidator;
        protected System.Web.UI.WebControls.RequiredFieldValidator
SexReqValidator;
        protected System.Web.UI.WebControls.RequiredFieldValidator
AgeReqValidator;
        protected System.Web.UI.WebControls.RangeValidator AgeRangeValidator;
        protected System.Web.UI.WebControls.RequiredFieldValidator
Requiredfieldvalidator5;
        protected System.Web.UI.WebControls.TextBox Age;
        protected System.Web.UI.WebControls.Button NoValidationSubmit;
        protected System.Web.UI.WebControls.ValidationSummary Summary;
```

```
private void Page_Load(object sender, System.EventArgs e)
{
   Status.Text = "";
}

#region Web Form Designer generated code
override protected void OnInit(EventArgs e)
{
   //
   // CODEGEN: This call is required by the ASP.NET Web Form Designer.
   //
   InitializeComponent();
   base.OnInit(e);
}

/// <summary>
/// Required method for Designer support - do not modify
/// the contents of this method with the code editor.
/// </summary>
private void InitializeComponent()
{
   this.NoValidationSubmit.Click += new
   System.EventHandler(this.NoValidationSubmit_Click);
   this.Submit.Click += new System.EventHandler(this.Submit_Click);
   this.Load += new System.EventHandler(this.Page_Load);

}
#endregion

private void ServerPhoneValidate(object source,
System.Web.UI.WebControls.ServerValidateEventArgs args)
{
   Regex expr = new Regex(@"^\(?\d{3}\)?(\s|-)\d{3}\-\d{4}$");
   MatchCollection matches = expr.Matches(args.Value, 0);
   args.IsValid = (matches != null && matches[0].Value == args.Value);

}

private void Submit_Click(object sender, System.EventArgs e)
{
   if (Page.IsValid)
      Status.Text = "Valid number: " + PhoneNumber.Text;
}

private void NoValidationSubmit_Click(object sender, System.EventArgs e)
{
   Status.Text = "Submitted without validation!";
}
   }
}
```

Examining the Phone Validation Using CustomValidator Web Form HTML

The generated HTML source code from the Phone Validation Using CustomValidator Web Form as viewed using View ➤ Source in Internet Explorer (IE) offers an excellent opportunity to learn how the ASP.NET client-side validation library ties together activities in the browser with the ASP.NET Web Form on the web server. It's well worth it to spend some time examining this, because it will allow you to debug and extend the validation framework with confidence. On a Web Form with validation controls that support client-side validation, we examine the process by breaking it into the following bite-sized sections:

- Registering the WebUIValidation.js script library

- Wiring up the HTML form's OnSubmit event

- Generating <SPAN> elements from validation controls

- Using dynamic script blocks for validation initialization

- Understanding the validation initialization process

- Using input control change event validation handling

- Examining ASP.NET Buttons and submitting the Web Form

- Performing specialized routines in the client validation library

We recommend using a JavaScript debugger such as the Microsoft Script Debugger to step through the client-side JavaScript code in the browser as a means to follow along with the initialization and validation event handling processes we describe in the following sections.

Registering the WebUIValidation.js Script Library

The first step taken by the ASP.NET client-side validation framework is to register the necessary script library via an HTML <SCRIPT> block:

```
<script language="javascript"
src="/aspnet_client/system_web/1_1_4322/WebUIValidation.js">
</script>
```

The preceding include declaration was generated on a machine with Visual Studio 2003 with the .NET Framework 1.1 RTM installed, so your version number folder may vary depending on the .NET Framework version your machine has installed. You can go to the root web site of your IIS installation to examine this WebUIValidation.js file in more detail. This relative path resolves to the following physical file location on a default installation of IIS on the C: drive for an RTM .NET Framework version 1.1 installation:

```
C:\Inetpub\wwwroot\aspnet_client\system_web\1_1_4322\WebUIValidation.js
```

The script block in this file brings in a host of functions and global variables to the HTML form. Table 9-3 shows the primary functions/variables used during the validation process that we examine in detail. It is a good reference for when you are deep within the call stack of client routines or trying to figure out why a certain function is wired to a button event handler. We cover the major routines in detail and examine the code as the chapter progresses.

Table 9-3. Primary JavaScript Functions/Variables in WebUIValidation.js

FUNCTION/VARIABLE	DESCRIPTION
Page_BlockSubmit	Global variable that determines whether to block the HTML form from posting back to the web server.
Page_ClientValidate	Function called by button elements to check on validation progress and update the global Page_BlockSubmit JavaScript variable. This function also causes the summary elements on the page to receive all error messages via invocation of ValidationSummaryOnSubmit. In addition, it causes the update of the Page_IsValid global variable due to invocation of the ValidatorUpdateIsValid function.
Page_IsValid	Global variable that represents whether the page validator elements have passed their client-side checks.
Page_ValidationVer	Global variable that determines the version number of the script library.
ValidatorCommonOnSubmit	Function called by the overridden onsubmit HTML form event handler before postback to ensure the page is valid before sending it back to the server. It checks on the value of the global Page_BlockSubmit JavaScript variable and cancels the page submit if necessary.
ValidatorGetValue	Function that returns the string value of the input element undergoing validation.
ValidatorGetValueRecursive	Recursively scans child HTML elements to find the value of an <INPUT>, <TEXTAREA>, or <SELECT> element.
ValidatorHookupControl	Function that attaches the ValidatorOnChange function to the onclick/onchange event of the input element and associates it with the validator element that has logic to check its values by adding a reference to that validator via a validators array attribute.
ValidatorHookupControlID	Top-level script function that wires up a validator element to an input element by calling the ValidatorHookupControl function. It does the job of retrieving the input element by its ID value before calling ValidatorHookupControl.

(Continued)

Table 9-3. Primary JavaScript Functions/Variables in WebUIValidation.js (Continued)

FUNCTION/VARIABLE	DESCRIPTION
ValidatorOnChange	Executes validation logic on an input element after a change occurs. It finds validators attached to the validators array attribute of an input element and invokes ValidatorValidate on each one. The final step calls ValidatorUpdateIsValid to update the status of the entire HTML form.
ValidatorOnLoad	Initialization method called to set up client-side validation on the HTML form, including hooking up validator elements to their input elements and setting global JavaScript variables.
ValidationSummaryOnSubmit	Updates the display of the validation summary elements on the HTML form if ValidationSummary controls are used on the Web Form. This function iterates through the Page_ValidationSummaries summary elements array and the Page_Validators array to find the correct validator element error messages and display them in the appropriate style.
ValidatorUpdateDisplay	Updates the dynamic display of error messages on a validator element if Dynamic is the Display attribute value and the browser supports DHTML.
ValidatorUpdateIsValid	Updates the Page_IsValid global JavaScript variable by checking the IsValid property of the validator elements in the Page_Validators array.
ValidatorValidate	Routine that executes the evaluation function attached to the evaluationfunction attribute of a validator element and assigns the results to the IsValid attribute. It also calls ValidatorUpdateDisplay to show/hide the inline validation error message.

Wiring Up the HTML Form's OnSubmit Event

The HTML form that hosts the validators is linked via its onsubmit handler to execute the ValidatorOnSubmit JavaScript function:

```
<form name="Form1" method="post" action="PhoneCustomValidator.aspx"
language="javascript" onsubmit="ValidatorOnSubmit();" id="Form1">
```

The code for ValidatorOnSubmit is emitted by the BaseValidator class that supports the built-in validation controls such as the RequiredFieldValidator and CustomValidator controls. This functionality is provided by inheriting from BaseValidator.

ValidatorOnSubmit is a simple function that checks to see if the validation system has been activated on the client by checking the `Page_ValidationActive` global variable. If the value is `true`, it forks back into the WebUIValidation.js script library function `ValidatorCommonOnSubmit`.

```
function ValidatorOnSubmit() {
   if (Page_ValidationActive) {
      ValidatorCommonOnSubmit();
   }
...
```

Because `ValidatorOnSubmit` is linked to the `onsubmit` event of the HTML form, it is called after any submitting element on the page has performed work that causes postback.

Generating <SPAN> Elements from Validator Controls

The next thing to look at is the HTML generated by the validation controls themselves. They all take the form of a `<SPAN>` tag because of the supported capability to display an inline error message. The `RequiredFieldValidator` and `RangeValidator` controls that are linked to the `Age` `TextBox` control look like the following:

```
<span id="AgeReqValidator" controltovalidate="Age" errormessage=
"Age is a required field" display="Dynamic"
evaluationfunction="RequiredFieldValidatorEvaluateIsValid" initialvalue=""
style="color:Red;display:none;">*</span><span id="AgeRangeValidator"
controltovalidate="Age" errormessage="Age must be in range 1-100"
display="Dynamic" type="Integer"
evaluationfunction="RangeValidatorEvaluateIsValid" maximumvalue="100"
minimumvalue="1" style="color:Red;display:none;">*</span>
```

`CompareValidator` renders in a similar manner. It is attached to the first `Password` `TextBox` to verify its input with the second `Password` `TextBox` control on the Web Form to ensure the values match:

```
<span id="CompareValidator1" controltovalidate="Password1"
errormessage="Passwords must match for confirmation" display="Dynamic"
evaluationfunction="CompareValidatorEvaluateIsValid"
controltocompare="Password2" controlhookup="Password2"
style="color:Red;display:none;">*</span>
```

We also have our `CustomValidator` control that is attached to our client-side evaluation routine to ensure a correct phone number:

```
<span id="CustomValidator" controltovalidate="PhoneNumber"
errormessage="PhoneNumber must be in format (xxx) xxx-xxxx or xxx-xxx-xxxx"
display="Dynamic" evaluationfunction="CustomValidatorEvaluateIsValid"
clientvalidationfunction="ClientPhoneValidate"
style="color:Red;display:none;">*</span>
```

Table 9-4 shows the attributes that are added to the <SPAN> tag by the BaseValidator class or its descendents to hook the validator elements to the rest of the client-side framework.

Table 9-4. BaseValidator *Client-Side Attributes*

ATTRIBUTE	DESCRIPTION
clientevalutionfunction	Custom client-side evaluation function for validation (CustomValidator)
controlhookup	ID of the input control to compare to (CompareValidator)
controltocompare	ID of the input control to compare to (CompareValidator —design-time)
controltovalidate	ID of the input control to validate
enabled	Attribute created as part of the loading of validation elements
errormessage	Error message to display via validation summary
evaluationfunction	Client-side function to invoke to validate the input control
initialvalue	Initial value of the input control; usually blank
isvalid	Boolean property that determines if the validator begins life as valid or not; usually not present, which resolves to true

When ASP.NET performs client-side validation, the evaluationfunction attribute is quite important. For the RequiredFieldValidator control, this attribute is set to RequiredFieldValidatorEvaluateIsValid. For the CustomValidator control, it is set to CustomValidatorEvaluateIsValid. The CustomValidator element also has an additional attribute, clientvalidationfunction, which points to the ClientPhoneValidate client-side function we specified to handle our custom client-side validation.

The controltovalidate attribute is an important piece of data as well for the validation system. It is what links the <SPAN> tag to the HTML element that represents the input control it validates. The CompareValidator extends this by adding the controltocompare and controlhookup attributes pointing to the HTML element that is the compared input control.

The validation controls in the example all take advantage of inline error message display by putting an asterisk (*) between the <SPAN> tags to indicate a problem with the input. The errormessage attribute is the text value that displays in the ValidationSummary control on the left side of the Web Form.

The DHTML style attribute on the <SPAN> tags provides access to CSS attributes of the HTML element representing the validator at execution time in the browser. Two key CSS attributes are critical to the inline error message display of the validator controls: display and visibility. When manipulated at runtime via JavaScript in the validation library, these two attributes permit the validation UI to react to changes visually inside the browser.

The CSS display attribute determines whether or not the flow layout engine in the browser should reserve space for the error message of the validation HTML element. If set to none, no space is reserved, whereas a value of block for the display CSS attribute will reserve the space regardless of the current visibility of the HTML element. This makes it possible to show and hide an element without the side effect of shifting elements to make room when it is required to report an error.

The CSS visibility attribute is responsible for making an element visible on the browser without regard to the layout. It's a binary switch: Either you see the element or you don't by setting visibility to a value of either visible or hidden. Because it doesn't change the document flow, visibility always reserves room in the HTML document, whether or not the element is visible. This is a good technique to use if you have a carefully aligned document you want to keep tightly confined.

Validation controls can take advantage of the two techniques described previously if the browser capabilities support the use of DHTML and JavaScript. This functionality is accessible in the Visual Studio .NET Designer by selecting the validator control and setting the Display property. It takes a value of None, Dynamic, or Static. None means the control will punt on inline display and will rely on an external control such as the ValidationSummary control to render error messages. Dynamic uses the display CSS attribute to make room for the error message inline with its location in the document. Static uses the visibility CSS attribute to show the message but also ensures that adequate space is reserved in the document.

In the Phone Validation Using CustomValidator example Web Form, the Name RequiredFieldValidator has a Display property set to Static, while the rest of the validation controls are set to Dynamic. You can see the difference in its style attribute:

```
style="color:Red;visibility:hidden;"
```

The rest of the validation controls have something similar to the following:

```
style="color:Red;display:none;"
```

JavaScript validation routines such as ValidatorUpdateDisplay change the display CSS attribute on the client in reaction to user input changes, which we examine later on in the chapter.

The ValidationSummary control emits a <DIV> tag that holds the results of the validation process for all the validation controls, as shown in the following code. The attribute displaymode lets the client-side validation framework know how to fill the <DIV> tag with error messages. This process occurs separately from the event handling attached to validation elements and is instead tied to initiation of the postback process for the HTML form.

```
<div id="Summary" displaymode="List" style="color:Red;display:none;">
```

In the next section, we discuss how the validation system uses dynamic script blocks to set up the client-side validation plumbing.

Using Dynamic Script Blocks for Validation Initialization

Scrolling down to the very bottom of the HTML source code, you see two script blocks added by the validation controls to the Web Form that initialize the client-side validation system. The first script block defines two arrays that are the data structures for the validation process. One of the arrays is named Page_ValidationSummaries. This array holds the representative summary elements for the `ValidationSummary` controls on the Web Form. The second array, `Page_Validators`, holds all the elements representing validation controls. You can see how it gains references to all the HTML elements that were emitted for validation purposes:

```
<script language="javascript">
<!--
    var Page_ValidationSummaries =  new Array(document.all["Summary"]);
    var Page_Validators = new Array(document.all["NameReqValidator"],
document.all["SexReqValidator"], document.all["AgeReqValidator"],
document.all["AgeRangeValidator"], document.all["Requiredfieldvalidator3"],
document.all["Requiredfieldvalidator4"], document.all["CompareValidator1"],
document.all["Requiredfieldvalidator5"],
document.all["RequiredFieldValidator6"], document.all["CustomValidator"],
document.all["Requiredfieldvalidator7"]);
        // -->
</script>
```

The next script block at the bottom of the HTML form kicks off logic to wire up the validation control system via the `ValidatorOnLoad` client function. The bulk of the client-side logic checks if the client browser is compatible with the validation library before initialization begins. Because the validation library uses the `document.all` construct to grab HTML element references, it ensures that IE is the browser before activating the validation system.

```
<script language="javascript">
<!--
var Page_ValidationActive = false;
if (typeof(clientInformation) != "undefined" &&
clientInformation.appName.indexOf("Explorer") != -1) {
    if (typeof(Page_ValidationVer) == "undefined")
        alert("Unable to find script library
'/aspnet_client/system_web/1_1_4322/WebUIValidation.js'. Try placing this file
manually, or reinstall by running 'aspnet_regiis -c'.");
    else if (Page_ValidationVer != "125")
        alert("This page uses an incorrect version of WebUIValidation.js. The
page expects version 125. The script library is " + Page_ValidationVer + ".");
    else
        ValidatorOnLoad();
}
```

The code also checks the value of the `Page_ValidationVer` global JavaScript variable from the WebUIValidation.js library to make sure that the currently loaded library is compatible with the .NET Framework code base of the control.

`Page_ValidationActive` is a global variable that determines if client-side validation is active. It is set to false until all the initialization code executed by the call to `ValidatorOnLoad` completes to prevent any race conditions from fouling things up.

The rest of the emitted script block includes a ValidatorOnSubmit function invoked from the HTML form onsubmit handler override discussed earlier. ValidatorOnSubmit is a thin wrapper function that ensures the page validation process is active before it calls ValidatorCommonOnSubmit:

```
function ValidatorOnSubmit() {
   if (Page_ValidationActive) {
      ValidatorCommonOnSubmit();
   }
}
// -->
</script>
```

In the next section, we discuss how the client-side validation process begins.

Understanding the Validation Initialization Process

The client-side validation process completes initialization when the embedded script code at the bottom of the page calls ValidatorOnLoad as shown in Listing 9-5. ValidatorOnLoad is a JavaScript function from the WebUIValidation.js library that iterates through the validation elements added to the Page_Validators array and proceeds to check their evaluationfunction attribute to see if it is defined in the web page. It also checks for the presence of an isvalid attribute and whether it is set to a false value on any of the validation elements. If this is the case, the overall status of the Web Form for validation, represented by the Page_IsValid JavaScript variable, is set to false.

Listing 9-5. The ValidatorOnLoad *JavaScript Function*

```
function ValidatorOnLoad() {
    if (typeof(Page_Validators) == "undefined")
        return;
    var i, val;
    for (i = 0; i < Page_Validators.length; i++) {
        val = Page_Validators[i];
        if (typeof(val.evaluationfunction) == "string") {
            eval("val.evaluationfunction = " + val.evaluationfunction + ";");
        }
        if (typeof(val.isvalid) == "string") {
            if (val.isvalid == "False") {
                val.isvalid = false;
                Page_IsValid = false;
            }
            else {
                val.isvalid = true;
            }
        } else {
            val.isvalid = true;
```

```
    }
    if (typeof(val.enabled) == "string") {
        val.enabled = (val.enabled != "False");
    }
    ValidatorHookupControlID(val.controltovalidate, val);
    ValidatorHookupControlID(val.controlhookup, val);
    }
    Page_ValidationActive = true;
}
```

Near the bottom of the script is the hookup process that links the validation element to its input control via a call to ValidatorHookupControlID. When reviewing the code, you may wonder why ValidatorHookupControlID is called twice, the second time with the mysterious controlhookup attribute as the source of the input element. The reason for this is the CompareValidator control and its need to have a control to validate and a control to compare against. The second call hooks into its system for resolving the second input control. For most of the validator elements, this code will fail to hook up anything because the controlhookup attribute will be blank.

Drilling into the code for ValidatorHookupControlID shown in Listing 9-6, you can see that it finds the ID of the input control via the ID value passed in and checks to see whether the input control is present. If it can't find the input control, it sets the validator element's isvalid attribute to true and sets its enabled value to false. (This is for the controlhookup attribute when processing non-CompareValidator validation elements.)

Listing 9-6. The ValidatorHookupControlID *JavaScript Function*

```
function ValidatorHookupControlID(controlID, val) {
    if (typeof(controlID) != "string") {
        return;
    }
    var ctrl = document.all[controlID];
    if (typeof(ctrl) != "undefined") {
        ValidatorHookupControl(ctrl, val);
    }
    else {
        val.isvalid = true;
        val.enabled = false;
    }
}
```

A successful search for the input control element causes an invocation of ValidatorHookupControl, as shown in Listing 9-7. The code in this function has the responsibility of recursively searching to find the innermost input element to ensure that it can work with the validation framework.

Listing 9-7. The ValidatorHookupControl *JavaScript Function*

```
function ValidatorHookupControl(control, val) {
   if (typeof(control.tagName) == "undefined" &&
       typeof(control.length) == "number") {
      var i;
      for (i = 0; i < control.length; i++) {
         var inner = control[i];
         if (typeof(inner.value) == "string") {
            ValidatorHookupControl(inner, val);
         }
      }
      return;
   }
   else if (control.tagName != "INPUT" && control.tagName != "TEXTAREA" &&
   control.tagName != "SELECT") {
      var i;
      for (i = 0; i < control.children.length; i++) {
         ValidatorHookupControl(control.children[i], val);
      }
      return;
   }
   else {
      if (typeof(control.Validators) == "undefined") {
      control.Validators = new Array;
         var ev;
         if (control.type == "radio") {
            ev = control.onclick;
         } else {
            ev = control.onchange;
         }
         if (typeof(ev) == "function" ) {
            ev = ev.toString();
            ev = ev.substring(ev.indexOf("{") + 1, ev.lastIndexOf("}"));
         }
         else {
            ev = "";
         }
         var func = new Function("ValidatorOnChange(); " + ev);
         if (control.type == "radio") {
            control.onclick = func;
         } else {
            control.onchange = func;
         }
      }
      control.Validators[control.Validators.length] = val;
   }
}
```

The recursive nature of the ValidatorHookupControl method is explained by the layout of the input control elements. For simple controls such as TextBox, this is either an <INPUT type="text">, <INPUT type="password">, or <TEXTAREA> HTML element:

```
<input name="Name" type="text" id="Name" />
<input name="Password1" type="password" id="Password1" />
<textarea name="Comments" rows="2" id="Comments"></textarea>
```

The DropDownList and ListBox controls are slightly more complicated but still have a top-level HTML element to manipulate for value retrieval and event handling:

```
<select name="Job" id="Job">
    <option value="Web Developer">Web Developer</option>
    <option value="Manager">Manager</option>
</select>
```

It gets trickier with the RadioButtonList control that emits a <TABLE> structure with <INPUT type="radio"> elements nested inside:

```
<table id="Sex" border="0">
    <tr><td><input id="Sex_0" type="radio" name="Sex" value="Male" />
    <label for="Sex_0">Male</label></td></tr>
    <tr><td><input id="Sex_1" type="radio" name="Sex" value="Female" />
    <label for="Sex_1">Female</label></td></tr>
</table>
```

The RadioButtonList control is found through the top-level check in ValidatorHookupControl that looks for controls with an "undefined" tagName attribute and with a length that resolves to a numeric value:

```
if (typeof(control.tagName) == "undefined" &&
    typeof(control.length) == "number")
```

Because both the <TABLE> and <INPUT type="radio"> tags resolve to the same id and name attributes previously, the document.all object returns a collection that ValidatorHookupControlID uses to find the innermost elements before it calls ValidatorHookupControl.

Once all the elements are in this collection, the code searches for radio elements identified by a string value. The final step is to wire up the <INPUT type="radio"> element with a recursive call to ValidatorHookupControl:

```
for (i = 0; i < control.length; i++) {
    var inner = control[i];
    if (typeof(inner.value) == "string") {
    ValidatorHookupControl(inner, val);
}
```

Scanning through the if-then structure in `ValidatorHookupControl`, you can see how it finds HTML input elements. This routine uses recursion to find the appropriate HTML element tag if the validation targets a higher-level structure:

```
else if (control.tagName != "INPUT" && control.tagName != "TEXTAREA" &&
control.tagName != "SELECT") {
   var i;
   for (i = 0; i < control.children.length; i++) {
      ValidatorHookupControl(control.children[i], val);
   }
   return;
}
```

Regardless of the path taken, the final if-then at the bottom of `ValidatorHookupControl` does the bulk of the work. It creates dynamic JavaScript event handlers that are triggered via the onchange or onclick JavaScript event. The onclick event is for <INPUT type="radio"> elements, and the onchange event is used for the rest of the validation control elements in the ASP.NET framework.

All the event handlers are wired up to call the `ValidatorOnChange` JavaScript function that is part of WebUIValidation.js. An array of validators is also attached to the input element attribute named validators to make it easier to execute all of the validation routines when the onchange event is raised. We discuss how validation client-side events are generated in the next section.

Using Input Control Validated Change Event Handling

At this point in the initialization process, the client-side validation system is prepared to handle client-side events. Validation action is triggered by two primary activities: changing the state of the input elements on the HTML form or attempting to submit the form via a button click or other postback mechanism. In this section, we step through the process for each triggering method, starting with input change event handling.

The validator input elements have had either their onchange or their onclick events mapped to the `ValidatorOnChange` method shown in Listing 9-8. This function grabs all of the validators attached to the input element and calls `ValidatorValidate` for each element. At the end of the process, it calls `ValidatorUpdateIsValid` to update the validation status of the HTML document.

Listing 9-8. The ValidatorOnChange *JavaScript Function*

```
function ValidatorOnChange() {
    var vals = event.srcElement.Validators;
    var i;
    for (i = 0; i < vals.length; i++) {
        ValidatorValidate(vals[i]);
    }
    ValidatorUpdateIsValid();
}
```

ValidatorValidate is the heart of the client-side validation system and is shown in Listing 9-9. It grabs the evaluationfunction and executes it dynamically using the JavaScript eval method. The results are transferred to the isvalid attribute of the validator element. It also kicks off the display of inline error messages by calling ValidatorUpdateDisplay.

Listing 9-9. The ValidatorValidate *JavaScript Function*

```
function ValidatorValidate(val) {
    val.isvalid = true;
    if (val.enabled != false) {
        if (typeof(val.evaluationfunction) == "function") {
            val.isvalid = val.evaluationfunction(val);
        }
    }
    ValidatorUpdateDisplay(val);
}
```

To further drill down into this example, we examine the evaluation function that is attached to a RequiredFieldValidator, which is aptly named RequiredFieldValidatorEvaluateIsValid and is shown in Listing 9-10.

Listing 9-10. The RequiredFieldValidatorEvaluateIsValid *JavaScript Function*

```
function RequiredFieldValidatorEvaluateIsValid(val) {
    return (ValidatorTrim(ValidatorGetValue(val.controltovalidate)) !=
ValidatorTrim(val.initialvalue))
}
```

RequiredFieldValidatorEvaluateIsValid uses the ValidatorGetValue function to grab the value of the input element it is attached to and then uses the ValidatorTrim function to remove extraneous spaces. If anything is left after the spaces are removed, the function returns the value.

ValidatorGetValue simplifies writing validation script, as it handles looking up the values of various input elements, whether they consist of <INPUT>, <TEXTAREA>, or <SELECT> tags. As shown in Listing 9-11, ValidatorGetValue calls upon the helper function GetValidatorGetValueRecursive shown in Listing 9-12 to retrieve the value from an element that holds the string value several layers down. It works in a manner similar to the ValidatorHookupControl code we examined earlier. Most of the code handles the case of the <INPUT type="radio"> HTML element emitted by the RadioButtonList control.

Listing 9-11. The ValidatorGetValue *JavaScript Function*

```
function ValidatorGetValue(id) {
   var control;
   control = document.all[id];
   if (typeof(control.value) == "string") {
      return control.value;
   }
   if (typeof(control.tagName) == "undefined" &&
       typeof(control.length) == "number") {
      var j;
      for (j=0; j < control.length; j++) {
         var inner = control[j];
         if (typeof(inner.value) == "string" &&
            (inner.type != "radio" || inner.status == true)) {
            return inner.value;
         }
      }
   }
   else {
      return ValidatorGetValueRecursive(control);
   }
   return "";
}
```

Listing 9-12. The ValidatorGetValueRecursive *JavaScript Function*

```
function ValidatorGetValueRecursive(control) {
   if (typeof(control.value) == "string" && (control.type != "radio" ||
control.status == true)) {
      return control.value;
   }
   var i, val;
   for (i = 0; i<control.children.length; i++) {
      val = ValidatorGetValueRecursive(control.children[i]);
      if (val != "") return val;
   }
   return "";
}
```

Now let's look at the evaluation function used by our phone number
CustomValidator element. As shown in Listing 9-13, the control emits the stock
CustomValidatorEvaluateIsValid JavaScript function that is designed to link up with
our custom code on the client, if present.

Listing 9-13. The `CustomValidatorEvaluateIsValid` *JavaScript Function*

```
function CustomValidatorEvaluateIsValid(val) {
    var value = "";
    if (typeof(val.controltovalidate) == "string") {
        value = ValidatorGetValue(val.controltovalidate);
        if (ValidatorTrim(value).length == 0)
            return true;
    }
    var args = { Value:value, IsValid:true };
    if (typeof(val.clientvalidationfunction) == "string") {
        eval(val.clientvalidationfunction + "(val, args) ;");
    }
    return args.IsValid;
}
```

`CustomValidatorEvaluateIsValid` links in the custom phone number–checking function `ClientPhoneValidate` by invoking this routine dynamically via the `clientvalidationfunction` attribute value and the JavaScript eval method. You can also see how it packages the dynamically created JavaScript object containing the `Value` and `IsValid` properties. The `Value` property is loaded from the input element by calling `ValidatorGetValue`. If the input value is null, the validation process is ignored. This goes along with the behavior exhibited by controls on the server where they ignore blank or null values. Checking to ensure a value is present is left to the domain of the validation logic emitted by the `RequiredFieldValidator` control.

After `ValidatorOnChange` has called the appropriate `evaluationfunction`, such as `CustomValidatorEvaluateIsValid`, its next task is to update the inline display of the validator element by invoking `ValidatorUpdateDisplay` shown in Listing 9-14. As we discussed earlier, it looks at the `display` attribute on the validation element to see how it will modify the correct CSS attributes. If the value is `None`, it does nothing. For a value of `Dynamic`, it modifies the `display` CSS attribute. For a value of `Static`, it causes the JavaScript routine to drop to the bottom, where it modifies the `visibility` CSS attribute.

Listing 9-14. The `ValidatorUpdateDisplay` *JavaScript Function*

```
function ValidatorUpdateDisplay(val) {
    if (typeof(val.display) == "string") {
        if (val.display == "None") {
            return;
        }
        if (val.display == "Dynamic") {
            val.style.display = val.isvalid ? "none" : "inline";
            return;
        }
    }
    val.style.visibility = val.isvalid ? "hidden" : "visible";
}
```

The final task of ValidatorOnChange is to update the HTML form validation status by calling ValidatorUpdateIsValid, as shown in Listing 9-15. It calculates this by examining all the validator's isvalid values and setting the global Page_IsValid variable, which holds the results. This becomes important when we examine what happens when a button or other form post–generating element attempts to post the HTML form.

Listing 9-15. The ValidatorUpdateIsValid *JavaScript Function*

```
function ValidatorUpdateIsValid() {
   var i;
   for (i = 0; i < Page_Validators.length; i++) {
      if (!Page_Validators[i].isvalid) {
         Page_IsValid = false;
         return;
      }
   }
   Page_IsValid = true;
}
```

A final item to note regarding ValidatorOnChange is that though it does display inline error messages for each validator, it does not update the summary display element emitted by the ValidationSummary control that aggregates messages for all client-side validation elements. It leaves that task for code wired to form-submitting elements on the HTML form, which we discuss in the next section.

Examining ASP.NET Buttons and Submitting the Web Form

The next part of the JavaScript validation library that we examine is the HTML emitted by the ASP.NET Button controls and the process used to send the Web Form back to the server via postback. ASP.NET Buttons emit different onclick event handlers when a Web Form includes validation controls:

```
<input type="submit" name="Submit" value="Submit" onclick=
"if (typeof(Page_ClientValidate) == 'function') Page_ClientValidate(); "
language="javascript" id="Submit" />
```

These different event handlers check for the presence of and invoke the Page_ClientValidate script function from WebUIValidation.js, initiating the client-side validation process. The source code for Page_ClientValidate is shown in Listing 9-16.

Listing 9-16. The Page_ClientValidate *JavaScript Function*

```
function Page_ClientValidate() {
   var i;
   for (i = 0; i < Page_Validators.length; i++) {
      ValidatorValidate(Page_Validators[i]);
```

```
    }
    ValidatorUpdateIsValid();
    ValidationSummaryOnSubmit();
    Page_BlockSubmit = !Page_IsValid;
    return Page_IsValid;
}
```

Page_ClientValidate first calls ValidatorValidate on each of the validators in the Page_Validator collection. Next, it calls ValidatorUpdateIsValid to harvest the isvalid properties for each validator and set the value of the Page_IsValid routine. ValidationSummaryOnSubmit, shown in Listing 9-17, is called to update the validation summary information on the HTML form. The <DIV> element emitted by the ValidatorSummary control has its contents created on the fly by this routine based on its displaystyle attribute.

Listing 9-17. The ValidationSummaryOnSubmit *JavaScript Function*

```
function ValidationSummaryOnSubmit() {
    if (typeof(Page_ValidationSummaries) == "undefined")
        return;
    var summary, sums, s;
    for (sums = 0; sums < Page_ValidationSummaries.length; sums++) {
        summary = Page_ValidationSummaries[sums];
        summary.style.display = "none";
        if (!Page_IsValid) {
            if (summary.showsummary != "False") {
                summary.style.display = "";
                if (typeof(summary.displaymode) != "string") {
                    summary.displaymode = "BulletList";
                }
                switch (summary.displaymode) {
                    case "List":
                        headerSep = "<br>";
                        first = "";
                        pre = "";
                        post = "<br>";
                        final = "";
                        break;
                    case "BulletList":
                        default:
                        headerSep = "";
                        first = "<ul>";
                        pre = "<li>";
                        post = "</li>";
                        final = "</ul>";
                        break;
                    case "SingleParagraph":
                        headerSep = " ";
                        first = "";
                        pre = "";
```

```
                    post = " ";
                    final = "<br>";
                    break;
            }
            s = "";
            if (typeof(summary.headertext) == "string") {
                s += summary.headertext + headerSep;
            }
            s += first;
            for (i=0; i<Page_Validators.length; i++) {
                if (!Page_Validators[i].isvalid &&
typeof(Page_Validators[i].errormessage) == "string") {
                    s += pre + Page_Validators[i].errormessage + post;
                }
            }
            s += final;
            summary.innerHTML = s;
            window.scrollTo(0,0);
        }
        if (summary.showmessagebox == "True") {
            s = "";
            if (typeof(summary.headertext) == "string") {
                s += summary.headertext + "<BR>";
            }
            for (i=0; i<Page_Validators.length; i++) {
                if (!Page_Validators[i].isvalid &&
typeof(Page_Validators[i].errormessage) == "string") {
                    switch (summary.displaymode) {
                        case "List":
                            s += Page_Validators[i].errormessage + "<BR>";
                            break;
                        case "BulletList":
                            default:
                            s += "  - " + Page_Validators[i].errormessage + "<BR>";
                            break;
                        case "SingleParagraph":
                            s += Page_Validators[i].errormessage + " ";
                            break;
                    }
                }
            }
            span = document.createElement("SPAN");
            span.innerHTML = s;
            s = span.innerText;
            alert(s);
        }
      }
    }
}
```

The final step for Page_ClientValidate is to set the form-blocking variable Page_BlockSubmit to the opposite value of Page_IsValid. Once Page_ClientValidate returns, the form validation process continues. The next step is execution of the HTML form's onsubmit handler, which calls ValidatorOnSubmit, displayed in Listing 9-18, which in turn calls ValidatorCommonOnSubmit.

Listing 9-18. The ValidatorOnSubmit *JavaScript Function*

```
function ValidatorOnSubmit() {
  if (Page_ValidationActive) {
    ValidatorCommonOnSubmit();
  }
}
```

The code in ValidatorCommonOnSubmit, shown in Listing 9-19, uses the event object available in IE to set the return value of the onclick event of the button that started the form submit in motion. If the Page_BlockSubmit is set to true, the return value is set to false and the onclick event does not send the form back to the web server.

Listing 9-19. The ValidatorCommonOnSubmit *JavaScript Function*

```
function ValidatorCommonOnSubmit() {
  event.returnValue = !Page_BlockSubmit;
  Page_BlockSubmit = false;
}
```

At this point, we have described the major functions present in the WebUIValidation.js script library provided by the .NET Framework. In the next section, we discuss server control–specific functionality built into the client-side validation framework.

Performing Specialized Routines in the Client Validation Library

Many controls require additional client-side script to perform successful validation. In this section, we examine the special-purpose routines in the script library that have control-specific functionality, as described in Table 9-5.

Most of the specialized functions in Table 9-5 deal with the evaluation capabilities of a specific validator control or help perform conversions, formatting, and comparison, as well as enable or disable the features of a validator control on the client side.

Table 9-5. Specialized JavaScript Functions in WebUIValidation.js

FUNCTION	DESCRIPTION
CompareValidatorEvaluateIsValid	Client-side validation function for CompareValidator.
CustomValidatorEvaluateIsValid	Client-side validation method for CustomValidator.
RangeValidatorEvaluateIsValid	Client-side validation function for RangeValidator.
RegularExpressionValidatorEvaluateIsValid	Client-side validation function for RegularExpressValidator.
RequiredFieldValidatorEvaluateIsValid	Client-side validation function for RequiredFieldValidator.
ValidatorCompare	Function to compare two values in client JavaScript. It uses ValidatorConvert to help with type conversions.
ValidatorConvert	Function to convert data types in JavaScript.
ValidatorEnable	Function to enable or disable a validator element.
ValidatorTrim	Function to trim extraneous spaces from a JavaScript string.

In the next section, we build our own custom control inheriting from BaseValidator. We reuse the client-script features of RegularExpressionValidator, specifically the RegularExpressionValidatorEvalutateIsValid client-side JavaScript function.

The BaseValidator and Validation Controls

The BaseValidator abstract class houses the core functionality of the built-in validator controls and, as you may surmise, represents a significant chunk of the validation feature set in ASP.NET. The overrides of this class that become the stock validator controls such as RequiredFieldValidator in ASP.NET are lightweight descendent classes that subtly enhance the heavy lifting BaseValidator provides.

Controls such as RequiredFieldValidation merely add properties and validation functions specific to their problem domain. When you build your own custom ASP.NET validator controls, it is highly recommended that you use BaseValidator as your base class unless you want to write a lot of low-level code. BaseValidator provides such key features as the following:

- Implementation of the necessary IValidator methods/properties

- Registration of a control in the Page class's Validators collection

- Interfacing with the validated control to get its value

- Determination of UpLevel/DownLevel client capabilities for client-side validation and rendering features

- Registration of the client-side ASP.NET script validation library

- Control registration to interact with the client-side ASP.NET script validation library

- Rendering of inline output for error messages

Interestingly, BaseValidator obtains some of its rendering capabilities by inheriting from the Label control. This is where BaseValidator obtains the Text property that displays inline error messages. Table 9-6 shows some of the additional properties and methods it adds to the Label base class.

Table 9-6. BaseValidator *Properties/Methods*

PROPERTY/METHOD	DESCRIPTION
ControlToValidate	String property to hold the name of the control that the validator control checks for compliance
Display	Enumeration property that determines how the control renders its errors: None, Static, or Dynamic
EnableClientScript	Manually turns on and off client-side rendering features
ErrorMessage	String property of the message to display in SummaryControl for invalid input
GetControlValidationValue	Method returns string value of the input control that is evaluated for compliance
IsValid	Boolean property that indicates whether or not the input is valid
RenderUpLevel	Boolean property that indicates whether or not the client browser supports client-side validation capabilities
Text	String property of the error message to display for invalid input in line with the validator control
Validate	Method to initiate the validator control user input check

ErrorMessage is the error message handed over to the ValidationSummary control that optionally can be used on the Web Form to summarize validation. We discussed the Display enumeration in the previous examination of the WebUIValidation.js JavaScript library, and we covered how it impacts whether or not the inline display of error messages is performed or if it takes advantage of DHTML effects if displayed.

GetControlValidationValue is a nice helper routine that obtains the ControlToValidate control ID string in the Page class's Controls collection and accesses the control to get the value that requires checking. It uses reflection on custom attributes of the control class to find a property adorned with ValidationPropertyAttribute in order to retrieve its validated value. For many of the controls in ASP.NET, this turns out to be the Text property of the control.

TIP ValidationPropertyAttribute *is an important attribute to apply to your custom controls when you want the controls to participate in the validation process. Place this attribute on the property you want to be validated.*

The RenderUpLevel Boolean property is a helper routine that encapsulates client capability checking by the BaseValidator class. BaseValidator checks specifically for MsDom version 4 and greater and EcmaScript 1.2 in the browser's capabilities in order to provide this Boolean value.

For all the features it provides, BaseValidator is not a complete solution as it is an abstract class. To demonstrate the foundational strength BaseValidator does provide and to further drill down into the validation process, we next build a CustomValidator control that inherits from it.

The PhoneValidator Custom Control

Now that you understand how client-side validation occurs with ASP.NET, with some work you can leverage and extend the system to your advantage. The PhoneValidator control will extend from BaseValidator and add the capability to validate phone numbers in either U.S. or international formats. Unlike the CustomValidator control from the previous example, all the grunge work with regular expressions is encapsulated within the control, which protects developers from these details and increases ease of use.

The first task in developing the control is to define an enum that allows the control consumer to select the U.S. or international format. We call this type PhoneNumberType:

```
public enum PhoneNumberType
{
    US = 0,
    Intl = 1
}
```

PhoneValidator will inherit from BaseValidator and add a property named NumberType that is of type PhoneNumberType and is backed via ViewState:

```
public virtual PhoneNumberType NumberType
{
    get
    {
        object numType = ViewState["NumberType"];
        if (numType == null)
            return PhoneNumberType.US;
        else
            return (PhoneNumberType) numType;
    }
    set
    {
        ViewState["NumberType"] = value;
    }
}
```

The primary task for a custom validator control that inherits from `BaseValidator` is to override the validation function named `EvaluateIsValid`. This is where we encapsulate the server-side regular expression code that we developed earlier for the `CustomerValidator` demonstration:

```
protected override bool EvaluateIsValid()
{
    // BaseValidator provides GetControlValidationValue
    // to make it easy to grab the control's value for you
    string number = base.GetControlValidationValue(base.ControlToValidate);

    // BaseValidator provides GetControlValidationValue
    // to make it easy to grab the control's value for you
    string number = base.GetControlValidationValue(base.ControlToValidate);
    // enforce the rule that we don't evaluate null
    // or empty values in non-RequiredFieldValidator
    // controls
    if (number.Trim() != "")
    {
        // use the regular expression engine of ASP.NET
        // to evaluate the phone number according to the
        // selected Phone type regular expression
        Regex expr = new Regex(PhoneRegex);
        MatchCollection matches = expr.Matches(number, 0);
        return (matches != null && matches[0].Value == number);
    }
    else
        return true;
}
```

To get the value from the validated input control, we use the `GetControlValidationValue` method exposed by `BaseValidator`. This method performs the acrobatics to examine the input control and find the correct property value.

That's all that's required to implement the server-side validation for our control. We now move on to implementing the client-side validation code within the framework provided by `BaseValidator`. With knowledge of how the client-side validation library works, we can leverage the features provided by ASP.NET for the `RegularExpressionValidator` control in our custom control.

We can add the needed client-side attributes using the `AddAttributesToRender` method available in `BaseValidator` as a result of its inheritance from the ASP.NET `Label` control. As shown in the following code, we first call `AddAttributesToRender` for the base class to make sure it adds attributes in our override of `AddAttributesToRender`. Next, we leverage the base class's `RenderUpLevel` property to check the browser's capabilities before proceeding.

```
protected override void AddAttributesToRender(HtmlTextWriter writer)
{
    base.AddAttributesToRender (writer);
```

```
   // BaseValidator has logic to determine the up-level browser
   // client capability
   if (base.RenderUplevel)
   {
      // link into the ClientValidation API of ASP.NET and
      // reuse its client-side Regex evaluation code
      writer.AddAttribute("evaluationfunction",
         "RegularExpressionValidatorEvaluateIsValid");
      writer.AddAttribute("validationexpression",PhoneRegex);
   }
}
```

The next step is to add evaluationfunction and validationexpresssion attributes, as shown in the following code. The PhoneRegex property used in this method abstracts the process of obtaining the international or U.S. phone number regular expression for use in the validationexpression attribute. The international phone number regular expression is probably oversimplified, but it works for demonstration purposes.

```
const string US_PHONE_REGEX = @"^\(?\d{3}\)?(\s|-)\d{3}\-\d{4}$";
const string INTL_PHONE_REGEX =@"^\d(\d|-){7,20}$";

private string PhoneRegex
{
   get
   {
      // read-only property selects the appropriate
      // regular expression to use for U.S. or
      // international phone based on the NumberType
      // property setting
      if (this.NumberType == PhoneNumberType.Intl)
            return INTL_PHONE_REGEX;
         else
            return US_PHONE_REGEX;
   }
}
```

The next step is to add the evaluationfunction and point it to the RegularExpressionValidatorEvaluateIsValid JavaScript function, as shown in Listing 9-20.

Listing 9-20. The RegularExpressionValidatorEvaluateIsValid *JavaScript Function*

```
function RegularExpressionValidatorEvaluateIsValid(val) {
    var value = ValidatorGetValue(val.controltovalidate);
    if (ValidatorTrim(value).length == 0)
        return true;
    var rx = new RegExp(val.validationexpression);
    var matches = rx.exec(value);
    return (matches != null && value == matches[0]);
}
```

The first step this JavaScript routine performs is to call `ValidatorGetValue` to look up the control's value. This function next trims this value to remove blank or null values. If the length of the input value is zero, then we follow the pattern outside of the `RequiredFieldValidator` and ignore blank or null values. The rest of the code contains regular expression work similar to our `CustomValidator` example using JavaScript regular expression support. At this point, our control is complete, as shown in Listing 9-21.

Listing 9-21. The `PhoneValidator` *Control Class*

```
using System;
using System.Web.UI;
using System.Web.UI.WebControls;
using System.Text.RegularExpressions;

namespace ControlsBookLib.Ch09
{
    public enum PhoneNumberType
    {
        US = 0,
        Intl = 1
    }

    [ ToolboxData("<{0}:PhoneValidator NumberType=US
runat=server></{0}:PhoneValidator>") ]
    public class PhoneValidator : BaseValidator
    {
        public virtual PhoneNumberType NumberType
        {
            get
            {
                object numType = ViewState["NumberType"];
                if (numType == null)
                    return PhoneNumberType.US;
                else
                    return (PhoneNumberType) numType;
            }
            set
            {
                ViewState["NumberType"] = value;
            }
        }

        const string US_PHONE_REGEX = @"^\(?\d{3}\)?(\s|-)\d{3}\-\d{4}$";
        const string INTL_PHONE_REGEX =@"^\d(\d|-){7,20}$";

        private string PhoneRegex
        {
            get
            {
                // read-only property selects the appropriate
                // regular expression to use for U.S. or
```

```
            // international phone based on the NumberType
            // property setting
            if (this.NumberType == PhoneNumberType.Intl)
                return INTL_PHONE_REGEX;
              else
                return US_PHONE_REGEX;
        }
    }

    protected override void AddAttributesToRender(HtmlTextWriter writer)
    {
        base.AddAttributesToRender (writer);

        // BaseValidator has logic to determine up-level browser
        // client capability
        if (base.RenderUplevel)
        {
            // link into the ClientValidation API of ASP.NET and
            // reuse its client-side Regex evaluation code
            writer.AddAttribute("evaluationfunction",
            "RegularExpressionValidatorEvaluateIsValid");
            writer.AddAttribute("validationexpression",PhoneRegex);
        }
    }

    protected override bool EvaluateIsValid()
    {
        // BaseValidator provides GetControlValidationValue
        // to make it easy to grab the control's value for you
        string number = base.GetControlValidationValue(
            base.ControlToValidate);

        // enforce the rule that we don't evaluate null
        // or empty values in non-RequiredFieldValidator
        // controls
        if (number.Trim() != "")
        {
            // use the regular expression engine of ASP.NET
            // to evaluate the phone number according to the
            // selected Phone type regular expression
            Regex expr = new Regex(PhoneRegex);
            MatchCollection matches = expr.Matches(number, 0);
            return (matches != null && matches[0].Value == number);
        }
        else
            return true;
    }
  }
}
```

In the next section, we exercise our newly created control to test its functionality.

The Phone Validation Using BaseValidator-Derived Control Web Form

The Phone Validation Using BaseValidator-Derived Control Web Form demonstrates our newly minted control testing for both U.S. and international phone numbers. It has a button to kick off validation and attempt a form post, as shown in Figure 9-5.

Figure 9-5. The Phone Validation Using BaseValidator-Derived Control Web Form

Attempt to input bogus values and you will get the error message shown in Figure 9-6.

Success is realized when you input valid U.S. and international phone numbers, as shown in Figure 9-7.

The full source code for the .aspx page and code-behind class for the Phone Validation Using BaseValidator-Derived Control Web Form is shown in Listings 9-22 and 9-23.

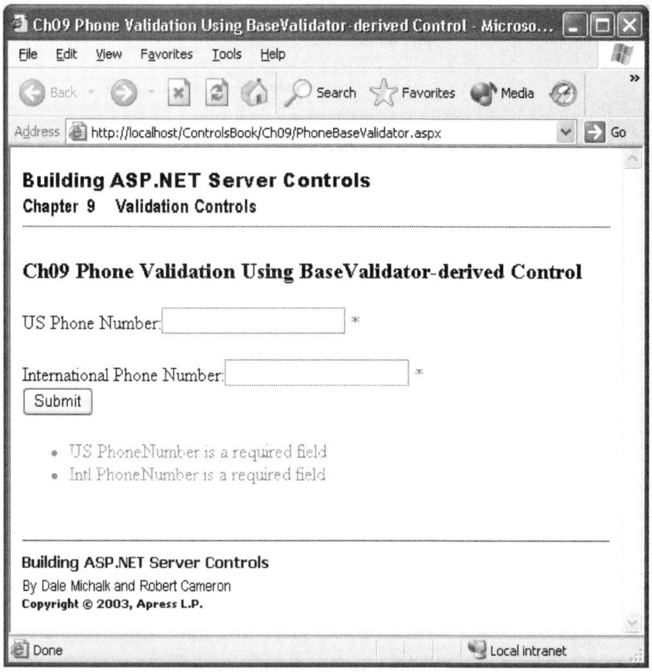

Figure 9-6. Testing the error detection capability of the PhoneValidator *control*

Figure 9-7. Successful result with validity checked by the PhoneValidator *control*

Listing 9-22. The Phone Validation Using BaseValidator-Derived Control Web Form
.aspx Page File

```
<%@ Page language="c#" Codebehind="PhoneBaseValidator.aspx.cs"
AutoEventWireup="false" Inherits="ControlsBookWeb.Ch09.PhoneBaseValidator" %>
<%@ Register TagPrefix="apressUC" TagName="ControlsBookFooter"
Src="..\ControlsBookFooter.ascx" %>
<%@ Register TagPrefix="apressUC" TagName="ControlsBookHeader"
Src="..\ControlsBookHeader.ascx" %>
<%@ Register TagPrefix="apress" Namespace="ControlsBookLib.Ch09"
Assembly="ControlsBookLib" %>
<!DOCTYPE HTML PUBLIC "-//W3C//DTD HTML 4.0 Transitional//EN" >
<HTML>
  <HEAD>
    <title>Ch09 Phone Validation Using BaseValidator-derived Control</title>
    <meta content="Microsoft Visual Studio .NET 7.1" name="GENERATOR">
    <meta content="C#" name="CODE_LANGUAGE">
    <meta content="JavaScript" name="vs_defaultClientScript">
    <meta content="http://schemas.microsoft.com/intellisense/ie5"
    name="vs_targetSchema">
  </HEAD>
  <body MS_POSITIONING="FlowLayout">
    <form id="Form1" method="post" runat="server">
      <apressuc:controlsbookheader id="Header" runat="server" chapternumber="9"
      chaptertitle="Validation Controls"></apressuc:controlsbookheader>
      <h3>Ch09 Phone Validation Using BaseValidator-derived Control</h3>
      US Phone Number:<asp:textbox id="USPhoneNumber" Runat="server"></asp:textbox>
      <asp:requiredfieldvalidator id="Requiredfieldvalidator" runat="server"
       ErrorMessage="US PhoneNumber is a required field"
        ControlToValidate="USPhoneNumber"
Display="Dynamic">*</asp:requiredfieldvalidator>
      <apress:phonevalidator id="PhoneValidatorUS" Runat="server"
ErrorMessage="PhoneNumber must be in format (xxx) xxx-xxxx or xxx-xxx-xxxx"
        NumberType="US" ControlToValidate="USPhoneNumber"
Display="Dynamic">*</apress:phonevalidator><BR>
      <br>
      International Phone Number:<asp:textbox id="IntlPhoneNumber"
Runat="server"></asp:textbox>
      <asp:requiredfieldvalidator id="Requiredfieldvalidator2" runat="server"
ErrorMessage="Intl PhoneNumber is a required field"
        ControlToValidate="IntlPhoneNumber"
Display="Dynamic">*</asp:requiredfieldvalidator>
      <apress:phonevalidator id="PhonevalidatorIntl" Runat="server"
ErrorMessage="Intl PhoneNumber must be in international format (8 to 20 digits
'-' separators)"
        NumberType="Intl" ControlToValidate="IntlPhoneNumber"
Display="Dynamic">*</apress:phonevalidator><BR>
      <asp:button id="Submit" Runat="server" Text="Submit"></asp:button><br>
      <BR>
      <asp:label id="Status" Runat="server"
Text=""></asp:label><asp:validationsummary id="Summary"
```

```
Runat="server"></asp:validationsummary><BR>
        <apressuc:controlsbookfooter id="Footer"
runat="server"></apressuc:controlsbookfooter></form>
    </FORM>
  </body>
</HTML>
```

Listing 9-23. The Phone Validation Using BaseValidator-Derived Control Web Form Code-Behind Class File

```
using System;
using System.Collections;
using System.ComponentModel;
using System.Data;
using System.Drawing;
using System.Web;
using System.Web.SessionState;
using System.Web.UI;
using System.Web.UI.WebControls;
using System.Web.UI.HtmlControls;

namespace ControlsBookWeb.Ch09
{
    public class PhoneBaseValidator : System.Web.UI.Page
    {
        protected System.Web.UI.WebControls.TextBox PhoneNumber;
        protected System.Web.UI.WebControls.Button Submit;
        protected System.Web.UI.WebControls.RequiredFieldValidator
                                        Requiredfieldvalidator;
        protected System.Web.UI.WebControls.Label Status;
        protected System.Web.UI.WebControls.TextBox IntlPhoneNumber;
        protected System.Web.UI.WebControls.RequiredFieldValidator
                                        Requiredfieldvalidator2;
        protected System.Web.UI.WebControls.TextBox USPhoneNumber;
        protected ControlsBookLib.Ch09.PhoneValidator PhoneValidatorUS;
        protected ControlsBookLib.Ch09.PhoneValidator PhonevalidatorIntl;
        protected System.Web.UI.WebControls.ValidationSummary Summary;

        private void Page_Load(object sender, System.EventArgs e)
        {
            Status.Text = "";
        }

        #region Web Form Designer generated code
        override protected void OnInit(EventArgs e)
        {
            //
            // CODEGEN: This call is required by the ASP.NET Web Form Designer.
            //
            InitializeComponent();
```

```
        base.OnInit(e);
    }


    /// <summary>
    /// Required method for Designer support - do not modify
    /// the contents of this method with the code editor.
    /// </summary>
    private void InitializeComponent()
    {
        this.Submit.Click += new System.EventHandler(this.Submit_Click);
        this.Load += new System.EventHandler(this.Page_Load);


    }
    #endregion

    private void Submit_Click(object sender, System.EventArgs e)
    {
        if (Page.IsValid)
            Status.Text = "Valid numbers US: " + USPhoneNumber.Text +
                " Intl: " + IntlPhoneNumber.Text;
    }
  }
}
```

Summary

Validation controls save ASP.NET web developers from having to write time-consuming client-side and server-side validation code. ASP.NET comes with a set of prebuilt validation-related controls: RequiredFieldValidator, RangeValidator, CompareValidator, RegularExpressionValidator, CustomValidator, and ValidationSummary.

ASP.NET provides several ways to extend the existing validation controls, which include implementing custom validation routines with the CustomValidator control, creating a control that inherits from the BaseValidator abstract class, and creating a control that implements the IValidator interface.

The IValidator interface defines the methods and properties a control must support to successfully interact with the Page class through a Validate method, the IsValid Boolean property, and the ErrorMessage string property.

WebUIValidation.js is the JavaScript client-side library used by controls that inherit from BaseValidator to perform client-side validation.

CHAPTER 10

Mobile Controls

THE ABILITY TO BUILD web applications that target mobile devices in additional to traditional desktop HTML browsers is becoming an important web application feature as the number of devices proliferates in a variety of form factors and display capabilities. An example of this is the fact that Microsoft produces versions of Pocket Internet Explorer for the Pocket PC, the Pocket PC Phone Edition, and the Smartphone mobile device platforms in addition to the traditional desktop IE product.

Many mobile phones sold today support Wireless Markup Language (WML), compact HTML (cHTML), or Extensible Hypertext Markup Language (XHTML) browsing as a core feature set, presenting a great opportunity for delivering mobile content. In addition to the increasing capabilities of recent mobile phone devices, wireless carriers in the United States have been building out their infrastructure for several years to provide increased data bandwidth capabilities in hopes of spurring demand as witnessed in other parts of the world, such as Europe and Japan.

TIP *Some older wireless networks can top out at 9600Kbps for data bandwidth. Also, wireless networks generally have higher latency when compared to wired networks. Keep this in mind when you design mobile web applications and server controls that support a wide range of devices and carriers.*

Developing mobile web applications has traditionally been a complex and tedious undertaking due to the need to address the plethora of device capabilities and ever-changing content markup specifications. Devices have different methods of sizing, positioning, and coloring information, and different methods of maintaining state on the client. Attempting to address these variations with custom code or XSLT scripts quickly becomes a maintenance nightmare. Add to that the task of keeping up with the actual content or business logic, and mobile web development can quickly become very costly to create and maintain. Having a powerful, flexible framework that provides an abstraction layer between application design and device-specific rendering can mean the difference between success and failure for a mobile development project.

Microsoft provides an integrated solution in the .NET Framework version 1.1 to ease these mobile development challenges and extend the ASP.NET platform to recognize and emit the appropriate markup tailored for many mobile devices. These extensions to ASP.NET, formerly a separate download called the Mobile Internet Toolkit for the 1.0 version of the .NET Framework, are called *mobile controls* and are located under the System.Web.UI.MobileControls namespace. Fortunately, mobile web application technology is based on the same fundamental model as ASP.NET with the Web Form construct and server control model, providing for a short learning curve to develop mobile web applications.

> **TIP** *The code in this chapter is built with the .NET Framework 1.1 Mobile Controls system with Device Update 2 installed. A device update is the method used by the ASP.NET mobile device team to periodically update the product to keep up with newer browsing protocols and devices. The biggest change in Device Update 2 is the support for XHTML devices. Search MSDN for "device update" for information on future device updates.*

As with building server controls for "regular" ASP.NET, it's necessary to understand the underlying technology architecture to successfully build controls that target mobile web development. In this chapter, we provide background on ASP.NET mobile web application technology and cover what's different as well as what's similar when compared to ASP.NET development targeting full-sized browsers. We also cover the various client-rendering technologies available in mobile development, including HTML, WML, and XHTML. Along the way, we explain the development, test, and debug cycle to use when developing mobile web applications and mobile controls with Visual Studio .NET and mobile device emulators. In Chapter 11, we dig into customization options with mobile controls as well as the nuts and bolts of building ASP.NET user and server controls for mobile applications.

Mobile Web Form Basics

ASP.NET mobile web applications are created using a descendent of the Page class that you are familiar with. The MobilePage class inherits from System.Web.UI.Page. Figure 10-1 shows the new mobile Web Form item available in the Visual Studio .NET 2003 IDE. This new MobilePage web page class is necessary because of how .aspx pages are constructed to support mobile development, which we discuss later in this chapter.

Visual Studio .NET 2003 also adds a project type named ASP.NET Mobile Web Application (see Figure 10-2). This project type adds new entries to the web.config file that set up mobile device development. Although it is possible to add MobilePage mobile web pages to standard ASP.NET web projects, it is recommended that you use the Mobile Web Application Wizard to automatically populate the web.config file with extra configuration settings to support mobile content generation and device detection.

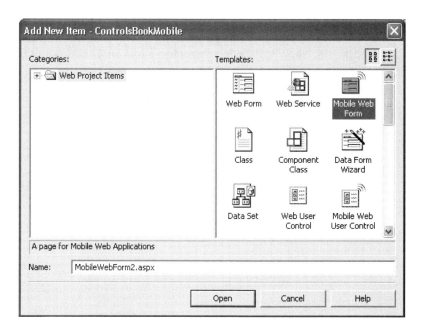

Figure 10-1. The Mobile Web Form page project item in Visual Studio .NET

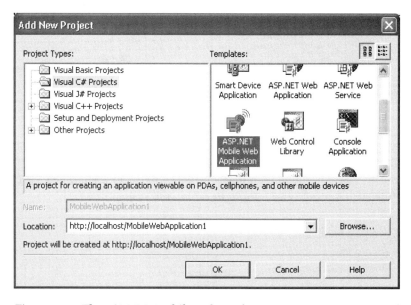

Figure 10-2. The ASP.NET Mobile Web Application project type in Visual Studio .NET

Figure 10-3 displays the MobileBasics mobile web page in the Visual Studio .NET 2003 Designer that serves as our launch point for explaining the ASP.NET mobile web application architecture. It is a simple "Hello, World" web application that takes input from a text box and displays a customized message.

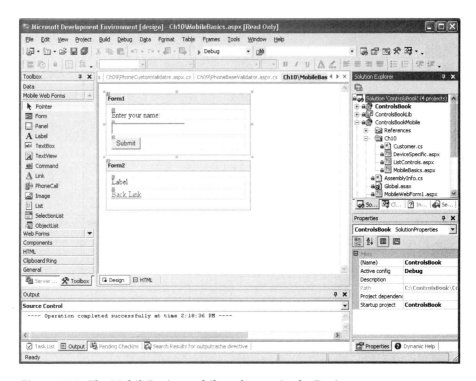

Figure 10-3. The MobileBasics mobile web page in the Designer

Mobile web pages are constructed using the same techniques as standard ASP.NET web applications in the Visual Studio .NET Designer. Drag and drop controls from the Mobile Web Forms section of the Toolbox to create the desired mobile UI. Listing 10-1 shows an .aspx page that should look familiar in form, if not structure.

Listing 10-1. The MobileBasics.aspx Mobile Web Form Page

```
<%@ Register TagPrefix="mobile" Namespace="System.Web.UI.MobileControls"
Assembly="System.Web.Mobile" %>
<%@ Page language="c#" Codebehind="MobileBasics.aspx.cs"
Inherits="ControlsBookMobile.Ch10.MobileBasics" AutoEventWireup="false" %>
<HEAD>
  <meta name="GENERATOR" content="Microsoft Visual Studio .NET 7.1">
  <meta name="CODE_LANGUAGE" content="C#">
  <meta name="vs_targetSchema" content="http://schemas.microsoft.com/Mobile/Page">
</HEAD>
<body Xmlns:mobile="http://schemas.microsoft.com/Mobile/WebForm">
  <mobile:Form id="Form1" runat="server">
    <mobile:Label id="Label1" runat="server">Enter your name:</mobile:Label>
    <mobile:TextBox id="TextBox1" runat="server"></mobile:TextBox>
    <mobile:Command id="cmdHello" runat="server">Submit</mobile:Command>
  </mobile:Form>
  <mobile:Form id="Form2" runat="server">
    <mobile:Label id="Label2" runat="server">Label</mobile:Label>
    <mobile:Link id="Link1" runat="server" NavigateUrl="#Form1">
    Back Link</mobile:Link>
  </mobile:Form>
</body>
```

The differences that spring to mind when comparing a regular ASP.NET Web Form with a mobile Web Form are that mobile application namespaces and tag prefixes are brought in by the topmost `Register` directive. The controls and the mobile Web Form import from the `System.Web.UI.MobileControls` namespace.

Another noticeable difference is that there is more than one Web Form tag in the .aspx page. The mobile .aspx page XML schema permits multiple mobile Web Forms on a single physical file to simplify the process of designing mobile web applications. Figure 10-4 shows the inheritance tree for the mobile `Form` class.

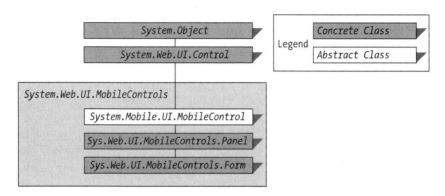

Figure 10-4. The mobile Form *class inheritance tree*

The recommended architecture for mobile web applications is to break down the content into bite-size chunks that are compatible with small screen displays. Although you could achieve this with multiple physical pages, it is more manageable to keep related content cohesively together on a single .aspx page, with a single `MobilePage` class, but in separate mobile Web Forms.

Another benefit of this design choice is that it mirrors the WML deck/card format that is prevalent on many mobile phones. The *deck* itself has multiple *cards* or forms that contain the content and is downloaded as a single entity. This allows for a fair amount of navigation and manipulation on the device without your having to go back to the server over the generally scarce bandwidth of the wireless carrier network.

Only the current active mobile Web Form is rendered, even when browsing a mobile Web Form using a traditional HTML browser. Also, despite multiple form tags within an .aspx page, mobile Web Form technology fully supports code-behind and server-side event handling.

The unification of these two completely different display models demonstrates how the mobile Web Form technology automatically accounts for the vast majority of display device types out of the box. The `MobileBasics` code-behind file in Listing 10-2 looks very much like a code-behind for a traditional ASP.NET Web Form, except for the additional mobile-related namespaces.

Listing 10-2. The `MobileBasics` *Code-Behind Class File*

```
using System;
using System.Collections;
using System.ComponentModel;
using System.Data;
using System.Drawing;
using System.Web;
using System.Web.Mobile;
using System.Web.SessionState;
using System.Web.UI;
using System.Web.UI.MobileControls;
using System.Web.UI.WebControls;
using System.Web.UI.HtmlControls;

namespace ControlsBookMobile.Ch10
{

    public class MobileBasics : System.Web.UI.MobileControls.MobilePage
    {
        protected System.Web.UI.MobileControls.Form Form2;
        protected System.Web.UI.MobileControls.TextBox TextBox1;
        protected System.Web.UI.MobileControls.Command cmdHello;
        protected System.Web.UI.MobileControls.Label Label1;
        protected System.Web.UI.MobileControls.Label Label2;
        protected System.Web.UI.MobileControls.Link Link1;
        protected System.Web.UI.MobileControls.Form Form1;
        private void Page_Load(object sender, System.EventArgs e)
        {
```

```
        // Put user code to initialize the page here
    }

    #region Web Form Designer generated code
    override protected void OnInit(EventArgs e)
    {
        //
        // CODEGEN: This call is required by the ASP.NET Web Form Designer.
        //
        InitializeComponent();
        base.OnInit(e);
    }

    /// <summary>
    /// Required method for Designer support - do not modify
    /// the contents of this method with the code editor.
    /// </summary>
    private void InitializeComponent()
    {
        this.cmdHello.Click += new System.EventHandler(this.cmdHello_Click);
        this.Load += new System.EventHandler(this.Page_Load);

    }
    #endregion

    private void cmdHello_Click(object sender, System.EventArgs e)
    {
        this.Label2.Text = "Hello " + TextBox1.Text;
        this.ActiveForm = Form2;
    }
  }
}
```

The code-behind class illustrates how the MobileBasics class inherits from the System.Web.UI.MobileControls.Page class instead of System.Web.UI.Page for the traditional ASP.NET Web Form. If you dig deeper into this inheritance tree, you will see that System.Web.UI.MobileControls.Page itself inherits from the System.Web.UI.Page class. This hints that the mobile web application architecture is similar to that of standard ASP.NET. The mobile Page class delivers increased functionality layered on top of the System.Web.UI.Page class.

On the MobileBasics .aspx, the controls are reachable via variable references, as are the two mobile Web Forms that contain them. You will notice that the controls themselves are in the UI namespace for mobile development, System.Web.UI.MobileControls. They have an inheritance tree that goes back to System.Web.UI.MobileControls.Control, which in turn inherits from System.Web.UI.Control. This also hints that you can apply all the tricks and techniques you learned from ASP.NET server control development in the mobile server control space, taking into account the smaller screen space and limited bandwidth. The major difference in developing mobile server controls is how control output is adapted by the mobile controls' framework to the specifics of the final device receiving the page output.

In the next section we cover how to browse mobile web forms during development and how to perform debugging when testing in an emulator.

Browsing Mobile Web Forms

Although it is convenient to browse a mobile Web Form in a desktop browser for basic testing, serious mobile web applications must be tested with all possible browsing devices. At the very least, a mobile web application should be tested with a sampling of device capabilities such as HTML, WML, and XHTML.

Using actual devices is ideal; however, testing with an emulator is the next best thing. Many of the popular mobile phone device manufacturers and other vendors provide a software development kit (SDK) with a phone emulator for testing purposes. It is possible to use an emulator for testing ASP.NET mobile web applications too. To display a mobile Web Form using the Pocket PC emulator, a Wireless Application Protocol (WAP) emulator, or an XHTML emulator, simply start the emulator, launch the web browser (if necessary), and enter the URL.

Once you have the desired emulators installed, you have a couple of options for debugging a mobile web application. One option is to simply run the web application using IE. Once the browser loads, minimize it and launch the desired emulator by entering the URL for the mobile web application. Because the application is in debug mode, you will hit breakpoints when viewing the web application in the emulator. When you have finished, close IE to stop debugging.

Another option is to integrate the emulator into Visual Studio .NET so that the emulator launches when you click Start Debug. To do this, right-click a mobile Web Form .aspx page and select Browse With from the context menu. Next, click Add, click Browse to locate the emulator .exe, click OK, provide a friendly name, and then click OK to return to the Browse With dialog box. Then select the newly added emulator and click Set As Default. Note that if the emulator takes a command-line argument, you can provide the URL as a parameter with this syntax:

```
"C:\pathToEmulator\emulator.exe %URL"
```

To have the emulator launch by default, you will need to change a project setting. Right-click the project in Solution Explorer and select Properties. Next, select Configuration Properties ➤ Debugging. Expand Start Options if it is not already expanded, and set Always Use Internet Explorer to false. This will cause the default browser for the start-up page to launch when Debug Start is selected. Note that if the emulator does not take a command-line parameter, you will have to manually enter the URL once the emulator is running. Once the emulator starts browsing the web application, the mobile web application will be in debug mode and will hit any breakpoints that are set and enabled.

In the following sections, we discuss how mobile web controls render in various mobile device emulators to help you better understand the target markup when you build custom mobile server controls in Chapter 11. We start with Pocket Internet Explorer (Pocket IE). Then we cover a WML client, and finally we look at an XHTML client. Many different emulator kits are available. We picked these three emulation environments as a representative mix of the device capabilities available.

Browsing with an HTML Client

As we mentioned previously, the mobile web application technology displays in a full-featured browser just as easily as in a WAP browser. Because Form1 is listed first in the tags on MobileBasics.aspx, it displays as the default "activated" mobile Web Form. Figure 10-5 shows what this mobile Web Form looks like when we browse to the MobileBasics.aspx URL from a mobile device HTML browser, such as the version of IE available with the Pocket PC emulator installed with Visual Studio .NET 2003.

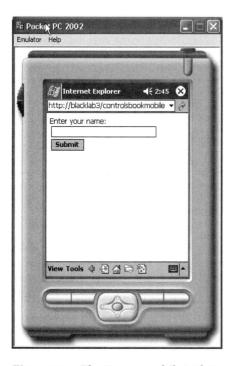

Figure 10-5. The Form1 mobile Web Form activated in the Pocket IE HTML browser

Looking at the HTML code in IE, you can see that only the first form is rendered in the HTML input, as you would expect:

```
<html>
<body>
<form id="Form1" name="Form1" method="post"
action="MobileBasics.aspx?__ufps=576914">
<input type="hidden" name="__EVENTTARGET" value="">
<input type="hidden" name="__EVENTARGUMENT" value="">
<script language=javascript><!--
function __doPostBack(target, argument){
  var theform = document.Form1
  theform.__EVENTTARGET.value = target
  theform.__EVENTARGUMENT.value = argument
  theform.submit()
}
// -->
</script>
Enter your name:<br>
<input name="TextBox1"/><br>
<input name="cmdHello" type="submit" value="Submit"/>
</form>
</body>
</html>
```

When we input a name and click Submit, the Web Form executes the postback cycle on the server and the code in cmdHello_Click executes:

```
private void cmdHello_Click(object sender, System.EventArgs e)
{
    this.Label2.Text = "Hello " + TextBox1.Text;
    this.ActiveForm = Form2;
}
```

Label2, which is nested inside the Form2 mobile Web Form, is configured to display a nice greeting that includes the name submitted by the TextBox control. We need to make this second mobile form visible in the click handler so that it is the form that renders. We do this by setting the ActiveForm property equal to Form2, which is an instance of the System.Web.UI.MobileControls.Page class. Figure 10-6 displays the resulting browser output.

The following is the HTML output rendered by Form2. You will notice there is no text box on the form, as compared to Form1.

```
<html>
<body>
<form id="Form2" name="Form2" method="post"
action="MobileBasics.aspx?__ufps=502021">
<input type="hidden" name="__VIEWSTATE"
value="aDxfX1A7QDxGb3JtMjvhlIrthYTsi5ngo4UsMjs+Oz7pttNd+vrN6KIXR74ekMPyJkCsiw
==">
```

```
<input type="hidden" name="__EVENTTARGET" value="">
<input type="hidden" name="__EVENTARGUMENT" value="">
<script language=javascript><!--
function __doPostBack(target, argument){
  var theform = document.Form2
  theform.__EVENTTARGET.value = target
  theform.__EVENTARGUMENT.value = argument
  theform.submit()
}
// -->
</script>
Hello Dale<br>
<a href="javascript:__doPostBack('Link1','Form1')">Back Link</a>
</form>
</body>
</html>
```

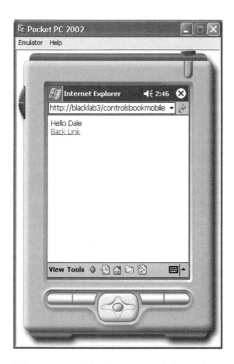

Figure 10-6. The Form2 mobile Web Form activated in the Pocket IE HTML browser

In the next section, we take our example page for a test drive in a WML client emulator.

Browsing with a WML Client

The next step in our basic mobile Web Form example is to examine how it renders WML. A useful environment for testing this is the WML emulator that comes with the Openwave SDK version 4.1.1. Figure 10-7 shows what opening the default Web Form, Form1, in the generic WML phone emulator configuration looks like.

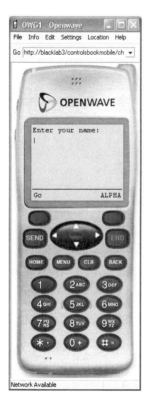

Figure 10-7. The Form1 mobile Web Form activated in the Openwave 4.1.1 WML browser

If we examine the WML content by using the source code option available in the simulator, we can see that the WML deck at this point has only a single card in it for gathering input:

```
<?xml version='1.0'?>
<!DOCTYPE wml PUBLIC '-//WAPFORUM//DTD WML 1.1//EN' 'http://www.wapforum.org/DTD
/wml_1.1.xml'><wml><head>
<meta http-equiv="Cache-Control" content="max-age=0" />
</head>
<card>
<onevent type="onenterforward">
```

```
<refresh><setvar name="TextBox1" value="" />
</refresh>
</onevent>
<do type="accept" label="Go">
<go href="/controlsbookmobile/(55iv1fqws5zwkk551et2
3y45)/ch10/mobilebasics.aspx?__ufps=6966851"
method="post">
<postfield
name="__EVENTTARGET" value="cmdHello" />
<postfield name="TextBox1" value="$(TextBox1)" />
</go>
</do>
<p>Enter your name:
<input name="TextBox1" />
</p>
</card>
</wml>
```

If we enter in a name value and click the soft key labeled Go, Form1 performs postback as before and the screen display changes to what is shown in Figure 10-8.

Figure 10-8. The Form2 mobile Web Form activated in the Openwave 4.1.1 WML browser

The WML source in the phone changes to include both cards in a single file deck:

```
<?xml version='1.0'?>
<!DOCTYPE wml PUBLIC '-//WAPFORUM//DTD WML 1.1//EN' 'http://www.wapforum.org/DTD
/wml_1.1.xml'>
<wml>
  <card id="Form2">
    <do type="accept" label="Link">
      <go href="#Form1"/>
    </do>
    <p>Hello Dale<br/><a href="#Form1" title="Link">Back Link</a>
    </p>
  </card>
  <card id="Form1">
    <onevent type="onenterforward">
      <refresh>
        <setvar name="TextBox1" value="Dale"/>
      </refresh>
    </onevent>
    <do type="accept" label="Go">
      <go href="/controlsbookmobile/(55iv1fqws5zwkk551et23y45)/ch10/mobilebasics
.aspx?Ooc=106&amp;__ufps=0782392" method="post">
        <postfield name="__VIEWSTATE" value="aDxfX1A7QDxGb3JtMjvlsajukZfsi5rgo4U
sMDs+Oz6lhnZPtmLWR8MTtwwOBTLkH8svUg=="/><postfield name="__EVENTTARGET" value="c
mdHello"/><postfield name="TextBox1" value="$$(TextBox1:noesc)"/>
      </go>
    </do>
    <p>Enter your name:<input name="TextBox1"/>
    </p>
  </card>
</wml>
```

The WML output is very efficient. It is aware that both cards are available on the client, so that when the Back Link is clicked, the device displays the original URL without making a request to the server. In the preceding WML output, you can see the link is deck oriented because the URL starts with a pound sign (#): #Form1. When the phone goes into the deck, the text box will have the previously entered value as a result of the onevent tag event handler setting its value.

Next, we show how our example mobile Web Form renders in an XHTML client emulator.

Browsing with an XHTML Client

Last but not least is the XHTML browsing client available by installing the Nokia Mobile Internet Toolkit 3.1. The default browser that comes with the toolkit may not have the greatest aesthetics, but it is reliable and it makes it easy to view WML or XHTML source. Figure 10-9 shows the rendered XHTML for Form1 in the Nokia emulator.

Figure 10-9. The Form1 mobile Web Form activated in the Nokia XHTML browser

As you can see, the following XHTML code is quite similar to the HTML markup generated for Pocket IE. The key difference is how the document follows the rules for well-formed XML, so the ‹TABLES›, ‹TR›, and ‹TD› tags are correctly nested, and so are single tags (for example, an HTML break is rendered as ‹BR /›). This makes life much easier for the browser developer, who can expect well-formed markup, and it is one of the benefits of XHTML.

```
<?xml version="1.0" encoding="utf-8"?>
<!DOCTYPE html PUBLIC "-//WAPFORUM//DTD XHTML Mobile 1.0//EN"
 "http://www.wapforum.org/DTD/xhtml-mobile10.dtd">
<html xmlns="http://www.w3.org/1999/xhtml">
<head>
<title></title></head>
<body><form id="Form1" method="post"
action="/controlsbookmobile/(rsk4mvidump3yqnw3bxq1pr4)/ch10/mobilebasics.aspx
?__ufps=93099">
<div><input type="hidden" name="__ET"/>
Enter your name:
<br/>
<input name="TextBox1"/>
<br/>
<input type="submit" name="cmdHello" value="Submit"/>
</div></form></body>
</html>
```

Figure 10-10 shows the rendered XHTML for Form2 in the Nokia emulator.

Figure 10-10. The Form2 mobile Web Form activated in the Nokia XHTML browser

The following rendered XHTML for Form2 is a close cousin of the HTML output rendered in Pocket IE. For this reason, in subsequent examples we stay with the Openwave WML browser and Pocket IE browser for comparing and contrasting the rendered output.

```
<?xml version="1.0"  encoding="utf-8"?>
<!DOCTYPE html PUBLIC "-//WAPFORUM//DTD XHTML Mobile 1.0//EN"
"http://www.wapforum.org/DTD/xhtml-mobile10.dtd">
<html xmlns="http://www.w3.org/1999/xhtml">
<head>
<title></title></head>
<body><form id="Form2" method="post"
action="/controlsbookmobile/(rsk4mvidump3yqnw3bxq1pr4)/ch10/mobilebasics.aspx
?__ufps=220257">
<div><input type="hidden" name="__VIEWSTATE"
value="aDxfX1A7QDxGb3JtMjvnuafmqrvsj6ngo4UsMDs+Oz4Fs7ASjjIrXly37XtRnwEVmfjlkw
=="/>
Hello Dale

<br/>
<a
href="/controlsbookmobile/(rsk4mvidump3yqnw3bxq1pr4)/ch10/mobilebasics.aspx?_
_VIEWSTATE=aDxfX1A7QDxGb3JtMjvnuafmqrvsj6ngo4UsMDs%2bOz4Fs7ASjjIrXly37XtRnwEV
mfjlkw%3d%3d&amp;__ET=Link1&amp;__EA=Form1&amp;__ufps=">
Back Link</a>
</div></form></body>

</html>
```

In the next section, we provide an overview of the mobile controls available in ASP.NET.

System.Web.UI.MobileControls Controls

Now that we've presented basic information on how the mobile Web Form works and demonstrated how ASP.NET can serve either HTML or WAP content, we can explore the System.Web.UI.MobileControls namespace to see what it has to offer from a control standpoint. A basic understanding of the capabilities provided by the built-in controls will serve you well when building custom user and composite mobile server controls.

In this section, we start off by discussing the various text controls available in the MobileControls namespace. As you would guess, we need a way to navigate through our mobile Web Forms and that is the topic of the section titled "Transfer Controls" in this section. We then dive into an example .aspx page to demonstrate these controls in action. After this, we cover list, rich, validation, and pagination mobile server controls, sprinkling in example demonstrations along the way.

After you read this section, you will have a strong sense of what's available in the MobileControls namespace and how mobile controls "work" as compared to regular server controls. This knowledge will serve you well in Chapter 11, when you dive into building custom mobile controls.

Text Controls

The workhorses of the ASP.NET mobile controls namespace are the controls that emit the textual content. Table 10-1 outlines the text-based control options in System.Web.UI.MobileControls.

Table 10-1. Simple Mobile Controls

NAME	HTML TAG	WML TAG	DESCRIPTION
Label	text	text	Displays text
TextBox	<INPUT type="text"> or <INPUT type="password">	<INPUT type="text"> or <INPUT type="password">	Gathers text input
TextView	text, <A>, <B>, <I>, 	text, <A>, <B>, <I>, 	Displays text with formatting, navigation, and pagination

The previous demonstration, MobileBasics.aspx, demonstrated the Label and TextBox controls in action. Label simply emits the text straight into the output stream without modification or processing. TextBox supports the ability to gather text input from a device, including a Password option that masks input.

The TextView is a supercharged version of the Label control that supports pagination to break up its content via the <P> or <BR> tag, offers navigation via the <A> tag, and provides additional support for font-related tags such as <B> and <I> in a similar manner to literal text within a Form tag.

Transfer Controls

Transfer controls support navigation and are listed in Table 10-2. The Link control is used in MobileBasics.aspx to navigate among the mobile Web Forms on the mobile page. The Link control can also be used to navigate to a new end-point URL. The PhoneCall control is for use with devices that have a wireless radio stack in them; it allows such a device to activate the dialing software. If the device doesn't support that, it will substitute either a text message or a clickable URL.

Table 10-2. Transfer Mobile Controls

NAME	HTML TAG	WML TAG	DESCRIPTION
Link	<a href="">	<GO>	Links to a URL
Command	<INPUT type="Submit">	<GO type="submit">	Posts to a URL
PhoneCall	<a href="">	<DO> and <GO>	Initiates a phone call or links to a URL

The Command control posts back the current Web Form to the web server for processing form data. Once the content is at the server, you can redirect it to a new URL or to one of the mobile Web Forms on a page by setting the Page.ActiveForm property.

The TxtandTransCtrl Web Form

The TxtandTransCtrl mobile Web Form demonstrates the text- and transfer-related controls in the mobile control arsenal. It consists of a login password page with the TextBox control's Password property set to true. The Command control renders as a button on an HTML display, but it renders as a soft key action on the mobile phone, as shown in Figure 10-11.

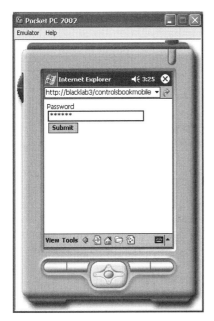

Figure 10-11. The TxtandTransCtrl Password form display

The code for the mobile web page and the code-behind class that generate the output for the preceding examples is shown in Listings 10-3 and 10-4.

Listing 10-3. The TxtandTransCtrls.aspx Mobile Web Form Page

```
<%@ Register TagPrefix="mobile" Namespace="System.Web.UI.MobileControls"
Assembly="System.Web.Mobile" %>
<%@ Page language="c#" Codebehind="TxtandTransCtrls.aspx.cs"
Inherits="ControlsBookMobile.Ch10.TextandTransCtrls" AutoEventWireup="false"
%>
<HEAD>
  <meta name="GENERATOR" content="Microsoft Visual Studio .NET 7.1">
  <meta name="CODE_LANGUAGE" content="C#">
  <meta name="vs_targetSchema" content="http://schemas.microsoft.com/Mobile/Page">
</HEAD>
<body Xmlns:mobile="http://schemas.microsoft.com/Mobile/WebForm">
  <mobile:Form id="Form1" runat="server">
    <mobile:Label id="Label1" runat="server">Password</mobile:Label>
    <mobile:TextBox id="TextBox1" runat="server" Password="True"></mobile:TextBox>
    <mobile:Command id="Command1" runat="server">Submit</mobile:Command>
  </mobile:Form>
  <mobile:Form id="Form2" runat="server">
    <mobile:Label id="Label2" runat="server"></mobile:Label>
    <mobile:TextView id="TextView1" runat="server"></mobile:TextView>
    <mobile:PhoneCall id="PhoneCall1" runat="server" PhoneNumber="555-1212"
```

```
AlternateUrl="http://www.microsoft.com"
      AlternateFormat="{0} ">Contact Microsoft</mobile:PhoneCall>
    <mobile:Link id="Link1" runat="server" NavigateUrl="#Form1">Back
Link</mobile:Link>
  </mobile:Form>
</body>
```

Listing 10-4. The TxtandTransCtrls.aspx Code-Behind Class File

```
using System;
using System.Collections;
using System.ComponentModel;
using System.Data;
using System.Drawing;
using System.Web;
using System.Web.Mobile;
using System.Web.SessionState;
using System.Web.UI;
using System.Web.UI.MobileControls;
using System.Web.UI.WebControls;
using System.Web.UI.HtmlControls;

namespace ControlsBookMobile.Ch10
{
    public class TextandTransCtrls : System.Web.UI.MobileControls.MobilePage
    {
        protected System.Web.UI.MobileControls.Label Label1;
        protected System.Web.UI.MobileControls.TextBox TextBox1;
        protected System.Web.UI.MobileControls.TextView TextView1;
        protected System.Web.UI.MobileControls.Command Command1;
        protected System.Web.UI.MobileControls.Label Label2;
        protected System.Web.UI.MobileControls.Form Form2;
        protected System.Web.UI.MobileControls.Link Link1;
        protected System.Web.UI.MobileControls.PhoneCall PhoneCall1;
        protected System.Web.UI.MobileControls.Form Form1;

        private void Page_Load(object sender, System.EventArgs e)
        {
            // Put user code to initialize the page here
        }

        #region Web Form Designer generated code
        override protected void OnInit(EventArgs e)
        {
            //
            // CODEGEN: This call is required by the ASP.NET Web Form Designer.
            //
            InitializeComponent();
            base.OnInit(e);
        }
```

```
        /// <summary>
        /// Required method for Designer support - do not modify
        /// the contents of this method with the code editor.
        /// </summary>
        private void InitializeComponent()
        {
            this.Command1.Click += new System.EventHandler(this.Command1_Click);
            this.Load += new System.EventHandler(this.Page_Load);

        }
        #endregion

        private void Command1_Click(object sender, System.EventArgs e)
        {
            this.ActiveForm = Form2;

            Label2.Text = "<b>Password:</b> <i>" + TextBox1.Text + "</i>";
            TextView1.Text = "<b>Password:</b> <i>" + TextBox1.Text + "</i>";
        }
    }
}
```

When you browse with Pocket IE, the HTML generated includes the simple `<INPUT>` tags for password and button generation:

```
Password<br>
<input name="TextBox1" type="password"/><br>
<input name="Command1" type="submit" value="Submit"/>
```

The WML rendered includes an `<INPUT>` tag and the `<DO>` and `<GO>` tags to post values back to the web server:

```
<do type="accept" label="Go">
<go href="/controlsbookmobile/(m5coxwi0txrxbd55h3if
ji45)/ch10/txtandtransctrls.aspx?__ufps=8249581" method="post">
<postfield name="__EVENTTARGET" value="Command1" />
<postfield name="TextBox1" value="$(mcsvcpese0)"/>
</go>
</do>
<p>Password<input name="mcsvcpese0" type="password" /></p>
```

Once you submit the password form and activate the second form via the `Command` control, the password is displayed. Figure 10-12 displays the output in Pocket IE and in a WML emulator.

Figure 10-12. The TxtandTransCtrl password form results in Pocket IE and a WML emulator

In the `Label` control, the embedded markup renders as text with the `<B>` and `<I>` tags appearing onscreen, whereas in the `TextView` control, the embedded markup renders as bold and italic. You can also see that instead of rendering a phone number, a link to `http://www.microsoft.com` is put in by the `PhoneCall` control:

```
&lt;b&gt;Password:&lt;/b&gt; &lt;i&gt;secret&lt;/i&gt;<br>
<b>Password:</b> <i>secret</i><br>
<a href="http://www.microsoft.com">Contact Microsoft </a><br>
<a href="javascript:__doPostBack('Link1','Form1')">
Back Link</a></form></body></html>
```

The WML results have the same effect on the differences between `Label` and `TextView` output. An interesting feature is how the `PhoneCall` control registers a `<GO>` tag with a special `href` that tells the mobile phone that the link should activate the dialing process:

```
  <card id="Form2">
    <do type="accept" label="Call">
      <go href="wtai://wp/mc;5551212"/>
    </do>
    <do type="options" label="Link">
      <go href="#Form1"/>
    </do>
    <p>&lt;b&gt;Password:&lt;/b&gt; &lt;i&gt;secret&lt;/i&gt;<br/>
<b>Password:</b><i>secret</i>
      <br/><a href="wtai://wp/mc;5551212" title="Call">Contact Microsoft</a>
      <br/><a href="#Form1" title="Link">Back Link</a>
    </p>
  </card>
```

The List Controls

The list controls are best used to display data in mobile device applications and are described in Table 10-3. As with their cousins in WebControl, the list controls make it simple to bind to a data source and display the information in an easily accessible format. As you would expect, these controls take into account the limited screen size of the majority of mobile phones. The controls do differ in their capability to paginate themselves, have static information linked to them, and provide a detailed view of the data they are linked to.

Table 10-3. List Mobile Controls

NAME	DESCRIPTION	STATIC/DYNAMIC	PAGINATION
List	Renders a list of items	Both	Yes
SelectionList	Renders a list of items Similar to a ListBox or a ComboBox	Both	No
ObjectList	Renders a list of items with multiple properties and item commands	Dynamic only	Yes

The ListControls Web Form

The ListControls Web Form is a mobile web page that demonstrates some of the capabilities of mobile server controls by exercising each list control type. As you'll see, these are miniature versions of their WebControl cousins designed for the smaller form factor of mobile devices.

The ListControls Web Form contains List, SelectionList, and ObjectList controls, with each hosted on a mobile form. The action is coordinated using Link controls hosted on the MainForm mobile Web Form. Listings 10-5 and 10-6 present the full .aspx file and code-behind class file, respectively. Listing 10-7 presents the CustDB data access class.

Listing 10-5. The ListControls.aspx Mobile Web Form Page

```
<%@ Page language="c#" Codebehind="ListControls.aspx.cs"
Inherits="ControlsBookMobile.Ch10.ListControls" AutoEventWireup="false" %>
<%@ Register TagPrefix="mobile" Namespace="System.Web.UI.MobileControls"
Assembly="System.Web.Mobile" %>
<HEAD>
  <meta content="Microsoft Visual Studio .NET 7.1" name="GENERATOR">
  <meta content="C#" name="CODE_LANGUAGE">
  <meta content="http://schemas.microsoft.com/Mobile/Page" name="vs_targetSchema">
</HEAD>
<body Xmlns:mobile="http://schemas.microsoft.com/Mobile/WebForm">
  <mobile:form id="MainForm" runat="server">
    <mobile:Link id="Link1" runat="server" NavigateUrl="#ListForm">
    List control</mobile:Link>
    <mobile:Link id="Link2" runat="server"
NavigateUrl="#SelectionListForm">SelectionList control</mobile:Link>
    <mobile:Link id="Link3" runat="server"
NavigateUrl="#ObjectListForm">ObjectList control</mobile:Link>
  </mobile:form>
  <mobile:form id="ListForm" runat="server">
    <mobile:Label id="ListResult" runat="server"></mobile:Label>
    <mobile:List id="List1" runat="server" Decoration="Bulleted"></mobile:List>
    <mobile:Link id="Link4" runat="server"
NavigateUrl="#MainForm">Back</mobile:Link>
  </mobile:form>
  <mobile:form id="SelectionListForm" runat="server">
    <mobile:Label id="SelectionListResults" runat="server"></mobile:Label>
    <mobile:SelectionList id="SelectionList1" runat="server"
SelectType="MultiSelectListBox"></mobile:SelectionList>
    <mobile:Command id="SelListCmd" runat="server">Submit</mobile:Command>
    <mobile:Link id="Link5" runat="server"
NavigateUrl="#MainForm">Back</mobile:Link>
  </mobile:form>
  <mobile:form id="ObjectListForm" runat="server">
    <mobile:ObjectList id="ObjectList1" runat="server" CommandStyle-
StyleReference="subcommand" LabelStyle-StyleReference="title"></mobile:ObjectList>
    <mobile:Link id="Link6" runat="server"
NavigateUrl="#MainForm">Back</mobile:Link>
  </mobile:form>
</body>
```

Listing 10-6. The ListControls.aspx Code-Behind Class File

```
using System;
using System.Collections;
using System.ComponentModel;
using System.Data;
using System.Drawing;
using System.Web;
```

```
using System.Web.Mobile;
using System.Web.SessionState;
using System.Web.UI;
using System.Web.UI.MobileControls;
using System.Web.UI.WebControls;
using System.Web.UI.HtmlControls;

namespace ControlsBookMobile.Ch10
{
    public class ListControls : System.Web.UI.MobileControls.MobilePage
    {
        protected System.Web.UI.MobileControls.Form ListForm;
        protected System.Web.UI.MobileControls.Form SelectionListForm;
        protected System.Web.UI.MobileControls.SelectionList SelectionList1;
        protected System.Web.UI.MobileControls.Form ObjectListForm;
        protected System.Web.UI.MobileControls.ObjectList ObjectList1;
        protected System.Web.UI.MobileControls.Form MainForm;
        protected System.Web.UI.MobileControls.Label ListResult;
        protected System.Web.UI.MobileControls.Command SelListCmd;
        protected System.Web.UI.MobileControls.Label SelectionListResults;
        protected System.Web.UI.MobileControls.Link Link1;
        protected System.Web.UI.MobileControls.Link Link2;
        protected System.Web.UI.MobileControls.Link Link3;
        protected System.Web.UI.MobileControls.List List1;

        #region Web Form Designer generated code
        override protected void OnInit(EventArgs e)
        {
            //
            // CODEGEN: This call is required by the ASP.NET Web Form Designer.
            //
            InitializeComponent();
            base.OnInit(e);
        }

        /// <summary>
        /// Required method for Designer support - do not modify
        /// the contents of this method with the code editor.
        /// </summary>
        private void InitializeComponent()
        {
            this.List1.ItemCommand += new
System.Web.UI.MobileControls.ListCommandEventHandler(this.List1_ItemCommand);
            this.ListForm.Activate += new System.EventHandler(this.Form1_Activate);
            this.SelListCmd.Click += new System.EventHandler(this.SelListCmd_Click);
            this.SelectionListForm.Activate += new
System.EventHandler(this.SelectionListForm_Activate);
            this.ObjectListForm.Activate += new
System.EventHandler(this.ObjectListForm_Activate);
```

```
         }
         #endregion


         private DataSet GetCustomersData()
         {
            return ControlsBookMobile.Ch10.CustDB.GetCustomersByName("[AB]","10");
         }

         private void Form1_Activate(object sender, System.EventArgs e)
         {
            DataSet ds = GetCustomersData();
            List1.DataSource = ds;
            List1.DataMember = "Customers";
            List1.DataTextField = "ContactName";
            List1.DataBind();
         }

         private void SelectionListForm_Activate(object sender, System.EventArgs e)
         {
            DataSet ds = GetCustomersData();
            SelectionList1.DataSource = ds;
            SelectionList1.DataMember = "Customers";
            SelectionList1.DataTextField = "ContactName";
            SelectionList1.DataBind();
         }

         private void ObjectListForm_Activate(object sender, System.EventArgs e)
         {
            DataSet ds = GetCustomersData();
            ObjectList1.DataSource = ds;
            ObjectList1.DataMember = "Customers";
            ObjectList1.DataBind();
         }

         private void List1_ItemCommand(object sender,
    System.Web.UI.MobileControls.ListCommandEventArgs e)
         {
            ListResult.Text = "Selected name:" + e.ListItem.Text;
         }

         private void SelListCmd_Click(object sender, System.EventArgs e)
         {
            string results = "";
            foreach (MobileListItem item in SelectionList1.Items)
            {
               if (item.Selected)
               {
                  if (results.Length == 0)
                     results += " " + item.Text;
                  else
```

```
                results += ", " + item.Text;
            }
        }
        SelectionListResults.Text = "Selected names:" + results;
    }
  }
}
```

Listing 10-7. The CustDB *Data Access Class*

```
using System;
using System.Data;
using System.Data.SqlClient;

namespace ControlsBookMobile.Ch10
{
   public class CustDB
   {
      public static DataSet GetCustomersByName(string Name, string TopAmount)
      {
         SqlConnection conn =
            new SqlConnection(
"Server=(local);Database=Northwind;Integrated Security=true;");
         conn.Open();

         SqlDataAdapter da =
            new SqlDataAdapter("SELECT TOP " + TopAmount + " CustomerID,
ContactName, ContactTitle, CompanyName FROM Customers WHERE ContactName LIKE
'%" + Name + "%'",
            conn);
         DataSet ds = new DataSet();
         da.Fill(ds,"Customers");

         return ds;
      }
   }
}
```

The first mobile Web Form on the page we examine is the ListForm containing the List control. Figure 10-13 shows how this control displays using HTML and WML.

Figure 10-13. The List *control rendered in Pocket IE and a WML emulator*

The List Control

The List control supports the ability to either bind to a data source or have its data specified statically via item elements in the .aspx page. You can put the data-binding server control techniques you learned in Chapter 7 to good use when you build your own custom mobile server controls, as demonstrated by the List controls covered in this section.

Our ListControls example chooses the dynamic route, data binding the List control to the Customers table in the Northwind SQL Server sample database through a helper routine that produces a DataSet called GetCustomersData. This is done in the Activate event that is raised when a mobile Web Form becomes the active form on a mobile page. This allows for form-specific initialization in the mobile Web Form's Page_Load event:

```
private void ListForm_Activate(object sender, System.EventArgs e)
{
    DataSet ds = GetCustomersData();
    List1.DataSource = ds;
    List1.DataMember = "Customers";
    List1.DataTextField = "ContactName";
    List1.DataBind();
}
```

The display can be configured to render a list without decoration, with bullets, or as a numbered list. The ListControls sample chooses to list out its items using bullets. Because an event handler is wired to the OnItemCommand event exposed by List, it adds the necessary steps to generate UI that posts the form back to the server:

```
private void List1_ItemCommand(object sender,
System.Web.UI.MobileControls.ListCommandEventArgs e)
{
   ListResult.Text = "Selected name:" + e.ListItem.Text;
}
```

You can see the results of this code in the rendered HTML, as each item is repre-sented by a hyperlink:

```
HTML
<ul>
<li><a href="javascript:__doPostBack('List1','0')" >Maria Anders</a></li>
<li><a href="javascript:__doPostBack('List1','1')" >Ana Trujillo</a></li>
<li><a href="javascript:__doPostBack('List1','2')" >Antonio Moreno</a></li>
<li><a href="javascript:__doPostBack('List1','3')" >Thomas Hardy</a></li>
<li><a href="javascript:__doPostBack('List1','4')" >Christina Berglund</a></li>
<li><a href="javascript:__doPostBack('List1','5')" >Hanna Moos</a></li>
<li><a href="javascript:__doPostBack('List1','6')" >Frederique Citeaux</a></li>
<li><a href="javascript:__doPostBack('List1','7')" >Martin Sommer</a></li>
<li><a href="javascript:__doPostBack('List1','8')" >Laurence Lebihan</a></li>
<li><a href="javascript:__doPostBack('List1','9')" >Elizabeth Lincoln</a></li>
</ul>
```

The control emits code that generates a post back to the web server when ren-dered for a WML browser as well. The generated WML content has a <SELECT> tag with embedded <TAGS> to describe the list information. The event functionality is handled by the <DO> and <GO> pair of tags to submit the content to the web server when a soft key is clicked:

```
<do type="accept" label="Go">
        <go href="#__pbc2">
           <setvar name="mcsvt" value="List1"/>
<setvar name="mcsva" value="$$(List1:noesc)"/>
        </go>
     </do>
     <select name="List1">
       <option value="0">Maria Anders</option>
       <option value="1">Ana Trujillo</option>
       <option value="2">Antonio Moreno</option>
       <option value="3">Thomas Hardy</option>
       <option value="4">Christina Berglund</option>
       <option value="5">Hanna Moos</option>
       <option value="6">Frederique Citeaux</option>
       <option value="7">Martin Sommer</option>
       <option value="8">Laurence Lebihan</option>
       <option value="9">Elizabeth Lincoln</option>
     </select>
```

Figure 10-14 shows what happens when an item is selected. The Label control at the top is changed to reflect the selection choice.

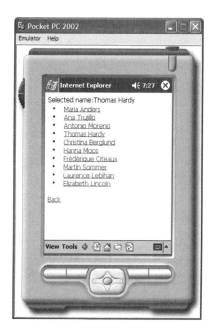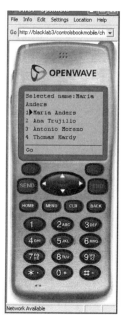

Figure 10-14. The List *control after selection, as rendered in Pocket IE and a WML emulator*

The SelectionList Control

The next stop on the list-type server control journey is the SelectionList control. This list control variant is designed to handle single selections like the List control as well as multiple selections. The SelectionList control can render a variety of ways. The SelectionList's SelectList property can take these options: DropDown, Radio, CheckBox, ListBox, and MultiSelectListBox. Figure 10-15 displays the SelectionList control.

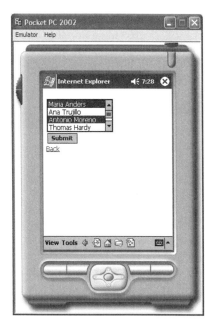 

Figure 10-15. The SelectionList *control rendered in Pocket IE and a WML emulator*

Unlike the List control, the SelectionList control does not generate its own commands, and it does not support pagination. This means you have to be cognizant of the size of its bound data list when it is rendered in a device and add a Command control to submit the selected data back to the web server. The following is the result of the output in our Pocket IE HTML browser:

```
<select multiple size="4" name="SelectionList1">
<option value="0">Maria Anders
<option value="1">Ana Trujillo
<option value="2">Antonio Moreno
<option value="3">Thomas Hardy
<option value="4">Christina Berglund
<option value="5">Hanna Moos
<option value="6">Frederique Citeaux
<option value="7">Martin Sommer
<option value="8">Laurence Lebihan
<option value="9">Elizabeth Lincoln
</select>
<br>
<input name="SelListCmd" type="submit" value="Submit"/>
```

Here is the rendered WML:

```
    <go href="/controlsbookmobile/(zeoknp553kychmmo2f1oqhre)/ch10/listcontrols
.aspx?Ooc=106&amp;__ufps=7795021" method="post">
        <postfield name="__VIEWSTATE" value="aDxfX1A7QDxTZWxlY3Rpb25MXNORm9ybTv
lnqnmobrskabgo4UsMTs+Oz4wgoihXbOTW6mZrbyMoJ9auczf3g=="/><postfield name="__EVENT
TARGET" value="SelListCmd"/><postfield name="SelectionList1" value="$$(Selection
List1:noesc)"/>
    </go>
  </do>
  <p> <select iname="SelectionList1" multiple="true">
      <option>Maria Anders</option>
      <option>Ana Trujillo</option>
      <option>Antonio Moreno</option>
      <option>Thomas Hardy</option>
      <option>Christina Berglund</option>
      <option>Hanna Moos</option>
      <option>Frederique Citeaux</option>
      <option>Martin Sommer</option>
      <option>Laurence Lebihan</option>
      <option>Elizabeth Lincoln</option>
    </select>
  </p>
```

The Submit command control event handling iterates through the Items collection, retrieves the names, and appends the item's Text value to the Label control's Text value:

```
private void SelListCmd_Click(object sender, System.EventArgs e)
{
    string results = "";
    foreach (MobileListItem item in SelectionList1.Items)
    {
        if (item.Selected)
        {
            if (results.Length == 0)
                results += " " + item.Text;
            else
                results += ", " + item.Text;
        }
    }
    SelectionListResults.Text = "Selected names:" + results;
}
```

The selected items are displayed at the top of the mobile Web Form in the contents of a Label control. You can see this by the display in the browsers in Figure 10-16.

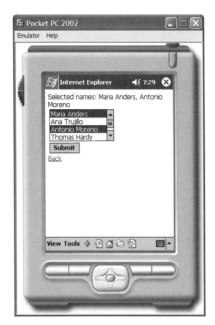

Figure 10-16. The SelectionList *control after selection in Pocket IE and a WML emulator*

The ObjectList Control

ObjectList is the most advanced list control and is recommended when you data-bind to a complex data source, such as a set of database rows. It is the closest mobile server control to the DataGrid control for mobile device development. Not only does it support command event generation and pagination, but it also provides two different displays modes in either a master list or detail format. The displayed fields from its data source are configurable, as is the final output via templates like those we discuss in Chapter 7.

Figure 10-17 shows the master list view of the ObjectList control when it is bound to the same Northwind Customers table list we used earlier. The resulting display is the default, which lets the ObjectList control figure out the fields to display in the list and detailed views.

Figure 10-17. The ObjectList *control rendered in Pocket IE and a WML emulator*

The ObjectList control renders as an HTML table in its master view:

```
<table border=0 width="100%">
<tr><td><font size="+1"><b>CustomerID</b></font></td></tr>
<tr><td colspan=2 bgcolor="#000000"></td></tr>
<tr><td><a href="javascript:__doPostBack('ObjectList1','__more0')" >
ALFKI</a></td></tr>
<tr><td><a href="javascript:__doPostBack('ObjectList1','__more1')" >
ANATR</a></td></tr>
<tr><td><a href="javascript:__doPostBack('ObjectList1','__more2')" >
ANTON</a></td></tr>
<tr><td><a href="javascript:__doPostBack('ObjectList1','__more3')" >
AROUT</a></td></tr>
<tr><td><a href="javascript:__doPostBack('ObjectList1','__more4')" >
BERGS</a></td></tr>
<tr><td><a href="javascript:__doPostBack('ObjectList1','__more5')" >
BLAUS</a></td></tr>
<tr><td><a href="javascript:__doPostBack('ObjectList1','__more6')" >
BLONP</a></td></tr>
<tr><td><a href="javascript:__doPostBack('ObjectList1','__more7')" >
BOLID</a></td></tr>
<tr><td><a href="javascript:__doPostBack('ObjectList1','__more8')" >
BONAP</a></td></tr>
<tr><td><a href="javascript:__doPostBack('ObjectList1','__more9')" >
BOTTM</a></td></tr>
<tr><td colspan=2 bgcolor="#000000"></td></tr>
</table>
```

The ObjectList control renders as a list in WML:

```
<card>
  <do type="accept" label="Go">
    <go href="#__pbc2">
      <setvar name="mcsvt" value="ObjectList1"/>
<setvar name="mcsva" value="$$(ObjectList1:noesc)"/>
    </go>
  </do>
  <p>
    <select name="ObjectList1">
      <option value="__more0">ALFKI</option>
      <option value="__more1">ANATR</option>
      <option value="__more2">ANTON</option>
      <option value="__more3">AROUT</option>
      <option value="__more4">BERGS</option>
      <option value="__more5">BLAUS</option>
      <option value="__more6">BLONP</option>
      <option value="__more7">BOLID</option>
      <option value="__more8">BONAP</option>
      <option value="__more9">BOTTM</option>
      <option value="Link6,MainForm">Back</option>
    </select>
  </p>
</card>
```

Clicking a link such as ALFKI brings up the screen shown in Figure 10-18. The list view has changed to a detail view that reveals the columns from the row of data on the customer contact.

Figure 10-18. The ObjectList *control rendered in Pocket IE and a WML emulator*

The HTML rendered is a table:

```
<table border=0 width="100%">
<tr><td colspan=2><font size="+1"><b>ALFKI</b></font></td></tr>
<tr><tr><td colspan=2 bgcolor="#000000"></td></tr>
<tr><td>CustomerID</td><td>ALFKI</td></tr>
<tr><td>ContactName</td><td>Maria Anders</td></tr>
<tr><td>ContactTitle</td><td>Sales Representative</td></tr>
<tr><td>CompanyName</td><td>Alfreds Futterkiste</td></tr>
<tr><td colspan=2 bgcolor="#000000"></td></tr>
<tr><td colspan=2><div align="Center"><font size="-1">[ 
<a href="javascript:__doPostBack('ObjectList1','__back')">Back</a> ]
</font></div></td></tr></table>
```

The WML renders as a card with both an embedded <A> tag for backward navigation and a <DO> with <GO> setup for soft key navigation back:

```
  <card>
    <do type="accept" label="Back">
      <go href="/controlsbookmobile/(dctdpwfxpqak5w4501x0op45)/ch10/listcontrols
.aspx?0oc=106&amp;__ufps=232790" method="post">
        <postfield name="__VIEWSTATE" value="aDxfX1A7QDxPYmplY3RMaXNORm9ybTvnp6P
gtJnskrvgo4UsMjs+O09iamVjdExpc3QxOOAwPHQ8O2k8Mj47aTwwPj47aTwyPjs+Oz7OEXX+LhB+g2F
I+nEUPsoCfOYM3w=="/><postfield name="__EVENTTARGET" value="ObjectList1"/><postfi
eld name="__EVENTARGUMENT" value="__back"/>
      </go>
    </do>
    <p>
      <b>
        <big>ALFKI</big>
      </b>
        <br/>CustomerID: ALFKI<br/>ContactName: Maria Anders<br/>ContactTitle: Sal
es Representative<br/>CompanyName: Alfreds Futterkiste<br/>
<anchor title="Back">Back<go
href="/controlsbookmobile/(dctdpwfxpqak5w4501x0op45)/ch10/listcontrols.a
spx?0oc=106&amp;__ufps=232790" method="post">
        <postfield name="__VIEWSTATE" value="aDxfX1A7QDxPYmplY3RMaXNORm9ybTvnp
6PgtJnskrvgo4UsMjs+O09iamVjdExpc3QxOOAwPHQ8O2k8Mj47aTwwPj47aTwyPjs+Oz7OEXX+Lh
B+g2FI+nEUPsoCfOYM3w=="/>
        <postfield name="__EVENTTARGET" value="ObjectList1"/><post
field name="__EVENTARGUMENT" value="__back"/>
      </go>
    </anchor>
    </p>
  </card>
```

This example shows that you get plenty of output for little input with the `ObjectList` control, and the output is tailored appropriately for the mobile client. We have yet to scratch the surface of this control's capabilities—it supports more advanced command generation, customizable display templates, and custom field selection to use on both its list and detail displays.

The Image, AdRotator, and Calendar Controls

The Image and AdRotator controls support the capability to display an image in the mobile device browser. The difference between the two controls is whether the choice is static or dynamic based on who is visiting for advertisement purposes. We have added the Calendar control to the discussion because this topic is as good as any to cover it in. It is probably the richest control in the mobile space outside of ObjectList. Table 10-4 describes these three controls.

Table 10-4. Image Mobile Controls

NAME	HTML TAG	WML TAG	DESCRIPTION
Image	`<a href="">`	`<DO>` and `<GO>`	Links to a new URL or deck
AdRotator	`<a href="">`	`<DO>` and `<GO>`	Links to a new URL or deck
Calendar	`<TABLE>`	`<DO>`, `<GO>`, and `<SELECT>`	Permits the selection of a date

Listings 10-8 and 10-9 present the ImageAdCalendar.aspx Web Form that demonstrates these controls. Listing 10-10 shows the advertisement file.

Listing 10-8. The ImageAdCalendar.aspx Mobile Web Form Page

```
<%@ Page language="c#" Codebehind="ImageAdCalendar.aspx.cs"
Inherits="ControlsBookMobile.Ch10.ImageAddCalendar" AutoEventWireup="false"
%>
<%@ Register TagPrefix="mobile" Namespace="System.Web.UI.MobileControls"
Assembly="System.Web.Mobile" %>
<HEAD>
  <meta name="GENERATOR" content="Microsoft Visual Studio .NET 7.1">
  <meta name="CODE_LANGUAGE" content="C#">
  <meta name="vs_targetSchema" content="http://schemas.microsoft.com/Mobile/Page">
</HEAD>
<body Xmlns:mobile="http://schemas.microsoft.com/Mobile/WebForm">
  <mobile:Form id="MainForm" runat="server">
    <mobile:Link id="Link1" runat="server" NavigateUrl="#ImageAdForm">
Image AdRotator Form</mobile:Link>
    <mobile:Link id="Link2" runat="server"
NavigateUrl="#CalendarForm">Calendar Form</mobile:Link>
  </mobile:Form>
  <mobile:Form id="ImageAdForm" runat="server">
    <mobile:AdRotator id="AdRotator1" runat="server"
AdvertisementFile="ads.xml"></mobile:AdRotator>
    <mobile:Image id="Image1" runat="server" AlternateText="Microsoft"
ImageUrl="mslogo.bmp"></mobile:Image>
  </mobile:Form>
  <mobile:Form id="CalendarForm" runat="server">
    <mobile:Label id="CalResult" runat="server"></mobile:Label>
    <mobile:Calendar id="Calendar1" runat="server"></mobile:Calendar>
  </mobile:Form>
</body>
```

Listing 10-9. The ImageAdCalendar.aspx Code-Behind Class

```
using System;
using System.Collections;
using System.ComponentModel;
using System.Data;
using System.Drawing;
using System.Web;
using System.Web.Mobile;
using System.Web.SessionState;
using System.Web.UI;
using System.Web.UI.MobileControls;
using System.Web.UI.WebControls;
using System.Web.UI.HtmlControls;
using System.Data.SqlClient;

namespace ControlsBookMobile.Ch10
{
    public class ImageAddCalendar : System.Web.UI.MobileControls.MobilePage
    {
        protected System.Web.UI.MobileControls.Form MainForm;
        protected System.Web.UI.MobileControls.Link Link1;
        protected System.Web.UI.MobileControls.Form ImageAdForm;
        protected System.Web.UI.MobileControls.Link Link2;
        protected System.Web.UI.MobileControls.Image Image1;
        protected System.Web.UI.MobileControls.AdRotator AdRotator1;
        protected System.Web.UI.MobileControls.Calendar Calendar1;
        protected System.Web.UI.MobileControls.Label CalResult;
        protected System.Web.UI.MobileControls.Label ChoiceLabel;
        protected System.Web.UI.MobileControls.Form CalendarForm;


        #region Web Form Designer generated code
        override protected void OnInit(EventArgs e)
        {
            //
            // CODEGEN: This call is required by the ASP.NET Web Form Designer.
            //
            InitializeComponent();
            base.OnInit(e);
        }

        /// <summary>
        /// Required method for Designer support - do not modify
        /// the contents of this method with the code editor.
        /// </summary>
        private void InitializeComponent()
        {
            this.Calendar1.SelectionChanged += new
System.EventHandler(this.Calendar1_SelectionChanged);
```

```
        }
        #endregion

        private void Calendar1_SelectionChanged(object sender, System.EventArgs e)
        {
            DateTime date = Calendar1.SelectedDate;
            CalResult.Text = "Selected " + date.ToShortDateString();
        }
    }
}
```

Listing 10-10. The ads.xml AdRotator *Advertisement File*

```xml
<?xml version="1.0" encoding="utf-8" ?>
<Advertisements>
  <Ad>
    <ImageUrl>microsoft.gif</ImageUrl>
    <NavigateUrl>http://www.microsoft.com</NavigateUrl>
    <AlternateText>Visit Microsoft's Site</AlternateText>
    <Impressions>80</Impressions>
    <Keyword>ProductInfo</Keyword>
  </Ad>
  <Ad>
    <ImageUrl>technet.gif</ImageUrl>
    <NavigateUrl>http://www.microsoft.com/technet</NavigateUrl>
    <AlternateText>Support for IT Professionals</AlternateText>
    <Impressions>40</Impressions>
    <Keyword>Support</Keyword>
  </Ad>
  <Ad>
    <ImageUrl>msdn.gif</ImageUrl>
    <NavigateUrl>http://msdn.microsoft.com</NavigateUrl>
    <AlternateText>Support for developers</AlternateText>
    <Impressions>40</Impressions>
    <Keyword>Support</Keyword>
  </Ad>
</Advertisements>
```

The mobile web page has two forms that demonstrate the image-related controls and the Calendar control. Figure 10-19 shows the ImageAd form in the HTML and WML browsers.

Figure 10-19. The Image *and* AdRotator *controls first hit, as rendered in Pocket IE and a WML emulator*

The HTML device was able to display images for both the AdRotator control and the Image control because they used the .gif and .bmp formats, respectively:

```
<a href="http://msdn.microsoft.com">
<img src="/controlsbookmobile/ch10/msdn.gif" alt="Support for developers"
border="0" />
</a>
<br>
<img src="mslogo.bmp" alt="Microsoft" border="0" />
```

Because the mobile phone WML browser uses a different image format—namely .wbmp, which is optimized for low-bandwidth networks—the WML browser opted to display the AlternateText property value for both controls:

```
<card id="ImageAdForm">
<do type="accept" label="Link">
<go href="http://msdn.microsoft.com" />
</do>
<p><a href="http://msdn.microsoft.com" title="Link">
<img src="/controlsbookmobile/ch10/msdn.gif" alt="Support for developers" />
</a>
<br/>
```

```
<img src="/controlsbookmobile/(k0jd32nx4e3caceu3wgw2qb4)/ch10/mslogo.bmp"
alt="Microsoft" />
</p>
</card>
```

If you recycle the form several times, you will get different values, as shown in Figure 10-20. This shows how the advertisement XML file is used to select different images and URLs for rendering by the AdRotator control.

Figure 10-20. The Image *and* AdRotator *controls recycled and rendered in Pocket IE and a WML emulator*

The other mobile Web Form in the ImageAdCalendar .aspx page hosts the Calendar control and is named CalendarForm. It generates a large amount of output for a small amount of input, as shown in Figure 10-21. This figure shows the wide dichotomy between the HTML and WML methods for displaying due to reduced screen real-estate. The figure shows the Calendar control before input is made on it to select a date.

Figure 10-21. The Calendar *control rendered in Pocket IE and a WML emulator*

The HTML calendar is rendered in markup as a fairly sophisticated HTML table:

```
<table cellspacing="0" cellpadding="2" border="0" style="border-
width:1px;border-style:solid;font-size:Medium;border-collapse:collapse;">
    <tr><td colspan="7" style="background-color:Silver;"><table cellspacing="0"
border="0" style="font-size:Medium;width:100%;border-collapse:collapse;">
        <tr><td style="width:15%;"><a
href="javascript:__doPostBack('_ctl2','V1096')"
style="color:Black">&lt;</a></td><td align="Center" style="width:70%;">February
2003</td><td align="Right" style="width:15%;"><a
href="javascript:__doPostBack('_ctl2','V1155')"
style="color:Black">&gt;</a></td></tr>
    </table></td></tr><tr><td align="Center">Sun</td><td
align="Center">Mon</td><td align="Center">Tue</td><td align="Center">Wed</td><td
align="Center">Thu</td><td align="Center">Fri</td><td
align="Center">Sat</td></tr><tr><td align="Center" style="width:14%;"><a
href="javascript:__doPostBack('_ctl2','1121')"
style="color:Black">26</a></td><td align="Center" style="width:14%;"><a
href="javascript:__doPostBack('_ctl2','1122')"
style="color:Black">27</a></td><td align="Center" style="width:14%;"><a
href="javascript:__doPostBack('_ctl2','1123')"
style="color:Black">28</a></td><td align="Center" style="width:14%;"><a
href="javascript:__doPostBack('_ctl2','1124')"
style="color:Black">29</a></td><td align="Center" style="width:14%;"><a
href="javascript:__doPostBack('_ctl2','1125')"
style="color:Black">30</a></td><td align="Center" style="width:14%;"><a
```

```
href="javascript:__doPostBack('_ctl2','1126')"
style="color:Black">31</a></td><td align="Center" style="width:14%;"><a
href="javascript:__doPostBack('_ctl2','1127')"
style="color:Black">1</a></td></tr><tr><td align="Center" style="width:14%;"><a
href="javascript:__doPostBack('_ctl2','1128')" style="color:Black">2</a></td><td
align="Center" style="width:14%;"><a
href="javascript:__doPostBack('_ctl2','1129')" style="color:Black">3</a></td><td
align="Center" style="width:14%;"><a
href="javascript:__doPostBack('_ctl2','1130')" style="color:Black">4</a></td><td
align="Center" style="width:14%;"><a
href="javascript:__doPostBack('_ctl2','1131')" style="color:Black">5</a></td><td
align="Center" style="width:14%;"><a
href="javascript:__doPostBack('_ctl2','1132')" style="color:Black">6</a></td><td
align="Center" style="width:14%;"><a
href="javascript:__doPostBack('_ctl2','1133')" style="color:Black">7</a></td><td
align="Center" style="width:14%;"><a
href="javascript:__doPostBack('_ctl2','1134')"
style="color:Black">8</a></td></tr><tr><td align="Center" style="width:14%;"><a
href="javascript:__doPostBack('_ctl2','1135')" style="color:Black">9</a></td><td
align="Center" style="width:14%;"><a
href="javascript:__doPostBack('_ctl2','1136')"
style="color:Black">10</a></td><td align="Center" style="width:14%;"><a
href="javascript:__doPostBack('_ctl2','1137')"
style="color:Black">11</a></td><td align="Center" style="width:14%;"><a
href="javascript:__doPostBack('_ctl2','1138')"
style="color:Black">12</a></td><td align="Center" style="width:14%;"><a
href="javascript:__doPostBack('_ctl2','1139')"
style="color:Black">13</a></td><td align="Center" style="width:14%;"><a
href="javascript:__doPostBack('_ctl2','1140')"
style="color:Black">14</a></td><td align="Center" style="width:14%;"><a
href="javascript:__doPostBack('_ctl2','1141')"
style="color:Black">15</a></td></tr><tr><td align="Center" style="width:14%;"><a
href="javascript:__doPostBack('_ctl2','1142')"
style="color:Black">16</a></td><td align="Center" style="width:14%;"><a
href="javascript:__doPostBack('_ctl2','1143')"
style="color:Black">17</a></td><td align="Center" style="width:14%;"><a
href="javascript:__doPostBack('_ctl2','1144')"
style="color:Black">18</a></td><td align="Center" style="width:14%;"><a
href="javascript:__doPostBack('_ctl2','1145')"
style="color:Black">19</a></td><td align="Center" style="width:14%;"><a
href="javascript:__doPostBack('_ctl2','1146')"
style="color:Black">20</a></td><td align="Center" style="width:14%;"><a
href="javascript:__doPostBack('_ctl2','1147')"
style="color:Black">21</a></td><td align="Center" style="width:14%;"><a
href="javascript:__doPostBack('_ctl2','1148')"
style="color:Black">22</a></td></tr><tr><td align="Center" style="width:14%;"><a
href="javascript:__doPostBack('_ctl2','1149')"
style="color:Black">23</a></td><td align="Center" style="width:14%;"><a
href="javascript:__doPostBack('_ctl2','1150')"
style="color:Black">24</a></td><td align="Center" style="width:14%;"><a
href="javascript:__doPostBack('_ctl2','1151')"
```

```
style="color:Black">25</a></td><td align="Center" style="width:14%;"><a
href="javascript:__doPostBack('_ctl2','1152')"
style="color:Black">26</a></td><td align="Center" style="width:14%;"><a
href="javascript:__doPostBack('_ctl2','1153')"
style="color:Black">27</a></td><td align="Center" style="width:14%;"><a
href="javascript:__doPostBack('_ctl2','1154')"
style="color:Black">28</a></td><td align="Center" style="width:14%;"><a
href="javascript:__doPostBack('_ctl2','1155')"
style="color:Black">1</a></td></tr><tr><td align="Center" style="width:14%;"><a
href="javascript:__doPostBack('_ctl2','1156')" style="color:Black">2</a></td><td
align="Center" style="width:14%;"><a
href="javascript:__doPostBack('_ctl2','1157')" style="color:Black">3</a></td><td
align="Center" style="width:14%;"><a
href="javascript:__doPostBack('_ctl2','1158')" style="color:Black">4</a></td><td
align="Center" style="width:14%;"><a
href="javascript:__doPostBack('_ctl2','1159')" style="color:Black">5</a></td><td
align="Center" style="width:14%;"><a
href="javascript:__doPostBack('_ctl2','1160')" style="color:Black">6</a></td><td
align="Center" style="width:14%;"><a
href="javascript:__doPostBack('_ctl2','1161')" style="color:Black">7</a></td><td
align="Center" style="width:14%;"><a
href="javascript:__doPostBack('_ctl2','1162')"
style="color:Black">8</a></td></tr>
</table>
```

The WML version renders as a series of cards that provide options to type in a date or choose a month and drill down to a date.

The Validation Controls

The incredibly useful validation controls have made the transition from the traditional ASP.NET Web Form to the mobile Web Form. They have the same names and functions, so not much review is necessary. Table 10-5 provides a high-level overview of these controls.

Table 10-5. Validation Mobile Controls

NAME	HTML TAG	WML TAG	DESCRIPTION
CompareValidator	`<a href="">`	`<DO>` and `<GO>`	Links to new URL or deck
CustomValidator	`<a href="">`	`<DO>` and `<GO>`	Links to new URL or deck
RangeValidator	`<a href="">`	`<DO>` and `<GO>`	Links to new URL or deck
RegularExpressionValidator	`<a href="">`	`<DO>` and `<GO>`	Links to new URL or deck
RequiredFieldValidator	`<a href="">`	`<DO>` and `<GO>`	Links to new URL or deck
ValidationSummary	`<a href="">`	`<DO>` and `<GO>`	Links to new URL or deck

What we do need to discuss is how these controls are designed to render on a mobile phone device. Because the display is limited on a mobile phone, the error message itself can take up the entire screen. For this reason, a common design pattern is to forego displaying the error message inline with the input tag. Instead, a separate mobile Web Form should be designated to host a ValidationSummary control to display the message.

The mobile version of the ValidationSummary control is enhanced with a Back link feature to better fit into the mobile design pattern. This is a nice example of the type of customization you should provide when designing your custom mobile server controls.

An example of using the RequiredFieldValidator, RangeValidator, and ValidationSummary controls is provided in Listings 10-11 and 10-12.

Listing 10-11. The ValidationControls.aspx Mobile Web Form Page

```
<%@ Register TagPrefix="mobile" Namespace="System.Web.UI.MobileControls"
Assembly="System.Web.Mobile" %>
<%@ Page language="c#" Codebehind="ValidationControls.aspx.cs"
Inherits="ControlsBookMobile.Ch10.ValidationControls" AutoEventWireup="false"
%>
<HEAD>
  <meta name="GENERATOR" content="Microsoft Visual Studio .NET 7.1">
  <meta name="CODE_LANGUAGE" content="C#">
  <meta name="vs_targetSchema" content="http://schemas.microsoft.com/Mobile/Page">
</HEAD>
<body Xmlns:mobile="http://schemas.microsoft.com/Mobile/WebForm">
  <mobile:Form id="InputForm" runat="server">
    <mobile:Label id="Label1" runat="server">
Enter a number between 1 and 10</mobile:Label>
    <mobile:TextBox id="NumberTextBox" runat="server"></mobile:TextBox>
    <mobile:Command id="Command1" runat="server">Submit</mobile:Command>
    <mobile:RequiredFieldValidator id="RequiredFieldValidator1"
runat="server" ErrorMessage="Number entry is required."
      ControlToValidate="NumberTextBox"></mobile:RequiredFieldValidator>
    <mobile:RangeValidator id="RangeValidator1" runat="server"
ErrorMessage="Number must be between 1 and 10."
      ControlToValidate="NumberTextBox" MaximumValue="10" MinimumValue="1"
Type="Integer"></mobile:RangeValidator>
  </mobile:Form>
  <mobile:Form id="ErrorForm" runat="server">
    <P>An Error Occurred:
<mobile:ValidationSummary id="ValidationSummary1" runat="server"
FormToValidate="InputForm"></mobile:ValidationSummary></P>
  </mobile:Form>
  <mobile:Form id="SuccessForm" runat="server">You have successfully entered:
<mobile:Label id="ResultNumber" runat="server"></mobile:Label></mobile:Form>
</body>
```

Listing 10-12. The ValidationControls.aspx Code-Behind Class

```
using System;
using System.Collections;
using System.ComponentModel;
using System.Data;
using System.Drawing;
using System.Web;
using System.Web.Mobile;
using System.Web.SessionState;
using System.Web.UI;
using System.Web.UI.MobileControls;
using System.Web.UI.WebControls;
using System.Web.UI.HtmlControls;

namespace ControlsBookMobile.Ch10
{
    public class ValidationControls : System.Web.UI.MobileControls.MobilePage
    {
        protected System.Web.UI.MobileControls.Form InputForm;
        protected System.Web.UI.MobileControls.RequiredFieldValidator
        RequiredFieldValidator1;
        protected System.Web.UI.MobileControls.RangeValidator RangeValidator1;
        protected System.Web.UI.MobileControls.Form ErrorForm;
        protected System.Web.UI.MobileControls.Label Label1;
        protected System.Web.UI.MobileControls.ValidationSummary ValidationSummary1;
        protected System.Web.UI.MobileControls.TextBox NumberTextBox;
        protected System.Web.UI.MobileControls.Form SuccessForm;
        protected System.Web.UI.MobileControls.Label ResultNumber;
        protected System.Web.UI.MobileControls.Command Command1;


        #region Web Form Designer generated code
        override protected void OnInit(EventArgs e)
        {
            //
            // CODEGEN: This call is required by the ASP.NET Web Form Designer.
            //
            InitializeComponent();
            base.OnInit(e);
        }

        /// <summary>
        /// Required method for Designer support - do not modify
        /// the contents of this method with the code editor.
        /// </summary>
        private void InitializeComponent()
        {
```

```
        this.SuccessForm.Activate += new
System.EventHandler(this.SuccessForm_Activate);
        this.Command1.Click += new System.EventHandler(this.Command1_Click);


    }
    #endregion

    private void Command1_Click(object sender, System.EventArgs e)
    {
        if (Page.IsValid)
            this.ActiveForm = SuccessForm;
        else
            this.ActiveForm = ErrorForm;
    }

    private void SuccessForm_Activate(object sender, System.EventArgs e)
    {
        ResultNumber.Text = NumberTextBox.Text;
    }
  }
}
```

The default active mobile Web Form contains a TextBox control to receive input from the user. The RequiredFieldValidator control ensures that a value is entered, and the RangeValidator control ensures that the value is a number between 1 and 10. When the user sends input to the server that fails validation, the result is transferred to the error mobile Web Form. As shown in the following code, we use the page-level validation property IsValid to determine the results of the validation effort. Figure 10-22 displays a validation error in Pocket IE and a WML emulator.

```
private void Command1_Click(object sender, System.EventArgs e)
{
    if (Page.IsValid)
        this.ActiveForm = SuccessForm;
    else
        this.ActiveForm = ErrorForm;
}
```

Figure 10-22. The validation control error rendered in Pocket IE and a WML emulator

The validation control, though placed on a different mobile Web Form named ErrorForm, is hooked up to the input of the original Web Form via its `FormToValidate` property. This allows it to capture the `ErrorMessage` properties from the `RequiredFieldValidator` and `RangeValidator` controls.

The display of the `ValidationSummary` control includes a Back link to the original input mobile Web Form. This forces the user to follow the Back link and input a valid value. Here is the rendered HTML that enforces this:

```
    An Error Occurred:
<font color="Red"><ul>
<li>Number must be between 1 and 10.</li>
</ul>
<a href="javascript:__doPostBack('_ctl4','InputForm')">Back</a></font>
```

The rendered WML is as follows:

```
  <card>
    <do type="accept" label="Back">
      <go href="/controlsbookmobile/(enrhy045kop2nn3bwtdi1w45)/ch10/validationco
ntrols.aspx?Ooc=106&amp;__ufps=709407" method="post">
        <postfield name="__VIEWSTATE" value="aDxfX1A7QDxFcnJvckZvcm077ZuI7Jed7JW
a4KOFLDA7Pjs+XyhCz/ONI3ZgdS9CRUJqjTX4RoU="/><postfield name="__EVENTTARGET" valu
e="_ctl4"/><postfield name="__EVENTARGUMENT" value="InputForm"/>
```

```
    </go>
  </do>
  <p>An Error Occurred: Number must be between 1 and 10.<br/>
<anchor title="Back">Back
<go href="/controlsbookmobile/(enrhy045kop2nn3bwtdi1w45)/ch10/validation
controls.aspx?Ooc=106&amp;__ufps=709407" method="post">
        <postfield name="__VIEWSTATE" value="aDxfX1A7QDxFcnJvckZvcmO77ZuI7Jed7
JWa4KOFLDA7Pjs+XyhCz/ONI3ZgdS9CRUJqjTX4RoU="/><postfield name="__EVENTTARGET" va
lue="_ctl4"/>
<postfield name="__EVENTARGUMENT" value="InputForm"/>
      </go>
    </anchor>
  </p>
</card>
```

Once input passes validation, a success message is displayed. The validation controls do their job well.

In the next section, we move on to cover container controls and pagination. Pagination is an especially important topic because most WML mobile phone devices are limited to displaying four lines of content at a time.

The Container Controls and Pagination

The controls discussed previously in this chapter display information. The controls covered in this section, however, provide content management via containment. Table 10-6 summarizes the container controls. You are already familiar with the Form control as a means of grouping together mobile server controls in a nice package on a MobilePage web page. The Panel control is an option for containing controls within a mobile Web Form.

Using a Panel control within a form is a handy way to group controls together. For instance, you may want to make a group of controls visible or not visible, en masse. Setting the Visible property on a Panel control to false will cause the controls contained by the Panel control to have the same value for their Visible property. In general, controls placed in a Panel control inherit style properties from the Panel container, although a control can override a particular style property if desired.

Table 10-6. Container Mobile Controls

NAME	HTML TAG	WML TAG	DESCRIPTION
Form	<a href="">	<DO> and <GO>	Links to a new URL or deck
Panel	<a href="">	<DO> and <GO>	Links to a new URL or deck

Pagination is an important capability in mobile server controls because most WML devices only support anywhere from two to ten lines of content onscreen, with each line containing just a few characters.

Controls that support pagination inherit from `PagedControl` instead of `MobileControl`. For example, the `List`, `ObjectList`, and `LiteralText` classes all inherit from `PagedControl`. When you build your own custom mobile server controls, consider inheriting form `PagedControl` if your control is capable of rendering a large amount of text.

The `Form` and `Panel` controls are containers that support pagination of their child control content. For example, the `Paginate` property of the `Panel` mobile server control is a suggestion to the runtime to keep the controls on the `Panel` together when paginating a mobile Web Form. Likewise, enabling pagination on a `Form` control provides support to mobile devices with limited screen area by permitting content to be spread across multiple views.

The ContainerControls sample is a mobile web page that demonstrates the use of two panels inside a single mobile Web Form as a way of managing content. It uses the `Visibility` property of the two `Panel` controls to determine which panel renders. The default `Panel` control, QueryPanel, takes as input a portion of a name that relates to a like-named customer in the SQL Server sample Northwind database. The second `Panel` control, ResultsPanel, is initially kept hidden but is made visible when a query is completed to display the search results in the contained data-bound `List` control. The code that accomplishes this is shown in Listings 10-13 and 10-14.

Listing 10-13. The ContainerControls.aspx Mobile Web Form Page

```
<%@ Page language="c#" Codebehind="ContainerControls.aspx.cs"
Inherits="ControlsBookMobile.Ch10.ContainerControls" AutoEventWireup="false"
%>
<%@ Register TagPrefix="mobile" Namespace="System.Web.UI.MobileControls"
Assembly="System.Web.Mobile" %>
<HEAD>
  <meta name="GENERATOR" content="Microsoft Visual Studio .NET 7.1">
  <meta name="CODE_LANGUAGE" content="C#">
  <meta name="vs_targetSchema" content="http://schemas.microsoft.com/Mobile/Page">
</HEAD>
<body Xmlns:mobile="http://schemas.microsoft.com/Mobile/WebForm">
  <mobile:Form id="PanelForm" runat="server" Paginate="True">
    <mobile:Panel id="QueryPanel" runat="server">
      <mobile:Label id="Label1" runat="server">Query by Contact
      Name:</mobile:Label>
      <mobile:TextBox id="PanelFormTextBox" runat="server"></mobile:TextBox>
      <mobile:Command id="PanelFormCmd" runat="server">Submit</mobile:Command>
    </mobile:Panel>
    <mobile:Panel id="ResultsPanel" Paginate="True" runat="server" Visible="False">
      <mobile:List id="PanelList" runat="server" ItemsPerPage="10"
Decoration="Numbered"></mobile:List>
    </mobile:Panel>
  </mobile:Form>
</body>
```

Listing 10-14. The ContainerControls.aspx Code-Behind Class

```
using System;
using System.Collections;
using System.ComponentModel;
using System.Data;
using System.Drawing;
using System.Web;
using System.Web.Mobile;
using System.Web.SessionState;
using System.Web.UI;
using System.Web.UI.MobileControls;
using System.Web.UI.WebControls;
using System.Web.UI.HtmlControls;


namespace ControlsBookMobile.Ch10
{
    public class ContainerControls : System.Web.UI.MobileControls.MobilePage
    {
        protected System.Web.UI.MobileControls.Form PanelForm;
        protected System.Web.UI.MobileControls.List PanelList;
        protected System.Web.UI.MobileControls.Panel ResultsPanel;
        protected System.Web.UI.MobileControls.Label Label1;
        protected System.Web.UI.MobileControls.TextBox PanelFormTextBox;
        protected System.Web.UI.MobileControls.Command PanelFormCmd;
        protected System.Web.UI.MobileControls.Panel QueryPanel;


        #region Web Form Designer generated code
        override protected void OnInit(EventArgs e)
        {
            //
            // CODEGEN: This call is required by the ASP.NET Web Form Designer.
            //
            InitializeComponent();
            base.OnInit(e);
        }

        /// <summary>
        /// Required method for Designer support - do not modify
        /// the contents of this method with the code editor.
        /// </summary>
        private void InitializeComponent()
        {
            this.PanelFormCmd.Click += new
System.EventHandler(this.PanelFormCmd_Click);
            this.PanelForm.Activate += new
System.EventHandler(this.PanelForm_Activate);
```

```
    }
    #endregion

    private DataSet GetCustomersData(string Name)
    {
        return CustDB.GetCustomersByName(Name,"20");
    }

    private void PanelForm_Activate(object sender, System.EventArgs e)
    {
        PanelList.DataSource = GetCustomersData(PanelFormTextBox.Text);
        PanelList.DataMember = "Customers";
        PanelList.DataTextField = "ContactName";
        PanelList.DataBind();
    }

    private void PanelFormCmd_Click(object sender, System.EventArgs e)
    {
        ActiveForm = PanelForm;
        QueryPanel.Visible = false;
        ResultsPanel.Visible = true;
    }
  }
}
```

Figure 10-23 shows the starting screen on both WML and HTML browsers.

Figure 10-23. The ContainerControls sample with the QueryPanel *visible on Pocket IE and a WML emulator*

Enter in a string and click the Submit button to launch a query that returns a maximum of 20 rows from the Customers table that match the characters of the input. The `Page` class and the `ResultsPanel Panel` control are configured with their `Paginate` property set to true. Additionally, the `List` control that binds to the data has its `ItemsPerPage` setting configured to 10. This breaks the first screen shown in Figure 10-24 into ten items.

Figure 10-24. The ContainerControls sample results, page 1

The controls are smart enough to render a Next link to manage the paging process for the developer. This happens both with the HTML and WML versions of content. Figure 10-25 shows what happens when you click the Next link. It shows the final ten results and gives you the ability to go back to the previous entries.

Figure 10-25. The ContainerControls sample results, page 2

If you examine the WML generated with the Panel-centric approach, you will see that there is just a single WML card rendered in each deck. This is a concern to keep in mind when you design the containment and organization of your mobile web pages. This section concludes our whirlwind tour of mobile ASP.NET development.

Summary

In this chapter, we examined the similarities and differences between mobile and traditional ASP.NET development. We discussed the idiosyncrasies of mobile development with respect to mobile device capabilities and how various UI mobile server controls render output in a device specific or optimized manner.

Developing mobile web applications has traditionally been a complex and tedious undertaking due to the need to address the plethora of device capabilities and ever-changing content markup specifications. Mobile controls in the ASP.NET framework provide a great foundation for building mobile web applications by allowing the mobile developer to focus on content instead of infrastructure. System.Web.UI.MobileControls is the primary namespace for mobile controls. The MobilePage class inherits fromSystem.Web.UI.Page and can contain multiple mobile Web Forms of the class System.Web.UI.MobileControls.Form.

Mobile web pages and mobile server controls provide a similar design and development experience to their traditional ASP.NET counterparts, yet they automatically take into account display limitations on mobile devices. The List, SelectionList, and ObjectList controls provide the ability to render a collection of data to support mobile web development. Pagination is an important capability to assist with rendering content on limited display sizes. The PagedControl class serves as the base class for controls that require pagination. Container controls such as the Panel and Form classes support pagination by helping to organize contained controls for rendering. You enable pagination on a mobile Web Form to prevent errors when web page size exceeds the capabilities of a mobile device to fit the form on a single screen.

In this chapter, we alluded to capabilities and behaviors of the built-in mobile server controls that you might want to include in your own custom mobile server control development efforts. In the next chapter, we cover how to implement custom mobile server controls and provide additional background on the architecture and design considerations when doing so.

CHAPTER 11

Customizing and Implementing Mobile Controls

ASP.NET MOBILE SERVER CONTROLS provide a rich, extensible framework for delivering content viewable on a wide array of mobile devices. In the previous chapter, we looked at out-of-the-box controls and the feature set available in .NET Framework version 1.1 as a means to examine mobile server control technology. In this chapter, we drill down into extensibility and customization mechanisms available to mobile server control developers. The extensibility hooks fall into the following categories:

- The StyleSheet control

- Templates

- Device-specific UI choices

- User controls

- Custom controls

- Device adapters

The StyleSheet class can provide a consistent look and feel in terms of styling objects such as Font across a set of controls, a mobile form, or mobile forms. Templates provide a mechanism to customize how content renders, such as what controls display content using the techniques discussed in Chapter 7. Device-specific UI customization is available with both of these techniques, as is customizing the attributes of a control based on the target device. Developers have the option to stay within the abstraction layer provide by the Framework or, if desired or required, they can specify alternate content to render on specific devices. The flexible detection engine built into ASP.NET makes this magic happen, greatly simplifying mobile web development without giving up fine-grained control.

The final two sections of this chapter cover the custom control opportunities discussed earlier in the book for traditional ASP.NET development: user controls and custom controls. Both techniques are available for mobile server control development, with the addition of mobile device capability management. The section covering mobile controls in this chapter examines how mobile controls emit device-specific output with the help of device adapters.

The StyleSheet Control

A couple of options are available to apply styles to controls in the mobile control framework. One option is to configure style attributes on individual controls. This yields increased maintenance as the number of individually configured controls increases, which is not optimal. The other option is the StyleSheet control, which provides a method to attach a consistent look and feel across multiple controls, centralizing style maintenance to one location. ASP.NET provides a default StyleSheet control with three styles elements named error, subcommand, and title. Table 11-1 shows how each is configured.

Table 11-1. Default StyleSheet *Styles Provided by ASP.NET*

STYLE	CONFIGURATION
error	ForeColor=red
subcommand	FontSize=small
title	Font-Bold=true, FontSize=large

As with other, similar style-handling mechanisms such as CSS, the StyleSheet class simplifies maintenance by providing a named Style element that represents a collection of style attributes. Due to widely varying device capabilities, StyleSheet Style elements provide access to common features that apply across a wide range of devices, particularly those relating to textual display.

Every mobile control contains an internal Style object inherited from the MobileControl class that is not directly accessible. Instead, Style attributes on the internal Style object can be customized through public properties:

- Font (Bold, Italic, Name, Size)

- Background color

- Foreground color

- Alignment (Left, Center, Right, NotSet)

- Wrapping (Wrap, NoWrap, NotSet)

- DeviceSpecific

Other controls, or your own custom mobile server controls, can have custom Style classes that inherit from the base Style class. For example, the Form class has a custom style class named PagerStyle that inherits from the default Style class to provide access to additional styling customization with respect to pagination. The ability to provide custom style classes to support custom control development is similar to traditional ASP.NET development, as covered in Chapter 6.

Once a StyleSheet object is placed on the mobile page from the Toolbox, you can configure it by right-clicking the StyleSheet object to display its context menu and selecting Edit Styles to display the ExternalStyleSheet – Styles Editor dialog box. This dialog box is shown in Figure 11-1.

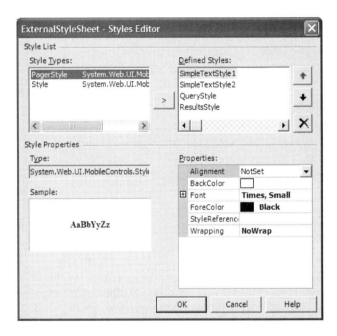

Figure 11-1. The Visual Studio .NET styles editor

 NOTE *You can place only one* StyleSheet *object on a mobile page. An error message will display if you try to add another* StyleSheet *object to a mobile page.*

After configuring a few styles on the StyleSheet object, we can apply these styles to controls. Controls gain access to StyleSheet styles through the StyleReference property inherited from MobileControl. The StyleReference drop-down list automatically populates with the default styles in addition to the custom styles we defined in the StyleSheet control.

Mobile controls apply configured styles during the rendering process with the help of device adapters, which we discuss later in this chapter. If a control is configured with a style that will not render on a particular device requesting the page, such as a WML browser that does not support color styles, the style will be ignored. This approach ensures that content is returned to the requesting device, albeit with less style.

As we mentioned previously, a control can accept the default style provided by MobileControl, or a control can require a custom style class in order to provide additional customization options for the control user. As an example, the mobile Web Form takes a custom style class named PagerStyle that provides an easy way for the control user to customize pagination behavior. PagerStyle provides the following attributes to customize the multipage navigation UI:

- NextPageText

- PageLabel

- PreviousPageText

These attributes permit you to customize the UI. For example, if you are programmatically creating a form with Next and Previous links to the appropriate pages, you can override the text for these links by setting the value of the properties previously mentioned. You can use methods such as GetNextPageText, GetPreviousPageText, or GetPageLabel to retrieve the current value of the properties.

The StyleSheetInline Mobile Web Page

The StyleSheet control can be made available to a Web Form and its controls by embedding it inside a mobile web page. The StyleSheet control provides a container for multiple named Style subelements. This section's example StyleSheet control embeds a single Style in the StyleSheet. Our StyleSheetInline.aspx Web Form has the following inline StyleSheet:

```
<mobile:stylesheet id="InlineStyleSheet" runat="server">
  <mobile:Style Font-Size="Small" Font-Name="Times" Font-Bold="True"
ForeColor="Black" Wrapping="NoWrap"
     Name="SimpleTextStyle1"></mobile:Style>
  <mobile:Style Font-Size="Small" Font-Name="Verdana" Font-Italic="True"
ForeColor="Black" Wrapping="NoWrap"
     Name="SimpleTextStyle2"></mobile:Style>
  <mobile:Style Font-Size="Small" Font-Name="Verdana" Font-Bold="True"
ForeColor="Black" Wrapping="NoWrap"
     Name="QueryStyle"></mobile:Style>
  <mobile:Style Font-Size="Small" Font-Name="Tahoma" Font-Bold="False"
Font-Italic="True" ForeColor="Black"
     Wrapping="NoWrap" Name="ResultsStyle"></mobile:Style>
</mobile:stylesheet>
```

StyleSheet Styles are referenced through the StyleReference attribute of a control. The control sets its StyleReference property to the desired Style's name. Styles can be applied at the control or container level, with styles applied to containers propagating down to contained controls unless specifically overridden in contained controls.

The .aspx page for the StyleSheetInline.aspx Web Form is shown in Listing 11-1. It contains several Web Forms that reference the defined StyleSheet section at the bottom of the .aspx page. For completeness, we also show the mechanics of the data-binding mechanisms in Listing 11-2 for the code-behind class.

Listing 11-1. The StyleSheetInline.aspx Mobile Web Form Page

```
<%@ Register TagPrefix="mobile" Namespace="System.Web.UI.MobileControls"
Assembly="System.Web.Mobile" %>
<%@ Page language="c#" Codebehind="StyleSheetInline.aspx.cs"
Inherits="ControlsBookMobile.Ch11.StyleSheetInline" AutoEventWireup="false" %>
<HEAD>
  <meta content="Microsoft Visual Studio .NET 7.1" name="GENERATOR">
  <meta content="C#" name="CODE_LANGUAGE">
  <meta content="http://schemas.microsoft.com/Mobile/Page" name="vs_targetSchema">
</HEAD>
<body Xmlns:mobile="http://schemas.microsoft.com/Mobile/WebForm">
  <mobile:form id="MainForm" runat="server">
    <mobile:Link id="Link1" runat="server" NavigateUrl="#LabelForm">
Label Styles</mobile:Link>
    <mobile:Link id="Link2" runat="server" NavigateUrl="#QueryForm">
Paging Style</mobile:Link>
  </mobile:form>
  <mobile:form id="LabelForm" runat="server">
    <mobile:Label id="Label3" runat="server"
StyleReference="SimpleTextStyle1">Some simple text.(BoldTimes)</mobile:Label>
    <mobile:Label id="Label5" runat="server" StyleReference="title">
Some Title text.(title default style)</mobile:Label>
    <mobile:Label id="Label4" runat="server"
StyleReference="SimpleTextStyle2">More simple text.(ItalicVerdana)</mobile:Label>
    <mobile:Label id="Label6" runat="server" StyleReference="subcommand">
Some subcommand Text.(subcommand default style)</mobile:Label>
    <mobile:Label id="Label7" runat="server" StyleReference="error">
Error: Some error text.(error default style)</mobile:Label>
  </mobile:form>
  <mobile:form id="QueryForm" runat="server" StyleReference="QueryStyle">
    <mobile:Label id="Label1" runat="server">Query by Contact Name:</mobile:Label>
    <mobile:TextBox id="NameTextBox" runat="server"></mobile:TextBox>
    <mobile:Command id="QueryCmd" runat="server">Submit</mobile:Command>
  </mobile:form>
  <mobile:form id="ResultsForm" runat="server" Paginate="True"
StyleReference="ResultsStyle" PagerStyle-NextPageText="Go To Next"
    PagerStyle-PreviousPageText="Go to Previous">
    <mobile:List id="CustList" runat="server" ItemsPerPage="10"
Decoration="Numbered"></mobile:List>
  </mobile:form>
```

```
    <mobile:stylesheet id="InlineStyleSheet" runat="server">
      <mobile:Style Font-Size="Small" Font-Name="Times" Font-Bold="True"
ForeColor="Black" Wrapping="NoWrap"
        Name="SimpleTextStyle1"></mobile:Style>
      <mobile:Style Font-Size="Small" Font-Name="Verdana" Font-Italic="True"
ForeColor="Black" Wrapping="NoWrap"
        Name="SimpleTextStyle2"></mobile:Style>
      <mobile:Style Font-Size="Small" Font-Name="Verdana" Font-Bold="True"
ForeColor="Black" Wrapping="NoWrap"
        Name="QueryStyle"></mobile:Style>
      <mobile:Style Font-Size="Small" Font-Name="Tahoma" Font-Bold="False"
Font-Italic="True" ForeColor="Black"
        Wrapping="NoWrap" Name="ResultsStyle"></mobile:Style>
    </mobile:stylesheet>
</body>
```

Listing 11-2. The StyleSheetInline.aspx Code-Behind Class

```
using System;
using System.Collections;
using System.ComponentModel;
using System.Data;
using System.Drawing;
using System.Web;
using System.Web.Mobile;
using System.Web.SessionState;
using System.Web.UI;
using System.Web.UI.MobileControls;
using System.Web.UI.WebControls;
using System.Web.UI.HtmlControls;

namespace ControlsBookMobile.Ch11
{
    public class StyleSheetInline : System.Web.UI.MobileControls.MobilePage
    {
        protected System.Web.UI.MobileControls.Label Label1;
        protected System.Web.UI.MobileControls.List CustList;
        protected System.Web.UI.MobileControls.TextBox NameTextBox;
        protected System.Web.UI.MobileControls.Form QueryForm;
        protected System.Web.UI.MobileControls.Form LabelForm;
        protected System.Web.UI.MobileControls.Label Label3;
        protected System.Web.UI.MobileControls.Label Label4;
        protected System.Web.UI.MobileControls.Form MainForm;
        protected System.Web.UI.MobileControls.Form ResultsForm;
        protected System.Web.UI.MobileControls.Link Link1;
        protected System.Web.UI.MobileControls.Link Link2;
        protected System.Web.UI.MobileControls.Label Label5;
        protected System.Web.UI.MobileControls.Label Label6;
        protected System.Web.UI.MobileControls.Label Label7;
        protected System.Web.UI.MobileControls.StyleSheet InlineStyleSheet;
        protected System.Web.UI.MobileControls.Command QueryCmd;
```

```csharp
private void Page_Load(object sender, System.EventArgs e)
{
    // Put user code to initialize the page here
}

#region Web Form Designer generated code
override protected void OnInit(EventArgs e)
{
    //
    // CODEGEN: This call is required by the ASP.NET Web Form Designer.
    //
    InitializeComponent();
    base.OnInit(e);
}

/// <summary>
/// Required method for Designer support - do not modify
/// the contents of this method with the code editor.
/// </summary>
private void InitializeComponent()
{
    this.QueryCmd.Click += new System.EventHandler(this.QueryCmd_Click);
    this.Load += new System.EventHandler(this.Page_Load);

}
#endregion

private DataSet GetCustomersByName(String Name)
{
    return ControlsBookMobile.Ch10.CustDB.GetCustomersByName(Name,"40");
}

private void QueryCmd_Click(object sender, System.EventArgs e)
{
    ActiveForm = ResultsForm;

    CustList.DataSource = GetCustomersByName(NameTextBox.Text);
    CustList.DataMember = "Customers";
    CustList.DataTextField = "ContactName";
    CustList.DataBind();
}
}
}
```

Figure 11-2 shows what this mobile web page looks like in the ASP.NET Design view.

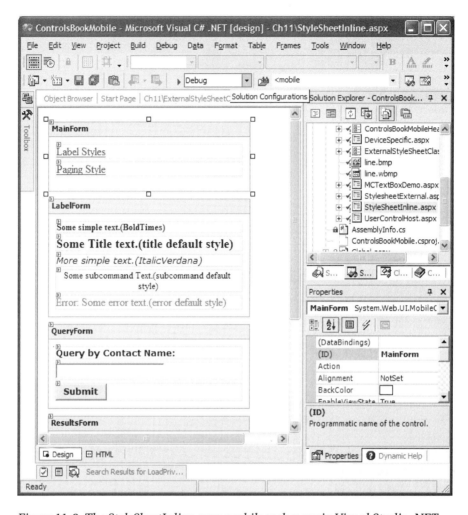

Figure 11-2. The StyleSheetInline.aspx mobile web page in Visual Studio .NET

The MainForm mobile form links to LabelForm, which displays Label controls with various Styles. LabelForm shows how easy it is to change the look and feel of the textual content by simply setting the StyleReference property to the desired Style object on the StyleSheet.

Figure 11-3 shows how LabelForm renders in both Pocket IE and in the WML browser emulator that comes with the Openwave SDK version 4.1.1.

Figure 11-3. LabelForm in Pocket IE and the WML emulator

The other link titled Paging Style on MainForm displays the QueryForm mobile Web Form. This form links to the ResultsForm Web Form and demonstrates applying Styles to a Web Form container. QueryWebForm has its StyleReference property set to QueryStyle:

```
<mobile:form id="QueryForm" runat="server" StyleReference="QueryStyle">
```

This form allows the user to search on the ContactName property of the sample SQL Server Northwind database's Customers table as we did in the previous chapter. The ResultsForm displays the results by data binding to the List control with its ItemsPerPage property set to 10. The ResultsForm has its StyleReference property set to the ResultsStyle style for rendering. In addition, you can see the PagerStyle settings that customize the Next and Previous buttons for navigating through the returned results:

```
<mobile:form id="ResultsForm" runat="server" Paginate="True"
StyleReference="ResultsStyle" PagerStyle-NextPageText="Go To Next"
    PagerStyle-PreviousPageText="Go to Previous">
```

Figure 11-4 shows the PageStyle attribute settings in action on both types of mobile devices.

Figure 11-4. ResultsForm in Pocket IE and the WML emulator

The StyleSheetExternal Mobile Web Page

In the previous example, we embedded a StyleSheet control into the mobile web page to make Styles available to mobile forms and controls. This model of embedding a StyleSheet into the mobile web page requires maintenance on each mobile page's StyleSheet object to keep all the mobile web pages in a web application consistent. A better model would be to maintain a single StyleSheet control instance that is shared by all of the mobile web pages in a web application.

The ASP.NET framework provides a method to store a StyleSheet instance in an external file. We provide an example of this in the StyleSheetExternal mobile web page. Instead of embedding a StyleSheet control hosting Style objects, the StyleSheet control references an external user control file. This is what the StyleSheet control looks like in the StyleSheetExternal mobile web page:

```
<mobile:StyleSheet id="ExternalStyleSheet" runat="server"
ReferencePath="ExternalStyleSheetClass.ascx" />
```

The file named ExternalStyleSheetClass.ascx is a mobile user control file that is similar to user controls in traditional ASP.NET development. We discuss mobile user controls in more detail later in this chapter. Listing 11-3 displays the source of this file.

Listing 11-3. The ExternalStyleSheetClass.ascx Mobile User Control File

```
<%@ Register TagPrefix="mobile" Namespace="System.Web.UI.MobileControls"
Assembly="System.Web.Mobile" %>
<%@ Control Language="c#" AutoEventWireup="false"
Codebehind="ExternalStyleSheetClass.ascx.cs"
Inherits="ControlsBookMobile.Ch11.ExternalStyleSheetClass"
TargetSchema="http://schemas.microsoft.com/Mobile/WebUserControl" %>
<mobile:stylesheet id="ExternalStyleSheet" runat="server">
  <mobile:Style Font-Size="Small" Font-Name="Times" Font-Bold="True"
ForeColor="Black" Wrapping="NoWrap"
    Name="SimpleTextStyle1"></mobile:Style>
  <mobile:Style Font-Size="Small" Font-Name="Verdana" Font-Italic="True"
ForeColor="Black" Wrapping="NoWrap"
    Name="SimpleTextStyle2"></mobile:Style>
  <mobile:Style Font-Size="Small" Font-Name="Verdana" Font-Bold="True"
ForeColor="Black" Wrapping="NoWrap"
    Name="QueryStyle"></mobile:Style>
  <mobile:Style StyleReference="QueryStyle" Font-Bold="False" Font-Italic="True"
Name="ResultsStyle"></mobile:Style>
</mobile:stylesheet>
```

As you can see, this mobile user control simply contains the StyleSheet control, renamed ExternalStyleSheet. One item to note is that this StyleSheet instance is not an exact duplicate of the instance in the StyleSheetInternal mobile web page. The ExternalStyleSheet instance modifies the ResultStyle Style object to look like this:

```
<mobile:Style StyleReference="QueryStyle" Font-Bold="False" Font-Italic="True"
Name="ResultsStyle"></mobile:Style>
```

This style declaration references another style via its own StyleReference attribute. This syntax makes it possible to build up a series of related styles to ease maintenance. In this example, we inherit the styling in the QueryStyle Style but override it setting Font-Bold to false and Font-Italic to true.

Using external StyleSheet references has a couple of drawbacks when compared to an inline or embedded StyleSheet control. Inline StyleSheets are applied to mobile controls when displayed in the Visual Studio .NET Designer, whereas externally referenced StyleSheets are not. The other design-time drawback is that Styles available in an externally referenced StyleSheet instance do not appear in the drop-down list for the StyleReference mobile control property.

Despite these two drawbacks, using externally referenced StyleSheets is recommended because of the greatly simplified Style maintenance of being able to maintain Styles in a single location.

Templates and Device-Specific Choices

As we discussed in Chapter 7, HTML or markup is a combination of content and appearance. In the previous section, we discussed how to modify appearance using styles. In this section, we discuss how to modify the document skeleton, or scaffold, on which control content hangs. Mobile templates offer similar capabilities to enhance the display of a mobile control or surround its data with markup that is driven via data binding. Mobile controls have the additional capability to select a template for rendering in a device-specific manner. This is a feature unique to mobile controls and is what we focus on in this chapter, as we covered the basics of templates and their incorporation in controls in Chapter 7.

The DeviceSpecific.aspx Mobile Web Page

The DeviceSpecific.aspx mobile web page demonstrates the use of templates and device-specific rendering to display a multiform web page that modifies its display based on the browsing device capabilities. The default Web Form activated on the mobile web page renders an input box for performing a search on the Northwind database's Customers table by ContactName, as we demonstrated previously in the book. The unique feature on the form is an image control that displays the correct image type for either an HTML or a WML browser, as shown in Figure 11-5.

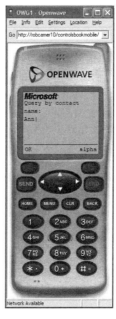

Figure 11-5. The DeviceSpecific.aspx InputForm mobile Web Form

Entering a value into the search text box and clicking Submit loads the second mobile Web Form, which renders a templated `ObjectList` mobile control. This control displays data from the search results in a manner customized for the target device. The mobile phone with the WML browser receives the more traditional text-based display, and the HTML browser receives a nice, colorized, visually appealing HTML table, as shown in Figure 11-6.

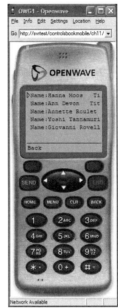

Figure 11-6. The DeviceSpecific.aspx ObjectListForm mobile Web Form

Listings 11-4 and 11-5 present the full code for the form. We next cover how an ASP.NET mobile control can detect device capabilities and render the correct UI accordingly.

Listing 11-4. The DeviceSpecific.aspx Mobile Page

```
<%@ Register TagPrefix="mobile" Namespace="System.Web.UI.MobileControls"
Assembly="System.Web.Mobile" %>
<%@ Page language="c#" Codebehind="DeviceSpecific.aspx.cs"
Inherits="ControlsBookMobile.Ch11.DeviceSpecific" AutoEventWireup="false" %>
<HEAD>
  <meta content="Microsoft Visual Studio .NET 7.1" name="GENERATOR">
  <meta content="C#" name="CODE_LANGUAGE">
  <meta content="http://schemas.microsoft.com/Mobile/Page" name="vs_targetSchema">
</HEAD>
<body Xmlns:mobile="http://schemas.microsoft.com/Mobile/WebForm">
```

```
    <mobile:form id="InputForm" runat="server">
      <P>
        <mobile:Image id="Image1" ImageUrl /ControlsBookMobile/Ch10/mslogo.bmp"
Runat="server">
          <DeviceSpecific>
            <Choice Filter="prefersWBMP" ImageUrl=
            " /ControlsBookMobile/Ch10/mslogo.wbmp"></Choice>
          </DeviceSpecific>
        </mobile:Image>
        <mobile:Label id="Label1" runat="server">
        Query by contact name:</mobile:Label>
        <mobile:TextBox id="NameTextBox" runat="server"></mobile:TextBox>
        <mobile:Command id="SelListCmd" runat="server">Submit</mobile:Command>
        <mobile:Label id="Label3" runat="server"
BreakAfter="False">Agent: </mobile:Label>
        <mobile:Label id="AgentLabel" runat="server"></mobile:Label>
        <mobile:Label id="Label2" runat="server"
BreakAfter="False">PreferredRenderingType: </mobile:Label>
        <mobile:Label id="PrefRendLabel" runat="server"></mobile:Label>
        <mobile:Label id="Label5" runat="server"
BreakAfter="False">PreferredImageMIME: </mobile:Label>
        <mobile:Label id="PrefImageLabel" runat="server"></mobile:Label>
      </P>
    </mobile:form>
    <mobile:form id="ObjectListForm" runat="server" Paginate="True">
      <mobile:ObjectList id="ObjectList1" runat="server" Wrapping="NoWrap"
CommandStyle-StyleReference="subcommand"
        LabelStyle-StyleReference="title" ItemsPerPage="10">
        <DeviceSpecific>
          <Choice Filter="isHTML32">
            <HeaderTemplate>
              <table>
                <tr bgcolor="#000084">
                  <td>
                    <font color="white">Contact Name</font>
                  </td>
                  <td>
                    <font color="white">Contact Title</font>
                  </td>
                  <td>
                    <font color="white">Company Name</font>
                  </td>
                </tr>
              </table>
            </HeaderTemplate>
            <ItemTemplate>
              <tr bgcolor="#EEEEEE">
                <td>
                  <%#((ObjectListItem)Container)["ContactName"]%>
                </td>
                <td>
                  <%#((ObjectListItem)Container)["ContactTitle"]%>
```

```
          </td>
          <td>
            <%#((ObjectListItem)Container)["CompanyName"]%>
          </td>
        </tr>
      </ItemTemplate>
      <AlternatingItemTemplate>
        <tr bgcolor="#DCDCDC">
          <td>
            <%#((ObjectListItem)Container)["ContactName"]%>
          </td>
          <td>
            <%#((ObjectListItem)Container)["ContactTitle"]%>
          </td>
          <td>
            <%#((ObjectListItem)Container)["CompanyName"]%>
          </td>
        </tr>
      </AlternatingItemTemplate>
      <FooterTemplate>
        </table>
      </FooterTemplate>
    </Choice>
    <Choice>
      <ItemTemplate>
        Name:<%#((ObjectListItem)Container)["ContactName"]%>  
Title:<%#((ObjectListItem)Container)["ContactTitle"]%>  
        Company:<%#((ObjectListItem)Container)["CompanyName"]%>
        <br />
      </ItemTemplate>
    </Choice>
  </DeviceSpecific>
  </mobile:ObjectList>
  </mobile:form>
</body>
```

Listing 11-5. The DeviceSpecific.aspx Mobile Page Code-Behind Class

```
using System;
using System.Collections;
using System.ComponentModel;
using System.Data;
using System.Drawing;
using System.Web;
using System.Web.Mobile;
using System.Web.SessionState;
using System.Web.UI;
using System.Web.UI.MobileControls;
using System.Web.UI.WebControls;
using System.Web.UI.HtmlControls;
```

```
namespace ControlsBookMobile.Ch11
{
    public class DeviceSpecific : System.Web.UI.MobileControls.MobilePage
    {
        protected System.Web.UI.MobileControls.ObjectList ObjectList1;
        protected System.Web.UI.MobileControls.Form ObjectListForm;
        protected System.Web.UI.MobileControls.Command SelListCmd;
        protected System.Web.UI.MobileControls.TextBox NameTextBox;
        protected System.Web.UI.MobileControls.Label Label1;
        protected System.Web.UI.MobileControls.Form InputForm;
        protected System.Web.UI.MobileControls.Label Label2;
        protected System.Web.UI.MobileControls.Label PrefRendLabel;
        protected System.Web.UI.MobileControls.Label Label3;
        protected System.Web.UI.MobileControls.Label AgentLabel;
        protected System.Web.UI.MobileControls.Label Label5;
        protected System.Web.UI.MobileControls.Label PrefImageLabel;
        protected System.Web.UI.MobileControls.Image Image1;

        private void Page_Load(object sender, System.EventArgs e)
        {
            // Put user code to initialize the page here
        }

        #region Web Form Designer generated code
        override protected void OnInit(EventArgs e)
        {
            //
            // CODEGEN: This call is required by the ASP.NET Web Form Designer.
            //
            InitializeComponent();
            base.OnInit(e);
        }

        /// <summary>
        /// Required method for Designer support - do not modify
        /// the contents of this method with the code editor.
        /// </summary>
        private void InitializeComponent()
        {
            this.SelListCmd.Click += new System.EventHandler(this.SelListCmd_Click);
            this.InputForm.Activate += new
System.EventHandler(this.InputForm_Activate);
            this.Load += new System.EventHandler(this.Page_Load);

        }
        #endregion

        private DataSet GetCustomersByName(String Name)
        {
            return ControlsBookMobile.Ch10.CustDB.GetCustomersByName(Name,"40");
        }
```

```
        private void SelListCmd_Click(object sender, System.EventArgs e)
        {
            ActiveForm = ObjectListForm;
            DataSet ds = GetCustomersByName(NameTextBox.Text);
            ObjectList1.DataSource = ds;
            ObjectList1.DataMember = "Customers";
            ObjectList1.DataBind();
        }

        private void InputForm_Activate(object sender, System.EventArgs e)
        {
            AgentLabel.Text = HttpContext.Current.Request.Headers["User-Agent"];
            MobileCapabilities caps = (MobileCapabilities)
                HttpContext.Current.Request.Browser;
            PrefRendLabel.Text = caps.PreferredRenderingType.ToString();
            PrefImageLabel.Text = caps.PreferredImageMime.ToString();
        }
    }
}
```

In our example, notice that we have a label that displays the user agent string obtained from the Request headers collection from the current request:

```
AgentLabel.Text = HttpContext.Current.Request.Headers["User-Agent"];
```

The value for our HTML browser was

```
Mozilla/2.0 (compatible; MSIE 3.02; Windows CE; PPC; 240x320)
```

For the WML browser, we saw

```
OWG1 UP/4.1.20a UP.Browser/4.1.20a-XXXX UP.Link/4.1.HTTP-DIRECT
```

The code for the Web Form displays the value from the MobileCapabilities object in two label values:

```
MobileCapabilities caps = (MobileCapabilities)
    HttpContext.Current.Request.Browser;
if (caps != null) //Cast succeeds
{
    PrefRendLabel.Text = caps.PreferredRenderingType.ToString();
    PrefImageLabel.Text = caps.PreferredImageMime.ToString();
}
```

MobileCapabilities inherits from HttpBrowserCapabilities. This allows us to cast the Browser object to the MobileCapabilities type. We next populate the labels with values based on the current request. The value of PreferredImageMIME for the HTML browser was

```
image/gif
```

The WML browser value for PreferredImageMIME was

```
image/vnd.wap.wbmp
```

The value of PreferredRenderingType for the HTML browser was

```
html32
```

The WML browser value for PreferredRenderingType was

```
wml11
```

As you can see, the device-detection engine succeeds in identifying Pocket IE and the WML emulator, and rendering the content appropriately. In the next sections, we cover how this process works in detail. We start off with a discussion on templates.

Templates

The easiest part of this example to understand is the templated content, especially if you are familiar with the concepts we discussed in Chapter 7. ObjectList has the following templates that you can override:

- HeaderTemplate

- FooterTemplate

- ItemTemplate

- AlternatingItemTemplate

- ItemDetailsTemplate

- SeparatorTemplate

The ObjectList control in the DeviceSpecific.aspx file has two sets of templates. One set of templates targets the textual WML display, and the other set of templates targets richer, HTML-oriented output. The mobile control template mechanism allows us to set up any number of templates for a control, with one getting chosen at runtime based on decisions made by the capability targeting engine.

The default template set with its ItemTemplate demonstrates how data-binding techniques used previously for regular ASP.NET controls function similarly in the mobile control world. The ItemTemplate data-binding expressions are careful to cast to the appropriate data type—in this case, the ObjectListItem class that represents each item in the ObjectList:

```
<ItemTemplate>
Name:<%#((ObjectListItem)Container)["ContactName"]%>  
Title:<%#((ObjectListItem)Container)["ContactTitle"]%>  
Company:<%#((ObjectListItem)Container)["CompanyName"]%>
<br />
</ItemTemplate>
```

Because of the ItemTemplate override, the ObjectList display is limited to our templated list. We forego the master/detail template that the ObjectList adheres to by default, which we examined in previous examples. Notice that there is not a link to a second page that displays the details of each item because we took things into our own hands. If you want to stick with the default list and just need to override the details page, the template you should target is ItemDetailsTemplate.

The DeviceSpecific and Choice Elements

The templates attached to the ObjectList control are not placed directly under the control's topmost element in the .aspx page as would be typical for an ASP.NET control. The mobile controls embed templates inside DeviceSpecific and Choice constructs under the ObjectList control.

The DeviceSpecific and Choice tags permit you to specify which templates to render in a device-specific manner. This feature is what sets mobile controls apart from their counterparts in traditional ASP.NET development with respect to templates. DeviceSpecific and Choice elements can do the following:

- Modify the text displayed for a control and text properties. For example, you may want message text to be short on a WML device but longer on a device with a larger display.

- Customize the styles applied, depending on detected device capabilities.

- Specify alternate image types that match detected device capabilities. We do this for the Image1 image mobile control in the next example.

This fine-grained tuning available also allows you to override control properties through the DeviceSpecific/Choice element mechanism. An example of this in the DeviceSpecific.aspx mobile web page is the Image control that overrides its ImageURL property:

```
<mobile:Image id="Image1" ImageUrl="../Ch10/mslogo.bmp" Runat="server">
  <DeviceSpecific>
    <Choice Filter="prefersWBMP" ImageUrl="../Ch10/mslogo.wbmp"></Choice>
  </DeviceSpecific>
</mobile:Image>
```

The default value is the .bmp file; however, there is a choice filter that states that a device that prefers a .wbmp file should use the .wbmp file in place of the .bmp file.

Any control that inherits from MobileControl can contain one—and only one—DeviceSpecific element. DeviceSpecific is a container element that hosts one or more Choice elements. The Choice element has a filter attribute that plugs into the device capability decision engine that is part of the mobile ASP.NET architecture.

In the case of the preceding Image control snippet of code, the Image control takes advantage of the built-in WML rendering features via the prefersWBMP filter attribute value to look for devices that prefer to render .wbmp bitmaps. The ObjectList control's Choice element has an isHTML32 filter value to ensure that the targeted device supports HTML 3.2 as a browsing language:

```
<DeviceSpecific>
    <Choice Filter="isHTML32">
      <HeaderTemplate>
        <table>
...
```

If the filter attribute looking for isHTML32 devices is satisfied, the Choice element selects the HeaderTemplate, ItemTemplate, AlternatingItemTemplate, and FooterTemplate templates for rendering by the ObjectList control. If not, the default Choice element is selected.

```
<Choice>
  <ItemTemplate>
    Name:<%#((ObjectListItem)Container)["ContactName"]%>  
Title:<%#((ObjectListItem)Container)["ContactTitle"]%>  
    Company:<%#((ObjectListItem)Container)["CompanyName"]%>
    <br />
  </ItemTemplate>
</Choice>
```

There can be many Choice elements with filters within a DeviceSpecific tag underneath a mobile control, each targeting a different filter or device capability. The first filter to match will stop the searching process for the appropriate Choice element. If there isn't a match, the Choice element without a filter attribute is selected as the default, and its child content is applied to the output.

In the example, the default `Choice` element is selected for the `ObjectList` control if the device filter for `isHTML32` never hits. There can be only one default `Choice` element within a `DeviceSpecific` element. Because the filter mechanism stops searching at the first match, it is recommended that you put the default `Choice` element last.

The Filter Attribute and deviceFilters Configuration Section

At this point you may be wondering how device detection is linked to the `DeviceSpecific/ Choice` element with its `filter` attribute in the mobile control. The `filter` attribute refers to a set of XML elements added to the standard web.config file when you select an ASP.NET mobile web application in Visual Studio .NET. You can also manually add these elements to an existing web.config file. The additional configuration section in web.config is appropriately named `deviceFilters`, as shown in Listing 11-6.

Listing 11-6. The deviceFilters *Section in the ASP.NET Mobile Web Application web.config File*

```
<deviceFilters>
  <filter name="isJPhone" compare="Type" argument="J-Phone" />
  <filter name="isHTML32" compare="PreferredRenderingType" argument="html32" />
  <filter name="isWML11" compare="PreferredRenderingType" argument="wml11" />
  <filter name="isCHTML10" compare="PreferredRenderingType" argument="chtml10" />
  <filter name="isGoAmerica" compare="Browser" argument="Go.Web" />
  <filter name="isMME" compare="Browser" argument="Microsoft Mobile Explorer" />
  <filter name="isMyPalm" compare="Browser" argument="MyPalm" />
  <filter name="isPocketIE" compare="Browser" argument="Pocket IE" />
  <filter name="isUP3x" compare="Type" argument="Phone.com 3.x Browser" />
  <filter name="isUP4x" compare="Type" argument="Phone.com 4.x Browser" />
  <filter name="isEricssonR380" compare="Type" argument="Ericsson R380" />
  <filter name="isNokia7110" compare="Type" argument="Nokia 7110" />
  <filter name="prefersGIF" compare="PreferredImageMIME" argument="image/gif" />
  <filter name="prefersWBMP" compare="PreferredImageMIME"
   argument="image/vnd.wap.wbmp" />
  <filter name="supportsColor" compare="IsColor" argument="true" />
  <filter name="supportsCookies" compare="Cookies" argument="true" />
  <filter name="supportsJavaScript" compare="Javascript" argument="true" />
  <filter name="supportsVoiceCalls" compare="CanInitiateVoiceCall"
   argument="true" />
</deviceFilters>
```

The `filter` XML element represents the comparison rules that controls link to for making their rendering choices. Each `filter` element has three main properties:

- Name

- Compare

- Argument

Name is used to uniquely identify the `filter` and is what the `Choice` element within a mobile control is matched against. The `compare` attribute is the name of the property of the `MobileCapabilties` object to test. The `argument` attribute is the value that should be matched to the capability property listed in the `compare` attribute. This is a simple Boolean comparison: If the `compare` attribute points to a capability property value that matches the `argument` attribute value, the `filter` is true and the `Choice` element on the control is picked.

Earlier we noted that the `Image` control was looking for `prefersWBMP`, whereas the `ObjectList` control wanted `isHTML32`. You can see from the preceding code listing that we need to see the `PreferredRenderingType` capability property set to a value of `html32`, and we need the `PreferredImageMIME` capability property equal to `image/vnd.wap.wbmp` for the `Choice` elements to match.

From a generic standpoint, the capability properties we have discussed need to come from somewhere concrete in ASP.NET, so in the next section we move on to discuss the `MobileCapabilities` class and the important role it plays.

MobileCapabilities, browserCaps, and Device Update 2

`MobileCapabilities` is a class from the `System.Web.Mobile` namespace that inherits from `HttpBrowserCapabilities` with strongly typed properties that represent device capabilities for traditional browsers and for a wide variety of mobile devices. It is mainly the receiver of gifts, as it is populated by the ASP.NET request mechanism when a client browser requests a page.

When a client requests a page, ASP.NET creates an instance of the `HttpRequest` class that exposes a browser property that exposes the `MobileCapabilities` object for that request. The `MobileCapabilities` object stores the device capabilities of the requestor. ASP.NET parses the request headers and uses a regular expression to match the `HTTP_USER_AGENT` contained in the headers. If a match is found, ASP.NET populates the `MobileCapabilities` object with information from the matching device in the `browserCapabilities` section of either web.config or machine.config, depending on where a match was found.

Adding support for a new device that accepts an existing rendering or markup technology such as WML, cHTML, and so on is a matter of adding a `<case>` to the `<browserCaps>` element and populating the attributes. The device manufacturer should have information on the capabilities of a particular device; however, rudimentary testing such as sending raw markup and testing with various mobile control configurations on a mobile page can assist in identifying capabilities.

Microsoft periodically publishes ASP.NET mobile control device updates to MSDN. These updates can include support for additional devices compatible with existing rendering technology and updates for additional devices compatible with new rendering or markup technology. For example, Device Update 2 includes support for XHTML markup.

The second type of update, support for new rendering technology, not only updates configuration files but also provides one or more additional device adapter assemblies. We discuss device adapter technology later in this chapter. Suffice it to say that support for a new rendering or markup technology requires a new device adapter.

For a device update, changes can be made to the following sections of the machine.config:

- `<assemblies>`

- `<browserCaps>`

- `<mobileControls>`

If a device update does not include adding support for new rendering or markup technology, only the `<browserCaps>` section is modified.

TIP *Because of configuration file inheritance or precedence rules, if you make application-specific customizations in an application's web.config file, these settings will take precedence if there are conflicts with settings in machine.conifig. Be sure to verify application-specific customizations after installing a device update.*

Device updates are available for both the .NET Framework version 1.0 and 1.1.

When you install a device update to .NET Framework 1.0, the device update replaces the existing `<browserCaps>` section with an update. A backup is made of the original machine.config file. If you customized the `<browserCaps>` section of machine.config from its original settings, you will need to manually transfer the custom changes to the updated machine.config file.

When you install a device update to .NET Framework 1.1, the device update adds a file reference to the existing `<browserCaps>` section to a file named deviceUpdate.config. If you make customizations to the `<browserCaps>` section, these changes are preserved. With Framework 1.1, you have additional options for further customizing the `<browserCaps>` section:

- Place custom changes in the deviceUpdate.config file. This file is placed at *systemdrive*\WindowsPath\Microsoft.NET\Framework\V1.1.432.

- Create a custom .config file such as deviceCustom.config and add additional `<browserCaps>` entries to machine.config. Order matters so files appearing later in this list take precedence. For example:

```
<file src="deviceUpdate.config" />
<file src="deviceCustom.config />
```

If support for a new device adapter is included in a device update, changes are made to the `<assemblies>` section of machine.config. Changes are also made to the `<mobileControls>` section of machine.config. This ensures that mobile controls use the correct device adapter to support the new rendering technology.

Custom Device Adapters and Mobile Controls

If you create or obtain a custom device adapter for a device that is not included with a Microsoft device update, you have two options. You can use the adapter provided in the device update, or you can manually update the references in the <mobileControls> section in machine.config after installing the device update.

For your custom mobile controls, device updates should not affect how they render with existing browsers. For new browsing clients added by a device update, your custom mobile controls should still render correctly, as long as the browser is compatible with your controls' requirements. The key takeaway is that you should test your custom mobile controls when a new device update is released to ensure compatibility.

New Capabilities in MobileCapabilities

As we mentioned in the last section, the System.Web.Mobile.MobileCapabilities class inherits from HttpBrowserCapabilities, so by default it supports the capabilities we discussed in Chapter 8. Table 11-2 recaps the base class properties.

Table 11-2. HttpBrowserCapabilities *Properties*

PROPERTY	DESCRIPTION
ActiveXControls	Browser support for ActiveX controls.
AOL	Is the browser an AOL version?
BackgroundSounds	Browser support for playing sounds.
Beta	Is the browser a beta version?
Browser	Full browser string from the request headers.
CDF	Browser support for Channel Definition Format (CDF).
ClrVersion	Version of the .NET CLR supported by browser.
Cookies	Browser support for cookies.
Crawler	Is the browser a web site crawler for search engines?
EcmaScriptVersion	Version of ECMAScript (JavaScript) supported by browser.
Frames	Browser support for frames.
JavaApplets	Browser support for Java applets.
JavaScript	Browser support for JavaScript.
MajorVersion	Major version of the browser.
MinorVersion	Minor version of the browser.
MSDomVersion	Microsoft version of the DOM supported by the browser.
Platform	Operating system (OS) platform that the browser is running on.
Tables	Browser support for tables.
TagWriter	Class used to emit HTML content from the control.
Type	Browser name and major version in a single string.
VBScript	Browser support for VBScript.
Version	Major.Minor version of the browser in single string.
W3CDomVersion	W3C version of the DOM supported by the browser.
Win16	Is the OS the browser is running on Win16 based?
Win32	Is the OS the browser is running on Win32 based?

This list is fairly short when compared to the `MobileCapabilities` class's properties. `MobileCapabilities` adds the new properties shown in Table 11-3.

Table 11-3. `MobileCapabilities` *Additional Properties*

PROPERTY	DESCRIPTION
CanCombineFormsInDeck	Browser on the device can handle decks that contain multiple forms, as separate cards.
CanInitiateVoiceCall	Indicates whether the device is capable of initiating a voice call.
CanRenderAfterInputOrSelectElement	Indicates whether the device can render a card that contains elements after an input or select element.
CanRenderEmptySelects	Indicates whether a device can render empty select markup statements.
CanRenderInputAndSelectElementsTogether	Indicates whether a device can render the <INPUT> and <SELECT> elements together.
CanRenderMixedSelects	Indicates whether the browser on the device can handle <SELECT> tags that include <OPTION> elements with both onpick and value attributes.
CanRenderOneventAndPrevElementsTogether	Indicates whether a device can handle <ONEVENT> and <DO type="prev" label="Back"></PREV></DO> elements when combined together.
CanRenderPostBackCards	Indicates whether a device supports postback cards.
CanRenderSetvarZeroWithMultiSelectionList	Indicates whether a device can accept WML <SETVAR> elements with the value attribute set to zero for the select/option construct of the multiselection list control.
CanSendMail	Indicates whether the browser supports the mailto tag for e-mail addresses.
DefaultSubmitButtonLimit	Stores the default number of soft keys for a device.
GatewayMajorVersion	Stores the major version number of the wireless gateway used by the mobile device to access a web application.
GatewayMinorVersion	Stores the minor version number of the wireless gateway used by the mobile device to access a web application.
GatewayVersion	Stores the version number of the wireless gateway used by the mobile device to access a web application.
HasBackButton	Indicates whether a device browser has a dedicated Back button.
HidesRightAlignedMultiselectScrollbars	Indicates whether the scrollbar of a right-aligned <SELECT MULTIPLE> element is obscured by the scrollbar for the page.

(Continued)

Table 11-3. MobileCapabilities *Additional Properties (Continued)*

PROPERTY	DESCRIPTION
InputType	Indicates the type of input supported on a device. The possible values are virtualKeyboard, telephoneKeypad, and keyboard.
IsColor	Indicates whether a device has a color display.
IsMobileDevice	Indicates whether a device is recognized as a mobile device.
MaximumRenderedPageSize	Stores the maximum length of a page, in bytes, that the device can display.
MaximumSoftkeyLabelLength	Stores the maximum length of text that a soft key label can display.
MobileDeviceManufacturer	Stores the name of the device manufacturer.
MobileDeviceModel	Stores the model name of the device, if available.
NumberOfSoftkeys	Stores the number of soft keys available on a device.
PreferredImageMime	Returns the MIME type preferred for images on a device.
PreferredRenderingMime	Returns the MIME type preferred for content on a device.
PreferredRenderingType	Returns the general name for the preferred type of content.
PreferredRenderingTypeChtml10	Static-source identifier to use for compact HTML 1.0.
PreferredRenderingTypeHtml32	Static-source identifier to use for HTML 3.2.
PreferredRenderingTypeWml11	Static-source identifier to use for WML 1.1.
PreferredRenderingTypeWml12	Static-source identifier to use for WML 1.2.
RendersBreakBeforeWmlSelectAndInput	Indicates whether a device inserts an additional break before rendering a WML <SELECT> or <INPUT> element.
RendersBreaksAfterHtmlLists	Indicates whether a device already renders breaks after HTML list tags.
RendersBreaksAfterWmlAnchor	Indicates whether a device or browser produces a break after a stand-alone anchor.
RendersBreaksAfterWmlInput	Returns whether a device automatically renders a break after input elements have been received.
RendersWmlDoAcceptsInline	Indicates whether a device renders a WML <DO>-based form accept construct as an inline button instead of a soft key.
RendersWmlSelectsAsMenuCards	Indicates whether a device renders the <SELECT> tag constructs as menu cards instead of a DropDownList.

(Continued)

Table 11-3. MobileCapabilities *Additional Properties (Continued)*

PROPERTY	DESCRIPTION
RequiredMetaTagNameValue	Returns a metatag that some devices require.
RequiresAttributeColonSubstitution	Indicates whether colons in tag name attributes need to substitute a different character for rendering.
RequiresContentTypeMetaTag	Indicates whether the device requires the content-type metatag.
RequiresDBCSCharacter	Indicates whether a device requires a double byte character set (DBCS) character.
RequiresHtmlAdaptiveErrorReporting	Indicates whether the HTML device should receive a default ASP.NET error message or an adaptive one for non-HTML devices such as WML.
RequiresLeadingPageBreak	Indicates that an additional break should render.
RequiresNoBreakInFormatting	Indicates that formatting tags should not include break ( ) tags.
RequiresOutputOptimization	Indicates that adapters should try to generate minimal output.
RequiresPhoneNumbersAsPlainText	Indicates whether a device supports phone dialing based on plain text only instead of special markup.
RequiresSpecialViewStateEncoding	Indicates whether a device requires special encoding for generated ViewState.
RequiresUniqueFilePathSuffix	Indicates whether a unique file path suffix is required so that WAP-cached pages process submitted forms correctly.
RequiresUniqueHtmlCheckboxNames	Indicates whether a device requires that the check box HTML <INPUT> tag contain unique name attribute values.
RequiresUniqueHtmlInputNames	Indicates whether a device requires that HTML <INPUT> tags contain unique name attribute values.
RequiresUrlEncodedPostfieldValues	Indicates whether a device encodes text in the value attribute of a posted field during postback.
ScreenBitDepth	Stores the display depth in bits per pixel of a device's display.
ScreenCharactersHeight	Stores the height of the display in character lines.
ScreenCharactersWidth	Stores the screen width in characters.
ScreenPixelsHeight	Stores the height of the display in pixels.
ScreenPixelsWidth	Stores the width of the display in pixels.
SupportsAccessKeyAttribute	Indicates that a device can handle the AccessKey attribute for the <A> and <INPUT> tags.

(Continued)

Table 11-3. MobileCapabilities *Additional Properties (Continued)*

PROPERTY	DESCRIPTION
SupportsBodyColor	Indicates whether a device supports the bgcolor attribute on the <BODY> tag.
SupportsBold	Indicates whether a device supports bold text as specified through the <B> tag.
SupportsCacheControlMetaTag	Indicates whether a device supports the <META> tag Cache-Control.
SupportsCss	Indicates whether a device supports CSS for styling.
SupportsDivAlign	Indicates whether a device supports the align attribute within the <DIV> tag.
SupportsDivNoWrap	Indicates whether a device supports the nowrap attribute within the <DIV> tag.
SupportsEmptyStringInCookieValue	Indicates whether a device supports an empty string for the value of a cookie.
SupportsFontColor	Indicates whether a device supports the color attribute for the <FONT> tag.
SupportsFontName	Indicates whether a device supports the name attribute for the <FONT> tag.
SupportsFontSize	Indicates whether a device supports the size attribute for the <FONT> tag.
SupportsImageSubmit	Indicates that a device can handle images submitting the form.
SupportsIModeSymbols	Indicates that a device supports i-Mode symbols.
SupportsInputIStyle	Indicates that a device supports the istyle attribute for the <INPUT> tag.
SupportsInputMode	Indicates that a device supports attribute mode for the <INPUT> tag.
SupportsItalic	Indicates that a device supports the <I> tag.
SupportsJPhoneMultiMediaAttributes	Indicates whether a device supports J-Phone multimedia attributes.
SupportsJPhoneSymbols	Indicates whether a device supports picture symbols specific to the J-Phone.
SupportsQueryStringInFormAction	Indicates whether a device supports a query string in the action attribute of a <FORM> tag.
SupportsRedirectWithCookie	Indicates whether a device honors the Set-Cookie header when the cookie is sent in conjunction with a redirect.
SupportsSelectMultiple	Indicates whether a device supports the multiple attribute for HTML select tags.
SupportsUncheck	Indicates whether a device returns the unselected status for an unchecked check box in posted data.

HttpBrowserCapabilities targets W3C standards that traditional desktop web browsers adhere to pretty well, keeping this class fairly simple. As you can see from Table 11-3, device capabilities vary widely in the mobile web application market, and standards are fractious. This size of this table demonstrates the challenges that arise when developers attempt to hand-code applications that target more than a couple of mobile devices. Either that or developers wrote their applications in plain-vanilla fashion as a one-size-fits-all design.

The ASP.NET mobile controls framework lends a helping hand by abstracting device differences while providing an extensible architecture that allows developers to add support for new devices as they become available.

The groundwork is laid to permit us to move on to control development. Mobile user controls are very similar to their cousins in traditional ASP.NET targeting desktop browsers. In the next section, we discuss mobile user controls, and then we round out this chapter with a discussion of custom server control development and device adapters.

User Controls

The ASP.NET mobile web application development system provides for modularity in control content in the same way as ASP.NET targets desktop browsers. User controls play an important role in this architecture. To recap information presented in Chapter 3, here is a list of important characteristics of user controls:

- User controls are a great way to package HTML and modularize web development. They are also a means of replacing the use of IIS include files.

- User controls support properties and methods that can be set either in the HTML as attributes or in the code-behind page of the hosting .ascx page.

- User controls can be cached in the ASP.NET cache based on a number of different parameters to speed web application performance (as detailed in the ASP.NET documentation).

- Certain tags are not permitted in a user control—specifically, the <HTML>, <HEAD>, <BODY>, and <FORM> tags. Using these tags would interfere with the functioning of the hosting .aspx page.

- User control tag declarations should appear between the hosting .aspx page's beginning and ending FORM tags to ensure proper operation.

We created user control samples in Chapter 3 to demonstrate how they work. In the next section, we build two user controls that mimic the header and footer user controls present in the traditional ASP.NET samples.

Mobile User Controls

Generally, the display constraints of mobile devices and the limited bandwidth available for data communication dictate that content take precedence over style or aesthetics. Mobile web applications tend to be more esoteric when compared to web applications that target desktop browsers.

With the efforts by wireless operators to upgrade their data bandwidth capacity and the release of more powerful mobile devices such as the Pocket PC Phone Edition and the Smartphone, this is changing. Designing mobile web applications that can grow as bandwidth and device capability improves warrants consideration.

Because mobile user controls provide a high degree of page modularity, they can help in this effort just as they can when targeting a desktop browser. For example, including header, footer, and left and right pane user controls in a web application is pretty easy to do up front. The application page template simply includes those user controls as part of normal development. User controls can act as placeholders for enriching the page experience as bandwidth and device capacity improve.

For instance, an esoteric one-line copyright statement in the footer could eventually be replaced with a footer you would expect to see in a traditional web application, with contact information, graphic logos, and so on. It is in this vein that we demonstrate mobile user controls.

Our example mobile page, UserControlHost.aspx, is a replica of the DeviceSpecific.aspx page that we discussed earlier in this chapter, except for the addition of two mobile user controls: a header user control and a footer user control. We wanted the mobile header and footer user controls to resemble their cousins designed for the desktop but at the same time take into account mobile device considerations.

Miniaturizing the Header and Footer

To start the conversion process, we add two mobile user control files named ControlsBookMobileFooter.ascx and ControlsBookMobileHeader.ascx. As you can see, the file extension for mobile user controls is the same. Next, we copy and paste the code from the desktop versions of the controls into the mobile versions, changing tag prefixes from "asp:" to "mobile:" and removing all HTML formatting so that we end up with four mobile Label controls on the header and three mobile Label controls on the footer.

Mobile Labels span the width of the mobile form—you can't put two mobile Labels side by side on a mobile form. Our first change, then, is to combine the Label containing "Chapter" and the placeholder Label containing the "Chapter Number" into a single Label to conserve one line on a mobile device.

Next, we modify Label styling to a size of Small and not Bold in an effort to compact the displayed information. Because <HR> tags do not have a WML equivalent, we switch to a .bmp image for HTML32 devices and a .wbmp for WML devices to display horizontal line separators in the header and footer controls. The results of our changes are shown in Listings 11-7 and 11-8 for the header user control and Listings 11-9 and 11-10 for the footer user control.

Listing 11-7. The ControlsBookMobileHeader .ascx File

```
<%@ Control Language="c#" AutoEventWireup="false"
Codebehind="ControlsBookMobileHeader.ascx.cs"
Inherits="ControlsBookMobile.Ch11.ControlsBookMobileHeader"
TargetSchema="http://schemas.microsoft.com/Mobile/WebUserControl" %>
<%@ Register TagPrefix="mobile" Namespace="System.Web.UI.MobileControls"
Assembly="System.Web.Mobile" %>
<mobile:label id="Label2" runat="server" Font-Name="Arial Narrow"
Font-Bold="False" Font-Size="Small">
Building ASP.NET Server Controls</mobile:label>
<mobile:label id="Label1" runat="server" Font-Name="Arial Narrow"
Font-Bold="False" Font-Size="Small">
<DeviceSpecific>
    <Choice Filter="isWML11" Visible="False"></Choice>
  </DeviceSpecific>Chapter</mobile:label>
<mobile:label id="Label4" runat="server" Font-Name="Arial Narrow"
Font-Bold="False" Font-Size="Small">
<DeviceSpecific>
    <Choice Filter="isWML11" Visible="False"></Choice>
  </DeviceSpecific>Chapter Title</mobile:label>
<mobile:Image id="Image1" runat="server" ImageUrl="line.bmp">
  <DeviceSpecific>
    <Choice Filter="isWML11" ImageUrl="line.wbmp"></Choice>
  </DeviceSpecific>
</mobile:Image>
```

Listing 11-8. The ControlsBookMobileHeader *Code-Behind Class File*

```
using System;
using System.Data;
using System.Drawing;
using System.Web;
using System.Web.Mobile;
using System.Web.UI.MobileControls;
using System.Web.UI.WebControls;
using System.Web.UI.HtmlControls;

namespace ControlsBookMobile.Ch11
{
   public abstract class ControlsBookMobileHeader :
System.Web.UI.MobileControls.MobileUserControl
   {
      protected System.Web.UI.MobileControls.Label Label1;
      protected System.Web.UI.MobileControls.Label Label4;
      protected System.Web.UI.MobileControls.Image Image1;
      protected System.Web.UI.MobileControls.Label Label2;

      //private members
      private string bookChapterTitle ;
      private int chapterNumber ;
```

```csharp
    private void Page_Load(object sender, System.EventArgs e)
    {
        Label1.Text = "Chapter " + chapterNumber.ToString() ;
        Label4.Text = bookChapterTitle ;
    }

    //properties
    public String ChapterTitle
    {
        get
        {
            return bookChapterTitle ;
        }
        set
        {
            bookChapterTitle = value;
        }
    }

    public int ChapterNumber
    {
        get
        {
            return chapterNumber ;
        }
        set
        {
            chapterNumber = value;
        }
    }

    #region Web Form Designer generated code
    override protected void OnInit(EventArgs e)
    {
        //
        // CODEGEN: This call is required by the ASP.NET Web Form Designer.
        //
        InitializeComponent();
        base.OnInit(e);
    }

    ///        Required method for Designer support - do not modify
    ///        the contents of this method with the code editor.
    /// </summary>
    private void InitializeComponent()
    {
        this.Load += new System.EventHandler(this.Page_Load);

    }
    #endregion
    }
}
```

Listing 11-9. The ControlsBookMobileFooter .ascx File

```
<%@ Register TagPrefix="mobile" Namespace="System.Web.UI.MobileControls"
Assembly="System.Web.Mobile" %>
<%@ Control Language="c#" AutoEventWireup="false"
Codebehind="ControlsBookMobileFooter.ascx.cs"
Inherits="ControlsBookMobile.Ch11.ControlsBookMobileFooter"
TargetSchema="http://schemas.microsoft.com/Mobile/WebUserControl" %>
<mobile:Image id="Image1" runat="server" ImageUrl="line.bmp">
  <DeviceSpecific>
    <Choice Filter="isWML11" ImageUrl="line.wbmp"></Choice>
  </DeviceSpecific>
</mobile:Image>
<mobile:label id="Label1" runat="server" Font-Bold="False" Font-Size="Small"
Font-Name="Tahoma">
<DeviceSpecific>
    <Choice Filter="isWML11" Visible="False"></Choice>
  </DeviceSpecific>Building ASP.NET Server Controls</mobile:label>
<mobile:label id="Label2" runat="server" Font-Size="Small"
Font-Name="Arial Narrow">
<DeviceSpecific>
    <Choice Filter="isWML11" Visible="False"></Choice>
  </DeviceSpecific>By Dale Michalk and Robert Cameron</mobile:label>
<mobile:label id="Label3" runat="server" Font-Bold="False" Font-Size="Small"
Font-Name="Tahoma">Copyright © 2003, Apress L.P. </mobile:label>
```

Listing 11-10. The ControlsBookMobileFooter *Code-Behind Class File*

```
using System;
using System.Data;
using System.Drawing;
using System.Web;
using System.Web.Mobile;
using System.Web.UI.MobileControls;
using System.Web.UI.WebControls;
using System.Web.UI.HtmlControls;

namespace ControlsBookMobile.Ch11
{
   public abstract class ControlsBookMobileFooter :
System.Web.UI.MobileControls.MobileUserControl
   {
      protected System.Web.UI.MobileControls.Label Label1;
      protected System.Web.UI.MobileControls.Label Label2;
      protected System.Web.UI.MobileControls.Image Image1;
      protected System.Web.UI.MobileControls.Label Label3;

      private void Page_Load(object sender, System.EventArgs e)
      {
```

```
        }

        #region Web Form Designer generated code
        override protected void OnInit(EventArgs e)
        {
            //
            // CODEGEN: This call is required by the ASP.NET Web Form Designer.
            //
            InitializeComponent();
            base.OnInit(e);
        }

        /// Required method for Designer support - do not modify
        /// the contents of this method with the code editor.
        /// </summary>
        private void InitializeComponent()
        {
            this.Load += new System.EventHandler(this.Page_Load);

        }
        #endregion
    }
}
```

We now focus our discussion on the header user control because it includes the functionality in the footer user control, but with a few additional wrinkles.

If you look at the header user control .aspx file, you will see a DeviceSpecific/Choice construct for each mobile Label. The default behavior is to display all three labels; however, if a WML11 device is detected, the user control displays only the first Label for the book title on the header control and the copyright Label for the footer control.

The other Labels have their Visible property set to false to prevent these labels from rendering. A .wbmp file is rendered for a WML11 device using a DeviceSpecific/Choice construct as well.

Next, we explore the mobile page that hosts our new mobile user controls.

Hosting the Header and Footer User Controls

The example mobile page, aptly named UserControlHost.aspx, is a copy of the DeviceSpecific.aspx page from the earlier example in this chapter. To add the header and footer user controls, we drag the user control files and drop them into the appropriate spot (top or bottom) on each mobile form. This results in the addition of the following lines to the .aspx page:

```
<%@ Register TagPrefix="ApressUCMobile" TagName="ControlsBookMobileHeader"
Src="ControlsBookMobileHeader.ascx" %>
<%@ Register TagPrefix="ApressUCMobile" TagName="ControlsBookMobileFooter"
Src="ControlsBookMobileFooter.ascx" %>
```

We changed the tag prefix from "uc1" to "ApressUCMobile". Also notice that we had to add the user controls to each mobile form. Here is what the tag declaration for the header control looks like:

```
<ApressUCMobile:ControlsBookMobileHeader id="ControlsBookMobileHeader1"
ChapterNumber="11" ChapterTitle="Customizing and Implementing Mobile Controls"
     runat="server"></ApressUCMobile:ControlsBookMobileHeader>
```

Here is what the tag declaration for the footer control looks like:

```
  <ApressUCMobile:ControlsBookMobileFooter id="ControlsBookMobileFooter1"
runat="server"></ApressUCMobile:ControlsBookMobileFooter>
```

Listing 11-11 presents the full listing for UserControlHost.aspx.

Listing 11-11. The UserControlHost.aspx File

```
<%@ Register TagPrefix="mobile" Namespace="System.Web.UI.MobileControls"
Assembly="System.Web.Mobile" %>
<%@ Page language="c#" Codebehind="UserControlHost.aspx.cs"
Inherits="ControlsBookMobile.Ch11.UserControlHost" AutoEventWireup="false" %>
<%@ Register TagPrefix="ApressUCMobile" TagName="ControlsBookMobileHeader"
Src="ControlsBookMobileHeader.ascx" %>
<%@ Register TagPrefix="ApressUCMobile" TagName="ControlsBookMobileFooter"
Src="ControlsBookMobileFooter.ascx" %>
<HEAD>
  <meta content="Microsoft Visual Studio .NET 7.1" name="GENERATOR">
  <meta content="C#" name="CODE_LANGUAGE">
  <meta content="http://schemas.microsoft.com/Mobile/Page" name="vs_targetSchema">
</HEAD>
<body Xmlns:mobile="http://schemas.microsoft.com/Mobile/WebForm">
  <mobile:form id="MainForm" runat="server">
    <ApressUCMobile:ControlsBookMobileHeader id="ControlsBookMobileHeader1"
ChapterNumber="11" ChapterTitle="Customizing and Implementing Mobile Controls"
     runat="server"></ApressUCMobile:ControlsBookMobileHeader>
    <mobile:Link id="Link1" runat="server" NavigateUrl="#LabelForm">
Label Styles</mobile:Link>
    <mobile:Link id="Link2" runat="server" NavigateUrl="#QueryForm">
Paging Style</mobile:Link>
    <ApressUCMobile:ControlsBookMobileFooter id="ControlsBookMobileFooter1"
runat="server"></ApressUCMobile:ControlsBookMobileFooter>
  </mobile:form>
  <mobile:form id="LabelForm" runat="server">
    <ApressUCMobile:ControlsBookMobileHeader id="ControlsBookMobileHeader2"
ChapterNumber="11" ChapterTitle="Customizing and Implementing Mobile Controls"
     runat="server"></ApressUCMobile:ControlsBookMobileHeader>
    <mobile:Label id="Label3" runat="server"
StyleReference="SimpleTextStyle1">Some simple text.(BoldTimes)</mobile:Label>
    <mobile:Label id="Label5" runat="server" StyleReference="title">
```

```
    Some Title text.(title default style)</mobile:Label>
        <mobile:Label id="Label4" runat="server"
    StyleReference="SimpleTextStyle2">More simple text.(ItalicVerdana)</mobile:Label>
        <mobile:Label id="Label6" runat="server" StyleReference="subcommand">
    Some subcommand Text.(subcommand default style)</mobile:Label>
        <mobile:Label id="Label7" runat="server" StyleReference="error">
    Error: Some error text.(error default style)</mobile:Label>
        <ApressUCMobile:ControlsBookMobileFooter id="ControlsBookMobileFooter2"
    runat="server"></ApressUCMobile:ControlsBookMobileFooter>
      </mobile:form>
      <mobile:form id="QueryForm" runat="server" StyleReference="QueryStyle">
        <ApressUCMobile:ControlsBookMobileHeader id="ControlsBookMobileHeader3"
    ChapterNumber="11" ChapterTitle="Customizing and Implementing Mobile Controls"
          runat="server"></ApressUCMobile:ControlsBookMobileHeader>
        <mobile:Label id="Label1" runat="server">Query by Contact Name:</mobile:Label>
        <mobile:TextBox id="NameTextBox" runat="server"></mobile:TextBox>
        <mobile:Command id="QueryCmd" runat="server">Submit</mobile:Command>
        <ApressUCMobile:ControlsBookMobileFooter id="ControlsBookMobileFooter3"
    runat="server"></ApressUCMobile:ControlsBookMobileFooter>
      </mobile:form>
      <mobile:form id="ResultsForm" runat="server" Paginate="True"
    StyleReference="ResultsStyle" PagerStyle-NextPageText="Go To Next"
        PagerStyle-PreviousPageText="Go to Previous">
        <ApressUCMobile:ControlsBookMobileHeader id="ControlsBookMobileHeader4"
    ChapterNumber="11" ChapterTitle="Customizing and Implementing Mobile Controls"
          runat="server"></ApressUCMobile:ControlsBookMobileHeader>
        <mobile:List id="CustList" runat="server" ItemsPerPage="10"
    Decoration="Numbered"></mobile:List>
        <ApressUCMobile:ControlsBookMobileFooter id="ControlsBookMobileFooter4"
    runat="server"></ApressUCMobile:ControlsBookMobileFooter>
      </mobile:form>
      <mobile:stylesheet id="InlineStyleSheet" runat="server">
        <mobile:Style Font-Size="Small" Font-Name="Times" Font-Bold="True"
    ForeColor="Black" Wrapping="NoWrap"
          Name="SimpleTextStyle1"></mobile:Style>
        <mobile:Style Font-Size="Small" Font-Name="Verdana" Font-Italic="True"
    ForeColor="Black" Wrapping="NoWrap"
          Name="SimpleTextStyle2"></mobile:Style>
        <mobile:Style Font-Size="Small" Font-Name="Verdana" Font-Bold="True"
    ForeColor="Black" Wrapping="NoWrap"
          Name="QueryStyle"></mobile:Style>
        <mobile:Style Font-Size="Small" Font-Name="Tahoma" Font-Bold="False"
    Font-Italic="True" ForeColor="Black"
          Wrapping="NoWrap" Name="ResultsStyle"></mobile:Style>
      </mobile:stylesheet>
    </body>
```

We did not make any modifications to the code-behind class file, so we do not show its listing here—it is exactly the same as in the DeviceSpecific.aspx.cs code-behind file except for the class name change. Figure 11-7 shows how the header and footer controls render in Pocket IE and in the WML emulator.

Figure 11-7. The header and footer user controls rendered in Pocket IE and the WML emulator

Now that we have covered mobile user controls with an example, we spend the rest of this chapter exploring custom mobile control development issues and device adapters. Much of control development process is the same as when you build mobile controls. Therefore, in the next section we focus on what is unique to custom mobile control development and develop an example to illustrate the differences between the two development models.

Custom Controls

Mobile server controls are developed in much the same manner as server controls designed for traditional ASP.NET web applications. In this section, we reinforce the similarities and identify the differences between them, starting with a discussion on mobile control rendering.

Rendering the Mobile Control

The level of standardization that exists in the desktop browser market, though not perfect by any means, is much better than what exists in the mobile device world in terms of device capabilities and markup technology.

There are a plethora of devices and more than a few rendering technologies, such as cHTML, WML, XHTML, and so on. This coupled with the rapidly growing and changing mobile device market means that a flexible architecture that isolates device and markup differences is required. Otherwise, the maintenance required to target multiple devices will prove cost prohibitive.

Luckily, ASP.NET provides a pluggable and extendible mobile control–rendering architecture that isolates device-specific rendering into device adapters while maintaining the fundamental server control architecture, as covered so far in this book.

Device Adapters

Mobile server controls encapsulate logic, events, and properties just like traditional server controls, but mobile controls do not render themselves. Instead of managing their own rendering, as with regular server controls, mobile controls offload that portion of the server control life cycle to helper classes or objects called *device adapters*.

Device adapters provide a nice abstraction layer between server control technology and the many devices and varied markup technology available. Each mobile server control can have several device adapters to render its content on supported devices. Likewise, when a new rendering technology becomes available, a new device adapter set is required for a mobile server control to render to that device, as described in Table 11-4.

Table 11-4. Device Adapter Set

ADAPTER	DESCRIPTION
Control adapter base class	Base class that all device adapters inherit from
Page adapter	Adapter for the mobile page
Form adapter	Adapter for each mobile form on the mobile page
Control adapter	Adapter for each mobile control available
Text writer	Writer that inherits from `MobileTextWriter` with device-specific methods

.NET Framework ASP.NET mobile controls with Device Update 2 include device adapter sets for the following types of devices:

- `HtmlDeviceAdapters`

- `ChtmlDeviceAdapters`

- `WmlDeviceAdapters`

- `XhtmlAdapters`

So, based on Table 11-4, the following device adapters handle rendering for WML devices that access a given mobile page:

- `WmlControlAdapter`

- `WmlFormAdapter`

- `WmlPageAdapter`

- `WmlMobileTextWriter`

`WmlControlAdapter` provides the base class for specific mobile control adapter classes. For each mobile server control, there is a class that inherits from `WmlControlAdapter` named `Wml`**`ControlName`**`Adapter`, where **`ControlName`** is something like `Image`, `Label`, `List`, and so on. These device adapters provide WML rendering services for the corresponding control.

All device adapters implement the `IControlAdapter` interface. Table 11-5 details this interface.

Table 11-5. `IControlAdapter` *Interface*

MEMBERS	DESCRIPTION
`Control`	Stores a reference to the associated control
`CreateTemplatedUI`	Creates a templated UI when called by base classes
`HandlePostBackEvent`	Returns true if the event is handled
`ItemWeight`	Stores the approximate weight of an item in the associated control
`LoadAdapterState`	Loads the adapter's private ViewState
`LoadPostData`	Returns true if the adapter loads posted data
`OnInit`	Called after a form or page initializes
`OnLoad`	Loads data for the control, page, or device adapter
`OnPreRender`	Performs adapter-specific logic prior to rendering
`OnUnload`	Unloads data for the control, page, or device adapter
`Page`	Stores a reference to the page associated with the device adapter
`Render`	Called by the associated control's `Render` method
`SaveAdapterState`	Saves the adapter's private ViewState
`VisibleWeight`	Stores the approximate weight of the control in characters

`ItemWeight` and `VisibleWeight` are two of the more interesting members of the `IControlAdapter` interface. The pagination system in ASP.NET mobile controls uses a weighting system to determine what controls to render on a page and how many items to render per page.

NOTE *The default unit system in ASP.NET mobile controls is based on a single line equal to 100 units based on the* DefaultWeight *static read-only property on the* ControlPager *class. The default* ItemWeight *is also the same value at 100 units.*

Device adapters implementing IControlAdapter maintain a reference to a specific control instance in its Control property. Device adapter instances are not shared among controls, as a device adapter can maintain instance-specific information or state.

The Mobile Control Life Cycle

The mobile control life cycle inherits the same general life cycle of regular server controls with a few twists related to rendering with device adapters and ViewState management. In Chapter 5, we stated that after the initial page request as an HTTP GET, each subsequent HTTP POST page request/response cycle generally consists of the following steps:

1. Instantiate the control tree, creating each server control object.

2. Unpack ViewState for each server control object.

3. Set the state from the previous server-side processing cycle for each object in the tree.

4. Process postback data.

5. Handle the Page_Load event.

6. Let controls know that data changed through postback, updating control state as necessary.

7. Execute server-side events based on data changes from postback.

8. Persist state back to ViewState.

9. Execute the render process for each server control.

10. Unload page and its control tree.

This process provides the illusion of a state-full application to the end user. During each request/response cycle, state is unpacked, changes are processed, and the UI is updated and rendered back to the client device. Because of the varied device capabilities in the mobile web world, two major differences exist in the mobile control life cycle—namely, rendering and ViewState management.

Mobile Control and Adapter Interaction

As we mentioned previously, mobile server controls do not render themselves. Mobile server control rendering is handled by device adapters. We also mentioned that each device type and/or markup technology has its own set of adapters ready to go when called into action. We describe exactly how this takes place next.

For each client request, ASP.NET populates the `HttpContext` object's `HttpRequest.Browser` property. This property maintains a reference to an object of type `MobileCapabilities`, which we discussed earlier in this chapter with respect to device detection.

As you may surmise, device detection leads to device adapter set selection. During the initialization phase of the mobile page's life cycle, the ASP.NET runtime maps information in the `MobileCapabilities` object to the device mappings in the `<mobileControls>` section of the web.config file. Once device adapters are selected and device-specific customizations are applied, the page life cycle continues. Table 11-6 details the mobile control specifics related to the server control life cycle.

Table 11-6. Mobile Server Control Events Related to the Control Execution Life Cycle

SERVER CONTROL EVENT	PAGE LIFE CYCLE PHASE	MOBILE CONTROL SPECIFICS
Init	Initialize	Device adapter selection and customizations `MobileControl.Init` is called. `Adapter.Init` is called.
LoadViewState	Unpack ViewState	`MobileControl.LoadPrivateViewState` is called. `Adapter.LoadAdapterState` is called.
LoadPostData	Handle form postback data	`MobileControl.LoadPostData` is called. `MobileControl.Load` is called.
Load	Page_Load event	`Adapter.Load` is called.
RaisePostDataChangedEvent	Notifies the page that the state of the control has changed	`MobileControl.RaisePostDataChangedEvent`.
RaisePostBackEvent	Execute server-side events	`MobileControl.RaisePostBackEvent` is called. Possibly call `Adapter.RaisePostBackEvent` if events can vary based on the client device.
PreRender	Render process	`MobileControl.PreRender` is called. `Adapter.PreRender` is called.
SaveViewState	Save ViewState	`MobileControl.SavePrivateViewState` is called. `Adapter.SaveAdapterState` is called.
Render	Render process	`MobileControl.Render` is called, which calls `Adapter.Render`. `MobileTextWriter` is called to actually output the required markup.
Unload	Unload process	`MobileControl.Unload` is called. `Adapter.Unload` is called.
Dispose	Dispose of control tree	`MobileControl.Dispose` is called.

As you can see, the mobile server control object and device adapter object are tightly coupled once the life cycle starts all the way through rendering. Figure 11-8 illustrates the entire device detection and rendering process.

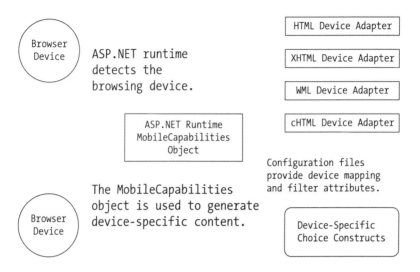

Figure 11-8. The capability detection and device-specific rendering process

Managing ViewState

Because of varied mobile device display capabilities and limited bandwidth available to mobile devices, the normal ViewState storage mechanism that uses a hidden form field on the client is not a viable option.

Instead, the mobile web application stores ViewState data into the Session object. Storing ViewState in the Session object provides a performance boost because ViewState is not transmitted over the wire during each postback cycle; however, this does incur additional memory demands on the server. This is something to keep in mind when you tune your mobile web applications.

Once a client device establishes a session with the web application, the session ID is embedded into the URL of the web application. For example, for the UserControlHost.aspx page, the client performs the initial HTTP GET with this URL:

```
http://localhost/ControlsBookMobile/ch11/usercontrolhost.aspx
```

When the page loads, a URL similar to this is returned:

```
http://localhost/ControlsBookMobile/(sttxgl55ofwsrl45by2l2i55)/Ch11/
UserControlHost.aspx
```

Notice the (sttxgl55ofwsrl45by2l2i55) string embedded into the URL. This string links the page to the session ID for the browsing device and is what associates the page's ViewState with the current session.

Because the ViewState is not physically stored with the page and given the stateless nature of HTTP, it is possible for a page to become out of sync with its current state. For instance, the user can click the Back button when viewing the latest page to bring up the previous page. The most recent ViewState on the server would be for the most recent page viewed—not the previous page brought up by the user clicking the Back button.

To alleviate this, the ASP.NET runtime keeps track of a limited number of ViewState pages in a ViewState history. The identifier in the preceding URL indicates what page the user is currently viewing in the history.

You can specify how many pages worth of ViewState should be cached in the web.config file, which can override the value stored in the machine.config file. On our machines, the machine.config file has this value:

```
<mobileControls
        sessionStateHistorySize="6"
...
```

ViewState can expire in mobile web applications because it is stored in the user's current session. If a page does not post back within the session expiration time, the OnViewStateExpire method fires for the page. The default implementation of this method is to throw an exception. An application has the option of overriding this method to prevent the exception if the application can restore ViewState manually.

As with traditional ASP.NET applications, each mobile control is responsible for managing its own ViewState. As we have alluded to, mobile controls differ from traditional server controls with respect to rendering and ViewState. We cover rendering in the next section, but suffice it to say that when a mobile control renders, it has help from device adapters to render its content appropriately for the device currently making the request.

One difference with server controls of type MobileControl is PrivateViewState. Mobile controls have an additional state-management mechanism in PrivateViewState that cannot be disabled as ViewState can be by setting EnableViewState to a value of false. To use PrivateViewState, a control overrides the LoadPrivateViewState and SavePrivateViewState methods.

PrivateViewState is stored in the page sent to the client, so state placed in PrivateViewState should be kept to a minimum due to both limited bandwidth and device capabilities. The main function of PrivateViewState is to make state information available across multiple pages. Here are some reasons why you would want to use PrivateViewState:

- To store the currently active form on a page

- To store pagination information about a form

- To store device-specific decisions made by a control's adapter

The device adapter object is closely tied to its associated mobile control instance, storing ViewState specific to the device adapter in addition to the mobile control's ViewState. All device adapters inherit from the IControlAdapter interface, which includes the following methods:

- LoadAdapterState

- SaveAdapterState

LoadAdapterState is called by the mobile control's LoadPrivateViewState method during the control's life cycle. Likewise, the mobile control's SavePrivateViewState method calls the device adapter's SaveAdapterState method. This extension of ViewState storage to the device adapter provides an opportunity for the device adapter to manage additional state with respect to control UI management. This is a great example of the flexibility this architecture provides.

Now that we have covered the differences between traditional server controls and mobile controls, and we have discussed the mobile control life cycle, we can move to discuss actually implementing mobile server controls. It is possible to create mobile server controls using the same techniques for traditional server control development, including

- Inheritance

- Composition

- Inheriting from MobileControl, the base class for all mobile controls

We cover these options in the next sections.

Inheritance

Customizing an existing server control through inheritance is an excellent option, especially for mobile controls because of the increased complexity with rendering. Unless you override the Render method in an inherited control, the base mobile control will still handle its own rendering.

Because inheritance in mobile server control development is performed in the same manner as with traditional server control development, we do not provide an example here. Instead, we refer you to Chapter 3, where we implemented an inherited control named TextBox3d.

Composition

Building composite mobile server controls is performed in a similar manner to developing traditional mobile control composite controls. As with inheritance, composition generally does not require any additional work due to the differences in rendering technology with mobile controls.

Composition in both traditional and mobile server control development relies on child controls to handle their own rendering. Also, there may be situations in which a composite control's behavior and appearance can be enhanced by altering the contained child controls in a device-specific manner. You can create a device-specific control adapter class that renders a device-specific control tree.

When you build composite mobile server controls, we recommend inheriting from `Panel` instead of `MobileControl`. This is similar to inheriting from a `<DIV>` tag in traditional composite control development, as it provides a nice container for the control. With composite mobile controls, this is especially important because the .NET Framework mobile architecture attempts to keep controls within a `Panel` displayed as a unit and not split controls in a `Panel` across pages whenever possible.

Because composite mobile control development is similar to building composite controls in traditional ASP.NET development, we do not provide an example but rather refer you to earlier chapters that include composite control samples, such as Chapter 8 with the `UpDown` composite control.

Inheriting from MobileControl

Now that you have a firm grasp of the inner workings of mobile server controls, you can see how similar in design they are to traditional ASP.NET server controls. You should now have a good understanding of what is unique to mobile server controls. We now move on to implementing a simple mobile server control that targets WML and HTML browsers.

The MCTextBox Control

The Mobile Control `TextBox` control, or `MCTextBox` sample, is a duplicate of the `TextBox` sample from Chapter 5. We first copied the `TextBox` control source code, changed the namespace to `ControlsBookLib.Ch11`, and changed the class name to `MCTextBox`. We also added a `using` statement for `System.Web.UI.MobileControls` and changed the inherited class from `Control` to `MobileControl`.

For our example, we keep the postback handling code and continue to use the `TextChangedEventHandler` class from Chapter 5. We add the property customizations listed in Table 11-7 to round out our mobile control implementation.

Table 11-7. Added Property Customizations

PROPERTY	DESCRIPTION
MaxLength	Maximum length permitted for the `Text` property
Numeric	Boolean value that indicates whether the `Text` property takes only numbers
Password	Boolean value that indicates whether the password characters are displayed
Size	Indicates the estimated size of `Text` property
Title	Stores the `Title` value for the control

Listing 11-12 is the listing for our mobile control.

Listing 11-12. The MCTextBox.cs File

```
using System;
using System.Web.UI;
using System.Collections.Specialized;
using System.Web.UI.MobileControls;
using System.ComponentModel;

namespace ControlsBookLib.Ch11
{
    [ToolboxData("<{0}:MCTextBox runat=server></{0}:MCTextBox>"),
    DefaultProperty("Text")]
    public class MCTextBox : MobileControl, IPostBackDataHandler
    {
        public string Text
        {
            get
            {
                object text = ViewState["text"];
                if (text == null)
                    return string.Empty;
                else
                    return (string) text;
            }
            set
            {
                ViewState["text"] = value;
            }
        }

        public string Title
        {
            get
            {
                object title = ViewState["title"];
                if (title == null)
                    return string.Empty;
                else
                    return (string) title;
            }
            set
            {
                ViewState["title"] = value;
            }
        }

        public int MaxLength
        {
            get
            {
                object maxLength = ViewState["maxLength"];
```

```
            if (maxLength == null)
                return 0 ;
            else
                return (int) maxLength;
        }
        set
        {
            ViewState["maxLength"] = value;
        }
    }

    public int Size
    {
        get
        {
            object size = ViewState["size"];
            if (size == null)
                return 0 ;
            else
                return (int) size;
        }
        set
        {
            ViewState["size"] = value;
        }
    }

    public bool Password
    {
        get
        {
            object password = ViewState["password"];
            if (password == null)
                return false ;
            else
                return (bool) password;
        }
        set
        {
            ViewState["password"] = value;
        }
    }

    public bool Numeric
    {
        get
        {
            object numeric = ViewState["numeric"];
            if (numeric == null)
                return false ;
            else
```

```
            return (bool) numeric;
         }
         set
         {
            ViewState["numeric"] = value;
         }
      }

      public event EventHandler TextChanged;

      public bool LoadPostData(string postDataKey,
         NameValueCollection postCollection)
      {
         string postedValue = postCollection[postDataKey];
         if (!Text.Equals(postedValue))
         {
            Text = postedValue;
            return true;
         }
         else
            return false;
      }

      public void RaisePostDataChangedEvent()
      {
         OnTextChanged(EventArgs.Empty);
      }

      protected virtual void OnTextChanged(EventArgs e)
      {
         if (TextChanged != null)
            TextChanged(this, e);
      }
   }
}
```

As we discussed previously, mobile controls do not render themselves. Instead, mobile controls are associated with device adapters to handle rendering tasks. In our example, we implement two device adapters: one for HTML devices and the other for WML devices.

The HTML Device Adapter

This device adapter was pretty easy to create because the rendering code is essentially the same as the sample server control in Chapter 5. Device adapters follow a naming convention of RenderingTechnologyControlNameAdapter, which translates to HtmlMCTextBoxAdapter for our sample. Listing 11-13 contains the source code for the HTML device adapter.

Listing 11-13. The HtmlMCTextBoxAdapter *Source File*

```
using System;
using System.Web.UI.MobileControls;
using System.Web.UI.MobileControls.Adapters;
using ControlsBookLib.Ch11;

namespace ControlsBookLib.Ch11.Adapters
{
   public class HtmlMCTextBoxAdapter : HtmlControlAdapter
   {
      protected new MCTextBox Control
      {
         get
         {
            return (MCTextBox)base.Control;
         }
      }

      public override void Render(HtmlMobileTextWriter writer)
      {
         // write out the HTML tag

         writer.Write("<input name=\""+Control.UniqueID+"\" ");
         writer.Write("value=\"" + Control.Text + "\" ");
         if (Control.Password)
         {
            writer.Write("type=\"password\" ");
         }
         if (Control.Size != 0)
         {
            writer.Write("size=\""+Control.Size+"\" ");
         }
         writer.Write("/>");

         if (Control.BreakAfter)
         {
            writer.Write("<br>");
         }
      }
   }
}
```

The device adapter inherits from HtmlControlAdapter and implements two methods. We replace the Control property using the new keyword with a strongly typed Control read-only property. ASP.NET populates this property with the associated MCTextBox control at runtime.

Render is the other method we implement, and it has a few enhancements when compared to the original rendering code from the TextBox control in Chapter 5. We have logic to add a <BR> tag if the BreakAfter property has a value of true. Similarly, we render the input tag as of type password if the Password property is set to true.

We also set the size for the <INPUT> tag. The Size property does not enforce a rule, but it does set the initial width in characters for the control. Following the convention for the mobile control TextBox, we ignore the Numeric and Title properties' settings when rendering HTML.

One difference from the rendering logic in Chapter 5 is that instead of using the this reference, we use the strongly typed reference stored in the Control property to get control data for rendering. Also, the writer parameter is a reference to HtmlMobileTextWriter to handle markup output.

The WML Device Adapter

The WML device adapter is nearly identical to the HTML device adapter, except of course for the Render method. Listing 11-14 presents the code for WmlMCTextBoxAdapter.

Listing 11-14. The WmlMCTextBoxAdapter.cs Source File

```
using System;
using System.Web.UI.MobileControls;
using System.Web.UI.MobileControls.Adapters;
using ControlsBookLib.Ch11;

namespace ControlsBookLib.Ch11.Adapters
{
    public class WmlMCTextBoxAdapter : WmlControlAdapter
    {
        protected new MCTextBox Control
        {
            get
            {
                return (MCTextBox)base.Control;
            }
        }

        public override void Render(WmlMobileTextWriter writer)
        {
            string Format;

            if (Control.Numeric)
            {
                Format = "*N"; //Set format to any number of numeric characters
            }
            else
            {
                Format = "*M"; //Set format to any number of characters
            }
            writer.RenderTextBox(Control.UniqueID,Control.Text,Format,Control.Title,
                Control.Password,Control.Size,
                Control.MaxLength,false,Control.BreakAfter);
        }
    }
}
```

The Render method takes advantage of a method on the WmlMobileTextWriter writer named RenderTextBox. This method takes a series of parameters for customizing the output. Table 11-8 lists the parameters for RenderTextBox.

Table 11-8. WmlMobileTextWriter.RenderTextBox *Parameters*

PARAMETER	DESCRIPTION
breakAfter	Indicates whether a tag should be rendered after the <INPUT> tag
format	Permits application of WML-specific formatting options
generateRandomID	Indicates whether the identifier for the control should be encrypted
id	Identifier of the associated mobile control
maxLength	Stores the maximum length permitted for the string
password	Indicates if the data should be masked with the password character *
size	Stores the size of the string
title	Stores the title for the text box
value	Value to initialize the control

When you compare the parameters of this method with the properties on the mobile TextBox and MCTextBox controls, you can see that the Numeric and Title properties are geared toward WML-capable devices.

The other logic in the Render method for the WmlMCTextBoxAdapter class modifies the format parameter for this method, setting it to *N for unlimited numeric characters or *M for unlimited any type of characters. These settings come from the WML specification for the <INPUT> tag. Table 11-9 details the available values for the format setting.

Table 11-9. Permitted Settings for the WML <INPUT> *Tag* format *Value*

FORMAT	DESCRIPTION
A	Punctuation or uppercase alphabetic characters.
a	Punctuation or lowercase alphabetic characters.
M	All characters permitted.
m	All characters permitted.
N	Numeric characters only.
X	Uppercase characters only.
x	Lowercase characters only.
nf	n indicates a number between 1 and 9 for the number of characters permitted. Replace f with one of the preceding letters to specify what characters are legal.
*f	* indicates any number of characters permitted. Replace f with one of the preceding letters to specify what characters are legal.

Creating device adapters requires a deep understanding of the nuances of the markup language. (Either that or a good reference close at hand!)

Mapping Device Adapters

Now that we have created our mobile server control and device adapters, it is time to modify a configuration file so that the ASP.NET runtime can select the correct device adapter to render the mobile control.

We can inherit from the machine.config file and create a new device mapping in the web.config file, or we can modify the machine.config file. The section of the configuration file we need to customize is the `<mobileControls>` element. For a given device target, we need to map the mobile control to a device adapter. Here is the syntax to map a mobile server control to a device adapter:

```
<control name= "controlName, assembly" adapter="adapterName, assembly" />
```

If the assembly is registered in the GAC, you can omit the assembly name. For our sample, we chose to modify the `<mobileControls>` tag in web.config by adding the following section:

```
<mobileControls cookielessDataDictionaryType=
"System.Web.Mobile.CookielessData">
<device name="ControlsBookHtml" inheritsFrom="HtmlDeviceAdapters">
    <control name=
    "ControlsBookLib.Ch11.MCTextBox,ControlsBookLib" adapter=
    "ControlsBookLib.Ch11.Adapters.HtmlMCTextBoxAdapter,ControlsBookLib" />
</device>
<device name="ControlsBookWml" inheritsFrom="WmlDeviceAdapters">
    <control name=
    "ControlsBookLib.Ch11.MCTextBox,ControlsBookLib" adapter=
    "ControlsBookLib.Ch11.Adapters.WmlMCTextBoxAdapter,ControlsBookLib" />
</device>
</mobileControls>
```

In the preceding section, we inherit from the standard device mappings listed in machine.config and can simply make the modifications we need for our control. This method makes it easy to add server controls to device adapter mappings.

Testing MCTextBox

Now that we have everything set up, we can put our new control through its paces. The sample mobile page is very similar to the sample in Chapter 5. Because the new control keeps the code the same as much as possible, it handles postback data and generates server-side events if the data changes in the MCTextBox. Listings 11-15 and 11-16 provide the source for MCTextBoxDemo.aspx and its code-behind file.

Listing 11-15. The MCTextBoxDemo.aspx File

```
<%@ Page language="c#" Codebehind="MCTextBoxDemo.aspx.cs"
Inherits="ControlsBookMobile.Ch11.MCTextBox" AutoEventWireup="false" %>
<%@ Register TagPrefix="mobile" Namespace="System.Web.UI.MobileControls"
Assembly="System.Web.Mobile" %>
<%@ Register TagPrefix="ApressMC" Namespace="ControlsBookLib.Ch11"
Assembly="ControlsBookLib" %>
<HEAD>
  <meta content="Microsoft Visual Studio .NET 7.1" name="GENERATOR">
  <meta content="C#" name="CODE_LANGUAGE">
  <meta content="http://schemas.microsoft.com/Mobile/Page" name="vs_targetSchema">
</HEAD>
<body>
  <mobile:form id="Form1" runat="server">
    <mobile:Label id="Label1" runat="server">Change the value:</mobile:Label>
    <ApressMC:MCTextBox id="MCTextBox1" runat="server" Text="Hi There!"
    Maxlength="15" Numeric="False" Password="False"
      Size="10"></ApressMC:MCTextBox>
    <mobile:Command id="Command1" runat="server">Command</mobile:Command>
    <mobile:Label id="ChangeLabel" runat="server">Message</mobile:Label>
  </mobile:form>
</body>
```

Listing 11-16. The MCTextBoxDemo.aspx File

```
using System;
using System.Collections;
using System.ComponentModel;
using System.Data;
using System.Drawing;
using System.Web;
using System.Web.Mobile;
using System.Web.SessionState;
using System.Web.UI;
using System.Web.UI.MobileControls;
using System.Web.UI.WebControls;
using System.Web.UI.HtmlControls;
using ControlsBookLib.Ch11;

namespace ControlsBookMobile.Ch11
{
    public class MCTextBox : System.Web.UI.MobileControls.MobilePage
    {
        protected ControlsBookLib.Ch11.MCTextBox MCTextBox1;
        protected System.Web.UI.MobileControls.Command Command1;
        protected System.Web.UI.MobileControls.Label ChangeLabel;
        protected System.Web.UI.MobileControls.Label Label1;
        protected System.Web.UI.MobileControls.TextBox TextBox1;
        protected System.Web.UI.MobileControls.Form Form1;
```

```
private void Page_Load(object sender, System.EventArgs e)
{
   ChangeLabel.Text = DateTime.Now.ToLongTimeString() +
   ": MCTextBox No change.";
}

#region Web Form Designer generated code
override protected void OnInit(EventArgs e)
{
   //
   // CODEGEN: This call is required by the ASP.NET Web Form Designer.
   //
   InitializeComponent();
   base.OnInit(e);
}

/// <summary>
/// Required method for Designer support - do not modify
/// the contents of this method with the code editor.
/// </summary>
private void InitializeComponent()
{
   this.MCTextBox1.TextChanged += new
   System.EventHandler(this.MCTextBox1_TextChanged);
   this.Load += new System.EventHandler(this.Page_Load);

}
#endregion

private void MCTextBox1_TextChanged(object sender, System.EventArgs e)
{
   ChangeLabel.Text = DateTime.Now.ToLongTimeString() +
   ": MCTextbox Changed! "+ MCTextBox1.Text ;
}
   }
}
```

The sample consists of MCTextBox, a Command button, and a Label to display a message. When the form first appears, the message label displays "No change". Change the value in the MCTextBox control and click the Command button. Figures 11-9 and 11-10 display the process in Pocket IE.

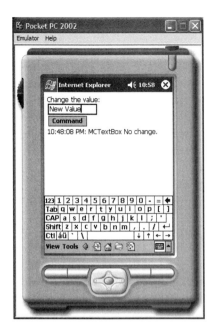

Figure 11-9. The initial state of the MCTextBoxDemo page

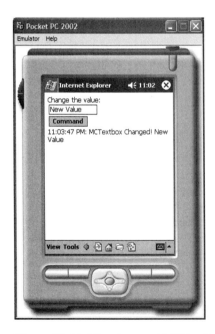

Figure 11-10. The changed MCTextBoxDemo page state

When the mobile form reloads after the postback process, the message label displays an updated time and a message stating that the value changed. This shows that the server-side event process is correctly implemented.

The MCTextBox control displays correctly in both Pocket IE and the WML emulator, demonstrating the extensibility of the ASP.NET framework mobile server control architecture.

Summary

In this chapter, you studied the extensibility hooks for mobile server controls, which are the StyleSheet control, templates, device-specific UI choices, user controls, custom controls, and device adapters. ASP.NET provides three default StyleSheet Styles in the StyleReference property: error, subcommand, and title.

Mobile control technology includes user controls, composite controls, and custom developed controls inherited from MobileControl. Creating custom mobile server controls is very similar to creating traditional mobile controls. The two major differences are ViewState management and the rendering process. Mobile server controls that inherit from MobileControl do not render themselves but instead rely on device adapters to handle their rendering.

There are a plethora of devices and more than a few rendering technologies, such as cHTML, WML, XHTML, and so on. Coupled with the rapidly growing and changing mobile device market, ASP.NET provides a flexible architecture that isolates device and markup differences. Device adapters render mobile controls on specific mobile devices. ASP.NET with Device Update 2 provides support for HTML, WML, cHTML, and XHTML. MobileCapabilties inherits from HttpBrowserCapabilities and aids in detecting the closest match of what device is currently browsing a web application.

Any control that inherits from MobileControl can contain one DeviceSpecific element. DeviceSpecific is a container element that hosts one or more Choice elements. The Choice element contained in the DeviceSpecific element has a filter attribute that plugs into the device capability decision engine that is part of the mobile ASP.NET architecture. The filter attribute refers to a set of XML elements added to the standard web.config file when you select an ASP.NET mobile web application in Visual Studio .NET.

With the information on the ASP.NET mobile control device capability detection system from Chapter 8 and this chapter, it is possible to modify machine configuration files to accommodate devices the ASP.NET team has not yet reached with the device update program. This architecture gives mobile control developers a wide range of options to modify built-in rendering behavior and enables them to create entirely new rendering engines targeting the latest and greatest mobile devices.

CHAPTER 12

Design-Time Support

DESIGN-TIME SUPPORT refers to working with server controls within the Visual Studio
.NET development environment. Dragging controls onto the web page Component
Designer surface from the Toolbox tool window, editing server control properties in the
Properties tool window, and right-clicking a control to bring up a context menu are all
examples of design-time support.

All these capabilities and more are made available to server control developers by
the .NET Framework. In this chapter, we explore the design-time capabilities and techniques available in the .NET Framework for inclusion in custom-developed server control development efforts.

Professional Quality

Support for visual controls in rapid application development (RAD) environments on
the Windows platform have existed since the early days of Visual Basic. As opposed to
just working with a class in code, controls enhance the development environment
experience and speed up development time. The qualities associated with a professional control include the following:

- Ease of installation

- High level of documentation

- Large amount of sample code that demonstrates control functionality

- Design-time support

In the remainder of this book, we aim to provide you with the requisite knowledge
to assist you in developing professional quality controls. In this chapter we cover
design-time support. We cover localization, help file integration, and deployment in
the follow-on chapters. In the next section, we take a look at the design-time architecture provided by the .NET Framework.

Design-Time Architecture

The .NET Framework provides design-time customizations for both Windows controls
and web controls. The customizations available in each environment differ mostly as a
result of rendering technology: ASP.NET server controls generate HTML, and Windows
Forms controls render using GDI+. This chapter focuses on design-time capabilities for
web controls, but many of the concepts discussed here apply to the Windows Forms
environment as well.

It is interesting to note that design-time support is not intrinsic to Visual Studio .NET. In the past, design-time support was built into editing tools or implemented on a component-by-component basis, such as ActiveX property pages. This is not the case with the .NET Framework.

For example, if you open a Web Form in Visual Studio .NET, drag a `DataGrid` onto the Component Designer surface, and select Property Builder, a powerful, UI type editor displays. Now perform the same steps in ASP.NET Web Matrix (available at `http://www.asp.net`). Open a Web Form, place a `DataGrid` on the Component Designer surface, click Property Builder, and the same design-time UI displays. The UI is part of the control, not the environment.

Certainly, the Visual Studio .NET UI is the more powerful development environment of the two. From a design-time support standpoint, Visual Studio .NET is more powerful mainly because ASP.NET Web Matrix does not fully implement all design-time interfaces. There are two primary facilities available for design-time programming:

- Design-time environment services

- Component-specific customizations

We next provide an overview of design-time environment services, and then we move on to cover component customization. As we implement component customization samples, we touch on the design-time environment services necessary to integrate into a design-time environment such as Visual Studio .NET.

Environment Services Overview

The .NET Framework design-time environment services extend the capabilities and level of integration with a designer such as Visual Studio .NET. To obtain a service, the `Component` class implements `IServiceProvider`, which has a method named `GetService` that can be used to obtain a reference to a service interface implemented by the design-time environment.

For example, a server control can use the `GetService` method in a UI type editor to obtain a reference to `IWindowsFormsEditorService`. Next, the control can call the `ShowDialog` method on the reference to have the design-time environment create a Windows Forms–based UI for editing a particular property. This is just one example of what is available in design-time environment services. Table 12-1 provides an overview of available design-time environment services.

Table 12-1. Design-Time Environment Interfaces

INTERFACE	DESCRIPTION
IComponentChangeService	Permits a designer to receive notifications when components are changed, added, or removed from the design-time environment.
IDesignerEventService	Permits a designer to receive notifications when designers are added or removed, and notifications when the selected component changes.

(Continued)

Table 12-1. Design-Time Environment Interfaces (Continued)

INTERFACE	DESCRIPTION
IDesignerFilter	Permits a designer to add to the set of properties displayed in the property browser and filter the properties.
IDesignerHost	Used to add and retrieve services available in the design-time environment and handle events related to designer state. It provides support for detecting that a designer is loading and helps manage component and designer transactions.
IDesignerOptionService	Permits a designer to get and set property values displayed in the Windows Forms Designer property grid displayed when Tools ➤ Options is selected.
IDictionaryService	Provides a key-based collection for user-defined data for designers.
IEventBindingService	Permits a designer to expose events at design time for the selected component in a property browser.
IExtenderListService	Makes the currently active extender providers available to a designer.
IExtenderProviderService	Permits a designer to add or remove extender providers at design time.
IHelpService	Permits a designer to create and remove help service contexts and attributes, and display help topics by keyword and URL.
IInheritanceService	Permits a designer to search for components of derived classes and identify any inheritance attributes for each.
IMenuCommandService	Permits a designer to search for, add, remove, and invoke menu commands at design time.
IReferenceService	Permits a designer to obtain a reference to an object by name and type, and obtain a reference to the desired object's parent.
IResourceService	Permits a designer to obtain a culture-specific resource reader or writer.
IRootDesigner	Permits a designer to replace the root designer view with a custom designer view display.
ISelectionService	Permits a designer to get a set of references to currently selected components, select components(s), and determine what components are currently selected.
IServiceContainer	Permits a component or designer to add or remove services for use by other components or designers.
ITypeDescriptorFilterService	Permits a component or designer to filter attributes, events, and properties exposed by a component.
ITypeResolutionService	Permits a designer to add an assembly reference to a project, obtain a type or assembly by name, and obtain the assembly's path.
IWindowsFormsEditorService	Permits a UI designer to create a Windows Form UI for editing a property at design time.

As Table 12-1 shows, the .NET Framework includes quite a few interfaces to permit a high level of integration between the framework, the components, and the design-time environment.

We now move our discussion to the primary method to implement design-time capabilities: customizing component behavior.

Customizing Component Behavior

The .NET Framework provides the necessary interfaces and services to enable a rich design-time experience when working with controls. As we mentioned previously, the design-time architecture is shared between Windows Forms and ASP.NET.

Windows Forms controls inherit from `System.ComponentModel.Component`, and we know that ASP.NET controls inherit from `System.Web.UI.Control`. Both classes implement the `IComponent` interface, which is in the `System.ComponentModel` namespace. The `System.ComponentModel.Design` namespace is where the majority of design-time classes exist.

Examine the design-time capabilities of the built-in `DataGrid` server control and you quickly see how extensive the support is. Customizations available at design time fall into the following categories:

- Designers

- Type converters

- UI type editors

The common root base class for both the Windows Forms and Web Forms custom designers is `System.ComponentModel.Design.ComponentDesigner`. Custom designers manage the UI and behavior of a component at design time. Customizations include changing the component's appearance, initialization, and interaction on the Component Designer surface. `DesignerAttribute` associates a designer with a type.

A custom designer can modify what properties display in the property browser and provide methods that can be linked to component events or fired through the developer/user clicking a menu command. Designers are only used by controls at design time.

The base class for type converters is `System.ComponentModel.TypeConverter`. Type converters are generally implemented for control properties that are not readily converted to the `string` type. Type converters are also implemented for types that include subproperties, such as the expand/collapse UI for the `Font` property. `TypeConverterAttribute` associates a type converter with a type or type member. `TypeConverters` can be used by controls both at design time and runtime.

The root base class for UI type editors for both Windows Forms and Web Forms is System.Drawing.Design.UITypeEditor. A *UI type editor* can provide a custom user interface for editing property values. It displays a custom representation of a property at design time. UI type editors are type specific. An example is the ForeColor property of type Color that displays the various colors available, which makes it much easier to select a particular color than with a hex value or name. EditorAttribute associates a UI type editor with a type or type member. A UI type editor can be used by controls both at design time and runtime.

For a Web Form's design-time support, ASP.NET-specific base class implementations exist in the System.Web.UI.Design namespace. For example, the base class for ASP.NET server control custom designers is System.Web.UI.Design.HtmlControlDesigner, which inherits from System.ComponentModel.Design.ComponentDesigner (discussed previously).

HtmlControlDesigner provides basic designer functionality for server controls. The class that developers extend when building custom designer classes for ASP.NET server controls is System.Web.UI.Design.ControlDesigner.

Though Windows Forms and Web Forms share a common architecture for design-time support, the recommendation here is to look to the rendering technology-specific design-time support namespaces first to ease development effort.

Attributes

As we mentioned previously, control customizations are applied using attributes. We provided an overview of attributes at the end of Chapter 3. Table 3-2 in Chapter 3 details basic design-time attributes such as DefaultProperty, DefaultValue, DescriptionAttribute, and so on. In the examples that follow, we apply several of these basic attributes as well as more advanced attributes related to this chapter's discussion. For more information on attributes, please refer to Chapter 3 or the .NET Framework documentation.

The TitledThumbnail Control

To demonstrate design-time behavior, we created a simple composite server control named TitledThumbnail. As you might have guessed, TitledThumbnail displays a thumbnail image with a title underneath. It has several custom properties including a complex property to help demonstrate design-time techniques. Figure 12-1 shows the control in a browser window.

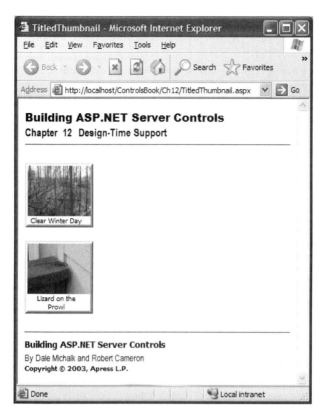

Figure 12-1. The TitledThumbnail *demonstration page in the browser*

There are two instances of the control displaying an image with a caption. We want to jump straight to our design-time discussion, and TitledThumbnail is so straightforward that we don't provide a discussion of how this control is constructed so we can go straight to the code. Listing 12-1 contains the source for the TitledThumbnail control.

Listing 12-1. The TitledThumbnail *Control*

```
using System;
using System.Web.UI;
using System.Web.UI.HtmlControls;
using System.Web.UI.WebControls;
using System.Text;
using System.Collections;
using System.Collections.Specialized;
using System.Web;
using System.Reflection;
using System.ComponentModel;
using ControlsBookLib.Ch12.Design;
```

```
namespace ControlsBookLib.Ch12
{
    public enum TitleAlignment {center,justify,left,right};

    [ToolboxData("<{0}:TitledThumbnail runat=server></{0}:TitledThumbnail>"),
EditorAttribute(typeof(TitledThumbnailComponentEditor),typeof(ComponentEditor)),
    Designer(typeof(TitledThumbnailDesigner)),
    DefaultProperty("ImageUrl")]
    public class TitledThumbnail : WebControl, INamingContainer
    {
        private Image imgThumbnail;
        private Label lblTitle;
        private ImageMetaData metaData;

        public TitledThumbnail() : base(System.Web.UI.HtmlTextWriterTag.Div)
        {

        }

        [DescriptionAttribute("Text to be shown as the image caption."),
        CategoryAttribute("Appearance")]
        public string Title
        {
            get
            {
                EnsureChildControls();
                object title = ViewState["title"];
                return (title == null) ? "" : (string) title;
            }
            set
            {
                EnsureChildControls();
                lblTitle.Text = value;
                ViewState["title"] = value;
            }
        }

        [DescriptionAttribute("The Url of the image to be shown."),
        CategoryAttribute("Appearance")]
        public string ImageUrl
        {
            get
            {
                EnsureChildControls();
                object imageUrl = ViewState["imageUrl"];
                return (imageUrl == null) ? "" : (string) imageUrl;
            }
            set
            {
                EnsureChildControls();
                imgThumbnail.ImageUrl = value;
```

611

```
          ViewState["imageUrl"] = value;
      }
   }

   [DescriptionAttribute("Set the alignment for the Image and Title."),
   CategoryAttribute("Layout"),DefaultValue("center")]
   public TitleAlignment Align
   {
      get
      {
         EnsureChildControls();
         object align = ViewState["align"];
         return (align == null) ? TitleAlignment.left : (TitleAlignment)align;
      }
      set
      {
         EnsureChildControls();
         this.Attributes.Add(
         "align",Enum.GetName(typeof(TitleAlignment),value));
         ViewState["align"] = value;
      }
   }

   [DesignerSerializationVisibility(DesignerSerializationVisibility.Content),
   NotifyParentProperty(true),CategoryAttribute("MetaData"),
   DescriptionAttribute(
   "Meta data that stores information about the displayed photo image.")]
   public ImageMetaData ImageInfo
   {
      get
      {
         EnsureChildControls();
         if (metaData == null)
         {
            metaData = new ImageMetaData();
         }
         return metaData;
      }
   }

   public override ControlCollection Controls
   {
      get
      {
         EnsureChildControls();
         return base.Controls;
      }
   }

   protected override void CreateChildControls()
   {
      Controls.Clear();
```

```
        imgThumbnail = new Image();
        this.Controls.Add(imgThumbnail);

        lblTitle = new Label();
        lblTitle.Width = 86;
        this.Controls.Add(lblTitle);
    }


  }
}
```

Listings 12-2 and 12-3 contain the source for the `TitledThumbnail` demonstration page and code-behind file.

Listing 12-2. The `TitledThumbnail` *Demonstration .aspx File*

```
<%@ Page language="c#" Codebehind="TitledThumbnail.aspx.cs"
AutoEventWireup="false" Inherits="ControlsBookWeb.Ch12.TitledThumbnail" %>
<%@ Register TagPrefix="apressUC" TagName="ControlsBookFooter"
Src="..\ControlsBookFooter.ascx" %>
<%@ Register TagPrefix="apressUC" TagName="ControlsBookHeader"
Src="..\ControlsBookHeader.ascx" %>
<%@ Register TagPrefix="apress" Namespace="ControlsBookLib.Ch12"
Assembly="ControlsBookLib" %>
<!DOCTYPE HTML PUBLIC "-//W3C//DTD HTML 4.0 Transitional//EN" >
<HTML>
  <HEAD>
    <title>TitledThumbnail</title>
    <meta content="Microsoft Visual Studio .NET 7.1" name="GENERATOR">
    <meta content="C#" name="CODE_LANGUAGE">
    <meta content="JavaScript" name="vs_defaultClientScript">
    <meta content="http://schemas.microsoft.com/intellisense/ie5"
     name="vs_targetSchema">
  </HEAD>
  <body MS_POSITIONING="GridLayout">
    <form id="Form1" method="post" runat="server">
      <apressuc:controlsbookheader id="Header" runat="server" chapternumber="12"
      chaptertitle="Design-Time Support"></apressuc:controlsbookheader>
      <br>
      <apress:titledthumbnail id="TitledThumbnail1" title="Clear Winter Day"
      runat="server" ImageInfo-ImageLocation="76N,101W"
      Align="center" ImageInfo-PhotographerFullName="Robert Cameron" ImageInfo-
ImageLongDescription="Winter outdoor scene in Februrary"
        ImageInfo-ImageDate="2003-04-02" BorderStyle="Outset" Font-Size="XX-
Small" Font-Names="Tahoma" ImageUrl="Outdoors.jpg"
        Height="88px" Width="88px" ImageInfo-
IsEmpty="False"></apress:titledthumbnail><br>
      <apress:titledthumbnail id="Titledthumbnail2" title="Lizard on the Prowl"
runat="server" ImageInfo-ImageLocation="34S,150E"
        Align="center" ImageInfo-PhotographerFullName="Rob Cameron" ImageInfo-
```

```
ImageLongDescription="A lizard on the side of the wood deck."
        ImageInfo-ImageDate="2003-04-08" BorderStyle="Outset" Font-Size="XX-
Small" Font-Names="Tahoma" ImageUrl="Lizard.jpg"
        Height="88px" Width="88px" ImageInfo-
IsEmpty="False"></apress:titledthumbnail>
    <br>
    <apressuc:controlsbookfooter id="Footer"
    runat="server"></apressuc:controlsbookfooter></form>
  </FORM>
 </body>
</HTML>
```

Listing 12-3. The TitledThumbnail *Demonstration Page Code-Behind File*

```
using System;
using System.Collections;
using System.ComponentModel;
using System.Data;
using System.Drawing;
using System.Web;
using System.Web.SessionState;
using System.Web.UI;
using System.Web.UI.WebControls;
using System.Web.UI.HtmlControls;
using ControlsBookLib;

namespace ControlsBookWeb.Ch12
{
    public class TitledThumbnail : System.Web.UI.Page
    {
        protected ControlsBookLib.Ch12.TitledThumbnail Titledthumbnail2;
        protected ControlsBookLib.Ch12.TitledThumbnail TitledThumbnail1;

        private void Page_Load(object sender, System.EventArgs e)
        {
        }

        #region Web Form Designer generated code
        override protected void OnInit(EventArgs e)
        {
            //
            // CODEGEN: This call is required by the ASP.NET Web Form Designer.
            //
            InitializeComponent();
            base.OnInit(e);
        }

        /// <summary>
        /// Required method for Designer support - do not modify
        /// the contents of this method with the code editor.
        /// </summary>
```

```
        private void InitializeComponent()
        {
            this.Load += new System.EventHandler(this.Page_Load);


        }
        #endregion
    }
}
```

The TitledThumbnail control implements properties such as ImageMetaData and Location that do not configure the control; rather, they store data about the thumbnail image. Though this may or may not be a useful design, the properties help us demonstrate design-time customizations, which is this chapter's focus.

The TitledThumbnail Control at Design Time

Figure 12-2 displays an annotated screen shot of the TitledThumbnail control at design time. Item 1 in Figure 12-2 highlights a couple of properties displayed in the Properties window. We discuss customizations for the Properties window in the next section.

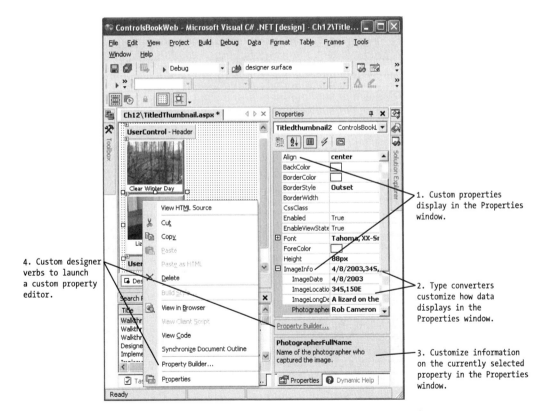

Figure 12-2. The TitledThumbnail *control in the Visual Studio .NET Designer*

The Properties Window

Without any work by the developer, a control that inherits from System.Web.UI.Control displays simple properties in the property browser. Simple properties include Boolean, string, integer, decimal, and so on. Although not a simple type, enumeration types also display automatically, as does a drop-down list in the property browser.

Some easy customizations include applying the basic design-time attributes listed in Chapter 3. Here is an example from the TitledThumbnail control:

```
[DescriptionAttribute("Set the alignment for the Image and Title."),
    CategoryAttribute("Layout"),DefaultValue("center")]
```

The DescriptionAttribute displays the passed-in string at the bottom of the property browser, as pointed out by item 3 in Figure 12-2. The CategoryAttribute places the property in the passed-in category in the Properties window. Example property browser categories are Layout, Behavior, and so on. The last attribute, DefaultValue, sets the default value for the property. For an enumeration property, set the Default-Value property to a string value representing the enumeration value, not the actual strongly typed enumeration value.

Attributes are generally named with the word "Attribute" appended at the end. However, the word "Attribute" is optional when applying the attribute. In the previous example, the text DescriptionAttribute("..") could be replaced with Description(""). Likewise, the actual class name of the DefaultVaue attribute is DefaultValueAttribute.

The ImageInfo property on the TitledThumbnail control is of type ImageMetaData. Listing 12-4 contains the source for the ImageMetaData class.

Listing 12-4. The ImageMetaData *Class*

```
using System;
using System.ComponentModel;
using System.Drawing.Design;
using System.Globalization;
using System.Text;
using ControlsBookLib.Ch12.Design;

namespace ControlsBookLib.Ch12
{
    [TypeConverter(typeof(ImageMetaDataConverter))]
    public class ImageMetaData
    {
        private DateTime imageDate;
        private Location imageLocation;
        private string imageLongDescription;
        private string photographerFullName;

        public ImageMetaData()
        {

        }
```

```
public ImageMetaData(DateTime PhotoDate,Location Loc,
   string ImageDescription,string FullName)
{
   photographerFullName = FullName;
   imageDate = PhotoDate;
   imageLongDescription = ImageDescription;
   imageLocation = Loc;
}

[NotifyParentProperty(true),
DescriptionAttribute("Name of the photographer who captured the image.")]
public string PhotographerFullName
{
   get
   {
      return photographerFullName;
   }
   set
   {
      photographerFullName = value;
   }
}

[NotifyParentProperty(true),
DescriptionAttribute("Date the image was captured.")]
public DateTime ImageDate
{
   get
   {
      return imageDate;
   }
   set
   {
      imageDate = value;
   }
}

[NotifyParentProperty(true),
DescriptionAttribute("Extended description of the image."),
EditorAttribute(typeof(ControlsBookLib.Ch12.Design.SimpleTextEditor),
typeof(UITypeEditor))]
public string ImageLongDescription
{
   get
   {
      return imageLongDescription;
   }
   set
   {
      imageLongDescription = value;
   }
}
```

```
        [NotifyParentProperty(true),
        DescriptionAttribute("Location where the image was captured.")]
        public Location ImageLocation
        {
          get
          {
            if (imageLocation == null)
            {
              imageLocation = new Location();
            }
            return imageLocation;
          }
          set
          {
            imageLocation = value;
          }
        }

        [Browsable(false)]
        public bool IsEmpty
        {
          get
          {
            return (photographerFullName.Length == 0
              && imageDate == DateTime.MinValue &&
              imageLongDescription.Length -- 0 &&
              imageLocation.IsEmpty);
          }
        }

        public override string ToString()
        {
          return ToString(CultureInfo.CurrentCulture);
        }

        public string ToString(CultureInfo Culture)
        {
          return
    TypeDescriptor.GetConverter(typeof(ImageMetaData)).ConvertToString(null,
          Culture, this);
        }
      }
    }
```

ImageMetaData is a class containing simple types and a complex type named Location. Listing 12-5 contains the source for the Location class.

Listing 12-5. The Location *Class*

```
using System;
using System.ComponentModel;
using System.Text;
using System.Globalization;
using ControlsBookLib.Ch12.Design;

namespace ControlsBookLib.Ch12
{
   [TypeConverter(typeof(LocationConverter))]
   public class Location
   {
      private double latitude;
      private double longitude;

      public Location()
      {
         latitude = 0;
         longitude = 0;
      }

      public Location(double Lat, double Long)
      {
         latitude = Lat;
         longitude = Long;
      }

      public double Latitude
      {
         get
         {
            return latitude;
         }
         set
         {
            latitude = value;
         }
      }

      public double Longitude
      {
         get
         {
            return longitude;
         }
         set
         {
            longitude = value;
         }
      }

   }

      public bool IsEmpty
```

```
    {
        get
        {
            return (latitude == 0 && longitude == 0);
        }
    }

    //override ToString so that it displays the values of
    //its members as opposed to its fully qualified type.
    public override string ToString()
    {
        return ToString(CultureInfo.CurrentCulture);
    }

    public string ToString(CultureInfo Culture)
    {
        return TypeDescriptor.GetConverter(typeof(Location)).ConvertToString(null,
            Culture, this);
    }

    public override bool Equals(object obj)
    {
        Location Loc = (Location) obj;

        if (Loc != null)
        {
            return (latitude == Loc.Latitude &&
                longitude == Loc.Longitude);
        }
        return false;
    }

    public override int GetHashCode()
    {
        //XOR the latitude and longitude coordinates
        return latitude.GetHashCode() ^ longitude.GetHashCode();
    }
    }
}
```

The Location class stores a latitude and longitude as a decimal. To help display these properties in the property browser, we implemented the ImageInfoConverter and LocationConverter type converters. Type converters are the subject of the next section.

Type Converters

Type converter attributes are applied to type class definitions to assist with converting the type to other data types and vice versa. Generally, this conversion is to/from the string type. Type converters can also alter how a type appears in the property browser at design time.

A custom type converter derives from `System.ComponentModel.TypeConverter` regardless of whether it is for a property of a Windows Forms or Web Forms control. The type converter for the `Location` class type has a type converter named `LocationConverter` that inherits from this class. The purpose of this type converter is to alter how the `Location` type displays in the property browser.

The LocationConverter Class

The `Location` class stores a latitude and longitude. An instance of this type is part of the `ImageMetaData` type. The `ImageMetaData` type uses the `Location` instance to store the location where the photo displayed by the `TitledThumbnail` control was taken. Latitude and longitude values are generally displayed using degrees/minutes/seconds notation or as a decimal with N/S, E/W appended to the decimal value.

Take a look again at Figure 12-2. Item 2 highlights the display for `ImageInfo` and `ImageLocation`. `ImageLocation` is of type `Location`. Notice the value displayed: 34S,150E. These values are easily understood to represent a latitude and longitude. If you look at the `Location` type, the underlying latitude and longitude values are of type `double` with a negative latitude representing south and a negative longitude representing east. The `LocationConverter` type converter makes this possible and is shown in Listing 12-6.

Listing 12-6. The LocationConverter *Source*

```
using System;
using System.Globalization;
using System.Reflection;
using System.ComponentModel;
using System.ComponentModel.Design.Serialization;
using ControlsBookLib.Ch12;

namespace ControlsBookLib.Ch12.Design
{
    public class LocationConverter : TypeConverter
    {
        public override bool CanConvertFrom(ITypeDescriptorContext
            context, Type sourceType)
        {
            if (sourceType == typeof(string))
            {
                return true;
            }

            return base.CanConvertFrom(context, sourceType);
        }

        public override bool CanConvertTo(ITypeDescriptorContext
            context, Type destinationType)
        {
            if ((destinationType == typeof(string)) ||
```

```
            (destinationType == typeof(InstanceDescriptor)))
      {
         return true;
      }

      return base.CanConvertTo(context, destinationType);
   }

   public override object ConvertFrom(ITypeDescriptorContext
      context, CultureInfo culture, object value)
   {
      if (value == null)
      {
         return new Location();
      }

      if (value is string)
      {
         string str = (string)value;
         if (str == "")
         {
            return new Location();
         }

         string[] propValues =
            str.Split(culture.TextInfo.ListSeparator[0]);

         if (propValues.Length != 2)
         {
            throw new ArgumentException("Invalid Location", "value");
         }

         //Peel off N/S for latitude and E/W for longitude
         string Lat = propValues[0];
         if (Lat.Substring(Lat.Length -1) == "N")
         {
            string[] latParts = Lat.Split("N".ToCharArray());
            Lat = latParts[0];
         }
         if (Lat.Substring(Lat.Length -1) == "S")
         {
            string[] latParts = Lat.Split("S".ToCharArray());
            Lat = "-" + latParts[0];
         }

         string Long = propValues[1];
         if (Long.Substring(Long.Length -1) == "W")
         {
            string[] longParts = Long.Split("W".ToCharArray());
            Long = longParts[0];
         }
```

```
            if (Long.Substring(Long.Length -1) == "E")
            {
                string[] longParts = Long.Split("E".ToCharArray());
                Long = "-" + longParts[0];
            }

            TypeConverter DoubleConverter =
                TypeDescriptor.GetConverter(typeof(double));

            return new
Location((double)DoubleConverter.ConvertFromString(context, culture, Lat),
                (double)DoubleConverter.ConvertFromString(context, culture, Long));
        }

        return base.ConvertFrom(context, culture, value);
    }

    public override object ConvertTo(ITypeDescriptorContext context,
CultureInfo culture, object value, Type destinationType)
    {
        if (value != null)
        {
            if (!(value is Location))
            {
                throw new ArgumentException("Not of type Location", "value");
            }
        }

        if (destinationType == typeof(string))
        {
            if (value == null)
            {
                return String.Empty;
            }

            Location Loc = (Location)value;
            string Lat ;
            string Long ;

            TypeConverter DoubleConverter =
                TypeDescriptor.GetConverter(typeof(double));

            //Add N/S for latitude, E/W for longitude
            if (Math.Round(Loc.Latitude) >= 0)
            {
                Lat =
                    DoubleConverter.ConvertToString(context,
                    culture, Loc.Latitude) + "N";
            }
            else
            {
```

```
      Lat =
         DoubleConverter.ConvertToString(context,
         culture, Math.Abs(Loc.Latitude)) + "S";
   }

   if (Math.Round(Loc.Longitude) >= 0)
   {
      Long =
         DoubleConverter.ConvertToString(context,
         culture, Loc.Longitude) + "W";
   }
   else
   {
      Long = DoubleConverter.ConvertToString(context,
         culture, Math.Abs(Loc.Longitude)) + "E";
   }

   // Display lat and long as concatenated string with
   //a comma as the separator based on the current culture
   return String.Join(culture.TextInfo.ListSeparator,
      new string[] {Lat,Long});
}
else if (destinationType == typeof(InstanceDescriptor))
{
   if (value == null)
   {
      return null;
   }

   MemberInfo memberInfo = null;
   object[] memberParameters = null;

   Location Loc = (Location)value;
   if (Loc.IsEmpty)
   {
      memberInfo =
         typeof(Location).GetConstructor(new Type[0]);
   }
   else
   {
      Type doubleType = typeof(double);
      memberInfo = typeof(Location).GetConstructor(new Type[]
         { doubleType, doubleType });
      memberParameters =
         new object[] { Loc.Latitude, Loc.Longitude };
   }

   if (memberInfo != null)
   {
      return new InstanceDescriptor(memberInfo,
         memberParameters);
```

```
        }
        else
        {
            return null;
        }
    }
    return base.ConvertTo(context, culture, value,
        destinationType);
    }
  }
}
```

When the page parser encounters a type that has a type converter associated with it via the following syntax, it uses the type converter's methods to assist with parsing the property to/from a string value:

```
[TypeConverter(typeof(LocationConverter))]
  public class Location
  {
...
```

The .NET Framework also uses TypeConverters to stream types to/from ViewState during the page life cycle. TypeConverters provide methods to check whether a type conversion is supported as well as a method to make the conversion. The Location type converter implements four methods:

- CanConvertFrom(..)

- CanConvertTo(..)

- ConvertFrom(..)

- ConvertTo(..)

CanConvertFrom has logic that checks what type is passed in and returns true if the type is a type, such as string, that can be converted into the class type. CanConvertTo has generally the same logic, returning true if the target type is a type that the class type can be converted to.

ConvertFrom for the LocationConverter class has logic to ensure that the N/S, E/W values are appropriately handled. Same for ConvertTo. This type converter provides nice functionality, altering how the type renders in the property browser so that it is more readable or in a format that makes more sense. Note that if the user decides to enter a latitude and longitude using this format, 34,–135 (34N,134E), the type converter logic is written in such a way to permit it.

We now move on to a discussion of the ImageMetaData class and its type converter.

The ImageMetaDataConverter Class

The ImageMetaData class is the type of the ImageInfo member on the TitledThumbnail control. The ImageMetaData class is a complex type that contains subproperties when viewed in the property browser, as shown in Figure 12-2. It contains the following properties:

- ImageDate

- ImageLocation

- ImageLongDescription

- PhotographerFullName

As we mentioned previously, unlike the other scalar types, ImageLocation is also a complex type of type Location. LocationConverter customizes how properties of type Location display in the Properties window.

Notice that the ImageMetaData class has a type converter associated with it:

```
[TypeConverter(typeof(ImageMetaDataConverter))]
    public class ImageMetaData
    {
```

This type converter inherits from System.ComponentModel.ExpandableObjectConverter, which provides functionality to display types with properties as subproperties similar to how the Font type displays in the Properties tool window. This type converter can also be used to alter what data shows for the value of the ImageInfo property listed in the property browser.

In Figure 12-2 you see that the data shown in the property field consists of ImageInfo's subproperties, separated by a comma. This behavior is also similar to what the Font property displays for its value in the property browser. Listing 12-7 lists the source for the ImageMetaDataConverter class.

Listing 12-7. The ImageMetaDataConverter Class

```
using System;
using System.ComponentModel;
using System.ComponentModel.Design.Serialization;
using System.Globalization;
using System.Reflection;
using ControlsBookLib.Ch12;

namespace ControlsBookLib.Ch12.Design
{
    public class ImageMetaDataConverter : ExpandableObjectConverter
    {
```

```
      public override bool CanConvertFrom(
                ITypeDescriptorContext context, Type sourceType)
      {
         if (sourceType == typeof(string))
         {
            return true;
         }
         return base.CanConvertFrom(context, sourceType);
      }

      public override bool CanConvertTo(
                ITypeDescriptorContext context, Type targetType)
      {
         if (targetType == typeof(string))
         {
            return true;
         }
         return base.CanConvertTo(context, targetType);
      }

      public override object ConvertFrom(
      ITypeDescriptorContext context, CultureInfo culture, object value)
      {
         if (value == null)
         {
            return new ImageMetaData();
         }

         if (value is string)
         {
            string str = (string)value;
            if (str == "")
            {
               return new ImageMetaData();
            }

            string[] propValues = str.Split(culture.TextInfo.ListSeparator[0]);

            if (propValues.Length != 4)
            {
               throw new ArgumentException("Invalid ImageMetaData", "value");
            }

         TypeConverter datetimeConverter =
TypeDescriptor.GetConverter(typeof(DateTime));
         TypeConverter locationConverter =
TypeDescriptor.GetConverter(typeof(Location));

         return new
ImageMetaData((DateTime)datetimeConverter.ConvertFromString(context,culture,prop
Values[0]),
```

```
            (Location)locationConverter.ConvertFromString(context, culture, propValues[1]),
                    (string)propValues[2],
                    (string)propValues[3]);
        }

        return base.ConvertFrom(context, culture, value);
    }

    public override object ConvertTo(ITypeDescriptorContext context,
CultureInfo culture, object value, Type targetType)
    {
        if (value != null)
        {
            if (!(value is ImageMetaData))
            {
                throw new ArgumentException("Not of type ImageMetaData", "value");
            }
        }

        if (targetType == typeof(string))
        {
            if (value == null)
            {
                return String.Empty;
            }

            ImageMetaData imageMetaData = (ImageMetaData)value;
            if (imageMetaData.IsEmpty)
            {
                return String.Empty;
            }

            TypeConverter datetimeConverter =
TypeDescriptor.GetConverter(typeof(DateTime));
            TypeConverter locationConverter =
TypeDescriptor.GetConverter(typeof(Location));

            return String.Join(culture.TextInfo.ListSeparator,
                new string[] {
                            datetimeConverter.ConvertToString(context,
culture, imageMetaData.ImageDate),
                            locationConverter.ConvertToString(context,
culture, imageMetaData.ImageLocation),
                            imageMetaData.ImageLongDescription,
                            imageMetaData.PhotographerFullName});
        }

        return base.ConvertTo(context, culture, value, targetType);
    }
}
}
```

Without this type converter, the value displayed for ImageInfo would be what you would expect if you called the ToString() method, which is the fully qualified type name:

```
ControlsBookLib.Ch12.ImageMetaData
```

This is not a very useful value to display, which is why it is recommended that you build a type converter that inherits from System.ComponentModel.ExpandableObjectConverter to provide expand/collapse functionality in the property browser for complex types such as properties with subproperties. This also provides a more useful value for the complex type in the property browser.

UI Type Editors

UI type editors provide a pop-up UI for editing properties listed in the Properties window. An example is the Color Picker dialog box that displays when you click the button that appears when you click or tab into the bgColor property of the Document object in the Visual Studio .NET property browser. This type editor provides a better UI than entering a hexadecimal color value by instead displaying the actual colors.

A UI type editor can have either a Windows Form or a drop-down configuration UI for setting a property of a specific type. An example of the drop-down UI is the editor that displays when you click the button for the BackColor property of a Label control.

With this short discussion of UI type editors out of the way, we now implement a UI type editor for the ImageInfo.ImageLongDescription property of the TitledThumbnail control.

The SimpleTextEditor Editor

The SimpleTextEditor UI type editor provides a large editing area for a property of type string. Figure 12-3 shows the Windows Form UI.

Figure 12-3. The SimpleTextEditor *Windows Form UI*

The Windows Form class is named `SimpleTextEditorDialog`. It has a single property named `TextValue`. Otherwise, the rest of the code is generated by Visual Studio .NET. Listing 12-8 shows the class listing.

Listing 12-8. The `ImageMetaDataConverter` *Class*

```
using System;
using System.Drawing;
using System.Collections;
using System.ComponentModel;
using System.Windows.Forms;

namespace ControlsBookLib.Ch12.Design
{
    public class formSimpleTextEditorDialog : System.Windows.Forms.Form
    {
        private System.Windows.Forms.TextBox textString;
        private System.Windows.Forms.Button buttonCancel;
        private System.Windows.Forms.Button buttonOK;

        private System.ComponentModel.Container components = null;

        public formSimpleTextEditorDialog()
        {
            InitializeComponent();
        }

        public string TextValue
        {
            get
            {
                return textString.Text;
            }
            set
            {
                textString.Text = value;
            }
        }

        protected override void Dispose( bool disposing )
        {
            if( disposing )
            {
                if(components != null)
                {
                    components.Dispose();
                }
            }
            base.Dispose( disposing );
        }

        #region Windows Form Designer generated code
        /// <summary>
```

```csharp
/// Required method for Designer support - do not modify
/// the contents of this method with the code editor.
/// </summary>
private void InitializeComponent()
{
    this.textString = new System.Windows.Forms.TextBox();
    this.buttonCancel = new System.Windows.Forms.Button();
    this.buttonOK = new System.Windows.Forms.Button();
    this.SuspendLayout();
    //
    // textString
    //
    this.textString.Location = new System.Drawing.Point(16, 16);
    this.textString.Multiline = true;
    this.textString.Name = "textString";
    this.textString.Size = new System.Drawing.Size(264, 200);
    this.textString.TabIndex = 0;
    this.textString.Text = "";
    //
    // buttonCancel
    //
    this.buttonCancel.DialogResult = System.Windows.Forms.DialogResult.Cancel;
    this.buttonCancel.Location = new System.Drawing.Point(200, 232);
    this.buttonCancel.Name = "buttonCancel";
    this.buttonCancel.TabIndex = 1;
    this.buttonCancel.Text = "&Cancel";
    //
    // buttonOK
    //
    this.buttonOK.DialogResult = System.Windows.Forms.DialogResult.OK;
    this.buttonOK.Location = new System.Drawing.Point(112, 232);
    this.buttonOK.Name = "buttonOK";
    this.buttonOK.TabIndex = 2;
    this.buttonOK.Text = "&Ok";
    //
    // formSimpleTextEditorDialog
    //
    this.AcceptButton = this.buttonOK;
    this.AutoScaleBaseSize = new System.Drawing.Size(5, 13);
    this.CancelButton = this.buttonCancel;
    this.ClientSize = new System.Drawing.Size(292, 266);
    this.Controls.Add(this.buttonOK);
    this.Controls.Add(this.buttonCancel);
    this.Controls.Add(this.textString);
    this.FormBorderStyle = System.Windows.Forms.FormBorderStyle.FixedDialog;
    this.Name = "formSimpleTextEditorDialog";
    this.StartPosition = System.Windows.Forms.FormStartPosition.CenterParent;
    this.Text = "Simple Text Editor";
    this.ResumeLayout(false);

}
#endregion
    }
}
```

Now that we have our UI built, we move on to create the UI type editor class. The SimpleTextEditor class inherits from UITypeEditor, the base class for type editors. The SimpleTextEditor includes two method overrides, EditValue and GetEditStyle. Listing 12-9 presents the source for SimpleTextEditor.

Listing 12-9. The SimpleTextEditor *Source*

```
using System;
using System.ComponentModel;
using System.Drawing;
using System.Drawing.Design;
using System.Windows.Forms;
using System.Windows.Forms.Design;

namespace ControlsBookLib.Ch12.Design
{
    public class SimpleTextEditor : UITypeEditor
    {
        public override object EditValue(ITypeDescriptorContext context,
            IServiceProvider serviceProvider, object value)
        {
            if ((context != null) && (serviceProvider != null))
            {
                IWindowsFormsEditorService editorService =
                    (IWindowsFormsEditorService)serviceProvider.GetService(
                    typeof(IWindowsFormsEditorService));

                if (editorService != null)
                {
                    formSimpleTextEditorDialog formEditor = new
formSimpleTextEditorDialog();
                    formEditor.TextValue = (string)value;

                    DialogResult DlgResult = editorService.ShowDialog(formEditor);
                    if (DlgResult == DialogResult.OK)
                    {
                        value = formEditor.TextValue;
                    }
                }
            }
            return value;
        }

        public override UITypeEditorEditStyle GetEditStyle(
            ITypeDescriptorContext context)
        {
            if (context != null)
            {
                return UITypeEditorEditStyle.Modal;
            }
            return base.GetEditStyle(context);
        }
    }
}
```

GetEditStyle takes ITypeDescriptorContext and returns UITypeEditorEditStyle. ITypeDescriptorContext implements IServiceProvider and is used for type conversion. In our case, though, we simply check to see whether or not it is null. If it is not null, then we know that it is design time and we return a UITypeEditorEditStyle constant. The UITypeEditorEditStyle enumeration has three possible values:

- DropDown

- Modal

- None

The default value in the base class implementation is to return None. Returning None indicates that the editor does not have a GUI interface. In our case, we return Modal to indicate that the type editor's style is a modal form dialog box.

The EditStyle method does the bulk of the work in our UI type editor example. It creates the SimpleTextEditorDialog UI and returns the value back to the callee—in this case, Visual Studio .NET. Earlier in this chapter, we discussed how Visual Studio .NET provides design-time environment services.

The EditStyle method takes as parameters ITypeDescriptorContext, IServiceProvider, and an object that represents the current value of the property. We use the context parameter to determine that we are in a design-time environment. We next ensure serviceProvider is valid. If it is, we call GetService on serviceProvider to obtain a reference to an object that implements IWindowsFormsEditorService.

To implement a UI type editor that has a UITypeEditorEditStyle of DropDown as in the BackColor property of a Label control, call the DropDownControl method of IWindowsFormsEditorService. We call ShowDialog on editorService to display the SimpleTextEditorDialog UI. This simple form class has a property named TextValue to set and get the property value.

The Collection Editor

A *collection editor* provides you with the ability to add values to or remove values from an item's collection, as in the DropDownList or ListBox controls. The base class for collection editors is CollectionEditor in the System.ComponentModel.Design namespace.

As an example, ListItemsCollectionEditor implements a descendent class of CollectionEditor to provide the UI editor for the ListItemCollection type used in ListControl, the base class for both the DropDownList and ListBox controls.

Implementing a collection editor involves creating a custom collection type appropriate for your control. In Chapter 7, we implemented the TagDataMenu control, which incorporated a custom collection class named MenuItemDataCollection. We implement a custom collection editor on the TagDataMenu control to provide a UI to edit the MenuItemDataCollection collection. We provided the full listing of MenuItemDataCollection in Chapter 7, but here is the class definition for your reference:

```
[Editor(typeof(ControlsBookLib.Ch12.Design.MenuItemDataCollectionEditor),
typeof(UITypeEditor))]
public sealed class MenuItemDataCollection : IList
{
 ...
```

As you can see, our custom collection editor is applied to the collection class using the Editor attribute. MenuItemDataCollection holds MenuItemData items. For the collection editor to provide the proper rendering and property access, we must apply a built-in type converter to the MenuItemData class like this:

```
[TypeConverter(typeof(ExpandableObjectConverter))]
public class MenuItemData
{
 ...
```

The built-in ExpandableObjectConverter type converter suffices for MenuItemData because this class consists of simple property types. If this class had more complex properties, as was the case with the ImageMetaData class and its ImageLocation property of type Location, we would need to implement a custom ExpandableObjectConverter type converter. Figure 12-4 displays the custom collection editor in action.

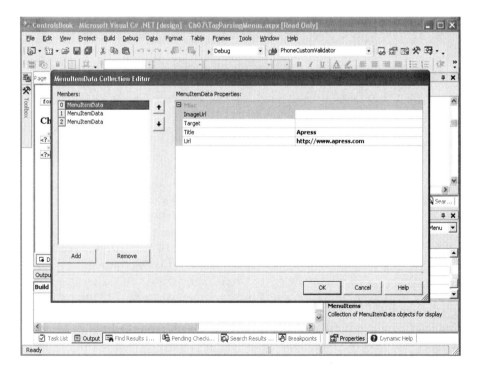

Figure 12-4. The custom collection editor Windows Form UI

Notice that the collection editor is centered over the parent window (Visual Studio .NET 2003) and is fairly wide. By default, the collection editor centers on the screen and is about 500 pixels wide. Because this collection takes a URL, it is more convenient to have a wider view. Also, we prefer that the collection editor center over Visual Studio .NET instead of the screen. Listing 12-10 presents the code for `MenuItemDataCollectionEditor`.

Listing 12-10. The `MenuItemDataCollectionEditor` *Source*

```
using System;
using System.ComponentModel;
using System.ComponentModel.Design;
using System.Design;
using System.Windows.Forms;
using System.Windows.Forms.Design;
using ControlsBookLib.Ch07;

namespace ControlsBookLib.Ch12.Design
{
    public class MenuItemDataCollectionEditor : CollectionEditor
    {
        public MenuItemDataCollectionEditor(Type type) : base(type)
        {
        }

        protected override
System.ComponentModel.Design.CollectionEditor.CollectionForm
CreateCollectionForm()
        {
            CollectionEditor.CollectionForm frm = base.CreateCollectionForm ();
            ((Form)frm).Width = 750;
            ((Form)frm).StartPosition = FormStartPosition.CenterParent;

            return frm;
        }
    }
}
```

The `CollectionEditor` class listing for `MenuItemDataCollectionEditor` is fairly short; it performs the one task of customizing how the collection editor displays, as noted previously. To modify the `Width` and `StartPosition` for the collection editing form, we cast the `CollectionForm` back to `Form` and perform the desired modifications.

Another potential customization would be to override the `CreateNewItemTypes` method in the event that the collection editor must be capable of editing multiple types. Another potential customization is to provide a custom collection editor form. With that covered, we next move on to another form of editor: the component editor.

Component Editors

A *component editor* is a modal dialog box that displays a property page similar to an ActiveX control's property page. Probably the most familiar component editor in ASP.NET is the DataGrid's component editor. It provides a convenient interface to quickly configure a DataGrid's numerous properties. You may have noticed this attribute on the previous TitledThumbnail server control:

```
EditorAttribute(typeof(TitledThumbnailComponentEditor),typeof(ComponentEditor))
```

This attribute is what associates the ComponentEditor with a server control. Building a component editor is different from what we have done so far because component editors are considered part of .NET Windows Forms based on its namespace. The namespace for the base class ComponentEditor is System.Windows.Forms.Design.

Component editors consist of a ComponentEditor-based class and a Component-EditorDlg Windows Form. The custom ComponentEditor class instantiates the component editor dialog box, initiates a DesignerTransaction, and either commits or rolls back any changes depending on whether the user clicks OK or Cancel on the component editor dialog box.

The Component Editor Dialog Box

Building the component editor dialog box is a matter of deciding what server control functionality to expose for configuration and laying out Windows Forms controls on the Windows Form that represents the editing dialog box on the Component Designer surface.

Because the component editor dialog box is a Windows Form, all the controls in .NET Windows Forms, such as the TabControl or TreeView, are available to provide a rich editing environment. For TitledThumbnailComponentEditorDlg, we expose the TitledThumbnail server control's main properties for editing on a simple form, as shown in Figure 12-5.

To create TitledThumbnailComponentEditorDlg, we start by adding a Windows Form to the project and setting the form's AcceptButton to buttonOK and CancelButton to ButtonCancel. Next, we edit its constructor to take a reference to a TitledThumbnail server control object. We need this reference to the TitledThumbnail server control in order to set its properties if the user clicks the OK button. Listing 12-11 shows the TitledThumbnailComponentEditorDlg class file.

Figure 12-5. The TitledThumbnail *component editor dialog box*

Listing 12-11. The TitledThumbnailComponentEditorDlg *Class File*

```
using System;
using System.Drawing;
using System.Collections;
using System.ComponentModel;
using System.Globalization;
using System.Windows.Forms;
using ControlsBookLib.Ch12.Design;

namespace ControlsBookLib.Ch12
{
    public class TitledThumbnailComponentEditorDlg : System.Windows.Forms.Form
    {
        private System.Windows.Forms.Button buttonCancel;
        private System.Windows.Forms.Button buttonOK;
        private System.ComponentModel.Container components = null;
        private System.Windows.Forms.Label label1;
        private System.Windows.Forms.Label label2;
        private System.Windows.Forms.GroupBox groupBox1;
        private System.Windows.Forms.Label label3;
        private System.Windows.Forms.Label label4;
        private System.Windows.Forms.Label label5;
        private System.Windows.Forms.Label label6;
        private System.Windows.Forms.DateTimePicker dtpImageTaken;
        private System.Windows.Forms.TextBox textLocation;
        private System.Windows.Forms.TextBox textLongImageDesc;
        private System.Windows.Forms.ComboBox cboAlignment;
```

```
        private System.Windows.Forms.TextBox textImageTitle;
        private System.Windows.Forms.TextBox textPhotographerFullName;

        private TitledThumbnail titledThumbnail;

        public TitledThumbnailComponentEditorDlg(TitledThumbnail component)
        {
           InitializeComponent();

           titledThumbnail = component;

           PopulateAlignment();

           cboAlignment.Text =
Enum.GetName(typeof(TitleAlignment),titledThumbnail.Align);
           textImageTitle.Text = titledThumbnail.Title;
           textLocation.Text = titledThumbnail.ImageInfo.ImageLocation.ToString();
           textPhotographerFullName.Text =
titledThumbnail.ImageInfo.PhotographerFullName;
           dtpImageTaken.Value = titledThumbnail.ImageInfo.ImageDate;
           textLongImageDesc.Text = titledThumbnail.ImageInfo.ImageLongDescription;
        }

        private void PopulateAlignment()
        {
           foreach (object Align in Enum.GetValues(typeof(TitleAlignment)))
           {
              cboAlignment.Items.Add(Align);
           }
        }

        protected override void Dispose( bool disposing )
        {
           if( disposing )
           {
              if(components != null)
              {
                 components.Dispose();
              }
           }
           base.Dispose( disposing );
        }

        #region Windows Form Designer generated code
        /// <summary>
        /// Required method for Designer support - do not modify
        /// the contents of this method with the code editor.
        /// </summary>
        private void InitializeComponent()
        {
           this.buttonCancel = new System.Windows.Forms.Button();
```

```
        this.buttonOK = new System.Windows.Forms.Button();
        this.label1 = new System.Windows.Forms.Label();
        this.cboAlignment = new System.Windows.Forms.ComboBox();
        this.textImageTitle = new System.Windows.Forms.TextBox();
        this.label2 = new System.Windows.Forms.Label();
        this.groupBox1 = new System.Windows.Forms.GroupBox();
        this.textLongImageDesc = new System.Windows.Forms.TextBox();
        this.label6 = new System.Windows.Forms.Label();
        this.label5 = new System.Windows.Forms.Label();
        this.textPhotographerFullName = new System.Windows.Forms.TextBox();
        this.label4 = new System.Windows.Forms.Label();
        this.textLocation = new System.Windows.Forms.TextBox();
        this.dtpImageTaken = new System.Windows.Forms.DateTimePicker();
        this.label3 = new System.Windows.Forms.Label();
        this.groupBox1.SuspendLayout();
        this.SuspendLayout();
        //
        // buttonCancel
        //
        this.buttonCancel.Anchor =
((System.Windows.Forms.AnchorStyles)((System.Windows.Forms.AnchorStyles.Bottom |
System.Windows.Forms.AnchorStyles.Right)));
        this.buttonCancel.DialogResult = System.Windows.Forms.DialogResult.Cancel;
        this.buttonCancel.Location = new System.Drawing.Point(384, 344);
        this.buttonCancel.Name = "buttonCancel";
        this.buttonCancel.TabIndex = 1;
        this.buttonCancel.Text = "&Cancel";
        //
        // buttonOK
        //
        this.buttonOK.Anchor =
((System.Windows.Forms.AnchorStyles)((System.Windows.Forms.AnchorStyles.Bottom |
System.Windows.Forms.AnchorStyles.Right)));
        this.buttonOK.DialogResult = System.Windows.Forms.DialogResult.OK;
        this.buttonOK.Location = new System.Drawing.Point(288, 344);
        this.buttonOK.Name = "buttonOK";
        this.buttonOK.TabIndex = 0;
        this.buttonOK.Text = "&OK";
        this.buttonOK.Click += new System.EventHandler(this.buttonOK_Click);
        //
        // label1
        //
        this.label1.Location = new System.Drawing.Point(16, 16);
        this.label1.Name = "label1";
        this.label1.Size = new System.Drawing.Size(100, 16);
        this.label1.TabIndex = 2;
        this.label1.Text = "Image Title:";
        //
        // cboAlignment
        //
        this.cboAlignment.DropDownStyle =
```

```
System.Windows.Forms.ComboBoxStyle.DropDownList;
         this.cboAlignment.Location = new System.Drawing.Point(344, 40);
         this.cboAlignment.Name = "cboAlignment";
         this.cboAlignment.Size = new System.Drawing.Size(121, 21);
         this.cboAlignment.TabIndex = 3;
         //
         // textImageTitle
         //
         this.textImageTitle.Location = new System.Drawing.Point(16, 40);
         this.textImageTitle.Name = "textImageTitle";
         this.textImageTitle.Size = new System.Drawing.Size(304, 20);
         this.textImageTitle.TabIndex = 4;
         this.textImageTitle.Text = "";
         //
         // label2
         //
         this.label2.Location = new System.Drawing.Point(344, 16);
         this.label2.Name = "label2";
         this.label2.Size = new System.Drawing.Size(100, 16);
         this.label2.TabIndex = 5;
         this.label2.Text = "Alignment";
         //
         // groupBox1
         //
         this.groupBox1.Controls.Add(this.textLongImageDesc);
         this.groupBox1.Controls.Add(this.label6);
         this.groupBox1.Controls.Add(this.label5);
         this.groupBox1.Controls.Add(this.textPhotographerFullName);
         this.groupBox1.Controls.Add(this.label4);
         this.groupBox1.Controls.Add(this.textLocation);
         this.groupBox1.Controls.Add(this.dtpImageTaken);
         this.groupBox1.Controls.Add(this.label3);
         this.groupBox1.Location = new System.Drawing.Point(16, 80);
         this.groupBox1.Name = "groupBox1";
         this.groupBox1.Size = new System.Drawing.Size(448, 248);
         this.groupBox1.TabIndex = 6;
         this.groupBox1.TabStop = false;
         this.groupBox1.Text = "Image Info";
         //
         // textLongImageDesc
         //
         this.textLongImageDesc.Location = new System.Drawing.Point(8, 120);
         this.textLongImageDesc.Multiline = true;
         this.textLongImageDesc.Name = "textLongImageDesc";
         this.textLongImageDesc.Size = new System.Drawing.Size(424, 112);
         this.textLongImageDesc.TabIndex = 14;
         this.textLongImageDesc.Text = "";
         //
         // label6
         //
         this.label6.Location = new System.Drawing.Point(8, 96);
```

```
this.label6.Name = "label6";
this.label6.Size = new System.Drawing.Size(136, 16);
this.label6.TabIndex = 13;
this.label6.Text = "Long Image Description:";
//
// label5
//
this.label5.Location = new System.Drawing.Point(272, 32);
this.label5.Name = "label5";
this.label5.Size = new System.Drawing.Size(152, 16);
this.label5.TabIndex = 12;
this.label5.Text = "Photographer Full Name:";
//
// textPhotographerFullName
//
this.textPhotographerFullName.Location = new
System.Drawing.Point(272, 56);
this.textPhotographerFullName.Name = "textPhotographerFullName";
this.textPhotographerFullName.Size = new System.Drawing.Size(160, 20);
this.textPhotographerFullName.TabIndex = 11;
this.textPhotographerFullName.Text = "";
//
// label4
//
this.label4.Location = new System.Drawing.Point(136, 32);
this.label4.Name = "label4";
this.label4.Size = new System.Drawing.Size(128, 16);
this.label4.TabIndex = 10;
this.label4.Text = "Location Image Taken:";
//
// textLocation
//
this.textLocation.Location = new System.Drawing.Point(136, 56);
this.textLocation.Name = "textLocation";
this.textLocation.Size = new System.Drawing.Size(112, 20);
this.textLocation.TabIndex = 9;
this.textLocation.Text = "ON,OW";
//
// dtpImageTaken
//
this.dtpImageTaken.Format =
System.Windows.Forms.DateTimePickerFormat.Short;
this.dtpImageTaken.Location = new System.Drawing.Point(8, 56);
this.dtpImageTaken.Name = "dtpImageTaken";
this.dtpImageTaken.Size = new System.Drawing.Size(112, 20);
this.dtpImageTaken.TabIndex = 8;
this.dtpImageTaken.Value = new System.DateTime(2003, 4, 8, 0, 0, 0, 0);
//
// label3
//
this.label3.Location = new System.Drawing.Point(8, 32);
```

```
            this.label3.Name = "label3";
            this.label3.Size = new System.Drawing.Size(100, 16);
            this.label3.TabIndex = 7;
            this.label3.Text = "Date Image Taken:";
            //
            // TitledThumbnailComponentEditorDlg
            //
            this.AcceptButton = this.buttonOK;
            this.AutoScaleBaseSize = new System.Drawing.Size(5, 13);
            this.CancelButton = this.buttonCancel;
            this.ClientSize = new System.Drawing.Size(480, 382);
            this.Controls.Add(this.groupBox1);
            this.Controls.Add(this.label2);
            this.Controls.Add(this.textImageTitle);
            this.Controls.Add(this.cboAlignment);
            this.Controls.Add(this.label1);
            this.Controls.Add(this.buttonOK);
            this.Controls.Add(this.buttonCancel);
            this.Name = "TitledThumbnailComponentEditorDlg";
            this.StartPosition = System.Windows.Forms.FormStartPosition.CenterParent;
            this.Text = "Titled Thumbnail Property Builder";
            this.groupBox1.ResumeLayout(false);
            this.ResumeLayout(false);

        }
        #endregion

        private void buttonOK_Click(object sender, System.EventArgs e)
        {
            PropertyDescriptorCollection properties =
                TypeDescriptor.GetProperties(titledThumbnail);

            PropertyDescriptor Title = properties["Title"];
            if (Title != null)
            {
                try
                {
                    Title.SetValue(titledThumbnail,textImageTitle.Text);
                }
                catch (Exception err)
                {
                    MessageBox.Show(this,
                        "Problem setting title property: Source:"+
                        err.Source+" Message: "+err.Message,"Error",
                        MessageBoxButtons.OK,MessageBoxIcon.Error);
                }
            }

            PropertyDescriptor alignment = properties["Align"];
            if (alignment != null)
            {
```

```
      try
      {
         alignment.SetValue(titledThumbnail,Enum.Parse(
         typeof(TitleAlignment),cboAlignment.Text));
      }
      catch (Exception err)
      {
         MessageBox.Show(this,"Problem setting align property: Source:"+
            err.Source+" Message: "+err.Message,"Error",
            MessageBoxButtons.OK,MessageBoxIcon.Error);
      }
   }


PropertyDescriptorCollection imageInfoProps =
   TypeDescriptor.GetProperties(titledThumbnail.ImageInfo);


PropertyDescriptor imageDescription =
imageInfoProps["ImageLongDescription"];
if (imageDescription != null)
{
   try
   {
      imageDescription.SetValue(titledThumbnail.ImageInfo,
      textLongImageDesc.Text);
   }
   catch (Exception err)
   {
      MessageBox.Show(this,
         "Problem setting image Long Description property: Source:"+
         err.Source+" Message: "+err.Message,"Error",
         MessageBoxButtons.OK,MessageBoxIcon.Error);
   }
}


PropertyDescriptor imageDate = imageInfoProps["ImageDate"];
if (imageDate != null)
{
   try
   {
      imageDate.SetValue(titledThumbnail.ImageInfo,dtpImageTaken.Value);
   }
   catch (Exception err)
   {
      MessageBox.Show(this,
         "Problem setting image date property: Source:"+err.Source+
         " Message: "
         +err.Message,"Error",
         MessageBoxButtons.OK,MessageBoxIcon.Error);
   }
}
```

```
            PropertyDescriptor photographerFullName =
            imageInfoProps["PhotographerFullName"];
            if (photographerFullName != null)
            {
               try
               {
                  photographerFullName.SetValue(
                  titledThumbnail.ImageInfo,textPhotographerFullName
.Text);
               }
               catch (Exception err)
               {
                  MessageBox.Show(this,
                     "Problem setting photographer's full name property: Source:"+
                     err.Source+" Message: "+err.Message,"Error",
                     MessageBoxButtons.OK,MessageBoxIcon.Error);
               }
            }

            PropertyDescriptor imageLocation = imageInfoProps["ImageLocation"];
            if (imageLocation != null)
            {
               try
               {
                  LocationConverter converter = new LocationConverter();
                  imageLocation.SetValue(
                  titledThumbnail.ImageInfo,converter.ConvertFrom(null,
Application.CurrentCulture,textLocation.Text));
               }
               catch (Exception err)
               {
                  MessageBox.Show(this,
                     "Problem setting image location property: Source:"+
                     err.Source+" Message: "+err.Message,"Error",
                     MessageBoxButtons.OK,MessageBoxIcon.Error);
               }
            }
         }
      }
   }
}
```

The first step in the code is to initialize the form's controls with the TitledThumbnail's current values. The string properties ImageTitle, ImageLongDescription, ImageDate, and PhotopgrapherFullName are simple string assignments. Initializing the Location TextBox takes advantage of the functionality provided by the LocationConverter type converter by calling the ToString() method on the Location object to get the customized display of the latitude and longitude. To initialize the Alignment ComboBox with values, we iterate over the custom enumeration TitleAlignment with this code:

```
private void PopulateAlignment()
{
    foreach (object Align in Enum.GetValues(typeof(TitleAlignment)))
    {
        cboAlignment.Items.Add(Align);
    }
}
```

This code sets the current value for `Alignment`:

```
cboAlignment.Text = Enum.GetName(typeof(TitleAlignment),titledThumbnail.Align);
```

The bulk of the other code in the `TitledThumbnailComponentEditorDlg` class is the OK button click method. This method starts by gaining a reference to the `TitledThumbnail` server control object's property collection. Next, for each property we obtain a `PropertyDescriptor` with code like this:

```
PropertyDescriptor Title = properties["Title"];
```

This code accesses the properties collection to obtain each property. The properties' `ImageTitle` and `TitleAlignment` are set by accessing the properties collection as follows:

```
alignment.SetValue(titledThumbnail,Enum.Parse(typeof(TitleAlignment),
cboAlignment.Text));
```

The `TitledThumbnail` server control contains a complex property of type `ImageMetaData`. To set these properties, another property collection is obtained for `ImageInfo` in this code:

```
PropertyDescriptorCollection imageInfoProps =
            TypeDescriptor.GetProperties(titledThumbnail.ImageInfo);
```

`ImageLongDescription`, `ImageDate`, and `PhotographerFullName` are straightforward assignments. For `ImageLocation`, we once again take advantage of its type converter to convert from the string entered in the `TextLocation` TextBox to a `Location` object:

```
LocationConverter converter = new LocationConverter();
imageLocation.SetValue(titledThumbnail.ImageInfo,converter.ConvertFrom(null,
Application.CurrentCulture,textLocation.Text));
```

That is all the relevant code in the `TitledThumbnailComponentEditorDlg` class. In the next section, we cover the component editor class that manages the editing dialog box.

The Component Editor Class

The TitledThumbnailComponentEditor class inherits from WindowsFormsComponentEditor and is fairly short. This class overrides a single method named EditComponent, which is the only required override. Listing 12-12 contains the class file for TitledThumbnailComponentEditor.

Listing 12-12. The TitledThumbnailComponentEditor *Class File*

```
using System;
using System.Design;
using System.ComponentModel;
using System.ComponentModel.Design;
using System.Windows.Forms;
using System.Windows.Forms.Design;
using ControlsBookLib.Ch12;

namespace ControlsBookLib.Ch12.Design
{
    public class TitledThumbnailComponentEditor : WindowsFormsComponentEditor
    {
        public override bool EditComponent(ITypeDescriptorContext context,
        object component, IWin32Window parent)
        {
            if ( !(component is TitledThumbnail) )
            {
                throw new ArgumentException("Must be a TitledThumbnail component",
                "component");
            }

            IServiceProvider serviceProviderSite = ((TitledThumbnail)component).Site;
            IComponentChangeService changeSrvc = null;

            DesignerTransaction trans = null;
            bool changed = false;

            try
            {
                if (null != serviceProviderSite)
                {
                    IDesignerHost designerHost =
(IDesignerHost)serviceProviderSite.GetService(typeof(IDesignerHost));
                    trans = designerHost.CreateTransaction("Property Builder");

                    changeSrvc =
(IComponentChangeService)serviceProviderSite.GetService(typeof(
IComponentChangeService));
                    if (null != changeSrvc)
                    {
                        try
                        {
```

```
                       changeSrvc.OnComponentChanging( (TitledThumbnail)component,
null);
                }
                catch (CheckoutException err)
                {
                    if (err == CheckoutException.Canceled)
                        return false;
                    throw err;
                }
            }
        }

        try
        {
            TitledThumbnailComponentEditorDlg propertyBuilderForm =
                new TitledThumbnailComponentEditorDlg(
(TitledThumbnail)component);
            if (propertyBuilderForm.ShowDialog(parent) == DialogResult.OK)
            {
                changed = true;
            }
        }
        finally
        {
            if (changed && (null != changeSrvc))
            {
                changeSrvc.OnComponentChanged( (TitledThumbnail)component,
null, null, null);
            }
        }
    }
    finally
    {
        if (trans != null)
        {
            if (changed)
            {
                trans.Commit();
            }
            else
            {
                trans.Cancel();
            }
        }
    }
    return changed;
    }
  }
}
```

EditComponent starts off by ensuring that the component editor is associated with is a TitledThumbnail server control. Next, EditComponent obtains a reference to the TitledThumbnail component's Site property. Every control has a Site property that is associated with the hosting designer environment, in this case Visual Studio .NET.

Site is of type ISite, which is an interface that derives from the IServiceProvider interface. IServiceProvider has a GetService method that permits the server control to gain access to design-time services, as described in Table 12-1. In our code, we get two services, one of type IDesignerHost and the other of type IComponentChangeService.

IDesignerHost is used to add and retrieve services available in the design-time environment and handle events related to designer state. IDesignerHost provides support for detecting a designer is loading and managing component and designer transactions. We use IDesignerHost to wrap component editing into a transaction of type DesignerTransaction.

IComponentChangeService permits a designer to receive notifications when components are changed, added, or removed from the design-time environment. We use IComponentChangeService to notify the hosting environment—in this case, Visual Studio .NET—that the component is being edited. Note that this code will cause Visual Studio .NET to want to check out the .aspx page for editing if the .aspx page is under source control:

```
changeSrvc.OnComponentChanging( (TitledThumbnail)component, null);
```

Once EditComponent initiates the DesignerTransaction and notifies Visual Studio .NET that the page is about to be edited, it displays the TitledThumbnailComponent-EditorDlg Windows Form. If the user clicks OK to set any changes, this code notifies Visual Studio .NET that the component has changed:

```
changeSrvc.OnComponentChanged( (TitledThumbnail)component, null, null, null);
```

The next step is to either commit or cancel the DesignerTransaction, depending on whether or not the user clicked OK or Cancel on the component editor dialog box. That's it for the TitledThumbnailComponentEditor class.

When the TitledThumbnail server control is selected in the Visual Studio .NET Designer, a hyperlink titled "Property Builder..." appears at the bottom of the Properties window. Also, if you right-click the TitledThumbnail server control, you will see a context menu item titled with the same text. A custom designer provides this functionality and is the topic of the next section.

Custom Designers

The Designer classes in .NET customize how components in Windows Forms and server controls in ASP.NET appear and behave at design time. You can implement custom designers to perform custom initialization, access design-time services such as template editing, add menu items to context menus, or to adjust the attributes, events, and properties available in a server control.

 NOTE *You can use type converters and UI type editors both at design time and at runtime. You can use designers only at design time.*

To associate a custom designer with a control, you apply the DesignerAttribute attribute. This is the code to apply the TitledThumbnailDesigner custom designer to the TitledThumbnail component:

```
Designer(typeof(TitledThumbnailDesigner))
```

All custom designers implement the IDesigner interface and provide customized methods and properties appropriate for the type of designer. IDesigner is a fairly simple interface, as you can see from Table 12-2.

Table 12-2. IDesigner *Interface*

MEMBER	DESCRIPTION
Component	Property that holds a reference to the component associated with the designer class
DoDefaultAction	Method that executes the default action for the designer class
Initialize	Method that initializes the designer instance with its associated component
Verbs	Property that references a collection of design-time verbs provided by a designer class

System.ComponentModel.Design.ComponentDesigner is the base class for all designers, and it implements the IDesign interface. Both Windows Forms and server controls can have designers; however, because of the difference in rendering technologies and architecture, separate base designer classes that inherit from ComponentDesigner are required.

System.Web.UI.Design.ControlDesigner is the base class for ASP.NET server control designers and is associated with System.Web.UI.Control. To implement a custom designer for a server control, you must inherit from ControlDesigner. Table 12-3 describes the virtual members that you must implement when you create a custom designer class.

Table 12-3. Required Overrides for a Custom Designer

METHOD	DESCRIPTION
GetDesignTimeHtml	This method returns a string that contains the HTML to render the control it is associated with at design time.
GetEmptyDesignTimeHtml	This method returns a string that contains the HTML to render when a control has not been configured to render itself. Often this text contains instructions on how to work with the control.
GetErrorDesignTimeHtml	This method returns a string that contains the HTML to render if the design-time parser encounters an error when parsing a control's tag
.Initialize	This method is invoked when the designer is initialized and applied to its associated component. This is the place to ensure that the designer has been associated with the correct control type.

The default behavior in ControlDesigner for GetEmptyDesignTimeHtml is to return the control type and its ID so that controls of the same type can be differentiated. You can customize this text by calling the helper method CreatePlaceHolderDesignTimeHtml. You can also use this method to customize the error message returned in GetErrorDesignTimeHtml. Otherwise, ControlDesigner returns an empty string for the error message.

For GetDesignTimeHtml, ControlDesigner calls the associated control's RenderControl method. For a composite control, this can cause a control to not render any design-time HTML if the control's child control collection, Controls, has not been created. We discuss a simple designer that addresses this issue in the next section.

The Composite Control Designer

A composite control depends on its children controls for proper rendering at runtime and at design time. Making a reference to a composite control's Controls property will cause its children controls to be created, and the control will render. At design time, this requirement may not be met, depending on how the control is constructed.

For example, TableCompCustomControl in Chapter 3 and TagDataMenu and BuilderMenu in Chapter 7 are composite controls that do not render at design time without some assistance. For this reason, we create a custom designer named CompCntrlDesigner to assist composite controls with proper rendering at design time. Listing 12-13 contains the source for CompCntrlDesigner.

Listing 12-13. The CompCntrlDesigner Class File

```
using System;
using System.ComponentModel;
using System.ComponentModel.Design;
using System.Web.UI;
using System.Web.UI.Design;
```

```
namespace ControlsBookLib.Ch12.Design
{
    public class CompCntrlDesigner : ControlDesigner
    {
        public override void Initialize(IComponent component)
        {
            if (!(component is Control) && !(component is INamingContainer))
            {
                throw new ArgumentException(
                    "This control is not a composite control.", "component");
            }
            base.Initialize(component);
        }

        protected override string GetEmptyDesignTimeHtml()
        {
            return CreatePlaceHolderDesignTimeHtml(Component.GetType()+" control.");
        }

        public override string GetDesignTimeHtml()
        {
            ControlCollection cntrls = ((Control)Component).Controls;
            return base.GetDesignTimeHtml();
        }

        protected override string GetErrorDesignTimeHtml(Exception e)
        {
            return CreatePlaceHolderDesignTimeHtml("There was an error rendering the"+
                this.Component.GetType() +" control."+
                "<br>Exception: "+e.Source+ " Message: "+e.Message);
        }
    }
}
```

The essential method in CompCntrlDesigner is GetDesignTimeHtml:

```
public override string GetDesignTimeHtml()
{
    ControlCollection cntrls = ((Control)Component).Controls;
    return base.GetDesignTimeHtml();
}
```

This method simply references the Controls property for the associated server control, which causes the control to create its Controls collection. Once the Controls collection is created, returning base.GetDesignTimeHtml calls Render on the control and the control displays correctly in the Visual Studio .NET Designer because its child controls are created and can render themselves.

Though `Pager` is a composite control and has `CompCntrlDesigner` as its
`DesignerAttribute`, `Pager` renders itself no problem without the custom designer.
This is because `Pager` had properties that call `EnsureChildControls()` in the get and
set methods, which is generally recommended. When Visual Studio .NET accesses
`Pager`'s properties so that it can populate the Properties window, this causes
`EnsureChildControls()` to be called. As its name suggests, the `EnsureChildControls()`
method provided by the `System.Web.UI.Control` class will call `CreateChildControls` to
instantiate the `Controls` collection both at runtime and at design time.

In contrast, `TableCompCustomControl` does not have any calls to `EnsureChildControls`
because its X and Y properties must be set before creating the control hierarchy. X and Y
tell `TableCompCustomControl` how many columns and rows to render. Calling
`EnsureChildControls` and causing control creation before these values are set does
not make sense in this case. Therefore, `TableCompCustomControl` requires the custom
designer shown in Listing 12-13 to render properly.

For `TagDataMenu` and `BuilderMenu`, these controls do not have any properties.
Therefore, their respective `Controls` collection does not get instantiated and these
controls do not have a design-time UI without the assistance of the `CompCntrlDesigner`
custom designer class as well.

The Control Designer and Designer Verbs

The `TitledThumbnail` component is a composite control that has a custom
control designer associated with it via the `DesignerAttribute` attribute named
`TitledThumbnailDesigner`. This control designer inherits from `CompCntrlDesigner`,
but with a couple of method overrides to further customize its functionality.

The first override is `Initialize`, in which we ensure that `TitledThumbnailDesigner`
is associated with a `TitledThumbnail` component:

```
public override void Initialize(IComponent comp)
{
    if (!(comp is TitledThumbnail))
    {
        throw new
        ArgumentException("Must be a TitledThumbnail component.", "component");
    }
    base.Initialize(comp);
}
```

The next override is GetDesignTimeHtml, in which we customize behavior to display a message that the developer/user should set the ImageUrl property as a helpful tip:

```
public override string GetDesignTimeHtml()
{
    ControlCollection cntrls = ((Control)Component).Controls;
    if (((TitledThumbnail)Component).ImageUrl == "")
    {
        return CreatePlaceHolderDesignTimeHtml(
        "Set ImageUrl to URL of desired thumbnail image.");
    }
    else
    {
        return base.GetDesignTimeHtml();
    }
}
```

When the ImageUrl property is empty for the TitledThumbnail control, it displays the broken link image at design time, as shown in Figure 12-6.

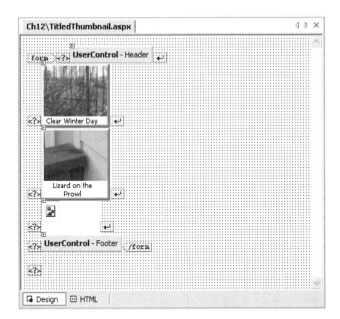

Figure 12-6. TitledThumbnail *at design time without the* GetDesignTimeHtml *override*

With the override of `GetDesignTimeHtml`, the design-time view changes to Figure 12-7.

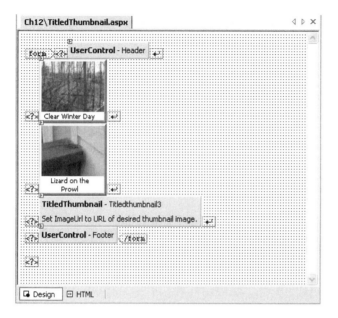

Figure 12-7. `TitledThumbnail` *at design time with the* `GetDesignTimeHtml` *override*

Instead of the broken image display, the developer/user now has a helpful hint as a guide to what the next step is to configure the control.

The final override in `TitledThumbnailDesigner` is the `Verbs` property of type `DesignerVerbCollection`. The `Verbs` collection is specified in the `IDesigner` interface as described in Table 12-2. Each designer verb represents a command usually presented to the developer/user by right-clicking the component. Visual Studio .NET also displays designer verbs at the bottom of the Properties window as pointed to by item 4 in Figure 12-2.

When the developer/user selects a menu item that represents a `DesignerVerb` object, an event handler associated with the designer verb is fired to execute the action. For `TitledThumbnail`, we want a menu item that when selected displays its custom component editor as described previously. To implement the desired menu item, we build an event handler to create the component editor UI:

```
private void OnPropertyBuilder(object sender, EventArgs e)
{
    TitledThumbnailComponentEditor TitledThumbnailPropsEditor = new
    TitledThumbnailComponentEditor();
    TitledThumbnailPropsEditor.EditComponent(Component);
}
```

The event handler creates a `TitledThumbnailComponentEditor` and calls its `EditComponent` method.

Listing 12-14 provides the source code for `TitledThumbnailDesigner`. In the listing, you find the override of the `Verbs` collection where a new `DesgnerVerbCollection` is created and the "Property Builder…" menu item is added to the collection and associated with the `OnPropertyBuilder` event handler.

Listing 12-14. The `TitledThumbnailDesigner` *Class File*

```
using System;
using System.Collections;
using System.ComponentModel;
using System.ComponentModel.Design;
using System.Diagnostics;
using System.Web.UI;
using System.Web.UI.Design;
using System.Web.UI.Design.WebControls;
using System.Web.UI.WebControls;
using ControlsBookLib.Ch12;

namespace ControlsBookLib.Ch12.Design
{
    public class TitledThumbnailDesigner : CompCntrlDesigner
    {
        private DesignerVerbCollection designTimeVerbs;
        public override DesignerVerbCollection Verbs
        {
            get
            {
                if (null == designTimeVerbs)
                {
                    designTimeVerbs = new DesignerVerbCollection();
                    designTimeVerbs.Add(new DesignerVerb(
"Property Builder...", new EventHandler(this.OnPropertyBuilder)));
                }
                return designTimeVerbs;
            }
        }

        private void OnPropertyBuilder(object sender, EventArgs e)
        {
            TitledThumbnailComponentEditor TitledThumbnailPropsEditor = new
TitledThumbnailComponentEditor();
            TitledThumbnailPropsEditor.EditComponent(Component);
        }

        public override void Initialize(IComponent comp)
        {
            if (!(comp is TitledThumbnail))
            {
```

```
            throw new ArgumentException(
"Must be a TitledThumbnail component.", "component");
        }
        base.Initialize(comp);
    }

    public override string GetDesignTimeHtml()
    {
        ControlCollection cntrls = ((Control)Component).Controls;
        if (((TitledThumbnail)Component).ImageUrl == "")
        {
            return CreatePlaceHolderDesignTimeHtml(
"Set ImageUrl to URL of desired thumbnail image.");
        }
        else
        {
            return base.GetDesignTimeHtml();
        }
    }
}
}
```

In Chapter 7, we discussed templates and data binding. In that chapter, we took advantage of a couple of designers to support our templated control, TemplateMenu, and our data-bound control, Repeater. In the next sections, we discuss these designer classes and how they support templates and data binding.

The Templated Control Designer

Earlier in this chapter, we covered the various services that a design-time environment such as Visual Studio .NET or ASP.NET Web Matrix can implement via interfaces to enhance the developer experience and reduce development time. One of these services is template editing by implementing the ITemplateEditingService service. We take advantage of this service to build a templated control designer.

The templated control TemplateMenu supports Header, Separator, and Footer templates. Although these templates can be manually edited by clicking the HTML tab in the Visual Studio .NET Designer, it is also possible to provide a drag-and-drop UI editing interface for template editing, and that is what the TemplateMenuDesigner implements for the TemplateMenu control. Figure 12-8 shows the editing interface for TemplateMenu.

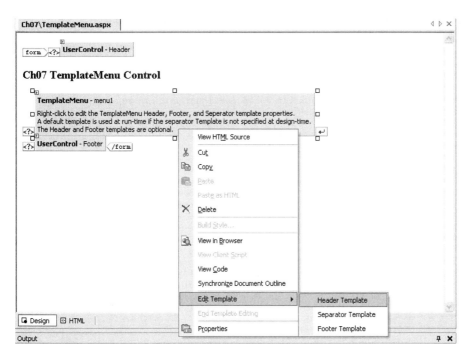

Figure 12-8. The menu interface for TemplateMenu *control template editing*

Figure 12-9 shows the editing UI for the Separator template after the developer/ user right-clicks and selects Edit Template ➤Separator Template on the TemplateMenu control.

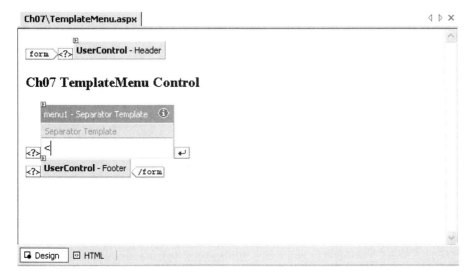

Figure 12-9. Template editing UI for the TemplateMenu *control* Separator *template*

The template editing interface allows the developer/user to drag and drop server controls from the Visual Studio .NET Toolbox into the template editing area. The developer/user can also configure the template UI by editing properties such as style in the Properties window.

The base class for TemplateMenuDesigner is TemplatedControlDesigner. TemplatedControlDesigner subclasses ControlDesigner, adding the key methods and properties listed in Table 12-4.

Table 12-4. Key TemplateControl *Designer Methods and Properties*

MEMBER	DESCRIPTION
CreateTemplateEditingFrame	Creates a frame for template editing according to the specified designer verb selected, as demonstrated in Figure 12-9
GetCachedTemplateEditingVerbs	Obtains a reference to the cached verbs of type TemplateEditingVerb for template editing
GetTemplateContent	Returns the current template's content from the control's child tags in the .aspx page
SetTemplateContent	Creates a new template instance and sets the template's content to the desired content

As with previous designer classes, we override the Initialize method to ensure that the TemplateMenuDesigner class is associated with a TemplateMenu server control via the Designer attribute.

Because template editing is initiated through clicking a menu item on the context menu for a control, we first must create the TemplateEditingVerbs, one for each template:

```
protected override TemplateEditingVerb[] GetCachedTemplateEditingVerbs()
{
    if (null == tmplEditingVerbs)
    {
        tmplEditingVerbs = new TemplateEditingVerb[3];
        tmplEditingVerbs[0] = new TemplateEditingVerb("Header Template", 0, this);
        tmplEditingVerbs[1] = new TemplateEditingVerb("Separator Template", 0, this);
        tmplEditingVerbs[2] = new TemplateEditingVerb("Footer Template", 0, this);
    }
    return tmplEditingVerbs;
}
```

The TemplateEditingVerb class subclasses DesignerVerb for the sole purpose of creating a template editing frame. By default, TemplateEditingVerbs appear as a submenu under the Edit Template menu item in the controls context menu. The template editing verbs are created in GetCachedTemplateEditingVerbs shown previously when the developer right-clicks the TemplateMenu control.

Note that unlike in the previous example, we do not create a custom event handler for each `TemplateEditingVerb`. Instead, when a `TemplateEditingVerb` menu item is selected, the `CreateTemplateEditingFrame` method is called the first time the menu item is selected. In this method, we obtain a reference to the `ITemplateEditingService`:

```
ITemplateEditingService tmplEditingService =
(ITemplateEditingService)GetService(typeof(ITemplateEditingService));
```

We next obtain a reference to the style of the associated control:

```
Style style = ((TemplateMenu)Component).ControlStyle;
```

Depending on which template was selected for editing, we use the `ITemplateEditingService` reference to create the editing frame using the control's style information and return the frame from this method:

```
frame = tmplEditingService.CreateFrame(this, verb.Text, new string[]
{ "Header Template" }, style, null);
```

After we create the editing frame, `GetTemplateContent` and `SetTemplateContent` are called. `GetTemplateContent` uses the `GetTextFromTemplate` method to retrieve the template's content from the declarative .aspx page and set the content into the template container. `SetTemplateContent` uses the `GetTemplateFromText` to set the template's content.

After editing the selected template, right-click the template editing surface to bring up the menu and select End Template Editing. This causes `SetTemplateContent` and then `GetDesignTimeHtml` to execute, rendering the control with its updated content on the Component Designer surface.

The other bit of code is the `OnComponentChanged` override. This event fires when the component has been changed. We check to see if any `Style`-related properties have been changed. If so, we dispose of the template editing verbs.

We noted previously that `CreateTemplateEditingFrame` is called the first time each template editing menu item is clicked. Subsequent clicks on a template editing menu item do not fire `CreateTemplateEditingFrame` for that menu item. However, anytime the template editing verbs are disposed, either when `TemplateMenu.Dispose` is called or in `OnComponentChanged`, the template editing verbs will be re-created the next time the developer/user right clicks the `TemplateMenu` control. This causes `GetCachedTemplateEditingVerbs` to execute and then `CreateTemplateEditingFrame` for the particular verb to be executed again.

This sequence of events is what permits changes to the server control's `BackColor`, `ForeColor`, and `Font` properties detected in `OnComponentChanged` to be applied to the template editing UI because the `TemplateEditingVerbs` are disposed. Disposing these verbs causes `CreateTemplateEditingFrame` to execute when template editing is invoked, re-creating the template editing frame with the updated `Style` information inherited from the server control.

If we did not dispose of the TemplateEditingVerbs in OnComponentChanged, the editing frame would not be "refreshed" with the server control's updated BackColor, ForeColor, or Font property. Listing 12-15 provides the full source for TemplateMenuDesigner.

Listing 12-15. The TemplateMenuDesigner *Source*

```
using System;
using System.ComponentModel;
using System.ComponentModel.Design;
using System.Web.UI;
using System.Web.UI.WebControls;
using System.Web.UI.Design;
using ControlsBookLib.Ch07;

namespace ControlsBookLib.Ch12.Design
{
    public class TemplateMenuDesigner : TemplatedControlDesigner
    {
        public override void Initialize(IComponent component)
        {
            if (!(component is TemplateMenu))
            {
                throw new ArgumentException(
"Component must be a TemplateMenu control for this custom designer."
                    , "component");
            }
            base.Initialize(component);
        }

        private TemplateEditingVerb[] tmplEditingVerbs;
        protected override TemplateEditingVerb[] GetCachedTemplateEditingVerbs()
        {
            if (null == tmplEditingVerbs)
            {
                tmplEditingVerbs = new TemplateEditingVerb[3];
                tmplEditingVerbs[0] = new TemplateEditingVerb(
"Header Template", 0, this);
                tmplEditingVerbs[1] = new TemplateEditingVerb(
"Separator Template", 0, this);
                tmplEditingVerbs[2] = new TemplateEditingVerb(
"Footer Template", 0, this);
            }
            return tmplEditingVerbs;
        }

        public override string GetTemplateContent(
        ITemplateEditingFrame editFrame, string tmplName, out bool
        allowTemplateEditing)
        {
            allowTemplateEditing = true;
```

```
        string templateContent = String.Empty;
        if (null  != tmplEditingVerbs)
        {
            if (editFrame.Verb == tmplEditingVerbs[0])
            {
                ITemplate existingTemplate =
((TemplateMenu)Component).HeaderTemplate;

                if (null  != existingTemplate)
                {
                    templateContent = GetTextFromTemplate(existingTemplate);
                }
            }

            if (editFrame.Verb == tmplEditingVerbs[1])
            {
                ITemplate existingTemplate =
((TemplateMenu)Component).SeparatorTemplate;

                if (null  != existingTemplate)
                {
                    templateContent = GetTextFromTemplate(existingTemplate);
                }
            }

            if (editFrame.Verb == tmplEditingVerbs[2])
            {
                ITemplate existingTemplate =
((TemplateMenu)Component).FooterTemplate;

                if (null  != existingTemplate)
                {
                    templateContent = GetTextFromTemplate(existingTemplate);
                }
            }
        }
        return templateContent;
    }

    public override string GetDesignTimeHtml()
    {
        if ((null == ((TemplateMenu)Component).HeaderTemplate ) &&
            (null  == ((TemplateMenu)Component).SeparatorTemplate) &&
            (null  == ((TemplateMenu)Component).FooterTemplate))
        {
            return GetEmptyDesignTimeHtml();
        }

        string designTimeHtml = String.Empty;
        try
        {
```

```
            ((TemplateMenu)Component).DataBind();
            designTimeHtml = base.GetDesignTimeHtml();
        }
        catch (Exception e)
        {
            designTimeHtml = GetErrorDesignTimeHtml(e);
        }

        return designTimeHtml;
    }

    public override void OnComponentChanged(object sender,
ComponentChangedEventArgs ceArgs)
    {
        base.OnComponentChanged(sender, ceArgs);

        if (null  != ceArgs.Member)
        {
            if (ceArgs.Member.Name.Equals("BackColor") ||
                ceArgs.Member.Name.Equals("ForeColor") ||
                ceArgs.Member.Name.Equals("Font"))
            {
                if (null  != tmplEditingVerbs)
                {
                    foreach (TemplateEditingVerb verb in tmplEditingVerbs)
                    {
                        verb.Dispose();
                    }
                }
            }
        }
    }

    protected override string GetErrorDesignTimeHtml(Exception e)
    {

        return CreatePlaceHolderDesignTimeHtml(
"There was an error rendering the TemplateMenu control."+
        "<br>Exception: "+e.Source+ "  Message: "+e.Message);
    }

    public override void SetTemplateContent(
ITemplateEditingFrame editingFrame, string tmplName, string tmplContent)
    {
        if (null  != tmplEditingVerbs)
        {
            if (tmplEditingVerbs[0] == editingFrame.Verb)
            {
                TemplateMenu control = (TemplateMenu)Component;
                ITemplate newHeader  = null;
```

```
                if ((null  != tmplContent) && (0  != tmplContent.Length))
                {
                    newHeader = GetTemplateFromText(tmplContent);
                }
                control.HeaderTemplate = newHeader;
            }

            if (tmplEditingVerbs[1] == editingFrame.Verb)
            {
                TemplateMenu control = (TemplateMenu)Component;
                ITemplate newSeparator = null;

                if ((null  != tmplContent) && (0 != tmplContent.Length))
                {
                    newSeparator = GetTemplateFromText(tmplContent);
                }
                control.SeparatorTemplate = newSeparator;
            }

            if (tmplEditingVerbs[2] == editingFrame.Verb)
            {
                TemplateMenu control = (TemplateMenu)Component;
                ITemplate newHeader = null;

                if ((null  != tmplContent) && (0 != tmplContent.Length))
                {
                    newHeader = GetTemplateFromText(tmplContent);
                }
                control.FooterTemplate = newHeader;
            }
        }
    }

    public override bool AllowResize
    {
        get
        {
            bool templateExists = null !=
((TemplateMenu)Component).HeaderTemplate ||
null != ((TemplateMenu)Component).SeparatorTemplate ||
null != ((TemplateMenu)Component).FooterTemplate;
            return templateExists || InTemplateMode;
        }
    }

    protected override ITemplateEditingFrame
CreateTemplateEditingFrame(TemplateEditingVerb verb)
    {
        ITemplateEditingFrame frame = null;

        if (null  != tmplEditingVerbs)
        {
```

```
            ITemplateEditingService tmplEditingService =
    (ITemplateEditingService)GetService(typeof(ITemplateEditingService));
            if (null  != tmplEditingService)
            {
                Style style = ((TemplateMenu)Component).ControlStyle;
                if (tmplEditingVerbs[0] == verb)
                {
                    frame = tmplEditingService.CreateFrame(this, verb.Text, new
  string[] { "Header Template" }, style, null);
                }
                if (tmplEditingVerbs[1] == verb)
                {
                    frame = tmplEditingService.CreateFrame(this, verb.Text, new
  string[] { "Separator Template" }, style, null);
                }
                if (tmplEditingVerbs[2] == verb)
                {
                    frame = tmplEditingService.CreateFrame(this, verb.Text, new
  string[] { "Footer Template" }, style, null);
                }
            }
        }
        return frame;
    }


    protected override string GetEmptyDesignTimeHtml()
    {
        return CreatePlaceHolderDesignTimeHtml(
"Right-click to edit the TemplateMenu Header, Footer," +
" and Separator template properties. " +
            "<br>A default template is used at runtime " +
"if the Separator template is not specified at design time."+
            "<br>The Header and Footer templates are optional.");
    }


    protected override void Dispose(bool disposing)
    {
        if (disposing)
        {
            if (null  != tmplEditingVerbs)
            {
                foreach (TemplateEditingVerb verb in tmplEditingVerbs)
                {
                    verb.Dispose();
                }
            }
        }
        base.Dispose(disposing);
    }
  }
}
```

The Data-Bound Control Designer

So far, we have built custom control designers to assist server controls with rendering at design time, to customize the context menu, to launch a custom property editor, and to demonstrate visual template editing for controls that support templates. Our next example includes some of those features, but the main focus is on interacting with other controls on the design surface to connect with design-time data sources.

In general, data-bound control designer classes inherit from ControlDesigner and may implement the IDataSourceProvider interface if a DataMember or DataField property is supported on the targeted server control for which the control designer needs to provide support. The Repeater control has a DataMember property, so it must implement IDataSourceProvider.

The IDataSourceProvider Interface

IDataSourceProvider is an interface for control designers to use to provide access to a data source at design time when the server control requires design-time support for DataMember or DataField. Table 12-5 lists the members of IDataSourceProvider and provides a short description of each.

Table 12-5. IDataSourceProvider *Members*

MEMBER	DESCRIPTION
GetResolvedSelectedDataSource	Obtains a reference to the selected member or data table for the selected DataSource identified in GetSelectedDataSource.
GetSelectedDataSource	Obtains a reference to the selected data source. This method is called when a DataSource is selected in the design-time environment for the control.

GetSelectedDataSource provides access to design-time data sources such as a DataSet component through design-time services. GetResolvedSelectedDataSource is the place where component developers implementing a data-bound control designer class can provide support for objects that implement IListSource (i.e., DataSet), which can contain multiple objects that implement IEnumerable (i.e., DataTable), mapping the selected IEnumerable object to the DataMember property for the server control. See Chapter 7 for more information on data binding.

The RepeaterDesigner Class

The Repeater server control in Chapter 7 works just fine at runtime and is able to data bind with all the expected data containers, including DataSet. However, without the RepeaterDesigner associated with it via the DesignerAttribute, the Repeater control is not able to data bind to a design-time data source such as a DataSet.

Before we discuss RepeaterDesigner, we should mention that there are a couple of things you must set on the Repeater class itself to make sure the design-time functionality works correctly. The first item is to override the DesignerSerializationVisibility attribute for the DataSource property on the Repeater control and change it to DesignerSerializationVisibility.Hidden. This causes the DataSource property to persist on the .aspx page like this:

```
<apress:repeater … " DataSource="<%# dataSetEmp %>" …>
```

The other item is to ensure that this event is fired in the DataBind method override in the Repeater class:

```
OnDataBinding(System.EventArgs.Empty);
```

If this event is not fired in the Repeater's DataBind method, the Repeater server control will not data bind to the design-time data source at runtime. An exception is not thrown. The Repeater simply renders blank, as if a DataSource was not set. With these items out of the way, we can now move on to our discussion of the RepeaterDesigner custom designer class.

The RepeaterDesigner class enables our Repeater to "see" DataSet objects at design time and bind to any available DataSet objects, displaying the data at runtime. The RepeaterDesigner also provides a design-time UI for the Repeater. Listing 12-16 provides the source for RepeaterDesigner.

Listing 12-16. The RepeaterDesigner *Class File*

```
using System;
using System.Collections;
using System.ComponentModel;
using System.ComponentModel.Design;
using System.Data;
using System.Web.UI;
using System.Web.UI.Design;
using ControlsBookLib.Ch07;

namespace ControlsBookLib.Ch12.Design
{
    public class RepeaterDesigner : ControlDesigner, IDataSourceProvider
    {
        public override void Initialize(IComponent component)
        {
            if (!(component is Ch07.Repeater))
            {
                throw new ArgumentException(
                "Component must be a Ch07.Repeater", "component");
            }
            base.Initialize(component);
        }

        public string DataSource
        {
```

```csharp
        get
        {
            DataBinding dataBinding = DataBindings["DataSource"];

            if (null != dataBinding)
            {
                return dataBinding.Expression;
            }
            else
            {
                return String.Empty;
            }
        }
        set
        {
            if ((0 == value.Length) || (null == value))
            {
                DataBindings.Remove("DataSource");
            }
            else
            {
                DataBinding dataBinding = DataBindings["DataSource"];

                if (null != dataBinding)
                {
                    dataBinding.Expression = value;
                }
                else
                {
                    dataBinding = new DataBinding("DataSource",
typeof(IEnumerable), value);
                }
                DataBindings.Add(dataBinding);
            }
            OnBindingsCollectionChanged("DataSource");
        }
    }

    public string DataMember
    {
        get
        {
            return ((Ch07.Repeater)Component).DataMember;
        }
        set
        {
            ((Ch07.Repeater)Component).DataMember = value;
        }
    }

    protected override string GetEmptyDesignTimeHtml()
```

```
            {
                return CreatePlaceHolderDesignTimeHtml(
        "Switch to HTML view to edit the control's templates.");
            }

            public override bool DesignTimeHtmlRequiresLoadComplete
            {
                get
                {
                    return !(0 == DataSource.Length);
                }
            }

            protected override void PreFilterProperties(IDictionary properties)
            {
                base.PreFilterProperties(properties);

                PropertyDescriptor propertyDescriptor =
        (PropertyDescriptor)properties["DataSource"];
                if (null != propertyDescriptor)
                {
                    System.ComponentModel.AttributeCollection runtimeAttributes =
        propertyDescriptor.Attributes;
                    Attribute[] attrs = new Attribute[runtimeAttributes.Count + 1];

                    runtimeAttributes.CopyTo(attrs, 0);
                    attrs[runtimeAttributes.Count] = new
        TypeConverterAttribute(typeof(DataSourceConverter));
                    propertyDescriptor = TypeDescriptor.CreateProperty(this.GetType(),
        "DataSource", typeof(string), attrs);
                    properties["DataSource"] = propertyDescriptor;
                }

                propertyDescriptor = (PropertyDescriptor)properties["DataMember"];
                if (null != propertyDescriptor)
                {
                    System.ComponentModel.AttributeCollection runtimeAttributes =
        propertyDescriptor.Attributes;
                    Attribute[] attrs = new Attribute[runtimeAttributes.Count + 1];

                    runtimeAttributes.CopyTo(attrs, 0);
                    attrs[runtimeAttributes.Count] = new
        TypeConverterAttribute(typeof(DataMemberConverter));
                    propertyDescriptor = TypeDescriptor.CreateProperty(this.GetType(),
        "DataMember", typeof(string),
                        attrs);
                    properties["DataMember"] = propertyDescriptor;
                }
            }

            object IDataSourceProvider.GetSelectedDataSource()
```

```
{
   object selectedDataSource = null;
   string dataSource = null;

   DataBinding binding = DataBindings["DataSource"];
   if (binding != null)
   {
      dataSource = binding.Expression;
   }

   if (dataSource != null)
   {
      ISite componentSite = Component.Site;
      if (componentSite != null)
      {
         IContainer container = (IContainer)componentSite.GetService(
            typeof(IContainer));

         if (container != null)
         {
            IComponent comp = container.Components[dataSource];
            if ((comp is IEnumerable) || (comp is IListSource))
            {
               selectedDataSource = comp;
            }
         }
      }
   }

   return selectedDataSource;
}

IEnumerable IDataSourceProvider.GetResolvedSelectedDataSource()
{
   object selectedDataSource =
      ((IDataSourceProvider)this).GetSelectedDataSource();

   DataView dataView = null;

   if (selectedDataSource is DataSet)
   {
      DataSet dataSet = (DataSet)selectedDataSource;
      DataTable dataTable = null;

      if ((DataMember != null) && (DataMember.Length>0))
         dataTable = dataSet.Tables[DataMember];
      else
         dataTable=dataSet.Tables[0];

      if (dataTable!=null)
      {
```

```
                dataView = dataTable.DefaultView;
            }
        }
        else if (selectedDataSource is DataTable)
        {
            dataView = ((DataTable)selectedDataSource).DefaultView;
        }
        else if (selectedDataSource is IEnumerable)
        {
            return selectedDataSource as IEnumerable;
        }

        return dataView as IEnumerable;
    }

    public override string GetDesignTimeHtml()
    {
        Ch07.Repeater repeater = (Ch07.Repeater)Component;
        string designerHTML = null;
        IEnumerable designerDataSource = GetDesignTimeDataSource(5);
        try
        {
            repeater.DataSource = designerDataSource;
            repeater.DataBind();
            designerHTML = base.GetDesignTimeHtml();
        }
        catch (Exception e)
        {
            designerHTML = GetErrorDesignTimeHtml(e);
        }
        finally
        {
            repeater.DataSource = null;
        }
        return designerHTML;
    }

    protected override string GetErrorDesignTimeHtml(Exception e)
    {
        return CreatePlaceHolderDesignTimeHtml(
"An error occurred rendering the Ch07.Repeater.");
    }

    private DataTable dummyTable;
    private IEnumerable GetDesignTimeDataSource(int minimumRows)
    {
        IEnumerable selectedDataSource =
((IDataSourceProvider)this).GetResolvedSelectedDataSource();

        DataTable dtTable = new DataTable() ;
```

```
        if (dtTable == null)
        {
            if (selectedDataSource != null)
            {
                dtTable = DesignTimeData.CreateSampleDataTable(selectedDataSource);
            }

            if (dtTable == null)
            {
                if (dummyTable == null)
                {
                    dummyTable = DesignTimeData.CreateDummyDataTable();
                }

                dtTable = dummyTable;
            }
        }

        IEnumerable realDataSource =
DesignTimeData.GetDesignTimeDataSource(dtTable, minimumRows);
        return realDataSource;
    }
  }
}
```

RepeaterDesigner has two properties: DataSource and DataMember. Both of these properties map themselves to the like-named properties for the associated Ch07.Repeater component. Designer classes change the behavior of server controls when manipulated in the design-time environment by shadowing the associated server control's properties.

When a developer/user changes the DataSource and DataMember properties of the Repeater control in Properties window, the custom designer class's versions of these properties are the actual properties that the developer/user configures. Naturally, the underlying Repeater's properties are set to the chosen values, but by hooking into these properties and the design-time services infrastructure, the custom designer class has an opportunity to make design-time data source objects available in the drop-down list for these properties.

Before the DataSource and DataMember properties can display design-time data source objects in a drop-down list in the Properties window for the associated Repeater control, the custom designer class must add the appropriate type converter attributes dynamically in the PreFilterProperties method. The PreFilterProperties method is part of the IDesignFilter interface, which we discuss next.

The IDesignFilter Interface

Our RepeaterDesigner class inherits from ControlDesigner, which inherits from ComponentDesigner. ComponentDesigner implements the IDesignFilter interface. The IDesignFilter interface provides the ability to modify the set of properties, events, and

attributes exposed by a component or server control at design time. Table 12-6 lists
IDesignFilter's members that can be overridden to customize a component (Windows
Form) or server control's (Web Form's) behavior.

Table 12-6. The IDesignFilter *Interface*

MEMBER	DESCRIPTION
PostFilterAttributes	Allows a custom designer class to change or remove the set of attributes on a component or server control at design time
PostFilterEvents	Allows a custom designer class to change or remove the set of events on a component or server control at design time
PostFilterProperties	Allows a custom designer class to change or remove the set of properties on a component or server control at design time
PreFilterAttributes	Allows a custom designer class to add attributes through an Attribute object or TypeID to a component or server control at design time
PreFilterEvents	Allows a custom designer class to add events through an EventDescriptor to a component or server control at design time
PreFilterProperties	Allows a custom designer class to add properties through a PropertyDescriptor to a component or server control at design time

Any overrides of the methods in Table 12-6 are in the associated control designer
class, but the actions affect the server control linked to the custom designer class
through the Designer attribute.

NOTE *When overriding methods of the* IDesignFilter *interface that begin with
"Pre," you should call* base.PreX *at the beginning of the override. For members that
begin with "Post," you should call* base.PostX *at the end of the override.*

As we mentioned previously, RepeaterDesigner overrides the PreFilterProperties
to add a type converter attribute to both the DataSource and DataMember properties.
Here is the code that alters the DataSource property in PreFilterProperties:

```
PropertyDescriptor propertyDescriptor =
(PropertyDescriptor)properties["DataSource"];
if (null != propertyDescriptor)
{
   System.ComponentModel.AttributeCollection runtimeAttributes =
propertyDescriptor.Attributes;
   Attribute[] attrs = new Attribute[runtimeAttributes.Count + 1];
```

```
    runtimeAttributes.CopyTo(attrs, 0);
    attrs[runtimeAttributes.Count] = new
TypeConverterAttribute(typeof(DataSourceConverter));
    propertyDescriptor = TypeDescriptor.CreateProperty(this.GetType(),
"DataSource", typeof(string),
        attrs);
    properties["DataSource"] = propertyDescriptor;
}
```

The first step in the preceding code snippet is to obtain a `PropertyDescriptor` reference for the `DataSource` property from the properties collection that is passed into `PreFilterProperties`. The next step is to obtain a reference to the `Attributes` collection from the `PropertyDescriptor` for the `DataSource`. These attributes are copied into a new `Attribute` collection that is one size larger to make room for adding the `DataSourceConverter` type converter attribute. Finally, the one-size-larger `Attributes` collection is copied back into the `PropertyDescriptor` for the `DataSource` property.

Adding this type converter permits the `DataSource` property to convert `DataSource` objects such as a `DataSet` to its string representation for display in the Visual Studio .NET Properties tool window in a `DropDownList` as well as for persistence on the control's tag.

The same steps are performed for the `DataMember` property in `PreFilterProperties` except that a `DataMemberConverter` type converter attribute is added to the `PropertyDescriptor` for `DataMember`.

`IDesignFilter` is not specific to data-bound controls. Server control developers can make use of `IDesignFilter` for all types of server controls as needed.

Supporting the DataTextField and DataValueField Properties

Though the `Repeater` control does not provide support for the `DataTextField` and `DataValueField` properties, the work required to support these properties is present. The implementation for `GetResolvedSelectedDataSource` in `RepeaterDesigner` could actually be reduced to this:

```
return null;
```

If you comment out the `GetResolvedSelectedDataSource` implementation and replace it with the preceding line of code, you will see that it still works as expected. This is because the full implementation of `GetResolvedSelectedDataSource` is only required if a server control supports the `DataTextField` and `DataValueField` properties. The more complete implementation of `GetResolvedSelectedDataSource` is provided as an example of what is required to support the `DataTextField` and `DataValueField` properties.

The next step to support the `DataTextField` and `DataValueField` properties would be to implement shadow properties for the `DataTextField` and `DataValueField` properties as we did for `DataMember`:

```
public string DataMember
{
   get
   {
      return ((Ch07.Repeater)Component).DataMember;
   }
   set
   {
      ((Ch07.Repeater)Component).DataMember = value;
   }
}
```

The final step would be the additional code in `PreFilterProperties` to modify the `Attributes` collection of the `PropertyDescriptor` for `DataTextField` and `DataValueField` to add the `DataFieldConverter` type converter attribute for each.

The DesignTimeData Class

The `DesignTimeData` class provides helper methods for control developers implementing data-bound control designers. We use the `DesignTimeData` class in `RepeaterDesigner` to create a design-time sample and dummy data by calling `CreateSampleDataTable` and `CreateDummyDataTable` in `RepeaterDesigner`'s `GetDesignTimeDataSource` member function.

In this chapter we showed you the long version of implementing the `IDataSourceProvider` interface. As a reminder, you are only required to implement `IDataSourceProvider` if a `DataMember` property is present. We can simplify `GetSelectedDataSource` and `GetResolvedSelectedDataSource` by taking advantage of `DesignTimeData`'s `GetSelectedDataSource` method. Here's a possible replacement for our `GetSelectedDataSource`:

```
object IDataSourceProvider.GetSelectedDataSource()
{
   DataBinding dataBinding;
   dataBinding = this.DataBindings["DataSource"];
   if (dataBinding != null)
   {
      return DesignTimeData.GetSelectedDataSource(
this.Component,dataBinding.Expression);
   }
   return null;
}
```

If your control needs to support the DataTextField and DataValueField properties, and you require a full implementation of GetResolvedSelectedDataSource, here's a potential replacement for our long version:

```
IEnumerable IDataSourceProvider.GetResolvedSelectedDataSource()
{
   DataBinding dataBinding;
   dataBinding= this.DataBindings["DataSource"];
   if (dataBinding!= null)
   {
      return DesignTimeData.GetSelectedDataSource(
this.Component,dataBinding.Expression, this.DataMember);
   }
   return null;
}
```

We provided the longer implementation in code so that you can see what is going on behind the scenes. Feel free to use the previous implementations in your own code to further take advantage of the facilities available in the .NET Framework.

Miscellaneous Design-Time Items

In this section, we tie up a couple of loose ends with respect to design-time support and development.

The Toolbox Icon

It is possible to provide a custom bitmap for the Toolbox icon for a custom server control. Simply add a 16~TMS16 pixel bitmap to the custom server control's project and give it the same name as the component. The next step is to set its Build Action to Embedded Resource by right-clicking the image and expanding Advanced. Under Advanced, change the value for Build Action to Embedded Resource.

Next, apply the ToolboxBitmapAttribute attribute to the control's class. First, add a reference to System.Drawing, which is the namespace where this attribute exists. The name of the resource is the name of the bitmap file. For a control named MyControl and a bitmap named MyControl.bmp, the attribute looks like this:

```
[ToolboxBitmap(typeof(MyControl), "MyControl.bmp")]
```

The constructor we use here takes the type for the MyControl server control and looks for an embedded resource named MyControl.bmp. When the control is added to the Visual Studio .NET Toolbox, it will display the custom bitmap instead of the default cog bitmap.

Debugging Design-Time Development

It is not possible to fully debug design-time code with a single instance of Visual Studio .NET. With a single instance of Visual Studio .NET, it is only possible to perform basic testing for design-time code. For example, to see if a custom designer renders the correct design-time HTML, you can create a custom designer class, apply the Designer attribute to the server control, recompile, and then flip to the test page hosting the desired server control to get a thumbs-up/thumbs-down judgment.

To fully debug design-time code with breakpoints, stepping through code, and so on, you must start up a second instance of Visual Studio .NET and open the same project in the second instance of Visual Studio .NET. Next, open the design-time code—for example, RepeaterDesigner—and set the desired breakpoints in one instance of Visual Studio .NET. In the instance of Visual Studio with RepeaterDesigner opened, select the Debug ➤ Processes menu item to display the Processes dialog box. Listed there is the other instance of devenv.exe, the filename for Visual Studio .NET.

Then you can either double-click devenv.exe or select devenv.exe and click Attach to display the Attach to Process dialog box. In this box, you just check Common Language Runtime. You should generally do this unless you have a need to select the other debugging program types. This speeds things up a bit. Next, click OK and then Close. You should now see the debug toolbar open with the Break All and Stop Debugging buttons enabled.

Now you are ready to flip to the other instance of Visual Studio .NET that is currently running under the debugger. In this example, if you bring up the Chapter 7 DataBound-Repeater.aspx sample test page and manipulate one of the Repeater controls at design-time, you hit the breakpoint that you set in the other instance of Visual Studio .NET, and you can step through code.

TIP *To quickly figure out which instance of Visual Studio .NET is debugging and which instance is being debugged in the Windows taskbar, click the program group to display both instances of Visual Studio .NET. The instance that has [run] in its caption is the instance that is debugging. The instance that has [design] in its caption is the instance being debugged.*

Note that if you attempt to rebuild the project while running multiple instances of Visual Studio .NET, you will get the following error message in the Output window in Visual Studio .NET:

```
Cannot copy assembly 'ControlsBookLib' to file
'c:\ControlsBook\bin\ControlsBookLib.dll'.  The process cannot access the file
because it is being used by another process.
```

To make changes and rebuild the project, close the project in one of the instances of Visual Studio .NET, make the desired changes, and then reopen the project in the second instance to begin debugging again.

Summary

Controls, as opposed to just working with a class in code, exist for the purpose of enhancing the development environment experience and speeding up development time. The .NET Framework provides design-time customizations for both Windows controls and web controls. The customizations available in each environment differ mostly as a result of rendering technology, with web controls generating HTML and Windows controls rendering using GDI+. Design-time customizations for controls are applied to a server control class through attributes primarily from the System.ComponentModel and System.Web.UI.Design namespaces.

The .NET Framework design-time environment services extend the capabilities and level of integration with a designer such as Visual Studio .NET. To obtain a service, the Component class implements IServiceProvider, which has a method named GetService that can be used to obtain a reference.

Custom designers manage the UI and behavior of a component at design time. Customizations include changing the component's appearance, initialization, and interaction on the Component Designer surface.

Type converters are generally implemented for control properties that are not readily converted to the string type. Type converters are also implemented for types that include subproperties such as the expand/collapse UI for the Font property.

A UI type editor can provide a custom user interface for editing property values. It displays a custom representation of a property at design time. UI type editors are type specific.

Type converters and UI type editors can be used both at design time and at runtime, whereas designers can be used only at design time.

Building a
Complex Control

AT THIS POINT in the book we have covered all the major concepts in developing server controls. In this chapter and the next we bring these concepts together and develop a powerful custom server control from the ground up to illustrate the techniques put forth in this book. This server control programmatically interacts with the Google Web APIs to provide a nice package that can be dropped into an ASP.NET application to provide search functionality. We hope that it provides a useful example and framework for building your own custom server controls and serves as a useful addition to your server control toolkit.

We break into two chapters our discussion of our complex control to keep things manageable, as there is a lot of functionality to cover. In this chapter, we focus on the following aspects of our complex control:

- Understanding the Google Web API

- Working with web services in server controls

- Using the global assembly cache (GAC) and strong named assemblies

- Using configuration files

- Integrating the custom web service proxy class

- Designing the Google control architecture

We round out the chapter with a discussion of the various server controls in the suite. In the next section we dive into a discussion of the Google API and web service.

The Problem Domain

The Google web site provides access to search engine services that let users search its store of over 3 billion URLs. To open this store to programmatic searches, Google released a web service API to search the information store from code. Our task in this and the next chapter is to demonstrate how to build a suite of server controls that make it easy to consume the search feature of Google and make it simple to incorporate into an ASP.NET web application. Here's a summary list of the requirements for our control project:

- Completely handle all web services communications with the Google web service.

- Provide the ability to either use the Google web service or redirect queries to the Google web site directly.

- Display a text box and button to gather search input from the end user.

- Display both the status information and the list of search results from the search query.

- Provide the Google look and feel out of the box while supporting complete UI customization.

- Provide the ability localize the look and feel.

- Handle paging through the search results.

- Provide the ability to display Google images with paging display or raw text, as well as the ability to turn off paging.

- Provide the ability to reconfigure the control without recompiling the control.

- Provide the ability to license access to the control.

The Google Web Service

Our first step when working with the Google web service is to understand what parameters we need to provide it and the data stream it returns. Google helps in this effort by providing a downloadable API from its main site that provides documentation and sample code for invoking the Google service. Figure 13-1 shows the download page for the Google Web APIs service.

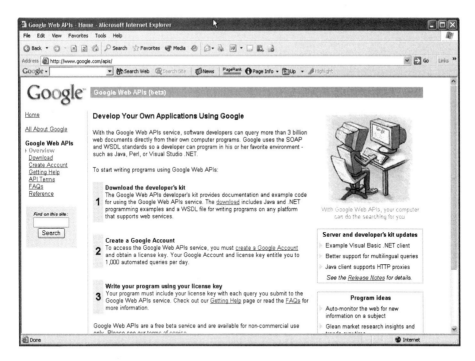

Figure 13-1. The Google Web APIs service download page

In Figure 13-1, you can see that three steps are involved in using the Google service:

1. Accept the terms and conditions to download the Google Web APIs developer's kit.

2. Create a Google Account to receive a license key for access to the Google Web APIs service.

3. Write code to access the Google Web APIs service.

It is a good idea to download the developer's kit and have the documentation for invoking the Google Web APIs service handy, as it helps in troubleshooting and understanding how the service works. The second item, getting a license key through Google's license download process, is a mandatory step because the Google Web APIs service requires authentication. The final step, programmatically accessing the Google Web APIs service, is what the example code and discussion in this and the next chapter cover.

Web Services Description Language and .NET Web Service Proxies

Web services are described in full detail through Web Services Description Language (WSDL) files. WSDL files provide information on what XML is sent over the wire to communicate with the web service, and they also determine the protocol bindings and addressing information for the web service. The Google Web APIs developer's kit includes a copy of its production WSDL file named GoogleSearch.wsdl as part of its download .zip file.

Because this is a book about building custom server controls, we do not examine the gory details of the XML contents of the WSDL file. Plenty of .NET web services books are available that cover that topic in depth. Instead, we show you how you can turn the WSDL file into a .NET class that handles the grunge work of working with XML and invoking the Google web service over the network.

One approach is to use the built-in feature "Add Web Reference" that comes with Visual Studio .NET. This feature provides an automated way of generating the proxy code and is the tool most developers are familiar with. All developers have to do is click through a set of menus to browse to the WSDL file, and the proxy code is created behind the scenes. We take a different route for our server control because we want more predictability in the generated code and we want to make changes to it without worrying about it being overridden by an automated process. We can use a command-line utility named wsdl.exe to generate a proxy class for a web service that is similar in its code-generation capabilities when compared to the "Add Web Reference" tool in Visual Studio .NET.

Make sure you use the command prompt that comes with Visual Studio .NET or make sure the binary wsdl.exe file is in your path before you try the following command on the GoogleSearch.wsdl description file:

```
wsdl.exe GoogleSearch.wsdl
```

Wsdl.exe takes the provided WSDL and produces a proxy class named GoogleSearchService.cs in the same directory where the tool was run. GoogleSearchService.cs encapsulates the web service into a programmatically easy-to-use package. At a later point in time, we will copy the code from the generated proxy class to our web control library project to add the necessary web service support for the server controls. If you peer inside the code file, you can see a class named GoogleSearchService that does the communication with the web service. You can also see the main web service method, doGoogleSearch, that we will invoke to do our searches with the Google web service. The code for doGoogleSearch is as follows:

```
public GoogleSearchResult doGoogleSearch(string key, string q, int start,
int maxResults, bool filter, string restrict, bool safeSearch, string lr,
string ie, string oe)
{
   object[] results = this.Invoke("doGoogleSearch", new object[] {
      key, q, start, maxResults, filter, restrict, safeSearch, lr, ie, oe});
   return ((GoogleSearchResult)(results[0]));
}
```

The internal implementation is not as important as understanding the types that are passed into the web service. Table 13-1 provides an explanation of the parameters that the doGoogleSearch method takes.

Table 13-1. Input Parameters for the Google Web Service Method doGoogleSearch

PARAMETER	TYPE	DESCRIPTION
filter	bool	Filters to hide similar results or duplicate results from web sites
ie	string	Input encoding (ignored parameter, defaults to UTF-8)
key	string	Google key for authenticating to a web service
lr	string	Restricts results to a certain language
maxResults	int	Maximum number of results to return from a search
oe	string	Output encoding (ignored parameter, defaults to UTF-8)
q	string	Query string for a web service search
restrict	string	Restricts search results to a subset according to the parameter
safeSearch	bool	Enables filtering of adult content
start	int	Zero-based starting index for web service search results

The two most important doGoogleSearch parameters are q and key. The q parameter represents the search criteria used by the Google service to look for matches and their URLs. The key parameter is the license key that authenticates requests and allows access to the web service. You obtain the license key by requesting one from Google. Other parameters of interest include the range of values that you will pull from the web service results, identified by the start and maxResults parameters. The start parameter is a zero-based index into the result set, and maxResults is the number of results returned by the service in the window on the data result set.

Figure 13-2 shows this concept graphically. For a given search represented by q, each call to the web service requests a number of entries identified by maxResults, starting at the position in the result set identified by the start parameter. We use these parameters to implement a sliding window that pages through the search results with the page size equaling maxResults, or less if it is the last page.

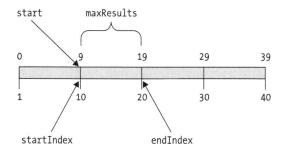

Figure 13-2. The Google service result page range

The result set returned from the doGoogleSearch method is of type
GoogleSearchResult. Table 13-2 describes this important class.

Table 13-2. The GoogleSearchResult *Class Returned by the* doGoogleSearch *Method*

PARAMETER	TYPE	DESCRIPTION
directoryCategories	directoryCategory	Open Directory Project (ODP) directory matches for this search.
documentFiltering	bool	Filtering was performed on search results.
endIndex	int	End index (one-based) of search results was returned.
estimateIsExact	bool	The results count estimate is accurate.
estimatedTotalResultsCount	int	Estimated number of results from this search.
resultElements	resultElement[]	Array of search result items.
searchQuery	string	String of search query.
searchTime	double	Amount of server time the search took to complete.
searchTips	string	Provides instructive information on how to use Google.
startIndex	int	Start index (one-based) of search results returned.

Observant readers will notice that the startIndex and endIndex fields of the
GoogleSearchResult class are one-based and not zero-based, as was the index that was
part of the request parameters. Make sure you heed this mathematical difference when
you are working with the result set. The result set also gives us an estimated count of all
the hits with the estimatedTotalResultsCount parameter. Google will tell us whether or
not this is an estimate with the estimateIsExact parameter.

The seminal piece of data inside the GoogleSearchResult class is the resultElements
property, which exposes an array of resultElement class instances. The resultElement
class holds the pertinent information for each URL match that was made against a
search query. Table 13-3 lists the resultElement class's fields.

Table 13-3. Google Web Service resultElement *Fields*

FIELD	TYPE	DESCRIPTION
cachedSize	string	If the cached page is available, this field returns the size of the page in kilobytes.
directoryCategory	directoryCategory	ODP category of the URL.
directoryTitle	string	Title of the category in the ODP directory.
hostname	string	Name of the host if filtering is turned on.
relatedInformationPresent	bool	Returns true if the "related:" query term is supported for the URL.
snippet	string	Snippet of HTML text that shows the context of where a query appears in a matched URL.
Summary	string	If the search result has a listing in the ODP directory, this field contains an ODP summary.
title	string	Title of a search result returned in HTML.
URL	string	Absolute path to the URL that matches the query.

We round out the discussion of the web service proxy to include the directoryCategory type. It provides ODP information about the Google search results. Table 13-4 contains a full explanation of the directoryCategory fields.

Table 13-4. Google Web Service directoryCategory *Fields*

FIELD	TYPE	DESCRIPTION
fullViewableName	string	ODP directory name for the current category
specialEncoding	string	Encoding scheme of the directory category

We do not discuss the doGetCachedPage and doSpellingSuggestion web service methods in the Google Web APIs service in this chapter because we do not use them as part of our control implementation. We can safely delete them from the proxy class created, as we ignore their functionality. For more information on how a web service proxy class works or how to work with WSDL from web services such as the Google Web APIs service, please consult the documentation or a .NET web services book.

Creating the Control Library Project

The first step in creating a control library is to ensure we have a well-organized namespace to identify and partition our controls from the rest of the control universe. A common paradigm for selecting such a namespace is to put business entities or organizations first, followed by a product or project title, followed by significant divisions within the actual product. For the Google web service control, we will use a namespace of Apress.GoogleControls. We give the Visual Studio .NET project the same name (i.e., "Apress.GoogleControls"), and we give the control assembly the output name of Apress.GoogleControls.dll. Keeping the namespace and the assembly name in sync like this is not a requirement, but it is a good design guideline to follow because it is mimicked by system DLLs such as System.Web.dll.

Strong-Named Assemblies and Versioning Attributes

After we decide on a namespace for our control project, the next step is to decide what sort of versioning policy we want to apply to it. We have two main options:

- Manually version code by releasing weak-named assemblies with documentation and hope consumers use the correct version.

- Take advantage of the built-in versioning in .NET available to strong-named assemblies, which ensures that the correct version of code is being used and provides a flexible policy for upgrade scenarios.

Although the process of taking a standard or weak-named assembly and converting it to a strong-named assembly isn't task-free, the extra work it entails is well worth the features it provides. An assembly gets this capability when you give it a version number, a culture, and a cryptographic key to identify the assembly beyond just its name. The extra work also provides built-in tampering protection, because the assembly can be signed with a digital signature of its hashed contents.

The first step in making a strong-named assembly is to create a cryptographic key to provide a unique identity. This key is easily created using the sn.exe command-line tool that comes with the rest of a .NET Framework or Visual Studio .NET installation. Find your favorite Visual Studio .NET command prompt or a command console window with sn.exe in its path and type the following to create the key:

```
sn -k Apress.GoogleControls.snk
```

Make note of the directory where the key pair file is created so you can copy it into the root of your control library project. To use the generated key, make a reference to it in the AssemblyInfo.cs file that comes with .NET projects in Visual Studio .NET by adding the following two attributes with the appropriate values:

```
// version the assembly using strong name
[assembly: AssemblyKeyFile(@"..\..\Apress.GoogleControls.snk")]
[assembly: AssemblyDelaySign(false)]
```

Notice that the reference to the key file uses two parent directories in its path statement. The reason for this is the structure that C# applications have in Visual Studio .NET. For a debug project, this is folder structure of the project showing executables two layers deep:

```
Projectfolder\
     Code.cs
     Mykey.snk
     bin\
             debug\
                     mydll.dll
```

After the key has been identified in the project, we fill out the rest of the information that makes up the strong "name" of an assembly. Of utmost importance to this process is the `AssemblyVersion` attribute:

```
[assembly: AssemblyVersion("1.0.0.0")]
```

The assembly version number is broken down into four separate numbers that can be versioned as the control author sees fit for his or her library. A recommended technique is to use this numerical representation as major, minor, build, and revision numbers. Builds and revisions will change more frequently during development cycles, whereas major and minor versions should be the public releases from the control developer.

Although the default configuration works in most settings, we recommend removing the two asterisks that mark the final two positions in the versioning scheme that is the default for Visual Studio .NET. Visual Studio .NET will generate a value for the final two numbers each time the project is compiled. This creates incompatibilities between versions for each compilation of the code project, even when a minor change is made to the source code. The .NET Framework requires an exact match on all four version numbers, so this default setting in AssemblyInfo.cs can cause strange versioning problems when you are implementing strong-named assemblies.

The final piece of information needed for making a strong-named assembly is the culture. The recommended culture setting for a primary assembly is the invariant culture, or a culture name with a blank string:

```
[assembly: AssemblyCulture("")]
```

We discuss in depth how this setting impacts localization in the next chapter in the "Globalization and Localization" section.

At this point we have specified full versioning information: name, public key, version, and culture. Clients that use our control will have metadata references using this strong name, and any changes to something (e.g., the version number) will cause a break in compatibility. Because of this, care should be taken when introducing bug fixes or new versions of a control library that supersede old versions. For more information on how to manage "breaking changes" please see the .NET Framework SDK documentation.

Bin Directory or Global Assembly Cache Deployment

Once we have compiled the control library with a strong name, we can install it in either the bin directory of a web site or in the *global assembly cache* (GAC), which is the .NET Framework–versioned code stored on a machine. The GAC provides for ease of installation and reuse if several web applications need the same control library on a machine.

Regardless of the location of deployment for a strong-named assembly, we recommend that you provide strong-named controls for ease of versioned updates and the side-by-side deployment capabilities they provide in .NET. Both have the potential to significantly improve the reliability of web applications and ease the maintenance burden on the web administrator.

The strong-named assembly has built-in tamper-proof features, as we alluded to earlier. During the build process for the assembly, the compiler performs a hash on the contents of the assembly to create a digital signature. The public key information is also stored inside the assembly so it can be verified by the runtime when it loads the assembly or when it is installed in the GAC. Any file tampering will cause an assembly load failure.

GAC installation provides a performance advantage over putting a strong-named assembly in the bin directory of the ASP.NET web application, because the verification process happens only once when the strong-named assembly is installed. If a strong-named assembly is loaded from an application's bin directory, the verification takes place each time on assembly load into an application.

Additional Assembly Attributes

Additional bookkeeping information about the control beyond the versioning and strong names can be entered into the AssemblyInfo.cs file via the use of assembly-level attributes. The following attributes are a subset of the full list available for giving a human-friendly description of the control library. This can be put to good use by tools that can read assembly metadata.

```
// General information about control assembly
[assembly: AssemblyTitle("Apress.GoogleControls")]
[assembly: AssemblyDescription(
"Apress ASP.NET Control Library for Google Web Service")]
[assembly: AssemblyCompany("Apress")]
[assembly: AssemblyProduct("Google ASP.NET Web Control Library")]
[assembly: AssemblyCopyright("")]
[assembly: AssemblyTrademark("")]
```

To help out the Toolbox support of a web control, it is best to add the TagPrefixAttribute at the assembly level. Here we use the Apress.GoogleControls namespace and default to google as the prefix to put in front of our tags when they are used in an .aspx page:

```
// configure the tag/namespace to be used in the toolbox
[assembly: TagPrefix("Apress.GoogleControls","google") ]
```

Another useful attribute to have in your AssemblyInfo.cs file is the CLSCompliantAttribute class set to true. This ensures that all Common Language Specification (CLS)–compliant languages can work seamlessly with your code. This attribute causes the compiler to generate a warning if a public non-CLS-compliant member is present. Think of it as a safety net that keeps you from doing things that would make your control incompatible with its consumers. The final list of attributes in the AssemblyInfo.cs file is shown in Listing 13-1.

Listing 13-1. The AssemblyInfo.cs Class File

```
using System;
using System.Web.UI;
using System.Reflection;
using System.Runtime.CompilerServices;

// version the assembly using strong name
[assembly: AssemblyKeyFile(@"..\..\Apress.GoogleControls.snk")]
[assembly: AssemblyDelaySign(false)]
[assembly: AssemblyVersion("1.0.0.0")]
[assembly: AssemblyCulture("")]

// General information about control assembly
[assembly: AssemblyTitle("Apress.GoogleControls")]
[assembly: AssemblyDescription(
"Apress ASP.NET Control Library for Google Web Service")]
[assembly: AssemblyCompany("Apress")]
[assembly: AssemblyProduct("Google ASP.NET Web Control Library")]
[assembly: AssemblyCopyright("")]
[assembly: AssemblyTrademark("")]

// configure the tag/namespace to be used in the toolbox
[assembly: TagPrefix("Apress.GoogleControls","google") ]

// ensure Common Language Specification (CLS) compliance
[assembly: CLSCompliant(true)]
```

Now that we have covered strong-named assemblies and how we implemented them in Google, in the next section we discuss how to store and retrieve configuration information using .config files.

Configuring the Search Settings

The Google search controls need a flexible way to retrieve configuration information that allows them to interact appropriately with the online web service. The following data is required:

- License key to authenticate with the Google web service

- URL of the Google search web service

- URL of a proxy server in situations in which the code is running behind a firewall

One approach to this sort of problem is hard-coding the configuration setting as string constants inside a control. Although simple in execution, this approach requires unnecessary recompilation steps that could hurt versioning and deployment maintenance of the web applications using the controls. A better approach is to use the XML configuration file mechanisms available to ASP.NET web applications.

Crafting the Configuration Section XML

Because we have several strings we want to use to configure our search controls, we decided to use a custom configuration section. This means we will have our own block of XML that is integrated as part of web.config. The following XML snippet is what we want to add to web.config:

```
<googleControls>
   <license
      googleLicenseKey="valid license key" />
   <url
      googleWebServiceUrl="http://api.google.com/search/beta2"
      proxyUrl="http://myproxyserver.com" />
</googleControls>
```

You can use whatever particular format suits your fancy as long as it is well-formed XML. Our custom configuration XML has the three configuration values that we need: googleLicenseKey, googleWebServiceUrl, and proxyUrl.

Building a Configuration Section Class

The first step in realizing this configuration information is to create a class that represents the main properties embodied by the XML configuration section. We name this class GoogleConfigSection, and it has a property for each of the three configuration values we discussed previously. Listing 13-2 presents the full code for the class file.

Listing 13-2. The GoogleConfigSection.cs Class File

```
using System.Configuration;
using System.Web;
using System.Xml;

namespace Apress.GoogleControls
{
    public class GoogleConfigSection
    {
        private string googleLicenseKey;
        private string googleWebServiceUrl;
        private string proxyUrl;

        public GoogleConfigSection(string googleLicenseKey,
        string googleWebServiceUrl, string proxyUrl)
        {
            this.googleLicenseKey = googleLicenseKey;
            this.googleWebServiceUrl = googleWebServiceUrl;
            this.proxyUrl = proxyUrl;
        }

        public string GoogleLicenseKey
        {
            get {return googleLicenseKey;}
        }

        public string GoogleWebServiceUrl
        {
            get {return googleWebServiceUrl;}
        }

        public string ProxyUrl
        {
            get {return proxyUrl;}
        }
    }
}
```

Registering the Configuration Section

Now that we have defined the XML format for our configuration data and the requisite class to provide an object-oriented representation of the XML data, we need a way to tell ASP.NET what we are up to. Our next task is to register a configuration section handler so that ASP.NET can process our custom XML configuration settings when servicing client requests.

The configuration section handler is brought into the picture via an XML section that is added to the top of the web.config file underneath the root-level configuration

XML element. `configSections` is a content-wrapping element that signifies we want to add additional content to the existing configuration sections, as shown here:

```
<configSections>
   <sectionGroup name="system.web">
     <section name="googleControls"
type="Apress.GoogleControls.GoogleConfigSectionHandler, Apress.GoogleControls,
Version=1.0.0.0, Culture=neutral, PublicKeyToken=9d0e1a77378e3a88" />
   </sectionGroup>
</configSections>
```

An interesting read is searching for `configSections` in the machine.config file that comes with the .NET Framework installation. You can see all of the configuration sections (such as for session state, authorization, and so on) familiar to web developers in this section of the machine.config file.

`sectionGroup` is used to group configuration section entries so there are no naming conflicts. If you choose an existing `sectionGroup` name that is already used, the new, custom `configSections` entry is nested under that configuration element. In our case, we choose to put the Google web service data under the `system.web` elements in the web.config file. We could also have chosen a unique name to be a root-level `sectionGroup` just as easily.

The final XML element in the preceding snippet, and the one that declares a binding to the code that handles the configuration parsing, is named `section`. Notice that we give `section` a name, `googleControls`, that corresponds to our top-level configuration section XML element. We also have to give it a fully qualified path to the class that implements the configuration section handler functionality, including the means to resolve the assembly containing the code.

Because we strongly named our control library project via the settings in the previously reviewed AssemblyInfo.cs file, we need to produce the name, version, culture, and public key token of the assembly. The easiest way to view this information is to use the shell extension GUI that is installed on a Windows machine along with the rest of the .NET Framework. Browse to the C:\windows\assembly folder. This folder has a special shell extension GUI that allows you to enumerate assemblies installed in the GAC, as shown in Figure 13-3.

Locate the assembly, right-click it, and select Properties. This action generates a pop-up dialog box with all the full versioning information of the assembly, as shown in Figure 13-4.

Building a Configuration Section Handler Class

Now that the configuration section handler is identified, ASP.NET will query the class that represents the new configuration section anytime a request is made for it. To satisfy this request, we need to build a configuration section handler class based on the `IConfigurationSection` interface. The primary method on this interface is the aptly named `Create` method:

```
public virtual object Create(object parent,object configContext, XmlNode section)
{ }
```

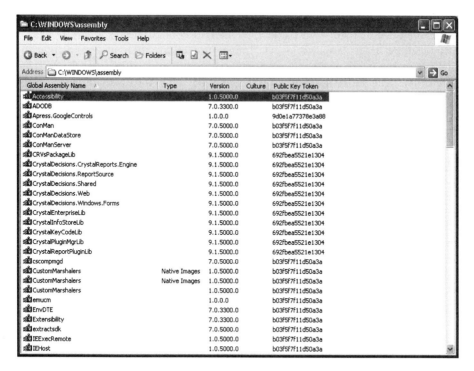

Figure 13-3. Finding your assembly in the Windows Explorer assembly viewer

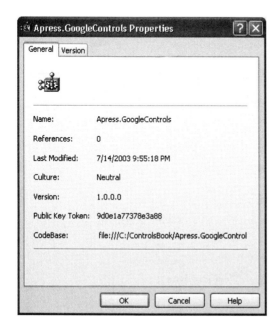

Figure 13-4. The Properties dialog box from an assembly discovered by the assembly viewer

The Create method provides access to any parent configuration information in the first parameter. ASP.NET operates differently than the configuration support for desktop applications in that it allows nested configuration information. It allows a child configuration section the capability to read parent settings and either pass them on or override them. The parent configuration section is passed in the first parameter. The second parameter is the HttpConfigurationContext instance that is also specific to ASP.NET configuration files. The sole bit of information it provides is a property named VirtualPath, which points to the web.config file that is the source of the configuration information. The final parameter is an XmlNode reference to the XML representing the configuration information for our configuration section. Those who have worked with XML in .NET will notice that this a Document Object Model (DOM)–based API for working with XML. You can use the standard techniques of XmlNode, XmlElement, and XmlAttribute to parse through the node tree to get the pertinent configuration data.

To make life easier on our configuration section handler for the Google controls, we build a helper class named ConfigHelper that abstracts the grunge work of parsing XML. ConfigHelper has a method called FindChildNode to grab a named node in the configuration section and a method named GetStringValue to pull string values from attributes. Listing 13-3 shows the full class listing for ConfigHelper.

Listing 13-3. The ConfigHelper.cs Class File

```
using System.Configuration;
using System.Web;
using System.Xml;

namespace Apress.GoogleControls
{
    public class ConfigHelper
    {
        public static XmlNode FindChildNode(XmlNode node, string element)
        {
            XmlNode e = node.SelectSingleNode("//" + element);
            if (e == null)
                throw new ConfigurationException(
                    "GoogleControl configuration element required: " + element);

            return e;
        }

        public static string GetStringValue(XmlNode node, string attribute,
        bool required, string defaultval)
        {
            string val = "";
            XmlNode a = node.Attributes.GetNamedItem(attribute);
            if (a == null)
            {
                if (required == true)
                {
                    throw new ConfigurationException(
```

```
                    "GoogleControl configuration attribute required: "
                    + attribute);
            }
            else
            {
                val = defaultval;
            }
        }
        else
        {
            val = a.Value;
        }
        return val;
    }
  }
}
```

Now that we have our helper code in place, we can implement the Create method of the IConfigurationSectionHandler interface. This is a straightforward process, as we already have done much of the hard work. We have a class to represent our data in GoogleConfigSection and an XML parsing utility class in ConfigHelper. All we have to do is locate the license and URL nodes to pull the googleLicenseKey, googleWebServiceUrl, and proxyUrl attributes.

One thing to keep in mind when you build configuration section handlers is to make sure they are implemented in a thread-safe fashion. ASP.NET has a thread pool to service its requests, and it can direct multiple threads against an instance of the configuration section handler at the same time. The best way to ensure thread safety is to stay away from member fields in the implementation of a configuration section handler or any blocking/synchronizing steps that could cause deadlock. Our implementation goes straight through its logic using only stack-based local variables in the Create method to stay out of trouble. Listing 13-4 presents the full listing for GoogleConfigSectionHandler.

Listing 13-4. The GoogleConfigSectionHandler.cs Class File

```
using System.Configuration;
using System.Web;
using System.Xml;

namespace Apress.GoogleControls
{
    public class GoogleConfigSectionHandler : IConfigurationSectionHandler
    {
        public virtual object Create(object parent,object configContext,
        XmlNode section)
        {
            string googleLicenseKey = "";
            string googleWebServiceUrl = "";
            string proxyUrl = "";
```

```
        XmlNode license = ConfigHelper.FindChildNode(section, "license");
        XmlNode url = ConfigHelper.FindChildNode(section, "url");

        googleLicenseKey =
            ConfigHelper.GetStringValue(license, "googleLicenseKey", true, "");

        googleWebServiceUrl =
            ConfigHelper.GetStringValue(url, "googleWebServiceUrl", true, "");

        proxyUrl =
            ConfigHelper.GetStringValue(url, "proxyUrl", true, "");

        return new GoogleConfigSection(
            googleLicenseKey, googleWebServiceUrl, proxyUrl);
      }
    }
}
```

Integrating the Configured Web Service Proxy

Implementing a custom configuration section does us little good if we don't put it to
use in our control library code. For this reason, we shift our attention back to our web
service proxy class that encapsulates the Google web service we created earlier in this
chapter. We modify its constructor to take both a web service URL and a proxy server
URL that will come from the configuration section data. The web service proxy uses
common sense when dealing with the proxy server URL parameter. We don't bother
with configuring a proxy server setup unless the proxy URL has a nonempty value.

   We next remove from the web service proxy class the autogenerated code that calls
the spelling suggestion method and the cached page retrieval web methods, and the
code that is added to call the web service asynchronously via delegates. Listing 13-5
contains the resulting web service proxy code.

Listing 13-5. The GoogleSearchService.cs Class File

```
namespace Apress.GoogleControls.Service
{
    using System.Diagnostics;
    using System.Xml.Serialization;
    using System;
    using System.Web.Services.Protocols;
    using System.ComponentModel;
    using System.Web.Services;
    using System.Net;

    [System.Diagnostics.DebuggerStepThroughAttribute()]
    [System.ComponentModel.DesignerCategoryAttribute("code")]
    [System.Web.Services.WebServiceBindingAttribute(Name="GoogleSearchBinding",
     Namespace="urn:GoogleSearch")]
```

```
[System.Xml.Serialization.SoapIncludeAttribute(typeof(ResultElement))]
internal class GoogleSearchService :
System.Web.Services.Protocols.SoapHttpClientProtocol
{
    public GoogleSearchService(string googleWebServiceUrl, string proxyUrl)
    {
        // default to the current Google Web Service Url if
        // none passed in
        if (googleWebServiceUrl.Length == 0)
            this.Url = "http://api.google.com/search/beta2";
        else
            this.Url = googleWebServiceUrl;

        // only configure proxy settings if passed in
        if (proxyUrl.Length != 0)
        {
            IWebProxy proxy = new WebProxy(proxyUrl, true);
            this.Proxy = proxy;
        }
    }
    [System.Web.Services.Protocols.SoapRpcMethodAttribute("urn:GoogleSearchAction",
RequestNamespace="urn:GoogleSearch", ResponseNamespace="urn:GoogleSearch")]
    [return: System.Xml.Serialization.SoapElementAttribute("return")]
    public GoogleSearchResult doGoogleSearch(string key, string q, int start,
int maxResults, bool filter, string restrict, bool safeSearch, string lr,
string ie, string oe)
    {
        object[] results = this.Invoke("doGoogleSearch", new object[] {
        key, q, start, maxResults, filter, restrict, safeSearch, lr, ie, oe});
        return ((GoogleSearchResult)(results[0]));
    }
}

[System.Xml.Serialization.SoapTypeAttribute("GoogleSearchResult",
"urn:GoogleSearch")]
public class GoogleSearchResult
{
    public bool documentFiltering;

    public string searchComments;

    public int estimatedTotalResultsCount;

    public bool estimateIsExact;

    public ResultElement[] resultElements;

    public string searchQuery;

    public int startIndex;
```

```
        public int endIndex;

        public string searchTips;

        public DirectoryCategory[] directoryCategories;

        public System.Double searchTime;
    }

    [System.Xml.Serialization.SoapTypeAttribute("ResultElement",
    "urn:GoogleSearch")]
    public class ResultElement
    {
        public string summary;

        public string URL;

        public string snippet;

        public string title;

        public string cachedSize;

        public bool relatedInformationPresent;

        public string hostName;

        public DirectoryCategory directoryCategory;

        public string directoryTitle;
    }

    [System.Xml.Serialization.SoapTypeAttribute("DirectoryCategory",
    "urn:GoogleSearch")]
    public class DirectoryCategory
    {
        public string fullViewableName;

        public string specialEncoding;
    }
}
```

Wrapping the Web Service Proxy in a Utility Method

To make it easier to work with the web service proxy, we wrap the creation and invocation process inside a utility class that abstracts all the details of communicating with the Google web service, as shown in Listing 13-6. This class also hides the work necessary to grab configuration information from the custom configuration section we created earlier in this chapter.

Listing 13-6. The SearchUtil.cs Class File

```csharp
using System;
using System.Configuration;
using System.Web;
using System.Web.Services.Protocols;

namespace Apress.GoogleControls.Service
{
    public class SearchUtil
    {
        const string ConfigSectionName = "system.web/googleControls";

        public static Service.GoogleSearchResult SearchGoogleService(
        string query, int startIndex, int maxResults, bool filtering)
        {
            string googleLicenseKey = "";
            string googleWebServiceUrl = "";
            string proxyUrl = "";

            // get <googleControl> config section from web.config
            // for search settings
            GoogleConfigSection config =
                ConfigurationSettings.GetConfig(
                ConfigSectionName) as GoogleConfigSection;
            if (config != null)
            {
                googleLicenseKey = config.GoogleLicenseKey;
                googleWebServiceUrl = config.GoogleWebServiceUrl;
                proxyUrl = config.ProxyUrl;
            }
                // if control is instantiated at runtime config section
                // should be present
            else if (HttpContext.Current != null)
            {
                throw new ConfigurationException(
                    "Apress.GoogleControls.Service.SearchUtil cannot find" + & +
                    "<googleControl> configuration section.");
            }

            // Create a Google Search object
            Service.GoogleSearchService service =
            new Service.GoogleSearchService(googleWebServiceUrl, proxyUrl);
            Service.GoogleSearchResult result = null;
            try
            {
                // Invoke the search method
                result = service.doGoogleSearch(
                    googleLicenseKey, query, startIndex, maxResults, filtering, "",
                    false, "", "", "");
```

```
        }
        catch (System.Web.Services.Protocols.SoapException ex)
        {
            throw new
                GoogleSearchException("Google web service query failed.",
                    ex);
        }
        return result;
    }
}

[Serializable]
public class GoogleSearchException : ApplicationException
{
    public GoogleSearchException(string message, SoapException e) :
    base(message, e)
    {

    }
}
}
```

The SearchUtil class provides a parameter list to its single static SearchGoogleService method that restricts some of the options available when calling the Google web service. In particular, it cuts out the restrict, safeSearch, lr, ie, and oe parameters. The net result of these changes is that our customized search is not restricted in terms of keywords, languages, or adult content. Consult Tables 13-1 through 13-4 for details on the parameters being defaulted to here.

For handling problems with the actual transmission of XML bits over the wire, we handle the SoapException exception that is thrown by the underlying web service proxy and instead create our own custom exception class named GoogleSearchException. This allows a web application developer to look for our specific GoogleSearchException instead of a generic SoapException in his or her error handling. The only constructor option given in our custom exception constructor requires an error message and the generated SoapException. We use the base functionality of ApplicationException, which stores the SoapException as an inner exception. This allows the consuming web application to reach in and retrieve the SoapException to display a more detailed error message regarding the communication problem.

Designing the Control Architecture

At this point, you have an understanding of how to access the Google web service, and you have some code to invoke it to return a set of search results. In the next phase of this chapter, you will learn how to display and interact with results from the Google web service.

The result set returned by the Google web service does not have the tabular structure that traditional data-bound controls such as the `Repeater` control or the `DataGrid` control expect. The top-level `GoogleSearchResult` class contains the overall status information about the search result, which would more likely be used as a header format. The `resultElements` array under `GoogleSearchResult` has a list of `resultElement` instances with the URL data for display in a repeating item format. The control we need to build has to work with the data on these two separate levels to display it appropriately. We achieve this by having templates that bind to different portions of the data source. We discussed how to create templates in Chapter 7.

Another major consideration is how to abstract communications with Google so that a developer can quickly add search capabilities to his or her application. To provide this ease of use, we encapsulate the Google web service searching inside of our control's code base. We provide a public data-binding method to load up the control UI from the result set, but the means to do it are abstracted away from the developer. All a developer needs to do is customize the UI and let the control do the heavy lifting of communicating with Google and paging the result set.

The first major architectural decision is to factor out the responsibilities of the control library. Instead of one supercontrol, we factor the functionality into three major controls: `Search`, `Result`, and `Pager`. We also have the `ResultItem` class, which contains the output templates as a utility control in support of the `Result` server control. The diagram in Figure 13-5 shows the breakdown of responsibilities.

The `Search` control has the primary responsibility of gathering input from the user and setting up the `Result` control with the first page of results in a new search. We want to separate `Search` from `Result` to allow flexible placement of the `Search` control's text boxes. The text boxes can be deployed in separate locations on a Web Form so as not to constrain the web application developer from a UI perspective.

The `Result` control handles the display of search results returned by the Google web service. On the first query to Google, the `Search` control will set up the `Result` control's `DataSource` property with an instance of `GoogleSearchResults` and call its `DataBind` method to have it bind its templates to the result set. This mimics the behavior of data-bound controls discussed in Chapter 7.

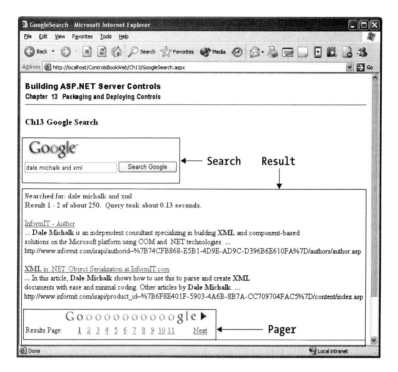

Figure 13-5. The architecture of the Google controls

The Pager control is the third main control in our control library and is embedded as a child control of the Result control. If paging is enabled, the Result control passes the Pager control the result set so that it calculates the starting index offsets based on page size and renders either images with links or just links.

Figure 13-6 shows the action that occurs with the Search, Result, and Pager controls on an initial search. The end result is a rendered page with embedded links that lets the page post back to itself to change the view of the search results.

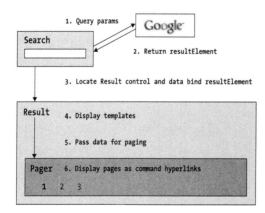

Figure 13-6. Controls in action on an initial search

Interacting with the paging features of the `Result` control is the next bit of functionality we discuss. When the links rendered by the `Pager` control are clicked, the control generates a server-side event. This event is mapped to the `Result` control, which then handles the process of going back to the Google web service and getting the desired page in the original result set. It sets its own `DataSource` property and calls `DataBind` on itself. This in turn starts the original binding process to render the new result set. Figure 13-7 shows the process graphically when the paging functionality of our control is exercised.

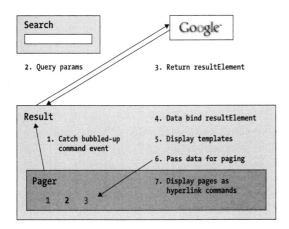

Figure 13-7. Controls in action after the paging link is clicked

Now that we have covered the overall design, we can move on to a more detailed analysis of the source code in each control, starting in the next section with the `Search` server control.

The `Search` Control

The `Search` control takes the input from the user to perform the search query. To accomplish this, we derive the control from the `WebControl` class and have it render its contents inside a `<DIV>` HTML tag. The `Query` property exposes the query string used to search the Google web service and is automatically set by the `TextBox` control, which is the primary input control for the `Search` control. The `Search` control does not expose a starting index property, as it assumes it will be on a one-based scale when it executes the query. `RedirectToGoogle` is a special property that provides the `Search` control the capability to ignore the Google web service and redirect the Web Form to the Google web site as if the user had typed in a query at the Google site directly.

The actual UI for the `Search` control is built in the composite control fashion of adding child controls from within the following `CreateChildControls` method. The first control added to the collection is a `HyperLink` control to hold the Google image and provide a clickable link back to Google as well. The `searchTextbox` control is a `TextBox` control that grabs the input from the user. The `searchButton` control is a `Button` control

that handles posting the page contents from the client back to the web server. Several
`LiteralControl` instances are also added to the `Controls` collection to fill in the HTML
spacing between the controls and provide breaks.

```
protected override void CreateChildControls()
{
    googleLinkImage = new HyperLink();
    googleLinkImage.ImageUrl = Google40PtLogoImageUrl;
    googleLinkImage.NavigateUrl = GoogleWebPageUrl;
    this.Controls.Add(googleLinkImage);

    LiteralControl br = new LiteralControl("<br>");
    this.Controls.Add(br);

    searchTextBox = new TextBox();
    searchTextBox.Width = SearchTextBoxWidth;
    searchTextBox.TextChanged +=new EventHandler(SearchTextBoxTextChanged);
    this.Controls.Add(searchTextBox);

    br = new LiteralControl(" ");
    this.Controls.Add(br);

    // search button Text is localized
    ResourceManager rm = ResourceFactory.Manager;
    searchButton = new Button();
    searchButton.Text = rm.GetString("Search.searchButton.Text");
    searchButton.Click += new EventHandler(SearchButtonClick);
    this.Controls.Add(searchButton);

    br = new LiteralControl("<br>");
    this.Controls.Add(br);
}
```

Events are wired up in `CreateChildControls` as well. The `Click` event of `searchButton`
and the `TextChanged` event of `searchTextBox` are the events of interest. These are routed
to the `SearchButtonClick` and `SearchTextBoxTextChanged` private methods, respectively.
All these events handlers really accomplish is passing the search query text over to the
`HandleSearch` method, which does the majority of the work inside the `Search` control.

Handling the Search

The top of `Search.HandleSearch` has code that checks an internal Boolean variable
named `searchHandled` to make sure that if both events fire on the same postback, we
don't get duplicate searches occurring on the same query value unnecessarily, as
shown here:

```
// check to see if search was handled on this postback
// (this prevents TextChanged and ButtonClicked from
// double-tapping the Google web service for the same query)
if (searchHandled == true)
   return;

// check for redirect of query processing to the Google web site
if (RedirectToGoogle == true)
{
   this.Page.Response.Redirect(
      GoogleWebSearchUrl + "?q=" +
      HttpContext.Current.Server.UrlEncode(Query), true);
}
```

In `HandleSearch` there is code that looks at the `RedirectToGoogle` property to decide whether to send the query back to the Google web site with `Response.Redirect`. The `Query` property is put on the URL string using the q variable on the HTTP GET string to accomplish this.

If we choose not to redirect the query to Google, then we use the `SearchUtil` class to receive a `GoogleSearchResult` from the web service proxy code it wraps. The `ResultControl` property of the `Search` control is used to do a dynamic lookup of the correct `Result` control via the `Page FindControl` method. We also use this control reference to infer the correct value for the `PageSize` and `Filtering` parameters used to query Google along with the `Query` property value.

```
// look up the Result control we are linked to
// and get the PageSize and Filtering property values
Result resControl = (Result) Page.FindControl(ResultControl);
int pageSize = resControl.PageSize;
bool filtering = resControl.Filtering;

// get search results from Google web service proxy
Service.GoogleSearchResult result =
   Service.SearchUtil.SearchGoogleService(
      Query,0,pageSize,filtering);
```

After getting the result data from the web service, we raise an event to any interested parties. The type of this event is named `GoogleSearched`. This allows someone to use the `Search` control as a data generator and build his or her own custom UI from the result sets. We follow the design pattern for invoking this event through a protected method with `On` as the prefix to the search name, `OnGoogleSearched`, as shown here:

```
// raise search results for any interested parties as well
OnGoogleSearched(new GoogleSearchedEventArgs(result));
```

The GoogleSearched event is a custom event we define in the class file
GoogleSearched.cs, as shown in Listing 13-7.

Listing 13-7. The GoogleSearched.cs Class File

```
using System;

namespace Apress.GoogleControls
{
    public class GoogleSearchedEventArgs : EventArgs
    {
        private Service.GoogleSearchResult result;

        public GoogleSearchedEventArgs(Service.GoogleSearchResult result)
        {
            this.result = result;
        }

        public Service.GoogleSearchResult Result
        {
            get
            {
                return result;
            }
        }
    }

    public delegate void GoogleSearchedEventHandler(object sender,
                        GoogleSearchedEventArgs e);
}
```

The GoogleSearchedEventArgs class wraps the results of a Google web service
query. We use that event argument's definition to create a GoogleSearchedEventHandler
delegate. If you go back to the Search control source code, you can see the code that
exposes the GoogleSearched event with this delegate definition. We use the manual
event declaration syntax that manages the delegate collection using an object key for
the event.

After the event is raised so that subscribers receive the Google web service search
results, we continue processing in the Search.HandleSearch method to bind data to the
Result control:

```
resControl.DataSource = result;
resControl.DataBind();
```

We set its DataSource property and call DataBind to have it fill its template structure with HTML that reflects the data of our web service query. The final step in the
HandleSearch method sets the searchHandled Boolean variable to ensure the control
does not fire two Google searches if both the TextBox TextChanged and the Button Click
events fire on the same postback, as shown here:

```
// set bool that tells us the search has been handled on this
// postback
searchHandled = true;
```

Listing 13-8 shows the source code for the Search control.

Listing 13-8. The Search.cs Class File

```
using System;
using System.Web.UI;
using System.Web.UI.HtmlControls;
using System.Web.UI.WebControls;
using System.Text;
using System.Collections;
using System.Collections.Specialized;
using System.Web;
using System.Reflection;
using System.ComponentModel;
using System.Configuration;
using System.Resources;

namespace Apress.GoogleControls
{
    [ParseChildren(true),
    ToolboxData("<{0}:Search runat=server></{0}:Search>"),
    Designer(typeof(SearchDesigner)),
#if LICENSED
    RsaLicenseData(
        "ffb30135-b07c-496b-8663-af996f7bff58",

"<RSAKeyValue><Modulus>tLMxOSJaiyTiEWtCWGuVVW7Q0aV59jDMvEIm4aILR9SlwD6DUG8FdnfbTf
tvMJZYGoI2XSaIyz5W6/20zjNyzZJdnNKN8V3zqT8BUBnVqrgyVAdA3mtjwdCk4MfpjEryeJAm19spgov
4dB5KUJOiDoKhbFVWZAyeXboHaE9uNWU=</Modulus><Exponent>AQAB</Exponent></RSAKeyValue
>"
        ),
    LicenseProvider(typeof(RsaLicenseProvider)),
#endif
    DefaultEvent("GoogleSearched")
    ]
    public class Search : WebControl, INamingContainer
    {
        private const string GoogleWebPageUrl = "http://www.google.com";
        private const string GoogleWebSearchUrl = "http://www.google.com/search";
        private const string Google25PtLogoImageUrl =
"http://www.google.com/logos/Logo_25wht.gif";
        private const string Google40PtLogoImageUrl =
"http://www.google.com/logos/Logo_40wht.gif";
        private const int SearchTextBoxWidth = 200;
        private const int DefaultPageSize = 10;
        private const bool DefaultFilteringValue = false;
```

```
            private const bool DefaultRedirectToGoogleValue = false;
            private bool searchHandled = false;

            private HyperLink googleLinkImage;
            private TextBox searchTextBox;
            private Button searchButton;
            private static readonly object GoogleSearchedKey = new object();

#if LICENSED
            private License license;
            private bool disposed = false;
#endif

            public Search()
            {

#if LICENSED
                // initiate license validation
                license =
                    LicenseManager.Validate(typeof(Search), this);
#endif

            }

            protected override HtmlTextWriterTag TagKey
            {
                get
                {
                    return HtmlTextWriterTag.Div;
                }
            }

#if LICENSED
            protected virtual void Dispose(bool disposing)
            {
                if (!disposed)
                {
                    // license resource cleanup
                    if (license != null)
                        license.Dispose();
                    license = null;
                }
                disposed = true;
            }

            public override void Dispose()
            {
                // clean up resources
                Dispose(true);

                // once disposed, no need to finalize
```

```
            GC.SuppressFinalize(this);
        }

        ~Search()
        {
           // clean up resources
           Dispose(false);
        }
#endif

        [DescriptionAttribute("Result control to bind search results for display."),
        CategoryAttribute("Search")]
        virtual public string ResultControl
        {
           get
           {
              object control = ViewState["ResultControl"];
              if (control == null)
                 return "";
              else
                 return (string) control;
           }
           set
           {
              ViewState["ResultControl"] = value;
           }
        }

        [DescriptionAttribute("Search query string."),
        CategoryAttribute("Search")]
        virtual public string Query
        {
           get
           {
              EnsureChildControls();
              return searchTextBox.Text;
           }
           set
           {
              EnsureChildControls();
              searchTextBox.Text = value;
           }
        }

        [DescriptionAttribute("Redirect search query to Google site web pages."),
        CategoryAttribute("Search")]
        virtual public bool RedirectToGoogle
        {
           get
           {
              object redirect = ViewState["RedirectToGoogle"];
```

```
            if (redirect == null)
                return DefaultRedirectToGoogleValue;
            else
                return (bool) redirect;
        }
        set
        {
            ViewState["RedirectToGoogle"] = value;
        }
    }

    protected void SearchButtonClick(object s, EventArgs e)
    {
        HandleSearch();
    }

    protected void SearchTextBoxTextChanged(object s, EventArgs e)
    {
        HandleSearch();
    }

    private void HandleSearch()
    {
        // check to see if search was handled on this postback
        // (this prevents TextChanged and ButtonClicked from
        // double-lapping Google web service for the same query)
        if (searchHandled == true)
            return;

        // check for redirect of query processing to Google web site
        if (RedirectToGoogle == true)
        {
            this.Page.Response.Redirect(
                GoogleWebSearchUrl + "?q=" +
                HttpContext.Current.Server.UrlEncode(Query), true);
        }

        if (ResultControl.Length != 0)
        {
            // look up the Result control we are linked to
            // and get the PageSize and Filtering property values
            Result resControl = (Result) Page.FindControl(ResultControl);
            int pageSize = resControl.PageSize;
            bool filtering = resControl.Filtering;

            // get search results from Google web service proxy
            Service.GoogleSearchResult result =
                Service.SearchUtil.SearchGoogleService(
                    Query,0,pageSize,filtering);

            // raise search results for any interested parties as well
            OnGoogleSearched(new GoogleSearchedEventArgs(result));
```

```
        // data bind search results with the Result control
        // we are linked with
        resControl.DataSource = result;
        resControl.DataBind();

    }


    // set bool that tells us the search has been handled on this
    // postback
    searchHandled = true;
}

public event GoogleSearchedEventHandler GoogleSearched
{
    add
    {
        Events.AddHandler(GoogleSearchedKey, value);
    }
    remove
    {
        Events.RemoveHandler(GoogleSearchedKey, value);
    }
}

protected virtual void OnGoogleSearched(GoogleSearchedEventArgs e)
{
    GoogleSearchedEventHandler del =
        (GoogleSearchedEventHandler) Events[GoogleSearchedKey];
    if (del != null)
    {
        del(this, e);
    }
}

protected override void CreateChildControls()
{
    googleLinkImage = new HyperLink();
    googleLinkImage.ImageUrl = Google40PtLogoImageUrl;
    googleLinkImage.NavigateUrl = GoogleWebPageUrl;
    this.Controls.Add(googleLinkImage);

    LiteralControl br = new LiteralControl("<br>");
    this.Controls.Add(br);
    searchTextBox = new TextBox();
    searchTextBox.Width = SearchTextBoxWidth;
    searchTextBox.TextChanged +=new EventHandler(SearchTextBoxTextChanged);
    this.Controls.Add(searchTextBox);
```

```
        br = new LiteralControl(" ");
        this.Controls.Add(br);

        // search button Text is localized
        ResourceManager rm = ResourceFactory.Manager;
        searchButton = new Button();
        searchButton.Text = rm.GetString("Search.searchButton.Text");
        searchButton.Click += new EventHandler(SearchButtonClick);
        this.Controls.Add(searchButton);

        br = new LiteralControl("<br>");
        this.Controls.Add(br);
    }

    public override ControlCollection Controls
    {
        get
        {
            EnsureChildControls();
            return base.Controls;
        }
    }
  }
}
```

Now that we have covered the search functionality, in the next section we discuss how the returned results are processed in the Result control.

The Result Control

The Result control is the most complex control of the Google controls library. It is a templated, data-bound control that has the capability to page itself as well as access the web service to update the page range. The Result server control takes its cue from the Repeater control we developed in Chapter 7. It provides a robust set of templates: HeaderTemplate, StatusTemplate, ItemTemplate, AlternatingItemTemplate, SeparatorTemplate, and FooterTemplate. Each template also has a like-named Style object to modify the HTML that is rendered for style content: HeaderStyle, StatusStyle, ItemStyle, AlternatingItemStyle, SeparatorStyle, and FooterStyle. The embedded Pager control has its style properties exposed by a Result class property named PagerStyle.

Each template is pushed into an instance of the ResultItem control. This is the primary child control of Result, and it provides the means for achieving access to search results from a template data-binding expression. As we mentioned previously, Result offloads most of the paging work to a control class named Pager, which handles offset and range calculations. We stuff the Pager control inside a ResultItem, so that it can page content. Figure 13-8 shows the structural architecture of the Result control, including the portion handed off to the Pager control.

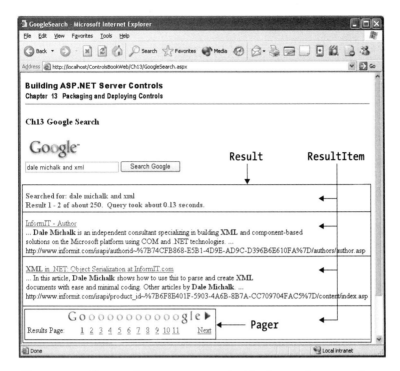

Figure 13-8. The ResultItem *structure inside the* Result *control*

In the next section, we discuss the details behind the ResultItem control class.

The ResultItem Control

The ResultItem class takes on a structure that is common to containers used as data-bound templates. It has the well-known DataItem property as well as an ItemIndex and ItemType property to store the index it occupies in the collection of ResultItem controls aggregated by its parent Result control. The ResultItemType enumeration matches up its usage with the templates and styles from the Result class as well.

Inside this file we also have a ResultItemEventHandler signature of ResultItem events. These provide interested clients with the capability to receive the creation (ItemCreated) and data-binding events (ItemDataBound) events of the parent Result control class. Listing 13-9 presents the full text listing for the ResultItem control.

Listing 13-9. The ResultItem.cs Class File

```
using System;
using System.Web;
using System.Web.UI;
using System.Web.UI.WebControls;
```

```
namespace Apress.GoogleControls
{
    public enum ResultItemType
    {
        Header = 0,

        Status,

        Item,

        AlternatingItem,

        Separator,

        Pager,

        Footer
    }

    public class ResultItem : WebControl, INamingContainer
    {
        private object dataItem;
        private ResultItemType itemType;
        private int itemIndex;

        public ResultItem(int index, ResultItemType type, object dataItem)
        {
            this.itemType = type;
            this.itemIndex = itemIndex;
            this.dataItem = dataItem;
        }

        public object DataItem
        {
            get
            {
                return dataItem;
            }
            set
            {
                dataItem = value;
            }
        }

        public int ItemIndex
        {
            get
            {
                return itemIndex;
            }
        }
```

```
      public ResultItemType ItemType
      {
         get
         {
            return itemType;
         }
      }

   }

   public delegate void ResultItemEventHandler(object sender,
   ResultItemEventArgs e);

   public class ResultItemEventArgs : EventArgs
   {
      private ResultItem item;

      public ResultItemEventArgs(ResultItem item)
      {
         this.item = item;
      }

      public ResultItem Item
      {
         get
         {
            return item;
         }
      }
   }
```
a

One thing to highlight regarding the Result control is how it binds different levels of data from the GoogleSearchResult data source to the ResultItem based on its associated control template in use. The data-binding expressions reach into a different data objects when they reference the Container.DataItem property depending on which ResultItem is referenced. The StatusTemplate is bound to the top-level GoogleSearchResult class through the DataItem property. The ItemTemplate and AlternatingItemItemTemplate are alternately bound to each ResultElement class that makes up the search results. HeaderTemplate, FooterTemplate, and SeparatorTemplate are not bound to any data source and have a null DataItem value.

Building the Result Control

To provide a pleasing UI experience out of the box and let the control render something when it is blank or when it is data bound, we have three primary modes that the Result control operates in: blank, data-binding, and postback. The blank mode is used for displaying a UI even when the user fails to link the control to a data source. Data-binding mode is used when a data source is provided and the user explicitly calls the DataBind method of the control. Postback is the mode the control takes on when it is sent back to the server from a postback event and the control hydrates its structure from ViewState.

The Blank Scenario

The default action of the Result control if you put it on a Web Form and leave it alone is triggered by code in its override of the following RenderContents method. If a Boolean named searchConducted is not set, it fires off a call to Result control's CreateBlankControlHierarchy method:

```
protected override void RenderContents(HtmlTextWriter writer)
{
    // if no search, create a hierarchy with header and
    // footer templates only
    if (!searchConducted)
    {
        CreateBlankControlHierarchy();
    }

    // prep all template styles
    PrepareControlHierarchy();

    // render all child controls
    base.RenderContents(writer);
}
```

After the call to the CreateBlankControlHierarchy method, the control next calls PrepareControlHierarchy to ensure all styles are applied to any user-provided templates. Lastly, the control calls the base class method of RenderContents to do its work of iterating through the child controls and rendering them.

If you look at CreateBlankControlHierarchy, you see that it looks for the HeaderTemplate and FooterTemplate templates and creates a ResultItem control to wrap them using the CreateResultItem helper method. We examine CreateResultItem in just a bit, but here is CreateBlankControlHierarchy:

```
private void CreateBlankControlHierarchy()
{
   if (HeaderTemplate != null)
   {
      ResultItem headerItem = CreateResultItem(-1, ResultItemType.Header, false,
                                               null);
      items.Add(headerItem);
   }

   if (FooterTemplate != null)
   {
      ResultItem footer = CreateResultItem(-1, ResultItemType.Footer,
                                           false, null);
      items.Add(footer);
   }
}
```

It adds the ResultItem control to an internal ArrayList collection. This is a
publicly reachable collection that is exposed via a top-level Items property on Result,
as shown in the following code. Notice that we didn't add the ResultItem controls to
the Controls collection of Result in CreateBlankControlHierarchy. This is handled by
CreateResultItem, along with other things such as data binding and raising item-related
events.

```
[Browsable(false)]
public ResultItemCollection Items
{
    get
    {
       return new ResultItemCollection(items);
    }
}
```

The ResultItemCollection type is a strongly typed collection of ResultItem controls.
Listing 13-10 contains the ResultItemCollection class.

Listing 13-10. The ResultItemCollection.cs Class File

```
using System;
using System.Collections;

namespace Apress.GoogleControls
{
   public class ResultItemCollection : CollectionBase
   {
      public ResultItemCollection(ArrayList list)
      {
         foreach (object item in list)
         {
```

```
              if (item is ResultItem)
                 List.Add(item);
           }
        }

        public int Add(ResultItem item)
        {
           return List.Add(item);
        }

        public void Insert(int index, ResultItem item)
        {
           List.Insert(index, item);
        }

        public void Remove(ResultItem item)
        {
           List.Remove(item);
        }

        public bool Contains(ResultItem item)
        {
           return List.Contains(item);
        }

        public inl IndexOf(ResultItem item)
        {
           return List.IndexOf(item);
        }

        public ResultItem this[int index]
        {
           get
           {
              return (ResultItem) List[index];
           }
           set
           {
              List[index] = value;
           }
        }

        public void CopyTo(ResultItemCollection col, int index)
        {
           for (int i=index; i < List.Count; i++)
           {
              col.Add(this[i]);
           }
        }
     }
  }
```

The Data-Bind Scenario

The next mode of creating child controls inside the Result control class focuses on what happens when the Search control executes a search, sets the DataSource property of the Result control, and invokes its DataBind method, as shown in the following code. The first task accomplished is clearing out child controls that might have been put into the collection manually and any information that might have been persisted to View-State. We also set the all-important searchConducted Boolean value to true so the control knows it is not in a blank control situation.

```
public override void DataBind()
{
    base.OnDataBinding(System.EventArgs.Empty);

    Controls.Clear();
    ClearChildViewState();
    TrackViewState();

    searchConducted = true;
    CreateControlHierarchy(true);
    ChildControlsCreated = true;
}
```

CreateControlHierarchy is used by DataBind to load up the control content and execute DataBind methods on each individual template. The Boolean value passed by DataBind is set to true to indicate to CreateControlHierarchy that we are in a data-bind scenario. We examine the details of CreateControlHierarchy later in this chapter after we have covered our third mode, which deals with a rendered Result control rehydrating at the beginning of postback.

The Postback Scenario

The Result control's CreateChildControls method shown in the following snippet is called when a server control needs to build its control structure. This could happen as part of the blank control-building scenario or as part of postback from a client round-trip.

```
override protected void CreateChildControls()
{
    Controls.Clear();

    if (searchConducted == false &&
        ViewState["ResultItemCount"] != null)
    {
        CreateControlHierarchy(false);
    }
}
```

The `CreateChildControls` method checks the `searchConducted` Boolean value to determine whether it has been called as part of the data-bind scenario. If the page has been manually data-bound, we do not need to create the control hierarchy. We also check to see whether there is content in the ViewState variable `ResultItemCount`. If this is present, the page is coming back via postback and we can call `CreateControlHierarchy` to have it repopulate the control structure based on `ResultItemControl` and have child controls retrieve their former values from ViewState. If the ViewState `ResultItemCount` variable is not present, we are in a blank control scenario and we let the code we have in `RenderContents` handle the blank mode situation.

Creating a Control Hierarchy for Data-Bind/Postback

Most of the heavy lifting to build the composite structure of the `Result` control occurs in the following `CreateControlHierarchy` for the data-bind and postback scenarios. This code is typical of your run-of-the-mill data-bound control.

```
private void CreateControlHierarchy(bool dataBind)
{
   Service.GoogleSearchResult result = null;

   // Result items
   items = new ArrayList();

   int count = 0;
   if (dataBind == true)
   {
      if (DataSource == null)
         return;
      result = (Service.GoogleSearchResult) DataSource;
      Query = result.searchQuery;
      StartIndex = result.startIndex-1;

      // set ViewState values for read-only props
      ViewState["TotalResultsCount"] = result.estimatedTotalResultsCount;
      ViewState["EndIndex"] = result.endIndex-1;

      count = result.resultElements.Length;
   }  else
   {
      object temp = ViewState["ResultItemCount"];
      if (temp != null)
         count = (int) temp;
   }

   if (HeaderTemplate != null)
   {
      ResultItem headerItem = CreateResultItem(-1, ResultItemType.Header,
      false, null);
      items.Add(headerItem);
   }
```

```
ResultItem statusItem = CreateResultItem(-1, ResultItemType.Status, dataBind,
result);
items.Add(statusItem);

// loop through and create ResultItem controls for each of the
// result elements from the Google web service result
ResultItemType itemType = ResultItemType.Item;
for (int i = 0; i < count; i++)
{
    if (separatorTemplate != null)
    {
        ResultItem separator =
        CreateResultItem(-1, ResultItemType.Separator, false, null);
        items.Add(separator);
    }

    Service.ResultElement resultElem = null;
    if (dataBind == true)
    {
        resultElem = result.resultElements[i];
    }

    ResultItem item = CreateResultItem(i, itemType, dataBind, resultElem);
    items.Add(item);

    // swap between Item and AlternatingItem types
    if (itemType == ResultItemType.Item)
        itemType = ResultItemType.AlternatingItem;
    else
        itemType = ResultItemType.Item;
}

// display pager if allowed by user and if results
// are greater than a page in length
if (DisplayPager == true && TotalResultsCount > PageSize)
{
    ResultItem pager = CreatePagerResultItem(dataBind, result);
    items.Add(pager);
}

if (FooterTemplate != null)
{
    ResultItem footer = CreateResultItem(-1, ResultItemType.Footer, false,
                                         null);
    items.Add(footer);
}
if (dataBind)
{
    ViewState["ResultItemCount"] = count;
}
}
```

If we are in data-binding mode based on the passed-in Boolean parameter, the
Result control examines the GoogleSearchResult instance linked to the DataSource
property of itself. DataSource is strongly typed in the implementation of Result to prevent someone from accidentally assigning a DataSet or other type of collection to it.

```
[Description("Data source that takes a GoogleSearchResult to build display."),
Category("Data"),
DesignerSerializationVisibility(DesignerSerializationVisibility.Hidden),
DefaultValue(null),
Bindable(true)]
public Service.GoogleSearchResult DataSource
{
   get
   {
      return dataSource;
   }
   set
   {
        dataSource = value;
   }
}
```

The code in DataBind pulls key parameters from the data source like the query, the
number of results, and the range of indexes from the result set. Notice that we account
for the EndIndex and StartIndex values being zero-based instead of the one-based
information provided by the result set returned from GoogleSearchResult. The count
variable is set to the size of the resultElement array returned to ensure accurate looping in the template creation process. The StartIndex and TotalResultsCount values are
not set via property accessors; rather, we directly input the ViewState values. The properties themselves are built to be read-only directly from the ViewState in order to prevent someone from overwriting them outside of the data-binding mechanism.

If we are not in a data-binding scenario, yet we are creating the control hierarchy,
we read ResultItemCount from the ViewState collection to set the count variable. Having a count is all we need because we go through a loop that creates the correct number of ResultItem controls for each of the search results and they then are able to pull
their previous information from ViewState.

When the code loops through the result set items, it creates the required template
for each item and data binds by calling the CreateResultItem method. As the result items
are processed, the HeaderTemplate, FooterTemplate, and SeparatorTemplates templates
are checked for a null value, whereas the StatusTemplate and ResultItemTemplate templates are not. The reason for this difference is that the ResultControl has two prewired
template classes as default templates for the StatusTemplate and ItemTemplate if they
are not specified by the user. You can see this by examining the CreateResultItem
method, which is responsible for creating the ResultItem control instances that house
the final template content.

Once we have looped through each ResultElement of the search query data set,
we turn to creating the paging structure. Here we call a different method to create the
ResultItem instance that houses the paging structure by calling the CreatePagerItem

method. We also set up the ViewState to remember the count of elements added so we can rehydrate them from ViewState during postback.

Creating ResultItem Controls

CreateControlHierarchy offloads most of the work to the CreateResultItem method, as shown in the following code. The CreateResultItem method is the true workhorse of the Result class. It creates the major structures, adds them to the Controls collection, and manages events and data binding.

```
private ResultItem CreateResultItem(int index, ResultItemType itemType,
                                    bool dataBind, object dataItem)
{
   ITemplate selectedTemplate;

   switch (itemType)
   {
      case ResultItemType.Header :
         selectedTemplate = HeaderTemplate;
         break;
      case ResultItemType.Status :
         if (StatusTemplate == null)
         {
            // if no StatusTemplate, pick up the default
            // template ResultStatusTemplate
            selectedTemplate = new ResultStatusTemplate();
         }
         else
            selectedTemplate = StatusTemplate;
         break;
      case ResultItemType.Item :
         if (ItemTemplate == null)
         {
            // if no ItemTemplate, pick up the default
            // template ResultItemTemplate
            selectedTemplate = new ResultItemTemplate();
         }
         else
            selectedTemplate = ItemTemplate;
         break;
      case ResultItemType.AlternatingItem :
         selectedTemplate = AlternatingItemTemplate;
         if (selectedTemplate == null)
         {
            // if no AlternatingItemTemplate, switch to Item type
            // and pick up ItemTemplate
            itemType = ResultItemType.Item;
            selectedTemplate = ItemTemplate;
            if (selectedTemplate == null)
            {
```

```
                    // if that doesn't work, pick up the default
                    // template ResultItemTemplate
                    selectedTemplate = new ResultItemTemplate();
                }
            }
            break;
        case ResultItemType.Separator :
            selectedTemplate = SeparatorTemplate;
            break;
        case ResultItemType.Footer :
            selectedTemplate = FooterTemplate;
            break;
        default:
            selectedTemplate = null;
            break;
    }

    ResultItem item = new ResultItem(index, itemType, dataItem);

    if (selectedTemplate != null)
    {
        selectedTemplate.InstantiateIn(item);
    }

    OnItemCreated(new ResultItemEventArgs(item));
    Controls.Add(item);

    if (dataBind)
    {
        item.DataBind();
        OnItemDataBound(new ResultItemEventArgs(item));
    }
    return item;
}
```

The first task for CreateResultItem is to determine what type of ResultItem it is creating using a switch statement. The end result of the process is grabbing the correct template from the Result control's template properties and assigning it to the selectedTemplate method variable. For the Status and Item types, it also handles the case of a blank template by instantiating the built-in default ResultStatusTemplate and ResultItemTemplate classes. If the AlternatingItemTemplate property is blank, the Item type ResultItemTemplate default template is used.

After template selection, a brand-new ResultItem control is created and is passed its index in the parent Result control's Item collection, as well as its type and a potentially valid data source. After the ResultItem is minted, it receives the template control content via the Instantiate method of the ITemplate interface.

The final step is to fire the required events. Once the control is created, we raise an ItemCreated event and add the control to the Controls collection. The final step is to call DataBind on the ResultItem if we are in a data-bind scenario, which then raises an ItemDataBound event.

Creating the Child Pager Control

The Pager control is added to the Controls collection of the parent Result control in CreatePagerResultItem. This special-purpose creation method creates a new ResultItem control and adds a configured Pager control to it as follows:

```
private ResultItem CreatePagerResultItem(bool dataBind, object dataItem)
{
    ResultItem item = new ResultItem(-1, ResultItemType.Pager, null);

    Pager pager = new Pager();
    pager.PageSize = PageSize;
    pager.PagerBarRange = PagerBarRange;
    pager.PagerLinkStyle = PagerLinkStyle;
    pager.TotalResultsCount = TotalResultsCount;
    pager.StartIndex = StartIndex;
    pager.EndIndex = EndIndex;

    item.Controls.Add(pager);

    Controls.Add(item);
    return item;
}
```

Pager is configured based on information from the web service query and information that is exposed by the parent Result control. The PageSize property is the number of entries listed per page that are returned from the Google search results. PagerBarRange is the number of pages to display in numeric form at the bottom of the page to go along with the Previous and Next buttons, if applicable. PagerLinkStyle is of type ResultPagerLinkStyle declared as follows. It determines whether images and text links are displayed or just images are displayed.

```
public enum ResultPagerLinkStyle
{
    Text = 0,
    TextWithImages
}
```

Notice that we don't have to explicitly pass GoogleSearchResult to Pager in the CreatePagerResultItem method. It has code inside of it to deal with calculating and displaying the correct page ranges based on the TotalResultsCount, StartingIndex, and EndIndex property values.

Managing Paging

The Pager control that is part of the child control structure of a paging Result control will raise the correct command events when an image or link is clicked to change the page of results displayed. The command event raised by the Pager control is intercepted by the parent Result control via the use of the OnBubbleEvent method override:

```
protected override bool OnBubbleEvent(object sender, EventArgs e)
{
    // Handle events raised by children by overriding OnBubbleEvent.
    // (main purpose is to detect paging events)
    bool handled = false;
    CommandEventArgs cea = e as CommandEventArgs;

    // handle Page event by extracting new start index
    // and calling HandleSearch method, which does the
    // work of rebinding this control to the results
    // from the web service
    if (cea.CommandName == "Page")
    {
        StartIndex = Convert.ToInt32(cea.CommandArgument);
        HandleSearch();

    }

    return handled;
}
```

The OnBubbleEvent implementation in Result grabs the index of the new page to display with the Result control and then calls HandleSearch, which actually talks to Google. HandleSearch is similar to the method of the same name in the Search control, except that it doesn't have to look up a Result control; it simply sets the DataSource and calls DataBind on itself.

Styling the Result Control

After all of the child controls are created, either by CreateBlankControlHierarchy or CreateControlHierarchy, the styles exposed by the Result control are applied. This is handled in the RenderContents override discussed earlier. At the end of RenderContents, the code invokes PrepareControlHierarchy to make this happen. It loops through all the ResultItem controls and applies the appropriate Style object if the style was set on the Result control, as shown here:

```
protected void PrepareControlHierarchy()
{
    // apply all the appropriate style attributes
    // to the items in the result output
    foreach (ResultItem item in this.Items)
```

```
    {
        if (item.ItemType == ResultItemType.Header)
        {
            if (HeaderStyle != null)
                item.ApplyStyle(HeaderStyle);
        }
        else if (item.ItemType == ResultItemType.Status)
        {
            if (StatusStyle != null)
                item.ApplyStyle(StatusStyle);
        }
        else if (item.ItemType == ResultItemType.Item)
        {
            if (ItemStyle != null)
                item.ApplyStyle(ItemStyle);

        }
        else if (item.ItemType == ResultItemType.AlternatingItem)
        {
            if (AlternatingItemStyle != null)
                item.ApplyStyle(AlternatingItemStyle);
            else if (ItemStyle != null)
                item.ApplyStyle(ItemStyle);
        }
        else if (item.ItemType == ResultItemType.Separator)
        {
            if (SeparatorStyle != null)
                item.ApplyStyle(SeparatorStyle);
        }
        else if (item.ItemType == ResultItemType.Pager)
        {
            if (PagerStyle != null)
            {
                Pager pager = (Pager) item.Controls[0];
                pager.ApplyStyle(PagerStyle);
            }
        }
        else if (item.ItemType == ResultItemType.Footer)
        {
            if (FooterStyle != null)
                item.ApplyStyle(FooterStyle);
        }
    }
}
```

Because we know there is only one instance of the Pager server control stored as a
ResultItem, we apply PagerStyle directly to this instance, as shown in the preceding
code. Listing 13-11 shows the full source for the Result control.

Listing 13-11. The Result.cs Class File

```
using System;
using System.Web.UI;
using System.Web.UI.HtmlControls;
using System.Web.UI.WebControls;
using System.Text;
using System.Collections;
using System.Collections.Specialized;
using System.Web;
using System.Reflection;
using System.ComponentModel;
using System.Configuration;
using System.Resources;

namespace Apress.GoogleControls
{
    public enum ResultPagerLinkStyle
    {
        Text = 0,

        TextWithImages
    }

    [ParseChildren(true),
    ToolboxData("<{0}:result runat=server></{0}:result>"),
    Designer(typeof(ResultDesigner)),
#if LICENSED
    RsaLicenseData(
        "ffb30135-b07c-496b-8663-af996f7bff58",
```
```
"<RSAKeyValue><Modulus>tLMxOSJaiyTiEWtCWGuVVW7QOaV59jDMvEIm4aILR9SlwD6DUG8FdnfbTf
tvMJZYGoI2XSaIyz5W6/2OzjNyzZJdnNKN8V3zqT8BUBnVqrgyVAdA3mtjwdCk4MfpjEryeJAm19spgov
4dB5KUJOiDoKhbFVWZAyeXboHaE9uNWU=</Modulus><Exponent>AQAB</Exponent></RSAKeyValue
>"
```
```
        ),
    LicenseProvider(typeof(RsaLicenseProvider)),
#endif
    DefaultEvent("GoogleSearched")
    ]
    public class Result : WebControl, INamingContainer, IDisposable
    {
        // constants
        private const int DefaultPageSize = 10;
        private const int DefaultPagerBarRange = 10;

        // style property fields
        private Style headerStyle;
        private Style statusStyle;
        private Style itemStyle;
        private Style alternatingItemStyle;
```

```
        private Style separatorStyle;
        private Style pagerStyle;
        private Style footerStyle;
        private ResultPagerLinkStyle pagerLinkStyle =
                ResultPagerLinkStyle.TextWithImages;

        // Template property fields
        private ITemplate headerTemplate;
        private ITemplate statusTemplate;
        private ITemplate itemTemplate;
        private ITemplate alternatingItemTemplate;
        private ITemplate separatorTemplate;
        private ITemplate footerTemplate;

        private bool searchConducted = false;
        private Service.GoogleSearchResult dataSource;
        private ArrayList items = new ArrayList();

        // event keys
        private static readonly object GoogleSearchedKey = new object();
        private static readonly object ItemCreatedKey = new object();
        private static readonly object ItemDataBoundKey = new object();

#if LICENSED
        private bool disposed = false;
        private License license;
#endif

        public Result()
        {
#if LICENSED
            // initiate license validation
            license =
                LicenseManager.Validate(typeof(Search), this);
#endif
        }

        protected override HtmlTextWriterTag TagKey
        {
            get
            {
                return HtmlTextWriterTag.Div;
            }
        }

        #region Dispose pattern

#if LICENSED

        protected virtual void Dispose(bool disposing)
        {
```

```
            if (!disposed)
            {
               // license resource cleanup
               if (license != null)
                  license.Dispose();
               license = null;
            }
            disposed = true;
         }

         public override void Dispose()
         {
            Dispose(true);
            GC.SuppressFinalize(this);
         }

         ~Result()
         {
            Dispose(false);
         }
#endif

      #endregion

      #region Search properties

/// <summary>
      /// Number of search results returned with query and displayed on page.
      /// </summary>
      [Description(
   "Number of search results returned with query and displayed on page."),
      Category("Search"),
      DefaultValue(DefaultPageSize)]
      virtual public int PageSize
      {
         get
         {
            object size = ViewState["PageSize"];
            if (size == null)
               return DefaultPageSize;
            else
               return (int) size;
         }
         set
         {
            ViewState["PageSize"] = value;
         }
      }

      /// <summary>
      /// Starting item index of search results.
```

```
/// </summary>
[Browsable(false)]
virtual public int StartIndex
{
   get
   {
      object index = ViewState["StartIndex"];
      if (index == null)
         return 1;
      else
         return (int) index;
   }
   set
   {
      ViewState["StartIndex"] = value;
   }
}

/// <summary>
/// Ending item index of search list results.
/// </summary>
[Browsable(false)]
virtual public int EndIndex
{
   get
   {
      object index = ViewState["EndIndex"];
      if (index == null)
         return 1;
      else
         return (int) index;
   }

}

/// <summary>
/// Estimated total results count from query.
/// </summary>
[Browsable(false)]
virtual public int TotalResultsCount
{
   get
   {
      object count= ViewState["TotalResultsCount"];
      if (count == null)
         return 0;
      else
         return (int) count;
   }

}
```

```
/// <summary>
/// Search query string.
/// </summary>
[Browsable(false)]
virtual public string Query
{
   get
   {
      object query = ViewState["Query"];
      if (query == null)
         return string.Empty;
      else
         return (string) query;
   }
   set
   {
      ViewState["Query"] = value;
   }
}

/// <summary>
/// Apply Google filtering of search result set.
/// </summary>
[Description("Apply Google filtering of search result set."),
Category("Search")]
virtual public bool Filtering
{
   get
   {
      object filter = ViewState["Filtering"];
      if (filter == null)
         return false;
      else
         return (bool) filter;
   }
   set
   {
      ViewState["Filtering"] = value;
   }
}
#endregion

#region Appearance properties

/// <summary>
/// Display paging links at bottom of search results.
/// </summary>
[Description("Display paging links at bottom of search results."),
Category("Appearance")]
virtual public bool DisplayPager
{
```

```csharp
      get
      {
         object pager = ViewState["DisplayPager"];
         if (pager == null)
            return true;
         else
            return (bool) pager;
      }
      set
      {
         ViewState["DisplayPager"] = value;
      }
}


/// <summary>
/// Style of Pager control link display.
/// </summary>
[Description("Style of Pager control link display."),
Category("Appearance")]
public ResultPagerLinkStyle PagerLinkStyle
{
   get
   {
      return pagerLinkStyle;
   }
   set
   {
      pagerLinkStyle = value;
   }
}


/// <summary>
/// Number of pages displayed in pager bar.
/// </summary>
[Description("Number of pages displayed in pager bar."),
Category("Appearance")]
virtual public int PagerBarRange
{
   get
   {
      object range = ViewState["PagerBarRange"];
      if (range == null)
         return DefaultPagerBarRange;
      else
         return (int) range;
   }
   set
   {
      ViewState["PagerBarRange"] = value;
   }
}
```

```
#endregion

#region Miscellaneous properties

[Description(
"Data source that takes a GoogleSearchResult to build display."),
Category("Data"),
DesignerSerializationVisibility(DesignerSerializationVisibility.Hidden),
DefaultValue(null),
Bindable(true)]
public Service.GoogleSearchResult DataSource
{
   get
   {
      return dataSource;
   }
   set
   {
      dataSource = value;
   }
}

[Browsable(false)]
public ResultItemCollection Items
{
   get
   {
      return new ResultItemCollection(items);
   }
}
#endregion

#region Style properties

[Category("Style"),
Description("The style to be applied to header template."),
DesignerSerializationVisibility(DesignerSerializationVisibility.Content),
NotifyParentProperty(true),
PersistenceMode(PersistenceMode.InnerProperty),
]
public virtual Style HeaderStyle
{
   get
   {
      if (headerStyle == null)
      {
         headerStyle = new Style();
         if (IsTrackingViewState)
            ((IStateManager)footerStyle).TrackViewState();
      }
      return headerStyle;
   }
}
```

```
[Category("Style"),
Description("The style to be applied to status template."),
DesignerSerializationVisibility(DesignerSerializationVisibility.Content),
NotifyParentProperty(true),
PersistenceMode(PersistenceMode.InnerProperty),
]
public virtual Style StatusStyle
{
   get
   {
      if (statusStyle == null)
      {
         statusStyle = new Style();
         statusStyle.ForeColor = System.Drawing.Color.Blue;
         statusStyle.Font.Bold = true;
         if (IsTrackingViewState)
            ((IStateManager)statusStyle).TrackViewState();
      }
      return statusStyle;
   }
}

[Category("Style"),
Description("The style to be applied to item template."),
DesignerSerializationVisibility(DesignerSerializationVisibility.Content),
NotifyParentProperty(true),
PersistenceMode(PersistenceMode.InnerProperty),
]
public virtual Style ItemStyle
{
   get
   {
      if (itemStyle == null)
      {
         itemStyle = new Style();
         if (IsTrackingViewState)
            ((IStateManager)itemStyle).TrackViewState();
      }
      return itemStyle;
   }
}

[ Category("Style"),
Description("The style to be applied to alternate item template."),
DesignerSerializationVisibility(DesignerSerializationVisibility.Content),
NotifyParentProperty(true),
PersistenceMode(PersistenceMode.InnerProperty),
]
public virtual Style AlternatingItemStyle
{
```

```
      get
      {
         if (alternatingItemStyle == null)
         {
            alternatingItemStyle = new Style();
            if (IsTrackingViewState)
               ((IStateManager)alternatingItemStyle).TrackViewState();
         }
         return alternatingItemStyle;
      }
   }

   [Category("Style"),
   Description("The style to be applied to the separator template."),
   DesignerSerializationVisibility(DesignerSerializationVisibility.Content),
   NotifyParentProperty(true),
   PersistenceMode(PersistenceMode.InnerProperty),
   ]
   public virtual Style SeparatorStyle
   {
      get
      {
         if (separatorStyle == null)
         {
            separatorStyle = new Style();
            if (IsTrackingViewState)
               ((IStateManager)separatorStyle).TrackViewState();
         }
         return separatorStyle;
      }
   }

   [Category("Style"),
   Description("The style to be applied to the pager."),
   DesignerSerializationVisibility(DesignerSerializationVisibility.Content),
   NotifyParentProperty(true),
   PersistenceMode(PersistenceMode.InnerProperty),
   ]
   public virtual Style PagerStyle
   {
      get
      {
         if (pagerStyle == null)
         {
            pagerStyle = new Style();
            if (IsTrackingViewState)
               ((IStateManager)pagerStyle).TrackViewState();
         }
         return pagerStyle;
      }
   }
```

```
    [Category("Style"),
    Description("The style to be applied to the footer template."),
    DesignerSerializationVisibility(DesignerSerializationVisibility.Content),
    NotifyParentProperty(true),
    PersistenceMode(PersistenceMode.InnerProperty),
    ]
    public virtual Style FooterStyle
    {
        get
        {
            if (footerStyle == null)
            {
                footerStyle = new Style();
                if (IsTrackingViewState)
                    ((IStateManager)footerStyle).TrackViewState();
            }
            return footerStyle;
        }
    }
    #endregion

    #region Style and ViewState management

    override protected object SaveViewState()
    {
        object baseState = base.SaveViewState();
        object headerStyleState = (headerStyle != null) ?
((IStateManager)HeaderStyle).SaveViewState() : null;
        object statusStyleState = (statusStyle != null) ?
((IStateManager)StatusStyle).SaveViewState() : null;
        object itemStyleState = (itemStyle != null) ?
((IStateManager)ItemStyle).SaveViewState() : null;
        object alternatingItemStyleState = (alternatingItemStyle != null) ?
((IStateManager)AlternatingItemStyle).SaveViewState() : null;
        object separatorStyleState = (separatorStyle != null) ?
((IStateManager)SeparatorStyle).SaveViewState() : null;
        object pagerStyleState = (pagerStyle != null) ?
((IStateManager)PagerStyle).SaveViewState() : null;
        object footerStyleState = (itemStyle != null) ?

((IStateManager)FooterStyle).SaveViewState() : null;

        object[] state = new object[8];
        state[0] = baseState;
        state[1] = headerStyleState;
        state[2] = statusStyleState;
        state[3] = itemStyleState;
        state[4] = alternatingItemStyleState;
        state[5] = separatorStyleState;
        state[6] = pagerStyleState;
        state[7] = footerStyleState;
```

```
      return state;
   }

   override protected void LoadViewState(object savedState)
   {
      if (savedState != null)
      {
         object[] state = (object[])savedState;

         if (state[0] != null)
            base.LoadViewState(state[0]);
         if (state[1] != null)
            ((IStateManager)HeaderStyle).LoadViewState(state[1]);
         if (state[2] != null)
            ((IStateManager)StatusStyle).LoadViewState(state[2]);
         if (state[3] != null)
            ((IStateManager)ItemStyle).LoadViewState(state[3]);
         if (state[4] != null)
            ((IStateManager)AlternatingItemStyle).LoadViewState(state[4]);
         if (state[5] != null)
            ((IStateManager)SeparatorStyle).LoadViewState(state[5]);
         if (state[6] != null)
            ((IStateManager)PagerStyle).LoadViewState(state[6]);
         if (state[7] != null)
            ((IStateManager)FooterStyle).LoadViewState(state[7]);
      }
   }

   protected void PrepareControlHierarchy()
   {
      // apply all the appropriate style attributes
      // to the items in the result output
      foreach (ResultItem item in this.Items)
      {
         if (item.ItemType == ResultItemType.Header)
         {
            if (HeaderStyle != null)
               item.ApplyStyle(HeaderStyle);
         }
         else if (item.ItemType == ResultItemType.Status)
         {
            if (StatusStyle != null)
               item.ApplyStyle(StatusStyle);
         }
         else if (item.ItemType == ResultItemType.Item)
         {
            if (ItemStyle != null)
               item.ApplyStyle(ItemStyle);

         }
         else if (item.ItemType == ResultItemType.AlternatingItem)
```

```
        {
            if (AlternatingItemStyle != null)
                item.ApplyStyle(AlternatingItemStyle);
            else if (ItemStyle != null)
                item.ApplyStyle(ItemStyle);
        }
        else if (item.ItemType == ResultItemType.Separator)
        {
            if (SeparatorStyle != null)
                item.ApplyStyle(SeparatorStyle);
        }
        else if (item.ItemType == ResultItemType.Pager)
        {
            if (PagerStyle != null)
            {
                Pager pager = (Pager) item.Controls[0];
                pager.ApplyStyle(PagerStyle);
            }
        }
        else if (item.ItemType == ResultItemType.Footer)
        {
            if (FooterStyle != null)
                item.ApplyStyle(FooterStyle);
        }
    }
}
#endregion

#region Template properties

[Browsable(false),
DefaultValue(null),
Description("The content to be shown at header of control."),
PersistenceMode(PersistenceMode.InnerProperty),
TemplateContainer(typeof(ResultItem))
]
public ITemplate HeaderTemplate
{
    get
    {
        return headerTemplate;
    }
    set
    {
        headerTemplate = value;
    }
}

[Browsable(false),
DefaultValue(null),
Description("The content to be shown in status area below header template."),
```

```
        PersistenceMode(PersistenceMode.InnerProperty),
        TemplateContainer(typeof(ResultItem))
        ]
        public ITemplate StatusTemplate
        {
           get
           {
              return statusTemplate;
           }
           set
           {
              statusTemplate = value;
           }
        }


        [Browsable(false),
        DefaultValue(null),
        Description(
        "The content to be shown with each item of the search result set."),
        PersistenceMode(PersistenceMode.InnerProperty),
        TemplateContainer(typeof(ResultItem))
        ]
        public ITemplate ItemTemplate
        {
           get
           {
              return itemTemplate;
           }
           set
           {
              itemTemplate = value;
           }
        }


        [Browsable(false),
        DefaultValue(null),
        Description(
        "The content to be shown with alternating items in the search result set."),
        PersistenceMode(PersistenceMode.InnerProperty),
        TemplateContainer(typeof(ResultItem))
        ]
        public ITemplate AlternatingItemTemplate
        {
           get
           {
              return alternatingItemTemplate;
           }
           set
           {
              alternatingItemTemplate = value;
           }
        }
```

```
        [Browsable(false),
        DefaultValue(null),
        Description(
"The content to be put between each item in the search result set."),
        PersistenceMode(PersistenceMode.InnerProperty),
        TemplateContainer(typeof(ResultItem))
        ]
        public ITemplate SeparatorTemplate
        {
           get
           {
              return separatorTemplate;
           }
           set
           {
              separatorTemplate = value;
           }
        }


        [Browsable(false),
        DefaultValue(null),
        Description(
"The content to be shown below search results at bottom of control."),
        PersistenceMode(PersistenceMode.InnerProperty),
        TemplateContainer(typeof(ResultItem))
        ]
        public ITemplate FooterTemplate
        {
           get
           {
              return footerTemplate;
           }
           set
           {
              footerTemplate = value;
           }
        }
        #endregion

        #region Events and Event Handling

        public event GoogleSearchedEventHandler GoogleSearched
        {
           add
           {
              Events.AddHandler(GoogleSearchedKey, value);
           }
           remove
           {
              Events.RemoveHandler(GoogleSearchedKey, value);
           }
        }
```

```
protected virtual void OnGoogleSearched(GoogleSearchedEventArgs e)
{
    GoogleSearchedEventHandler del =
        (GoogleSearchedEventHandler) Events[GoogleSearchedKey];
    if (del != null)
    {
        del(this, e);
    }
}

public event ResultItemEventHandler ItemCreated
{
    add
    {
        Events.AddHandler(ItemCreatedKey, value);
    }
    remove
    {
        Events.RemoveHandler(ItemCreatedKey, value);
    }
}

protected virtual void OnItemCreated(ResultItemEventArgs e)
{
    ResultItemEventHandler del =
        (ResultItemEventHandler) Events[ItemCreatedKey];
    if (del != null)
    {
        del(this, e);
    }
}

public event ResultItemEventHandler ItemDataBound
{
    add
    {
        Events.AddHandler(ItemDataBoundKey, value);
    }
    remove
    {
        Events.RemoveHandler(ItemDataBoundKey, value);
    }
}

protected virtual void OnItemDataBound(ResultItemEventArgs e)
{
    ResultItemEventHandler del =
        (ResultItemEventHandler) Events[ItemDataBoundKey];
    if (del != null)
    {
        del(this, e);
    }
}
```

```
    protected override bool OnBubbleEvent(object sender, EventArgs e)
    {
        // Handle events raised by children by overriding OnBubbleEvent.
        // (main purpose is to detect paging events)
        bool handled = false;
        CommandEventArgs cea = e as CommandEventArgs;

        // handle Page event by extracting new start index
        // and calling HandleSearch method, which does the
        // work of rebinding this control to the results
        // from the web service
        if (cea.CommandName == "Page")
        {
            StartIndex = Convert.ToInt32(cea.CommandArgument);
            HandleSearch();

        }

        return handled;
    }

    private void HandleSearch()
    {
        Service.GoogleSearchResult result =
            Service.SearchUtil.SearchGoogleService(
            Query, StartIndex, PageSize, Filtering);

        OnGoogleSearched(new GoogleSearchedEventArgs(result));

        this.DataSource = result;
        this.DataBind();
    }
    #endregion

    #region Control Creation/Rendering

    private ResultItem CreateResultItem(int index, ResultItemType itemType,
bool dataBind, object dataItem)
    {
        ITemplate selectedTemplate;

        switch (itemType)
        {
            case ResultItemType.Header :
                selectedTemplate = HeaderTemplate;
                break;
            case ResultItemType.Status :
                if (StatusTemplate == null)
                {
                    // if no StatusTemplate, pick up the default
                    // template ResultStatusTemplate
                    selectedTemplate = new ResultStatusTemplate();
```

```
            }
            else
               selectedTemplate = StatusTemplate;
            break;
        case ResultItemType.Item :
            if (ItemTemplate == null)
            {
               // if no ItemTemplate, pick up the default
               // template ResultItemTemplate
               selectedTemplate = new ResultItemTemplate();
            }
            else
               selectedTemplate = ItemTemplate;
            break;
        case ResultItemType.AlternatingItem :
            selectedTemplate = AlternatingItemTemplate;
            if (selectedTemplate == null)
            {
               // if no AlternatingItemTemplate, switch to Item type
               // and pick up ItemTemplate
               itemType = ResultItemType.Item;
               selectedTemplate = ItemTemplate;
               if (selectedTemplate == null)
               {
                  // if that doesn't work, pick up the default
                  // template ResultItemTemplate
                  selectedTemplate = new ResultItemTemplate();
               }
            }
            break;
        case ResultItemType.Separator :
            selectedTemplate = SeparatorTemplate;
            break;
        case ResultItemType.Footer :
            selectedTemplate = FooterTemplate;
            break;
        default:
            selectedTemplate = null;
            break;
    }

    ResultItem item = new ResultItem(index, itemType, dataItem);

    if (selectedTemplate != null)
    {
       selectedTemplate.InstantiateIn(item);
    }

    OnItemCreated(new ResultItemEventArgs(item));
    Controls.Add(item);
```

```
    if (dataBind)
    {
        item.DataBind();
        OnItemDataBound(new ResultItemEventArgs(item));
    }
    return item;
}

private ResultItem CreatePagerResultItem(bool dataBind, object dataItem)
{
    ResultItem item = new ResultItem(-1, ResultItemType.Pager, null);

    Pager pager = new Pager();
    pager.PageSize = PageSize;
    pager.PagerBarRange = PagerBarRange;
    pager.PagerLinkStyle = PagerLinkStyle;
    pager.TotalResultsCount = TotalResultsCount;
    pager.StartIndex = StartIndex;
    pager.EndIndex = EndIndex;

    item.Controls.Add(pager);

    Controls.Add(item);

    return item;
}

private void CreateControlHierarchy(bool dataBind)
{
    Service.GoogleSearchResult result = null;

    // Result items
    items = new ArrayList();

    int count = 0;

    if (dataBind == true)
    {
        if (DataSource == null)
            return;
        result = (Service.GoogleSearchResult) DataSource;
        Query = result.searchQuery;
        TotalResultsCount = result.estimatedTotalResultsCount;
        EndIndex = result.endIndex-1;
        StartIndex = result.startIndex-1;
        count = result.resultElements.Length;
    }
    else
    {
        object temp = ViewState["ResultItemCount"];
        if (temp != null)
```

```
            count = (int) temp;
        }

        if (HeaderTemplate != null)
        {
            ResultItem headerItem = CreateResultItem(-1, ResultItemType.Header,
            false, null);
            items.Add(headerItem);
        }

        ResultItem statusItem = CreateResultItem(-1, ResultItemType.Status,
        dataBind, result);
        items.Add(statusItem);

        // loop through and create ResultItem controls for each of the
        // result elements from the Google web service result
        ResultItemType itemType = ResultItemType.Item;
        for (int i = 0; i < count; i++)
        {
            if (separatorTemplate != null)
            {
                ResultItem separator =
                    CreateResultItem(-1, ResultItemType.Separator, false, null);
                items.Add(separator);
            }

            Service.ResultElement resultElem = null;
            if (dataBind == true)
            {
                resultElem = result.resultElements[i];
            }

            ResultItem item = CreateResultItem(i, itemType, dataBind, resultElem);
            items.Add(item);

            // swap between Item and AlternatingItem types
            if (itemType == ResultItemType.Item)
                itemType = ResultItemType.AlternatingItem;
            else
                itemType = ResultItemType.Item;
        }

        // display pager if allowed by user and if results
        // are greater than a page in length
        if (DisplayPager == true && TotalResultsCount > PageSize)
        {
            ResultItem pager = CreatePagerResultItem(dataBind, result);
            items.Add(pager);
        }

        if (FooterTemplate != null)
```

```
      {
         ResultItem footer = CreateResultItem(-1, ResultItemType.Footer,
         false, null);
         items.Add(footer);
      }
      if (dataBind)
      {
         ViewState["ResultItemCount"] = count;
      }
   }

   private void CreateBlankControlHierarchy()
   {
      if (HeaderTemplate != null)
      {
         ResultItem headerItem = CreateResultItem(-1, ResultItemType.Header,
         false, null);
         items.Add(headerItem);
      }

      if (FooterTemplate != null)
      {
         ResultItem footer = CreateResultItem(-1, ResultItemType.Footer,
         false, null);
         items.Add(footer);
      }
   }

   override protected void CreateChildControls()
   {
      Controls.Clear();

      if (searchConducted == false &&
         ViewState["ResultItemCount"] != null)
      {
         CreateControlHierarchy(false);
      }
   }

   public override void DataBind()
   {
      base.OnDataBinding(System.EventArgs.Empty);

      Controls.Clear();
      ClearChildViewState();
      TrackViewState();

      searchConducted = true;
      CreateControlHierarchy(true);
      ChildControlsCreated = true;
   }
```

```
    public override ControlCollection Controls
    {
       get
       {
          EnsureChildControls();
          return base.Controls;
       }
    }

    protected override void RenderContents(HtmlTextWriter writer)
    {
       // if no search, create a hierarchy with header and
       // footer templates only
       if (!searchConducted)
       {
          CreateBlankControlHierarchy();
       }

       // prep all template styles
       PrepareControlHierarchy();

       // render all child controls
       base.RenderContents(writer);
    }
    #endregion
  }
}
```

Now that we have covered the Search and Result server controls, in the next section we discuss the Pager control.

The Pager Control

The Pager control wraps the cumbersome logic of calculating page ranges in the pager bar and determining whether or not to display a Previous or Next button. It takes the properties we discussed earlier—PageSize, PagerBarRange, TotalResultsCount, StartingIndex, and Index—and builds a composite child control structure to render the paging functionality. The interesting work it does is centered on its CreateControlHierarchy implementation.

The actual scaffolding for the Pager control is an HTML table that has a row for images and row for text links. You can break it down into the following sections: Results, Previous button/image, Page button/image, and Next button/image. In special cases, there will be a first image, as shown in Figure 13-9, in which there are no previous pages to navigate to.

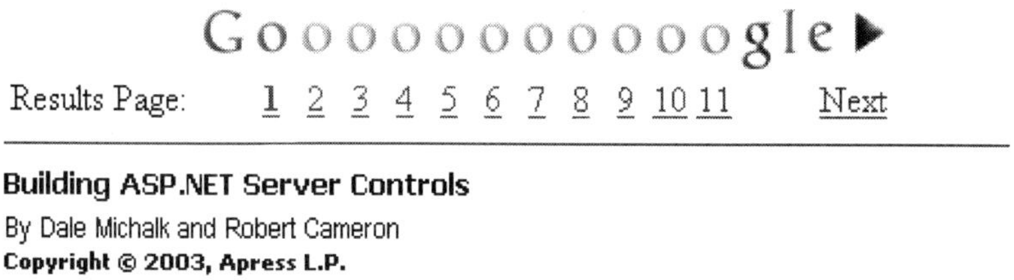

Goooooooooogle ▶

Results Page: 1 2 3 4 5 6 7 8 9 10 11   Next

Building ASP.NET Server Controls

By Dale Michalk and Robert Cameron
Copyright © 2003, Apress L.P.

Figure 13-9. A Pager *control with a first image*

Figure 13-10 shows the situation in which there are pages before and after the current page.

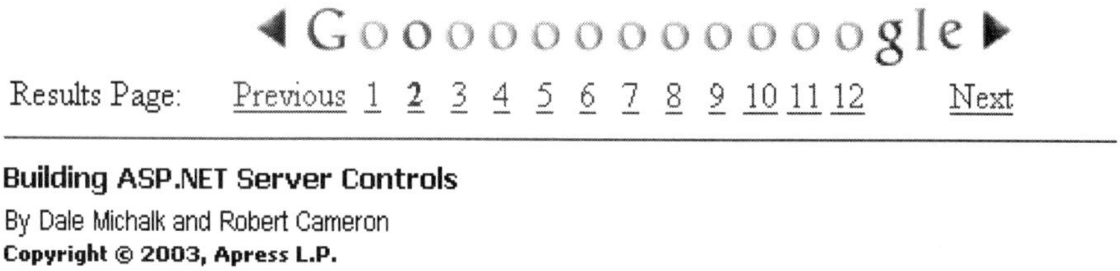

◀ Goooooooooooogle ▶

Results Page: Previous 1 **2** 3 4 5 6 7 8 9 10 11 12   Next

Building ASP.NET Server Controls

By Dale Michalk and Robert Cameron
Copyright © 2003, Apress L.P.

Figure 13-10. A Pager *control with Previous and Next links*

In the scenario in which there are no next pages in the page range, as shown in Figure 13-11, there is the use of a last image.

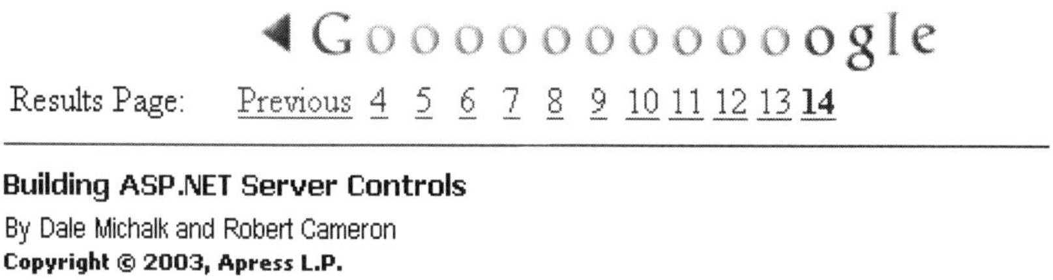

◀ Goooooooooooogle

Results Page: Previous 4 5 6 7 8 9 10 11 12 13 **14**

Building ASP.NET Server Controls

By Dale Michalk and Robert Cameron
Copyright © 2003, Apress L.P.

Figure 13-11. A Pager *control with a last image*

Creating the Pager Results

The Pager control, like the Result and Search controls, is built using a composite control architecture. Because of this, it overrides the CreateControlHierarchy method to build up its HTML table structure:

```
private void CreateControlHierarchy()
{
    table = new Table();

    TableRow imageRow = new TableRow();
    imageRow.VerticalAlign = VerticalAlign.Bottom;

    TableRow textRow = new TableRow();
    textRow.VerticalAlign = VerticalAlign.Top;

    // insert localized "Page Results:" text
    CreatePagerResults(imageRow, textRow, PagerLinkStyle);
```

The first part of this method adds the Results text section. You can see that it puts an HTML nonbreaking space in the top image row of the HTML table while putting the Results text in the bottom text row of the table.

```
private void CreatePagerResults(TableRow imageRow, TableRow textRow,
ResultPagerLinkStyle style)
{
    TableCell cell;
    if (style == ResultPagerLinkStyle.TextWithImages)
    {
        cell = new TableCell();
        cell.Text = " ";
        imageRow.Cells.Add(cell);
    }

    cell = new TableCell();

    ResourceManager rm = ResourceFactory.Manager;

    cell.Text = rm.GetString("Pager.resultsPageCell.Text");
    cell.Wrap = false;
    cell.HorizontalAlign = HorizontalAlign.Center;
    textRow.Cells.Add(cell);
}
```

Creating the Pager Previous Button

The next piece of code calculates the total number of pages based on the EndIndex and PageSize values. The current page is also determined by looking at the StartIndex of the current web service search and dividing it by PageSize:

```
// calculate the total number of pages based on the
// page size and the TotalResultsCount from the
// search service query
int numPages = (int) System.Math.Ceiling(
   (double) TotalResultsCount / PageSize);

// Because the TotalResultsCount is not infallible
// for calculating the bounding of the size of a
// result set, check to see that a page's worth
// of data is coming back with each request.
// If the ending index of that result is less than
// the TotalResultsCount, you know there is a shortage
// in what Google will give you.
if (EndIndex - StartIndex < PageSize - 1 &&
   EndIndex < TotalResultsCount)
{
   // if so, recalculate page number on EndIndex value
   // instead of the estimated count
   numPages = (int) System.Math.Ceiling(
   (double) EndIndex / PageSize);
}


int currentPage = (int) System.Math.Floor(
   (double) StartIndex / PageSize) + 1;
```

After we have the currentPage and numPages variables defined, we run some logic to see whether we need a Previous button link inserted. If we need it, we add the necessary linkage via CreatePagerPreviousButton:

```
// if the page number is greater than 1 you can put in a previous page
// link
if (currentPage > 1)
{
   // use indexes of the result items as the value of the
   // navigation (bounded at zero, of course)
   int prevIndex = StartIndex - PageSize;
   if (prevIndex < 0)
      prevIndex = 0;

   // insert Previous text and Google image with left arrow
   CreatePagerPreviousButton(imageRow, textRow, PagerLinkStyle, prevIndex);
}
```

The following `CreatePagerPreviousButton` method has code to determine whether to add just text links or text links with a previous image via the `PagerLinkStyle` parameter that is passed into it. The images are adding using an `ImageButton` control to make them clickable to activate the postback and associated command event. We use a `LinkButton` for the text link as well.

```
private void CreatePagerPreviousButton(TableRow imageRow, TableRow textRow,
ResultPagerLinkStyle style, int prevIndex)
{

    TableCell cell;

    if (style == ResultPagerLinkStyle.TextWithImages)
    {
        cell = new TableCell();
        ImageButton prevImgButton = new ImageButton();
        prevImgButton.ImageUrl = GoogleNavPreviousImageUrl;
        prevImgButton.CommandName = "Page";
        prevImgButton.CommandArgument = prevIndex.ToString();

        cell.Controls.Add(prevImgButton);
        imageRow.Cells.Add(cell);
    }

    ResourceManager rm = ResourceFactory.Manager;

    cell = new TableCell();
    LinkButton prevButton = new LinkButton();
    prevButton.ID = "PrevButton";
    prevButton.Text = rm.GetString("Pager.prevButton.Text");
    prevButton.CommandName = "Page";
    prevButton.CommandArgument = prevIndex.ToString();
    cell.HorizontalAlign = HorizontalAlign.Right;
    cell.Controls.Add(prevButton);

    textRow.Cells.Add(cell);
}
```

Crucial to the functioning of the parent `Result` control are the `ImageButton` and `LinkButton` that are configured to raise a specific command event named "Page". The `CommandArgument` to the event is set to the numeric index of the page and is received by the `Result` control in its `OnBubbleEvent` override.

Creating the Pager First Image

Within the `CreateControlHierarchy` method, the if-then code construct that checks for the necessary conditions to display a Previous button has an else clause that is responsible for executing code to display the Google image without a Previous button. This code runs only if we set `ResultPagerLinkStyle` to `TextWithImages`. It calls `CreatePagerFirstImage` to render the *G* of the Google image without a hyperlink, as shown here:

```
else if (PagerStyle == ResultPagerLinkStyle.TextWithImages)
{
    CreatePagerFirstImage(imageRow, textRow);
}
```

This code does not generate a hyperlink because the Google *G* is generated with an Image control instead of an `ImageLink` control. There is also a no-break HTML space added to the text row, as shown here:

```
private void CreatePagerFirstImage(TableRow imageRow, TableRow textRow)
{
    TableCell cell = new TableCell();
    cell.HorizontalAlign = HorizontalAlign.Left;
    Image lastImg = new Image();
    lastImg.ImageUrl = GoogleNavFirstImageUrl;
    cell.Controls.Add(lastImg);
    imageRow.Cells.Add(cell);

    cell = new TableCell();
    cell.Text = " ";
    textRow.Cells.Add(cell);
}
```

Creating the Pager Bar Pages

The next section of code in `CreateControlHierarchy` deals with the page numbers that are directly displayed by the `Pager` control. The `PagerBarRange` property controls the size of this bar. Inside the code, we loop through each page, creating its content by invoking `CreatePagerPageButton`:

```
// calculate starting and ending pages for the
// page index links (bound at 1 and max pages)
int startPage = currentPage - pagerBarRange;
if (startPage < 1)
    startPage = 1;
int endPage = currentPage + pagerBarRange;
if (endPage > numPages)
    endPage = numPages;
```

```
// loop through each page and spit out the page link
for (int pageNum = startPage; pageNum <= endPage; pageNum++)
{
    // result index number is used for navigation to
    // specific page
    int pageIndex = ((pageNum - 1) * PageSize);

    // insert Page number text and Google O image
    CreatePagerPageButton(imageRow, textRow, PagerLinkStyle,
    pageNum, pageIndex,
    (currentPage == pageNum));
}
```

The code in the following `CreatePagerPageButton` checks to see whether the page it is rendering as a Google *o* image is the current one based on the `currentPage` Boolean parameter. If it is, it will appear in red.

```
private void CreatePagerPageButton(TableRow imageRow, TableRow textRow,
    ResultPagerLinkStyle style, int pageNum, int pageIndex, bool currentPage)
{
    TableCell cell;
    LiteralControl lit;

    if (style == ResultPagerLinkStyle.TextWithImages)
    {
        cell = new TableCell();
        ImageButton pageImgButton = new ImageButton();
        pageImgButton.Width = 16;
        if (currentPage == true)
            pageImgButton.ImageUrl = GoogleNavCurrentImageUrl;
        else
            pageImgButton.ImageUrl = GoogleNavPageImageUrl;

        pageImgButton.CommandName = "Page";
        pageImgButton.CommandArgument = pageIndex.ToString();

        cell.Controls.Add(pageImgButton);
        imageRow.Cells.Add(cell);
    }

    cell = new TableCell();
    cell.HorizontalAlign = HorizontalAlign.Center;

    // add extra separation between page numbers
    // if text, only paging is used
    if (style == ResultPagerLinkStyle.Text)
    {
        lit = new LiteralControl();
        lit.Text = " ";
        cell.Controls.Add(lit);
    }
```

```
LinkButton pageButton = new LinkButton();
pageButton.ID = "page" + pageIndex.ToString() + "Button";
pageButton.Text = pageNum.ToString();
pageButton.CommandName = "Page";
pageButton.CommandArgument = pageIndex.ToString();
pageButton.CausesValidation = true;
if (currentPage == true)
   pageButton.ControlStyle.Font.Bold = true;

cell.Controls.Add(pageButton);
textRow.Cells.Add(cell);
}
```

Creating the Pager Next Button

After we are done creating the page number links, we have code that is similar to
the Previous button code. However, this code creates the Next button with a call
to CreatePagerNextButton:

```
// insert a next link if less than max number of pages
if (currentPage < numPages)
{
   // calculate the next index to link to
   // (bounded by totalresultscount)
   int nextIndex = StartIndex + PageSize;
   if (nextIndex > TotalResultsCount)
      nextIndex = TotalResultsCount;

   // insert Next text and Google image with right arrow
   CreatePagerNextButton(imageRow, textRow, PagerLinkStyle, nextIndex);
}
```

The code for CreatePagerNextButton is as follows:

```
private void CreatePagerNextButton(TableRow imageRow, TableRow textRow,
   ResultPagerLinkStyle style, int nextIndex)
{
   TableCell cell = new TableCell();
   LiteralControl lit;

   if (style == ResultPagerLinkStyle.TextWithImages)
   {
      cell = new TableCell();
      cell.HorizontalAlign = HorizontalAlign.Left;
      ImageButton nextImgButton = new ImageButton();
      nextImgButton.ImageUrl = GoogleNavNextImageUrl;
      nextImgButton.CommandName = "Page";
      nextImgButton.CommandArgument = nextIndex.ToString();
```

```
        cell.Controls.Add(nextImgButton);
        imageRow.Cells.Add(cell);
    }

    cell = new TableCell();

    // add extra separation between page numbers
    // if text only paging is used
    if (style == ResultPagerLinkStyle.Text)
    {
        lit = new LiteralControl();
        lit.Text = " ";
        cell.Controls.Add(lit);
    }

    ResourceManager rm = ResourceFactory.Manager;

    LinkButton nextButton = new LinkButton();
    nextButton.ID = "nextButton";
    nextButton.Text = rm.GetString("Pager.nextButton.Text");
    nextButton.CommandName = "Page";
    nextButton.CommandArgument = nextIndex.ToString();
    cell.HorizontalAlign = HorizontalAlign.Center;
    cell.Controls.Add(nextButton);

    textRow.Cells.Add(cell);
}
```

Creating the Pager Last Image

If there is no Next button, we call CreatePagerLastImage to create the *gle* of the Google image without hyperlinks, as shown here:

```
// if there is no next button, insert the trailing
    // Google image without a right arrow
else if (PagerLinkStyle == ResultPagerLinkStyle.TextWithImages)
{
    CreatePagerLastImage(imageRow, textRow);
}
```

As with CreatePagerFirstImage, we use an Image control to put the image in the table:

```
private void CreatePagerLastImage(TableRow imageRow, TableRow textRow)
{
    TableCell cell = new TableCell();
    cell.HorizontalAlign = HorizontalAlign.Left;
    Image lastImg = new Image();
    lastImg.ImageUrl = GoogleNavLastImageUrl;
```

```
    cell.Controls.Add(lastImg);
    imageRow.Cells.Add(cell);

    cell = new TableCell();
    cell.Text = " ";
    textRow.Cells.Add(cell);
}
```

The final part of CreateControlHierarchy adds the created image and text rows to the HTML table and then adds it to the Controls collection:

```
    // only add the image row links if we have selected them
    // for paging
    if (PagerLinkStyle == ResultPagerLinkStyle.TextWithImages)
    {
        table.Rows.Add(imageRow);
    }

    // always display text links
    table.Rows.Add(textRow);

    Controls.Add(table);
}
```

Ensuring Pager Style Rendering

The Pager server control overrides the RenderContents methods for two primary reasons. First, it ensures that all child controls are correctly created in a design-time situation. It does that by having code that calls EnsureChildControls in the rendering override. Second, it ensures that the PagerStyle property maintained by the Result control and specifically passed by the code in its PrepareControlHierarchy implementation is rendered correctly as part of the internal structure of the Pager control.

```
protected override void RenderContents(HtmlTextWriter writer)
{
    EnsureChildControls();

    PrepareControlHierarchy();

    base.RenderContents (writer);
}
```

It uses a `PrepareControlHierarchy` implementation to grab the `Table` control, which is the major child structure, and applies its `ControlStyle` property to it if it has been set:

```
protected void PrepareControlHierarchy()
{
   // apply the Pager style attributes to the
   // table if they were specified by Result control
   if (this.ControlStyleCreated)
      table.ApplyStyle(this.ControlStyle);
}
```

At this point, we have a fully functional `Pager` control. Listing 13-12 presents the complete class file.

Listing 13-12. The Pager.cs Class File

```
using System;
using System.Web.UI;
using System.Web.UI.HtmlControls;
using System.Web.UI.WebControls;
using System.Text;
using System.Collections;
using System.Collections.Specialized;
using System.Web;
using System.Reflection;
using System.ComponentModel;
using System.Resources;

namespace Apress.GoogleControls
{
    internal class Pager : WebControl, INamingContainer
    {
        private const string GoogleNavPreviousImageUrl =
 "http://www.google.com/nav_previous.gif";
        private const string GoogleNavFirstImageUrl =
"http://www.google.com/nav_first.gif";
        private const string GoogleNavNextImageUrl =
"http://www.google.com/nav_next.gif";
        private const string GoogleNavPageImageUrl =
"http://www.google.com/nav_page.gif";
        private const string GoogleNavCurrentImageUrl =
"http://www.google.com/nav_current.gif";
        private const string GoogleNavLastImageUrl =
"http://www.google.com/nav_last.gif";

        private Table table;
        private ResultPagerLinkStyle pagerLinkStyle;
        private int pagerBarRange;
        private int pageSize;
```

```
private int startIndex;
private int endIndex;
private int totalResultsCount;

protected override HtmlTextWriterTag TagKey
{
    get
    {
        return HtmlTextWriterTag.Span;
    }
}

public int PageSize
{
    get
    {
        return pageSize;
    }
    set
    {
        pageSize = value;
    }
}

public int PagerBarRange
{
    get
    {
        return pagerBarRange;
    }
    set
    {
        pagerBarRange = value;
    }
}

public ResultPagerLinkStyle PagerLinkStyle
{
    get
    {
        return pagerLinkStyle;
    }
    set
    {
        pagerLinkStyle = value;
    }
}

public int StartIndex
{
    get
```

```
      {
         return startIndex;
      }
      set
      {
         startIndex = value;
      }
   }

   public int EndIndex
   {
      get
      {
         return endIndex;
      }
      set
      {
         endIndex = value;
      }
   }

   public int TotalResultsCount
   {
      get
      {
         return totalResultsCount;
      }
      set
      {
         totalResultsCount = value;
      }
   }

   private void CreatePagerResults(TableRow imageRow, TableRow textRow,
      ResultPagerLinkStyle style)
   {
      TableCell cell;
      if (style == ResultPagerLinkStyle.TextWithImages)
      {
         cell = new TableCell();
         cell.Text = " ";
         imageRow.Cells.Add(cell);
      }

      cell = new TableCell();

      ResourceManager rm = ResourceFactory.Manager;

      cell.Text = rm.GetString("Pager.resultsPageCell.Text");
      cell.Wrap = false;
      cell.HorizontalAlign = HorizontalAlign.Center;
```

```
        textRow.Cells.Add(cell);
}

private void CreatePagerFirstImage(TableRow imageRow, TableRow textRow)
{
    TableCell cell = new TableCell();
    cell.HorizontalAlign = HorizontalAlign.Left;
    Image lastImg = new Image();
    lastImg.ImageUrl = GoogleNavFirstImageUrl;
    cell.Controls.Add(lastImg);
    imageRow.Cells.Add(cell);

    cell = new TableCell();
    cell.Text = " ";
    textRow.Cells.Add(cell);
}

private void CreatePagerPreviousButton(TableRow imageRow, TableRow textRow,
    ResultPagerLinkStyle style, int prevIndex)
{

    TableCell cell;

    if (style == ResultPagerLinkStyle.TextWithImages)
    {
        cell = new TableCell();
        ImageButton prevImgButton = new ImageButton();
        prevImgButton.ImageUrl = GoogleNavPreviousImageUrl;
        prevImgButton.CommandName = "Page";
        prevImgButton.CommandArgument = prevIndex.ToString();

        cell.Controls.Add(prevImgButton);
        imageRow.Cells.Add(cell);
    }

    ResourceManager rm = ResourceFactory.Manager;

    cell = new TableCell();
    LinkButton prevButton = new LinkButton();
    prevButton.ID = "PrevButton";
    prevButton.Text = rm.GetString("Pager.prevButton.Text");
    prevButton.CommandName = "Page";
    prevButton.CommandArgument = prevIndex.ToString();
    cell.HorizontalAlign = HorizontalAlign.Right;
    cell.Controls.Add(prevButton);

    textRow.Cells.Add(cell);
}

private void CreatePagerPageButton(TableRow imageRow, TableRow textRow,
    ResultPagerLinkStyle style, int pageNum, int pageIndex, bool currentPage)
```

```csharp
{
   TableCell cell;
   LiteralControl lit;

   if (style == ResultPagerLinkStyle.TextWithImages)
   {
      cell = new TableCell();
      ImageButton pageImgButton = new ImageButton();
      pageImgButton.Width = 16;
      if (currentPage == true)
         pageImgButton.ImageUrl = GoogleNavCurrentImageUrl;
      else
         pageImgButton.ImageUrl = GoogleNavPageImageUrl;

      pageImgButton.CommandName = "Page";
      pageImgButton.CommandArgument = pageIndex.ToString();

      cell.Controls.Add(pageImgButton);
      imageRow.Cells.Add(cell);
   }

   cell = new TableCell();
   cell.HorizontalAlign = HorizontalAlign.Center;

   // add extra separation between page numbers
   // if text-only paging is used
   if (style == ResultPagerLinkStyle.Text)
   {
      lit = new LiteralControl();
      lit.Text = " ";
      cell.Controls.Add(lit);
   }

   LinkButton pageButton = new LinkButton();
   pageButton.ID = "page" + pageIndex.ToString() + "Button";
   pageButton.Text = pageNum.ToString();
   pageButton.CommandName = "Page";
   pageButton.CommandArgument = pageIndex.ToString();
   pageButton.CausesValidation = true;
   if (currentPage == true)
      pageButton.ControlStyle.Font.Bold = true;

   cell.Controls.Add(pageButton);
   textRow.Cells.Add(cell);
}

private void CreatePagerNextButton(TableRow imageRow, TableRow textRow,
   ResultPagerLinkStyle style, int nextIndex)
{
   TableCell cell = new TableCell();
   LiteralControl lit;
```

```
         if (style == ResultPagerLinkStyle.TextWithImages)
         {
            cell = new TableCell();
            cell.HorizontalAlign = HorizontalAlign.Left;
            ImageButton nextImgButton = new ImageButton();
            nextImgButton.ImageUrl = GoogleNavNextImageUrl;
            nextImgButton.CommandName = "Page";
            nextImgButton.CommandArgument = nextIndex.ToString();

            cell.Controls.Add(nextImgButton);
            imageRow.Cells.Add(cell);
         }

         cell = new TableCell();

         // add extra separation between page numbers
         // if text-only paging is used
         if (style == ResultPagerLinkStyle.Text)
         {
            lit = new LiteralControl();
            lit.Text = " ";
            cell.Controls.Add(lit);
         }

         ResourceManager rm = ResourceFactory.Manager;

         LinkButton nextButton = new LinkButton();
         nextButton.ID = "nextButton";
         nextButton.Text = rm.GetString("Pager.nextButton.Text");
         nextButton.CommandName = "Page";
         nextButton.CommandArgument = nextIndex.ToString();
         cell.HorizontalAlign = HorizontalAlign.Center;
         cell.Controls.Add(nextButton);

         textRow.Cells.Add(cell);
      }

      private void CreatePagerLastImage(TableRow imageRow, TableRow textRow)
      {
         TableCell cell = new TableCell();
         cell.HorizontalAlign = HorizontalAlign.Left;
         Image lastImg = new Image();
         lastImg.ImageUrl = GoogleNavLastImageUrl;
         cell.Controls.Add(lastImg);
         imageRow.Cells.Add(cell);

         cell = new TableCell();
         cell.Text = " ";
         textRow.Cells.Add(cell);
      }
```

```
private void CreateControlHierarchy()
{
   table = new Table();

   TableRow imageRow = new TableRow();
   imageRow.VerticalAlign = VerticalAlign.Bottom;

   TableRow textRow = new TableRow();
   textRow.VerticalAlign = VerticalAlign.Top;

   // insert localized "Page Results:" text
   CreatePagerResults(imageRow, textRow, PagerLinkStyle);

   // calculate the total number of pages based on the
   // page size and the TotalResultsCount from the
   // search service query
   int numPages = (int) System.Math.Ceiling(
      (double) TotalResultsCount / PageSize);

   // Since the TotalResultsCount is not infallible
   // for calculating bounding of the size of a
   // result set, check to see that a page's worth
   // of data is coming back with each request.
   // If the ending index of that result is less than
   // the TotalResultsCount, you know there is a shortage
   // in what Google will give you.
   if (EndIndex - StartIndex < PageSize - 1 &&
      EndIndex < TotalResultsCount)
   {
      // if so, recalculate page number on EndIndex value
      // instead of the estimated count
      numPages = (int) System.Math.Ceiling(
         (double) EndIndex / PageSize);
   }


   int currentPage = (int) System.Math.Floor(
      (double) StartIndex / PageSize) + 1;

   // if the page number greater than 1 you can put in a previous page
   // link
   if (currentPage > 1)
   {
      // use indexes of the result items as the value of the
      // navigation (bounded at zero, of course)
      int prevIndex = StartIndex - PageSize;
      if (prevIndex < 0)
         prevIndex = 0;

      // insert Previous text and Google image with left arrow
      CreatePagerPreviousButton(imageRow, textRow,
```

```
        PagerLinkStyle, prevIndex);
    }
    else if (PagerLinkStyle == ResultPagerLinkStyle.TextWithImages)
    {
        CreatePagerFirstImage(imageRow, textRow);
    }


    // calculate starting and ending pages for the
    // page index links (bound at 1 and max pages)
    int startPage = currentPage - pagerBarRange;
    if (startPage < 1)
        startPage = 1;
    int endPage = currentPage + pagerBarRange;
    if (endPage > numPages)
        endPage = numPages;



    // loop through each page and spit out the page link
    for (int pageNum = startPage; pageNum <= endPage; pageNum++)
    {
        // result index number is used for navigation to
        // specific page
        int pageIndex = ((pageNum - 1) * PageSize);

        // insert Page number text and Google O image
        CreatePagerPageButton(imageRow, textRow, PagerLinkStyle,
            pageNum, pageIndex,
            (currentPage == pageNum));
    }

    // insert a next link if less than max number of pages
    if (currentPage < numPages)
    {
        // calculate the next index to link to
        // (bounded by totalresultscount)
        int nextIndex = StartIndex + PageSize;
        if (nextIndex > TotalResultsCount)
            nextIndex = TotalResultsCount;

        // insert Next text and Google image with right arrow
        CreatePagerNextButton(imageRow, textRow, PagerLinkStyle, nextIndex);
    }
        // if there is no next button, insert the trailing
        // Google image without a right arrow
    else if (PagerLinkStyle == ResultPagerLinkStyle.TextWithImages)
    {
        CreatePagerLastImage(imageRow, textRow);
    }

    // only add the image row links if we have selected them
    // for paging
```

```
            if (PagerLinkStyle == ResultPagerLinkStyle.TextWithImages)
            {
                table.Rows.Add(imageRow);
            }

            // always display text links
            table.Rows.Add(textRow);

            Controls.Add(table);
        }

        override protected void CreateChildControls()
        {
            Controls.Clear();
            CreateControlHierarchy();
        }

        public override ControlCollection Controls
        {
            get
            {
                EnsureChildControls();
                return base.Controls;
            }
        }

        protected void PrepareControlHierarchy()
        {
            // apply the Pager style attributes to the
            // table if they were specified by Result control
            if (this.ControlStyleCreated)
                table.ApplyStyle(this.ControlStyle);
        }

        protected override void RenderContents(HtmlTextWriter writer)
        {
            EnsureChildControls();

            PrepareControlHierarchy();

            base.RenderContents (writer);
        }
    }
}
```

This completes the first part of our discussion of the Google server control. In the next chapter, we dive deeper into the implementation details and test the functionality of the control.

Summary

In this chapter, we focused on putting together a full-featured control based on the Google web service. We covered the web service API and the design decisions that went into the control, and we provided detailed discussion of the individual controls. The discussion included information on building a control library in a strong-named assembly to allow it to deploy into the global assembly cache (GAC) for easy machine-level deployment and to provide built-in tamper-resistant facilities. We also demonstrated how to use the web.config configuration file system for our own purposes by developing a custom configuration section for our control library.

We rounded out this chapter with a detailed discussion of the individual controls that make up the Google control library. We also set the stage for the next chapter by implementing configuration management for licensing and deployment. In the next chapter, we finish our discussion of the Google control by covering design-time functionality, template support, globalization, localization, and tools to assist with quality and deployment.

Packaging and Deployment

THIS CHAPTER IS second in our two-part discussion of the Google control. In the previous chapter, we covered the design of each control, configuration management and, of course, the Google API and the design decisions that went into the control to interact with the Google API. In this chapter, we start off with a discussion of design-time support in the Google control and then jump into the packaging and deployment process with server controls using our Google control as an example control. We focus on the following topics for packaging and deploying server controls:

- Design-time support (data binding and templates)

- Testing the Google controls

- Licensing

- Implementing globalization and localization

- Using FxCop to check design decisions and coding conventions

- Using XML comments in code to generate documentation

Designer Support

Oftentimes, what separates a good control from a great control is the design-time experience for users of a server control, or any component for that matter. In this section, we discuss the design-time support built into the Google web control library to provide a pleasant UI when working with the controls at design time.

Designers and Dummy Data Source

The designer support for the Google web control library centers on support for the two primary controls that are visible and reachable in the design-time environment. Both Result and Search have a designer built specifically for them. SearchDesigner is the simpler of the two. As shown in Listing 14-1, it is a typical composite control designer that implements the bare minimum to get it rendered correctly.

Listing 14-1 The SearchDesigner.cs Class File

```csharp
using System;
using System.ComponentModel;
using System.ComponentModel.Design;
using System.Web.UI;
using System.Web.UI.Design;

namespace Apress.GoogleControls
{
    public class SearchDesigner : ControlDesigner
    {
        public override void Initialize(IComponent component)
        {
            if (!(component is Control) && !(component is INamingContainer))
            {
                throw new ArgumentException(
                    "This control is not a composite control.", "component");
            }
            base.Initialize(component);
        }

        public override string GetDesignTimeHtml()
        {
            ControlCollection cntrls = ((Control)Component).Controls;
            return base.GetDesignTimeHtml();
        }

        protected override string GetEmptyDesignTimeHtml()
        {
            return CreatePlaceHolderDesignTimeHtml(
                Component.GetType()+" control.");
        }

        protected override string GetErrorDesignTimeHtml(Exception e)
        {
            return CreatePlaceHolderDesignTimeHtml(
                "There was an error rendering the"+
                this.Component.GetType() +" control."+
                "<br>Exception: "+e.Source+ " Message: "+e.Message);
        }
    }
}
```

ResultDesigner is more complex. Because it handles the large number of templates that the Result control exposes, we decided to give it a designer verb for each of the templates: HeaderTemplate, StatusTemplate, ItemTemplate, AlternatingItemTemplate, SeparatorTemplate, and FooterTemplate. Figure 14-1 shows the template menu options.

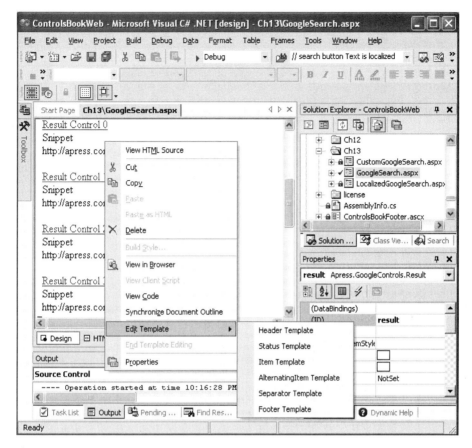

Figure 14-1. The ResultDesigner *template verb options*

The GetDesignTimeHtml method also uses a dummy data source instead of actually invoking the Google web service in the designer. ResultDummyDataSource has a method named GetGoogleSearchResults that takes as a parameter the page size so that it will create that many elements in the result set. ResultDesigner queries the Result control for its PageSize property value before invoking GetGoogleSearchResults to make the design-time display more reflective of the execution display.

The full code for ResultDesigner is shown in Listing 14-2, and the code for ResultDummyDataSource is in Listing 14-3.

Listing 14-2. The ResultDesigner.cs Class File

```
using System;
using System.Collections;
using System.ComponentModel;
using System.ComponentModel.Design;
using System.Data;
```

```csharp
using System.Diagnostics;
using System.Web.UI;
using System.Web.UI.Design;
using System.Web.UI.WebControls;

namespace Apress.GoogleControls
{
    public class ResultDesigner : TemplatedControlDesigner
    {
        private TemplateEditingVerb[] templateVerbs;
        private bool templateVerbsDirty = true;

        public override void Initialize(IComponent component)
        {
            if (!(component is Result) && !(component is INamingContainer))
            {
                throw new ArgumentException(
                    "This control is not a Result control.", "component");
            }
            base.Initialize(component);
        }

        public override bool AllowResize
        {
            get
            {
                // When templates are not defined, render a read-only fixed-
                // size block. Once templates are defined or are being edited,
                // the control allows resizing
                return TemplatesExist || InTemplateMode;
            }
        }

        public override string GetDesignTimeHtml()
        {
            Result control = (Result)Component;
            string designTimeHTML = null;

            // bind Result control to dummy data source
            // that has the appropriate page size
            control.DataSource =
                ResultDummyDataSource.GetGoogleSearchResults(control.PageSize);
            control.DataBind();

            // let base class designer call Render() on
            // data-bound control to get HTML
            designTimeHTML = base.GetDesignTimeHtml();

            return designTimeHTML;
        }
```

```csharp
protected override string GetEmptyDesignTimeHtml()
{
   string text;

   if (CanEnterTemplateMode)
   {
      text =
      "Right-click and choose a set of templates to edit their content.";
   }
   else
   {
      text = "Switch to HTML view to edit the control's templates.";
   }
   return CreatePlaceHolderDesignTimeHtml(text);
}

protected override string GetErrorDesignTimeHtml(Exception e)
{
   return CreatePlaceHolderDesignTimeHtml(
"There was an error rendering the control.<br>Check to make sure all properties "
& + "are valid.");
}

protected bool TemplatesExist
{
   get
   {
      return (
         ((Result)Component).HeaderTemplate != null ||
         ((Result)Component).StatusTemplate != null ||
         ((Result)Component).ItemTemplate != null ||
         ((Result)Component).AlternatingItemTemplate != null ||
         ((Result)Component).SeparatorTemplate != null ||
         ((Result)Component).FooterTemplate != null
      );
   }
}

protected override ITemplateEditingFrame
CreateTemplateEditingFrame(TemplateEditingVerb verb)
{
   ITemplateEditingService teService =
   (ITemplateEditingService)GetService(typeof(ITemplateEditingService));

   string [] templateNames = new string[1];
   Style[] templateStyles = new Style[1];

   switch (verb.Index)
   {
      case 0:
         templateNames[0] = "HeaderTemplate";
```

```
            templateStyles[0] = ((Result)Component).HeaderStyle;
            break;
        case 1:
            templateNames[0] = "StatusTemplate";
            templateStyles[0] = ((Result)Component).StatusStyle;
            break;
        case 2:
            templateNames[0] = "ItemTemplate";
            templateStyles[0] = ((Result)Component).ItemStyle;
            break;
        case 3:
            templateNames[0] = "AlternatingItemTemplate";
            templateStyles[0] = ((Result)Component).AlternatingItemStyle;
            break;
        case 4:
            templateNames[0] = "SeparatorTemplate";
            templateStyles[0] = ((Result)Component).SeparatorStyle;
            break;
        case 5:
            templateNames[0] = "FooterTemplate";
            templateStyles[0] = ((Result)Component).FooterStyle;
            break;
    }

    ITemplateEditingFrame editingFrame =
        teService.CreateFrame(this, verb.Text, templateNames,
            ((Result)Component).ControlStyle, templateStyles);
    return editingFrame;
}

protected override void Dispose(bool disposing)
{
    if (disposing)
    {
        DisposeTemplateVerbs();
    }
    base.Dispose(disposing);
}

private void DisposeTemplateVerbs()
{
    if (templateVerbs != null)
    {
        templateVerbs[0].Dispose();
        templateVerbs[1].Dispose();
        templateVerbs[2].Dispose();
        templateVerbs[3].Dispose();
        templateVerbs[4].Dispose();
        templateVerbs[5].Dispose();

        templateVerbs = null;
```

```
            templateVerbsDirty = true;
        }
    }

    protected override TemplateEditingVerb[] GetCachedTemplateEditingVerbs()
    {
        if (templateVerbsDirty == true)
        {
            DisposeTemplateVerbs();

            templateVerbs = new TemplateEditingVerb[6];
            templateVerbs[0] = new TemplateEditingVerb("Header Template", 0,
            this);
            templateVerbs[1] = new TemplateEditingVerb("Status Template", 1,
            this);
            templateVerbs[2] = new TemplateEditingVerb("Item Template", 2, this);
            templateVerbs[3] = new TemplateEditingVerb(
            "AlternatingItem Template", 3, this);
            templateVerbs[4] = new TemplateEditingVerb("Separator Template", 4,
            this);
            templateVerbs[5] = new TemplateEditingVerb("Footer Template", 5,
            this);

            templateVerbsDirty = false;
        }
        return templateVerbs;
    }

    public override string GetTemplateContent(ITemplateEditingFrame
    editingFrame, string templateName, out bool allowEditing)
    {
        allowEditing = true;
        ITemplate template = null;
        string templateContent = String.Empty;

        if (templateName.Equals("HeaderTemplate") &&
            editingFrame.Verb.Index == 0)
        {
            template = ((Result)Component).HeaderTemplate;
        }
        else if (templateName.Equals("StatusTemplate") &&
                editingFrame.Verb.Index == 1)
        {
            template = ((Result)Component).StatusTemplate;
        }
        else if (templateName.Equals("ItemTemplate") &&
                editingFrame.Verb.Index == 2)
        {
            template = ((Result)Component).ItemTemplate;
        }
        else if (templateName.Equals("AlternatingItemTemplate") &&
```

```
                editingFrame.Verb.Index == 3)
    {
       template = ((Result)Component).AlternatingItemTemplate;
    }
    else if (templateName.Equals("SeparatorTemplate") &&
             editingFrame.Verb.Index == 4)
    {
       template = ((Result)Component).SeparatorTemplate;
    }
    else if (templateName.Equals("FooterTemplate") &&
             editingFrame.Verb.Index == 5)
    {
       template = ((Result)Component).FooterTemplate;
    }

    if (template != null)
    {
       templateContent = GetTextFromTemplate(template);
    }
    return templateContent;
}

public override void OnComponentChanged(object sender,
                      ComponentChangedEventArgs e)
{
    if (e.Member != null)
    {
       string memberName = e.Member.Name;
       if (memberName.Equals("HeaderStyle") ||
          memberName.Equals("StatusStyle") ||
          memberName.Equals("ItemStyle") ||
          memberName.Equals("AlternatingItemStyle") ||
          memberName.Equals("SeparatorStyle") ||
          memberName.Equals("PagerStyle") ||
          memberName.Equals("FooterStyle"))
       {
          OnStylesChanged();
       }
    }

    base.OnComponentChanged(sender, e);
}

protected void OnStylesChanged()
{
    OnTemplateEditingVerbsChanged();
}

protected void OnTemplateEditingVerbsChanged()
{
    templateVerbsDirty = true;
```

```
        }

        public override void SetTemplateContent(ITemplateEditingFrame editingFrame,
                            string templateName, string templateContent)
        {

            ITemplate template = null;

            if ((templateContent != null) && (templateContent.Length != 0))
            {
                template = GetTemplateFromText(templateContent);
            }

            if (templateName.Equals("HeaderTemplate") &&
                editingFrame.Verb.Index == 0)
            {
                ((Result)Component).HeaderTemplate = template;
            }
            else if (templateName.Equals("StatusTemplate") &&
                    editingFrame.Verb.Index == 1)
            {
                ((Result)Component).StatusTemplate = template;
            }
            else if (templateName.Equals("ItemTemplate") &&
                    editingFrame.Verb.Index == 2)
            {
                ((Result)Component).ItemTemplate = template;
            }
            else if (templateName.Equals("AlternatingItemTemplate") &&
                    editingFrame.Verb.Index == 3)
            {
                ((Result)Component).AlternatingItemTemplate = template;
            }
            else if (templateName.Equals("SeparatorTemplate") &&
                    editingFrame.Verb.Index == 4)
            {
                ((Result)Component).SeparatorTemplate = template;
            }
            else if (templateName.Equals("FooterTemplate") &&
                    editingFrame.Verb.Index == 5)
            {
                ((Result)Component).FooterTemplate = template;
            }
        }
    }
}
```

Listing 14-3. The ResultDummyDataSource.cs Class File

```csharp
using System;

namespace Apress.GoogleControls
{
    public class ResultDummyDataSource
    {
        private const int TotalResultsCount = 100;

        public static Service.GoogleSearchResult GetGoogleSearchResults(int pageSize)
        {
            Service.GoogleSearchResult result = new Service.GoogleSearchResult();

            result.estimatedTotalResultsCount = TotalResultsCount;
            result.estimateIsExact = true;
            result.documentFiltering = false;
            result.startIndex = 1;
            result.endIndex = pageSize;
            result.searchTime = 0.09;
            result.searchQuery = "Result Control";
            result.searchComments = "";
            result.searchTips = "";
            result.directoryCategories = new Service.DirectoryCategory[1];
            result.directoryCategories[0] =
            ResultDummyDataSource.GetDirectoryCategory();

            // fill up 10 result elements
            result.resultElements = new Service.ResultElement[pageSize];
            for (int i = 0; i < pageSize; i++)
            {
                result.resultElements[i] = GetResultElement(i);
            }

            return result;
        }

        public static Service.ResultElement GetResultElement(int index)
        {
            Service.ResultElement elem = new Service.ResultElement();
            elem.title = "Result Control " + index;
            elem.URL = "http://apress.com/resultcontrol" + index;
            elem.summary = "Summary";
            elem.snippet = "Snippet";
            elem.hostName = "apress";
            elem.cachedSize = "2k";
            elem.relatedInformationPresent = false;
            elem.directoryTitle = "Test";
            elem.directoryCategory = ResultDummyDataSource.GetDirectoryCategory();
            return elem;
        }
```

```
    public static Service.DirectoryCategory GetDirectoryCategory()
    {
        Service.DirectoryCategory dirCat = new Service.DirectoryCategory();
        dirCat.fullViewableName = "Test Category";
        dirCat.specialEncoding = "";
        return dirCat;
    }
  }
}
```

In the next section, we discuss the default template support provided in the Result control.

Template Support in the Result Control

The Result control is able to display a decent stock Google look and feel even when directly dropped from the Toolbox. This is achieved through the use of two templates, ResultStatusTemplate and ResultItemTemplate, which are added to the control if the template structure is not set in the .aspx page containing the control. To provide implementation of the default templates, the template classes must implement the ITemplate interface and its InstantiateIn method. The signature for this method is as follows:

```
public void InstantiateIn(Control container)
{}
```

The template is given the container in which to instantiate its controls. In ResultStatusTemplate, we use InstantiateIn to add a Label control and a LiteralControl, which represents an HTML break:

```
public void InstantiateIn(Control container)
{
    Label header = new Label();
    header.DataBinding +=new EventHandler(BindResultHeader);
    container.Controls.Add(header);
    LiteralControl lit = new LiteralControl();
    lit.Text = "<br>";
    container.Controls.Add(lit);
}
```

We also map the DataBinding event exposed by the Label control to BindResultHeader. This allows us to later insert the correct information into our Label control when a data source is attached to the StatusTemplate of the Result control in its data-binding process. BindResultHeader uses a help method named GetResultControl, which is able to cast from the Label control upward to get at the Result control. We then use the GetResult helper method to grab the search result data from in the form of the GoogleSearchResult class. The rest of the method is a process of building up a string that depicts the range of the search results, the number of total results, and the time it took for the query to happen. Listing 14-4 shows the full source code for ResultStatusTemplate.

Listing 14-4. The ResultStatusTemplate.cs Class File

```csharp
using System;
using System.Web;
using System.Web.UI;
using System.Web.UI.WebControls;
using System.Text;
using System.Resources;

namespace Apress.GoogleControls
{
    public class ResultStatusTemplate : ITemplate
    {
        public void InstantiateIn(Control container)
        {
            Label header = new Label();
            header.DataBinding +=new EventHandler(BindResultHeader);
            container.Controls.Add(header);
            LiteralControl lit = new LiteralControl();
            lit.Text = "<br>";
            container.Controls.Add(lit);
        }

        private Service.GoogleSearchResult GetResult(Control container)
        {
            ResultItem item = (ResultItem) container;
            return (Service.GoogleSearchResult) item.DataItem;
        }

        private Result GetResultControl(Control container)
        {
            ResultItem itemControl = (ResultItem) container.Parent;
            Result resultControl = (Result) itemControl.Parent;
            return resultControl;
        }

        private void BindResultHeader(object source, EventArgs e)
        {
            Label header = (Label) source;
            Result resultControl = GetResultControl(header);
            Service.GoogleSearchResult result = GetResult(header.NamingContainer);

            StringBuilder section = new StringBuilder();
```

```
        // get ResourceManager for localized format strings
        ResourceManager rm = ResourceFactory.Manager;

        // Searched for: <searchQuery>
        section.Append(
        String.Format(
            rm.GetString("ResultStatusTemplate.SearchFor"),
            result.searchQuery));
        section.Append("<br>");

        // Result <StartIndex+1> - <EndIndex+1> of about
        // <TotalResultsCount> records
        // (accounting for zero based index)
        section.Append(
        String.Format(
            rm.GetString("ResultStatusTemplate.ResultAbout"),
        resultControl.StartIndex+1,
        resultControl.EndIndex+1,
        resultControl.TotalResultsCount));
        section.Append("  ");

        // Query took about <searchTime> seconds.
        section.Append(
            String.Format(
                rm.GetString("ResultStatusTemplate.QueryTook"),
                System.Math.Round(result.searchTime, 2)));
        section.Append("<br>");

        header.Text = section.ToString();
    }
  }
}
```

ResultItemTemplate provides the default display for each item from the search results. The control content added inside the container includes a hyperlink displaying the title field Google resultElement and providing a hyperlink to the value of its URL field. It also adds a label to display the snippet field and a label to display the URL field. It uses three separate data-binding routines to accomplish the data loading: BindLink, BindSnippet, and BindUrl. Listing 14-5 presents the full source code.

Listing 14-5. The ResultItemTemplate.cs Class File

```
using System;
using System.Web;
using System.Web.UI;
using System.Web.UI.WebControls;
```

```
namespace Apress.GoogleControls
{
    /// <summary>
    /// Default ResultItemTemplate implementation used by a
    ///  stock GoogleLib Result control without a ItemTemplate
    /// </summary>
    public class ResultItemTemplate : ITemplate
    {
        /// <summary>
        /// Method puts template controls into container control
        /// </summary>
        /// <param name="container">Outside control container to
        /// template items</param>
        public void InstantiateIn(Control container)
        {
            HyperLink link = new HyperLink();
            link.DataBinding += new EventHandler(BindLink);
            container.Controls.Add(link);
            container.Controls.Add(new LiteralControl("<br>"));

            Label snippet = new Label();
            snippet.DataBinding += new EventHandler(BindSnippet);
            container.Controls.Add(snippet);
            container.Controls.Add(new LiteralControl("<br>"));

            Label url = new Label();
            url.DataBinding += new EventHandler(BindUrl);
            container.Controls.Add(url);
            container.Controls.Add(new LiteralControl("<br>"));
            container.Controls.Add(new LiteralControl("<br>"));
        }

        private Service.ResultElement GetResultElement(Control container)
        {
            ResultItem item = (ResultItem) container;
            return (Service.ResultElement) item.DataItem;
        }

        private void BindLink(object source, EventArgs e)
        {
            HyperLink link = (HyperLink) source;
            Service.ResultElement elem = GetResultElement(link.NamingContainer);
            link.Text = elem.title;
            link.NavigateUrl = elem.URL;
        }

        private void BindSnippet(object source, EventArgs e)
        {
            Label snippet = (Label) source;
            Service.ResultElement elem = GetResultElement(snippet.NamingContainer);
            snippet.Text = elem.snippet;
        }
```

```
    private void BindUrl(object source, EventArgs e)
    {
        Label url = (Label) source;
        Service.ResultElement elem = GetResultElement(url.NamingContainer);
        url.Text = elem.URL;
    }
  }
}
```

Toolbox Image Icons

After the controls are built, we can ensure a nice experience in the Toolbox used by
Visual Studio .NET Web Forms when in design mode by adding Toolbox image icons.
This task is accomplished by putting a 16×16 bitmap file with the same name as the
control and settings its Build Action property in the Visual Studio .NET Properties window to Embedded Resource. Once this is complete and the DLL representing the control library is built, you can add the controls in the DLL into the Toolbox via the Visual
Studio .NET Tools menu's Customize Toolbox dialog box, as shown in Figure 14-2.

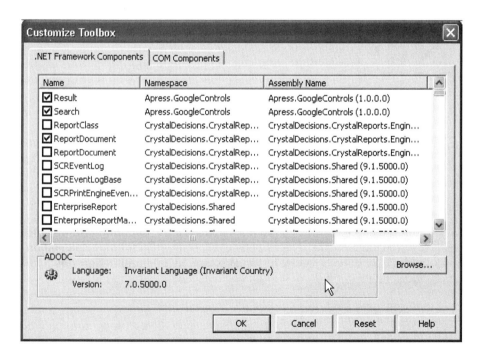

Figure 14-2. The Customize Toolbox dialog box

The end result of adding the new controls is a Toolbox tab like the one shown in
Figure 14-3.

Figure 14-3. Toolbox icons for the Google controls library

In the next section, we put all the Google controls to work in a couple of demonstration Web Forms.

Testing the Google Controls

The default look and feel of the Google controls displays if you drag and drop the controls onto a Web Form. Both the `Search` and `Result` controls require little configuration effort to provide a pleasing display in the Visual Studio .NET Control Designer, as shown in Figure 14-4.

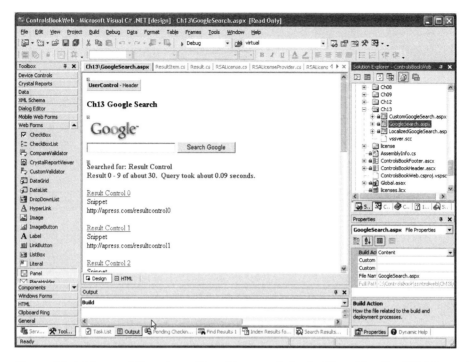

Figure 14-4. The stock `Search` *and* `Result` *controls in the Visual Studio .NET Control Designer*

The Default Look and Feel

The same default look and feel is generated in the browser. Figure 14-5 shows the initial page with just the `Search` control rendering its output. Type in a search query and you can see the results in Figure 14-6.

TIP *Remember to replace the settings in the web.config file of the web application project that relate to the proxy URL and the Google license file in order to get the samples shown in Figures 14-5 and 14-6 working.*

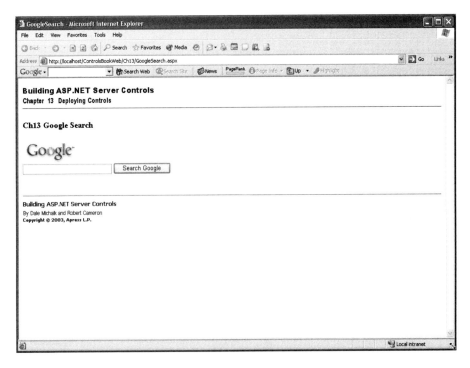

Figure 14-5. A blank GoogleSearch.aspx page

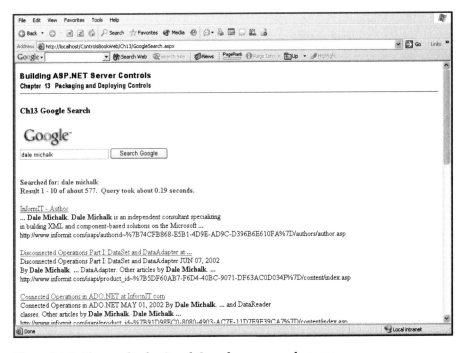

Figure 14-6. The result of a GoogleSearch.aspx search query

Listings 14-6 and 14-7 contain the Web Form and the code-behind, respectively.

Listing 14-6. The GoogleSearch.aspx Page File

```
<%@ Register TagPrefix="apressUC" TagName="ControlsBookHeader"
Src="..\ControlsBookHeader.ascx" %>
<%@ Register TagPrefix="apressUC" TagName="ControlsBookFooter"
Src="..\ControlsBookFooter.ascx" %>
<%@ Page language="c#" Codebehind="GoogleSearch.aspx.cs" AutoEventWireup="false"
 Inherits="ControlsBookWeb.Ch13.GoogleSearch" %>
<%@ Register TagPrefix="google" Namespace="Apress.GoogleControls"
Assembly="Apress.GoogleControls, Version=1.0.0.0, Culture=neutral,
PublicKeyToken=9d0e1a77378e3a88" %>
<!DOCTYPE HTML PUBLIC "-//W3C//DTD HTML 4.0 Transitional//EN" >
<HTML>
    <HEAD>
        <title>GoogleSearch</title>
        <meta content="Microsoft Visual Studio .NET 7.1" name="GENERATOR">
        <meta content="C#" name="CODE_LANGUAGE">
        <meta content="JavaScript" name="vs_defaultClientScript">
        <meta content="http://schemas.microsoft.com/intellisense/ie5"
        name="vs_targetSchema">
    </HEAD>
    <body MS_POSITIONING="FlowLayout">
        <form id="Form1" method="post" runat="server">
            <apressuc:controlsbookheader id="Header" runat="server"
chapternumber="13" chaptertitle=
"Packaging and Deploying Controls"></apressuc:controlsbookheader>
            <h3>Ch13 Google Search</h3>
            <google:search id="search" runat="server" ResultControl="result"
RedirectToGoogle="false"></google:search><br>
            <br>
            <google:result id="result" runat="server" PagerStyle="TextWithImages">
                <STATUSSTYLE ForeColor="Blue" Font-Bold="True"></STATUSSTYLE>
            </google:result><apressuc:controlsbookfooter id="Footer"
            runat="server"></apressuc:controlsbookfooter>
            <P> </P>
        </form>
    </body>
</HTML>
```

Listing 14-7. The GoogleSearch.cs Code-Behind Class File

```
using System;
using System.Collections;
using System.ComponentModel;
using System.Data;
using System.Drawing;
using System.Web;
using System.Web.SessionState;
```

```
using System.Web.UI;
using System.Web.UI.WebControls;
using System.Web.UI.HtmlControls;

namespace ControlsBookWeb.Ch13
{
   public class GoogleSearch : System.Web.UI.Page
   {
      protected Apress.GoogleControls.Result result;
      protected Apress.GoogleControls.Search Search1;
      protected Apress.GoogleControls.Search Search2;
      protected Apress.GoogleControls.Search search;

      private void Page_Load(object sender, System.EventArgs e)
      {

      }

      #region Web Form Designer generated code
      override protected void OnInit(EventArgs e)
      {
         //
         // CODEGEN: This call is required by the ASP.NET Web Form Designer.
         //
         InitializeComponent();
         base.OnInit(e);
      }

      /// <summary>
      /// Required method for Designer support - do not modify
      /// the contents of this method with the code editor.
      /// </summary>
      private void InitializeComponent()
      {
         this.Load += new System.EventHandler(this.Page_Load);

      }
      #endregion
   }
}
```

Customizing the Google Controls' Appearance

The Google controls we produced provide extensive support for customization
through styles, templates, and data-binding overrides. The next Web Form demonstration takes advantage of all three features. The CustomGoogleSearch Web Form implements its own version of ItemTemplate, AlternatingItemTemplate, and StatusTemplate
to show a numbered list of the search results on the left side and a different color for
each alternating row.

The work of keeping the item index is performed in the code-behind class file that links up to events exposed by the Search and Result controls. It resets a count variable when either Search or Result raises the GoogleSearched event. Then on each ItemCreated event raised by the Result control, it increments its counter and inserts the number at the head of the ResultItem content for each row. Figure 14-7 shows the result.

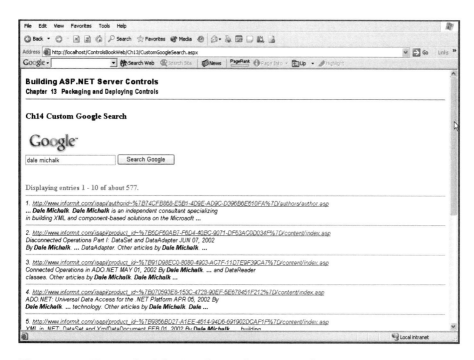

Figure 14-7. The result of the GoogleSearch.aspx search query

Listings 14-8 and 14-9 show the Web Form and the code-behind, respectively.

Listing 14-8. The CustomGoogleSearch.aspx Page File

```
<%@ Import Namespace="Apress.GoogleControls.Service" %>
<%@ Page language="c#" Codebehind="CustomGoogleSearch.aspx.cs"
AutoEventWireup="false" Inherits="ControlsBookWeb.Ch13.CustomGoogleSearch" %>
<%@ Register TagPrefix="apressUC" TagName="ControlsBookFooter"
Src="..\ControlsBookFooter.ascx" %>
<%@ Register TagPrefix="apressUC" TagName="ControlsBookHeader"
Src="..\ControlsBookHeader.ascx" %>
<%@ Register TagPrefix="google" Namespace="Apress.GoogleControls"
Assembly="Apress.GoogleControls, Version=1.0.0.0, Culture=neutral,
PublicKeyToken=9d0e1a77378e3a88" %>
<!DOCTYPE HTML PUBLIC "-//W3C//DTD HTML 4.0 Transitional//EN" >
<HTML>
```

```
        <HEAD>
            <title>CustomGoogleSearch</title>
            <meta content="Microsoft Visual Studio .NET 7.1" name="GENERATOR">
            <meta content="C#" name="CODE_LANGUAGE">
            <meta content="JavaScript" name="vs_defaultClientScript">
            <meta content="http://schemas.microsoft.com/intellisense/ie5"
             name="vs_targetSchema">
        </HEAD>
        <body MS_POSITIONING="FlowLayout">
            <form id="Form1" method="post" runat="server">
                <apressuc:controlsbookheader id="Header" runat="server"
                chapternumber="13" chaptertitle="Packaging and Deploying
                Controls"></apressuc:controlsbookheader>
                <h3>Ch14 Custom Google Search</h3>
                <google:search id="search" runat="server" ResultControl="result"
                 RedirectToGoogle="false"></google:search><br>
                <br>
                <google:result id="result" runat="server" DisplayPager="false">
                    <ItemTemplate>
                        <A href="<%# ((ResultElement) Container.DataItem).URL  %>">
                            <%# ((ResultElement) Container.DataItem).URL  %>
                        </A>
                        <BR>
                        <%# ((ResultElement) Container.DataItem).snippet  %>
                        <BR>
                    </ItemTemplate>
                    <ItemStyle Font-Size="X-Small" Font-Names="Arial"
                    Font-Italic="True"></ItemStyle>
                    <StatusStyle Font-Bold="True" ForeColor="Red"></StatusStyle>
                    <AlternatingItemTemplate>
                        <A href="<%# ((ResultElement) Container.DataItem).URL  %>">
                            <%# ((ResultElement) Container.DataItem).URL  %>
                        </A>
                        <BR>
                        <%# ((ResultElement) Container.DataItem).snippet  %>
                        <BR>
                    </AlternatingItemTemplate>
                    <AlternatingItemStyle Font-Size="X-Small" Font-Names="Arial"
                    Font-Italic="True"></AlternatingItemStyle>
                    <StatusTemplate>
Displaying entries <%# ((GoogleSearchResult)
Container.DataItem).startIndex.ToString()  %> - <%# ((GoogleSearchResult)
Container.DataItem).endIndex.ToString()  %> of about <%# ((GoogleSearchResult)
Container.DataItem).estimatedTotalResultsCount.ToString()  %>.<BR>
</StatusTemplate>
                    <SeparatorTemplate>
                        <HR>
                    </SeparatorTemplate>
                </google:result><apressuc:controlsbookfooter id="Footer"
                runat="server"></apressuc:controlsbookfooter></form>
        </body>
</HTML>
```

Listing 14-9. The CustomGoogleSearch.cs Code-Behind Class File

```csharp
using System;
using System.Collections;
using System.ComponentModel;
using System.Data;
using System.Drawing;
using System.Web;
using System.Web.SessionState;
using System.Web.UI;
using System.Web.UI.WebControls;
using System.Web.UI.HtmlControls;
using Apress.GoogleControls;

namespace ControlsBookWeb.Ch13
{
    public class CustomGoogleSearch : System.Web.UI.Page
    {
        protected Search search;
        protected Result result;
        private int resultIndex = 0;

        private void Page_Load(object sender, System.EventArgs e)
        {
        }

        #region Web Form Designer generated code
        override protected void OnInit(EventArgs e)
        {
            //
            // CODEGEN: This call is required by the ASP.NET Web Form Designer.
            //
            InitializeComponent();
            base.OnInit(e);
        }

        /// <summary>
        /// Required method for Designer support - do not modify
        /// the contents of this method with the code editor.
        /// </summary>
        private void InitializeComponent()
        {
            this.search.GoogleSearched += new
Apress.GoogleControls.GoogleSearchedEventHandler(this.search_GoogleSearched);
            this.result.ItemCreated += new
Apress.GoogleControls.ResultItemEventHandler(this.result_ItemCreated);
            this.result.GoogleSearched += new
Apress.GoogleControls.GoogleSearchedEventHandler(this.result_GoogleSearched);
            this.Load += new System.EventHandler(this.Page_Load);

        }
        #endregion
```

```
        private void result_ItemCreated(object o,
Apress.GoogleControls.ResultItemEventArgs rie)
        {
            ResultItem item = rie.Item;

            if (item.ItemType == ResultItemType.Item ||
                item.ItemType == ResultItemType.AlternatingItem)
            {
                item.Controls.AddAt(0, new LiteralControl(resultIndex.ToString() +
                                        "."));
                resultIndex++;
            }
        }

        private void search_GoogleSearched(object o,
Apress.GoogleControls.GoogleSearchedEventArgs gsea)
        {
            resultIndex = gsea.Result.startIndex;
        }

        private void result_GoogleSearched(object o,
Apress.GoogleControls.GoogleSearchedEventArgs gsea)
        {
            resultIndex = gsea.Result.startIndex;
        }
    }
}
```

Now that we have a fully functioning search server control, in the next section we discuss how to add licensing support to a custom server control.

Licensing Support

We ignored two key aspects of the source code for the Search and Result controls to streamline our discussion: globalization and licensing. We start the process by drilling down into licensing. The licensing system that we provide for the Google control is based upon the licensing framework that is already in place for .NET.

Several core classes provide the architecture and base foundation for adding licensing to components in the .NET Framework environment, as shown in Figure 14-8.

The primary class is the abstract LicenseProvider class, which ensures that a particular component has the necessary licensing information. To do its job, the LicenseProvider class relies on another abstract base class, the License class, to physically represent the licensing information. LicenseProvider has a key abstract method called GetLicense that validates and returns a License instance if it passes inspection. To link LicenseProvider to a component that needs license validation, the LicenseProviderAttribute attribute is provided to attach at the class level of the component. Once this is done, code is also manually added to the constructor to kick off the license validation process through the Validate method of the LicenseManager class.

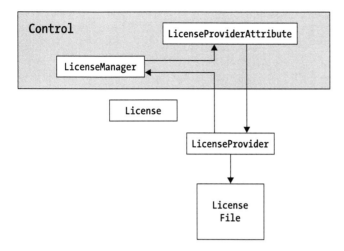

Figure 14-8. The .NET licensing architecture

The .NET Framework provides a trivial implementation of the abstract LicenseProvider class named LicFileLicenseProvider that provides a minimal licensing enforcement check. The only check it performs is for the presence of a .lic file with a text string in it, but it serves as a good starting point. We improve on this simple scheme in the following sections by writing a custom implementation of LicenseProvider and other related licensing classes using more advanced cryptographic techniques.

The RsaLicense License

The License class from the System.ComponentModel namespace represents the information used to direct the behavior of the license validation system and control feature enablement. For our licensing system, we rely on the following information stored in our custom license class:

- System.Type value of the control the license applies to

- Globally unique identifier (GUID) for the particular build of the control for licensing purposes

- Expiration date for the license

- Full key string from the license file

The resulting class is simple because it is primarily a structure for information transport. Listing 14-10 shows the full code for our RsaLicense class.

Listing 14-10. The RsaLicense.cs Class File

```
using System;
using System.ComponentModel;

namespace Apress.GoogleControls
{
    public class RsaLicense : License
    {
        private Type type;
        private string licenseKey;
        private string guid;
        private DateTime expireDate;

        public RsaLicense(Type type, string key, string guid, DateTime expireDate)
        {
            licenseKey = key;
            this.type = type;
            this.guid = guid;
            this.expireDate = expireDate;
        }

        public override string LicenseKey
        {
            get
            {
                return licenseKey;
            }
        }

        public Type Type
        {
            get
            {
                return type;
            }
        }

        public string Guid
        {
            get
            {
                return guid;
            }
        }

        public DateTime ExpireDate
        {
            get
            {
                return expireDate;
```

```
        }
    }

    public override void Dispose()
    {

        }
    }
}
```

License Cryptography

Now that we have reviewed the .NET representation of the licensing information, we next focus on the cryptographic techniques used by our system to authorize use of our control. We present a cursory review of public key cryptography and how it is used to secure the license file information in a tamper-proof manner. For a more detailed look at cryptography features in the .NET Framework SDK and for more information on this topic in general, please consult a text on cryptography.

Public key cryptography is a relatively new technique in the world of cryptography that helps with the traditional problem of exchanging private keys used for encryption and decryption. Instead of using a single private key that is shared by both parties—which is subject to interception or loss because it must be distributed to both parties—you use two keys that have different capabilities. Generally speaking, you can use one key to encrypt and the other key to read without knowing the private key. Figure 14-9 illustrates the differences between public and private key cryptography.

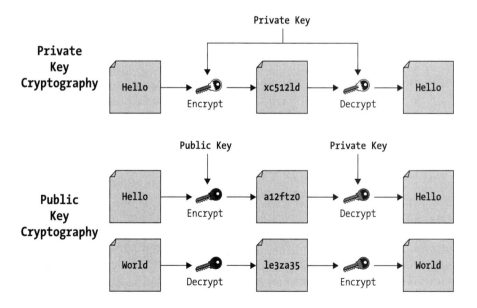

Figure 14-9. Public and private key cryptography

The asymmetric nature of the keys provides us with the ability to distribute one side of the keys without compromising the other, meaning that the public key cannot be readily used to figure out the private key.

The general usage of public key cryptography falls into two patterns, encryption and digital signature, as shown in Figure 14-10. In *encryption,* someone is able to send an encrypted message using the public key that only the private key holder can read. A *digital signature* comes into play when the holder of the private key encrypts something to prove possession of that key to anyone holding the public key. This is traditionally the signature of a hash value to make that process as computationally friendly as possible. This public key technology is the basis of the technology we discussed earlier that is used by the .NET Framework to sign assemblies to prevent tampering.

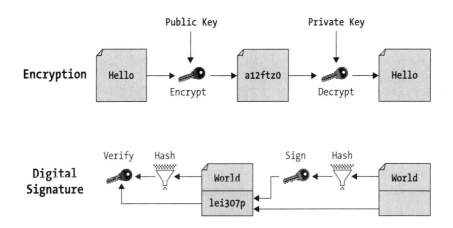

Figure 14-10. Public key cryptography usage patterns

We could have chosen a private key system for use with our control system. We moved away from this for two reasons. First, we want to demonstrate how to use public key cryptography in building control license schemes, and second, we want to solve the problem of how to embed the key in the code without giving away the secrets to the operation. This is not to say our approach is infallible or that private key techniques are any worse. Any technique chosen can be broken with patience through a brute-force attack or other means on the part of the attacker. The purpose of licensing is to provide enough barriers to deter the effort for enough time to make attack less likely.

The starting point with building the licensing system is to generate a public and private key pair. An organization building a control library can use a tool such as the one we provide in the sample code project to generate all the necessary data. The control provider then keeps the generated private key in a secure location so it is safe from loss and is not compromised. The public key is inserted into the metadata of the control in an XML format for it to use as part of the license validation process. We also take the extra step of inserting a GUID metadata value into the control to give us a way to version licenses without having to continually regenerate public/private key pairs.

The second process is the generation of the license file. It has the following format:

```
guid#expiration date#signature
```

The GUID matches up to the specific GUID that was embedded in the control library metadata. The expiration date puts an upper bound on how long the control can be used before the license is invalid. The signature of this licensing information is what makes the license file valid and tamper-proof through public key cryptography.

To create the signature for the license file string, we run a bytecode value that represents the license data for the GUID and expiration data through the SHA-1 algorithm to generate a hash value. This algorithm has a reasonable guarantee of a unique output for its input to prevent someone from tampering to get the correct output value. For each change in the input, such as a single character, the output bytes will vary wildly.

After the hash is calculated, it is signed with the RSA algorithm using the private key of the control provider to protect the licensing values against tampering by including this digital signature. The process of verifying integrity when the control is deployed also unlocks the control functionality.

The process of validating the license file occurs in reverse order of the process for creating the digital signature. The first action the control licensing code takes is to locate and read the license file from a well-known location. In our case, we chose to put the license file into a directory of the web application for easy deployment. Once the licensing code locates the file, the control licensing code takes the clear text portion of the license string to parse its value. If the GUID in the license file equals the GUID in the metadata for the control and the expiration date has not been met, the process continues with verification of the digital signature. To do the verification, the licensing code calculates a hash of the clear text license key. After the hash is completed, the licensing code reaches into the metadata of the control to find the public key used to unlock the signature present in the license file. The public key is able to decrypt the signature and check to make sure that the decrypted hash and the separately computed hash are identical. If the two are equal, we make the assumption that the information the license file contains is valid and the control is allowed to continue its normal execution process.

Generating the License

To make this process easy on the control developer, we have included source code for a rudimentary Windows Form license generator that does the grunge work of creating the license file and handling the cryptography. It also makes it easy to reverify previously generated license data. Figure 14-11 shows what the application looks like.

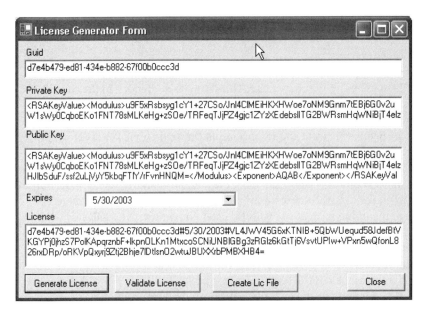

Figure 14-11. The License Generator application

The application is fairly simple to use. Click the Generate License button to populate the text box fields on the form with a new private/public key pair, a GUID, and a digital signature based on the expiration date. Make sure to copy and paste the public and private keys to a safe location for storage and use with the control building process. Click the Create Lic File button once this initialization step has occurred to enable you to save the licensing data in the correct .lic file format. Listing 14-11 shows the key code from the application.

Listing 14-11. The License Generator Application Code

```
private string GetLicenseText()
{
   return GUID.Text + "#" + Expires.Value.ToShortDateString() + "#";
}

private void btnGenLicense_Click(object sender, System.EventArgs e)
{
   GUID.Text = Guid.NewGuid().ToString();
   byte[] clear = ASCIIEncoding.ASCII.GetBytes(GetLicenseText());
   SHA1Managed provSHA1 = new SHA1Managed();
   byte[] hash = provSHA1.ComputeHash(clear);
```

```
RSACryptoServiceProvider provRSA = new RSACryptoServiceProvider();
PublicKey.Text = provRSA.ToXmlString(false);
PrivateKey.Text = provRSA.ToXmlString(true);

byte[] signature = provRSA.SignHash(hash, CryptoConfig.MapNameToOID("SHA1"));

License.Text = GetLicenseText() +
Convert.ToBase64String(signature,0,signature.Length);
}
```

The first thing the License Generator application does is create a new GUID. It then calls `GetLicenseText` to get the clear text license string with the expiration date. Next, it passes this as an array of bytes to `SHA1Managed`, the .NET-managed implementation of the SHA-1 hash algorithm, to create byte array for the hash with its `ComputeHash` method.

The byte array hash is passed to `RSACryptoServiceProvider`, which is initialized shortly afterward in the code. Notice how we use its `ToXmlString` methods to easily grab the newly generated public and private keys that are created when `RSACryptoServiceProvider` is initialized in a convenient-to-handle format.

The `SignHash` method on `RSACryptoServiceProvider` creates the digital signature needed to ensure integrity and validate the license information. The resulting final license text is put back together to include GUID, expiration date, and signature at the very end. The default license file that is included with the source code for the book (you can download the source code from the Downloads area of the Apress web site, `http://www.apress.com`) contains the following data after all is said and done with the License Generator application:

ffb30135-b07c-496b-8663-af996f7bff58#7/28/2005#AeddSLAjrD3zUjE6FabGOfqhnWafXITcmu
UjW+GifPnySV+DWRoNes8mwZXGHfq59qyyoqhK+gsfv3cND1vdjeChxt1LJk3hDTXgAcAuIL1/OnYLolW
uS9UQLy5/FwfdO7xHXRbDKnZnOTaBDl1KzZl3TqmXNbBTdjyKhC52xRI=

The RsaLicenseDataAttribute Custom Attribute

After the license data is generated, we bind some of the information to the control itself to ensure linkage between the signature in the license file and the control. The important information is the GUID and the public key. Instead of putting them in hidden fields inside the control, we chose to store them in metadata that is easily accessible, because the public information in them does not compromise the integrity of the license system. `RsaLicenseDataAttribute` is a custom attribute that is built specifically for this purpose.

NOTE *You can override the control implementation and replace the custom* License *attribute with a new value. One way to handle this situation is to make the* Search *and* Result *classes sealed. This requires some additional code rework to remove the virtual/protected modifiers from several of the methods. We do not do this work here; rather, we leave it open for extension and further customization.*

Listing 14-12 presents the full code for the custom attribute.

Listing 14-12. The RsaLicenseDataAttribute *Class File*

```
using System;

namespace Apress.GoogleControls
{
    /// <summary>
    /// Custom attribute for annotating licensing data on GoogleLib controls
    /// </summary>
    [AttributeUsage(AttributeTargets.Class, Inherited = false,
        AllowMultiple = false)
    ]
    public sealed class RsaLicenseDataAttribute : Attribute
    {
        private string guid;
        private string publicKey;

        /// <summary>
        /// Constructor for RsaLicenseDataAttribute
        /// </summary>
        /// <param name="guid"></param>
        /// <param name="publicKey"></param>
        public RsaLicenseDataAttribute(string guid, string publicKey)
        {
            this.guid = guid;
            this.publicKey = publicKey;
        }

        /// <summary>
        /// Guid representing specific build of server control type
        /// </summary>
        public string Guid
        {
            get
            {
                return guid;
            }
        }
    }
```

```
    /// <summary>
    /// Public key representing specific build of server control type
    /// </summary>
    public string PublicKey
    {
        get
        {
            return publicKey;
        }
    }
}
}
```

Next, we discuss how to apply licensing to the Search and Result custom server controls.

Adding Licensing to the Search and Result Controls

The RsaLicenseDataAttribute attribute is applied with the appropriate values to both the Search and Result controls to provide the means of accessing the GUID and public key for validation. We add LicenseProviderAttribute to link in our custom license provider, RsaLicenseProvider, which we cover in a moment. We use the following code:

```
#if LICENSED
   RsaLicenseData(
      "ffb30135-b07c-496b-8663-af996f7bff58",

"<RSAKeyValue><Modulus>tLMxOSJaiyTiEWtCWGuVVW7QOaV59jDMvEIm4aILR9SlwD6DUG8FdnfbTf
tvMJZYGoI2XSaIyz5W6/2OzjNyzZJdnNKN8V3zqT8BUBnVqrgyVAdA3mtjwdCk4MfpjEryeJAm19spgov
4dB5KUJOiDoKhbFVWZAyeXboHaE9uNWU=</Modulus><Exponent>AQAB</Exponent></RSAKeyValue
>"
      ),
   LicenseProvider(typeof(RsaLicenseProvider)),
#endif
```

The LICENSED keyword is a conditional compilation constant available in the C# language that allows the project to quickly and easily be compiled with or without licensing if needed. The default setting for LICENSED is defined in the Visual Studio .NET project that comes with the book's source code.

You can change this setting by going to the GoogleControls project in the Visual Studio .NET Solution Explorer, right-clicking, and selecting the Properties menu item to bring up the project Properties dialog box. Under the project configuration dialog box, look for the Configuration Properties ~TRA Build ~TRA Conditional compilation constants section. Figure 14-12 shows what the dialog box for this build setting looks like. Remove LICENSED from the list and the code between #if and #endif is ignored in the compile process.

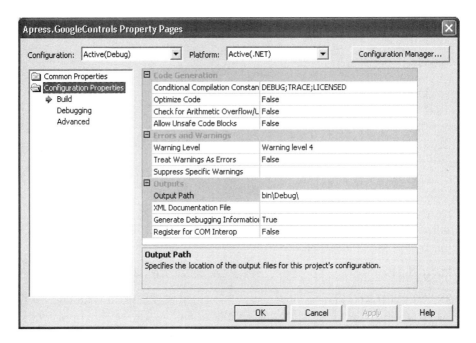

Figure 14-12. Conditional compilation constant for licensing

The RsaLicenseProvider Class

The heart of the validation process exists inside the RsaLicenseProvider class. It inherits from the base LicenseProvider class to implement the GetLicense method, which validates licensing data and then returns a valid license if successful in that process. The signature for GetLicense is as follows:

```
public override License GetLicense(LicenseContext context, Type type, object
                            instance, bool allowExceptions)
{
```

The first parameter is an instance of LicenseContext that informs the LicenseProvider implementation what the current environment is. We use it to determine whether the server control is executing within a design-time environment. The Type parameter and the Object parameter provide access to the control type and instance that is validated. AllowExceptions is a Boolean that indicates whether LicenseProvider should throw a LicenseException to indicate that the control was unable to obtain a valid license. In our code this is ignored, and instead of raising an exception it returns a null value. The full implementation for GetLicense is as follows:

```
public override License GetLicense(LicenseContext context, Type type, object
instance, bool allowExceptions)
{
    string attrGuid = "";
    string publicKey = "";
```

```
// pull licensing data (guid/publickey) from custom attributes
// on the control
RsaLicenseDataAttribute licDataAttr = GetRsaLicenseDataAttribute(type);
if (licDataAttr == null)
    return null;
publicKey = licDataAttr.PublicKey;
attrGuid = licDataAttr.Guid;

// if in Design mode create and return nonexpiring license
// so design-time ASP.NET is always working
if (context.UsageMode == LicenseUsageMode.Designtime)
{
    return new RsaLicense(type, "", attrGuid, DateTime.MaxValue);
}

// check cache for cached license information
RsaLicense license =  licenseCache.GetLicense(type);
string keyValue = "";
if (license == null)
{
    // check the license folder under the web root for a
    // license file and parse key data from it
    keyValue = LoadLicenseData(type);

    // validate the new license data key value
    DateTime expireDate = new DateTime();
    if (IsKeyValid(keyValue, publicKey, attrGuid, type, ref expireDate))
    {
        license = new RsaLicense(type, keyValue, attrGuid, expireDate);
        licenseCache.AddLicense(type, license);
    }

}
    return license;
}
```

The first bit of code in GetLicense is responsible for grabbing the information from the custom attributes. This is handled by the GetRsaLicenseDataAttribute helper method:

```
private RsaLicenseDataAttribute GetRsaLicenseDataAttribute(System.Type type)
{
    RsaLicenseDataAttribute licDataAttr;
    object[] attrs = type.GetCustomAttributes(false);
    foreach (object attr in attrs)
    {
        licDataAttr = attr as RsaLicenseDataAttribute;
        if (licDataAttr != null)
            return licDataAttr;
    }
    return null;
}
```

Once GetLicense retrieves the licensing information, it obtains the public key and GUID value from the metadata and stores them in instance variables. Afterward, GetLicense checks to see if the control itself is running in design-time mode and, if so, it creates a valid license to permit the class to work in the designer.

After verifying that the server control is running in the design-time environment, GetLicense checks whether the license is in a custom cache class that holds licenses based on the type of the executing control. The cache class is named RsaLicenseCache and is based on a Hashtable collection with strongly typed methods. This is a static field of RsaLicenseProvider to save on the resource-intensive task of going to disk to examine and parse license information for each control instance. If the license is in the cache, GetLicense returns immediately to save on processing time. If not, GetLicense executes the validation process by examining the data in the license file. LoadLicense-Data is the method responsible for looking up the control information:

```
protected string LoadLicenseData(Type type)
{
    // format of license files in web app folder structure
    // web root\
    // license\
    // Apress.GoogleControls.lic

    string keyValue = "";
    string assemblyName = type.Assembly.GetName().Name;
    string relativePath = "~\\license\\" + assemblyName + ".lic";
    string licFilePath = HttpContext.Current.Server.MapPath(relativePath);

    if (File.Exists(licFilePath))
    {
        // grab the first line that contains license data
        FileStream file = new FileStream(licFilePath,
            FileMode.Open, FileAccess.Read, FileShare.ReadWrite);
        StreamReader rdr = new StreamReader(file);
        keyValue = rdr.ReadLine();
        rdr.Close();
        file.Close();
    }

    return keyValue;
}
```

The location at which LoadLicenseData looks for the licensing information is a directory named "license" off of the web application directory. It looks for a file with the same name as the assembly but with a .lic extension. For our control library, this would be Apress.GoogleControls.lic.

After the code returns from GetLicense, we have the license string ready for verification. The following IsKeyValid method takes care of this. If IsKeyValid returns true, GetLicense adds the license to the cache and returns a valid instance to signify the process was successful. The IsKeyValid method uses the String.Split method to separate the license string by the hash mark character (#) and checks compliance by validating against the date timestamp and the GUID returned from the control metadata.

```
protected bool IsKeyValid(string keyValue, string publicKey, string attrGuid,
System.Type type, ref DateTime expireDate)
{
    if (keyValue.Length == 0)
        return false;

    char[] separators = { '#' };
    string[] values = keyValue.Split(separators);
    string signature = values[2];
    string licGuid = values[0];
    string expires = values[1];

    // Convert the expiration date using the neutral
    // culture of the assembly(en-US)
    expireDate = Convert.ToDateTime(expires,
        DateTimeFormatInfo.InvariantInfo);

    // do a date comparison for expiration and make
    // sure we are matching control with right license data
    return (licGuid == attrGuid &&
        expireDate > DateTime.Now &&
        VerifyHash(publicKey, licGuid, expires, signature));
}
```

The IsKeyValid method then calls the VerifyHash method to perform the cryptographic work that verifies the digital signature:

```
private bool VerifyHash(string publicKey, string guid, string expires,
                        string signature)
{
    // recompute the hash value
    byte[] clear = ASCIIEncoding.ASCII.GetBytes(guid + "#" + expires + "#");
    SHA1Managed provSHA1 = new SHA1Managed();
    byte[] hash = provSHA1.ComputeHash(clear);

    // reload the RSA provider based on the public key only
    CspParameters paramsCsp = new CspParameters();
    paramsCsp.Flags = CspProviderFlags.UseMachineKeyStore;
    RSACryptoServiceProvider provRSA = new RSACryptoServiceProvider(paramsCsp);
    provRSA.FromXmlString(publicKey);

    // verify the signature on the hash
    byte[] sigBytes= Convert.FromBase64String(signature);
    bool result = provRSA.VerifyHash(hash, CryptoConfig.MapNameToOID("SHA1"),
        sigBytes);

    return result;
}
```

The SHA1Managed implementation of the SHA-1 hashing algorithm is used to create a computed hash value on the contents of the license file. Once this is complete, an instance of RSACryptoServiceProvider is initialized using the public key from the control metadata. The VerifyHash and RSACryptoServiceProvider methods next verify that the signature in the license file is valid according to the separately computed hash. The result of this check is returned from RSACryptoServiceProvider.VerifyHash to IsKeyValid, which in turn notifies the parent GetLicense of success or failure.

At this point, we have completed our discussion of license validation. Listings 14-13 and 14-14 contain the code for RsaLicenseCache and RsaLicenseProvider.

Listing 14-13. The RsaLicenseCache.cs Class File

```
using System;
using System.ComponentModel;
using System.Collections;

namespace Apress.GoogleControls
{
    /// <summary>
    ///    Custom cache collection built on Hashtable for storing RsaLicense
    ///    instances
    /// </summary>
    internal class RsaLicenseCache
    {
        private Hashtable hash = new Hashtable();

        public void AddLicense(Type type, RsaLicense license)
        {
            hash.Add(type, license);
        }

        public RsaLicense GetLicense(Type type)
        {
            RsaLicense license = null;
            if (hash.ContainsKey(type))
                license = (RsaLicense) hash[type];
            return license;
        }

        public void RemoveLicense(Type type)
        {
            hash.Remove(type);
        }
    }
}
```

Listing 14-14. The RsaLicenseProvider.cs Class File

```csharp
using System;
using System.Reflection;
using System.ComponentModel;
using System.ComponentModel.Design;
using System.IO;
using System.Text;
using System.Security.Cryptography;
using System.Web;
using System.Collections;
using System.Globalization;

namespace Apress.GoogleControls
{
    public class RsaLicenseProvider : LicenseProvider
    {
        static RsaLicenseCache licenseCache = new RsaLicenseCache();

        public override License GetLicense(LicenseContext context, Type type,
        object instance, bool allowExceptions)
        {
            string attrGuid = "";
            string publicKey = "";

            // pull licensing data (guid/publickey) from custom attributes
            // on the control
            RsaLicenseDataAttribute licDataAttr = GetRsaLicenseDataAttribute(type);
            if (licDataAttr == null)
                return null;
            publicKey = licDataAttr.PublicKey;
            attrGuid = licDataAttr.Guid;

            // if in Design mode create and return nonexpiring license
            // so design-time ASP.NET is always working
            if (context.UsageMode == LicenseUsageMode.Designtime)
            {
                return new RsaLicense(type, "", attrGuid, DateTime.MaxValue);
            }

            // check cache for cached license information
            RsaLicense license = licenseCache.GetLicense(type);
            string keyValue = "";
            if (license == null)
            {
                // check the license folder under the web root for a
                // license file and parse key data from it
                keyValue = LoadLicenseData(type);

                // validate the new license data key value
                DateTime expireDate = new DateTime();
```

```
      if (IsKeyValid(keyValue, publicKey, attrGuid, type, ref expireDate))
      {
         license = new RsaLicense(type, keyValue, attrGuid, expireDate);
         licenseCache.AddLicense(type, license);
      }

   }
   return license;
}

private RsaLicenseDataAttribute GetRsaLicenseDataAttribute(System.Type type)
{
   RsaLicenseDataAttribute licDataAttr;
   object[] attrs = type.GetCustomAttributes(false);
   foreach (object attr in attrs)
   {
      licDataAttr = attr as RsaLicenseDataAttribute;
      if (licDataAttr != null)
         return licDataAttr;
   }
   return null;
}

protected string LoadLicenseData(Type type)
{
   // format of license files in web app folder structure
   // web root\
   // license\
   // Apress.GoogleControls.lic

   string keyValue = "";
   string assemblyName = type.Assembly.GetName().Name;
   string relativePath = "~\\license\\" + assemblyName + ".lic";
   string licFilePath = HttpContext.Current.Server.MapPath(relativePath);

   if (File.Exists(licFilePath))
   {
      // grab the first line that contains license data
      FileStream file = new FileStream(licFilePath,
         FileMode.Open, FileAccess.Read, FileShare.ReadWrite);
      StreamReader rdr = new StreamReader(file);
      keyValue = rdr.ReadLine();
      rdr.Close();
      file.Close();
   }

   return keyValue;
}
```

```
protected bool IsKeyValid(string keyValue, string publicKey,
string attrGuid, System.Type type, ref DateTime expireDate)
{
    if (keyValue.Length == 0)
        return false;

    char[] separators = { '#' };
    string[] values = keyValue.Split(separators);
    string signature = values[2];
    string licGuid = values[0];
    string expires = values[1];

    // Convert the expiration date using the neutral
    // culture of the assembly(en-US)
    expireDate = Convert.ToDateTime(expires,
        DateTimeFormatInfo.InvariantInfo);

    // do a date comparison for expiration and make
    // sure we are matching control with right license data
    return (licGuid == attrGuid &&
        expireDate > DateTime.Now &&
        VerifyHash(publicKey, licGuid, expires, signature));
}

private bool VerifyHash(string publicKey, string guid, string expires,
string signature)
{
    // recompute the hash value
    byte[] clear = ASCIIEncoding.ASCII.GetBytes(guid + "#" + expires + "#");
    SHA1Managed provSHA1 = new SHA1Managed();
    byte[] hash = provSHA1.ComputeHash(clear);

    // reload the RSA provider based on the public key only
    CspParameters paramsCsp = new CspParameters();
    paramsCsp.Flags = CspProviderFlags.UseMachineKeyStore;
    RSACryptoServiceProvider provRSA = new
    RSACryptoServiceProvider(paramsCsp);
    provRSA.FromXmlString(publicKey);

    // verify the signature on the hash
    byte[] sigBytes= Convert.FromBase64String(signature);
    bool result = provRSA.VerifyHash(hash, CryptoConfig.MapNameToOID("SHA1"),
        sigBytes);

    return result;
}
}
}
}
```

Globalization and Localization

In this section of the chapter, we discuss issues surrounding developing server controls that work nicely in an ASP.NET application that is localized to cultures other than U.S. English. A key feature of a server control library is the capability to support modification techniques that make it easy to deploy to the appropriate culture. Two key definitions crystallize what needs to be done: globalization and localization. *Globalization* is the process of designing an application so that it can be easily modified or updated to support different cultures. *Localization* is the actual work it takes to modify the application for a specific culture. An application designed with globalization in mind makes the localization process very easy.

The CultureInfo Class

The international support in .NET focuses on the `CultureInfo` class in the `System.Globalization` namespace. The `CultureInfo` class stores information required by the rest of the .NET Framework to correctly process string, numeric, and date formats, as well as load resources based on current culture settings. To create an instance of the `CultureInfo` class, developers typically invoke its constructor by passing in a culture string. The format of the string is a two-part structure based on the RFC 1766 format that contains a language and a country/region in a primary two-digit format. The language is specified in lowercase letters, and the country/region is specified in uppercase letters. An example for Spanish as spoken in Mexico is as follows:

```
CultureInfo culture = new CultureInfo("es-MX");
```

In order for code that is currently executing to use the settings of an instance of `CultureInfo`, that `CultureInfo` instance must be assigned to the currently executing thread. The easiest way to do this is to use the static helper method `CurrentThread` of the `Thread` class in the `System.Threading` namespace:

```
Thread.CurrentThread.CurrentCulture = culture;
Thread.CurrentThread.CurrentUICulture = culture;
```

The demonstration code shows that the `Thread` class has both a `CurrentCulture` and a `CurrentUICulture` property that can be assigned by an instance of `CultureInfo`. The instance assigned to the `CurrentCulture` affects the formatting and comparisons of string, numeric, and date formats. The `CurrentUICulture` property setting affects resources such as strings and images that are loaded from assemblies. Setting both to the same value for a thread ensures that consistent culture settings are applied.

The ResourceManager Class

A key consideration when designing ASP.NET controls that support localization is to ensure that static control layouts accommodate for potential size changes due to language differences. You should avoid hard-coding any textual values; instead, you should rely on a resource-based approach. This approach supports localization with the side benefit of not requiring a full recompile of a control library just to modify language support.

With that in mind, we switch to looking at a snippet of the Search control, which loads the string for the Text property using the ResourceManager class:

```
// search button Text is localized
ResourceManager rm = ResourceFactory.Manager;
searchButton = new Button();
searchButton.Text = rm.GetString("Search.searchButton.Text");
searchButton.Click += new EventHandler(SearchButtonClick);
this.Controls.Add(searchButton);
```

The ResourceManager class exists in the System.Resources namespace and is responsible for locating the correct resources requested based on the CurrentUICulture setting on the thread that is executing. The preceding code indicates that the ResourceManager instance should retrieve a string value that is identified by the name "Search.searchButton.Text". Once it is located, the string value is assigned to the Text property.

The ResourceManager instance created in the preceding code snippet is retrieved by a utility class named ResourceFactory in the Google control library code. Listing 14-15 shows the full listing for this utility class.

Listing 14-15. The ResourceFactory.cs Class File

```
using System;
using System.Resources;
using System.Reflection;

namespace Apress.GoogleControls
{
    internal class ResourceFactory
    {
        internal const string ResourceName = "Apress.GoogleControls.LocalStrings";
        static ResourceManager rm;

        public static ResourceManager Manager
        {
            get
            {
                if (rm == null)
                {
                    // Load the LocalStrings resource bound to the
```

```
        // main assembly or one of the language-specific
        // satellite assemblies
        rm = new ResourceManager(ResourceName,
        Assembly.GetExecutingAssembly(), null);
      }
      return rm;
    }
  }
}
```

ResourceFactory exists to provide easy, efficient access to an instance of the ResourceManager class. It does this through a static factory method approach so that each time we go for a localized resource we don't have to pay the price of initializing an instance of ResourceManager. The code also specifies the desired resource name for the ResourceManager instance:

```
internal const string ResourceName = "Apress.GoogleControls.LocalStrings";
```

The namespace of the control assembly is the prefix to the LocalStrings resource name. To create this resource, we add a resource file named LocalStrings.resx to the control project. LocalStrings.resx has an XML structure with a schema definition at the top and a data section at the bottom for holding pertinent text strings needed to localize the controls' textual output. Listing 14-16 shows the complete LocalStrings.resx file.

Listing 14-16. The LocalStrings.resx Resource File

```
<?xml version="1.0" encoding="utf-8" ?>
<root>
    <xsd:schema id="root" xmlns="" xmlns:xsd="http://www.w3.org/2001/XMLSchema"
    xmlns:msdata="urn:schemas-microsoft-com:xml-msdata">
      <xsd:element name="root" msdata:IsDataSet="true">
        <xsd:complexType>
          <xsd:choice maxOccurs="unbounded">
            <xsd:element name="data">
              <xsd:complexType>
                <xsd:sequence>
                  <xsd:element name="value" type="xsd:string" minOccurs="0"
                    msdata:Ordinal="1" />
                  <xsd:element name="comment" type="xsd:string"
                    minOccurs="0" msdata:Ordinal="2" />
                </xsd:sequence>
                <xsd:attribute name="name" type="xsd:string" />
                <xsd:attribute name="type" type="xsd:string" />
                <xsd:attribute name="mimetype" type="xsd:string" />
              </xsd:complexType>
            </xsd:element>
            <xsd:element name="resheader">
              <xsd:complexType>
```

```
                <xsd:sequence>
                  <xsd:element name="value" type="xsd:string" minOccurs="0"
                  msdata:Ordinal="1" />
                </xsd:sequence>
                <xsd:attribute name="name" type="xsd:string" use="required" />
              </xsd:complexType>
            </xsd:element>
          </xsd:choice>
        </xsd:complexType>
      </xsd:element>
    </xsd:schema>
    <resheader name="ResMimeType">
      <value>text/microsoft-resx</value>
    </resheader>
    <resheader name="Version">
      <value>1.0.0.0</value>
    </resheader>
    <resheader name="Reader">
      <value>System.Resources.ResXResourceReader, System.Windows.Forms,
Version=1.0.5000.0, Culture=neutral, PublicKeyToken=b77a5c561934e089</value>
    </resheader>
    <resheader name="Writer">
      <value>System.Resources.ResXResourceWriter, System.Windows.Forms,
Version=1.0.5000.0, Culture=neutral, PublicKeyToken=b77a5c561934e089</value>
    </resheader>
    <data name="Search.searchButton.Text">
      <value>Search Google</value>
    </data>
    <data name="ResultStatusTemplate.SearchFor">
      <value>Searched for: {0}</value>
    </data>
    <data name="ResultStatusTemplate.ResultAbout">
      <value>Result {0} - {1} of about {2}.</value>
    </data>
    <data name="ResultStatusTemplate.QueryTook">
      <value>Query took about {0} seconds.</value>
    </data>
    <data name="Pager.nextButton.Text">
      <value>Next</value>
    </data>
    <data name="Pager.prevButton.Text">
      <value>Previous</value>
    </data>
    <data name="Pager.resultsPageCell.Text">
      <value>Results Page: </value>
    </data>
</root>
```

The controls that store values inside LocalStrings include the Search control and its button's Text property, and the Pager control and its Next/Previous buttons and Results text. The ResultStatusTemplate template also uses LocalStrings to build its content for search results.

Culture Types and Localizing Resource Files

The LocalStrings.resx resource file is an embedded resource for the primary culture of the assembly. To make this happen as part of the Visual Studio .NET assembly build process, the Properties window for the LocalStrings.resx file has its Build Action property set to embedded resource. Figure 14-13 shows the compilation process and how it converts the .resx file to a binary resource file before it embeds it in the assembly.

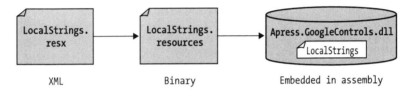

Figure 14-13. Compiling a resource file and embedding it in an assembly

The default culture for the LocalStrings resource is determined by the value of the AssemblyCulture assembly-level attribute:

```
[assembly: AssemblyCulture("")]
```

The blank value specified in the control library code indicates the use of the invariant culture. The *invariant culture* is the ultimate fallback culture that is used to resolve a lookup by ResourceManager if no other culture is specified or a culture cannot be matched using available resources.

Because we want to provide more than just an English version of output for our controls, we have to provide additional resource files that are localized for the appropriate culture. We do this by creating a resource file with the same resource name as LocalStrings but with a language and/or culture/region as part of the filename right before the filename extension. To add Spanish spoken in Mexico, we would use the following filename:

```
LocalStrings.en-MX.resx
```

When we specify the full culture with both the language and the country/region, the culture we are targeting is called a *specific culture*. We can also specify just the language to create a neutral culture such as the following for the neutral German culture:

```
LocalStrings.de.resx
```

Once you have added the desired resource files to the project, you need to copy the XML data section from the invariant culture resource file to ensure that the identifiers are the same. Once you have the structure for the resource files in place, unless you have language specialists on your staff, you will probably need the services of a translation agency. There are several commercial vendors who will accept a .NET .resx resource file and return a localized version for the desired culture.

The data section for the Spanish as spoken in Mexico es-MX file translates to the following content:

```
<data name="Search.searchButton.Text">
   <value>Búsqueda Google</value>
</data>
<data name="ResultStatusTemplate.SearchFor">
   <value>Buscado para: {0}</value>
</data>
<data name="ResultStatusTemplate.ResultAbout">
   <value>Resultado {0} - {1} de alrededor {2}.</value>
</data>
<data name="ResultStatusTemplate.QueryTook">
   <value>Pregunta tomó sobre {0} segundos. </value>
</data>
<data name="Pager.nextButton.Text">
   <value>Después</value>
</data>
<data name="Pager.prevButton.Text">
   <value>Anterior</value>
</data>
<data name="Pager.resultsPageCell.Text">
   <value>Página De los Resultados: </value>
</data>
```

The data section for the neutral German file looks like this:

```
<data name="Search.searchButton.Text">
        <value>Suche Google</value>
</data>
<data name="ResultStatusTemplate.SearchFor">
   <value>Gesucht nach: {0}</value>
</data>
<data name="ResultStatusTemplate.ResultAbout">
   <value>Resultat {0} - {1} von ungefähr {2}.</value>
</data>
<data name="ResultStatusTemplate.QueryTook">
   <value>Frage nahm über {0} Sekunden.</value>
</data>
<data name="Pager.nextButton.Text">
   <value>Zunächst</value>
</data>
<data name="Pager.prevButton.Text">
   <value>Vorhergehend</value>
```

```
    </data>
    <data name="Pager.resultsPageCell.Text">
      <value>Resultat Seite: </value>
    </data>
```

Now that we have our resource files in place, we next explore how to incorporate the localized resource files into a server control.

Satellite Assemblies and Resource Fallback

The localized resource files we add to the control project are not compiled by Visual Studio .NET as resources to be embedded in the primary assembly. Instead, they become part of what is called a *satellite assembly,* which contains just the localized resources as part of its content. It does this in an organized fashion using a specific file folder structure so the `ResourceManager` class can find it. For the two preceding files, LocalStrings.en-MX.resx and LocalStrings.de.resx are located in the folder structure shown in Figure 14-14.

The `ResourceManager` resource resolution process first attempts to take an exact match if it is provided with a specific culture. An example of this type of specific culture string is es-MX. In this case, there is a matching satellite assembly, so `ResourceManager` will pull the localized text from it.

The globalization support has a fallback mechanism in the event that an exact match cannot be found, as shown in Figure 14-15. If the fallback process cannot find an exact match, it continues until it either finds a suitable neutral culture match or winds up with the invariant culture in the main assembly. For example, if we specify a culture string of fr-FR for French spoken in France, we would end up with the English string from the main assembly because we do not have a satellite assembly for the French language.

If we specify a culture string of de-AU for German spoken in Austria, the `ResourceManager` would miss on the specific culture but pick up the German neutral culture (de) satellite assembly, as shown in Figure 14-16.

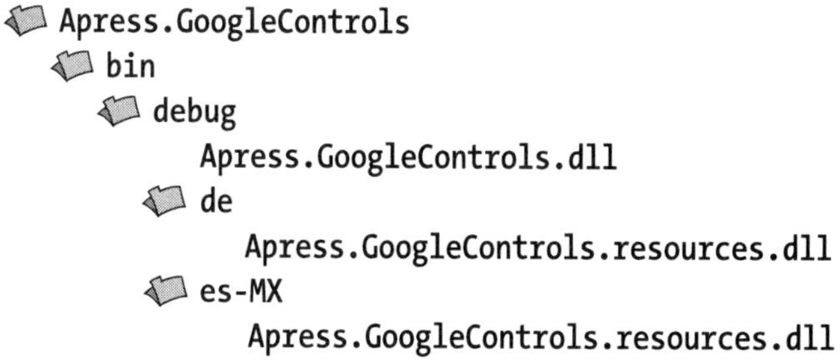

Apress.GoogleControls
bin
debug
Apress.GoogleControls.dll
de
Apress.GoogleControls.resources.dll
es-MX
Apress.GoogleControls.resources.dll

Figure 14-14. The satellite assembly folder structure

Apress.GoogleControls
bin
debug
Apress.GoogleControls.dll
de
Apress.GoogleControls.resources.dll
es-MX
Apress.GoogleControls.resources.dll
de-AU
de-AU (Not Present)

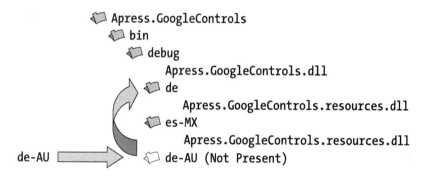

Figure 14-15. The resource fallback process in action, part 1

Apress.GoogleControls
bin
debug
Apress.GoogleControls.dll
de
Apress.GoogleControls.resources.dll
es-MX
Apress.GoogleControls.resources.dll
fr (Not Present)
fr-FR
Fr-FR (Not Present)

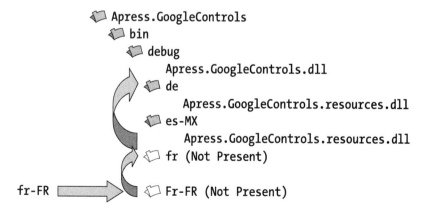

Figure 14-16. The resource fallback process in action, part 2

Setting Thread Culture in the Global.asax File

To test the localization features, you must configure ASP.NET to identify the desired culture specified by the browser. This is best done in a centralized manner by overriding the `Application_BeginRequest` event in the global.asax file, as shown here:

```
protected void Application_BeginRequest(Object sender, EventArgs e)
{
    // find the preferred culture from the browser
    string culture = HttpContext.Current.Request.UserLanguages[0];

    CultureInfo info = null;

    // check for a neutral culture of length 2 (i.e., de or es)
    if (culture.Length == 2)
        // use CultureInfo to convert from neutral to specific culture
        // so we can assign to both CurrentCulture and CurrentUI Culture
        info = CultureInfo.CreateSpecificCulture(culture);
    else
        info = new CultureInfo(culture);

    // set it for both formatting/comparisons (CurrentCulture)
    // and resource lookup (CurrentUICulture)
    Thread.CurrentThread.CurrentCulture = info;
    Thread.CurrentThread.CurrentUICulture = info;
}
```

The first thing the code does is look at the HTTP client request variables for culture information that are available via the `Request` object's `UserLanguages` array. The array is populated from the web browser's `HTTP_ACCEPT_LANGUAGE` HTTP request header, and it has culture values that match those in RFC 1766, which is what the `CultureInfo` class expects. As a simplification to the process, we take the first language in the array. More robust code could be written to check if the site supported the first language and, if not, to walk along the array until a supported language was found.

The language header is manually controllable in Internet Explorer to allow you to easily test the localized resources built into the Google controls library. You control this by selecting Tools ~TRA Internet Options to open the Internet Options dialog box. At the very bottom of the Internet Options dialog box is a Languages button. Click the Languages button to open another dialog box that presents the language settings (see Figure 14-17).

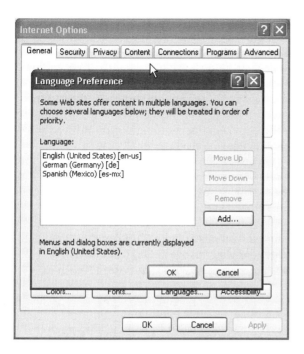

Figure 14-17. Changing language settings in Internet Explorer

The Language Preference box gives you the option of adding languages and prioritizing the accepted languages in order. Now you can test different language settings.

Once the culture setting is retrieved from the browser, the Application.BeginRequest event handler checks to see if a specific culture with the language identifier is present. The CurrentUICulture Thread class property works with a neutral culture, and the CurrentCulture property requires a specific culture to function correctly to do its formatting job, so we must account for the differences. We use the static helper method on the CultureInfo class named CreateSpecificCulture to do the conversion to a default specific culture from a neutral culture that might be passed in from the browser. The end result is a culture such as "de" getting transformed to "de-DE." Lastly, we assign the culture to the currently executing thread for the web application page to set up localized page rendering, which also sets the culture for the custom server control.

Viewing a Localized Web Form

LocalizedGoogleSearch.aspx is a slightly modified Web Form from our previous
GoogleSearch Web Form that has additional controls on it to show the current culture
settings that the browser is providing to the web server. It has code in it to check the
`Thread` for the `CurrentCulture` and display it in a `Label` control along with the current
time to show the formatting differences:

```
private void Page_Load(object sender, System.EventArgs e)
{
  CultureLabel.Text = Thread.CurrentThread.CurrentCulture.DisplayName;
  DateTimeLabel.Text = DateTime.Now.ToLongDateString();
}
```

Figures 14-18, 14-19, and 14-20 show the various results with different cultures.
Notice how the button text and the status template change among cultures. In
Figure 14-21, notice how we fall back to the English invariant culture for a French
culture setting.

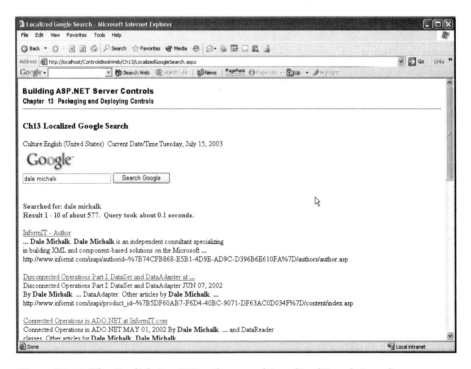

Figure 14-18. The English (en-US) culture and LocalizedGoogleSearch.aspx

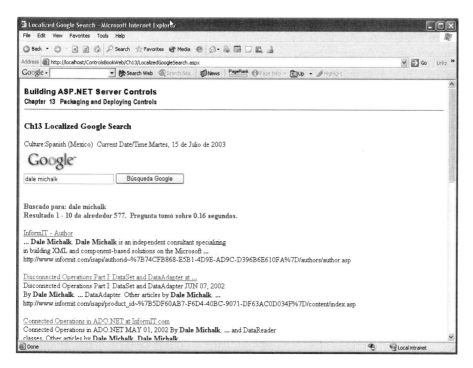

Figure 14-19. The Spanish (es-MX) culture and LocalizedGoogleSearch.aspx

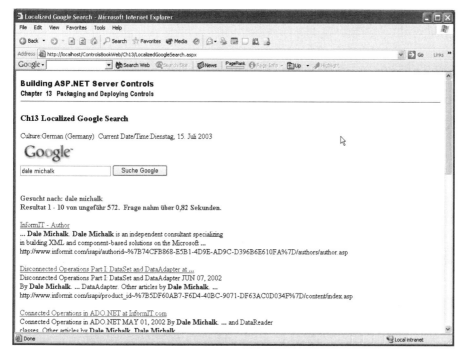

Figure 14-20. The German (de) culture and LocalizedGoogleSearch.aspx

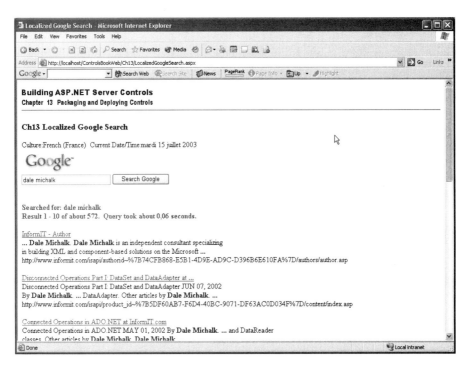

Figure 14-21. The French (fr) culture and LocalizedGoogleSearch.aspx

Listings 14-17 and 14-18 present the source code for the Localized Google Search Web Form.

Listing 14-17. The LocalizedGoogleSearch.aspx Page File

```
<%@ Page language="c#" Codebehind="LocalizedGoogleSearch.aspx.cs"
AutoEventWireup="false" Inherits="ControlsBookWeb.Ch13.LocalizedGoogleSearch" %>
<%@ Register TagPrefix="apressUC" TagName="ControlsBookFooter"
Src="..\ControlsBookFooter.ascx" %>
<%@ Register TagPrefix="apressUC" TagName="ControlsBookHeader"
Src="..\ControlsBookHeader.ascx" %>
<%@ Register TagPrefix="google" Namespace="Apress.GoogleControls"
Assembly="Apress.GoogleControls, Version=1.0.0.0, Culture=neutral,
PublicKeyToken=9d0e1a77378e3a88" %>
<!DOCTYPE HTML PUBLIC "-//W3C//DTD HTML 4.0 Transitional//EN" >
<HTML>
    <HEAD>
        <title>Localized Google Search</title>
        <meta content="Microsoft Visual Studio .NET 7.1" name="GENERATOR">
        <meta content="C#" name="CODE_LANGUAGE">
        <meta content="JavaScript" name="vs_defaultClientScript">
        <meta content="http://schemas.microsoft.com/intellisense/ie5"
        name="vs_targetSchema">
```

```
        </HEAD>
    <body MS_POSITIONING="FlowLayout">
        <form id="Form1" method="post" runat="server">
            <apressuc:controlsbookheader id="Header" runat="server"
chapternumber="13" chaptertitle="Packaging and Deploying
Controls"></apressuc:controlsbookheader>
            <h3>Ch13 Localized Google Search</h3>
            Culture:<asp:Label ID="CultureLabel" Runat="server">
            </asp:Label>  Current
            Date/Time:<asp:Label ID="DateTimeLabel" Runat="server">
            </asp:Label>
            <br>
            <google:search id="search" runat="server" ResultControl="result"
            RedirectToGoogle="false"></google:search><br>
            <br>
            <google:result id="result" runat="server" PagerStyle="TextWithImages">
                <StatusStyle Font-Bold="True" ForeColor="Blue"></StatusStyle>
            </google:result><apressuc:controlsbookfooter id="Footer"
            runat="server"></apressuc:controlsbookfooter>
            <P> </P>
        </form>
    </body>
</HTML>
```

Listing 14-18. The LocalizedGoogleSearch.cs Code-Behind Class File

```
using System;
using System.Collections;
using System.ComponentModel;
using System.Data;
using System.Drawing;
using System.Web;
using System.Web.SessionState;
using System.Web.UI;
using System.Web.UI.WebControls;
using System.Web.UI.HtmlControls;
using System.Threading;
using System.Globalization;

namespace ControlsBookWeb.Ch13
{
    public class LocalizedGoogleSearch : System.Web.UI.Page
    {
        protected Apress.GoogleControls.Result result;
        protected Apress.GoogleControls.Search Search1;
        protected Apress.GoogleControls.Search Search2;
        protected System.Web.UI.WebControls.DropDownList CultureList;
        protected System.Web.UI.WebControls.Label CultureLabel;
        protected System.Web.UI.WebControls.Label DateTimeLabel;
        protected Apress.GoogleControls.Search search;
```

```
        private void Page_Load(object sender, System.EventArgs e)
        {
            CultureLabel.Text = Thread.CurrentThread.CurrentCulture.DisplayName;
            DateTimeLabel.Text = DateTime.Now.ToLongDateString();
        }

        #region Web Form Designer generated code
        override protected void OnInit(EventArgs e)
        {
            //
            // CODEGEN: This call is required by the ASP.NET Web Form Designer.
            //
            InitializeComponent();
            base.OnInit(e);
        }

        /// <summary>
        /// Required method for Designer support - do not modify
        /// the contents of this method with the code editor.
        /// </summary>
        private void InitializeComponent()
        {
            this.Load += new System.EventHandler(this.Page_Load);

        }
        #endregion
    }
}
```

This completes our discussion of globalization and localization. In the next sections, we discuss a few tools that can help you write robust, .NET Framework–friendly custom server controls.

FxCop

FxCop is a tool developed by the .NET Framework team at Microsoft to help ensure compliance with name and coding conventions. It consists of a robust desktop application with a rules engine to check for common violations and errors. Figure 14-22 shows the application's user interface.

You can configure FxCop to adjust the level of reporting it provides or the guidance it offers. It is a great automated form of code review, and you can adapt it by adding new rules to the system. You can find FxCop on the Microsoft GotDotNet site at http://www.gotdotnet.com/team/fxcop/.

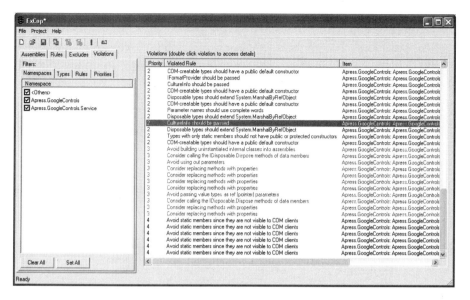

Figure 14-22. The FxCop application

Documentation

The downloadable code for the book has additional content for the source code listed in this chapter because it contains XML comments that were pared to shorten the chapter text. We took advantage of the XML comment system built into the C# language and Visual Studio .NET to generate documentation for us once we were finished coding.

This functionality is configured by going into the Visual Studio .NET project properties for the Google controls library. Go to Configuration Properties, select the Build section, and look for the XML Documentation File setting. We decided to generate an XML file with all the comments named Apress.GoogleControls.Doc.xml, as shown in Figure 14-23. Now when the project is built, Visual Studio .NET will parse the XML comments out of the code and insert it into our XML file. The content looks like the snippet in Figure 14-24.

Raw XML is not the best documentation form, but fortunately for us, Visual Studio .NET has the capability to generate a set of HTML pages that present our comment pages in a professional format. The Build Comment Pages option on the Tools menu kicks off the process and gives you a choice about where to build the HTML content. Figure 14-25 shows the menu and Figure 14-26 shows the dialog box that provides options for the location of the generated HTML. A screenshot of the final HTML product is shown in Figure 14-27.

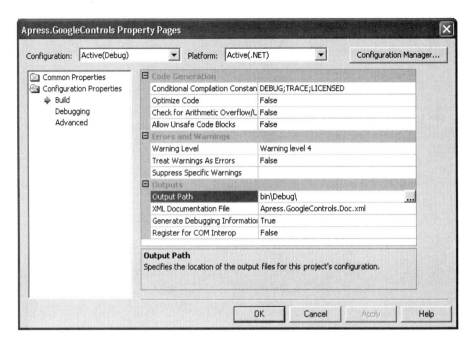

Figure 14-23. The XML Documentation File setting

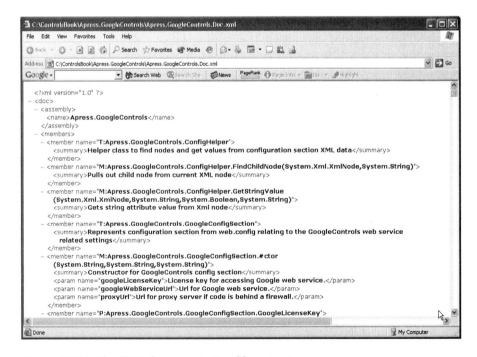

Figure 14-24. The XML documentation file output

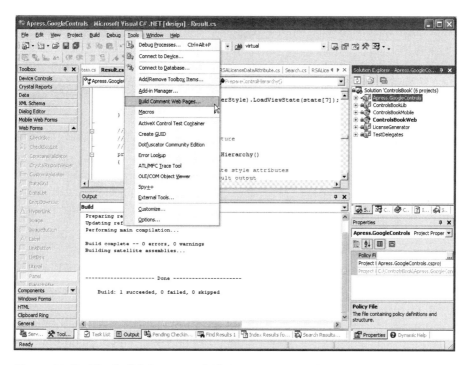

Figure 14-25. The Build Comment Web Pages menu option

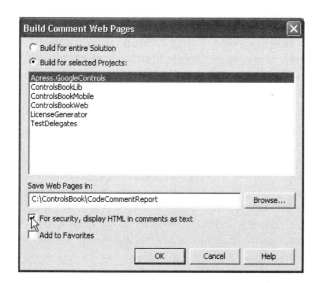

Figure 14-26. The Build Comment Web Pages dialog box

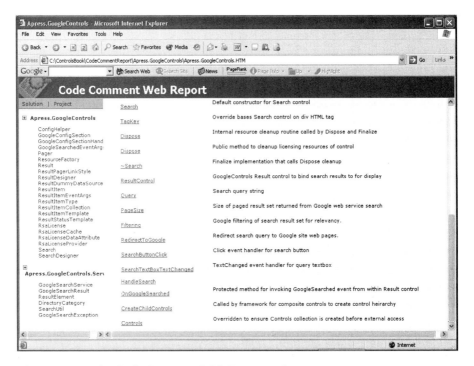

Figure 14-27. The Code Comment Web Report web page

The savvy developer has additional options to improve the documentation generated beyond the simple HTML pages built by Visual Studio .NET. For advanced help and direct integration with the new help system of Visual Studio .NET, there is a tool named Custom Help Builder that is bundled with the rest of the PowerToys for Visual Studio .NET 2003 (http://www.gotdotnet.com/team/ide).

Summary

In this chapter, we started off with a discussion of design-time support to include data binding and template support. After testing out the Google control, we next covered how to implement licensing as part of server control deployment. We also covered the globalization/localization features available when building custom server controls and provided an example of how to add these features to the Google control. Finally, we discussed the use of the XML comment system in ASP.NET to easily generate documentation based on source code comments.

Index

Symbols

(hash) character, 225
#region preprocessor directive, 26
$ assertion, 390
* quantifier, 390
. character class, 389
.Initialize method, 650
? quantifier, 390
@Page directive, 247
[^abc] character class, 389
[abc] character class, 389
[d-f1-3] character class, 389
\B assertion, 390
\b assertion, 390
\d character class, 389
\D character class, 389
\f\n\r\t\v] character class, 389
\s character class, 389
\w character class, 389
\W character class, 389
^ assertion, 390
__doPostBack function, 193
__VIEWSTATE field, 123, 124, 216
{n} quantifier, 390
{n,} quantifier, 390
{n,m} quantifier, 390
+ quantifier, 390

A

<a href=""> tag, 510, 536, 541
<a> tag, 32, 41, 509
AccessKey attribute, 575
action attribute, 120
Active Server Pages. *See* ASP (Active Server Pages)
ActiveX controls, 8, 14, 393, 572
ActiveXControls property, 393, 572
Add Style Rule dialog box, 228
AddAttribute method, 95, 236
AddAttributesToRender method, 235–36
    and CursorStyle enumeration, 268, 269
    overriding, 236, 412
and PhoneValidator custom control, 484
and rendering FancyLabel Control, 274
and styled Textbox control, 237
AddParsedSubObject method, 284, 310
AddStyleAttribute method, 249, 269
ADO Recordset, 4
AdRotator control, 529–33
AfterLabel control, 172, 176, 177
AlternateItemStyle property, 249
AlternatingItemTemplate property, 724
AlternatingItemTemplate template, 49, 316–17, 361
AOL property, 393, 572
AppDomains object, 113
Application Center 2000, 117
Application object, 114, 115–16
Application property, 116
Application variables, 112, 116
Application_BeginRequest event, 818
ApplicationInstance property, 116
ApplyStyle class method, 255, 269
Apress web site, 124
ArrayList collection, 23, 286, 289, 310, 336, 349, 717
ASP (Active Server Pages), 2
    vs. ASP.NET, 11–14
    development model, 3–6
    state management techniques, 112
ASP.NET
    vs. ASP, 11–14
    development model, 8–11
ASP.NET Page Handler, 115
ASP.NET Service Handler, 115
aspnet_isapi.dll library, 113
aspnet_wp.exe worker process, 113
AssemblyVersion attribute, 687
asynchronous handlers, 115
Attribute collection, 673
attributes. *See also names of specific attributes*
    design-time, 109–10
    what they are, 108–9
Attributes collection, 274, 373, 374
AutoPostBack property, 153, 360

GoogleSearchService class, 682
GotDotNet site, 824
GridLayout setting, 229

H

<H3> tag, 94, 95, 100
HandleSearch method, 704, 706
HasBackButton property, 573
hash (#) character, 225
Hashtable collection, 804
<HEAD> section, 64–65, 226
Header user control, 71, 73
HeaderTemplate property, 286, 287
HeaderTemplate template, 49, 287, 290, 326
Height property, 231
"Hello,World" Web Form, 17–29
    control events, 24–27
    control methods, 23–24
    control properties, 21–22
    overview, 17–21
    web page as control tree, 27–29
helper methods, 89
HidesRightAlignedMultiselectScrollbars
    property, 573
hostname field, 685
<href=""> tag, 529
HTML controls demonstration, 32–36
HTML (HyperText Markup Language),
    223–30. *See also names of specific
    HTML tags*
    hidden variables, 120–22
    HTML controls vs. Web controls,
        65–66
    overview, 223
    style properties and Visual Studio
        .NET, 227–30
    styling using Cascading Style Sheets,
        224–27
    styling using tags, 224
    version 3.2, 247–49
<HTML> tag, 29, 70
Html32TextWriter, 249
HtmlControls namespace, 82
HtmlEncode, 195
HtmlForm control, 29, 32, 66
HtmlGenericControl server control, 31,
    35–36, 39, 100
HtmlHidden control, 129
HtmlInputFile control, 37, 39, 66
HtmlInputText control, 30, 35, 65
HtmlTable control, 82, 100
HtmlTableCell control, 35
HtmlTableRow control, 35
HtmlTextArea control, 41

HtmlTextWriter class, 140, 217, 393
    and down-level browser style render-
        ing, 249
    and MenuCustomControl server con-
        trol, 89, 90
    string fields exposed by, 95
    and TableCustomControl server con-
        trol via rendering, 96
    Write methods of, 94
HtmlTextWriter method, 236, 268
HtmlTextWriterTag method, 96
HtmlTextWriterTag.Span enumeration
    value, 235
HTTP GET request, 125, 132
HTTP header, 388
HTTP (Hypertext Transfer Protocol), 4,
    111–12
HTTP postback mechanism, 9
HTTP POST mechanism, 120, 125, 140
HTTP_USER_AGENT header, 387
HttpApplication object, 113
HttpApplicationFactory object, 113
HttpApplicationState, 116
HttpBrowserCapabilities class, 387
    and down-level browser style render-
        ing, 249
    and JavaScript detection, 379
    properties of, 393, 394, 572
HttpContext class, 116
HttpContext.Current property, 117
HttpHandler class, 114, 115
HttpHandlers, 112, 115
HttpModule class, 114, 115
HttpModules, 112, 115
HttpPostedFile object, 39
HttpRequest class, 118, 119, 120–21, 570
HttpRequest.Browser property, 589
HttpResponse class, 119
HttpRuntime object, 113
HttpSessionState, 116
HyperLink control, 41, 129, 703
HyperText Markup Language. *See* HTML
    (HyperText Markup Language)
Hypertext Transfer Protocol. *See* HTTP
    (Hypertext Transfer Protocol)

I

<I> tag, 224, 509
ICollection interface, 122
IComponent interface, 608
IComponentChangeService interface, 606
IConfigurationSection interface, 692
IControlAdapter interface, 587, 592
id attributes, 225
id parameter, 599